Most people have three things in common when they buy a car.

"Edmund's® arms you with more facts. In addition to reviews and specs, new-car buyers will find each car's invoice price, sticker price, destination charge and dealer holdback (profit the dealer makes even if the car sells at invoice)."

—Kristin Davis, **Kiplinger's Personal Finance Magazine,** December, 1997

"Edmund's® ... provides an amazing compilation of facts, details and evaluations about (a) car. You will be able to read honest and direct evaluations of (a) vehicle. You have the information at your fingertips to put together your dream car at invoice price."

—Ron Raisglid, **Buying & Leasing Cars on the Internet** (Los Angeles, CA: Renaissance Books, 1998)

"Edmund's®...is jam-packed with valuable information on virtually every new and used vehicle model as well as tips and safety information."

—Glenn Fannick, **Dow Jones Business Directory** (http://bd.dowjones.com), April 20, 1998

"The Edmund's® car buying guide print version...is an excellent product for consumers to use...(and is) one of the best auto information sources."

—Paul Maghielse, **The Motley Fool** (http://www.fool.com/car/step5car.htm), March 8, 1998

"Another resource of general auto pricing information can be found in bookstores, called the Edmund's® New Car Price Books. *Make sure you get their latest quarterly edition..."*

—Darrell Parrish, **The Car Buyer's Art** (Bellflower, CA: Book Express, 1998)

"Edmund's® has built a solid reputation for providing objective, reliable, new and used car and truck prices."

—Ron Raisglid, **Buying & Leasing Cars on the Internet** (Los Angeles, CA: Renaissance Books, 1998)

"Using the percent factor to figure dealer cost is not as accurate as using specific information published in Edmund's® New Car Prices.*"*

—Mark Eskeldson, **What Car Dealers Don't Want You to Know** (Fair Oaks, CA: Technews Publishing, 1997)

"Edmund's® Automobile Buyers Guides are among the most respected new car books around...they're well-written, too, even entertaining. You'll also find detailed pricing information, as well as information about how dealers structure their prices. Ever heard of 'dealer holdback'? You can use this kind of knowledge in bargaining for a great price."

—**Houston Chronicle,** January 23, 1998

"Edmund's® provides engaging descriptions of many models of cars, plus important specifications, (and) a straightforward description of the calculus leading to a fair price for both dealer and consumer."

—**The Wall Street Journal,** April 15, 1999

"If you really want the nitty-gritty, you're going to have to ... (get) ... Edmund's® New Car Prices. *This little book is a gold mine for the curious car buyer... It is an automobile fancier's delight, a straightforward, meaty compendium of raw facts. Buy the book, follow the steps outlined ... and you will determine the exact cost of just about any car."*

—Remar Sutton, **Don't Get Taken Every Time** (New York, NY: Penguin Books, 1997)

2000

edmunds.com
consumer driven

NEW TRUCKS

PRICES & REVIEWS

"THE ORIGINAL CONSUMER PRICE AUTHORITY"

Cover photo:
2000 GMC Yukon

ISBN: 0-87759-655-7
ISSN: 1089-8735

TABLE OF CONTENTS

SPRING 2000 **VOL S3401-0006**

Special offer from 1-800-CAR-CLUB - details on page 3

2001 Ford Explorer Sport

What's with the new name and logo?

"Consumer driven" is our motto. It accompanies our new logo, which was redesigned after we changed our name, and will serve as an advertising tagline. Call us Edmunds.com, your faithful servant since 1966, bringing you the scoop on car and truck pricing for nearly 35 years.

edmunds.com
consumer driven

If you've been living without cable TV in an Airstream trailer on the outskirts of Quartzsite, Ariz., for the past couple of years, you might wonder what all this "dot com" stuff is about. In a word, the Internet. It's the future of publishing, of retailing, of banking, of investing, of education, and likely a number of things car hacks like us haven't dreamed of.

We publish a free Web site at http://www.edmunds.com, hence the new name of our company. At this Web site, you can gather all the same facts and figures on mainstream cars and trucks sold in the U.S. that you can by using this book. But there's more than just invoice and retail pricing, reviews, specifications, and how-to-buy articles. The photos are in color. We print the results of full road tests on a weekly basis. Plus, we can direct you to companies that can help you buy or finance a car, obtain an extended warranty, or provide you with aftermarket accessories.

Our free Web site is updated daily. This book you're holding is updated quarterly. That means our Web site can be more accurate if pricing on a vehicle has changed recently. We also publish timely incentive and rebate data on the Web site, required information for anyone looking to buy a new car. Finally, because this book is constrained by size and printing costs and the Web site is not, you get more detail on the vehicle you're considering when you visit the Internet than when you visit the local bookstore.

Why do we give all of the information in this book, and more, away for free on our Web site? Because we're consumer driven. It's our motto.

But I don't have a computer. What does this book provide me?

Not everyone owns a computer or has a desire to surf the Web. Others like to have all the available data gathered in one easy-to-read volume that's small enough to be carried around but large enough to offer thorough coverage. Some even like to collect and archive our printed compendiums of automotive facts and figures. If you fit this description, this edition of our traditional print buyer's guide is for you.

Within these pages, we provide you with pricing and specifications for models currently sold in the U.S. that cost less than $55,000. You'll also find editorial about the vehicles, crash-test data, a list of frequently asked questions about cars and the car-buying process and tutorials that will help you should you decide to haggle with the dealer.

There's also a list of our editorial staff's favorite vehicles in a variety of size and type classes, a full road test of the vehicle on the cover, and customer-assistance phone numbers for the major automakers so you can obtain more information on the models contained in this book.

How do I use this guide?

If you're new to Edmunds.com, or are new to the car-buying experience, here is how to use this guide. Your first step should be to visit a car dealership.

Take a pad of paper with you, and write down all pertinent information from the window sticker of the car you like. Then, go home and snuggle up with this buyer's guide to start figuring out how to get the best deal on the car of your dreams.

Read the articles about **dealer holdbacks**, **buying your next new automobile**, and **leasing tips**. Then study the make and model that you're interested in. You'll find a representative photo of the vehicle, followed by a synopsis of "What's New?" for the model year. Then, a short review provides our opinion of the car. An extensive listing of standard equipment for each trim level comes next, telling you what items are included in the base price of the vehicle. The first paragraph pertains to the base model, and if more than one trim level is available, successive paragraphs will explain what additional features the additional trim levels include over the base model.

"All things considered equal, your target price should include a 3 percent profit to the dealer."

Next is the meat of this guide: the pricing data. Each vehicle has base invoice price and base MSRP listed for each trim level, and the destination charge, which is the cost of shipping the vehicle from the factory to the dealer. Don't forget to add the destination charge, which is non-negotiable, when pricing a vehicle. Following the base prices and destination charge is a listing of all the optional equipment available on the vehicle from the factory. Along the left margin you'll find a factory code for each option. The dealer invoice price and the MSRP are listed near the right margin. Some option listings have short descriptions that tell you, for example, what might be included in a particular option package, or what trim level the option is available on, or if there are restrictions and requirements regarding availability.

You'll notice that some models do not have option listings. This is because the automaker includes the most popular accessories as standard equipment on a particular trim level, and any additional items that you might like to add to the vehicle will have to be purchased from and installed by the dealer, or are installed at the port of entry. Generally, you can haggle about 25 percent off dealer-installed accessories with little effort.

Looking for the exact specifications of your dream car? Check the back of this book, where you'll find charts displaying the length of the vehicle, the curb weight of the vehicle, and how much horsepower the base engine makes, among others. This format allows you to easily locate and compare specifications between different models and trim levels.

I've followed your advice. Why won't the dealer sell me the car?

Keep in mind that the laws of supply and demand apply to automobiles as much as they apply to any other material commodity. If a vehicle is in great demand and short supply, don't expect to get much of a discount. On the other hand, inflated inventories and tough competition mean that deals are readily available on models that aren't selling well. If a rebate is available on the car or truck you're shopping for, that's an indicator that the dealer will slash the price to the bone to get the car off the lot.

INTRODUCTION

If you've got to be the first on your block with a hot new model, you'll pay for the privilege. In fact, dealers sometimes demand profit above the MSRP on ultra-hot models, and they expect to get it. Meanwhile, it is not uncommon for older, stale models to sell below invoice, thanks to hefty incentive programs and rebates, particularly at year-end clearance time. All things considered equal, your target price should include a 3 percent profit to the dealer. But hot cars will cost more. Sometimes much more.

Contact us.

We strive to give you precise, accurate information so that you can make your very best deal, and we invite your comments. Your best bet for a response is to send email to: editor@edmunds.com. Otherwise, try snail mail to the attention of the Automotive Editors at Edmunds.com, P.O. Box 18827; Beverly Hills, CA, 90209-4827.

2000 Chrysler Town & Country

STEP-BY-STEP COST WORKSHEET

edmunds.com consumer driven

MAKE: EXTERIOR COLOR:

MODEL: INTERIOR COLOR:

TRIM LEVEL: ENGINE/TRANSMISSION:

ITEMS	INVOICE
Basic Vehicle Price:	
Optional Equipment:	
1.	
2.	
3.	
4.	
5.	
6.	
7.	
8.	
9.	
10.	
11.	
12.	
13.	
14.	
15.	
TOTAL	
SUBTRACT Holdback Amount (if ordering car)	
ADD 3% Fair Profit	
ADD Destination Charge	
ADD Advertising Fees (1.5% of MSRP maximum)	
ADD Documentation and D&H fees ($100 maximum)	
SUBTRACT Trade-In Value or Cash Down Payment	
or, if you own more on your existing car than it is worth,	
ADD Difference Between Trade Value and Loan Balance	
ADD Sales Taxes (and Registration fees, if applicable in your region)	
SUBTRACT Rebates and/or Incentives	
FINAL Price for Purchase or Capitalized Cost for Lease	
TOTAL COST	

HOW TO BUY YOUR NEXT NEW AUTOMOBILE

Every automobile buyer has but one thought in mind — to save money by getting a good deal. Your goal should be to pay 3 percent over the dealer's true cost, not the 10-15 percent the dealer wants you to pay. Use the following guide to help you plan your purchase:

Step 1 Know what type of vehicle you need, and study the different models available.

Step 2 Test-drive, as extensively as possible, each model you're interested in. Pay special attention to safety features, design, comfort, braking, handling, acceleration, ride quality, ease of entry and exit, etc.

Step 3 Check insurance rates on the models you're interested in to make sure the premiums fall within your budget.

Step 4 Contact several financial institutions to obtain loan rate information. Later on, you can compare their arrangement with the dealer's financing plan.

Step 5 Find the exact vehicle you want, and copy all of the contents listed on the window sticker onto a pad of paper. Then, use our pricing information to determine actual dealer cost (if ordering the vehicle from the factory, just use our data to determine what the order will cost when you place it):

a) Total the dealer invoice column for the model and equipment you want using our step-by-step costing form.

b) If ordering the vehicle, determine the value of the holdback and subtract this amount. If the dealer orders the vehicle, he won't pay floorplanning (the charge to stock the vehicle), or advertising (an expected cost of business), which the holdback is designed to subsidize.

c) Add 3 percent fair profit. Keep in mind that hot-selling models in high demand and short supply will command additional profit, sometimes in excess of MSRP in extreme situations.

d) Add the destination charge, which is non-negotiable. Also expect to be charged advertising fees by the auto manufacturer to help pay for those MTV-style TV commercials that got you thinking about a new car in the first place. You should pay no more than 1.5 percent of the vehicle's MSRP.

e) Some dealers charge a delivery and handling (D&H) fee. Negotiate this fee. It's just added profit.

f) Add sales taxes.

g) Deduct any incentives or rebates.

Step 6 Shop this price around to several different dealerships. The dealer who meets or comes closest to your target price should get your business. Be sure that the dealer's price quote will be your final cost. Get it in writing!

Step 7 If your present vehicle will be used as a trade-in, negotiate the highest possible value for it. Try not to accept a value that is less than Edmunds.com's trade-in value for your car. When trading in your vehicle, you should deduct the trade value from the cost of the new vehicle. If you owe the bank more money than the trade-in is worth to the dealer, you are upside-down on your trade and must add the difference between what you owe and the trade value to the cost of the new vehicle. If you're making a cash down payment, either with or without a trade-in, be sure to deduct this amount from the cost of the new vehicle as well.

Step 8 To the final vehicle cost, add documentation fees and, in some areas, license plate charges.

Step 9 When talking to the finance manager as you close the deal, he or she will try to sell you rustproofing, undercoating, protection packages, dealer-added options, and an extended warranty or service contract. Forget about this stuff. Dealers charge a substantial markup on these usually useless items to fatten the profit margin on your deal.

Step 10 Enjoy your new vehicle, knowing that you did everything possible to get the best deal.

EDMUND'S® MOST WANTED

by Automotive Editors, Edmund Publications

Our staff members get the same question over and over: What's the "best" car or truck? There are many ways to answer this question, because there isn't a single "best" car or truck that will meet everyone's needs. When somebody asks us what the "best" of the crop is, we respond by quizzing the inquiring mind about her needs and wants in a vehicle.

Still, readers want to know what cars and trucks we'd buy given the resources. So our editorial staff recently gathered to hash over the roster of 2000 models available to the public. We picked our favorites under $55,000 in a variety of vehicle classes, resulting in a list of cars and trucks we'd want in our own garages.

When reviewing our selections, keep in mind that we're a group of men and women that enjoys driving. Our staff of writers ranges in age from the mid-twenties to the mid-forties. Half of us have kids. We enjoy long road trips. Some of us lead active lifestyles while the rest of us chomp chocolate chip cookie dough and eagerly await "Must See TV" each Thursday night. We need vehicles that fit this kind of lifestyle.

How did we select the Most Wanted? Only 2000 models were eligible, and at least one member of our editorial team had to have driven the vehicle prior to our deadline of October 1, 1999. Nominations were accepted, and votes were counted. Majority rule determined the winner. On some occasions there was unanimous agreement, such as our election of the Mercedes-Benz CLK for best luxury coupe. On others we engaged in heated discussions, such as when deciding if the Toyota Land Cruiser's steep price was worth skipping the redesigned GMC Yukon for best large SUV honors.

Our selections were guided as much by our hearts as our heads. We eat, breathe and dream automobiles, and in many instances, this love for the car overruled common sense during our selection process. But that's the great thing about Edmunds.com's Most Wanted list. It's guided by passion, not science.

Small Coupe: Honda Civic

Hey there, old man. In an amazing display of virility, the Honda Civic once again made the Edmunds.com Most Wanted list. By far the oldest car on our list (the current Civic platform dates back to 1996), the Civic Coupe continues to impress us with numerous attributes. Despite a higher initial price than many other cars, the Civic makes up for it with a superior reputation for reliability and resale. The DX and HX are the two entry-level models, the main difference between the two being the HX's more fuel-efficient engine. The Civic Coupe EX features a 127-horsepower VTEC engine, plus goodies like standard air conditioning, a CD player, and a moonroof. While the coupe's styling is still attractive, the main charge leveled against Civics in general is that they are rather boring. Honda's answer to that is the Civic Si. Available only in the coupe body style, the Si packs a 160-horsepower engine, a stiffer suspension, special 15-inch wheels, and four-wheel disc brakes. With MSRPs ranging from $12,680 for a DX Coupe to $17,545 for the Si, the Civic Coupe continues to be one of the best small cars on the market.

Small Sedan: Ford Focus

Focus? Never heard of it, you say? Don't worry; it's brand-new! Built by Ford, the Focus has performed a giant cannonball dive into the wading pool of small sedans. Not only have our initial impressions been good enough to elevate the Focus to the top of the best Small Sedan category, but we'd also say that it's Ford's best small car ever. What impresses us about the Focus is its intelligent design and how it surpasses expectations. The interior offers considerable room and comfort and the handling and steering actually make the Focus fun to drive. Safety has been addressed with a stiff body structure, standard front airbags, and optional side airbags. Trim levels for the sedan are LX, SE and ZTS. The LX and SE use a 110-horsepower engine for power, while a 130-horsepower engine is optional on the SE and standard on the ZTS. The MSRPs start at $12,125 for the LX Sedan and end up at $15,165 for the ZTS. For the money, you'll be hard pressed to find another sedan that offers as much as the Focus.

Midsize Coupe: Toyota Camry Solara

Torn between your need to have a practical car and your desire to drive something with a bit of pizzazz? One couldn't ask for a more sensible automobile than Toyota's Camry. Offering Toyota's long-standing attributes of reliability and refinement, the Camry quietly and competently goes about its business. The only problem is that it's rather boring in terms of style, both inside and out. Enter the Camry Solara Coupe. Now you can have your cake and eat it too, as the Solara keeps all the goodness of the

Camry four-door and adds more than a touch of style with its rakish coupe body. And the interior, capable of carrying four adults comfortably, is more attractive as well, with a cockpit feel and faux wood trim that could pass for the real thing. The Solara is available in two trim levels: SE and SLE. SE models come well equipped with A/C, power windows/locks/mirrors, antilock brakes and a four-cylinder engine with 135 horsepower. An ultra-smooth, 200-hp V6 is optional on the SE and standard on the upscale, leather-clad SLE. Transmission choices include a five-speed manual or four-speed automatic on the SEs and auto tranny only on the SLE.

Midsize Sedan: Volkswagen Passat

Yes, you can enjoy driving a family sedan, thanks to the existence of the Volkswagen Passat. Moreover, it comes in an artfully styled wrapper, which helps you stand apart from the crowd. Roomy and comfortable, with top-notch offset crash-test scores, the Passat is well equipped right out of the box. Basic GLS trim includes a torquey 150-hp turbocharged four-cylinder engine and all the creature comforts you'll need. Spend a few extra grand and you can get leather, sunroof, alloy wheels and a substantial V6 engine in zooty GLX trim. A five-speed manual transmission is standard, while a Tiptronic-style automanual is optional. Inside you'll find materials and switchgear that is shared with higher-end Audi products, but you'll have to live with small stereo controls and one of the worst cupholder designs we've seen in years. Nevertheless, this VW will put a smile on your face for miles to come, and is equipped with one of the best powertrain warranties in the business for peace of mind. Carting the family around town isn't a chore anymore.

Large Sedan: Dodge Intrepid

Sedan buyers desiring interior and trunk space need look no further than the affordable Dodge Intrepid. This car is gargantuan, with plenty of room for five adults and much of their luggage. It's a good-looking car too, as long as cab-forward architecture and modern lines appeal to you. There are shortcomings, mainly in terms of refinement, but the low price and high value quotient make it easy to live with cheap interior materials and intrusive road rumble. Choose from base or sporty ES trim levels, and you'll get a well-equipped and comfortable family hauler. A 2.7-liter V6 mated to an automatic transmission is standard on both cars. Base Intrepids include all the usual goodies, but ABS, remote keyless entry and a power driver's seat are options. ES has the gimmicky AutoStick automanual standard, and can be equipped with an optional 3.2-liter V6. ES is also your ticket to traction control, aluminum wheels, in-dash CD changer, fog lights and leather upholstery. Either way you go the Intrepid will serve your needs capably if buying a big car is on your "to do" list.

Station Wagon: Audi A4 Avant

Here's a vehicle that truly lets you have it all. Looking for a sporty ride with telepathic steering, minimal body roll and a penchant for dusting sport coupes in the twisties? The A4 Avant handles performance needs in a most un-station-wagon-like manner. But wait, your spouse needs a car that can haul the kids and groceries in a comfortable yet safe environment. The A4 comes standard with air conditioning and climate control. It also gets top marks in crash testing, is equipped with Audi's sure-footed Quattro all-wheel-drive system, and features standard front and side airbags. A 1.8-liter four-cylinder engine makes 150 horsepower while the larger 2.8-liter V6 makes 190 ponies. Check the sport package and cold weather package on your option sheet and you'll have the ultimate family truckster for any and all situations.

Sport Coupe: Ford SVT Mustang Cobra

Sure, the Ford SVT Mustang Cobra was at the center of controversy when some 1999 Cobra motors were found NOT to be making the 320 horsepower they are advertised as having. But Ford had initiated a fix and pushed engine performance higher on the Special Vehicle Team's priority list. With that issued solved, enthusiasts are left reaping the driving-enjoyment benefits of the Cobra's exclusive Independent Rear Suspension system (or IRS). When you add in its five-speed manual, beefy four-wheel discs with ABS and traction control and 17-inch rubber, the Cobra attacks twisty ribbons of pavement like few others in its class. With fresh styling, improved steering and a long list of standard equipment and creature comforts, its surprising that this kind of performance prowess can be this much fun to drive. While other manufacturers are thinking of putting their pony car models out to pasture, Ford's IRS-equipped SVT Mustang Cobra raises the bar on handling while keeping sales at a full gallop. And when it comes to value, where else can you get a 300-odd horse V8 and IRS handling for less than 35,000?

Sport Sedan: Audi S4

The Audi A4 has always been one of our favorite cars. It's affordable, comfortable, supportive, stealthy, and sexy. Kind of like great underwear, you might say. And now there's a new version of the A4, this time with little blue and yellow rocket ships on it. Ooh, baby! Think of the $37,900 Audi S4 as an A4 2.8 Quattro on massive doses of illegal steroids. Power comes from a 2.7-liter, 30-valve, twin-turbo V6 engine. Horsepower is rated at 250. More impressively, 258 foot-pounds of torque are available as low as 1,850 rpm. Take your choice of either a six-speed manual or five-speed automatic transmission. The S4's suspension is performance-tuned, and the brakes are more powerful than a standard A4's. To visually separate the S4, there are special wheels, larger air-intake openings, different interior materials, and two exclusive colors—Imola Yellow and Nogaro Blue. If you need a four-door sedan that is equally apt at city cruising or back-road roosting, our choice for 2000 is overwhelmingly the S4.

Entry-Luxury Coupe: BMW 3 Series

Last year we were blown away by BMW's redesigned 3 Series sedan. This year the company follows up with its exceptional 3 Series coupe, building them on the same E46 platform. Yet the new 323Ci and 328Ci Coupes are more than just two-door versions of the sedan. They have slightly altered exterior dimensions that make them longer, lower and wider than the four-door cars. A 2.5-liter inline six, creating 170 horsepower, propels the 323Ci while a 2.8-liter six, making 193 horsepower, scoots the 328Ci. These silky-smooth engines can be mated to either a slick-shifting five-speed manual or a new Steptronic five-speed automatic transmission. Of course, the real driving pleasure, when talking BMWs, comes not from straightline blasts but from back-road barnstorming, where the real magic of these ultimate driving machines can be experienced. If you're a performance enthusiast seeking a touch of class at a reasonable price, the sub-$30,000 323Ci deserves a test drive.

Entry-Luxury Sedan: Lincoln LS

The rear-drive LS is a huge departure for Ford's traditionally stodgy Lincoln brand and we've been sufficiently impressed during initial test-drives to name it our pick of the entry-luxury sedan litter. Sharing a platform with Jaguar's impressive S-Type, LS is available with either a strong 210-hp Duratec V6 or a delicious 252-hp V8. The V6 model can be equipped with a manual transmission (!), which is bundled with a sport package that includes a tighter suspension and less brightwork on the bumpers. LS V8 Sport models come only with an automanual transmission called SelectShift, and attractive five-spoke 17-inch wheels and tires. As expected, LS comes loaded with luxury accoutrements, and the options list is short. A power sunroof, Alpine sound, traction control and Lincoln's RESCU emergency messaging system are notable extras. Tuned to go head to head with the best from Europe, the LS is fun to drive. It's also a good-looking car, with strongly chiseled flanks and tastefully incorporated Lincoln styling cues. Though unproven, the new Lincoln LS is decidedly different in a market segment awash with overseas nameplates, and represents a dramatic turning point for this American luxury brand.

Luxury Coupe: Mercedes-Benz CLK

Luxury-car buyers demand brand cachet, real wood trim, sumptuous leather, stylish good looks and plenty of doodads to fiddle with during the drive. This Benz meets and exceeds expectations on all fronts. First, you've got the three-pointed star hood ornament, reminding you each and every time you get behind the wheel that you're driving a Mercedes. Burled walnut trim decorates interior surfaces, and high-quality leather is stretched tautly over firm and supportive seats. The exterior of the CLK screams class, with tasteful chrome accents, a traditional grille, trademark round headlamps and ribbed taillights. Loaded with luxury, the CLK comes standard with everything you could want except heated seats, a power sunroof, xenon gas discharge headlamps, CD changer, integrated telephone and rain-sensing windshield wipers. Two models are available: a speedy and sophisticated CLK320 with a smooth-revving 3.2-liter V6, or the beefy V8-powered CLK430 that was seemingly modeled after American muscle cars of yore. With 270 horsepower, 17-inch wheels and stability control, the CLK430 is the rougher-riding and better performing model of the two.

Luxury Sedan: BMW 5 Series

The 5 Series is a favorite of enthusiasts everywhere, and for good reason. Perhaps more than any other carmaker, BMW has the best balance of luxury and performance. Throw in rock-solid build quality, aggressive styling and safety features galore and it's no wonder why this is our favorite luxury sedan. Whether gobbling up hundreds of miles of interstate or dispatching decreasing-radius turns on your favorite canyon run, the 5 Series is unflappable. Sharing the same body, the main difference between the two 5 Series models is the powerplant. The 528i comes with a 2.8-liter, inline six making 193 hp, whereas the 540i has a mighty 4.4-liter, 282-horse V8. Either car can be fitted with a manual or automatic transmission and both offer excellent performance in terms of acceleration, braking, handling and ride. For those with deeper pockets and an even greater need for speed, the 540i offers sports car level athleticism, such as a sub-6-second zero-to-60 time.

Luxury Station Wagon: BMW 5 Series

Station wagons are actually cool these days, appealing to the growing contingent of anti-SUV consumers that wants cargo-carrying capability but none of the compromises in performance and ride that come with most truck-based sport-utes. BMW's excellent, but expensive, 5 Series wagon is the antithesis of the sport-utility vehicle. Choose either the 528i with its 193-hp, twin-cam inline six, or the ground pounding 540i for its 282-hp V8. The stiff premium paid for the 540 may be worth it to enthusiasts who can brag that they own the fastest station wagon sold in America. Others will be happy with the smooth, refined and significantly less expensive 528, the only BMW wagon available with either a stick or automatic. By selecting the 5 Series wagon, you get all the benefits of owning a BMW, with none of the detriments of the traditional station wagon. This family truckster behaves just like the 5 Series sedan; the only indication from behind the wheel that you're piloting a vehicle capable of carrying up to 65 cubic feet of cargo is the reflection you find in the rearview mirror. If we were to buy a luxury station wagon, this Bimmer would be ours.

Convertible: Mazda Miata

Introduced as a 1990 model, Mazda's back-to-basics sports car was a smash success right out of the box. With peppy performance from its four-cylinder engine and handling like that of a go-kart, the small two-seater offered all the fun of the old British roadsters, such as Triumphs and MGs, coupled to superior Japanese reliability and build quality. Mazda redesigned the Miata last year, keeping all the car's inherent goodness while still making some worthwhile changes. The most noteworthy improvements are increased engine output (now rated at 140 hp) and a change from a plastic back window to a glass unit. Exposed headlights and more aggressive body contours freshened up the car's

looks. For a base price of around $20,000, the Miata offers up a fun driving experience unmatched by any other car near its price range.

Sports Car: Chevrolet Corvette

Bet you wish you had a dollar for every time you read some auto scribe blab, "This is the best 'Vette yet!" It seems each time this classic American sports car has gone in for a remake, reviewers come back with that same old saw. But we're here to tell you that (gasp!) this is the best 'Vette yet! Really! Cross-our-hearts, hope-to-die, stick a needle in our eye! Without getting into a discussion of age, let's just say that we're including our experience with big blocks, LT1 small blocks, pace cars, LT5-powered ZR-1s, anniversary editions, second-generation LT1s - you name 'em. And toss in countless hours sampling rides at Bloomington Gold and Corvettes at Carlisle. Granted, the new, 345-horsepower LS1 V8 is not the most awe-inspiring 'Vette engine ever made. But its smoothness almost belies its pushrod architecture. And its delivery of power—when experienced in concert with this car's improved shift action, steering, brakes, suspension, rigidity, comfort, ergonomics and features—positions the Corvette on the top tier of American performance. Its looks might not stoke everybody's fire, but one drive will convince you there's never been a more capable Corvette built than the C5.

Small Pickup: Ford Ranger

Despite a few character flaws, Ford's best-selling Ranger is the truck we'd buy if we needed a small, reliable hauler. We like its rugged good looks, ergonomically correct cabin, and available four-door extended-cab body. A large selection of drivetrains is available to serve a wide variety of needs. You can get your choice of three engines mated to manual or automatic transmissions with two-wheel drive or shift-on-the-fly four-wheel drive. Two trim levels, XL or XLT, are available in regular-cab short- or longbed and extended-cab shortbed configurations. Optional sport appearance and off-road packages dress up a Ranger nicely, and you can even get a stylish FlareSide bed. Rangers work hard and play hard while delivering comfort and convenience in a dependable package. Regardless of what Ranger you choose, you'll be getting one rewarding pickup.

Full-size Pickup: Ford F-Series

Despite the recent introduction of new full-size GM and Toyota pickups, Ford's versatile F-Series lineup offers pickup-truck buyers superior selection from a wide range of light- and heavy-duty models. F-150 light-duty trucks are the best-selling vehicles in the world. Availability ranges from sturdy work trucks to luxurious four-wheelers with four-door extended cabs to a true 360-hp muscle truck that can spank many sport coupes on the street and at the track. Curvaceous sheetmetal, a carlike interior, comfortable seats and powerful overhead-cam engines are hallmarks of the F-150. Super duty F-250 and F-350 pickups have rugged big-rig styling and an interior with an industrial ambience. Regular-, extended- and crew-cab body styles are available; you can tow as much as 10,000 pounds and benefit from GVWRs reaching above 11,200 pounds. Optional on Super Duty trucks is a torque-pig turbodiesel V8 making 500 ft-lbs. of twist at 1,600 rpm, but to get this added grunt you've gotta spend some big green. Yep, Ford's got everyone's pickup needs covered with the incredibly popular F-Series trucks.

Small Van: Honda Odyssey

Just when it was beginning to look like Chrysler had an unbreakable stranglehold on the minivan market, Honda punts them, and everyone else, into oblivion with its all-new Odyssey. If it were just a matter of having that great 3.5-liter VTEC engine, complete with 210 horsepower and 229 foot-pounds of torque, the Odyssey would not be our choice for this category. And the dual power sliding doors on the EX models, while potentially convenient, didn't sway us immediately to the Honda camp either. But once inside, where we could drop the third-row seat into the floor and remove both second-row seats (all in less than 60 seconds), it became apparent where the future of minivans was going, and that Honda was already there. The Odyssey also offers safety, with top scores in frontal-impact, side-impact, and offset-impact crash testing. A stellar engine, functional and roomy interior, along with benchmark safety and Honda quality at a great price. Sorry Chrysler, your reign has ended.

Large Van: Ford Econoline

For sheer people-hauling ability, it doesn't get any better than a domestically built van/wagon. And although sales of large vans are heavily biased towards commercial use, the Edmunds.com staff would choose Ford's

Econoline if given the choice. The current lineup is quite extensive. Depending on what version you pick, the Econoline can haul between seven to 15 passengers and tow from 4,700 to 10,000 pounds. For engines, the main gasoline choices are a 5.4-liter V8 with 255 horsepower and 350 foot-pounds of torque, or a 6.8-liter V10 with 305 horsepower and 420 foot-pounds of torque. There's also a myriad of options and configurations to choose from, ensuring that you can find the exact model to match your needs.

Small SUV: Honda CR-V

How can the CR-V be Edmunds.com's Most Wanted small SUV when the hot-selling Nissan Xterra won our recent comparison test? Simple, our editors are willing to deal with a harsh ride, cramped rear seat and "creative" styling elements in return for a truly capable off-road vehicle with plenty of ground clearance and a torquey six-cylinder engine...at least for the duration of a comparison test that involves extensive off-road driving. However, when it's time to drive a small SUV the way most of us really do (on paved roads with multiple passengers), the Xterra fades fast while the CR-V rises to the occasion. The only small SUV currently on the market with a fully functional rear seat, the CR-V also boasts top-notch ergonomics, quality interior materials, and a pleasant, carlike ride. Don't get us wrong, we love Lenny Kravitz and first-aid kits as much as the next guy. But when it comes to how most of us drive our mini-SUVs most of the time, Honda's CR-V leads the way.

Midsize SUV: Jeep Grand Cherokee

Jeep did an amazing job of updating an already great SUV when it redesigned the Grand Cherokee in 1999. For 2000 the JGC continues to rule the midsize SUV field with its powerful engine offerings, luxurious interior appointments, comfortable and confident on-road ride, and class-leading off-road ability. The 4.0-liter, inline six-cylinder engine that comes standard in the Laredo models was refined in 1999 and makes a healthy 195 horsepower. The optional 4.7-liter V8 bumps peak horsepower to a neck snapping 235 with 295 ft-lbs. of torque. Jeep's Quadra-Drive four-wheel-drive system makes quick work of slippery surfaces while its high-travel suspension allows for "billy-goat" class rock climbing. If your demands for a midsize SUV run to the extremes in both on and off-road capabilities, Jeep's Grand Cherokee is simply the only vehicle worth considering.

Large SUV: GMC Yukon

You've got stuff. You need something to haul your stuff. An '83 Subaru Brat isn't going to cut it. What are you going to get? There are plenty of contestants in the full-size SUV market. All of them are good. But the freshly minted models from GM—the GMC Yukon and Yukon XL, as well as the Chevrolet Tahoe and Suburban—are our top choices. While both the Yukon and Yukon XL are, of course, large, the XL's longer wheelbase endows it with a considerably bigger cargo capacity. Both SUVs can seat up to nine passengers. Visually, the new Yukons don't look considerably different than the ones before. The changes underneath and inside, however, are substantial. GMC has improved both handling and braking. There is more headroom and legroom. The interior design is better. For power, your choices are three different V8s, ranking from 275 to 300 horsepower. Four-wheel drive is available on all models. For most families, we feel the Yukon is plenty big enough. But for those families whose needs and desires exceed a piddly Yukon, the Yukon XL should serve nicely.

Luxury SUV: Lexus LX 470

In the luxury SUV class, excessive is clearly the name of the game. Excessive size, excessive chrome, excessive engine displacement. Interesting then that our pick for the ultimate luxury SUV is a model that is relatively moderate in most respects (except for the excessive price). The Lexus LX 470 is not the biggest, gaudiest or most powerful SUV in the luxury class, but it is easily the most talented. You want a cushy and comfortable on-road ride, plus a palatial interior with high-tech options and you still want it to cross the Rubicon Trail? No problem. Heck, it will even drop down to allow easier entry and egress for passengers, and raise up to offer increased ground clearance during extreme off-road maneuvers. Its adaptive variable suspension can stiffen or loosen up the shock valving in 2.5 milliseconds, depending on road conditions, and its third-row seat is a snap to fold up for additional cargo capacity. We still love Toyota's Land Cruiser and feel it is a better value, but for pure luxury combined with pure utility, see your Lexus dealer today.

Abbreviations

8V	8-valve
12V	12-valve
16V	16-valve
24V	24-valve
2WD	two-wheel drive
4WD	four-wheel drive
ABS	antilock braking system
A/C	air conditioning
ALR	automatic locking retractor
Amp	ampere
AS	all-season
ASR	automatic slip regulation
AT	automatic
Auto	automatic
AWD	all-wheel drive
BSW	black sidewall
Cass.	cassette
CD	compact disc
CFC	chloroflourocarbon
Conv.	convertible
Cpe	coupe
Cu. Ft.	cubic foot (feet)
Cyl.	cylinder
DOHC	dual overhead cam
DRL	daytime running light(s)
DRW	dual rear wheels
DSC	dynamic stability control
EDL	electronic differential lock
EFI	electronic fuel injection
ELR	emergency locking retractor
EQ	equalizer
ETR	electronically-tuned radio
Ext.	extended
ft-lbs.	foot-pounds (measurement of torque)
FWD	front-wheel drive
Gal.	gallon(s)
GAWR	gross axle weight rating
GVW	gross vehicle weight
GVWR	gross vehicle weight rating
GPS	global positioning satellite
Hbk.	hatchback
HD	heavy duty
Hp	horsepower
HUD	heads-up display
HVAC	heating, ventilation and air conditioning
I-4	inline four
I-5	inline five
I-6	inline six
L	liter
LB	longbed
lb(s).	pound(s)
LCD	liquid crystal display
LED	light emitting diode
LEV	low emission vehicle
LH	left hand
LWB	long wheelbase
M&S	mud and snow
mpg	miles per gallon
mph	miles per hour
MPI	multi-port injection
MSRP	manufacturer's suggested retail price
N/A	not available OR not applicable
NC	no charge
NHTSA	National Highway and Traffic Safety Administration
NVH	noise, vibration and harshness
OD	overdrive
OHC	overhead cam
OHV	overhead valve
Opt.	option OR optional
OWL	outline white-letter
Pass.	passenger
Pkg.	package
PRNDL	Park, Reverse, Neutral, Drive, Low
RBL	raised black-letter
Reg.	regular
RH	right hand
r/l	right and left
rpm	revolutions per minute
RWD	rear-wheel drive
SB	shortbed
SBR	steel-belted radial
Sdn	sedan
SFI	sequential fuel injection
SLA	short/long arm
SMPI	sequential multi-port injection
SOHC	single overhead cam
SPI	sequential port injection
SRW	single rear wheels
Std.	standard
SUV	sport utility vehicle
SWB	short wheelbase
TDI	turbocharged direct injection
TOD	torque on demand
V6	V-type six
V8	V-type eight
V10	V-type ten
V12	V-type twelve
VR	v-rated
VSC	vehicle skid contrl
VTEC	variable valve timing and lift electronic control
VVT-i	variable valve timing, intelligence
Wgn.	wagon
WOL	white outline-letter
WS	work series
WSW	white sidewall
W/T	work truck
X-cab	extended cab

GMC's BIG SUV Gets Better, Not Bigger

by Brent Romans
photos courtesy of GMC

If you wanted to be a fly on a wall (and hey, who wouldn't these days?), one of the more interesting places to be the last few years would be General Motors' headquarters. For years, GM had the end-all, be-all, mack-daddy supreme of hauling brood/toys/stuff. Yes, that would be the Suburban. But in 1997, a pesky little thing called the Ford Expedition came along. Bigger than the popular Ford Explorer, the Expedition went head-to-head with the Suburban. And what was surely causing major ants-in-the-pants for GM execs, the Expedition began selling quite well.

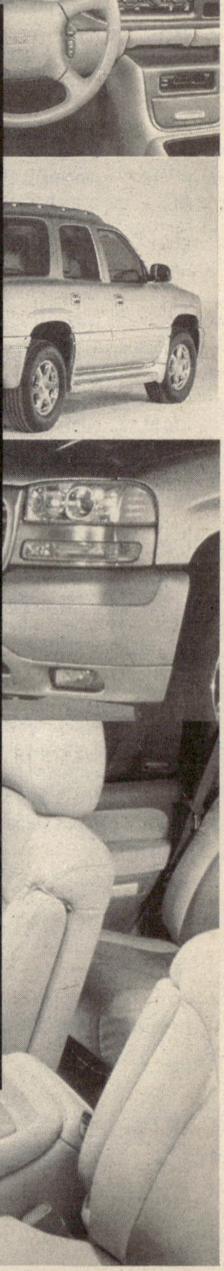

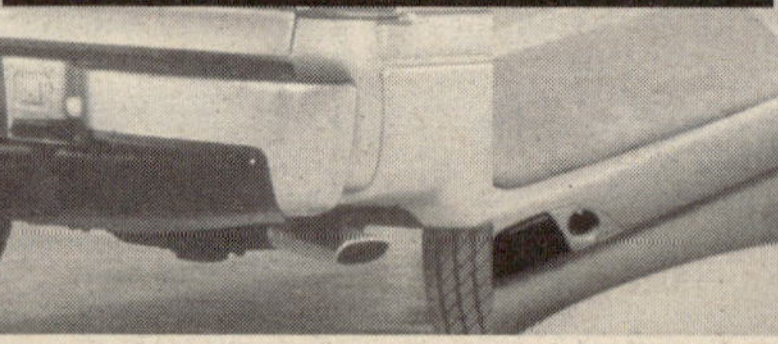

As of July '99, the Expedition had reached a 34 percent segment share. While this number is still below GM's total segment share (at that same July '99 point, GM's full-sized 'utes combined to over 50 percent) we're sure there is welcome relief about having a redesigned 2000 full-sized SUV to bring to the market.

GMC gets two versions of the full-sized 'ute: the Yukon, and the larger Yukon XL. The Yukon XL also comes in two variations, the 1500 (half-ton) and the 2500 (three-quarter ton). The 2500 is the heavy-duty version, with increased towing and hauling capacities. One thing to note is that the Yukon XL name is new. Previously, there was the Yukon and the larger Suburban. But the Suburban tag is now reserved exclusively for Chevrolet, so GMC will use Yukon XL to signify the longer-wheelbase version.

The 2000 Yukon and Yukon XL are based off the Sierra full-sized pickup-truck platform that debuted in 1999. Many of the improvements found on the Sierra can be found on the new full-sized 'ute. GMC has wisely avoided a "We've got the biggest sport-ute!" arms race against Ford and its 2000 Excursion. Instead, GMC has added capability and size where needed.

Like the Sierra update, the 2000 Yukon's looks are evolutionary rather than revolutionary. The overall shape still looks like a Yukon, and the swept-up headlight and front turn-signal assemblies are the most noticeable sign of the pickup truck's lineage. But it looks more muscular than it did before; the hood, fenders, and bumpers are more aggressively styled. GMC's sheetmetal is also different compared to Chevrolet's 2000 Tahoe and Suburban. The Yukon checks in at 76.7 inches in height, 78.9 inches in width, and 198.9 inches in length. The Yukon XL is slightly smaller in height, but 20 inches longer in length. The XL's wheelbase is 130 inches and the Yukon's is 116. All of these numbers are very similar to the '99 models with the exception of height, as both models are now about 4 inches taller.

GMC claims that both Yukons will fit into standard garages. In what was a mildly amusing moment at press introduction, GMC officials trotted out a replica of a garage-door frame and drove a Yukon through it to prove their point. We'll take their word for it until we get our own paws on one, but make no mistake—the Yukon XL ain't no Metro.

Then again, a Metro wouldn't exactly be up to the task of hauling family, cargo, and gear for a week-long vacation. This is something that GM's full-sized 'utes have always excelled at, and things only get better for 2000. The increase in height has positively affected the interior. There is more headroom, legroom, and hip room at almost every position. GMC also says that all of the seats are more comfortable than before. Both the Yukon and the Yukon XL have a maximum carrying capacity of nine people. New for the 2000 Yukon is an optional third-row 50/50 split-folding bench seat. Either of the third-row seat's halves can be flipped and folded to increase cargo space. The seat halves can either be stowed inside the vehicle or removed. With the second- and third-row seats removed, the Yukon provides up to 104.6 cubic feet of cargo space. Doing the same to the XL provides 131.6 cubic feet of space.

GMC has also done a good job of adding content to the interior. Its general feel and layout is considerably better than before. Yukons and XLs equipped with front bucket seats receive a new center console that includes a large lockable storage compartment and four cupholders. The new audio system sounds very impressive. Standard on all Yukons and XLs, the system comes with a CD player and nine speakers (complete with an 8-inch rear-mounted subwoofer!). Other new items that made our "this is cool" list include a more comprehensive gauge cluster, optional rear-seat audio controls, and rear heater ducts on Yukon XLs (optional on Yukons). The luxury package includes heated seats, automatic climate control, and GM's OnStar system. GMC says the new frame has been considerably improved for occupant safety. Side airbags are standard.

While the interior is noticeably improved, driving dynamics are where the Yukon and XL truly shine. Thanks to a body structure that is 23 percent stiffer than '99 models, GMC engineers have been able to better dial in the suspension. All models now have a torsion-bar independent front suspension (from the Sierra pickup) and a five-link coil-spring rear suspension (except for 2500-series XLs, which still use a leaf-spring rear suspension). Simply put, the Yukon and XL don't act their size. On the road, they feel much smaller and lighter than the actual specs would indicate. Wider front and rear tracks enhance stability, and all models feature tighter turning circles than before. During our brief evaluation period at the press intro, the steering seemed to be quicker and more responsive than the versions found on the previous model. A variable-effort power steering system is standard on 4x4 Yukons and 4x4 XL 1500s.

The brakes have also been improved. All four wheels use disc brakes, and the brake components themselves are considerably larger than before. GMC says the 2000 Yukon's brakes should provide shorter stopping distances and better brake pad life. There are also a couple of electronic braking systems to improve braking traction at the rear of the vehicle.

Four-wheel drive is optional on all Yukons and XLs. Models so equipped also get GMC's AutoTrac as standard. This active transfer case normally diverts all power to the rear wheels until slippage is detected. At that point, AutoTrac automatically switches power between the rear and front wheels until the vehicle regains traction. Two-wheel-drive Yukons and XLs offer a new traction control system for more controlled acceleration and stability on slippery surfaces.

One more interesting aspect of the 2000 Yukon platform is the optional Autoride suspension. The Autoride suspension uses special shocks that are automatically adjusting for proper damping. The truck's computer monitors road and vehicle conditions, and can change the shock damping on a continual, 20-millisecond basis, if needed. This system also includes a compressed-air, rear-leveling feature that automatically maintains the vehicle's proper height under all load conditions. As a simple test of the Autoride suspension, we drove a Yukon XL with two total adults and then with six total adults. The Autoride suspension did seem to keep the extra weight in check, though using both extra passengers and a fully loaded trailer would be a truer test.

The 2000 Yukon platform features improved towing ability, thanks to a new selection of V8 engines. The 4.8-liter is the Yukon's standard engine. It provides 275 horsepower at 5,200 rpm and 290 foot-pounds of torque at 4,000 rpm. The 5.3-liter V8 (optional on the Yukon and standard on the XL 1500) generates 285 horsepower and 325 foot-pounds of torque. The topline 6.0-liter V8 found on the XL 2500 makes 300 horsepower at 4,800 rpm and 355 foot-pounds of torque at 4,000 rpm. All three engines are mated to four-speed automatic transmissions. Maximum trailering capacity for the Yukon 4x4 is 8,800 pounds. The 4x2 XL 2500 has a maximum trailering capacity of 10,500 pounds.

There has never been a doubt that GM's full-sized SUVs were the kings of hauling. In our 1999 full-size SUV comparison test, a Chevrolet Suburban K2500 and a GMC Yukon Denali (which, incidentally, takes a one-year hiatus) both beat out a Ford Expedition, but lost to a Toyota Land Cruiser. The Toyota, despite its cost, was superior in interior luxury, highway performance, off-road prowess, and all-around livability. Given that the 2000 GMC Yukon and Yukon XL are improved in many of these areas, it looks like GMC has a solid full-sized SUV on its hands. ■

2000 X5

2000 BMW X5

What's New?

BMW joins the SUV craze with its all-new X5 SAV (sport activity vehicle).

Review

With the success of SUVs in recent years, it was only a matter of time before BMW added their own version to the mix. This year the X5 debuts as the first BMW SAV, or sport activity vehicle. In typical BMW fashion, the German automaker has decided to follow its own path in designing such a vehicle and create one that accurately represents the company's philosophy. What they've come up with is the ultimate, uh, activity machine?

Actually, BMW's goal was to design an SUV that performed extraordinarily on every surface. Thus far that distinction would have been reserved for the Toyota Land Cruiser/Lexus LX 470 twins. But with a powerful 4.4-liter eight-cylinder engine, along with an advanced four-wheel independent suspension and electronic wizardry like dynamic stability control the new X5 blows the Land Cruiser into the weeds as far as on-road performance goes.

Once into the weeds, however, the BMW's unibody design and refined suspension components are outgunned by the Toyota, Land Rover, and GM luxury SUVs, all of which offer superior abilities when the road gets ugly (or simply disappears). BMW freely admits that the X5 is not meant for extreme off-road adventuring, and we'd advise any potential buyers preparing to drop $50K on one to listen.

But BMW knows that most luxury SUV buyers spend about as much time off-roading as they do in the 99-cent store. These customers are looking for a palatial and secure environment to carry them between business meetings and soccer games. Here the X5 scores, with leather and wood grain interior surfaces, a sophisticated all-wheel-drive system, front and rear electric seating adjustments, a navigation system, advanced ABS, rear climate controls, and a total of 10 airbags. Crash testing of the X5 has shown it to set new standards in front- and side-impact protection. From a pure safety standpoint, contends BMW, the X5 is unmatched by anything currently available.

Exterior dimensions for the X5 put it at roughly the same size as the Jeep Grand Cherokee. Its short overhangs and compact size (it's 4.5 inches shorter than a 5 Series sedan) add to the SAV's maneuverability claims. Of course it still features the BMW styling cues we've come to expect, including a twin kidney grille, quad headlights and L-shaped taillights.

The X5 is produced at the Spartanburg plant in South Carolina and will be initially available with the 4.4-liter eight-cylinder engine. Performance from this engine is brisk with a sub-8-second zero-to-60 time. A six-cylinder model will appear in the not-too-distant future and we're certain an M-badged X5, similar in philosophy to the Mercedes ML55, is in the works. Until then, we'll try to get used to the idea of a BMW SUV while simultaneously preparing our automotive psyche for a Porsche-badged utility vehicle in the near future.

Standard Equipment

BASE (5A): 4.4L V8 DOHC SMPI with variable valve timing 32-valve engine, requires premium unleaded fuel; 5-speed electronic OD auto transmission with lock-up; 120-amp alternator; automanual transmission; full-time 4-wheel drive, traction control; dual stainless steel exhaust; electronic stability, front independent strut suspension with anti-roll bar, front coil springs, gas-pressurized front shocks, rear independent multi-link suspension with anti-roll bar, rear coil springs, gas-pressurized rear shocks; power re-circulating ball steering with engine speed-sensing assist; 4-wheel disc brakes with 4-wheel antilock braking system; rear lip spoiler, side impact bars; tailgate rear cargo door; roof rack; front and rear body-colored bumpers with black rub strip; black bodyside molding, rocker panel extensions, black wheel well molding; clearcoat monotone paint; projector beam halogen headlamps with delay-off feature; additional exterior lights include front fog/driving lights; driver's and passenger's power remote body-colored heated folding outside mirrors; front and rear 18" x 8" silver alloy wheels; P255/55HR18 A/S BSW front and rear tires; inside under cargo mounted full-size alloy spare wheel; dual zone front air conditioning with climate control, air filter, rear heat ducts, auto air recirculation; AM/FM stereo, seek-scan, cassette, CD changer pre-wiring, in-dash CD pre-wiring, 10 speakers, theft deterrent, and window grid diversity antenna, radio steering wheel controls; cruise control with steering wheel controls; power heated door locks with 2 stage unlock, remote keyless entry, child safety rear door locks, power remote hatch/trunk release; cell phone pre-wiring, 1 power accessory outlet, driver's foot rest, retained accessory power, smokers' package; instrumentation display includes tachometer, water temperature gauge, in-dash clock, systems monitor, trip odometer; warning indicators include oil pressure, water temp, battery, low oil level, low coolant, lights on, key in ignition, low fuel, low washer fluid, bulb failure, door ajar, trunk ajar, service interval, brake fluid, check control; driver's and passenger's front airbags, driver's and front passenger's door mounted side airbags, overhead airbag; ignition disable, panic alarm, security system; tinted windows, power front and rear windows with front and rear 1-touch down; variable intermittent front windshield wipers with heated jets, sun visor strip, fixed interval rear wiper, rear window defroster, flip up rear window; seating capacity of 5, front bucket seats, adjustable headrests, center armrest with storage, driver's seat includes 6-way power seat, passenger's seat includes 6-way power seat; 50-50 folding rear bench seat with adjustable headrests, center armrest, with storage; front height adjustable seatbelts with front pretensioners; leather seats, leather door trim insert, full cloth headliner, full carpet floor covering, genuine wood trim on instrument panel, leather/wood gear shift knob; memory on driver's seat with 3 memory setting(s) includes settings for exterior mirrors, steering wheel; interior lights include dome light with fade, front and rear reading lights, illuminated entry; leather-wrapped steering wheel with power tilt and telescopic adjustment; dual illuminated vanity mirrors; day/night rearview mirror; full floor console, locking glove box with light, front and rear cupholders, 2 seat back storage pockets, driver's and passenger's door bins, rear door bins; carpeted cargo floor, plastic trunk lid, cargo cover, cargo light; chrome grille, chrome side window moldings, black front windshield molding, black rear window molding and black door handles.

Base Prices

0062	X5 (5A)	44620	49400
Destination Charge:		570	570

Accessories

CODE	DESCRIPTION	INVOICE	MSRP
248	Heated Steering Wheel	130	150
	REQUIRES 383.		
261	Rear Side Impact Airbags	325	385
330	Sport Package	2100	2470
	Includes a black headliner, white blinkers and side marker lights, tires: front P255/50R19 performance, rear P285/45R19 performance, sport seats, sport suspension, Shadowline trim, black chrome exhaust pipes and titanium colored grille insert.		
383	Activity Package	725	850
	Includes heated front seats, headlamp washer, rain-sensing wipers and ski sack.		
403	Power Glass Moonroof	895	1050
412	Retractable Load Floor	325	380
417	Rear Side Window Sunshades	155	180
430	Self-Dimming Interior and Exterior Mirrors	255	300
488	Front Lumbar Support	340	400
508	Park Distance Control	300	350
522	Xenon Headlamps	425	500
555	Multi-Information Display	255	300
	Includes an upgraded on-board computer.		
609	BMW Navigation System	1690	1990
	Includes multi-information display. NOT AVAILABLE with 662.		
662	Radio with CD Player	170	200
	NOT AVAILABLE with 609.		
677	Premium Audio System with DSP	1020	1200
	Includes 12 speakers.		
761	Privacy Glass	235	275

2000 ESCALADE

2000 Cadillac Escalade

What's New?

The big change for 2000 is the availability of vertical-split rear cargo doors in addition to the standard split-tailgate rear-hatch design.

Review

After Cadillac dealers grew tired of watching thousands of new luxury sport-utility customers walk into rival Lincoln showrooms and snap up the big Navigator SUV, General Motors had to do something, and fast. Sure, GM had been working on a new, full-size Cadillac sport-utility project, but engineers couldn't promise it before the 2000 model year. So the marketing guys came up with an idea to clone GMC's new-for-'99 premium SUV, the Yukon Denali, and rebadge it as a Cadillac to give those dealers something to sell until the big new Caddy SUV is ready next year.

Enter the Escalade. As the first truck-based vehicle in Cadillac's 96-year history, Escalade is meant to combine the best features of a luxury car with those of an all-weather, all-terrain vehicle. Exterior styling differs from the donor Denali by the use of a more distinct grille with bright chrome bezel and the Cadillac logo affixed smack dab in the middle. Reflector-optic halogen headlamps and recessed projector-beam fog lamps reside in a smoothie-style front fascia. Body-color cladding and integrated running boards spruce up the flanks, with textured body-color door handles, outside rearview mirrors and color-keyed rails on the flush roof rack completing the monotone look. Out back, a functional step bumper conceals a standard trailer hitch.

The Escalade's interior features upper and lower consoles packed with storage cubbies and other conveniences such as reading lamps, cupholders, a rear power point and audio controls. Instrumentation is backlit in blue with white pointers and includes a tachometer. Luxury touches abound, with Zebrano wood trim, leather front and rear heated seats, and a premium Bose sound system with six-CD changer and single-CD in-dash player. GM's OnStar mobile communications system is standard, as are dual front next-generation airbags and keyless remote entry with an adjustable, shock-sensing anti-theft system.

Powering all this opulence is 5.7-liter pushrod V8 packing 255 horsepower. The Vortec 5700 puts its 330 foot-pounds of torque to the ground via a four-speed automatic transmission and the AutoTrac full-time four-wheel-drive system. When activated, the AutoTrac transfer case will automatically shift from two-wheel drive to 4WD when it senses wheel slippage. Escalade rides on unique six-spoke chromed aluminum wheels wearing Firestone 265/70R-16 touring tires designed especially for sport-utility applications on- and off-road in both wet and dry conditions.

The Escalade provides a "look-at-me" driving experience around town and a king-of-the-road feel out on the highway. There's no question that the big Caddy SUV has gobs of curb appeal, but understand that it is all riding atop a 10-year-old pickup truck design, with all the flaws inherent to its humble underpinnings. The steering is vague, brakes are on the numb side and the ride quality is not as highly tuned as the price tag.

Luxo SUVs are the hot ticket right now, and Escalade fits the bill. But the price walk from an optioned-out GMC Yukon to the dolled-up Cadillac Escalade is rather steep. We think the Escalade will lose much of its luster every time you see a GMC Yukon Denali pass by. It might be wiser to just wait and see what the next-generation big luxury SUV GM is working on will be like.

Standard Equipment

ESCALADE (4A): 5.7L V8 OHV SMPI 16-valve engine; 4-speed electronic OD auto transmission with lock-up; 600-amp battery with run down protection; engine oil cooler; 140-amp alternator; transmission, oil cooler; part-time 4-wheel drive, auto locking hub control and electronic shift, limited slip differential, 3.73 axle ratio; stainless steel exhaust with chrome tip; front independent torsion suspension with anti-roll bar, front torsion springs, front torsion bar, premium front shocks, rigid rear axle suspension with anti-roll bar, rear leaf springs, premium rear shocks; power re-circulating ball steering with vehicle speed-sensing assist; front disc/rear drum brakes with 4-wheel antilock braking system; 30 gal. capacity fuel tank; front license plate bracket, running boards, side impact bars; tailgate rear cargo door; HD class III trailering, trailer harness, trailer hitch; roof rack; front and rear body-colored bumpers with front tow hooks, rear step; body-colored bodyside cladding, body-colored fender flares; clearcoat monotone paint; aero-composite halogen fully auto headlamps with daytime running lights, delay-off feature; additional exterior lights include front fog/driving lights, underhood light; driver's and passenger's power remote body-colored heated folding outside mirrors; front and rear 16" x 7" chrome alloy wheels; P265/70SR16 A/S BSW front and rear tires; underbody mounted full-size steel spare wheel; air conditioning, rear air conditioning with separate controls, rear heat ducts; AM/FM stereo, clock, seek-scan, cassette 6-disc CD changer, 7 premium speakers, amplifier, auto equalizer, theft deterrent, and fixed antenna rear controls; cruise control; power door locks, remote keyless entry, child safety rear door locks, power remote hatch/trunk release; 5 power accessory outlets, retained accessory power, garage door opener, smokers' package, emergency "S.O.S"; instrumentation display includes tachometer, oil pressure gauge, water temperature gauge, volt gauge, compass, exterior temp, trip odometer; warning indicators include battery, lights on, key in ignition, door ajar; driver's and passenger's front airbags; ignition disable, panic alarm, tracker system, security system; deep tinted windows, power front and rear windows with driver's 1-touch down, fixed 1/4 vent windows; variable intermittent front windshield wipers, sun visor strip, flip-up rear window, rear window wiper, rear window defroster; seating capacity of 5, heated-cushion front bucket seats, adjustable tilt headrests, center armrest with storage, driver's seat includes 4-way power seat, 8-way direction control, power 2-way lumbar support, passenger's seat includes 4-way power seat, 8-way direction control, power 2-way lumbar support; heated 60-40 folding rear split-bench seat with adjustable headrests, center armrest with storage; front and rear height adjustable seatbelts; leather seats, leather door trim insert, full cloth headliner, full carpet floor covering with carpeted floor mats, deluxe sound insulation, genuine wood trim on instrument panel, leather-wrapped gear shift knob; interior lights include dome light with fade, front and rear reading lights, 4 door curb lights, illuminated entry; steering wheel with tilt adjustment; dual illuminated vanity mirrors, dual auxiliary visors; auto-dimming day/night rearview mirror; full floor console, full overhead console with storage, glove box with light, front and rear cupholders, 2 seat back storage pockets, driver's and passenger's door bins; carpeted cargo floor, carpeted trunk lid, cargo cover, cargo net, cargo light; chrome grille, black side window moldings, black front windshield molding, black rear window molding and body-colored door handles.

CODE	DESCRIPTION	INVOICE	MSRP
	Base Prices		
6K10706	Escalade 4WD (4A)	42451	46225
Destination Charge:		675	675
	Accessories		
RM6	New Jersey Cost Surcharge	83	NC

2000 ASTRO

2000 Chevrolet Astro

What's New?

Retained accessory power and additional warning chimes are added to this ancient van for 2000. Also new are automatic headlights with a flash-to-pass feature, remote keyless entry, battery rundown protection, lockout protection, and a tow/haul trailering mode for the transmission. The ABS, engine and exhaust have been improved, and a plastic 27-gallon fuel tank is standard.

Review

Models that have been around for a while can still deliver impressive value - and valor. That's true of the long-lived Astro van, a staple in Chevy's lineup since 1985. This hard-working passenger van, sporting a conventionally boxy shape, has - if anything - mellowed with age.

No, you don't get the curvaceous contours or the ergonomics of a Chrysler mini or a Ford Windstar. What you do acquire is a highly practical carrier that can be equipped to suit just about any family, trimmed in any of three levels. Depending on configuration, Astros can seat up to eight passengers and haul as much as three tons.

Out on the road, rolling hour after hour, is where the Astro demonstrates its true worth. Taller than its likely rivals, Astros are admittedly more truck-like in temperament, but deliver a pleasant highway ride with competent handling for long journeys. Seats are a little short, but comfortable, in both the front and center positions. Unfortunately, overly small front footwells drop the comfort level a notch, especially after long stints behind the wheel. A 190-horsepower, 4.3-liter V6 is standard, putting power through a smooth-shifting, four-speed electronically controlled automatic transmission to drive the rear wheels.

Dual depowered airbags and antilock brakes are standard. You get only one body choice: the extended-length version. The lower-priced rear-drive rendition is the ticket for hauling plenty of weight. All-wheel-drive costs more and delivers improved wet-pavement traction, but slurps up more fuel along the route.

For 2000, Chevy has made improvements to the engine, antilock braking system, and exhaust system in an effort to make the Astro quieter and more reliable. A plastic fuel tank is new, and Astro is now equipped with retained accessory power and battery rundown protection. A tow/haul mode on the transmission holds revs longer when Astro is laden with cargo or a trailer, and remote keyless entry is standard on LS and LT models. Headlights that automatically activate in low-light situations have been added, along with a flash-to-pass feature for those interested in inciting road rage. Additional warning chimes remind the driver if the keys have been left in the ignition, among other things, and lockout protection comes with power door locks this year.

Solid and substantial, Astros remain tempting - if dated - choices, whether for hauling passengers or cargo. This is one small van that can boast big-van capacity and versatility.

Standard Equipment

BASE RWD PASSENGER VAN (4A): 4.3L V6 OHV SMPI 12-valve engine; 4-speed electronic OD auto transmission with lock-up; 600-amp battery with run down protection; engine oil cooler, HD radiator; 100-amp alternator; transmission, oil cooler; rear-wheel drive, 3.23 axle ratio; partial stainless steel exhaust; front independent suspension with anti-roll bar, front coil springs, rigid rear axle suspension with rear leaf springs; power re-circulating ball steering with engine speed-sensing assist; front disc/rear drum brakes with 4-wheel antilock braking system; 27 gal. capacity fuel tank; front license plate bracket, side impact bars; 3 doors with sliding right rear passenger's door, split swing-out rear cargo door; trailer harness; front and rear body-colored bumpers with rear step; monotone paint; sealed beam halogen fully auto headlamps with daytime running lights; driver's and passenger's manual black folding outside mirrors; front and rear 15" x 6" painted styled steel wheels; P215/75SR15 A/S BSW front and rear tires; underbody mounted compact steel spare wheel; air conditioning, rear heat ducts; AM/FM stereo, clock, seek-scan, 6 speakers, and fixed antenna; child safety rear door locks; 4 power accessory outlets, retained accessory power, smokers' package; instrumentation display includes oil pressure gauge, water temperature gauge, volt gauge, trip odometer; warning indicators include battery, lights on, key in ignition; driver's and passenger's front airbags; ignition disable; tinted windows, vented rear windows, fixed 1/4 vent windows; variable intermittent front windshield wipers; seating capacity of 8, front captain's seats, fixed headrests, driver's and passenger's armrests, driver's seat includes 4-way direction control, lumbar support, passenger's seat includes 4-way direction control, lumbar support; removable 2nd row bench seat with adjustable headrests; removable 3rd row bench seat with adjustable headrest; front height adjustable seatbelts; cloth seats, cloth door trim insert, full cloth headliner, full carpet floor covering, deluxe sound insulation; interior lights include dome light with delay; vanity mirrors, dual auxiliary visors; day/night rearview mirror; engine cover console with storage, front and rear cupholders, 2 seat back storage pockets, driver's and passenger's door bins; carpeted cargo floor, plastic trunk lid, cargo light; argent grille, black side window moldings, black front windshield molding, black rear window molding and black door handles.

BASE AWD PASSENGER VAN (4A) (in addition to or instead of BASE RWD PASSENGER VAN (4A) equipment): Full-time all-wheel drive, 3.42 axle ratio; front independent torsion suspension with anti-roll bar, front torsion springs and front torsion bar.

Base Prices

CM11006-ZW9	Base RWD Passenger Van (4A)	19536	21587
CL11006-ZW9	Base AWD Passenger Van (4A)	21618	23887
Destination Charge:		620	620

Accessories

—	Leather Seat Trim *REQUIRES 1SE.*	817	950
1SA	Preferred Equipment Group 1SA *Includes Base Decor package and 8-person seating.*	NC	NC
1SC	Preferred Equipment Group 1SC (AWD)	2860	3326
	Manufacturer Discount	(2247)	(2613)
	Net Price *Includes 8-person seating, LS Decor package: uplevel chrome grille with accents, aero-composite headlamps, custom cloth seat trim, carpet trunk lid trim, rear vented*	613	713

CODE	DESCRIPTION	INVOICE	MSRP
	window, swing-out rear door windows, lower body side cladding, front and rear color-keyed floor mats, dual illuminated visor vanity mirrors, overhead console, cargo net, convenience group: tilt steering wheel, speed control; power convenience group: power windows, power door lock system; deep tinted solar-ray glass, electric remote black mirrors, AM/FM stereo with cassette and seek/scan, black luggage carrier, remote keyless entry, remote panic alarm, roof console with electronics, compass, exterior temperature instrumentation and wheels: styled steel chrome-cladded.		
1SC	**Preferred Equipment Group 1SC (RWD)**	2860	3326
	Manufacturer Discount	(1817)	(2113)
	Net Price	1043	1213
	Includes 8-person seating, LS Decor package: uplevel chrome grille with accents, aero-composite headlamps, custom cloth seat trim, carpet trunk lid trim, rear vented window, swing-out rear door windows, lower body side cladding, front and rear color-keyed floor mats, dual illuminated visor vanity mirrors, overhead console, cargo net, convenience group: tilt steering wheel, speed control; power convenience group: power windows, power door lock system; deep tinted solar-ray glass, electric remote black mirrors, AM/FM stereo with cassette and seek/scan, black luggage carrier, remote keyless entry, remote panic alarm, roof console with electronics, compass, exterior temperature instrumentation and wheels: styled steel chrome-cladded.		
1SC	**Preferred Equip. Grp. 1SC with Passenger's Storage Compartment (AWD)**	2886	3356
	Manufacturer Discount	(2247)	(2613)
	Net Price	639	743
	Includes 8-person seating, LS Decor package: uplevel chrome grille with accents, aero-composite headlamps, custom cloth seat trim, carpet trunk lid trim, rear vented window, swing-out rear door windows, lower body side cladding, front and rear color-keyed floor mats, dual illuminated visor vanity mirrors, overhead console, cargo net, convenience group: tilt steering wheel, speed control; power convenience group: power windows, power door lock system; deep tinted solar-ray glass, electric remote black mirrors, AM/FM stereo with cassette and seek/scan, black luggage carrier, remote keyless entry, remote panic alarm, roof console with electronics, compass, exterior temperature instrumentation and wheels: styled steel chrome-cladded.		
1SC	**Preferred Equip. Grp. 1SC with Passenger's Storage Compartment (RWD)**	2886	3356
	Manufacturer Discount	(1817)	(2113)
	Net Price	1069	1243
	Includes 8-person seating, LS Decor package: uplevel chrome grille with accents, aero-composite headlamps, custom cloth seat trim, carpet trunk lid trim, rear vented window, swing-out rear door windows, lower body side cladding, front and rear color-keyed floor mats, dual illuminated visor vanity mirrors, overhead console, cargo net, convenience group: tilt steering wheel, speed control; power convenience group: power windows, power door lock system; deep tinted solar-ray glass, electric remote black mirrors, AM/FM stereo with cassette and seek/scan, black luggage carrier, remote keyless entry, remote panic alarm, roof console with electronics, compass, exterior temperature instrumentation and wheels: styled steel chrome-cladded.		

CODE	DESCRIPTION	INVOICE	MSRP
1SE	Preferred Equipment Group 1SE	5722	6653
	Manufacturer Discount	(688)	(800)
	Net Price	5034	5853
	Includes 8-person seating, LT Decor package: cargo net, convenience group: tilt steering wheel, speed control; power convenience group: power windows, power door lock system; deep tinted solar-ray glass, electric remote black mirrors, black luggage carrier, remote keyless entry, remote panic alarm, roof console with electronics, compass, exterior temperature instrumentation, black leather-wrapped steering wheel, uplevel chrome grille with accents, aero-composite headlamps, body side accent stripe, dual illuminated visor vanity mirrors, front and rear reading lights, dual door curb/courtesy lights, carpet trunk lid trim, power windows, special cloth seat trim, swing-out rear door windows, lower body side cladding, front and rear color-keyed floor mats, keyless remote lock, cargo dutch doors, rear window wiper/ washer, electric rear window defogger, AM/FM stereo with CD and cassette, front and rear air conditioning, 105-amp alternator, rear heater, wheels: brushed aluminum and 6-way power driver's seat.		
1SE	Preferred Equipment Group 1SE with Passenger's Storage Compartment	5747	6683
	Manufacturer Discount	(688)	(800)
	Net Price	5059	5883
	Includes 8-person seating, LT Decor package: cargo net, convenience group: tilt steering wheel, speed control; power convenience group: power windows, power door lock system; deep tinted solar-ray glass, electric remote black mirrors, black luggage carrier, remote keyless entry, remote panic alarm, roof console with electronics, compass, exterior temperature instrumentation, black leather-wrapped steering wheel, uplevel chrome grille with accents, aero-composite headlamps, body side accent stripe, dual illuminated visor vanity mirrors, front and rear reading lights, dual door curb/courtesy lights, carpet trunk lid trim, power windows, special cloth seat trim, swing-out rear door windows, lower body side cladding, front and rear color-keyed floor mats, keyless remote lock, cargo dutch doors, rear window wiper/ washer, electric rear window defogger, AM/FM stereo with CD and cassette, front and rear air conditioning, 105-amp alternator, rear heater, wheels: brushed aluminum and 6-way power driver's seat.		
AG1	6-Way Power Driver's Seat	206	240
	REQUIRES 1SC. INCLUDED in 1SE.		
AG2	6-Way Power Passenger's Seat	206	240
	Includes front underseat storage delete. REQUIRES 1SC or 1SE.		
AJ1	Deep Tinted Solar-Ray Glass	249	290
	INCLUDED in 1SC, 1SE.		
AN0	Seat Package	144	168
	Includes inboard/outboard armrests and manually adjustable lumbar support.		
AP9	Cargo Net	26	30
	INCLUDED in 1SC, 1SE.		
AU0	Remote Keyless Entry	146	170
	Includes remote panic alarm. INCLUDED in 1SC, 1SE.		
AU3	Power Door Lock System	192	223
B37	Front and Rear Color-Keyed Floor Mats	59	69

CODE	DESCRIPTION	INVOICE	MSRP
B88	Body Side Molding *NOT AVAILABLE with BVE.*	104	121
BVE	Running Boards *Includes cladding. REQUIRES PF3 or Z82 or AG2 or Z82 and (1SA or 1SC). NOT AVAILABLE with B88.*	344	400
BX2	Lower Body Side Cladding *REQUIRES 1SC or 1SE.*	190	221
BX2	Lower Body Side Cladding *REQUIRES ZY2 and (1SC or 1SE).*	301	350
C36	Rear Heater *REQUIRES 1SA or 1SC. INCLUDED in 1SE.*	176	205
C69	Front and Rear Air Conditioning *Includes 105-amp alternator. REQUIRES 1SA or 1SC. INCLUDED in 1SE.*	450	523
C95	Reading Lamps *REQUIRES 1SA. NOT AVAILABLE with DK8.*	28	33
D48	Electric Remote Black Mirrors *Below-eye-line exterior. REQUIRES ZQ2 and 1SA. INCLUDED in 1SC, 1SE.*	84	98
DK6	Overhead Console *REQUIRES 1SA.*	71	83
DK6	Overhead Console with Illuminated Sunshades *REQUIRES 1SA.*	137	159
DK8	Roof Console with Electronics *Includes compass and exterior temperature instrumentation. REQUIRES 1SA. NOT AVAILABLE with C95. INCLUDED in 1SC, 1SE.*	192	223
E54	Cargo Dutch Doors *Includes rear window wiper/washer and electric rear window defogger. REQUIRES 1SA. INCLUDED in 1SE.*	445	518
G80	Locking Differential	217	252
GT4	3.73 Axle Ratio	NC	NC
GU6	3.42 Axle Ratio	NC	NC
NP5	Black Leather-Wrapped Steering Wheel *REQUIRES 1SC.*	46	54
PA6	Wheels: Styled Steel Painted Silver *REQUIRES 1SA. NOT AVAILABLE with PC2, PF3.*	79	92
PC2	Wheels: Styled Steel Chrome-Cladded *REQUIRES 1SA. NOT AVAILABLE with PA6, PF3. INCLUDED in 1SC.*	292	340
PC2	Wheels: Styled Steel Chrome-Cladded *REQUIRES 1SE. INCLUDED in 1SC.*	(22)	(25)
PF3	Wheels: Brushed Aluminum *REQUIRES 1SC. INCLUDED in 1SE.*	22	25
PF3	Wheels: Brushed Aluminum *REQUIRES 1SC. NOT AVAILABLE with PA6, PC2. INCLUDED in 1SE.*	314	365
QCM	Tires: P215/75R15 AS WOL SBR *Includes front, rear and compact spare.*	76	88
R6M	New Jersey Cost Surcharge	64	NC
TL1	Uplevel Chrome Grille with Accents *Includes aero-composite headlamps. REQUIRES 1SA.*	189	220

CODE	DESCRIPTION	INVOICE	MSRP
UG1	3-Channel Garage Door Opener *REQUIRES DK8.*	99	115
UK6	Rear Seat Audio Controls *Includes jacks. REQUIRES (ULO or UPO) and (1SC or 1SE). NOT AVAILABLE with UNO.*	108	125
ULO	Radio: AM/FM Stereo with Cassette and Automatic Tone Control *Includes digital clock, theft lock and speed compensated volume. REQUIRES 1SC. NOT AVAILABLE with UPO, UNO.*	138	160
ULO	Radio: AM/FM Stereo with Cassette and Automatic Tone Control *Includes digital clock, theft lock and speed compensated volume. REQUIRES 1SE. NOT AVAILABLE with UNO, UPO.*	264	307
UM6	Radio: AM/FM Stereo with Cassette *Includes digital clock. REQUIRES 1SA. INCLUDED in 1SC.*	126	147
UNO	Radio: AM/FM Stereo with CD *Includes seek-scan, auto tone control, digital clock, theft lock and speed compensated volume. REQUIRES 1SC. NOT AVAILABLE with UK6, ULO, UPO.*	224	260
UNO	Radio: AM/FM Stereo with CD *Includes seek-scan, auto tone control, digital clock, theft lock and speed compensated volume. REQUIRES 1SE. NOT AVAILABLE with ULO, UPO, UK6.*	350	407
UPO	Radio: AM/FM Stereo with CD and Cassette *Includes seek-scan, auto tone control, digital clock, cassette tape with search and repeat, theft lock and speed compensated volume. REQUIRES 1SA. NOT AVAILABLE with ULO, UNO. INCLUDED in 1SE.*	436	507
UPO	Radio: AM/FM Stereo with CD and Cassette *Includes seek-scan, auto tone control, digital clock, cassette tape with search and repeat, theft lock and speed compensated volume. REQUIRES 1SC. NOT AVAILABLE with ULO, UNO. INCLUDED in 1SE.*	310	360
V10	Cold Climate Package *Includes coolant protection and engine block heater.*	40	46
V54	Black Luggage Carrier *REQUIRES 1SA. INCLUDED in 1SC, 1SE.*	108	126
Z82	HD Trailering Special Equipment *Includes platform trailer hitch and 8-lead wiring harness.*	266	309
ZP7	7-Person Seating *Includes 4 high back buckets with seat back recliner, 3-passenger bench and seat package. REQUIRES 1SA.*	494	574
ZP7	7-Person Seating *Includes 4 high back buckets with seat back recliner, 3-passenger bench and seat package. REQUIRES 1SC.*	273	318
ZP7	7-Person Seating *Includes 4 high back buckets with seat back recliner, 3-passenger bench and seat package. REQUIRES 1SE.*	NC	NC
ZQ2	Power Convenience Group *Includes power windows and power door lock system. REQUIRES 1SA. INCLUDED in 1SC, 1SE.*	408	474

CODE	DESCRIPTION	INVOICE	MSRP
ZQ3	Convenience Group *Includes tilt steering wheel and speed control. REQUIRES 1SA. INCLUDED in 1SC, 1SE.*	329	383
ZY2	Two-Tone Appearance Paint *REQUIRES BVE.*	NC	NC

2000 BLAZER

2000 Chevrolet Blazer

What's New?

Base models are dropped as Chevy learns SUV buyers prioritize goodies and a luxury image rather than rugged go-anywhere capability. The engine, exhaust and ABS are refined for increased durability, and exterior trim on some models is cosmetically modified. Two new colors are available.

Review

Back in 1982, Chevrolet rolled out the S-10 Blazer, the first modern compact sport-utility vehicle. Eighteen years later, the Blazer remains a strong seller in one of the hottest automotive markets. Take only one good look and it's easy to see why the attractive Blazer has such lasting appeal. Powered by a stout 4.3-liter, 190-horsepower V6 and available with several suspension choices, the Blazer can be tailored to specific needs, with either two-wheel or four-wheel drive, with two doors or four.

There are accommodations for as many as six passengers in the bigger Blazer, if they don't mind squeezing. There's lots of cargo space too, with the spare tire mounted underneath the cargo floor on four-door models. Chevy claims that with the rear seat folded, a washing machine box will fit into the cargo bay. Sadly, the Blazer's interior is marred by acres of chintzy plastic and precious little rear foot room in front of a rather low and mushy seat. Adult rear-seat riders are likely to complain loudly.

Off road is not where the Blazer shines brightest, despite the availability of a ZR2 super-duty suspension package. Offered only on two-door 4WD models, the ZR2 Blazer has a special chassis with a wider track, huge 31-inch tires, specially tuned Bilstein 46mm shocks, and an underbody shield package. Regular Blazers are capable enough for two-track dirt, but serious off-road adventures would be better handled by something with a little more wheel travel.

On the other hand, as a road-going hauler the Blazer is quite capable. All 4x4 models can be equipped with the available AutoTrac push-button electronic transfer case. AutoTrac automatically senses wheel slippage and sends power to the axle with the most traction, which makes those old full-time all-wheel-drive systems obsolete. This setup takes the guesswork out of sure-footed travel over wet or snowy pavement.

GM's PassLock anti-theft system, automatic headlight control and four-wheel disc brakes are all standard. Heated exterior mirrors and an electrochromic rearview mirror are standard on LT models, and optional on the LS. TrailBlazers come fully stocked with a long list of standard equipment.

For 2000, Chevrolet has dropped base models from the roster, leaving three trim levels: LS, LT and TrailBlazer. The automaker also has enhanced the durability of several key components ranging from the engine and airbag system to the brakes and exhaust. Other changes are limited to minor trim modifications, two new colors and the addition of a CD player to uplevel sound systems.

When the current Blazer debuted for the 1995 model year, it won the North American Truck of the Year award. Smart styling, a powerful drivetrain and reasonable pricing made it an instant hit. Lately, however, the bar has been raised over the Blazer, as most competitors have been completely redesigned or substantially improved since its debut. Simply put, with the new product in the compact-SUV world, this Chevy isn't the value it used to be.

Standard Equipment

LS 2WD 2-DOOR (5M): 4.3L V6 OHV SMPI 12-valve engine; 5-speed OD manual transmission; 525-amp HD battery with run down protection; engine oil cooler; 100-amp alternator; transmission oil cooler; rear-wheel drive, limited slip differential, 3.42 axle ratio; stainless steel exhaust; touring ride suspension, front independent suspension with anti-roll bar, front coil springs, rigid rear axle suspension with anti-roll bar, rear leaf springs; power re-circulating ball steering; 4-wheel disc brakes with 4-wheel antilock braking system; 19 gal. capacity fuel tank; front license plate bracket, side impact bars; tailgate rear cargo door; trailer harness; front and rear body-colored bumpers with front black rub strip, rear step; monotone paint; aero-composite halogen fully auto headlamps with daytime running lights; additional exterior lights include underhood light; driver's and passenger's manual black folding outside mirrors; front and rear 15" x 7" painted styled steel wheels; P235/70SR15 A/S BSW front and rear tires; inside mounted full-size steel spare wheel; air conditioning, rear heat ducts; AM/FM stereo, clock, seek-scan, cassette, 4 speakers, and fixed antenna; rear window power remote release; 1 power accessory outlet, retained accessory power; instrumentation display includes tachometer, oil pressure gauge, water temperature gauge, volt gauge, trip odometer; warning indicators include battery, lights on, key in ignition; driver's and passenger's front airbags; ignition disable; deep tinted windows, fixed 1/4 vent windows; variable intermittent front windshield wipers, flip-up rear window; seating capacity of 5, front bucket seats, fixed headrests, center armrest with storage, driver's seat includes 4-way direction control, lumbar support, passenger's seat includes 4-way direction control, lumbar support, easy entry; 50-50 folding rear split-bench seat with adjustable headrests; cloth seats, cloth door trim insert, full cloth headliner, full carpet floor covering with carpeted floor mats; interior lights include dome light with delay; passenger's side vanity mirror; day/night rearview mirror; full floor console, glove box with light, front and rear cupholders, instrument panel bin, interior concealed storage, driver's and passenger's door bins; carpeted cargo floor, cargo tie downs, cargo light; chrome grille, black side window moldings, black front windshield molding, black rear window molding and black door handles.

LS 2WD 4-DOOR (4A) (in addition to or instead of LS 2WD 2-DOOR (4A) equipment): 4-speed electronic OD auto transmission with lock-up; 3.08 axle ratio; comfort ride suspension, 18 gal. capacity fuel tank; front chrome bumper with black rub strip, rear body-colored bumper; child safety rear door locks; seating capacity of 6, 60-40 split-bench front seat, fixed headrests, driver's seat includes 4-way direction control, passenger's seat includes 4-way direction control; 60-40 folding rear split-bench seat with adjustable headrests; 2 seat back storage pockets and rear door bins.

LT 2WD (4A) (in addition to or instead of LS 2WD 4-DOOR (4A) equipment): Touring ride suspension; black bodyside molding; driver's and passenger's power remote black heated folding outside mirrors; AM/FM stereo, clock, seek-scan, single CD, 6 speakers, auto equalizer, theft deterrent, and fixed antenna; power door locks with 2 stage unlock, power remote hatch/trunk release, power rear window remote release; 2 power accessory outlets; ignition disable, panic alarm; driver's seat includes 4-way power seat, 8-way direction control and power 2-way lumbar support.

TRAILBLAZER 2WD (4A) (in addition to or instead of LT 2WD (4A) equipment): Front and rear body-colored bumpers with front black rub strip; body-colored bodyside molding; P235/70SR15 A/T BSW front and rear tires; air conditioning with climate control, rear heat ducts; leatherette door trim insert and auto-dimming day/night rearview mirror.

LS 4WD (in addition to or instead of LS 2WD equipment): Part-time 4-wheel drive, auto locking hub control and electronic shift, 3.42 axle ratio; front torsion springs, front torsion bar and front tow hooks.

LT 4WD/TRAILBLAZER 4WD (in addition to or instead of LT 2WD/TRAILBLAZER 2WD equipment): AutoTrac part-time 4-wheel drive, auto locking hub control and electronic shift, 3.42 axle ratio; front torsion springs, front torsion bar and front tow hooks.

Base Prices

CS10516-E55	LS 2WD 2-Door (5M)	17168	18970
CT10516-E55	LS 4WD 2-Door (5M)	19883	21970
CS10506-YC5	LS 2WD 4-Door (4A)	22236	24570
CS10506-YC6	LT 2WD 4-Door (4A)	23865	26370
CT10506-YC5	LS 4WD 4-Door (4A)	24046	26570
CT10506-YC6	LT 4WD 4-Door (4A)	25856	28570
CS10506-CTB	Trailblazer 2WD 4-Door (4A)	26761	29570
CT10506-CTB	Trailblazer 4WD 4-Door (4A)	28571	31570
Destination Charge:		550	550

Accessories

1SA	Preferred Equipment Group 1SA (LS) *Includes vehicle with standard equipment. REQUIRES PNV or P16. NOT AVAILABLE with DK8, UL0, UP0, UQ3, U1Z, CF5, UK3, ZY7, RYJ.*	NC	NC
1SB	Preferred Equipment Group 1SB (LS 2-Door) *Includes AM/FM stereo with seek/scan, auto tone control, clock and cassette, power windows, power locks, exterior remote heated mirrors, electric rear window release, rear window defogger, rear wiper/washer, tilt steering wheel, cruise control and deep tinted glass with dark tint. NOT AVAILABLE with U1Z.*	903	1050
1SB	Preferred Equipment Group 1SB (LS 4-Door) *Includes AM/FM stereo with seek/scan, auto tone control, clock and cassette, power windows, power locks, exterior remote heated mirrors, electric rear window release, rear window defogger, rear wiper/washer, tilt steering wheel, cruise control, body side moldings and deep tinted glass with dark tint. REQUIRES PNV or P16. NOT AVAILABLE with UP0, ZR2.*	1032	1200
1SC	Preferred Equipment Group 1SC (LS 2-Door) *Includes AM/FM stereo with seek/scan, auto tone control, clock and CD, power windows, power locks, exterior remote heated mirrors, electric rear window release, rear window defogger, rear wiper/washer, tilt steering wheel, cruise control, deep tinted glass with dark tint, remote keyless entry with content theft alarm, 6-way*	1978	2300

CODE	DESCRIPTION	INVOICE	MSRP
	power driver's seat, overhead console including compass and outside temperature gauge. REQUIRES PNV or P16.		
1SC	Preferred Equipment Group 1SC (LS 4-Door) *Includes AM/FM stereo with seek/scan, auto tone control, clock and cassette, power windows, power locks, exterior remote heated mirrors, electric rear window release, rear window defogger, rear wiper/washer, tilt steering wheel, cruise control, body side moldings, deep tinted glass with dark tint, overhead console including compass and outside temperature gauge and bucket seats with center console.*	1247	1450
1SD	Preferred Equipment Group 1SD (LT) *Includes vehicle with standard equipment. NOT AVAILABLE with KA1.*	NC	NC
1SE	Preferred Equipment Group 1SE (LT) *Includes 8-way leather power driver's seat and auto electronic air conditioning.*	860	1000
1SF	Preferred Equipment Group 1SF (LT) *Includes 8-way leather power driver's seat, auto electronic air conditioning, 2-position memory driver's seat, 8-way power passenger's seat, deluxe overhead console, Homelink 3-channel programmable garage door opener, enhanced electronic display with compass and temperature gauge, trip computer, fog lamps, electrochromic interior rear view mirror and electrochromic exterior outside rear view mirrors with heater.*	1634	1900
1SG	Preferred Equipment Group 1SG (TrailBlazer) *Includes vehicle with standard equipment.*	NC	NC
ANL	Fog Lamps (LS Except 2-Door 4WD/LT) *NOT AVAILABLE with 1SA. INCLUDED in 1SG, 1SF.*	99	115
CF5	Electric Tilt and Slide Sunroof *Includes mini console. NOT AVAILABLE with 1SA.*	645	750
DK7	Custom Overhead Console (LS 2-Door) *Includes compass/exterior temperature display. NOT AVAILABLE with 1SA, DK8. INCLUDED in 1SC.*	126	147
DK8	Deluxe Overhead Console (LS) *Includes Homelink 3-channel programmable transmitter, enhanced electronic display and trip computer. NOT AVAILABLE with 1SA. INCLUDED in 1SG, 1SF.*	238	277
DK8	Deluxe Overhead Console (LS/LT) *Includes Homelink 3-channel programmable transmitter, enhanced electronic display and trip computer. REQUIRES 1SC. NOT AVAILABLE with 1SA. INCLUDED in 1SG, 1SF.*	112	130
FE9	Federal Emission Requirements	NC	NC
G80	Locking Differential	240	270
GT4	3.73 Axle Ratio (4WD) *REQUIRES G80. NOT AVAILABLE with Z83, Z82, ZQ1, GU4.*	NC	NC
GU4	3.08 Axle Ratio (All Except TrailBlazer 4WD) *REQUIRES Z83 or ZQ1. NOT AVAILABLE with G80, ZR2, GT4.*	NC	NC
KA1	Driver's and Passenger's Heated Seats (LT/TrailBlazer) *NOT AVAILABLE with 1SD.*	215	250
M30	Transmission: 4-Speed Automatic with OD (2-Door) *Includes brake-transmission shift interlock.*	860	1000

CODE	DESCRIPTION	INVOICE	MSRP
NP8	Autotrac Active Transfer Case (LS 4WD)	194	225
P16	Spare Wheel and Tire Carrier (LS 4WD 2-Door) *Includes spare tire and cover. NOT AVAILABLE with PNV.*	137	159
PNV	Outside Spare Tire Carrier Not Desired (LS 2-Door) *NOT AVAILABLE with P16, QEB.*	NC	NC
QBG	Tires: P235/70R15 AS WOL SBR (All Except LS 4-Door) *NOT AVAILABLE with QCA, QCE, Z83, QEB, QJJ, ZR2, ZQ1.*	114	133
QBG	Tires: P235/70R15 AS WOL SBR (LS 4-Door) *NOT AVAILABLE with QCA, QCE, ZQ1, QEB.*	114	133
QCA	Tires: P205/75R15 AS WOL (All Except LS 2-Door) *REQUIRES ZQ1. NOT AVAILABLE with QBG, QCE, QEB.*	NC	NC
QCA	Tires: P205/75R15 AS WOL SBR (LS 2-Door) *REQUIRES Z83. NOT AVAILABLE with QBG, QCE, QEB, QJJ, ZR2.*	NC	NC
QCE	Tires: P205/75R15 AS BSW (LS 4-Door/LT/2WD TrailBlazer) *REQUIRES ZQ1. NOT AVAILABLE with QBG, QCA, QEB.*	NC	NC
QCE	Tires: P205/75R15 AS BSW SBR (LS 2-Door) *REQUIRES Z83. NOT AVAILABLE with QBG, QCA, QEB, QJJ, ZR2.*	NC	NC
QEB	Tires: P235/75R15 AT WOL (LS 4WD 2-Door/LT 4WD) *REQUIRES P16. NOT AVAILABLE with QBG, QCE, QCA, QJJ, PNV, ZR2, Z83, ZQ1.*	144	168
R6M	New Jersey Cost Surcharge	70	NC
RYJ	Rear Compartment Shade (4WD - LT/TrailBlazer)	NC	NC
RYJ	Rear Compartment Shade (LS 4-Door) *NOT AVAILABLE with 1SA.*	59	69
U1Z	Remote 6-Disc CD Changer *REQUIRES UL0 or 1SC. NOT AVAILABLE with UP0, 1SA, 1SB.*	340	395
UA1	690 CCA HD Delco Freedom Battery	48	56
UK3	Redundant Steering Wheel Audio Controls *NOT AVAILABLE with 1SA.*	108	125
UL0	Radio: AM/FM Stereo with Cassette and Automatic Tone Control *Includes enhanced performance speaker system, seek/scan, auto tone control, digital clock, theft lock and speed compensated volume. NOT AVAILABLE with UP0, 1SA. INCLUDED in 1SB, 1SC.*	NC	NC
UN0	Radio: AM/FM Stereo with CD and Automatic Tone Control (LS) *Includes enhanced performance speaker system, seek/scan, auto tone control, digital clock, theft lock and speed compensated volume. REQUIRES 1SB or 1SC. NOT AVAILABLE with 1SA, UL0, UP0, U1Z. INCLUDED in 1SD, 1SG, 1SE, 1SF, 1SC.*	86	100
UP0	Radio: AM/FM Stereo with CD and Cassette and ATC (LS 2-Door) *Includes enhanced performance speaker system, seek/scan, auto tone control, digital clock, theft lock and speed compensated volume. REQUIRES 1SB. NOT AVAILABLE with U1Z, UQ3, UL0, 1SA, 1SC.*	172	200
UP0	Radio: AM/FM Stereo with CD and Cassette and ATC (LS 2-Door) *Includes enhanced performance speaker system, seek/scan, auto tone control, digital clock, theft lock and speed compensated volume. REQUIRES 1SC. NOT AVAILABLE with U1Z, UQ3, UL0, 1SA, 1SB.*	86	100
UP0	Radio: AM/FM Stereo with CD, Cassette and ATC (LS 4-Door) *Includes seek/scan, auto tone control, digital clock, theft lock and speed compensated volume. NOT AVAILABLE with 1SA, U1Z, UQ3.*	172	200

CODE	DESCRIPTION	INVOICE	MSRP
UPO	Radio: AM/FM Stereo with CD, Cassette and Automatic Tone Control (LT) ...... *Includes seek/scan, auto tone control, digital clock, theft lock and speed compensated volume. NOT AVAILABLE with U1Z, UQ3, ULO.*	86	100
UQ3	Bose Premium Sound System ... *REQUIRES ULO or 1SC or 1SD or 1SE or 1SF or 1SG. NOT AVAILABLE with UPO, 1SA.*	426	495
V10	Cold Climate Package ... *Includes 690-cca HD Delco freedom battery and engine block heater.*	77	89
YF5	California Emission Requirements ...	NC	NC
Z82	HD Trailering Special Equipment ... *Includes weight distribution hitch platform. REQUIRES GU4. NOT AVAILABLE with G80, ZR2, GT4.*	181	210
Z83	Smooth Ride Suspension (LS 2-Door) ... *REQUIRES GU4 and (QCA or QCE). NOT AVAILABLE with QBG, QJJ, QEB, ZR2, GT4.*	NC	NC
ZM5	Shield Package (4WD) ... *Includes transfer case and front differential skid plates and fuel tank and steering linkage shield.*	108	126
ZQ1	Smooth Ride Suspension Package (LS 4-Door/LT/TrailBlazer) ... *REQUIRES QCA or QCE or GU4. NOT AVAILABLE with QBG, QEB, GT4.*	NC	NC
ZR2	Wide Stance Sport Performance Package (LS 4WD 2-Door) ... *Includes unique revised frame for wide tread, unique strengthened front differential gears and drive axles, unique rear axle with 8.5" ring gear, larger wheel bearings, longer and larger diameter axle shafts, unique rear suspension with revised multi-leaf springs, rear axle track bar, unique 28mm vs 25mm diameter front stabilizer bar, modified jack and tire stowage winch, shield package, 46 mm Bilstein shocks, gvwr: 5,000 lbs and gawr: 2500/2700. The body is 3" higher than standard, front tread 61.2"/rear tread 59.1". REQUIRES QJJ and G80. NOT AVAILABLE with QBG, QCA, QCE, QEB, Z82, Z83, GU4, 1SB.*	1720	2000
ZY7	Custom Two-Tone Paint (4-Door LS/LT) ... *NOT AVAILABLE with 1SA.*	194	225

2000 C/K PICKUP

What's New?

Literally, one new paint color. The C/K is a dead duck after this model year.

Review

General Motors' best-selling vehicles, as truck loyalists know full well, are the full-size pickups: half- three-quarter- and one-tonners with a reputation as reliable workhorses. Ford's similar-sized F-Series grabs the higher sales totals each year, but faithful Chevrolet buyers are seldom swayed. The pickup that feels right at home to a Chevy fan tends to send prickles up the spine of a Ford fan, and vice-versa. Each is likely to declare the other's truck to be harder riding or anemic in acceleration, even if an impartial observer discerns little difference between the two.

Most truck lovers know by now that an all-new Chevrolet pickup is in showrooms. Dubbed Silverado, this model is currently available as 1500 and 2500 light-duty models, with the heavy-duty 2500 and 3500 trucks following next year. So it's not surprising that no changes are on tap for the carryover 2000 heavy-duty C/K pickup. In fact, only a single exterior paint color change, from Meadow Green to Emerald Green, separates these new C/Ks from the 1999 versions.

Four-wheel antilock braking is standard fare. Correctly fitted, a C/K pickup can tow as much as 10,000 pounds. Long-life engine components extend service intervals up to 100,000 miles on some items. For luxury-oriented truckers, a C/K can be trimmed in leather when the top LS trim package is specified.

When selecting a full-size Chevy truck, you have to face the usual bewildering selection of models, which vary by wheelbase, cab design, and short box or long box cargo-bed size. Don't stop yet: you also have to choose from three different engines (including a diesel), and then decide whether you want two- or four-wheel drive. After that, you still have the dizzying single-option list to ponder.

We get tired just thinking about all those possibilities, but they come with the territory when you're heading into big-pickup range. Truck customers don't want the same hauler that everybody else is buying, they want one tailored to their own specific needs. Chevrolet provides these customers with myriad possibilities to create that special, one-of-a-kind heavy-duty truck.

2000 Chevrolet K2500

2000 C/K 2500 PICKUP

Standard Equipment

BASE 2WD REGULAR CAB HD (5M): 5.7L V8 OHV SMPI 16-valve engine; 5-speed OD manual transmission; 600-amp HD battery; engine oil cooler; 100-amp alternator; rear-wheel drive, 3.73 axle ratio; stainless steel exhaust; front independent suspension with anti-roll bar, front coil springs, rigid rear axle suspension with rear leaf springs; power re-circulating ball steering with vehicle speed-sensing assist; front disc/rear drum brakes with 4-wheel antilock braking system; 34 gal. capacity fuel tank; side impact bars; trailer harness; front chrome bumper, rear black bumper with rear step; monotone paint; sealed beam halogen headlamps with daytime running lights; additional exterior lights include pickup cargo box light, underhood light; driver's and passenger's manual black folding outside mirrors; front and rear 16" x 6.5" painted styled steel wheels; LT245/75SR16 A/S BSW front and rear tires; underbody mounted full-size steel spare wheel with crankdown; AM/FM stereo, clock, seek-scan, 4 speakers, and fixed antenna; 3 power accessory outlets; instrumentation display includes tachometer, oil pressure gauge, water temperature gauge, volt gauge, trip odometer; warning indicators include oil pressure, water temp, battery, lights on, key in ignition, door ajar; ignition disable; tinted windows;

variable intermittent front windshield wipers; seating capacity of 3, bench front seat, adjustable headrests, driver's seat includes 2-way direction control, passenger's seat includes 2-way direction control; front height adjustable seatbelts; vinyl seats, full cloth headliner, full vinyl floor covering, cabback insulator; interior lights include dome light with delay, front reading lights; sport steering wheel; passenger's side vanity mirror; day/night rearview mirror; glove box with light, front cupholder, dashboard storage, driver's and passenger's door bins; cargo concealed storage; black grille, black side window moldings, black front windshield molding, black rear window molding and black door handles.

BASE 2WD EXTENDED CAB HD (5M) (in addition to or instead of BASE 2WD REGULAR CAB HD (5M) equipment): Rear heat ducts; seating capacity of 6, 60-40 split-bench front seat, adjustable headrests, driver's seat includes 4-way direction control, easy entry, passenger's seat includes 4-way direction control, easy entry; full folding rear bench seat with adjustable headrests.

BASE 2WD CREW CAB HD (4A) (in addition to or instead of BASE 2WD EXTENDED CAB HD (5M) equipment): Four-speed electronic OD auto transmission with lock-up; transmission oil cooler; 25 gal. capacity fuel tank; chrome wheel well molding; bench front seat, adjustable headrests, driver's seat includes 2-way direction control, passenger's seat includes 2-way direction control; interior lights include rear reading lights and rear door bins.

4WD (in addition to or instead of 2WD equipment): Part-time 4 wheel drive, auto locking hub control and manual shift; front torsion springs, front torsion bar; HD trailering, trailer harness; front tow hooks and black fender flares.

Base Prices

CODE	DESCRIPTION	INVOICE	MSRP
CC20903	Base 2WD Regular Cab HD (5M)	17059	19497
CC20953	Base 2WD Extended Cab HD (5M)	18550	21201
CC20743	Base 2WD Crew Cab HD (4A)	20720	23681
CK20903	Base 4WD Regular Cab HD (5M)	19470	22252
CK20753	Base 4WD Extended Cab HD SB (5M)	21268	24307
CK20953	Base 4WD Extended Cab HD LB (5M)	21379	24434
CK20743	Base 4WD Crew Cab HD (4A)	23585	26955
Destination Charge:		665	665

Accessories

CODE	DESCRIPTION	INVOICE	MSRP
—	Cloth Seat Trim (Reg Cab/X-Cab) *NOT AVAILABLE with A95.*	NC	NC
—	Leather Seat Trim (Crew Cab) *REQUIRES 1SB. INCLUDED in 1SC.*	946	1100
—	Leather Seat Trim (Reg Cab/X-Cab) *REQUIRES 1SB. NOT AVAILABLE with A95. INCLUDED in 1SC.*	860	1000
1SA	Preferred Equipment Group 1SA (2WD X-Cab) *Includes vehicle with standard equipment. REQUIRES C60. NOT AVAILABLE with R9A, R9B.*	NC	NC
1SA	Preferred Equipment Group 1SA (All Except 2WD X-Cab) *Includes vehicle with standard equipment. REQUIRES C60. NOT AVAILABLE with R9B.*	NC	NC
1SA	Preferred Equipment Group 1SA (Reg Cab/X-Cab) *Includes vehicle with standard equipment. REQUIRES R9A, R9B. NOT AVAILABLE with UL5, YG6.*	(602)	(700)

CODE	DESCRIPTION	INVOICE	MSRP
1SA	**Preferred Equipment Group 1SA (Reg Cab/X-Cab)** *Includes vehicle with standard equipment. REQUIRES C60 and R9B. NOT AVAILABLE with R9A.*	(172)	(200)
1SA	**Preferred Equipment Group 1SA (Reg Cab/X-Cab)** *Includes vehicle with standard equipment. REQUIRES R9A. NOT AVAILABLE with YG6, R9B, UL5.*	(430)	(500)
1SB	**Preferred Equipment Group 1SB (Crew Cab)** *Includes LS Decor equipment: air conditioning, power windows, power door locks, cruise control, tilt steering, full carpet floor covering, floor mats, storage tray behind seat, AM/FM stereo with cassette, clock and seek/scan; leather-wrapped steering wheel, custom cloth seat trim, electrochromic rearview mirror with 8 point compass, rally wheel trim, bright wheel opening moldings, appearance package: chrome grille, composite halogen headlamps and dual note horn; chrome front bumper with rub strip, body side moldings with bright trim and dual power remote exterior mirrors. NOT AVAILABLE with A95.*	3156	3670
1SB	**Preferred Equipment Group 1SB (Reg Cab/X-Cab)**	2611	3036
	Manufacturer Discount	(645)	(750)
	Net Price *Includes LS Decor equipment: air conditioning, power windows, power door locks, cruise control, tilt steering, full carpet floor covering, floor mats, storage tray behind seat, AM/FM stereo with cassette, clock and seek/scan; leather-wrapped steering wheel, custom cloth seat trim, electrochromic rearview mirror, rally wheel trim, bright wheel opening moldings, appearance package: chrome grille, composite halogen headlamps and dual note horn; chrome front bumper with rub strip, body side moldings with bright trim and dual power remote exterior mirrors.*	1966	2286
1SC	**Preferred Equipment Group 1SC (Crew Cab)** *Includes LS Decor equipment: air conditioning, power windows, power door locks, cruise control, tilt steering, full carpet floor covering, floor mats, storage tray behind seat, AM/FM stereo with cassette, clock and seek/scan; leather-wrapped steering wheel, electrochromic rearview mirror with 8-point compass, rally wheel trim, bright wheel opening moldings, appearance package: chrome grille, composite halogen headlamps and dual note horn; chrome front bumper with rub strip, body side moldings with bright trim and dual power remote exterior mirrors; remote keyless entry, power driver's seat, 60/40 reclining split-bench seat and leather seat trim. NOT AVAILABLE with A95.*	4524	5260
1SC	**Preferred Equipment Group 1SC (Reg Cab)**	3874	4505
	Manufacturer Discount	(645)	(750)
	Net Price *Includes LS Decor equipment: air conditioning, power windows, power door locks, cruise control, tilt steering, full carpet floor covering, floor mats, storage tray behind seat, AM/FM stereo with cassette, clock and seek/scan; leather-wrapped steering wheel, electrochromic rearview mirror with 8-point compass, rally wheel trim, bright wheel opening moldings, appearance package: chrome grille, composite halogen headlamps and dual note horn; chrome front bumper with rub strip, body side moldings with bright trim and dual power remote exterior mirrors; remote keyless entry, 60/40 reclining split-bench seat and leather seat trim. NOT AVAILABLE with A95.*	3229	3755

CODE	DESCRIPTION	INVOICE	MSRP
1SC	Preferred Equipment Group 1SC (X-Cab)	3931	4571
	Manufacturer Discount	(645)	(750)
	Net Price	3286	3821
	Includes LS Decor equipment: air conditioning, power windows, power door locks, cruise control, tilt steering, full carpet floor covering, floor mats, storage tray behind seat, AM/FM stereo with cassette, clock and seek/scan; leather-wrapped steering wheel, electrochromic rearview mirror with 8-point compass, rally wheel trim, bright wheel opening moldings, appearance package: chrome grille, composite halogen headlamps and dual note horn; chrome front bumper with rub strip, body side moldings with bright trim and dual power remote exterior mirrors; remote keyless entry, power driver's seat, 60/40 reclining split-bench seat and leather seat trim.		
A28	Sliding Rear Window	99	115
	NOT AVAILABLE with C49.		
A95	Reclining High Back Bucket Seats (Crew Cab)	364	423
	Includes power lumbar, floor console and overhead console. REQUIRES 1SB. NOT AVAILABLE with AE7, 1SC.		
A95	Reclining High Back Bucket Seats (Reg Cab)	332	386
	Includes power lumbar and floor console. REQUIRES 1SB. NOT AVAILABLE with 1SC, AE7, Leather Seat Trim.		
A95	Reclining High Back Bucket Seats (X-Cab)	232	270
	Includes power lumbar, floor console and overhead console. REQUIRES 1SB. NOT AVAILABLE with AE7.		
A95	Reclining High Back Bucket Seats with Leather (Crew Cab)	1310	1523
	Includes power lumbar, floor console and overhead console. REQUIRES 1SB. NOT AVAILABLE with AE7.		
A95	Reclining High Back Bucket Seats with Leather (X-Cab)	232	270
	Includes power lumbar, floor console and overhead console. REQUIRES 1SC. NOT AVAILABLE with AE7.		
A95	Reclining High Back Bucket Seats with Leather Trim (Crew Cab)	278	323
	Includes power lumbar, floor console and overhead console. REQUIRES 1SC. NOT AVAILABLE with AE7.		
A95	Reclining High Back Bucket Seats with Leather (X-Cab)	1092	1270
	Includes power lumbar, floor console and overhead console. REQUIRES 1SB. NOT AVAILABLE with AE7.		
AE7	60/40 Reclining Split Beach Seat with Leather (Crew Cab)	1032	1200
	Includes storage armrest and power lumbar. REQUIRES 1SB. NOT AVAILABLE with A95. INCLUDED in 1SC.		
AE7	60/40 Reclining Split-Bench Seat (Crew Cab)	86	100
	Includes storage armrest and power lumbar. NOT AVAILABLE with A95. INCLUDED in 1SC.		
AE7	60/40 Reclining Split-Bench Seat (Reg Cab)	150	174
	Includes storage armrest and power lumbar. NOT AVAILABLE with A95. INCLUDED in 1SC.		
AE7	60/40 Reclining Split-Bench Seat with Leather (Reg Cab)	1010	1174
	Includes storage armrest and power lumbar. REQUIRES 1SB. NOT AVAILABLE with A95. INCLUDED in 1SC.		

CODE	DESCRIPTION	INVOICE	MSRP
AG9	Power Driver's Seat (X-Cab/Crew Cab) *REQUIRES 1SB, AE7 or A95. NOT AVAILABLE with A52 (Crew Cab). INCLUDED in 1SC.*	206	240
AJ1	Deep Tinted Solar-Ray Glass (Crew Cab) *Includes light tint glass rear window. REQUIRES C49.*	155	180
AJ1	Deep Tinted Solar-Ray Glass (Crew Cab) *NOT AVAILABLE with C49.*	185	215
AJ1	Deep Tinted Solar-Ray Glass (Reg Cab) *REQUIRES A28.*	30	35
AJ1	Deep Tinted Solar-Ray Glass (X-Cab) *Includes light tint glass rear window. REQUIRES C49.*	62	72
AJ1	Deep Tinted Solar-Ray Glass (X-Cab) *NOT AVAILABLE with C49.*	92	107
AU0	Remote Keyless Entry *REQUIRES 1SB. INCLUDED in 1SC.*	129	150
AU3	Power Door Locks (Crew Cab) *INCLUDED in 1SB or 1SC.*	192	223
AU3	Power Door Locks (Reg Cab/X-Cab) *INCLUDED in 1SB or 1SC.*	134	156
B30	Carpet Floor Covering (Reg Cab) *INCLUDED in 1SB or 1SC.*	30	35
B30	Carpet Floor Covering (X-Cab) *INCLUDED in 1SB or 1SC.*	44	51
B32	Front Floor Mats (Reg Cab/X-Cab) *REQUIRES B30. INCLUDED in 1SB or 1SC.*	17	20
B33	Rear Floor Mats (X-Cab) *REQUIRES B32 & B30. NOT AVAILABLE with YG4. INCLUDED in 1SB or 1SC.*	14	16
B85	Bright Bodyside and Wheel Opening Moldings (2WD - Reg Cab/X-Cab) *INCLUDED in 1SB or 1SC.*	92	107
B85	Bright Bodyside and Wheel Opening Moldings (4WD - Reg Cab/X-Cab) *INCLUDED in 1SB or 1SC.*	65	76
BG9	Full Rubber Color-Keyed Flooring (Reg Cab) *Replaces carpeting and floor mats.*	(30)	(35)
BG9	Full Rubber Color-Keyed Flooring (X-Cab) *Replaces carpeting and floor mats.*	(44)	(51)
BZY	Under Rail Bedliner *NOT AVAILABLE with KL6.*	194	225
C49	Electric Rear Window Defogger (X-Cab/Crew Cab) *REQUIRES C60 (Crew Cab with 1SA) or R9A. NOT AVAILABLE with A28, 1SA (X-Cab).*	150	175
C60	Air Conditioning *NOT AVAILABLE with YG6. INCLUDED in R9A, 1SB or 1SC.*	692	805
DD7	10" Electrochromic ISRV Mirror *Includes 8-point compass. REQUIRES 1SB (Reg Cab/X-Cab). INCLUDED in 1SB (Crew Cab), 1SC.*	125	145
DF2	Stainless Steel Camper Type Mirrors (Reg Cab/X-Cab) *Includes 7.5" width x 10.5" height heads.*	46	53

CODE	DESCRIPTION	INVOICE	MSRP
DF2	Stainless Steel Camper Type Mirrors (Reg Cab/X-Cab) *Includes 7.5" width x 10.5" height heads. REQUIRES 1SB or 1SC.*	(39)	(45)
EF1	Rear Bumper Delete Provisions *Vehicles registered in certain states must have a rear bumper to be operated on their roads. Consult your local laws. NOT AVAILABLE with Z82, R9B, 1SB, 1SC.*	(112)	(130)
EF1	Rear Bumper Delete Provisions *Vehicles registered in certain states must have a rear bumper to be operated on their roads. Consult your local laws. REQUIRES 1SB or 1SC. NOT AVAILABLE with Z82.*	(172)	(200)
F60	HD Front Springs (4WD)	54	63
G80	Locking Differential	245	285
GT5	4.10 Axle Ratio *Includes engine oil cooler. NOT AVAILABLE with KL6.*	NC	NC
K47	High Capacity Air Cleaner	22	25
KL5	Alternative Fuel Conversion (Reg Cab/X-Cab) *Liquid propane gas and compressed natural gas conversion ready. NOT AVAILABLE with L29, L65.*	108	125
KL6	Natural Gas Provisions (Reg Cab 4WD) *NOT AVAILABLE with L29, L65, GT5, BZY.*	4988	5800
L29	Engine: Vortec 7400 V8 SFI *REQUIRES F60 (4WD). NOT AVAILABLE with KL5, VYU, KL6.*	516	600
L65	Engine: 6.5L V8 Turbo Diesel *Includes HD auxiliary battery, engine block heater and front bumper guards (only with 1SB or 1SC). REQUIRES F60. NOT AVAILABLE with KL5, TP2, V10, VYU, KL6.*	2460	2860
MT1	Transmission: 4-Speed Automatic OD HD (Reg Cab/X-Cab)	942	1095
MW3	Transmission: 5-Speed Manual OD HD (Crew Cab) *Includes auxiliary transmission cooler delete. REQUIRES L29. NOT AVAILABLE with NP1, UP0.*	(942)	(1095)
NP1	Electronic Shift Transfer Case (4WD) *Includes 2 speeds. REQUIRES ZQ3 or R9A.*	129	150
NZZ	Skid Plate Package (4WD) *Includes fuel tank, front differential and transfer case shields.*	82	95
P06	Rally Wheel Trim *INCLUDED in R9B, 1SB or 1SC.*	52	60
R6M	New Jersey Cost Surcharge	74	NC
R9A	Comfort and Convenience Package *Includes air conditioning, convenience group: speed control, tilt wheel; AM/FM stereo with cassette and seek/scan. REQUIRES 1SA. NOT AVAILABLE with YG6, UL5, 1SB, 1SC.*	1150	1337
R9B	Bright Appearance Package (2WD - Reg Cab/X-Cab) *Includes bright bodyside moldings, appearance package, composite halogen headlamps, chrome grille, dual note horn, chrome deluxe front bumper with rub strip and rally wheel trim. REQUIRES 1SA. NOT AVAILABLE with 1SB, 1SC, EF1.*	415	483
R9B	Bright Appearance Package (4WD - Reg Cab/X-Cab) *Includes bright bodyside moldings, appearance package, composite halogen headlamps, chrome grille, dual note horn, chrome deluxe front bumper with rub strip and rally wheel trim. REQUIRES 1SA. NOT AVAILABLE with 1SB, 1SC, EF1.*	389	452

CODE	DESCRIPTION	INVOICE	MSRP
R9B	Bright Appearance Package (Crew Cab) *Includes appearance package: composite halogen headlamps, chrome grille, dual note horn and rally wheel trim. NOT AVAILABLE with EF1.*	301	350
TP2	Auxiliary Battery *NOT AVAILABLE with L65.*	115	134
U01	Roof Marker Lamps	47	55
UL0	Radio: AM/FM Stereo with Cassette and Automatic Tone Control *Includes seek/scan, digital clock, auto tone control, theft lock and speed compensated volume. REQUIRES 1SB or 1SC. NOT AVAILABLE with UN0, UP0.*	77	90
UL5	Radio Delete *Includes clock delete. REQUIRES 1SA. NOT AVAILABLE with 1SB, 1SC, R9A, UM6.*	(247)	(287)
UM6	Radio: AM/FM Stereo with Cassette *Includes digital clock. NOT AVAILABLE with UL5. INCLUDED in 1SB, 1SC.*	126	147
UN0	Radio: AM/FM Stereo with CD and Automatic Tone Control *Includes seek/scan, digital clock, auto tone control, theft lock and speed compensated volume. REQUIRES 1SB or 1SC. NOT AVAILABLE with UL0, UP0.*	163	190
UP0	Radio: AM/FM Stereo with CD, Cassette and Automatic Tone Control *Includes seek/scan, digital clock, theft lock, speed compensated volume, remote CD and auto tone control. REQUIRES MT1 and (1SB or 1SC). NOT AVAILABLE with UL0, UN0, MW3.*	249	290
V10	Cold Climate Package *Includes engine block heater. NOT AVAILABLE with L65.*	28	33
V22	Appearance Package *Includes composite halogen headlamps, chrome grille and dual note horn. INCLUDED in 1SB, 1SC.*	164	191
V76	Recovery Hooks (4WD)	33	38
VB3	Chrome Rear Step Bumper (X-Cab/Crew Cab) *NOT AVAILABLE with EF1. INCLUDED in 1SB, 1SC and R9B.*	85	99
VB3	Chrome Rear Step Bumper with Rub Strip (Reg Cab) *NOT AVAILABLE with EF1. INCLUDED in 1SB, 1SC.*	85	99
VG3	Chrome Deluxe Front Bumper with Rub Strip (Reg Cab/X-Cab) *INCLUDED in 1SB, 1SC and R9B.*	22	26
VYU	Snow Plow Prep Package (4WD - Reg Cab/X-Cab) *Includes HD front springs. REQUIRES L31 (X-Cab). NOT AVAILABLE with L29, L65.*	101	118
XGK	Tires: Front LT245/75R16E AT BSW (4WD) *REQUIRES YGK.*	19	23
YG4	Rear Seat Delete (X-Cab) *REQUIRES 1SA. NOT AVAILABLE with A95.*	(374)	(435)
YG6	Air Conditioning Not Desired *REQUIRES 1SA. NOT AVAILABLE with R9A, C60.*	NC	NC
YGK	Tires: Rear LT245/75R16E AT BSW	19	23
Z82	HD Trailering Special Equipment *Includes trailer hitch platform. REQUIRES GT5. NOT AVAILABLE with EF1.*	141	164
ZQ3	Convenience Group *Includes speed control and tilt wheel. INCLUDED in 1SB, 1SC and R9A.*	331	385

2000 C/K 3500 PICKUP

Standard Equipment

BASE 2WD REGULAR CAB HD LB (5M): 5.7L V8 OHV SMPI 16-valve engine; 5-speed OD manual transmission; 600-amp HD battery; engine oil cooler; 100-amp alternator; rear-wheel drive, power take-off provision, 4.1 axle ratio; stainless steel exhaust; front independent suspension with anti-roll bar, front coil springs, rigid rear axle suspension with rear leaf springs; power re-circulating ball steering with vehicle speed-sensing assist; front disc/rear drum brakes with 4-wheel antilock braking system; 34 gal. capacity fuel tank; side impact bars; trailer harness; front chrome bumper, rear black bumper, rear step; monotone paint; sealed beam halogen headlamps with daytime running lights; additional exterior lights include pickup cargo box light, underhood light; driver's and passenger's manual black folding outside mirrors; front and rear 16" x 6.5" painted styled steel wheels; LT245/75SR16 A/S BSW front and rear tires; underbody mounted full-size steel spare wheel with crankdown; AM/FM stereo, clock, seek-scan, 4 speakers, and fixed antenna; 3 power accessory outlets; instrumentation display includes tachometer, oil pressure gauge, water temperature gauge, volt gauge, trip odometer; warning indicators include battery, lights on, key in ignition, door ajar; ignition disable; tinted windows; variable intermittent front windshield wipers, sun visor strip; seating capacity of 3, bench front seat, adjustable headrests, driver's seat includes 2-way direction control, passenger's seat includes 2-way direction control; front height adjustable seatbelts; vinyl seats, full cloth headliner, full vinyl floor covering, plastic/rubber gear shift knob, cabback insulator; interior lights include dome light with delay, front reading lights; sport steering wheel; passenger's side vanity mirror; day/night rearview mirror; glove box with light, front cupholder, dashboard storage, driver's and passenger's door bins; argent grille, black side window moldings, black front windshield molding, black rear window molding and black door handles.

BASE 2WD EXTENDED CAB HD LB (5M) (in addition to or instead of BASE 2WD REGULAR CAB HD LB (5M) equipment): Additional exterior lights include cab clearance lights; front and rear 16" x 6" painted steel wheels; LT225/75SR16 A/S BSW front and rear tires; vented rear windows; seating capacity of 6, 60-40 split-bench front seat, adjustable headrests, driver's seat includes 4-way direction control, easy entry, passenger's seat includes4-way direction control, easy entry and full folding rear bench seat with adjustable headrests.

BASE 2WD CREW CAB SB (5M) (in addition to or instead of BASE 2WD EXTENDED CAB LB (5M) equipment): 7.4L V8 OHV SMPI 16-valve engine; 26 gal. capacity fuel tank; chrome bumper insert; manual front and rear windows; child safety rear door locks, bench front seat, adjustable headrests, driver's seat includes 2-way direction control, passenger's seat includes 2-way direction control; full folding rear bench seat with reclining adjustable headrests and rear door bins.

BASE 2WD CREW CAB LB (5M) (in addition to or instead of BASE 2WD CREW CAB SB (5M) equipment): 5.7L V8 OHV SMPI 16-valve engine; chrome wheel well molding; front and rear 16" x 6.5" painted styled steel wheels; LT245/75SR16 A/S BSW front and rear tires; rear heat ducts; manual front and rear windows; seating capacity of 6; full folding rear bench seat with reclining adjustable headrests and rear door bins.

4WD (5M) (in addition to or instead of 2WD (5M) equipment): Part-time 4-wheel drive, auto locking hub control and manual shift; front torsion springs, front torsion bar; front tow hooks and black fender flares.

Base Prices

CC30903	Base 2WD Regular Cab HD LB (5M)	17495	19995
CC30953	Base 2WD Extended Cab HD LB (5M)	20493	23421
CC30743	Base 2WD Crew Cab HD SB (5M)	21704	24805

CODE	DESCRIPTION	INVOICE	MSRP
CC30943	Base 2WD Crew Cab HD LB (5M)	20409	23325
CK30903	Base 4WD Regular Cab HD LB (5M)	20120	22995
CK30953	Base 4WD Extended Cab HD LB (5M)	22953	26232
CK30743	Base 4WD Crew Cab HD SB (5M)	24482	27979
CK30943	Base 4WD Crew Cab HD LB (5M)	23186	26499
Destination Charge:		640	640

Accessories

CODE	DESCRIPTION	INVOICE	MSRP
—	Cloth Seat Trim (Reg Cab/X-Cab) *NOT AVAILABLE with A95.*	NC	NC
—	Leather Seat Trim (Reg Cab/X-Cab) *Leather on seating surface only. REQUIRES 1SB. NOT AVAILABLE with 1SJ, A95. INCLUDED in 1SC.*	860	1000
1SA	Preferred Equipment Group 1SA (Reg Cab/X-Cab) *Includes vehicle with standard equipment.*	(602)	(700)
1SA	Preferred Equipment Group 1SA (Reg Cab/X-Cab) *Includes vehicle with standard equipment. NOT AVAILABLE with R9B.*	(430)	(500)
1SA	Preferred Equipment Group 1SA (Reg Cab/X-Cab) *Includes vehicle with standard equipment. REQUIRES YG6. NOT AVAILABLE with R9A.*	(172)	(200)
1SA	Preferred Equipment Group 1SA *Includes vehicle with standard equipment. REQUIRES YG6. NOT AVAILABLE with R9B.*	NC	NC
1SB	Preferred Equipment Group 1SB (Crew Cab) *Includes LS Decor: front air conditioning, power windows with driver's one touch down, power door locks, convenience group: tilt wheel, speed control; AM/FM stereo with seek, scan and cassette, leather-wrapped steering wheel, full width behind seat storage tray, deluxe chrome rear bumper, appearance package: chrome grille, dual composite halogen headlamps; electric remote control black mirrors and rally wheel trim. NOT AVAILABLE with A95.*	3156	3670
1SB	Preferred Equipment Group 1SB (Reg Cab)	2611	3036
	Manufacturer Discount	(645)	(750)
	Net Price *Includes LS Decor: front air conditioning, power windows, power door locks, convenience group: tilt wheel, cruise control; AM/FM stereo with cassette, leather-wrapped steering wheel, seatback storage pockets, chrome rear step bumper, appearance package: chrome grille, composite halogen headlamps; electric remote control painted mirrors and rally wheel trim. NOT AVAILABLE with R05.*	1966	2286
1SB	Preferred Equipment Group 1SB (Reg Cab/X-Cab)	2526	2937
	Manufacturer Discount	(645)	(750)
	Net Price *Includes LS Decor: front air conditioning, power windows, power door locks, convenience group: tilt wheel, cruise control; AM/FM stereo with cassette, leather-wrapped steering wheel, seatback storage pockets, chrome rear step bumper, appearance package: chrome grille, composite halogen headlamps; electric remote*	1881	2187

CODE	DESCRIPTION	INVOICE	MSRP
	control painted mirrors and rally wheel trim. REQUIRES R05. NOT AVAILABLE with APC, APD, BNP.		
1SC	**Preferred Equipment Group 1SC (Crew Cab)**	4524	5260
	Includes LS Premium Decor, front air conditioning, power windows with driver's one touch down, power door locks, convenience group: tilt wheel, speed control; AM/FM stereo with seek, scan and cassette, leather-wrapped steering wheel, full width behind seat storage tray, deluxe chrome rear bumper, appearance package: chrome grille, dual composite halogen headlamps; electric remote control black mirrors, rally wheel trim, remote keyless entry, illuminated entry, power driver's seat, reclining 60/40 split bench seat and leather seat trim.		
1SC	**Preferred Equipment Group 1SC (Reg Cab)**	3874	4505
	Manufacturer Discount	(645)	(750)
	Net Price	3229	3755
	Includes LS Premium Decor: front air conditioning, power windows, power door locks, convenience group: tilt wheel, cruise control; AM/FM stereo with cassette, leather-wrapped steering wheel, seatback storage pockets, chrome rear step bumper, appearance package: chrome grille, composite halogen headlamps; electric remote control painted mirrors, rally wheel trim, remote keyless entry, illuminated entry, 10" electrochromic inside rear view mirror, 8-point compass, reclining 60/40 split bench seat and leather seat trim. NOT AVAILABLE with R05.		
1SC	**Preferred Equipment Group 1SC (Reg Cab)**	3789	4406
	Manufacturer Discount	(645)	(750)
	Net Price	3144	3656
	Includes LS Premium Decor: front air conditioning, power windows, power door locks, convenience group: tilt wheel, cruise control; AM/FM stereo with cassette, leather-wrapped steering wheel, seatback storage pockets, chrome rear step bumper, appearance package: chrome grille, composite halogen headlamps; electric remote control painted mirrors, rally wheel trim, remote keyless entry, illuminated entry, 10" electrochromic inside rear view mirror, 8-point compass, reclining 60/40 split bench seat and leather seat trim. REQUIRES R05.		
1SC	**Preferred Equipment Group 1SC (X-Cab)**	3846	4472
	Manufacturer Discount	(645)	(750)
	Net Price	3201	3722
	Includes LS Premium Decor: front air conditioning, power windows, power door locks, convenience group: tilt wheel, cruise control; AM/FM stereo with cassette, leather-wrapped steering wheel, seatback storage pockets, chrome rear step bumper, appearance package: chrome grille, composite halogen headlamps; electric remote control painted mirrors, rally wheel trim, remote keyless entry, illuminated entry, 10" electrochromic inside rear view mirror, 8-point compass, reclining 60/40 split bench seat and leather seat trim. NOT AVAILABLE with APC, APD, BNP.		
A28	**Sliding Rear Window**	99	115
	NOT AVAILABLE with C49, AJ1.		
A95	**Reclining High Back Bucket Seats (Crew Cab)**	364	423
	Includes power lumbar and floor and overhead console. REQUIRES 1SB. NOT AVAILABLE with AE7, 1SC.		

CODE	DESCRIPTION	INVOICE	MSRP
A95	**Reclining High Back Bucket Seats (Crew Cab)** *Includes power lumbar and floor and overhead console. REQUIRES 1SC. NOT AVAILABLE with AE7, 1SB.*	278	323
A95	**Reclining High Back Bucket Seats (Reg Cab)** *Includes power lumbar and floor console. REQUIRES 1SB. NOT AVAILABLE with 1SC, 1SJ, ~~2, AE7, Leather Seat Trim.*	332	386
A95	**Reclining High Back Bucket Seats (X-Cab)** *Includes power lumbar, floor console and overhead console. REQUIRES 1SB. NOT AVAILABLE with 1SC, 1SJ.*	232	270
AE7	**Reclining 60/40 Split Bench Seat (Crew Cab)** *Includes storage armrest and power lumbar. REQUIRES 1SB. NOT AVAILABLE with A95. INCLUDED in 1SC.*	86	100
AE7	**Reclining 60/40 Split Bench Seat (Reg Cab)** *Includes storage armrest and power lumbar. REQUIRES 1SB. NOT AVAILABLE with A95, 1SJ. INCLUDED in 1SC.*	150	174
AG9	**Power Driver's Seat (X-Cab/Crew Cab)** *REQUIRES 1SB and (AE7 or A95) or 1SC (X-Cab). INCLUDED in 1SC (Crew Cab).*	206	240
AJ1	**Deep Tinted Solar-Ray Glass (Crew Cab)** *NOT AVAILABLE with A28.*	185	215
AJ1	**Deep Tinted Solar-Ray Glass (Crew Cab)** *NOTE: with A28 sliding rear window the rear window is light tint glass.*	155	180
AJ1	**Deep Tinted Solar-Ray Glass (Reg Cab)**	30	35
AJ1	**Deep Tinted Solar-Ray Glass (X-Cab)** *NOT AVAILABLE with C49.*	92	107
AJ1	**Deep Tinted Solar-Ray Glass (X-Cab)** *NOTE: when C49 defogger is specified the rear window is light tint glass. REQUIRES 1SB or 1SC.*	62	72
AU0	**Remote Keyless Entry** *Includes illuminated entry. REQUIRES 1SB. INCLUDED in 1SC.*	129	150
AU3	**Power Door Locks (Crew Cab)** *REQUIRES 1SA.*	192	223
AU3	**Power Door Locks (Reg Cab/X-Cab)** *REQUIRES 1SA.*	134	156
B30	**Carpet Floor Covering (Reg Cab)** *REQUIRES 1SA.*	30	35
B30	**Carpet Floor Covering (X-Cab)** *REQUIRES 1SA.*	44	51
B32	**Front Floor Mats (Reg Cab/X-Cab)** *REQUIRES 1SA, B30.*	17	20
B33	**Rear Floor Mats (X-Cab)** *REQUIRES 1SA, B30 and B32. NOT AVAILABLE with YG4.*	14	16
B85	**Bright Exterior Moldings (Reg Cab 2WD)** *Includes bodyside and wheel opening moldings. NOT AVAILABLE with R05, YYK, YHP, YHR.*	92	107
B85	**Bright Exterior Moldings (Reg Cab 4WD)** *Includes bodyside molding. NOT AVAILABLE with R05, YYK, YHP, YHR, YYL.*	65	76

CODE	DESCRIPTION	INVOICE	MSRP
BG9	Full Rubber Color-Keyed Flooring (Reg Cab) *Replaces carpeting and floor mats. REQUIRES 1SB or 1SC.*	(30)	(35)
BG9	Full Rubber Color-Keyed Flooring (X-Cab) *Replaces carpeting and floor mats. REQUIRES 1SB and 1SC.*	(44)	(51)
BZY	Under Rail Bedliner	194	225
C49	Electric Rear Window Defogger *NOT AVAILABLE with A28.*	150	175
C60	Front Air Conditioning *REQUIRES 1SA. NOT AVAILABLE with YG6.*	692	805
C7A	GVWR: 10,000 Lbs *REQUIRES R05 and (XYK or XYL or XHR) or YYK or YHP or YHR or YYL. NOT AVAILABLE with XGK, YGK, ZGK, KL5.*	NC	NC
DD7	10" Electrochromic ISRV Mirror (Reg Cab/X-Cab) *Includes 8-point compass. REQUIRES 1SB. INCLUDED in 1SC.*	125	145
DF2	Stainless Steel Camper Type Mirrors *Exterior stainless steel 7.5" wide x 10.5" high mirrors. REQUIRES 1SB or 1SC.*	(39)	(45)
DF2	Stainless Steel Camper Type Mirrors *REQUIRES 1SA. Exterior stainless steel 7.5" wide x 10.5" high mirrors.*	46	53
EF1	Rear Bumper Delete *REQUIRES 1SA. NOT AVAILABLE with R9B, Z82, VB3.*	(112)	(130)
EF1	Rear Bumper Delete *REQUIRES 1SB or 1SC. NOT AVAILABLE with Z82.*	(172)	(200)
F60	HD Front Springs (4WD)	54	63
FE9	Federal Emission Requirements	NC	NC
G80	Locking Differential	245	285
HC4	4.56 Axle Ratio *Includes locking differential. REQUIRES (C7A and MT1) or C7A. NOT AVAILABLE with L65, YF5, VYU, KL5.*	245	285
K47	High Capacity Air Cleaner	22	25
KL5	Alternative Fuel Conversion (Reg Cab/X-Cab) *LPG and CNG conversion ready. REQUIRES MT1. NOT AVAILABLE with L65, C7A, R05, YF5, XYK, YYK, YHP, YHR, YYL, XYL, ZYL, XHR, ZHR, HC4.*	108	125
KL6	Natural Gas Conversion (Crew Cab LB)	4988	5800
L29	Engine: Vortec 7400 V8 SFI (All Except Crew Cab SB) *REQUIRES F60. NOT AVAILABLE with KL5, VYU.*	516	600
L65	Engine: 6.5L V8 Turbo Diesel (All Except Crew Cab SB) *Includes engine block heater and HD auxiliary battery. REQUIRES F60. NOT AVAILABLE with HC4, TP2, KL5, VYU, V10.*	2460	2860
L65	Engine: 6.5L V8 Turbo Diesel (Crew Cab SB) *Includes engine block heater and HD auxiliary battery. NOT AVAILABLE with HC4, TP2, V10.*	1944	2260
MT1	Transmission: Electronic 4-Speed HD Auto with OD *Includes auxiliary transmission oil cooler.*	856	995
NZZ	Skid Plate Package (4WD) *Includes fuel tank shield, front differential and transfer case shields.*	82	95
P06	Rally Wheel Trim *REQUIRES 1SA.*	52	60

CODE	DESCRIPTION	INVOICE	MSRP
R05	Dual Rear Wheels (Crew Cab LB) *Includes tailgate lamps and roof marker lamps. REQUIRES C7A and (YYK or YHP or YHR or YYL). NOT AVAILABLE with XGK, YGK, ZGK.*	737	857
R05	Dual Rear Wheels (Reg Cab) *Includes tailgate lamps and roof marker lamps. REQUIRES C7A and (YYK or YHP or YHR or YYL). NOT AVAILABLE with KL5, XGK, YGK, ZGK.*	821	955
R6M	New Jersey Cost Surcharge	74	NC
R9A	Comfort and Convenience Package *Includes front air conditioning, AM/FM stereo with cassette, speed control and tilt wheel. REQUIRES 1SA. NOT AVAILABLE with UL5, YG6.*	1150	1337
R9B	Bright Appearance Package (2WD - Reg Cab/X-Cab) *Includes bright exterior moldings, appearance package: chrome grille, composite halogen headlamps; chrome rear step bumper, deluxe chrome front bumper and rally wheel trim. REQUIRES 1SA. NOT AVAILABLE with R05, EF1.*	415	483
R9B	Bright Appearance Package (4WD - Reg Cab/X-Cab) *Includes bright exterior moldings, appearance package: chrome grille, composite halogen headlamps; chrome rear step bumper, deluxe chrome front bumper and rally wheel trim. REQUIRES 1SA. NOT AVAILABLE with R05, EF1.*	389	452
R9B	Bright Appearance Package (Crew Cab) *Includes appearance package: chrome grille, dual composite halogen headlamps; deluxe chrome rear bumper and rally wheel trim. REQUIRES 1SA. NOT AVAILABLE with EF1.*	301	350
R9B	Bright Appearance Package (Reg Cab/X-Cab) *Includes appearance package: chrome grille, composite halogen headlamps; chrome rear step bumper, deluxe chrome front bumper and rally wheel trim. REQUIRES 1SA and R05. NOT AVAILABLE with EF1.*	323	376
TP2	Auxiliary Battery *NOT AVAILABLE with L65.*	115	134
U01	Roof Marker Lamps (Reg Cab/Crew Cab LB) *NOT AVAILABLE with YF5.*	47	55
UL0	Radio: AM/FM Stereo with Cassette and ATC (Crew Cab) *Includes digital clock, theft lock, speed compensated volume and auto tone control. REQUIRES 1SB or 1SC. NOT AVAILABLE with UN0, UP0.*	77	90
UL0	Radio: AM/FM Stereo with Cassette and ATC (Reg Cab/X-Cab) *Includes seek-scan, digital clock, theft lock, and speed compensated volume. REQUIRES 1SB or 1SC. NOT AVAILABLE with UN0, UP0.*	77	90
UL5	Radio Delete *REQUIRES 1SA. NOT AVAILABLE with R9A, UM6.*	(247)	(287)
UM6	Radio: AM/FM Stereo with Cassette (Crew Cab) *Includes digital clock. REQUIRES 1SA. NOT AVAILABLE with UL5.*	126	147
UM6	Radio: AM/FM Stereo with Cassette (Reg Cab/X-Cab) *Includes seek-scan and digital clock. REQUIRES 1SA. NOT AVAILABLE with UL5.*	126	147
UN0	Radio: AM/FM Stereo with CD and Automatic Tone Control (Crew Cab) *Includes digital clock, theft lock, speed compensated volume and auto tone control. REQUIRES 1SB or 1SC. NOT AVAILABLE with UL0, UP0.*	163	190

CODE	DESCRIPTION	INVOICE	MSRP
UN0	Radio: AM/FM Stereo with CD and Automatic Tone Control (Reg Cab/X-Cab) *Includes seek-scan, digital clock, theft lock, and speed compensated volume. REQUIRES 1SB or 1SC. NOT AVAILABLE with UL0, UP0.*	163	190
UP0	Radio: AM/FM Stereo with CD and Cassette (Crew Cab) *Includes remote compact disc, digital clock, theft lock, speed compensated volume and auto tone control. REQUIRES MT1 and (1SB or 1SC). NOT AVAILABLE with UL0, UN0.*	249	290
UP0	Radio: AM/FM Stereo with CD and Cassette (Reg Cab/X-Cab) *Includes seek-scan, digital clock, theft lock, auto tone control and speed compensated volume. REQUIRES MT1 and (1SB or 1SC). NOT AVAILABLE with UL0, UN0.*	249	290
V10	Cold Climate Package *Includes engine block heater. NOT AVAILABLE with L65.*	28	33
V22	Deluxe Front Appearance Package *Includes composite halogen headlamps and chrome grille. REQUIRES 1SA.*	164	191
V76	Recovery Hooks (2WD)	33	38
VB3	Chrome Rear Step Bumper (Reg Cab/X-Cab) *Includes rubber step pad. REQUIRES VG3 and 1SA. NOT AVAILABLE with EF1.*	85	99
VB3	Deluxe Chrome Rear Bumper (Crew Cab) *Includes rub strip. REQUIRES 1SA. NOT AVAILABLE with EF1.*	85	99
VG3	Deluxe Chrome Front Bumper (Reg Cab/X-Cab) *Includes rubber strip. REQUIRES 1SA.*	22	26
VYU	Snow Plow Prep Package (4WD - Reg Cab/X-Cab) *Includes HD front springs. NOT AVAILABLE with L65, HC4.*	101	118
XGK	Tires: Front LT245/75R16E AT BSW (4WD - Reg Cab/Crew Cab LB) *REQUIRES YGK and ZGK. NOT AVAILABLE with R05, C7A, XHR, XYK, XYL, YHP, YHR, YYK, YYL, ZHR, ZYK, ZYL.*	19	23
XHP	Tires: Front LT225/75R16D AS BSW (Reg Cab/Crew Cab LB) *REQUIRES YHP. NOT AVAILABLE with KL5, XGK, XHR, XYK, XYL, YGK, YYK, YYL, ZGK, ZYK, ZYL.*	(58)	(68)
XHR	Tires: Front LT225/75R16D AT BSW (4WD - Reg Cab/Crew Cab LB) *REQUIRES YHR and ZHR. NOT AVAILABLE with KL5, XGK, XYK, XYL, YGK, YHP, YYK, YYL, ZGK, ZYK, ZYL.*	(40)	(46)
XHR	Tires: Front LT225/75R16D AT BSW (4WD - X-Cab/Crew Cab SB) *REQUIRES YHR and ZHR. NOT AVAILABLE with KL5, XYK, YYK, ZYK, XYL, YYL, ZYL.*	19	22
XYK	Tires: Front LT215/85R16D Highway BSW (Reg Cab/Crew Cab LB) *REQUIRES YYK and ZYK. NOT AVAILABLE with KL5, XGK, XHR, XYL, YGK, YHP, YHR, YYL, ZGK, ZHR, ZYL.*	64	74
XYK	Tires: Front LT215/85R16D Highway BSW (X-Cab/Crew Cab SB) *REQUIRES YYK and ZYK. NOT AVAILABLE with KL5, XHR, YHR, ZHR, XYL, YYL, ZYL.*	122	142
XYL	Tires: Front LT215/85R16D AT BSW (4WD - Reg Cab/Crew Cab LB) *REQUIRES F60 and YYL and ZYL. NOT AVAILABLE with KL5, XGK, XHR, XYK, YGK, YHP, YHR, YYK, ZGK, ZHR, ZYK.*	112	130
XYL	Tires: Front LT215/85R16D AT BSW (4WD - X-Cab/Crew Cab SB) *REQUIRES F60 and YYL and ZYL. NOT AVAILABLE with KL5, XHR, YHR, ZHR, XYK, YYK, ZYK.*	170	198

CODE	DESCRIPTION	INVOICE	MSRP
YF5	California Emission Requirements *REQUIRES L65 or MT1. NOT AVAILABLE with HC4, KL5, U01.*	NC	NC
YG4	Rear Seat Delete (X-Cab) *REQUIRES 1SA.*	(374)	(435)
YG6	Air Conditioning Not Desired *REQUIRES 1SA. NOT AVAILABLE with R9A.*	NC	NC
YGK	Tires: Rear LT245/75R16E AT BSW (Reg Cab/Crew Cab LB) *REQUIRES XGK and ZGK. NOT AVAILABLE with R05, C7A, XHR, XYK, XYL, YHP, YHR, YYK, YYL, ZHR, ZYK, ZYL.*	19	23
YHP	Tires: Rear LT225/75R16D AS BSW (Reg Cab/Crew Cab LB) *REQUIRES R05 and C7A. NOT AVAILABLE with KL5, XGK, XHR, XYK, XYL, YGK, YHR, YYK, YYL, ZGK, ZHR, ZYK, ZYL.*	370	430
YHR	Tires: Rear LT225/75R16D AT BSW (Reg Cab/Crew Cab LB) *REQUIRES R05 and C7A and XHR and ZHR. NOT AVAILABLE with KL5, XGK, XYK, XYL, YGK, YHP, YYK, YYL, ZGK, ZYK, ZYL.*	408	474
YHR	Tires: Rear LT225/75R16D AT BSW (X-Cab/Crew Cab SB) *REQUIRES ZHR and XHR. NOT AVAILABLE with KL5, XYK, YYK, ZYK, XYL, YYL, ZYL.*	38	44
YYK	Tires: Rear LT215/85R16D Highway BSW (Reg Cab/Crew Cab LB) *REQUIRES R05 and C7A and XYK and ZYK. NOT AVAILABLE with KL5, XGK, XHR, XYL, YGK, YHP, YHR, YYL, ZGK, ZHR, ZYL.*	614	714
YYK	Tires: Rear LT215/85R16D Highway BSW (X-Cab/Crew Cab SB) *REQUIRES XYK and ZYK. NOT AVAILABLE with KL5, XHR, YHR, ZHR, XYL, YYL, ZYL.*	244	284
YYL	Tires: Rear LT215/85R16D AT BSW (4WD - Reg Cab/Crew Cab LB) *REQUIRES R05 and C7A and XYL and ZYL. NOT AVAILABLE with KL5, XGK, XHR, XYK, YGK, YHP, YHR, YYK, ZGK, ZHR, ZYK.*	710	826
YYL	Tires: Rear LT215/85R16D AT BSW (4WD - X-Cab/Crew Cab SB) *REQUIRES XYL and ZYL. NOT AVAILABLE with KL5, XHR, YHR, ZHR, XYK, YYK, ZYK.*	341	396
Z82	HD Trailering Special Equipment (Crew Cab) *Includes platform trailer hitch. NOT AVAILABLE with EF1.*	141	164
Z82	HD Trailering Special Equipment (Reg Cab/X-Cab) *Includes trailer hitch platform. NOT AVAILABLE with EF1.*	141	164
ZGK	Tire: Spare LT245/75R16E AT BSW (Reg Cab/Crew Cab LB) *REQUIRES XGK and YGK. NOT AVAILABLE with C7A, R05, XHR, XYK, XYL, YHP, YHR, YYK, YYL, ZHR, ZYK, ZYL.*	9	11
ZHP	Tire: Spare LT225/75R16D AS BSW (Reg Cab/Crew Cab LB) *REQUIRES YHP. NOT AVAILABLE with KL5, XGK, XHR, XYK, XYL, YGK, YHR, YYK, YYL, ZGK, ZHR, ZYK, ZYL.*	(29)	(34)
ZHR	Tire: Spare LT225/75R16D AT BSW (Reg Cab/Crew Cab LB) *REQUIRES YHR or XHR. NOT AVAILABLE with KL5, XGK, XYK, XYL, YGK, YHP, YYK, YYL, ZGK, ZYK, ZYL.*	(20)	(23)
ZHR	Tire: Spare LT225/75R16D AT BSW (X-Cab/Crew Cab SB) *REQUIRES YHR and XHR. NOT AVAILABLE with XYK, YYK, ZYK, XYL, YYL, ZYL.*	9	11
ZQ3	Convenience Group *Includes tilt wheel and speed control. REQUIRES 1SA.*	331	385

CODE	DESCRIPTION	INVOICE	MSRP
ZYK	Tire: Spare LT215/85R16D Highway BSW (Reg Cab/Crew Cab LB) .... *REQUIRES YYK or XYK. NOT AVAILABLE with XGK, XHR, XYL, YGK, YHP, YHR, YYL, ZGK, ZHR, ZYL.*	32	37
ZYK	Tire: Spare LT215/85R16D Highway BSW (X-Cab/Crew Cab SB) .... *REQUIRES YYK and XYK. NOT AVAILABLE with XHR, YHR, ZHR, XYL, YYL, ZYL.*	61	71
ZYL	Tire: Spare LT215/85R16D AT BSW (4WD - Reg Cab/Crew Cab LB) .... *REQUIRES YYL or XYL. NOT AVAILABLE with KL5, XGK, XHR, XYK, YGK, YHP, YHR, YYK, ZGK, ZHR, ZYK.*	56	65
ZYL	Tire: Spare LT215/85R16D AT BSW (4WD - X-Cab/Crew Cab SB).................. *REQUIRES YYL and XYL. NOT AVAILABLE with XHR, YHR, ZHR, XYK, YYK, ZYK.*	85	99
~~2	Leather Seat Trim (Crew Cab) .... *Includes leather surface on seating only. REQUIRES 1SB. INCLUDED in 1SC.*	946	1100

2000 EXPRESS

2000 Chevrolet Express

What's New?

Chevy updates the basic V6 for quieter operation, enhanced durability and reduced emissions. New exterior colors and side striping debut, and a new rear defogger for models with fixed rear glass and swing-out vent windows improves visibility.

Review

When Chevy dealers received a brand-new, full-size van to sell in 1996, it marked the first time in 25 years that GM had completely redesigned its big vans. The Chevy Express comes standard with lots of cargo space, dual airbags and four-wheel antilock brakes. And it can be equipped with a variety of powerful engines. With this modern design and body-on-frame construction, Chevrolet is stealing some of Ford's thunder in the full-size van market.

Because most full-size vans are bought for conversion into rolling motel rooms, engineers decided to put the Chevy Express on a full-frame platform for improved stability. Regular-length models carry 267 cubic feet of cargo, and extended-length vans can haul 317 cubic feet of stuff. Trick rear doors open 180 degrees to make loading and unloading easier. Up to 15 passengers can ride in the extended-length version, making it perfect for use as an airport shuttle. Other seating options include five-, eight- and 12-passenger arrangements. And G3500s can tow up to 10,000 pounds when properly equipped.

For convenience, the full-size spare is stored underneath the cargo floor. A 31-gallon fuel tank keeps this thirsty vehicle from frequent fill-ups, but topping off an empty tank will quickly empty your wallet. Engine choices are sourced from the Chevrolet family of Vortec gasoline motors, or if you prefer, a turbocharged diesel. The Vortec 4300 V6 has been updated for 2000 to provide quieter operation, reduced emissions and improved durability. Other powerplants include the 5000, 5700, and 7400 V8s, and a 6.5-liter turbodiesel V8. Standard side cargo doors are a 60/40 panel arrangement, but a traditional slider is a no-cost option on 135-inch wheelbase vans.

Two trim levels are available: base and LS. Child safety locks are standard on the rear and side doors. Handy assist handles help folks climb in and out. Base Express vans include front air conditioning (front and rear air conditioning is optional), vinyl seats, AM/FM stereo, and daytime running lights. LS adds power windows and locks, cruise control and tilt wheel.

Exterior styling is an interesting mix of corporate Chevrolet, Astro Van and old Lumina Minivan. We'll admit the high, rear pillar-mounted taillights are odd looking, but at least they're functional. They can easily be seen even if the van is operated with the rear doors open. Low-mounted bumpers and moldings make the Chevy Express look much taller than it is. An attractively sculpted body side gives the van's smooth, slab-sided flanks a dose of character, as does the quad-lamp grille arrangement. For 2000, new exterior colors and side striping debut, as a new rear defogger is available for models with fixed or vented rear glass.

Overall, Chevrolet's latest rendition of the traditional full-size van appears to be right on target, giving Ford's Econoline/Club Wagon its only real competition.

Standard Equipment

G1500 BASE PASSENGER VAN LD (4A): 4.3L V6 OHV SMPI 12-valve engine; 4-speed electronic OD auto transmission with lock-up; 600-amp battery; engine block heater; 100-amp alternator; rear-wheel drive, 3.42 axle ratio; stainless steel exhaust; front independent suspension with anti-roll bar, front coil springs, rigid rear axle suspension with rear leaf springs; power re-circulating ball steering with vehicle speed-sensing assist; front disc/rear drum brakes with 4-wheel antilock braking system; 30.9 gal. capacity fuel tank; front license plate bracket, side impact bars; 3 doors with split swing-out right rear passenger's door, split swing-out rear cargo door; front and rear argent bumpers with rear step; monotone paint; sealed beam halogen headlamps with daytime running lights; driver's and passenger's manual black folding outside mirrors; front and rear 15" x 7" painted styled steel wheels; P235/75SR15 A/S BSW front and rear tires; underbody mounted full-size steel spare wheel with crankdown; air conditioning; AM/FM stereo, clock, seek-scan, 4 speakers, and fixed antenna; child safety rear door locks; 2 power accessory outlets, smokers' package; instrumentation display includes oil pressure gauge, water temperature gauge, volt gauge, trip odometer; warning indicators include battery, lights on, key in ignition; driver's and passenger's front airbags; ignition disable; tinted windows, vented rear windows; variable intermittent front windshield wipers, vented rear window; seating capacity of 8, front bucket seats, fixed headrests, driver's seat includes 4-way direction control, passenger's seat includes 4-way direction control; removable 2nd row bench seat; removable 3rd row bench seat; front height adjustable seatbelts; vinyl seats, full cloth headliner, full vinyl floor covering, plastic/rubber gear shift knob; interior lights include dome light; day/night rearview mirror; engine cover console with storage, front cupholder, instrument panel covered bin, 2 seat back storage pockets; vinyl cargo floor, plastic trunk lid, cargo light; argent grille, black side window moldings, black front windshield molding, black rear window molding and black door handles.

G2500 BASE PASSENGER VAN HD/ G2500 BASE EXTENDED PASSENGER VAN HD (4A) (in addition to or instead of G1500 BASE PASSENGER VAN LD (4A) equipment): 5.7L V8 OHV SMPI 16-valve engine; 124-amp alternator; transmission oil cooler; 3.73 axle ratio; front and rear 16" x 6.5" painted styled steel wheels; LT225/75SR16 A/S BSW front and rear tires; seating capacity of 12 and cloth door trim insert.

G3500 BASE PASSENGER VAN HD/ G3500 BASE EXTENDED PASSENGER VAN HD (4A) (in addition to or instead of G2500 BASE PASSENGER VAN HD/ G2500 BASE EXTENDED PASSENGER VAN HD (4A) equipment): LT245/75SR16 A/S BSW front and rear tires.

Base Prices

Code	Description	Invoice	MSRP
CG11406-ZW9	G1500 Base LD (4A)	20361	23270
CG21406-ZW9	G2500 Base HD (4A)	22549	25770
CG31406-ZW9	G3500 Base HD (4A)	22798	26059
CG21706-ZW9	G2500 Base Extended HD (4A)	23336	26670
CG31706-ZW9	G3500 Base Extended HD (4A)	23625	27004
Destination Charge:		640	640

Accessories

— **Custom Cloth Seat Trim** .... NC NC
REQUIRES AS5 and (1SA or 1SB).

1SA **Preferred Equipment Group 1SA** .... NC NC
Includes vehicle with standard equipment. NOT AVAILABLE with UNO, ULO, UPO.

1SB **Preferred Equipment Group 1SB** 739 859
Includes convenience group: power door locks, power windows, tilt-wheel and cruise control.

1SC **Preferred Equipment Group 1SC** 1423 1655
Includes convenience group: power door locks, power windows, tilt-wheel, cruise control; LS Decor package: chrome bumpers, rear step, chrome grille, aero-composite headlamps, body side molding, trim rings, bright center hub caps, auxiliary lighting package: reading lamps, underhood lamp, front and side door step well lights; carpeted cargo area, vinyl floor mats, custom cloth seat trim, driver's and passenger's arm rests and full floor carpeting.

1SD **Preferred Equipment Group 1SD (1500)** 2841 3303
Includes convenience group, power door locks, power windows, tilt-wheel, cruise control, LS Decor package: chrome bumpers, rear step, chrome grille, aero-composite headlamps, body side molding, trim rings, bright center hub caps, auxiliary lighting package: reading lamps, underhood lamp, front and side door step well lights; carpeted cargo area, vinyl floor mats, custom cloth seat trim, driver's and passenger's arm rests and full floor carpeting; front and rear air conditioning, rear heater, deep-tinted glass, remote keyless entry, dual illuminated visor mirrors and leather-wrapped steering wheel.

1SD **Preferred Equipment Group 1SD (Extended)** 2101 2443
Includes convenience group, power door locks, power windows, tilt-wheel, cruise control, LS Decor package: chrome bumpers, rear step, chrome grille, aero-composite headlamps, body side molding, trim rings, bright center hub caps, auxiliary lighting package: reading lamps, underhood lamp, front and side door step well lights; carpeted cargo area, vinyl floor mats, custom cloth seat trim, driver's and passenger's arm rests and full floor carpeting; front and rear air conditioning, rear heater, deep-

CODE	DESCRIPTION	INVOICE	MSRP
	tinted glass, remote keyless entry, dual illuminated visor mirrors and leather-wrapped steering wheel.		
1SD	Preferred Equipment Group 1SD (Regular - 2500/3500)	2792	3247
	Includes convenience group, power door locks, power windows, tilt-wheel, cruise control, LS Decor package: chrome bumpers, rear step, chrome grille, aero-composite headlamps, body side molding, trim rings, bright center hub caps, auxiliary lighting package: reading lamps, underhood lamp, front and side door step well lights; carpeted cargo area, vinyl floor mats, custom cloth seat trim, driver's and passenger's arm rests and full floor carpeting; front and rear air conditioning, rear heater, deep-tinted glass, remote keyless entry, dual illuminated visor mirrors and leather-wrapped steering wheel.		
AG1	6-Way Power Driver's Seat	206	240
	REQUIRES AS5.		
AG2	6-Way Power Passenger's Seat	206	240
	REQUIRES AG1 and AS5.		
AJ1	Deep-Tinted Glass	335	390
	INCLUDED in 1SD.		
AS5	Front Bucket Deluxe Seat	NC	NC
	Includes inboard armrest.		
AU0	Remote Keyless Entry	129	150
	REQUIRES 1SC. INCLUDED in 1SD.		
B30	Full Floor Carpeting	126	147
	REQUIRES 1SA or 1SB. Includes front and rear vinyl mats.		
C36	Rear Heater	206	240
C49	Rear Defogger	132	154
	REQUIRES AG1.		
C69	Front and Rear Air Conditioning (1500)	740	860
	Includes rear heater and 124-amp alternator. INCLUDED in 1SD.		
C69	Front and Rear Air Conditioning (Extended)	NC	NC
	Includes rear heater. INCLUDED in 1SD.		
C69	Front and Rear Air Conditioning (Regular - 2500/3500)	691	804
	Includes rear heater. INCLUDED in 1SD.		
DE5	Electric Remote Fold-Away Mirrors	97	113
	Includes defog feature. REQUIRES ZQ2. INCLUDED in 1SD.		
DH6	Dual Illuminated Visor Mirrors	64	75
	REQUIRES 1SC. INCLUDED in 1SD.		
G80	Locking Differential	217	252
GT4	3.73 Axle Ratio	NC	NC
	NOT AVAILABLE with L30, GT5.		
GT5	4.10 Axle Ratio (All Except 1500)	NC	NC
KL5	Alternative Fuel Conversion (All Except 1500)	108	125
	NOT AVAILABLE with L65, L29.		
KW2	124-Amp Alternator (1500)	52	60
L29	Engine: Vortec 7400 V8 SFI (3500)	516	600
	NOT AVAILABLE with KL5.		
L30	Engine: Vortec 5000 V8 SFI (1500)	426	495
	NOT AVAILABLE with GT4.		

CODE	DESCRIPTION	INVOICE	MSRP
L31	Engine: Vortec 5700 V8 SFI (1500)	1028	1195
L65	Engine: 6.5L V8 Turbo Diesel (All Except 1500/2500 Regular) *NOT AVAILABLE with KL5, V10.*	2460	2860
N90	Wheels: Aluminum (1500) *Spare is steel. REQUIRES 1SA or 1SB.*	267	310
N90	Wheels: Aluminum (1500) *Spare is steel. REQUIRES 1SC or 1SD*	215	250
NC7	Federal Emission Override	NC	NC
NP5	Leather-Wrapped Steering Wheel *INCLUDED in 1SD.*	52	60
P06	Trim Rings and Bright Center Hub Caps *REQUIRES 1SA or 1SB.*	52	60
R6M	New Jersey Cost Surcharge	64	NC
TR9	Auxiliary Lighting *Includes reading lamps, underhood lamp and front and side door step well lights. REQUIRES 1SA or 1SB.*	138	160
U75	Power Antenna	73	85
UL0	Radio: AM/FM Stereo with Cassette and Automatic Tone Control *Includes digital clock, seek-scan, theft lock, speed compensated volume, 8 speakers and power antenna. NOT AVAILABLE with 1SA, UM6, UN0, UP0.*	380	442
UM6	Radio: AM/FM Stereo with Cassette *Includes digital clock. NOT AVAILABLE with UL0, UN0, UP0.*	126	147
UN0	Radio: AM/FM Stereo with CD and Automatic Tone Control *Includes digital clock, seek-scan, theft lock, speed compensated volume, 8 speakers and power antenna. NOT AVAILABLE with 1SA, UM6, UL0, UP0.*	466	542
UP0	Radio: AM/FM Stereo with CD, Cassette and Automatic Tone Control *Includes digital clock, seek-scan, theft lock, search and repeat, speed compensated volume, 8 speakers and power antenna. NOT AVAILABLE with 1SA, UM6, UL0, UN0.*	552	642
V10	Cold Climate Package *Includes engine block heater. NOT AVAILABLE with L65.*	41	48
XHB	Tires: P235/75R15X AS WSW (1500) *Includes front, rear and spare. NOT AVAILABLE with XHM.*	86	100
XHM	Tires: P235/75R15XL AS WOL (1500) *Includes front, rear and spare. NOT AVAILABLE with XHB.*	108	125
YA2	Sliding Side Rear Door	NC	NC
Z82	HD Trailering Special Equipment *Includes platform trailer hitch and 8-wire harness. (Additional cooling not required.).*	267	310
ZP3	15-Passenger Seating (3500)	319	371
ZP5	5-Passenger Seating (1500)	(319)	(371)
ZP8	8-Passenger Seating (Regular - 2500/3500)	(319)	(371)
ZQ2	Convenience Group *Includes power door locks and power windows. REQUIRES 1SA. INCLUDED in 1SB, 1SC, 1SD.*	408	474
ZQ3	Convenience Group *Includes tilt-wheel and cruise control. REQUIRES 1SA. INCLUDED in 1SB, 1SC, 1SD.*	331	385

2000 S-10

2000 Chevrolet S-10

What's New?

Performance and durability enhancements have been made to the engine, exhaust system, manual transmission, and antilock braking system, but they don't result in more horsepower. Trucks equipped with the ZR2 package get a new axle ratio designed to improve acceleration. Extended cabs come in Base trim this year, and LS models have revised exterior moldings.

Review

Like most of today's compact trucks, Chevrolet's S-Series has been growing more carlike, especially since its last redesign in 1994. That's the trend, and Chevy has continued transforming its small-scale pickups into everyday vehicles, without blurring their identity as practical machines. S-10 brand manager Debra Kelly-Ennis says, "It's a durable, rugged pickup, yet it has comfortable carlike qualities." Indeed, grasping the S-10's long manual-transmission gearshift lever makes it easy to imagine you're piloting a big rig, while enjoying the blissful comforts of a compact.

Four-cylinder models need that manual shift to gain top performance, but the available V6 engine (optional on 2WD S-10 and standard on 4WD models) is strong with either manual or automatic transmissions. The 180-horsepower Vortec 4300 V6 cranks out 245 foot-pounds of twist (190 horsepower and 250 ft-lbs. of torque in 4WD models). New are roller rocker arms, a roller timing chain and a powdered metal timing-chain sprocket that help the engine run more quietly and durably.

Extended cab trucks, newly available in Base trim, can be equipped with a handy access panel that opens wide to allow for easier access to the rear of the cab. Located on the driver's side, this optional third door deletes one of the extended cab's jump seats, but makes it much easier to load cargo, a friend, or your pal Spot into the S-10. But be warned, the third door makes for aggravating rattles on broken pavement.

Two- and four-wheel-drive trucks come in several configurations, with a short or long bed, a Fleetside box or Sportside box, and a short or extended wheelbase available. Ride comfort varies from car-smooth to strictly firm, depending on the choice of suspensions and tires.

Headroom is ample and seats are supportive, but the driver sits low, facing a tall steering wheel and cowl. In theory, three people fit across an S-Series bench seat, but only someone as slim as TV's Ally McBeal could fit comfortably in the space allotted. Surprisingly, the extended cab's rear jump seats are comfortable enough for short trips, as long as only one adult occupies the space behind the front seats.

The full complement of gauges is excellent and easy to read, but the upright dashboard is constructed of cheap- and brittle-looking plastic. Despite a low-height windshield, visibility is super, helped by huge side mirrors. Dual airbags and daytime running lamps are standard, as well as a theft deterrent system and four-wheel ABS. Off-roaders will want the burly ZR2 package with its wider track and taller ride height, featuring special wheel flares, tough suspension components, aggressive rubber and 3.73 rear-axle ratio.

The sporty Xtreme package can be had as a regular or extended cab, with a Fleetside or Sportside box, a four- or six-cylinder engine, manual or automatic transmission, and in base or LS trim. Riding on a special ZQ8 suspension that is lowered 2 full inches, the two-wheel-drive only Xtreme aims to be a factory sport truck that can be custom tailored to meet a variety of needs and budgets. No matter how you configure it, Xtreme stands out from the crowd with body-color grille and bumpers, front air dam with fog lamps, full ground effects with wheel flares, and unique 16-inch aluminum wheels wearing P235/55 blackwall tires. While we'd pick an extended cab LS Sportside with the V6 and a five-speed, this truck rides sports-car firm and handles superbly any way you package it.

Also new for '00 are improvements to the exhaust system, manual transmission, and antilock braking system. There's even revised LS exterior moldings, and a fresh paint color called Space Blue.

Like many Chevrolets, the S-10 is loaded with value, but we've never quite warmed up to it. Occasional squeaks and rattles and the low-buck interior don't provide the feeling of brawny quality that we've experienced in the S-10's major competitor, Ford's Ranger. Couple this lack of substantive feel with lousy crash-test scores, and we cannot find reason to recommend this GM compact over more capable and refined models.

Standard Equipment

BASE 2WD REGULAR CAB SB/LB (5M): 2.2L I4 OHV SMPI 8-valve engine; 5-speed OD manual transmission; 525-amp HD battery with run down protection; 100-amp alternator; rear-wheel drive, 3.73 axle ratio; stainless steel exhaust; comfort ride suspension (SB), firm ride suspension (LB), front independent suspension with anti-roll bar, front coil springs, rigid rear axle suspension with rear leaf springs; speed sensing power re-circulating ball steering; front disc/rear drum brakes with 4-wheel antilock braking system; 19 gal. capacity fuel tank; front license plate bracket, side impact bars; front and rear black bumpers with rear step; clearcoat monotone paint; aero-composite halogen fully auto headlamps with daytime running lights; driver's and passenger's manual black folding outside mirrors; front and rear 15" x 7" silver steel wheels; P205/75SR15 A/S BSW front and rear tires; underbody mounted compact steel spare wheel; AM/FM stereo, clock, seek-scan, 4 speakers, and fixed antenna; 1 power accessory outlet, retained accessory power, smokers' package; instrumentation display includes oil pressure gauge, water temperature gauge, volt gauge, trip odometer; warning indicators include battery, lights on, key in ignition; driver's front airbag, passenger's cancelable front airbag; ignition disable; tinted windows; variable intermittent front windshield wipers, sun visor strip; seating capacity of 3, bench front seat, fixed headrests, driver's seat includes 2-way direction control, passenger's seat includes 2-way direction control; vinyl seats, full cloth headliner, full vinyl floor covering, cabback insulator; interior lights include dome light with delay; day/night rearview mirror; glove box with light, front cupholder, driver's and passenger's door bins; cargo concealed storage; chrome grille, black side window moldings, black front windshield molding, black rear window molding and black door handles.

BASE 2WD EXTENDED CAB (5M) (in addition to or instead of BASE 2WD REGULAR CAB SB/LB (5M) equipment): 4.1 axle ratio; seating capacity of 5, 60-40 split-bench front seat, fixed headrests, center armrest with storage, driver's seat includes 4-way direction control, lumbar support, passenger's seat includes 4-way direction control, easy entry; 50-50 folding side facing rear jump seats; premium cloth seats, rear cupholders and 2 seat back storage pockets.

LS (in addition to or instead of BASE equipment): Front and rear body-colored bumpers with rear step; 3 power accessory outlets, front reading lights, 60-40 split-bench front seat, fixed headrests, center armrest with storage, driver's seat includes 4-way direction control, lumbar support, passenger's seat includes 4-way direction control; premium cloth seats, cloth door trim insert and full color-keyed carpet floor covering.

4WD (in addition to or instead of 2WD equipment): 4.3L V6 OHV SMPI 12-valve engine; engine oil cooler; transmission oil cooler; part-time 4 wheel drive, auto locking hub control and manual shift, 3.42 axle ratio; front torsion springs, front torsion bar, front tow hooks and P235/70SR15 A/S BSW front and rear tires.

Base Prices

CODE	DESCRIPTION	INVOICE	MSRP
CS10603-E63	Base 2WD Regular Cab SB (5M)	11912	12605
CS10803-E63	Base 2WD Regular Cab LB (5M)	12243	12956
CS10603-E63-YC3	LS 2WD Regular Cab SB (5M)	12332	13627
CS10803-E63-YC3	LS 2WD Regular Cab LB (5M)	12650	13978
CS10653-E63	Base 2WD Extended Cab SB (5M)	14020	15492
CS10653-E63-YC3	LS 2WD Extended Cab SB (5M)	14415	15928
CT10603-E63	Base 4WD Regular Cab SB (5M)	15913	16839
CT10603-E63-YC3	LS 4WD Regular Cab SB (5M)	16318	18031
CT10653-E63	Base 4WD Extended Cab SB (5M)	16318	17730
CT10653-E63-YC3	LS 4WD Extended Cab SB (5M)	18173	20081
Destination Charge:		535	535

Accessories

CODE	DESCRIPTION	INVOICE	MSRP
—	Custom Cloth Seat Trim (Base Reg Cab)	NC	NC
1SA	Preferred Equipment Group 1SA (2WD Reg Cab SB)	(430)	(500)
	Includes fleetside box. REQUIRES C60 or R6G. NOT AVAILABLE with UM7, ZQ6, ZQ8, UM6.		
1SA	Preferred Equipment Group 1SA (Base)	(387)	(450)
	Includes fleetside box. REQUIRES C60 or R6G. NOT AVAILABLE with UM7, ZQ6, UM6, ZQ8.		
1SA	Preferred Equipment Group 1SA (Base 2WD Reg Cab LB)	(688)	(800)
	Includes fleetside box. REQUIRES C60 or R6G. NOT AVAILABLE with UM7, ZQ6, UM6, L43, L35, M50.		
1SA	Preferred Equipment Group 1SA (Base 4WD Reg Cab)	(344)	(400)
	Includes fleetside box. REQUIRES C60 or R6G. NOT AVAILABLE with UM7, ZQ6, UM6.		
1SB	Preferred Equipment Group 1SB (LS 2WD Except LB)	1214	1412
	Manufacturer Discount	(1140)	(1325)
	Net Price	74	87
	Includes LS Decor package, fleetside box, air conditioning and floor mats. REQUIRES LN2 and MW2. NOT AVAILABLE with R6G, UM7, YC5, UPO, ZQ8, L35, L43, M50, GT5, G80.		
1SB	Preferred Equipment Group 1SB (LS 2WD Reg Cab LB)	126	147
	Manufacturer Discount	(989)	(1150)
	Net Price	(863)	(1003)
	Includes LS Decor package, fleetside box and floor mats. REQUIRES LM2 and MW2. NOT AVAILABLE with R6G, UM7, UPO, L43, L35, M50.		

CODE	DESCRIPTION	INVOICE	MSRP
1SB	Preferred Equipment Group 1SB (LS 2WD Reg Cab LB)	281	327
	Manufacturer Discount	(1140)	(1325)
	Net Price	(859)	(998)
	Includes LS Decor package, fleetside box and floor mats. REQUIRES M30. NOT AVAILABLE with R6G, UM7, M50, UP0.		
1SB	Preferred Equipment Group 1SB (LS 2WD Reg Cab LB)	126	147
	Manufacturer Discount	(860)	(1000)
	Net Price	(734)	(853)
	Includes LS Decor package, fleetside box and floor mats. REQUIRES MW2 or M50. NOT AVAILABLE with R6G, UM7, UP0.		
1SB	Preferred Equipment Group 1SB (LS SB)	1257	1412
	Manufacturer Discount	(860)	(1000)
	Net Price	397	412
	Includes LS Decor package, fleetside box, air conditioning and floor mats. REQUIRES (MW2 or M50) (2WD). NOT AVAILABLE with R6G, UM7, YC5, UP0, ZQ8, C5A, ZR2.		
1SB	Preferred Equipment Group 1SB (LS SB)	1214	1412
	Manufacturer Discount	(860)	(1000)
	Net Price	354	412
	Includes LS Decor package, fleetside box, air conditioning and floor mats. REQUIRES M30. NOT AVAILABLE with R6G, UM7, M50, YC5, UP0, ZQ8, C5A, ZR2.		
1SC	Preferred Equipment Group 1SC (LS 4WD X-Cab)	4533	5271
	Manufacturer Discount	(1140)	(1325)
	Net Price	3393	3946
	Includes ZR2 wide stance suspension package, front tread 61.2"/rear tread 59.1", unique 28mm front stabilizer bar, 46mm gas Bilstein shock absorbers, shield package, extra wide wheel flares, tachometer, AM/FM stereo with seek/scan and cassette, air conditioning, floor mats, wheels: bright aluminium, locking differential, comfort convenience group: cruise control, comfortilt steering wheel; sliding rear window, deep tinted glass and leather-wrapped steering wheel. NOT AVAILABLE with AM6, ANL, B84, N90, QEB, R6G, UM6, UM7, YC5, ZBF, ZEB, UP0.		
1SC	Preferred Equipment Group 1SC (LS 4WD X-Cab)	4533	5271
	Manufacturer Discount	(860)	(1000)
	Net Price	3673	4271
	Includes ZR2 wide stance suspension package, front tread 61.2"/rear tread 59.1", unique 28mm front stabilizer bar, 46mm gas Bilstein shock absorbers, shield package, extra wide wheel flares, tachometer, AM/FM stereo with seek/scan and cassette, air conditioning, floor mats, wheels: bright aluminium, locking differential, comfort convenience group: cruise control, comfortilt steering wheel; sliding rear window, deep tinted glass and leather-wrapped steering wheel. REQUIRES M50. NOT AVAILABLE with AM6, ANL, B84, N90, QEB, R6G, UM6, UM7, YC5, ZBF, ZEB, M30, UP0.		
1SD	Preferred Equipment Group 1SD (Base 2WD SB)	2743	3189
	Manufacturer Discount	(860)	(1000)
	Net Price	1883	2189
	Includes Xtreme sport appearance package: sport suspension package: wheels: 16" x 8" unique aluminum, tires: P235/55R16 A/S BSW SBR, 2" lowered ride		

CODE	DESCRIPTION	INVOICE	MSRP
	height; body color grille, body colored front and rear bumpers, body colored facia with removable license plate pocket, 270 degree ground effects, Xtreme badging, integral fog lamps, wheel flares, air conditioning, tachometer and leather-wrapped steering wheel. NOT AVAILABLE with A28, AJ1, C5D, G80, GU4, GU6, L35, M50, R6G, UL5, UM7, Z85, ZCE, ZQ6, ZQ8, UM6.		
1SE	Preferred Equipment Group 1SE (LS 2WD - Reg Cab SB/X-Cab)	3024	3516
	Manufacturer Discount	(1140)	(1325)
	Net Price	1884	2191
	Includes Xtreme sport appearance package: sport suspension package: wheels: 16" x 8" unique aluminum, tires: P235/55R16 A/S BSW SBR, 2" lowered ride height; body color grille, body colored front and rear bumpers, body colored facia with removable license plate pocket, 270 degree ground effects, Xtreme badging, integral fog lamps, wheel flares, air conditioning, tachometer, leather-wrapped steering wheel, LS Decor package and floor mats. NOT AVAILABLE with ANL, B84, C5D, QCA, R6G, UM7, Z85, ZCA, ZCE, YC5, ZQ8, M50, UPO, C3A.		
1SE	Preferred Equipment Group 1SE (LS 2WD - Reg Cab SB/X-Cab)	3024	3516
	Manufacturer Discount	(860)	(1000)
	Net Price	2164	2516
	Includes Xtreme sport appearance package: sport suspension package: wheels: 16" x 8" unique aluminum, tires: P235/55R16 A/S BSW SBR, 2" lowered ride height; body color grille, body colored front and rear bumpers, body colored facia with removable license plate pocket, 270 degree ground effects, Xtreme badging, integral fog lamps, wheel flares, air conditioning, tachometer, leather-wrapped steering wheel, LS Decor package and floor mats. NOT AVAILABLE with ANL, B84, C5D, QCA, R6G, UM7, Z85, ZCA, ZCE, YC5, ZQ8, UPO, C3A.		
1SE	Preferred Equipment Group 1SE (LS 2WD Reg Cab SB)	2869	3336
	Manufacturer Discount	(860)	(1000)
	Net Price	2009	2336
	Includes Xtreme sport appearance package: sport suspension package: wheels: 16" x 8" unique aluminum, tires: P235/55R16 A/S BSW SBR, 2" lowered ride height; body color grille, body colored front and rear bumpers, body colored facia with removable license plate pocket, 270 degree ground effects, Xtreme badging, integral fog lamps, wheel flares, air conditioning, tachometer, leather-wrapped steering wheel, LS Decor package and floor mats. REQUIRES MW2 or M50. NOT AVAILABLE with ANL, B84, C5D, QCA, R6G, UM7, Z85, ZCA, ZCE, YC5, ZQ8, UPO, L43.		
1SE	Preferred Equipment Group 1SE (LS 2WD Reg Cab SB)	2783	3236
	Manufacturer Discount	(731)	(850)
	Net Price	2052	2386
	Includes Xtreme sport appearance package: sport suspension package: wheels: 16" x 8" unique aluminum, tires: P235/55R16 A/S BSW SBR, 2" lowered ride height; body color grille, body colored front and rear bumpers, body colored facia with removable license plate pocket, 270 degree ground effects, Xtreme badging, integral fog lamps, wheel flares, air conditioning, tachometer, leather-wrapped steering wheel, LS Decor package and floor mats. REQUIRES MW2. NOT AVAILABLE with ANL, B84, C5D, QCA, R6G, UM7, Z85, ZCA, ZCE, YC5, ZQ8, UPO, M50, GT5, G80, L35.		

CODE	DESCRIPTION	INVOICE	MSRP
1SE	Preferred Equipment Group 1SE (LS 2WD X-Cab)	2783	3236
	Manufacturer Discount	(769)	(894)
	Net Price	2014	2342
	Includes Xtreme sport appearance package: sport suspension package: wheels: 16" x 8" unique aluminum, tires: P235/55R16 A/S BSW SBR, 2" lowered ride height; body color grille, body colored front and rear bumpers, body colored facia with removable license plate pocket, 270 degree ground effects, Xtreme badging, integral fog lamps, wheel flares, air conditioning, tachometer, leather-wrapped steering wheel, LS Decor package and floor mats. REQUIRES M50. NOT AVAILABLE with ANL, B84, C3A, QCA, R6G, UM7, ZCA, ZCE, YC5, ZQ8, UP0.		
A28	Sliding Rear Window	103	120
	NOT AVAILABLE with 1SD. INCLUDED in 1SC.		
AJ1	Deep Tinted Glass (Reg Cab)	64	75
	NOT AVAILABLE with 1SD. INCLUDED in 1SC.		
AJ1	Deep Tinted Glass (X-Cab)	99	115
	INCLUDED in 1SC.		
AM6	60/40 Split Bench Seat (LS 4WD - Reg Cab SB/X-Cab)	(215)	(250)
	Includes arm rest. REQUIRES M30, 1SB. NOT AVAILABLE with UP0, 1SC, ZR2.		
ANL	Fog Lamps (LS)	99	115
	NOT AVAILABLE with 1SE, 1SC, C5A, QJJ, ZJJ, ZR2.		
AV5	High Back Reclining Bucket Seats (2WD)	293	341
	REQUIRES L35 and M50. NOT AVAILABLE with L43, M30. INCLUDED in 1SC.		
B84	Body Side Moldings (LS Except LB)	86	100
	Black with bright accent, mounted between front and rear wheels. NOT AVAILABLE with YC5, 1SE, ZQ8, 1SC, ZR2.		
C3A	GVWR: 4,400 Lbs (2WD X-Cab)	NC	NC
	All GVWR options contain brake, suspension and chassis enhancements to achieve GVWR rating. REQUIRES ZQ8. NOT AVAILABLE with 1SE.		
C5A	GVWR: 4,900 Lbs (2WD LB/LS 4WD X-Cab)	NC	NC
	All GVWR options contain brake, suspension and chassis enhancements to achieve GVWR rating. NOT AVAILABLE with L43, GT5, 1SB, ANL, QEB, ZBF, ZEB.		
C5D	GVWR: 4,600 Lbs (2WD)	NC	NC
	All GVWR options contain brake, suspension and chassis enhancements to achieve GVWR rating. REQUIRES Z85. NOT AVAILABLE with ZQ8, 1SD, 1SE, C5A, L35, M50, GU4, GU6, G80, C3A.		
C60	Air Conditioning	692	805
	NOT AVAILABLE with R6G. INCLUDED in 1SB, 1SC.		
E24	Third Door (X-Cab)	271	315
	INCLUDED in 1SC.		
G80	Locking Differential	232	270
	NOT AVAILABLE with L43, 1SD, GT5, 1SB, 1SE. INCLUDED in 1SC.		
GT5	4.10 Axle Ratio (2WD)	NC	NC
	NOT AVAILABLE with L35, M50, G80, 1SB, 1SE, C5A.		
GU4	3.08 Axle Ratio (2WD)	NC	NC
	REQUIRES M30 or M50. NOT AVAILABLE with L43, 1SD.		
GU6	3.42 Axle Ratio	NC	NC
	REQUIRES G80. NOT AVAILABLE with M50, L43, 1SD, 1SC, C5A.		

CODE	DESCRIPTION	INVOICE	MSRP
L35	Engine: Vortec 4300 V6 SFI (2WD) *Includes engine oil cooler, transmission oil cooler and tachometer. REQUIRES (M30 and GU4) or (M50 and GU4) or (M30 and GU6) or C5A. NOT AVAILABLE with GT5, 1SD, 1SB, 1SE, 1SA.*	1114	1295
M30	Transmission: Electronic 4-Speed Automatic with OD *Includes brake-transmission shift interlock. REQUIRES GU4 or GU6 or GT5 or C60 or R6G. NOT AVAILABLE with AV5, 1SC, ZR2.*	942	1095
M50	Transmission: 5-Speed Manual with OD *REQUIRES GU4 or AV5 or C5A. NOT AVAILABLE with GU6, GT5, L43, 1SD, UP0, 1SB, 1SA, AM6, 1SC.*	NC	NC
N60	Wheels: Aluminum (Base 2WD X-Cab) *REQUIRES 1SA and M30 and C60. NOT AVAILABLE with L35, L43, M50. INCLUDED in 1SB.*	241	280
N60	Wheels: Aluminum Argent (LS 2WD) *NOT AVAILABLE with 1SE, YC5. INCLUDED in 1SB.*	241	280
N90	Wheels: Cast Aluminum (LS 4WD) *NOT AVAILABLE with PA3, 1SC, ZR2.*	241	280
NC7	Federal Emission Override	NC	NC
NP5	Leather-Wrapped Steering Wheel (LS) *INCLUDED in 1SC.*	46	54
PA3	Wheels: Bright Aluminium (LS 4WD) *Includes gray accent. NOT AVAILABLE with N90. INCLUDED in 1SC.*	241	280
QCA	Tires: P205/75R15 AS WOL SBR (LS 2WD) *Includes front, rear and compact spare. NOT AVAILABLE with ZCE, ZQ8, 1SE.*	104	121
QEB	Tires: P235/75R15 AT WOL SBR (LS 4WD) *Includes front, rear and compact spare. NOT AVAILABLE with ZBF, 1SC, QJJ, C5A, ZJJ, ZR2.*	123	143
QJJ	Tires: 31 x 10.5/15R AT BSW SBR (LS 4WD) *Includes full size spare. REQUIRES C5A. NOT AVAILABLE with QEB, ZBF, ZEB, ANL.*	NC	NC
R6G	Air Conditioning Not Desired *NOT AVAILABLE with C60, 1SB, 1SD, 1SE, 1SC.*	NC	NC
R6M	New Jersey Cost Surcharge	46	NC
U16	Tachometer (2WD)	51	59
UL0	Radio: AM/FM Stereo with Cassette (LS 2WD Reg Cab SB) *Includes seek-scan, digital clock, theft lock, speed compensated volume and auto tone control. NOT AVAILABLE with UN0, UP0, UM7, UM6, 1SB, 1SE. INCLUDED in 1SC.*	174	202
UL0	Radio: AM/FM Stereo with Cassette (LS 2WD Reg Cab SB) *Includes seek-scan, digital clock, theft lock, speed compensated volume and auto tone control. NOT AVAILABLE with UN0, UP0, UM7, UM6. INCLUDED in 1SC.*	NC	NC
UL0	Radio: AM/FM Stereo with Cassette (LS Except 2WD Reg Cab SB) *Includes digital clock, theft lock, speed compensated volume and auto tone control. NOT AVAILABLE with UN0, UP0, UM7, UM6, 1SB, 1SE. INCLUDED in 1SC.*	174	202
UL0	Radio: AM/FM Stereo with Cassette (LS Except 2WD Reg Cab SB) *Includes digital clock, theft lock, speed compensated volume and auto tone control. NOT AVAILABLE with UN0, UP0, UM7, UM6. INCLUDED in 1SC.*	69	80

CODE	DESCRIPTION	INVOICE	MSRP
UL5	Radio Delete (Base) *NOT AVAILABLE with UM6, UM7, 1SD.*	(194)	(226)
UM6	Radio: AM/FM Stereo with Cassette (Base) *Includes seek-scan and digital clock. NOT AVAILABLE with UM7, UL5, 1SA, 1SD. INCLUDED in 1SB, 1SE.*	299	348
UM6	Radio: AM/FM Stereo with Cassette (Base) *Includes seek-scan and digital clock. REQUIRES 1SA. NOT AVAILABLE with UM7, UL5, UL0, UN0, UP0, 1SC. INCLUDED in 1SB, 1SE.*	105	122
UN0	Radio: AM/FM Stereo with CD (LS) *Includes seek-scan, digital clock, theft lock, speed compensated volume and auto tone control. REQUIRES 1SB or 1SE. NOT AVAILABLE with UL0, UP0, UM7, UM6.*	155	180
UN0	Radio: AM/FM Stereo with CD (LS 4WD X-Cab) *Includes seek-scan, digital clock, theft lock, speed compensated volume and auto tone control. REQUIRES 1SC. NOT AVAILABLE with UL0, UP0, UM7, UM6.*	NC	NC
UP0	Radio: AM/FM Stereo with Cassette and CD (LS) *Includes seek-scan, digital clock, theft lock, speed compensated volume and auto tone control. REQUIRES 1SB or 1SE, (AV5 and M30). NOT AVAILABLE with UL0, UN0, M50, UM7, UM6, AM6, 1SC.*	86	100
UP0	Radio: AM/FM Stereo with Cassette and CD (LS 4WD X-Cab) *Includes seek-scan, digital clock, theft lock, speed compensated volume and auto tone control. REQUIRES M30 and 1SC. NOT AVAILABLE with UL0, UN0, UM7, UM6, AM6, 1SB.*	172	200
V10	Cold Climate Package *Includes HD battery and engine block heater.*	77	89
YC5	Exterior Appearance Package (LS Except Reg Cab LB) *Includes front and rear chrome bumpers, bright wheel opening moldings and body side moldings. NOT AVAILABLE with ZQ8, B84, 1SE, 1SB, 1SC, ZR2.*	494	575
YC5	Exterior Appearance Package (LS Except Reg Cab LB) *Includes front and rear chrome bumpers, bright wheel opening moldings and body side moldings. REQUIRES 1SB, 1SC or 1SE. NOT AVAILABLE with ZQ8, B84, ZR2.*	254	295
Z85	Increased Capacity Suspension Package (2WD - Reg Cab SB/X-Cab) *NOT AVAILABLE with ZQ8, 1SD, 1SE.*	55	64
ZBF	Tire: Spare P235/70R15 AS BSW SBR (4WD) *Includes steel wheel. NOT AVAILABLE with ZEB, QEB, 1SC, QJJ, C5A, ZJJ, ZR2.*	82	95
ZCA	Tire: Spare P205/75R15 AS WL SBR (LS 2WD) *Includes steel wheel. REQUIRES QCA. NOT AVAILABLE with ZQ8, ZCE, 1SE.*	82	95
ZCE	Tire: Spare P205/75R15 AS BW SBR (2WD) *Includes steel wheel. NOT AVAILABLE with QCA, ZCA, ZQ8, 1SD, 1SE.*	82	95
ZEB	Tire: Spare P235/75R15 AT WOL SBR (LS 4WD) *Includes steel wheel. REQUIRES QEB. NOT AVAILABLE with ZBF, 1SC, QJJ, C5A, ZJJ, ZR2.*	82	95
ZJJ	Tire: Spare 31 x 10.5/15R AT BSW SBR (LS 4WD X-Cab) *Includes steel wheel. REQUIRES QJJ and C5A. NOT AVAILABLE with QEB, ZBF, ZEB, ANL.*	NC	NC
ZM5	Shield Package (4WD) *INCLUDED in 1SC.*	108	126

CODE	DESCRIPTION	INVOICE	MSRP
ZQ3	Comfort Convenience Group *Includes cruise control and comfortilt steering wheel. INCLUDED in 1SC.*	340	395
ZQ6	Power Convenience Group *Includes power windows, power door locks, heated outside rearview mirrors and remote keyless entry. NOT AVAILABLE with 1SA, 1SD. INCLUDED in 1SC.*	684	795
ZQ8	Sport Suspension Package (LS 2WD - Reg Cab SB/X-Cab) *Full size spare tire not available. Includes wheels: 16" aluminum and tires: P235/55R16 A/S BSW SBR. NOT AVAILABLE with 1SA, C5D, Z85, ZCE, 1SD, QCA, ZCA, YC5, B84, 1SE, 1SB.*	675	785
ZQ8	Sport Suspension Package (LS 2WD - Reg Cab SB/X-Cab) *Full size spare tire not available. Includes wheels: 16" aluminum and tires: P235/55R16 A/S BSW SBR. REQUIRES 1SB. NOT AVAILABLE with Z85, QCA, ZCA, ZCE, YC5, C5D, B84, 1SE.*	434	505
ZR2	Wide Stance Suspension Package (LS 4WD X-Cab) *Includes unique revised frame for wide tread, unique strengthened front differential gears and drive axles, unique rear axle with 8.5" gear ring, larger wheel bearings, longer, larger diameter rear axle shafts, unique rear suspension with revised multi-leafed springs and added rear axle track bar, gray and chrome grille, unique front fenders and pickup box outer panels, modified jack and spare tire stowage winch, full size spare tire, front tread 61.2"/rear tread 59.1", unique 28mm front stabilizer bar, 46mm gas Bilstein shock absorbers, shield package, extra wide wheel flares and tachometer. Body is 3" higher. NOT AVAILABLE with B84, YC5, AM6, 1SB, QEB, ZBF, ZEB, ANL, N90, M30. INCLUDED in 1SC.*	1630	1895

2000 SILVERADO

What's New?

After a complete redesign last year, few changes make news for 2000. Most substantial is the addition of a fourth access door to extended cab models, but it's optional, unlike the standard quad-portal arrangement on the Ford F-150. The already potent Vortec 4800 and 5300 V8 engines make more power, and programmable door locks can be instructed to unlock automatically when the Silverado is shut off, solving an irritating problem on 1999 trucks. A Sportside cargo box is available on 1500 LT models, and 1500 4WD trucks can be equipped with wheel flares this year. LS and LT trucks get a standard electrochromic self-dimming rearview mirror with compass and exterior temperature display, and a soft tonneau cover is available from the factory.

Review

Imagine the pressure engineers and designers suffered when they undertook the task of completely revising the best-selling model that General Motors produces. Success would insure that GM could continue to reap large benefits from a booming truck industry. Failure would reduce market share, profits and credibility. Making matters worse, the existing platform was already a hot seller. How to fix something that wasn't broken?

They started by asking Chevy truck customers what they wanted in a new full-size pickup. More power, better handling, more interior room, better fuel economy and a stronger chassis were the answers. What they most certainly did not want was cartoonish or carlike styling, which Chevy owners felt the Dodge and Ford stores were selling.

So Chevrolet gave the customer what they asked for. Looking at the Silverado, some might be hard-pressed to discern differences between it and the old C/K model. But under the skin, GM served up a heaping pile of massive improvement, and that's where it counts.

Several engine choices are available, ranging from a newly improved 4.3-liter V6 to a turbodiesel 6.5-liter V8. Most buyers select 4800 and 5300 Vortec V8 engines, and they make more power for 2000. The 4.8-liter and 5.3-liter units each generate 15 more ponies than they did in '99, but only the 5300 motor gets a boost in torque, from 315 foot-pounds at 4,000 rpm to 325 ft-lbs. at the same revs. The 6.0-liter V8 gets a new high-extension torque converter when equipped with the available automatic transmission. Automatics also come equipped with a tow-haul mode that improves performance under heavy loads.

Holding all this together is a three-section frame that is stiff, light and easy to assemble. It contributes to class-leading impact absorption, a smooth ride and a quiet interior. Payload capacity is stout as well. State-of-the-art steering, suspension and braking systems help make driving the Silverado a joy. Four-wheel disc antilock brakes are standard, and steering feel is tight for a large truck, thanks in part to the power rack-and-pinion gear on models under 6,400 GVWR. The turning circle is relatively small and a wide rear track contributes to stability on the highway. Optional is Adjustable Electronic Ride Control, the first selective damping system ever offered on a pickup.

Inside, Silverado buyers will find logically laid out switchgear, though the plastics feel like they're sourced from the same supplier contracted by Fisher Price. The cabin is roomy, particularly on extended cab models. A standard third door on the latter makes entry and exit to the rear bench seat easy, and if front passengers are willing to sacrifice a bit of legroom, the back of the extended cab is quite comfortable. Front seatbelts are mounted to the seats themselves so rear passengers don't need to chop through a web of fabric to get in and out. Optional for '00 is a fourth door on the driver's side of the truck.

Other changes this year include power door locks that can be programmed to unlock automatically when the Silverado is shut off, solving an irritating problem on 1999 trucks. A Sportside cargo box is available on 1500 LT models, and 1500 4WD trucks can be equipped with wheel flares this year. Optional on the LS and standard on the LT trucks are an electrochromic self-dimming rearview mirror with compass and exterior temperature display. A soft tonneau cover is available on the LT Fleetside Box version only.

The bar was raised with the introduction of the Chevy Silverado, and GM bean counters needn't worry about their bonuses at year's end. This truck will continue to be a huge success.

2000 Chevrolet Silverado

2000 SILVERADO 1500

Standard Equipment

BASE 2WD REGULAR CAB SB/LB (5M): 4.3L V6 OHV SMPI 12-valve engine; 5-speed OD manual transmission; 600-amp HD battery; 105-amp alternator; rear-wheel drive, 3.08 axle ratio; stainless steel exhaust; front independent suspension with anti-roll bar, front coil springs, rigid rear axle suspension with rear leaf springs; power rack-and-pinion steering with vehicle speed-sensing assist; 4-wheel disc brakes with 4-wheel antilock braking system; 26 gal. (34 gal. - LB) capacity fuel tank; side impact bars; trailer harness; front and rear bumper black rub strip, front chrome bumper, rear argent bumper, rear step; monotone paint; aero-composite halogen fully auto headlamps with daytime running lights; additional exterior lights include pickup cargo box light, underhood light; driver's and passenger's manual black folding outside mirrors; front and rear 16" x 6.5" silver styled steel wheels; P235/75SR16 A/S BSW front and rear tires; underbody mounted full-size steel spare wheel with crankdown; AM/FM stereo, clock, seek-scan, 4 speakers, and fixed antenna; 3 power accessory outlets; instrumentation display includes tachometer, oil pressure gauge, water temperature gauge, volt gauge, compass, exterior temp, trip odometer; warning indicators include oil pressure, water temp, battery, low oil level, low coolant, lights on, key in ignition, low fuel, door ajar, service interval; driver's front airbag, passenger's cancelable front airbag; ignition disable; tinted windows; variable intermittent front windshield wipers, sun visor strip; seating capacity of 3, 40-20-40 split-bench front seat, adjustable headrests, driver's seat includes 4-way direction control, passenger's seat includes 2-way direction control; vinyl seats, full cloth headliner, full vinyl floor covering, cabback insulator; interior lights include dome light with delay, front reading lights; sport steering wheel with tilt adjustment; passenger's side vanity mirror; auto-dimming day/night rearview mirror; glove box with light, front cupholder, driver's and passenger's door bins; argent grille, black side window moldings, black front windshield molding, black rear window molding and black door handles.

LS 2WD REGULAR CAB SB/LB (5M) (in addition to or instead of BASE 2WD REGULAR CAB SB/LB (5M) equipment): Front and rear chrome bumpers with black rub strip; colored bodyside molding with chrome bodyside insert; driver's and passenger's power remote chrome folding outside mirrors; air conditioning; AM/FM stereo, clock, seek-scan, single CD, 6 performance speakers, auto equalizer, theft deterrent, and fixed antenna; cruise control; power door locks with 2 stage unlock, remote keyless entry; retained accessory power; ignition disable, panic alarm, security system; power front windows with driver's 1-touch down; center armrest with storage, driver's seat includes 4-way direction control, lumbar support, passenger's seat includes, 4-way direction control, lumbar support; premium cloth seats, cloth door trim insert, full color-keyed carpet floor covering with floor mats; interior lights include illuminated entry; leather-wrapped sport steering wheel with tilt adjustment and chrome grille.

BASE 2WD EXTENDED CAB SB (5M) (in addition to or instead of BASE 2WD REGULAR CAB SB (5M) equipment): 3.42 axle ratio; rear heat ducts; seating capacity of 6 and full folding rear bench seat with adjustable headrests.

BASE 2WD EXTENDED CAB LB (5M) (in addition to or instead of BASE 2WD EXTENDED CAB SB (5M) equipment): 4.8L V8 OHV SMPI 16-valve engine and warning indicators include low washer fluid.

LS 2WD EXTENDED CAB SB (5M) (in addition to or instead of LS 2WD REGULAR CAB SB (5M) equipment): 3.42 axle ratio; rear heat ducts; seating capacity of 6 and full folding rear bench seat with adjustable headrests and 2 seat back storage pockets.

LS 2WD EXTENDED CAB LB (5M) (in addition to or instead of LS 2WD REGULAR CAB LB (5M) equipment): 4.8L V8 OHV SMPI 16-valve engine; 3.42 axle ratio; rear heat ducts; seating capacity of 6, full folding rear bench seat with adjustable headrests; warning indicators include low washer fluid and 2 seat back storage pockets.

CODE	DESCRIPTION	INVOICE	MSRP

LT 2WD EXTENDED CAB SB/LB (4A) (in addition to or instead of LS 2WD EXTENDED CAB LB (4A) equipment): 5.3L V8 OHV SMPI 16-valve engine; 4-speed electronic OD auto transmission with lock-up; driver's selectable multi-mode transmission; HD ride suspension, 26 gal. (34 gal. ? LB) capacity fuel tank; body-colored bodyside molding with chrome bodyside insert; additional exterior lights include front fog/driving lights; driver's and passenger's power remote chrome heated folding outside mirrors; P255/70SR16 A/S BSW front and rear tires; AM/FM stereo, clock, seek-scan, cassette, single CD, 6 performance speakers, auto equalizer, theft deterrent, and fixed antenna; deep tinted windows; variable intermittent front windshield wipers, sun visor strip, rear window defroster; seating capacity of 5, heated-cushion front bucket seats, adjustable headrests, driver and passenger armrests, driver's seat includes 6-way power seat, power 2-way lumbar support, passenger's seat includes 6-way power seat power 2-way lumbar support; leather seats; memory on driver's seat with 2 memory setting(s); full floor console, full overhead console with storage and front and rear cupholders.

BASE/LS 4WD REGULAR CAB SB/LB (5M) (in addition to or instead of BASE/LS 2WD REGULAR CAB SB/LB (5M) equipment): Part-time 4 wheel drive, auto locking hub control and manual shift, 3.73 axle ratio; front independent torsion suspension with anti-roll bar, front torsion springs, front torsion bar; power re-circulating ball steering with vehicle speed-sensing assist; front and rear tow hooks and P245/75SR16 A/S BSW front and rear tires.

BASE/LS 4WD EXTENDED CAB SB/LB (5M) (in addition to or instead of BASE/LS 2WD EXTENDED CAB LB (5M) equipment): Part-time 4 wheel drive, auto locking hub control and manual shift, 3.73 axle ratio; front independent torsion suspension with anti-roll bar, front torsion springs, front torsion bar; power re-circulating ball steering with vehicle speed-sensing assist; 26 gal. (34 gal. LB) capacity fuel tank; rear tow hooks and P245/75SR16 A/S BSW front and rear tires.

LT 4WD EXTENDED CAB SB/LB (4A) (in addition to or instead of LT 2WD EXTENDED CAB SB/LB (4A) equipment): Auto full-time 4 wheel drive, auto locking hub control and electronic shift, 3.73 axle ratio; front independent torsion suspension with anti-roll bar, front torsion springs, front torsion bar; power re-circulating ball steering with vehicle speed-sensing assist; rear tow hooks, and P245/75SR16 A/S BSW front and rear tires.

Base Prices

CC15703	Base 2WD Regular Cab SB (5M)	14168	15655
CC15903	Base 2WD Regular Cab LB (5M)	14439	15955
CK15703	Base 4WD Regular Cab SB (5M)	16987	18770
CK15903	Base 4WD Regular Cab LB (5M)	17258	19070
CC15753	Base 2WD Extended Cab SB (5M)	17263	19729
CC15703	LS 2WD Regular Cab SB (5M)	17282	19751
CC15903	LS 2WD Regular Cab LB (5M)	17545	20051
CC15953	Base 2WD Extended Cab LB (5M)	18134	20724
CC15753	LS 2WD Extended Cab SB (5M)	19688	22501
CK15703	LS 4WD Regular Cab SB (5M)	19995	22851
CK15903	LS 4WD Regular Cab LB (5M)	20257	23151
CC15953	LS 2WD Extended Cab LB (5M)	20559	23496
CK15753	Base 4WD Extended Cab SB (5M)	20584	23524
CK15953	Base 4WD Extended Cab LB (5M)	20846	23824
CK15753	LS 4WD Extended Cab SB (5M)	23009	26296
CK15953	LS 4WD Extended Cab LB (5M)	23272	26596
CC15753	LT 2WD Extended Cab SB (4A)	24596	28110

CODE	DESCRIPTION	INVOICE	MSRP
CC15953	LT 2WD Extended Cab LB (4A)	24859	28410
CK15753	LT 4WD Extended Cab SB (4A)	27405	31320
CK15953	LT 4WD Extended Cab LB (4A)	27668	31620
Destination Charge:		665	665

Accessories

—	Cloth Seat Trim (Base)	NC	NC
—	Custom Cloth Seat Trim (Base)	NC	NC
—	Leather Seat Trim (LS) *Includes 6-way power driver/passenger seats.*	1273	1480
1SA	Preferred Equipment Group 1SA (Base) *Includes vehicle with standard equipment.*	NC	NC
1SB	Preferred Equipment Group 1SB (LS) *Includes vehicle with standard equipment.*	NC	NC
1SC	Preferred Equipment Group 1SC (LT) *Includes vehicle with standard equipment.*	NC	NC
A28	Sliding Rear Window (Base/LS) *NOT AVAILABLE with C49.*	108	125
A95	Reclining Bucket Seats (LS) *Includes inboard armrests and manual lumbar and floor and overhead console.*	366	425
AG2	6-Way Power Driver's/Passenger's Seats (LS)	413	480
AJ1	Deep Tinted Solar Ray Glass (Reg Cab - Base/LS) *REQUIRES A28 or C49.*	43	50
AJ1	Deep Tinted Solar Ray Glass (X-Cab - Base/LS)	92	107
AU3	Power Door Locks (Base)	139	162
B71	Black Wheel Opening Flares (Base 4WD)	155	180
B71	Wheel Opening Flares (4WD - LS/LT)	155	180
BG9	Color-Keyed Rubber Floor Covering (LS) *Replaces carpeting and floor mats.*	(86)	(100)
C49	Electric Rear Window Defogger (Base/LS) *REQUIRES C60. NOT AVAILABLE with A28.*	150	175
C60	Front Air Conditioning (Base)	710	825
DF2	Camper Type Mirrors (Base) *Retractable with wide field of vision.*	52	60
DF2	Camper Type Mirrors (LS) *Retractable with wide field of vision. NOT AVAILABLE with DL8.*	(33)	(38)
DF5	10" Electrochromic ISRV Mirror (LS) *Includes 8-point compass and temperature.*	150	175
DL8	OSRV with Heater (LS) *REQUIRES C49. NOT AVAILABLE with DF2.*	36	42
E25	Fourth Door (X-Cab)	289	330
E62	Sportside Body (Base) *X-Cab REQUIRES LM7 or (LR4 and M30). NOT AVAILABLE with UY2 and E95. INCLUDES VB3.*	770	895

CODE	DESCRIPTION	INVOICE	MSRP
E62	Sportside Body (LS/LT) *LS X-Cab REQUIRES LM7 or (LR4 and M30). NOT AVAILABLE with ZY2 (LS), UY2 and E95.*	684	795
E95	Tonneau Cover	206	240
G80	Locking Differential *REQUIRES GT4 or GU6.*	245	285
GT4	3.73 Axle Ratio *REQUIRES LR4 or LM7. NOT AVAILABLE with GT5.*	NC	NC
GT5	4.10 Axle Ratio (4WD) *REQUIRES LM7 or LR4.*	NC	NC
GU6	3.42 Axle Ratio (2WD) *NOT AVAILABLE with GT4.*	NC	NC
K05	Engine Block Heater	30	35
K34	Cruise Control (Base)	206	240
K47	High Capacity Air Cleaner	22	25
LM7	Engine: Vortec 5300 SFI V8 (Reg Cab - Base/LS) *REQUIRES GT4 or GU6.*	1286	1495
LM7	Engine: Vortec 5300 SFI V8 (X-Cab - Base/LS)	688	800
LR4	Engine: Vortec 4800 SFI V8 (Reg Cab/X-Cab SB - Base/LS) *REQUIRES GT4 or GU6.*	598	695
M30	Transmission: 4-Speed Automatic (Base/LS)	942	1095
NC7	Federal Emission Override	NC	NC
NP8	Autotrac Active Transfer Case (LS 4WD) *REQUIRES M30.*	322	375
NZZ	Skid Plate Package (4WD - Base/LS) *Includes front differential and transfer case shields.*	82	95
PF9	Wheels: 16" Cast Aluminum (LS) *Includes spare wheel not matching.*	95	110
QBN	Tires: LT245/75R16C On/Off Road BSW (4WD) *REQUIRES Z71 (LS/LT). NOT AVAILABLE with QBX, QGA, QGB, QNL, QGC, QGD.*	138	161
QBX	Tires: LT245/75R16C On/Off Road OWL (4WD) *REQUIRES Z71 (LS/LT). NOT AVAILABLE with QBN, QGA, QGB, QNL, QGC, QGD.*	245	286
QCC	Tires: P255/70R16 AS BSW (2WD) *REQUIRES ZX3 (LS/LT). NOT AVAILABLE with QCJ, QNG.*	146	170
QCJ	Tires: P255/70R16 AS WOL (2WD) *REQUIRES ZX3 (LS/LT). NOT AVAILABLE with QNG.*	254	295
QCJ	Tires: P255/70R16 AS WOL (2WD)	108	125
QGA	Tires: P245/75R16 BSW AT (4WD) *NOT AVAILABLE with QBN, QBX, QGB, QGC, QGD, QNL, Z71.*	90	105
QGB	Tires: P245/75R16 AT WOL (4WD) *NOT AVAILABLE with QBN, QBX, QGA, QGC, QGD, QNL, Z71.*	198	230
QGC	Tires: P265/75R16 AT BSW (4WD - LS/LT) *REQUIRES Z71 and PF9 (LS). NOT AVAILABLE with QBN, QBX, QGA, QGB, QGD, QNL.*	206	240
QGD	Tires: P265/75R16 AT WOL (4WD - LS/LT) *REQUIRES Z71 and PF9 (LS). NOT AVAILABLE with QBN, QBX, QGA, QGB, QGC, QNL.*	314	365

CODE	DESCRIPTION	INVOICE	MSRP
QNG	Tires: P235/75R16 AS WOL (2WD - Base/LS) *NOT AVAILABLE with QCJ, ZX3, Z82.*	108	125
QNL	Tires: P245/75R16 AS OWL (4WD) *NOT AVAILABLE with QBN, QBX, QGA, QGB, QGC, QGD, Z71.*	108	125
R6M	New Jersey Cost Surcharge	74	NC
R9D	Exterior Appearance Package (Base) *Includes black bodyside moldings, chrome grille, wheels: chrome and chrome rear step bumper. NOT AVAILABLE with VF7.*	538	625
R9D	Exterior Appearance Package (Base) *Includes black bodyside moldings, chrome grille, wheels: chrome and chrome rear step bumper. REQUIRES E62. NOT AVAILABLE with VF7.*	452	525
R9E	Floor Covering Package (Base) *Includes floor carpeting with rubber mats.*	86	100
T96	Fog Lamps (LS)	120	140
UL0	Radio: AM/FM Stereo with Cassette (LS) *Includes digital clock, theft lock, speed compensated volume and auto tone control. NOT AVAILABLE with UP0.*	NC	NC
UL5	Radio Delete (Base) *Stowage tray, base speaker system and antenna remain. NOT AVAILABLE with UM6.*	(215)	(250)
UM6	Radio: AM/FM Stereo with Cassette (Base Reg Cab) *Includes seek-scan and digital clock. NOT AVAILABLE with UL5.*	146	170
UM6	Radio: AM/FM Stereo with Cassette (Base X-Cab) *Includes seek-scan and digital clock. NOT AVAILABLE with UL5.*	129	150
UP0	Radio: AM/FM Stereo with CD and Cassette (LS X-Cab) *Includes digital clock, auto tone control, search, repeat, theft lock, speed compensated volume, remote CD and an enhanced performance speaker system. REQUIRES NP8 (4WD). NOT AVAILABLE with UL0.*	86	100
UV8	Cellular Telephone Wiring Provisions *Includes wiring for remote mircrophone and cellular phone.*	43	50
UY2	Camper and Fifth Wheel Wiring Provisions *REQUIRES Z82.*	22	25
V76	Two Front Recovery Hooks (2WD)	33	38
VB3	Chrome Rear Step Bumper (Base) *NOT AVAILABLE with VF7.*	86	100
VF7	Rear Bumper Delete Provisions (Base) *Vehicles registered in certain states must have a rear bumper to be operated on their roads. Consult your local laws. NOT AVAILABLE with Z82, VB3, R9D.*	(86)	(100)
VF7	Rear Bumper Delete Provisions (LS) *Vehicles registered in certain states must have a rear bumper to be operated on their roads. Consult your local laws. NOT AVAILABLE with Z82.*	(172)	(200)
VYU	Snow Plow Prep Package (4WD Reg Cab - Base/LS) *Includes electrical connections, increased capacity cooling and 130-amp alternator. REQUIRES (1SA and Z82 and (LR4 or LM7)) or (1SA and (LR4 or LM7)) (Base) or 1SB (LS).*	163	190

CODE	DESCRIPTION	INVOICE	MSRP
VYU	Snow Plow Prep Package (Base 4WD Reg Cab) *Includes electrical connections, increased capacity cooling and 130-amp alternator. REQUIRES 1SA and (LM7 or LR4).*	245	285
Z71	Off-Road Package (4WD - LS/LT) *Includes 46mm shocks, off-road jounce bumpers, stabilizer bars, Z71 Decal and high capacity air cleaner. REQUIRES (LM7 or LR4) and (QBN or QBX or QGC or QGD). NOT AVAILABLE with QGA, QGB, QNL.*	340	395
Z82	HD Trailering Special Equipment *Includes 7-lead wiring harness, trailer hitch platform and transmission oil cooler. REQUIRES (LM7 or LR4) or ZX3 or Z71. NOT AVAILABLE with VF7, QNG.*	245	285
Z85	HD Suspension *Includes 36mm shocks. REQUIRES QCJ. NOT AVAILABLE with QNG, ZX3, Z71.*	82	95
ZX3	Smooth Ride Suspension (LS 2WD) *Includes 46mm shocks. Provides 2-position electronic control for shock setting and smooth road/trailering. REQUIRES (LM7 or LR4) and QCJ. NOT AVAILABLE with L35, VYU or QNG.*	361	420
ZX3	Smooth Ride Suspension (LT 2WD) *Includes 46mm shocks. Provides 2-position electronic control for shock setting and smooth road/trailering.*	280	325
ZY2	Two Tone Paint Application (LS)	215	250

2000 SILVERADO 2500

Standard Equipment

BASE 2WD REGULAR CAB LB HD (5M): 6.0L V8 OHV SMPI 16-valve engine; 5-speed OD manual transmission; 600-amp HD battery with run down protection; 105-amp alternator; rear-wheel drive, power take-off provision, 3.73 axle ratio; stainless steel exhaust; front independent suspension with anti-roll bar, front coil springs, rigid rear axle suspension with rear leaf springs; power re-circulating ball steering with vehicle speed-sensing assist; 4-wheel disc brakes with 4-wheel antilock braking system; 34 gal. capacity fuel tank; side impact bars; trailer harness; front and rear black rub strip, front chrome bumper, rear argent bumper, rear step; monotone paint; aero-composite halogen auto on headlamps with daytime running lights; additional exterior lights include pickup cargo box light, underhood light; driver's and passenger's manual black folding outside mirrors; front and rear 16" x 6.5" silver styled steel wheels; LT245/75SR16 A/S BSW front and rear tires; underbody mounted full-size steel spare wheel; AM/FM stereo, clock, seek-scan, 4 speakers, and fixed antenna; 3 power accessory outlets, retained accessory power; instrumentation display includes tachometer, oil pressure gauge, water temperature gauge, volt gauge, trip odometer; warning indicators include oil pressure, water temp, battery, low oil level, low coolant, lights on, key in ignition, low fuel, low washer fluid, door ajar, service interval; driver's front airbag, passenger's cancelable front airbag; ignition disable; tinted windows; variable intermittent front windshield wipers, sun visor strip; seating capacity of 3, 40-20-40 split-bench front seat, adjustable headrests, driver's seat includes 4-way direction control, passenger's seat includes 2-way direction control; vinyl seats, full cloth headliner, full vinyl floor covering, cabback insulator; interior lights include dome light, front reading lights; sport steering wheel with tilt adjustment; passenger's side vanity mirror; day/night rearview mirror; glove box with light, front cupholder, driver's and passenger's door bins; argent grille, black side window moldings, black front windshield molding, black rear window molding and black door handles.

CODE	DESCRIPTION	INVOICE	MSRP

BASE 2WD REGULAR CAB LB (4A) (in addition to or instead of BASE 2WD REGULAR CAB LB HD (4A) equipment): 5.3L V8 OHV SMPI 16-valve engine; 4-speed electronic OD auto transmission with lock-up; driver's selectable multi-mode transmission; LT225/75SR16 A/S BSW front and rear tires.

BASE 2WD EXTENDED CAB SB (4A) (in addition to or instead of BASE 2WD REGULAR CAB LB (4A) equipment): 3.42 axle ratio; 26 gal. capacity fuel tank; underbody mounted full-size steel spare wheel with crankdown; rear heat ducts; seating capacity of 6; full folding rear bench seat with adjustable headrests and interior lights include dome light with delay.

BASE 2WD EXTENDED CAB LB (5M) (in addition to or instead of BASE 2WD EXTENDED CAB SB (5M) equipment): 6.0L V8 OHV SMPI 16-valve engine; 5-speed OD manual transmission; power take-off provision, 3.73 axle ratio; 34 gal. capacity fuel tank; LT245/75SR16 A/S BSW front and rear tires; and interior lights include 2 door curb lights.

LS 2WD (in addition to or instead of BASE DECOR equipment): Front and rear chrome bumpers with black rub strip; colored bodyside molding with chrome bodyside insert, colored fender flares; driver's and passenger's power remote chrome folding outside mirrors; air conditioning, air filter; AM/FM stereo, clock, seek-scan, single CD, 6 performance speakers, auto equalizer, theft deterrent, and fixed antenna; cruise control; power door locks with 2 stage unlock, remote keyless entry; panic alarm, security system; power windows with driver's 1-touch down; rear quarter swing-out windows (X-Cab); center armrest with storage, driver's seat includes 4-way direction control, lumbar support, passenger's seat includes 4-way direction control, lumbar support; premium cloth seats, cloth door trim insert, full color-keyed carpet floor covering with floor mats; interior lights include 2 door curb lights, illuminated entry; leather-wrapped sport steering wheel with tilt adjustment; mini overhead console with storage, 2 seat back storage pockets and chrome grille.

LT 2WD (in addition to or instead of LS DECOR equipment): 4-speed electronic OD auto transmission with lock-up; oil cooler; body-colored bodyside molding with chrome bodyside insert, body-colored fender flares; additional exterior lights include front fog/driving lights; driver's and passenger's power remote chrome heated folding outside mirrors; AM/FM stereo, clock, seek-scan, cassette, single CD, 6 performance speakers, auto equalizer, theft deterrent, and fixed antenna; instrumentation display includes compass, exterior temp; deep tinted windows; rear window defroster; seating capacity of 5, heated-cushion front bucket seats, driver and passenger armrests, driver's seat includes 6-way power seat, power 2-way lumbar support, passenger's seat includes 6-way power seat, power 2-way lumbar support; leather seats; memory on driver's seat with 2 memory setting(s); auto-dimming day/night rearview mirror; full floor console, full overhead console with storage and rear cupholders.

BASE/LS 4WD (5M) (in addition to or instead of BASE/LS 2WD equipment): 6.0L V8 OHV SMPI 16-valve engine; 5-speed OD manual transmission; part-time 4 wheel drive, auto locking hub control and manual shift, power take-off provision; 3.73 axle ratio, front independent torsion suspension with anti-roll bar, front torsion springs, front torsion bar, front tow hooks and LT245/75SR16 A/S BSW front and rear tires.

LT 4WD (in addition to or instead 2WD LT equipment): Driver's selectable multi-mode transmission; auto full-time 4 wheel drive, auto locking hub control and electronic shift; front independent torsion suspension with anti-roll bar, front torsion springs and front torsion bar.

Base Prices

CODE	DESCRIPTION	INVOICE	MSRP
CC25903-C6P	Base 2WD Regular Cab LB HD (5M)	17665	20189
CC25903	Base 2WD Regular Cab LB (4A)	18012	20585
CC25903-C6P	LS 2WD Regular Cab LB HD (5M)	19960	22811
CC25953	Base 2WD Extended Cab LB (5M)	20072	22939
CC25753	Base 2WD Extended Cab SB (4A)	20156	23035

CODE	DESCRIPTION	INVOICE	MSRP
CC25903	LS 2WD Regular Cab LB (4A)	20306	23207
CK25903	Base 4WD Regular Cab LB (5M)	20378	23289
CC25953	LS 2WD Extended Cab LB (5M)	22366	25561
CC25753	LS 2WD Extended Cab SB (4A)	22450	25657
CK25753	Base 4WD Extended Cab SB (5M)	22522	25739
CK25903	LS 4WD Regular Cab LB (5M)	22672	25911
CK25953	Base 4WD Extended Cab LB (5M)	22784	26039
CK25753	LS 4WD Extended Cab SB (5M)	24816	28361
CK25953	LS 4WD Extended Cab LB (5M)	25078	28661
CC25753	LT 2WD Extended Cab SB (4A)	25079	28662
CC25953	LT 2WD Extended Cab LB (4A)	25865	29560
CK25753	LT 4WD Extended Cab SB (4A)	28731	32835
CK25953	LT 4WD Extended Cab LB (4A)	28993	33135
Destination Charge:		665	665

Accessories

—	Cloth Seat Trim (Base)	NC	NC
—	Custom Cloth Seat Trim (Base)	NC	NC
—	Custom Leather Seat Trim (LS) *Includes 6-way power driver's/passenger's seats.*	1273	1480
—	Fourth Door (X-Cab)	289	330
1SA	Preferred Equipment Group 1SA (Base) *Includes vehicle with standard equipment.*	NC	NC
1SB	Preferred Equipment Group 1SB (LS) *Includes vehicle with standard equipment.*	NC	NC
1SC	Preferred Equipment Group 1SC (LT) *Includes vehicle with standard equipment.*	NC	NC
A28	Sliding Rear Window (Base/LS) *NOT AVAILABLE with C49.*	108	125
A95	Reclining Bucket Seats (LS) *Includes inboard armrests, manual lumbar, floor console and overhead console.*	322	375
AG2	6-Way Power Driver/Passenger Seats (LS)	413	480
AJ1	Deep Tinted Solar Ray Glass (Reg Cab - Base/LS) *REQUIRES A28 or C49.*	43	50
AJ1	Deep Tinted Solar Ray Glass (X-Cab - Base/LS)	92	107
AU3	Power Door Locks (Base)	139	162
BG9	Color-Keyed Rubber Floor Covering (LS) *Replaces carpeting and floor mats.*	(86)	(100)
C49	Electric Rear Window Defogger (Base/LS) *REQUIRES C60. NOT AVAILABLE with A28.*	150	175
C60	Front Air Conditioning (Base)	710	825
DF2	Camper Type Mirrors (Base) *Retractable with wide field of vision.*	52	60
DF2	Camper Type Mirrors (LS) *Retractable with wide field of vision. NOT AVAILABLE with DL8.*	(33)	(38)

CODE	DESCRIPTION	INVOICE	MSRP
DF5	10" Electrochromic ISRV Mirror (LS) *Includes 8-point compass and temperature display.*	150	175
DL8	OSRV Mirror with Heater (LS) *REQUIRES C49. NOT AVAILABLE with DF2.*	36	42
E95	Tonneau Cover	206	240
G80	Locking Differential *REQUIRES GT5.*	245	285
GT5	4.10 Axle Ratio	NC	NC
K05	Engine Block Heater	30	35
K34	Cruise Control (Base)	206	240
K47	High Capacity Air Cleaner (2WD Base/LS - Reg Cab LD/X-Cab SB)	22	25
KC4	Engine Oil Cooling *REQUIRES LQ4. NOT AVAILABLE with VYU.*	116	135
LQ4	Engine: Vortec 6000 V8 SFI (2WD Base/LS - Reg Cab LD/X-Cab SB) *Includes high capacity air cleaner. REQUIRES MT1. NOT AVAILABLE with VYU.*	305	355
MT1	Transmission: 4-Speed Automatic (All Except LT) *Includes transmission oil cooler.*	942	1095
MT1	Transmission: 4-Speed Automatic (LT) *Includes transmission oil cooler. NOT AVAILABLE with VYU, Z82.*	NC	NC
NC7	Federal Emission Override *REQUIRES MT1.*	NC	NC
NP8	Autotrac Active Transfer Case (LS 4WD) *REQUIRES MT1.*	322	375
NZZ	Skid Plate Package (4WD) *Includes front differential and transfer case shields.*	82	95
PY0	Wheels: Forged Polished Aluminum (LS) *Includes wheel: spare not matching.*	95	110
QIW	Tires: LT245/75R16E AT BSW (All Except HD) *NOT AVAILABLE with QIZ.*	241	280
QIW	Tires: LT245/75R16E AT BSW (HD)	47	55
QIZ	Tires: LT245/75R16E AS BSW (All Except HD) *NOT AVAILABLE with QIW.*	194	225
R6M	New Jersey Cost Surcharge	74	NC
R9D	Exterior Appearance Package (Base) *Includes body side molding, chrome rear step bumper, chrome grille and wheels: chrome. NOT AVAILABLE with VF7.*	538	625
R9E	Floor Covering Package (Base) *Includes floor carpeting with rubber mats.*	86	100
T96	Front Fog Lamps (LS)	120	140
TP2	Auxiliary Battery *NOT AVAILABLE with (YF5 and (M30 or MT1))*	116	135
UL0	Radio: AM/FM Stereo with Cassette (LS) *Includes digital clock, theft lock, speed compensated volume and auto tone control. NOT AVAILABLE with UP0.*	NC	NC
UL5	Radio Delete (Base) *Includes stowage tray. Base speaker system and antenna remain. NOT AVAILABLE with UM6.*	(215)	(250)

CODE	DESCRIPTION	INVOICE	MSRP
UM6	Radio: AM/FM Stereo with Cassette (Base Reg Cab) *Includes digital clock and seek/scan. NOT AVAILABLE with UL5.*	146	170
UM6	Radio: AM/FM Stereo with Cassette (Base X-Cab) *Includes digital clock and seek/scan. NOT AVAILABLE with UL5.*	129	150
UP0	Radio: AM/FM Stereo with Cassette and CD (LS X-Cab) *Includes seek-scan, digital clock, theft lock, speed compensated volume and auto tone control. REQUIRES MT1 and A95 and NP8 (4WD). NOT AVAILABLE with UL0.*	86	100
UV8	Cellular Telephone Wiring Provisions *Includes wiring for remote microphone and cellular phone.*	43	50
UY2	Camper and Fifth Wheel Wiring Provisions *REQUIRES Z82.*	22	25
V76	Two Front Recovery Hooks (2WD)	33	38
VB3	Chrome Rear Step Bumper (Base) *NOT AVAILABLE with VF7.*	86	100
VF7	Rear Bumper Delete Provisions (Base) *Vehicles registered in certain states must have a rear bumper to be operated on their roads. Consult your local laws. NOT AVAILABLE with Z82, VB3, R9D.*	(86)	(100)
VF7	Rear Bumper Delete Provisions (LS) *Vehicles registered in certain states must have a rear bumper to be operated on their roads. Consult your local laws. NOT AVAILABLE with Z82.*	(172)	(200)
VYU	Snow Plow Prep Package (2WD Base/LS Except HD/X-Cab LB) *Includes increased cooling, electrical connections and 130-amp alternator. REQUIRES LM7. NOT AVAILABLE with Z82, MT1, KC4.*	245	285
VYU	Snow Plow Prep Package (Base/LS/LT X-Cab 4WD) *Includes increased cooling, electrical connections and 130-amp altemator. NOT AVAILABLE with Z82.*	280	325
VYU	Snow Plow Prep Package (Base/LS/LT X-Cab 4WD) *Includes increased cooling, electrical connections and 130-amp alternator. REQUIRES Z82.*	163	190
Z82	HD Trailering Special Equipment (Base/LS 2WD Except HD/X-Cab LB) *Includes 7-lead wiring hamess, trailer hitch platform and transmission oil cooler. REQUIRES LM7. NOT AVAILABLE with MT1.*	245	285
Z82	HD Trailering Special Equipment *Includes 7-lead wiring harness and trailer hitch platform. NOT AVAILABLE with VF7, VYU.*	280	325
Z85	HD Suspension *Includes 36 mm shocks. REQUIRES QIW or QIZ.*	82	95
ZY2	Two Tone Paint Application (LS)	215	250

2000 SUBURBAN

What's New?

The 2000 Chevrolet Suburban is completely redesigned. It's roomier, safer, more comfortable and a more powerful ride.

2000 Chevrolet Suburban

Review

In the war of the SUVs, Ford took the lead for largest competitor. But in war, bigger is not always better — just ask Goliath. While the 2000 Chevrolet Suburban may have David aspirations in this vehicular tete-a-tete, being small isn't part of its character. More importantly, this Suburban is completely redesigned and the engineers took that opportunity to capitalize on their long history of truck building by changing as much as they could. This 2000 model offers more comfort from a stiffer frame and upgraded interiors, more power with two new small-block V8 engines, and more safety from side-impact airbags and larger brake pads.

All Excursions aside, this vehicle is big. Coming in at a length of 18.3 feet, the heavy-duty 2500 weighs in at an impressive 5760 pounds — almost 3 tons of truck. The body shape hasn't changed considerably, staying close to the fairly nondescript image this SUV has had for years. Towering above 6 feet for the four-wheel-drive models, it poses no less a threat than Ford's monster, which is 7 inches taller. However, 7 inches can make a difference — a Suburban will fit in a standard garage.

The 2000 Suburban comes in two models, the 1500 and the 2500, both offering two- and four-wheel-drive configurations. The 1500s come with a 285-horsepower, 5.3-liter V8 engine, while the 2500s have a 300-horsepower 6.0-liter V8. Both come from the new Vortec family of small-block engines and have more horsepower than previous Suburban engines. Fronting a four-speed automatic transmission, this combination proves to be a great workhorse, but not much of a sprinter.

Ride and handling have been improved, with body strength and stiffness increasing 400 percent over last year's model. The 1500s are equipped with a new five-link coil rear suspension, allowing the truck to track better on gravel or washboard roads and giving you more wheel control. If you do lose control and end up in a moderate speed front-end collision, the 1500s are fitted with a new front crush cap, allowing the repair shop to simply swap it out without having to replace the entire front frame. The suspension on the 2500s comes with the same rear leaf springs as their Silverado stablemates, giving them heavy-duty towing capacities to go with that stronger V8.

The interior has been changed substantially, making it more comfortable and convenient. More efficient placement of air ducts and moving the spare from inside to underneath the cargo floor have increased useable space, allowing better movement throughout. All the seats have improved seatback angles and upgrades include second-row captain's chairs and a driver's seat with more options than some near-luxury cars provide.

This Suburban has a lot to offer. There are more cupholders for the soccer team and increased headroom for the business associates. The engineers took the time to change and modify everything that needed improvement. It's not the most stylish, nor the biggest SUV on the market, but a lot of time and effort seems to have paid off.

Standard Equipment

1500 BASE 2WD (4A): 5.3L V8 OHV SMPI 16-valve engine; 4-speed electronic OD auto transmission with lock-up; 600-amp HD battery with run down protection; 130-amp alternator; driver's selectable multi-mode transmission; rear-wheel drive, 3.73 axle ratio; stainless steel exhaust; front independent torsion suspension with HD anti-roll bar, front torsion springs, rigid rear axle multi-link suspension with anti-roll bar, rear coil springs; power re-circulating ball steering; 4-wheel disc brakes with 4-wheel antilock braking system; 32.5 gal. capacity fuel tank; side impact bars; split swing-out rear cargo door; trailer harness; front and rear chrome bumpers with colored rub strip, rear step; monotone paint; aero-composite halogen fully auto headlamps with daytime running lights; additional exterior lights include underhood light; driver's and passenger's manual black folding outside mirrors; front and rear 16" x 7" silver styled steel wheels; P245/75SR16 A/S BSW front and rear tires; underbody mounted full-size steel spare wheel with crankdown; rear heat ducts; AM/FM stereo, clock, seek-scan, 4 speakers, theft deterrent, and fixed antenna; power door locks, child safety rear door locks; 3 power accessory outlets, front cigar lighter(s), smokers' package; instrumentation display includes tachometer, oil pressure gauge, water temperature gauge, volt gauge, trip odometer; warning indicators include oil pressure, water temp, battery, low oil level, low coolant, lights on, key in ignition, low fuel, low washer fluid, door ajar, trunk ajar, service interval; driver's and passenger's front airbags, driver's and front passenger's seat mounted side airbags; ignition disable; tinted windows, manual front and rear windows, fixed 1/4 vent windows; variable intermittent front windshield wipers, sun visor strip; seating capacity of 3, 40-20-40 split-bench front seat, adjustable headrests, driver's seat includes 2-way direction control, passenger's seat includes, 2-way direction control; front height adjustable seatbelts; vinyl seats, full cloth headliner, full vinyl floor covering, plastic/rubber gear shift knob; interior lights include dome light with delay; sport steering wheel with tilt adjustment; passenger's side vanity mirror; day/night rearview mirror; glove box with light, front and rear cupholders, instrument panel bin, driver's and passenger's door bins; vinyl cargo floor, plastic trunk lid, cargo tie downs, cargo light; argent grille, black side window moldings, black front windshield molding, black rear window molding and colored door handles.

2500 BASE 2WD (4A) (in addition to or instead of 1500 BASE 2WD (4A) equipment): 6.0L V8 OHV SMPI 16-valve engine; transmission oil cooler; front independent suspension with HD anti-roll bar, front coil springs, rigid rear axle suspension with anti-roll bar, rear leaf springs; 38.5 gal. capacity fuel tank; front and rear 16" x 6.5" silver styled steel wheels and LT245/75SR16 A/S BSW front and rear tires.

BASE 4WD (4A) (in addition to or instead of BASE 2WD (4A) equipment): Part-time 4-wheel drive, auto locking hub control and electronic shift; power re-circulating ball steering with vehicle speed-sensing assist, front tow hooks and colored fender flares (2500).

Base Prices

CC15906	1500 Base 2WD (4A)	22497	25711
CC25906	2500 Base 2WD (4A)	24146	27595
CK15906	1500 Base 4WD (4A)	25049	28627
CK25906	2500 Base 4WD (4A)	26771	30595
Destination Charge:		710	710

Accessories

—	Leather Seat Trim *Includes driver's and passenger's 6-way power seats. REQUIRES 1SB.*	1746	2030

CODE	DESCRIPTION	INVOICE	MSRP
1SA	**Preferred Equipment Group 1SA** *Includes Base Decor.*	NC	NC
1SB	**Preferred Equipment Group 1SB** *Includes LS Decor: AM/FM stereo with CD, seek, scan and auto tone control, short overhead console, remote keyless entry, keyfob remote release, illuminated entry, color-keyed carpet with vinyl floor mats, deep-tinted glass, electrochromic rerview mirror, 8-point compass, exterior temperature display, front and rear air conditioning and heater, 60/40 split bench second row seat, leather-wrapped steering wheel, dual illuminated visor vanity mirrors, power windows, rear defogger, chrome deluxe grille, luggage rack, dual power heated foldaway mirrors, spectra gray body side moldings and wheels: stainless steel clad.*	6384	7423
1SC	**Preferred Equipment Group 1SC (1500)** *Includes LT Decor: AM/FM stereo with seek, scan, cassette and CD, rear seat audio controls, short overhead console, OnStar communications system, remote keyless entry, keyfob remote release, illuminated entry, color-keyed carpet with carpeted floor mats, deep-tinted glass, electrochromic rearview mirror, 8-point compass, exterior temperature display, front and rear air conditioning and heater, custom power reclining bucket seats, driver's and passenger's 6-way power seats, 60/40 split bench second row seat, leather-wrapped steering wheel, dual illuminated visor vanity mirrors, Homelink universal garage door opener, power windows, assist steps, rear defogger, chrome deluxe grille, fog lamps, luggage rack, dual power heated foldaway mirrors and tires: P265/70R16 AT BW SBR.*	9790	11384
1SC	**Preferred Equipment Group 1SC (1500)** *Includes LT Decor: AM/FM stereo with seek, scan, cassette and CD, rear seat audio controls, short overhead console, OnStar communications system, remote keyless entry, keyfob remote release, illuminated entry, color-keyed carpet with carpeted floor mats, deep-tinted glass, electrochromic rearview mirror, 8-point compass, exterior temperature display, front and rear air conditioning and heater, custom power reclining bucket seats, driver's and passenger's 6-way power seats, 60/40 split bench second row seat, leather-wrapped steering wheel, dual illuminated visor vanity mirrors, Homelink universal garage door opener, power windows, assist steps, rear defogger, chrome deluxe grille, fog lamps, luggage rack, dual power heated foldaway mirrors and tires: P265/70R16 AT BW SBR. NOT AVAILABLE with CF5.*	9683	11259
1SC	**Preferred Equipment Group 1SC (2500)** *Includes LT Decor: AM/FM stereo with seek, scan, cassette and CD, rear seat audio controls, short overhead console, OnStar communications system, remote keyless entry, keyfob remote release, illuminated entry, color-keyed carpet with carpeted floor mats, deep-tinted glass, electrochromic rearview mirror, 8-point compass, exterior temperature display, front and rear air conditioning and heater, custom power reclining bucket seats, driver's and passenger's 6-way power seats, 60/40 split bench second row seat, third row bench seat, leather-wrapped steering wheel, dual illuminated visor vanity mirrors, Homelink universal garage door opener, power windows, assist steps, rear defogger, chrome deluxe grille, fog lamps, luggage rack, dual power heated foldaway mirrors and wheels: forged aluminum.*	9415	10948
1SC	**Preferred Equipment Group 1SC (2500)** *Includes LT Decor: AM/FM stereo with seek, scan, cassette and CD, rear seat audio controls, short overhead console, OnStar communications system, remote keyless*	9308	10823

CODE	DESCRIPTION	INVOICE	MSRP
	entry, keyfob remote release, illuminated entry, color-keyed carpet with carpeted floor mats, deep-tinted glass, electrochromic rearview mirror, 8-point compass, exterior temperature display, front and rear air conditioning and heater, custom power reclining bucket seats, driver's and passenger's 6-way power seats, 60/40 split bench second row seat, third row bench seat, leather-wrapped steering wheel, dual illuminated visor vanity mirrors, Homelink universal garage door opener, power windows, assist steps, rear defogger, chrome deluxe grille, fog lamps, luggage rack, dual power heated foldaway mirrors and wheels: forged aluminum. NOT AVAILABLE with CF5.		
A95	**Reclining Bucket Seats (2500)** *Includes driver's and passenger's inboard armrest and manual lumbar and floor console. REQUIRES 1SB.*	322	375
A95	**Reclining High Back Bucket Seats (1500)** *Includes driver's and passenger's inboard armrest and manual lumbar and floor console. REQUIRES 1SB.*	322	375
AG2	**Driver's and Passenger's 6-Way Power Seats** *REQUIRES 1SB.*	413	480
AL4	**Second Row Bucket Seats** *REQUIRES 1SB or 1SC.*	249	290
AS3	**Third Row Bench Seat (2500)** *Includes 60/40 split bench second row seat. REQUIRES 1SA.*	1058	1230
AS3	**Third Row Bench Seat (1500)** *Includes 60/40 split bench second row seat. REQUIRES 1SA.*	1058	1230
AT5	**60/40 Split Bench Second Row Seat** *REQUIRES 1SA.*	542	630
B71	**Wheel Flares (All Except 2500 4WD)**	155	180
BVE	**Assist Steps** *REQUIRES 1SB.*	280	325
CF5	**Power Sunroof** *REQUIRES 1SB or 1SC. NOT AVAILABLE with V53, VYU.*	856	995
E52	**Liftgate with Wiper** *Includes flip-up rear window with wiper. REQUIRES 1SB or 1SC.*	NC	NC
G80	**Locking Differential (4WD)**	217	252
GT5	**4.10 Axle Ratio (1500)**	NC	NC
GT5	**4.10 Axle Ratio (2500)**	NC	NC
KC4	**Auxiliary Engine Oil Cooling (2500)**	116	135
K05	**Engine Block Heater**	28	33
NZZ	**Skid Plate Package (4WD)** *Includes oil pan, differential case and transfer case shields.*	82	95
QIW	**Tires: LT245/75R16E AT BW SBR (2500 4WD)**	124	144
QMJ	**Tires: P265/70R16 AT BW SBR (1500)** *REQUIRES ZW7 and 1SB. NOT AVAILABLE with QMK, QNL. INCLUDED in 1SC.*	NC	NC
QMK	**Tires: P265/70R16 WOL SBR AT (1500)** *REQUIRES ZW7 and (1SB or 1SC). NOT AVAILABLE with QNL, QMJ.*	108	125
QNL	**Tires: P245/75R16 WOL SBR AS (1500)** *REQUIRES 1SA or 1SB. NOT AVAILABLE with ZW7, QMK, QMJ.*	108	125
R6M	**New Jersey Cost Surcharge**	94	NC

CODE	DESCRIPTION	INVOICE	MSRP
R9F	Traction Package (2WD) *Includes locking differential and recovery hooks.*	249	290
R9F	Traction Package (2WD) *Includes traction assist, cruise control, locking differential and recovery hooks. NOT AVAILABLE with R9H.*	454	528
R9G	Appearance Package *Includes uplevel grille, spectra gray body side moldings, wheels: stainless steel clad and luggage rack. REQUIRES 1SA.*	617	717
R9H	Climate Package *Includes deep-tinted glass, front air conditioning and rear defogger. REQUIRES 1SA.*	1326	1542
R9I	Trailering Package (1500) *Includes trailer hitch platform, 7-lead wiring connector, high capacity air cleaner, trailer brake pre-wire harness and transmission oil cooler.*	245	285
R9I	Trailering Package (2500) *Includes trailer hitch platform, 7-lead wiring connector, trailer brake pre-wire harness and auxiliary engine oil cooling.*	257	299
R9K	Convenience Package *Includes carpeted floor mats and Homelink transmitter. REQUIRES 1SB. NOT AVAILABLE with CF5.*	294	342
R9K	Convenience Package *Includes carpeted floor mats and Homelink transmitter. REQUIRES 1SB.*	202	235
T96	Fog Lamps *REQUIRES 1SB.*	73	85
U01	Roof Marker Lamps (5) (2500) *REQUIRES 1SA.*	47	55
UK6	Rear Seat Audio Controls *REQUIRES A95 and 1SB.*	142	165
UL0	Radio: AM/FM Stereo with Cassette *Includes digital clock, theft lock, speed compensated volume and auto tone control. REQUIRES 1SB.*	NC	NC
UM6	Radio: AM/FM Stereo with Cassette *Includes digital clock. REQUIRES 1SA.*	126	147
UP0	Radio: AM/FM Stereo with Cassette and CD *Includes digital clock, theft lock, speed compensated volume and auto tone control. REQUIRES A95 and 1SB. NOT AVAILABLE with UL0.*	108	125
V53	Luggage Rack Delete *REQUIRES 1SB. NOT AVAILABLE with CF5.*	NC	NC
VYU	Snow Plow Prep Package (2500 2WD) *Includes instrument panel switch, roof beacon wiring, forward lamp wiring, increased capacity front coil springs and auxiliary engine oil cooling. REQUIRES 1SA or 1SB. NOT AVAILABLE with CF5.*	163	190
VYU	Snow Plow Prep Package (2500 4WD) *Includes instrument panel switch, roof beacon wiring, forward lamp wiring, torsion bar adjuster and auxiliary engine oil cooling. REQUIRES 1SA or 1SB. NOT AVAILABLE with CF5.*	218	253

CODE	DESCRIPTION	INVOICE	MSRP
Z55	Autoride (1500) *Includes bi-state variable shock dampening and rear air assisted load leveling. REQUIRES 1SC.*	602	700
Z55	Autoride (2500) *Includes bi-state variable shock dampening. REQUIRES 1SB. NOT AVAILABLE with Z85.*	645	750
Z85	Firm Ride Suspension (2500) *NOT AVAILABLE with Z55.*	34	40
ZW7	Premium Ride Suspension (1500) *REQUIRES 1SB and (QMJ or QMK). NOT AVAILABLE with QNL.*	315	366
ZY2	Two-Tone Paint (1500) *REQUIRES 1SB.*	172	200
ZY2	Two-Tone Paint (2500) *REQUIRES 1SB.*	172	200

2000 TAHOE

2000 Chevrolet Tahoe LT

What's New?

The engineers at Chevy redesigned the Tahoe from top to bottom, making it safer, more powerful and a more pleasurable vehicle to drive.

Review

Chevrolet is calling their new Tahoe a "real" sport utility, implying that sport-utes are more about getting things done than doing them in style. With nearly every automaker offering an SUV these days, it takes a lot of effort to be unique. However, despite differing opinions of what does and what does not constitute a good SUV (i.e., BMW's X5), the 2000 Tahoe has a whole lot going for it. This is courtesy of the full redesign it got this year. For 2000, the Tahoe is stronger, is easier to drive on and off the road, and gets some new seats and safety features.

Available with either two- or four-wheel-drive, this Tahoe has a redesigned frame and body that are similar in appearance, but stronger and more rigid, than previous models. The body is made of more durable exterior sheetmetal, thanks to improved corrosion protection and stronger dent-resistant steel. The engineers rethought everything, even redesigning the door hinges so they last four times as long and putting a unique crush cap on the front so you don't have to replace the whole front end in a moderate-speed accident with a slow-moving tree.

Under the hood, the 2000 Tahoe comes with Chevy's powerful new Vortec V8 engines, offering 275 horsepower from the 4.8-liter motor on the base model and 285 horsepower from the 5.3-liter motor on the LS and LT models. All that power runs through an electronically controlled four-speed automatic transmission. While these engines are stronger than last year, they lead their competition in fuel economy and are compliant with low-emission vehicle (LEV) standards, making them safer for driving in Mother Nature's backyard.

The powertrain has been beefed up for 2000, offering a more durable rear axle, strengthened differential case, and stiffer axle shafts. But Chevy didn't bump up its off-road durability at the expense of the highway drive. With a 400 percent increase in body-mount structure stiffness and a five-link rear suspension, this redesign provides a smoother, quieter and more stable ride on virtually all road surfaces.

Inside all the new metal is an innovative 50/50 split third-row seat that provides greater cargo flexibility and the possibility to boost passenger capacity to nine. Those eight other people will be better protected in the 2000 model because this Tahoe has a host of advanced safety features, including four-wheel, ventilated disc antilock brakes, front-seat side-impact airbags, seat-mounted safety belts in the first- and third-row outboard positions, and an energy-absorbing foam on the interior surfaces, reducing the chances that your less-than-bright friends will hurt their heads while exiting.

Built on the same foundation as the Chevy Silverado pickup, this Tahoe is a tough SUV, redesigned to be stronger and safer than it's ever been. There are plenty of reasons to buy an SUV these days and many of them have nothing to do with unpaved roads. If you want a sport utility that can handle a ditch better than many, the redesigned 2000 Chevrolet Tahoe should be on your short list.

Standard Equipment

BASE 2WD (4A): 4.8L V8 OHV SMPI 16-valve engine; 4-speed electronic OD auto transmission with lock-up; 600-amp HD battery with run down protection; 130-amp alternator; driver's selectable multi-mode transmission; rear-wheel drive, 3.42 axle ratio; stainless steel exhaust; front independent torsion suspension with anti-roll bar, front torsion springs, front torsion bar, rigid rear axle multi-link suspension with rear coil springs; power re-circulating ball steering; 4-wheel disc brakes with 4-wheel antilock braking system; 26 gal. capacity fuel tank; side impact bars; split swing-out rear cargo door; trailer harness; front and rear chrome bumpers with colored rub strip, rear step; monotone paint; aero-composite halogen fully auto headlamps with daytime running lights; additional exterior lights include underhood light; driver's and passenger's manual black folding outside mirrors; front and rear 16" x 7" silver styled steel wheels; P245/75SR16 A/S BSW front and rear tires; underbody mounted full-size steel spare wheel with crankdown; air conditioning; AM/FM stereo, clock, seek-scan, 8 speakers, auto equalizer, theft deterrent, and fixed antenna; power door locks with 2 stage unlock, child safety rear door locks; 3 power accessory outlets, front cigar lighter(s), smokers' package; instrumentation display includes tachometer, oil pressure gauge, water temperature gauge, volt gauge, trip odometer; warning indicators include oil pressure, battery, low oil level, low coolant, lights on, key in ignition, low fuel, door ajar, trunk ajar, service interval; driver's and passenger's front airbags, driver's and front passenger's seat mounted side airbags; ignition disable; tinted windows, manual front and rear windows, fixed 1/4 vent windows; variable intermittent front windshield wipers, sun visor strip; seating capacity of 6, 40-20-40 split-bench front seat, adjustable headrests, driver's seat includes 4-way direction control, passenger's seat includes 4-way direction control; 60-40 folding rear split-bench seat with adjustable headrests, center armrest with storage; front and rear height adjustable seatbelts; vinyl seats, cloth door trim insert, full cloth headliner, full vinyl floor covering, deluxe sound insulation; interior lights include dome light with delay, 4 door curb lights; sport steering wheel with tilt adjustment; passenger's side vanity mirror; day/night rearview mirror; glove box with light, front and rear cupholders, instrument panel bin, driver's and passenger's door bins; carpeted cargo floor, plastic trunk lid, cargo light; argent grille, black side window moldings, black front windshield molding, black rear window molding and colored door handles.

BASE 4WD (4A) (in addition to or instead of BASE 2WD (4A) equipment): Part-time 4-wheel drive, auto locking hub control and electronic shift, 3.73 axle ratio; rigid rear axle multi-link suspension with anti-roll bar; power re-circulating ball steering with vehicle speed-sensing assist and front tow hooks.

Base Prices

Code	Description	Invoice	MSRP
CC15706	Base 2WD (4A)	21813	24929
CK15706	Base 4WD (4A)	24364	27845
Destination Charge:		675	675

Accessories

Code	Description	Invoice	MSRP
1SA	**Preferred Equipment Group 1SA** *Includes Base Decor package.*	NC	NC
1SB	**Preferred Equipment Group 1SB** *Includes LS Decor package: engine: Vortec 5300 V8 SFI, AM/FM stereo with seek, scan, CD, and auto tone control, enhanced 9-speaker system, retractable/removable cargo shade, cargo net, short overhead console, cruise control, programmable power door locks, content theft alarm, color-keyed carpet with vinyl floor mats, deep tint glass, illuminated entry, electrochromic inside rearview mirror, front and rear air conditioning, 40/20/40 split front bench seat, custom cloth seat trim, leather-wrapped steering wheel, lighted vanity mirrors, power windows with lockout feature, electric rear window defogger, deluxe chrome grille, roof mounted black luggage rack, electric heated exterior mirrors, body side moldings with chrome strip, wheels: machined cast aluminum and tires: P245/75R16 SBR A/S BW.*	5301	6164
1SC	**Preferred Equipment Group 1SC** *Includes LT Decor package: engine: Vortec 5300 V8 SFI, AM/FM stereo with seek, scan, auto tone control, CD and cassette, rear seat audio controls, enhanced 9-speaker system, retractable/removable cargo shade, cargo net, short overhead console, OnStar communications system, cruise control, programmable power door locks, content theft alarm, color-keyed carpet with carpeted floor mats, deep tint glass, illuminated entry, electrochromic inside rearview mirror, air conditioning with rear heater, power reclining front bucket seats, custom leather seat trim, leather-wrapped steering wheel, lighted vanity mirrors, Homelink universal garage door opener, power windows with lockout feature, side step running boards, chrome front bumper with body color top pad, electric rear window defogger, color-keyed door handles, deluxe chrome grille, fog lamps, roof mounted black luggage rack, electric heated exterior mirrors, body side moldings with chrome strip, wheels: polished cast aluminum, tires: P265/70R16 SBR AT BW and premium ride suspension. NOT AVAILABLE with CF5.*	9105	10587
1SC	**Preferred Equipment Group 1SC** *Includes LT Decor package: engine: Vortec 5300 V8 SFI, AM/FM stereo with seek, scan, auto tone control, CD and cassette, rear seat audio controls, enhanced 9-speaker system, retractable/removable cargo shade, cargo net, short overhead console, OnStar communications system, cruise control, programmable power door*	8729	10150

CODE	DESCRIPTION	INVOICE	MSRP
	locks, content theft alarm, color-keyed carpet with carpeted floor mats, deep tint glass, illuminated entry, electrochromic inside rearview mirror, air conditioning with rear heater, power reclining front bucket seats, custom leather seat trim, leather-wrapped steering wheel, lighted vanity mirrors, Homelink universal garage door opener, power windows with lockout feature, side step running boards, chrome front bumper with body color top pad, electric rear window defogger, color-keyed door handles, deluxe chrome grille, fog lamps, roof mounted black luggage rack, electric heated exterior mirrors, body side moldings with chrome strip, wheels: polished cast aluminum, tires: P265/70R16 SBR AT BW and premium ride suspension. REQUIRES CF5.		
8X7	**Gas Shock Absorbers**	206	240
	Includes Delco/Bilstein 46mm gas shock absorbers.		
A95	**Reclining High Back Bucket Seats**	322	375
	Includes driver's and passenger's inboard armrest and manual lumbar and floor console. REQUIRES 1SB.		
AG2	**Driver's and Passenger's 6-Way Power Seats**	413	480
	REQUIRES 1SB.		
B71	**Wheel Flares**	155	180
	Spectra Gray only.		
BVE	**Assist Steps**	280	325
	REQUIRES 1SB. NOT AVAILABLE with R9L.		
C5H	**GVWR: 6900 Lbs (4WD)**	NC	NC
	Includes 3600 lbs. front GAWR and 4000 lbs. rear GAWR. REQUIRES R9J and (1SB or 1SC). NOT AVAILABLE with C5U.		
C5U	**GVWR: 6,800 Lbs**	NC	NC
	Includes 3150 lbs. front GAWR and 4000 lbs. rear GAWR. REQUIRES R9J. NOT AVAILABLE with C5H or 1SA (2WD).		
CF5	**Electric Sliding Sunroof**	856	995
	Includes Homelink 3-channel transmitter. REQUIRES 1SB or 1SC. NOT AVAILABLE with V53.		
E52	**Liftgate with Liftglass Rear Door System**	NC	NC
	REQUIRES 1SB or 1SC.		
G80	**Locking Differential (4WD)**	217	252
GT4	**3.73 Axle Ratio**	NC	NC
	NOT AVAILABLE with GT5.		
GT5	**4.10 Axle Ratio (4WD)**	NC	NC
	NOT AVAILABLE with GT4.		
K05	**Engine Block Heater**	28	33
LM7	**Engine: Vortec 5300 V8 SFI**	602	700
	REQUIRES 1SA.		
NZZ	**Skid Plate Package (4WD)**	82	95
	Includes oil pan, differential case and transfer case shields.		
QMJ	**Tires: P265/70R16 SBR AT BW**	NC	NC
	REQUIRES 1SB. NOT AVAILABLE with QNL, QMK, R9J, R9L.		
QMK	**Tires: P265/70R16 SBR AT WOL**	108	125
	REQUIRES 1SB. NOT AVAILABLE with QNL, R9J, R9L.		

CODE	DESCRIPTION	INVOICE	MSRP
QMK	Tires: P265/70R16 SBR AT WOL *REQUIRES 1SC. NOT AVAILABLE with QNL, R9J.*	108	125
QNK	Tires: P245/70R16 SBR AS BW *REQUIRES 1SC and R9J. NOT AVAILABLE with QNL, QMJ, QMK, Z55.*	(100)	(116)
QNL	Tires: P245/75R16 SBR AS WOL *REQUIRES R9J. NOT AVAILABLE with QNK, QMK, QMJ, Z55, R9L.*	8	9
R6M	New Jersey Cost Surcharge	83	NC
R91	Trailer Package *Includes 7-lead wiring connector, trailer brake pre-wire harness, trailer hitch platform, high capacity air cleaner and transmission oil cooler. NOT AVAILABLE with LR4 or GU6.*	245	285
R9F	Traction Package (2WD) *Includes locking differential and recovery hooks.*	249	290
R9F	Traction Package (2WD) *Includes traction assist, locking differential and recovery hooks. NOT AVAILABLE with R9H.*	454	528
R9G	Appearance Package *Includes uplevel grille, spectra gray body side moldings, wheels: stainless steel clad and luggage rack. REQUIRES 1SA.*	617	717
R9H	Climate Package *Includes deep-tinted glass, front air conditioning, cruise control and rear defogger. REQUIRES 1SA.*	1326	1542
R9J	Third Row Seat Package *Includes third row 50/50 split seat, liftgate with liftglass rear door system and rear heat and load floor mat delete. REQUIRES 1SB and (C5U or C5H). NOT AVAILABLE with QMK, R9L.*	792	921
R9J	Third Row Seat Package *Includes third row 50/50 split seat, liftgate with liftglass rear door system and rear heat and load floor mat delete. REQUIRES 1SB and (~~2 or C5H). NOT AVAILABLE with QMJ, QMK, R9L.*	1136	1321
R9J	Third Row Seat Package *Includes third row 50/50 split seat, liftgate with liftglass rear door system and rear heat and load floor mat delete. REQUIRES 1SB, C5H. NOT AVAILABLE with QMJ, QMK, R9L.*	792	921
R9J	Third Row Seat Package *Includes third row 50/50 split seat, liftgate with liftglass rear door system, rear heat and load floor mat delete. REQUIRES 1SC, C5H. NOT AVAILABLE with Z55, QMK, QMJ.*	821	955
R9K	Convenience Package *Includes Homelink 3-channel transmitter, heated outside rearview mirrors and carpeted floor mats. REQUIRES 1SB. NOT AVAILABLE with CF5.*	294	342
R9K	Convenience Package *Includes Homelink 3-channel transmitter, heated outside rearview mirrors and carpeted floor mats. REQUIRES 1SB.*	202	235
R9L	Z71 Off-Road Package (4WD) *Includes off-road suspension, high capacity air cleaner, wheel flares, skid plate package, tires: LT265/75R16 SBR BW on/off road, reclining high back bucket*	1257	1462

CODE	DESCRIPTION	INVOICE	MSRP
	seats, floor console, locking differential, OnStar communications system and wheels: stainless steel clad. REQUIRES 1SB. NOT AVAILABLE with BVE, ZW7, QNL, QMK, R9J.		
T96	Fog Lamps *REQUIRES 1SB.*	73	85
T96	Fog Lamps *REQUIRES 1SC.*	NC	NC
UK6	Rear Seat Audio Controls *REQUIRES A95 and 1SB.*	142	165
ULO	Radio: AM/FM Stereo with Cassette and Automatic Tone Control *Includes digital clock, theft lock and speed compensated volume. REQUIRES 1SB.*	NC	NC
UM6	Radio: AM/FM Stereo with Cassette and Clock *REQUIRES 1SA.*	126	147
UPO	Radio: AM/FM Stereo with Automatic Tone Control, CD and Cassette *Includes electronic tuning, digital clock, theft lock, speed compensated volume and remote CD player. REQUIRES A95 and 1SB. NOT AVAILABLE with ULO.*	108	125
V53	Luggage Rack Delete *REQUIRES 1SB. NOT AVAILABLE with CF5.*	NC	NC
Z55	Autoride *Includes bi-state variable shock dampening and rear air assisted load leveling. REQUIRES 1SC. NOT AVAILABLE with R9J, ZW7.*	602	700
ZW7	Premium Ride Suspension *REQUIRES 1SB. NOT AVAILABLE with R9J.*	315	366
ZW7	Premium Ride Suspension *REQUIRES 1SB. NOT AVAILABLE with R9L.*	NC	NC
ZY2	Two-Tone Paint *REQUIRES 1SB.*	172	200
~~2	Custom Leather Seat Trim *Includes driver's and passenger's 6-way power seats. REQUIRES 1SB.*	1187	1380

2000 TAHOE LIMITED/Z71

What's New?

All old-style Tahoes are dropped, except these two four-door special editions. The rugged 4WD Z71 is for the rock-hopping weekend warrior set, while the swanky 2WD Limited appeals to those who'd otherwise have a truck reworked by Earl Sheib and Tirerack.com.

Review

A new Tahoe is in town. Based on the redesigned Silverado pickup platform, the new truck is more powerful, more efficient, more sturdy, and roomier to boot. The Z71 and Limited are not a part of this equation. These two special-edition Tahoes are based on the old C/K platform that's been the foundation for millions of vehicles since 1988.

Produced in the same Arlington, Texas, assembly plant as the Cadillac Escalade and the GMC Yukon Denali (all carryover models for 2000), Chevy concocted the Z71 and Limited to appeal to buyers who like the old styling better than the new, and to take up some slack in the production schedule while the Texas plant prepares to change over to the redesigned Caddy and GMC. So if you like what you see here, 2000 is likely your only chance to snag one.

Let's start with the Limited. Based on the 2WD Tahoe, it's powered by the evergreen 5.7-liter Vortec V8 that makes 255 horsepower and 330 ft-lbs. of torque at 2,800 rpm. The standard equipment list is long, and includes all the goodies from last year's leather-lined LT model plus high-gloss black monotone paint, beautiful five-spoke polished aluminum wheels, sporty ground effects and a front air dam, integrated front fog lights, and two-tone leather seats. Options are, uh, limited to a 3.73 rear axle ratio, a trailering package, and a comfort and security package that includes heated dual power seats, HomeLink transmitter and electrochromic heated outside mirrors.

The Z71, like the Limited, has the Vortec 5.7-liter V8 and the contents of last year's LT trim level. But it's based on the 4WD Tahoe chassis, costs $5,000 more, and gets macho off-road garb in the form of a brush guard, taillight protectors, side rails, recovery hooks, color-keyed wheel flares, and a roof rack. Chrome wheels, fog lights, and a monotone paint treatment in one of four different colors round out the appearance package. Options mirror the Limited's, except the 3.73 rear axle ratio is standard.

Inside, both models are lined with leather and nearly every option available. You get front and rear air conditioning, deep-tinted glass, self-dimming rearview mirror with compass and outside temperature display, combination CD and cassette deck, cruise, tilt, and a bunch of power operated doo-dads. Rear cargo doors are standard, but if you don't like that center pillar blocking your view, you can opt for a conventional fold-down tailgate at no charge.

Tahoes, even the oldie moldy ones, are pretty decent trucks. They're adequately powerful, adequately comfortable, and adequately reliable. Just the right size inside for a family of five, they're still more manageable around town and in the woods than a hulking Expedition or Suburban. But with the newly redesigned and greatly improved versions sharing showroom floor space in LS and LT trim, you'll likely want to skip these leftovers for more modern machinery.

2000 Chevrolet Tahoe Z71

Standard Equipment

LIMITED 2WD (4A): 5.7L V8 OHV SMPI 16-valve engine; 4-speed electronic OD auto transmission with lock-up; 600-amp HD battery; 100-amp alternator; rear-wheel drive, 3.42 axle ratio; stainless steel exhaust; front independent suspension with anti-roll bar, front coil springs, rigid rear axle suspension with rear leaf springs; power re-circulating ball steering with vehicle speed-sensing assist; front disc/rear drum brakes with 4-wheel antilock braking system; 30 gal. capacity fuel tank; side impact bars; split swing-out rear cargo door; trailer harness; front and rear chrome bumpers with black rub strip, front chrome bumper insert, rear step; black bodyside molding with chrome bodyside insert, chrome wheel well molding; monotone paint; aero-composite halogen headlamps with daytime running lights; additional exterior lights include underhood light; driver's and passenger's power remote black folding outside mirrors; front and rear 15" x 7" silver alloy wheels; P235/75SR15 A/S BSW front and rear tires; underbody mounted full-size steel spare wheel with crankdown; air conditioning, rear heat ducts; AM/FM stereo, clock, seek-scan, cassette, single CD, 8 performance speakers, auto equalizer, theft deterrent, and fixed antenna; cruise control; power door locks with 2 stage unlock, remote keyless entry, child safety rear door locks, power remote hatch/trunk release; 3 power accessory outlets, smokers' package; instrumentation display includes tachometer, oil pressure gauge, water temperature gauge, volt gauge, compass, exterior temp, trip odometer; warning indicators include battery, lights on, key in ignition, door ajar; driver's and passenger's front airbags; ignition disable, panic alarm; deep tinted windows, power front and rear windows with driver's 1-touch down, fixed 1/4 vent windows; variable intermittent front windshield wipers, sun visor strip, rear window defroster; seating capacity of 5, front bucket seats, adjustable headrests, driver's and passenger's armrests, driver's seat includes 4-way power seat, 8-way direction control, power 2-way lumbar support, passenger's seat includes 4-way direction control, power 2-way lumbar support; 60-40 folding rear split-bench seat with adjustable headrests, center armrest with storage; front and rear height adjustable seatbelts; leather seats, cloth door trim insert, full cloth headliner, full color-keyed carpet floor covering with rubber front and rear floor mats, deluxe sound insulation, plastic/rubber gear shift knob; interior lights include dome light with delay, front and rear reading lights, 4 door curb lights, illuminated entry; leather-wrapped sport steering wheel with tilt adjustment; dual illuminated vanity mirrors, dual auxiliary visors; auto-dimming day/night rearview mirror; partial floor console, full overhead console with storage, glove box with light, front and rear cupholders, 2 seat back storage pockets, driver's and passenger's door bins; carpeted cargo floor, carpeted trunk lid, cargo cover, cargo light; chrome grille, black side window moldings, black front windshield molding, black rear window molding and black door handles.

Z71 4WD (4A) (in addition to or instead of LIMITED 2WD (4A) equipment): Auto full-time 4-wheel drive, auto locking hub control and electronic shift, 3.73 axle ratio; front torsion springs, front torsion bar; front tow hooks; front and rear 16" x 7" silver alloy wheels and P245/75SR16 AT BSW front and rear tires.

Base Prices

CC10706	Limited 2WD (4A)	29688	33929
CK10706	Z71 4WD (4A)	34032	38894
Destination Charge:		675	675

Accessories

1SC	Preferred Equipment Group 1SC *Includes vehicle with standard equipment.*	NC	NC
R6B	Front Brush Guard Not Desired (Z71)	(150)	(175)
R6M	New Jersey Cost Surcharge	83	NC
Z82	HD Trailering Equipment (Z71) *Includes trailer hitch platform and wiring harness.*	NC	NC
ZM9	Comfort and Security Package (Limited) *Includes carpeted front/rear floor mats, rear air conditioning, 46mm Bilstein shocks, heated driver's and front passenger's seats, power passenger's front seat, reversible rear cargo mat, heated electrochromic exterior mirrors and Homelink 3-channel transmitter.*	900	1047
ZM9	Comfort and Security Package (Z71) *Includes carpeted front/rear floor mats, rear air conditioning, 46mm Bilstein shocks, heated driver's and front passenger's seats, power passenger's front seat, reversible*	1373	1597

rear cargo mat, heated electrochromic exterior mirrors and Homelink 3-channel transmitter.

2000 TRACKER

2000 Chevrolet Tracker

What's New?

After a complete redesign in 1999, new colors sum up the changes for 2000.

Review

An all-new Tracker arrived last year, with a fresh look and revamped interior that made it more attractive to folks cross-shopping the Kia Sportage, Toyota RAV4 and Honda CR-V mini-utes. Only the name and a handful of components carried over from the previous-generation Tracker.

Unlike many of today's unibody mini-SUVs built off car platforms, Tracker boasts full ladder-type frame construction. But suspension and steering upgrades hide the rigid chassis, resulting in improved ride and handling, with better stability and more substantial road feel. Power front disc brakes with rear drums bring things to a halt, while four-wheel ABS is optional. A "shift-on-the-fly" four-wheel-drive system with automatic locking front hubs is standard on all 4WD models.

With its lower roofline, sloping hood and rounded flanks, Tracker's design is more modern than its chunky predecessor, whether you choose the two-door soft-top model or four-door hardtop. Better still, Tracker's interior is more comfortable and features better ergonomics. Four-door Trackers can be equipped with power windows, door locks and mirrors, while child security rear door locks are standard. Rear seating is surprisingly comfortable for two adults. Stowing the rear seat provides a nearly flat load floor, but maximum cargo space still trails primary competitors.

The two-door convertibles have a two-piece "easy-opening" top that opens up the front section, rear section or both to the sun, but you'll still utilize the uncouth parts of your vocabulary while raising or lowering the roof. Dealer-installed exterior accessory packages can also be added to custom-tailor your Tracker for more serious on- or off-road duty, if you so desire.

A 2.0-liter, 16-valve, DOHC four-cylinder engine is standard on the four-door and optional on convertibles. It puts out 127 horsepower at 6,000 rpm and 134 foot-pounds of torque at 3,000 revs through a five-speed manual or optional four-speed automatic transmission. The base motor on the two-door is a 1.6-liter inline four available only with the stick shift - but the little motor's 97 tortured ponies and mere 100 foot-pounds of torque demand that you opt for the bigger engine mated to the five-speed. But even with its more powerful engine, the Tracker is woefully wheezy while under hard acceleration — buzzing and complaining well before redline.

Power-hungry drivers aside, there's no denying that fun-in-the-sun motoring takes on fresh meaning behind the wheel of a little Tracker convertible — even more so with the go-anywhere attitude afforded by four-wheel drive. And more practical-minded folks will no doubt appreciate the blend of good utility and fuel economy afforded by a Tracker four-door.

Standard Equipment

2WD CONVERTIBLE (5M): 1.6L I4 SOHC MPI 16-valve engine; 5-speed OD manual transmission; 390-amp battery with run down protection; 55-amp alternator; rear-wheel drive, 5.12 axle ratio; stainless steel exhaust; front independent strut suspension with anti-roll bar, front coil springs, rigid rear axle multi-link suspension with rear coil springs; power rack-and-pinion steering; front disc/rear drum brakes; 14.8 gal. capacity fuel tank; skid plate(s), side impact bars; conventional rear cargo door; manual convertible roof with roll-over protection; front and rear black bumpers with front and rear tow hooks, rear step; black bodyside molding; monotone paint; aero-composite halogen fully auto headlamps with daytime running lights; driver's and passenger's manual black outside mirrors; front and rear 15" x 5.5" silver styled steel wheels; P195/75SR15 A/S BSW front and rear tires; outside rear mounted full-size steel spare wheel; rear heat ducts; AM/FM stereo, clock, seek-scan, 4 speakers, and manual retractable antenna; 2 power accessory outlets, smokers' package; instrumentation display includes tachometer, water temperature gauge, trip odometer; warning indicators include oil pressure, battery, lights on, key in ignition; driver's and passenger's front airbags; tinted windows; variable intermittent front windshield wipers; seating capacity of 4, front bucket seats, adjustable headrests, driver's seat includes 4-way direction control, easy entry, passenger's seat includes 4-way direction control, easy entry; full folding rear bench seat with adjustable headrests; front height adjustable seatbelts; cloth seats, cloth door trim insert, full carpet floor covering with carpeted floor mats, plastic/ rubber gear shift knob; interior lights include dome light with delay, front reading lights; dual auxiliary visors, passenger's side vanity mirror; day/night rearview mirror; full floor console, locking glove box, front and rear cupholders, instrument panel bin, 2 seat back storage pockets, driver's and passenger's door bins; carpeted cargo floor, plastic trunk lid; chrome grille, black side window moldings, black front windshield molding and black door handles.

2WD HARD TOP (5M) (in addition to or instead of 2WD CONVERTIBLE (5M) equipment): 2.0L I4 DOHC MPI 16-valve engine; 550-amp battery with run down protection; 4.62 axle ratio; 17.4 gal. capacity fuel tank; child safety rear door locks; tinted windows, manual front and rear windows, fixed 1/4 vent windows; variable intermittent front windshield wipers, rear window defroster; seating capacity of 5, driver's seat includes 4-way direction control, passenger's seat includes 4-way direction control; 50-50 folding rear bench seat with adjustable headrests; cargo cover, cargo net and cargo light.

4WD (5M) (in addition to or instead of 2WD (5M) equipment): Part-time 4 wheel drive, auto locking hub control and manual shift, 5.12 (Convertible)/4.62 (Hardtop) axle ratio; P205/75SR15 A/S BSW front and rear tires.

Base Prices

CE10367	2WD Convertible (5M)	13117	13925
CJ10367	4WD Convertible (5M)	14154	15025
CE10305	2WD Hard Top (5M)	14271	15150
CJ10305	4WD Hard Top (5M)	15308	16250
Destination Charge:		400	400

CODE	DESCRIPTION	INVOICE	MSRP

Accessories

CODE	DESCRIPTION	INVOICE	MSRP
1SA	Preferred Equipment Group 1SA *Includes vehicle with standard equipment. REQUIRES (10T or 41T or 61T) and (R6G or C60). NOT AVAILABLE with Z05.*	NC	NC
1SB	Preferred Equipment Group 1SB *Includes air conditioning, cruise control, AM/FM stereo with cassette and tilt steering wheel. NOT AVAILABLE with R6G, U1C.*	1375	1545
C60	Air Conditioning *NOT AVAILABLE with R6G. INCLUDED in 1SB.*	832	935
FE9	Federal Emission Requirements	NC	NC
JM4	4-Wheel Antilock Brakes	530	595
L34	Engine: 2.0L 4 Cylinder DOHC MPI (Convertible) *Includes 4.62 axle ratio.*	356	400
MX0	Transmission: 4-Speed Automatic with OD *Includes 4.87 axle ratio.*	890	1000
P17	Black Vinyl Spare Tire and Wheel Cover	44	50
QA4	Wheels: 15" Alloy	325	365
R6G	Air Conditioning Not Desired *NOT AVAILABLE with 1SB, C60.*	NC	NC
R6M	New Jersey Cost Surcharge	46	NC
U1C	Radio: AM/FM Stereo with CD *Includes seek-scan, digital clock, theft lock and 4 speakers. NOT AVAILABLE with UM6, 1SA.*	89	100
U1C	Radio: AM/FM Stereo with CD *Includes seek-scan, digital clock, theft lock and 4 speakers. NOT AVAILABLE with UM6, 1SB.*	236	265
UM6	Radio: AM/FM Stereo with Cassette *Includes seek-scan, digital clock and 4 speakers. NOT AVAILABLE with U1C. INCLUDED in 1SB.*	147	165
V54	Painted Black Luggage Carrier (Hardtop)	112	126
YF5	California Emission Requirements	NC	NC
Z05	Convenience Package (Hardtop) *Includes power windows, power door locks and power mirrors. NOT AVAILABLE with 1SA.*	650	730

2000 VENTURE

What's New?

Chevy adds two new models on either end of the price spectrum for 2000. On the low end, a new Value Van includes basic equipment for a low price, while on the high end, a Warner Bros. Edition provides leather and an in-van entertainment system. New radios include RDS (radio data system) on uplevel versions. Three-door models die this year, while remaining models get new interior fabric patterns and a redesigned gauge cluster with a scratch-resistant lens. Smokey Carmel is a new paint color.

2000 Chevrolet Venture

Review

It should be no surprise that Venture has surpassed previous Chevrolet minivan sales records, given the limited appeal of its mini-vac shaped, plastic-bodied predecessor, the Lumina Minivan. Developed in concert with GM's European Opel division, Venture enters its fourth model year wearing conservative, yet modern, sheetmetal capped by a toothy chrome grille. Looks aside, this minivan's appeal is measured by a number of functional family features, including a standard driver's-side sliding door, optional passenger's-side power sliding door, available modular seating, optional integrated child seats, standard four-wheel antilock brakes, optional traction control, standard side airbags, and the ability to pull a 3,500-pound trailer.

Value Van, Base, LS, LT or Warner Bros. Edition versions are available. New-for-2000, the Value Van includes seven-passenger bench seating, air conditioning, rear-seat heat ducts, a tilt steering wheel, and an AM/FM stereo. Base models add split-bench seating, map pockets, overhead consolette, particle and odor filter, cargo net, and rear window defogger. LS provides items like upgraded cloth upholstery, remote keyless entry, power windows, tinted glass, driver information center, cruise control, alloy wheels and cassette stereo. Pop for LT trim and you'll get a power driver's seat, second-row captain's chairs, rear audio controls and air conditioning, and a combination CD/cassette deck. Warner Bros. Edition vans (not available in Minn.) are loaded with leather, an integrated child safety seat, modular bucket seating, and a three-mode audio and visual entertainment system that includes a VCP and overhead flip-down LCD screen.

Choose a short or long wheelbase van with four doors. All Ventures come equipped with a 3.4-liter V6 that makes 185 horsepower and 210 foot-pounds of torque. A four-speed automatic transmission with overdrive transmits power to the front wheels. Standard P215/70R-15 tires provide a big footprint for better roadholding. Designed to satisfy consumers on either side of the Atlantic Ocean, the Venture treats drivers with a communicative chassis, sharp steering, and almost nimble handling, all while providing room inside for up to eight passengers and a good amount of their belongings.

Updates for 2000 include new radios with revised controls and graphics, as well as RDS technology on higher-level systems. Revised interior fabrics and a new gauge cluster help spruce up the cabin. One new exterior color, Smokey Carmel, is added to the color palette. Some carryover features worth noting are the optional dual-mode audio unit, which allows rear passengers to listen to a CD via headphones while front passengers catch traffic reports on the radio, and a load-leveling suspension complete with an auxiliary air hose.

Yes, we like the Venture, and whether you prefer the Chevy flavor or the Pontiac (Montana) and Oldsmobile (Silhouette) versions of the same van, we think any of the three have the credentials to go toe-to-toe with Chrysler, Ford and Honda minivans.

Standard Equipment

VALUE (4A): 3.4L V6 OHV SMPI 12-valve engine; 4-speed electronic OD auto transmission with lock-up; 600-amp battery with run down protection; 105-amp alternator; front-wheel drive, 3.29 axle ratio; stainless steel exhaust; comfort ride suspension, front independent strut suspension with anti-roll bar, front coil springs, rear non-independent torsion suspension with anti-roll bar, rear coil springs; power rack-and-pinion steering with vehicle speed-sensing assist; front disc/rear drum brakes with 4-wheel antilock braking system; 20 gal. capacity fuel tank; side impact bars; 4 doors with sliding left rear passenger door, sliding right rear passenger door, liftback rear cargo door; front and rear body-colored bumpers with black rub strip, rear step; black bodyside molding; clearcoat monotone paint; aero-composite halogen fully auto headlamps with daytime running lights, delay-off feature; additional exterior lights include underhood light; driver's and passenger's manual black folding outside mirrors; front and rear 15" x 6" steel wheels; P215/70SR15 A/S BSW front and rear tires; underbody mounted compact steel spare wheel with crankdown; air conditioning; AM/FM stereo, clock, seek-scan, 4 speakers, and window grid antenna; power door locks with 2 stage unlock, child safety rear door locks, remote hatch/trunk release; 3 power accessory outlets, smokers' package; instrumentation display includes water temperature gauge, systems monitor, trip odometer; warning indicators include oil pressure, water temp, battery, low oil level, low coolant, lights on, key in ignition, low fuel, service interval; driver's and passenger's front airbags, driver's and front passenger's seat mounted side airbags; ignition disable; tinted windows, manual 1/4 vent windows; variable intermittent front windshield wipers, sun visor strip; seating capacity of 7, front bucket seats, fixed headrests, driver's and passenger's armrests, driver's seat includes 6-way direction control, passenger's seat includes 4-way direction control; removable full folding 2nd row bench seat with reclining adjustable headrests; removable full folding 3rd row bench seat with reclining adjustable headrest; front height adjustable seatbelts; cloth seats, cloth door trim insert, full cloth headliner, full carpet floor covering, deluxe sound insulation; interior lights include dome light, front reading lights; steering wheel with tilt adjustment; vanity mirrors; day/night rearview mirror; locking glove box with light, front and rear cupholders, instrument panel covered bin, dashboard storage, 2 seat back storage pockets, driver's and passenger's door bins, front underseat tray; carpeted cargo floor, plastic trunk lid, cargo tie downs, cargo light; argent grille, black side window moldings, black front windshield molding, black rear window molding and black door handles.

BASE PASSENGER (4A) (in addition to or instead of VALUE (4A) equipment): Rear coil springs; 20 gal. capacity fuel tank; AM/FM stereo, clock, seek-scan, 4 speakers, and window grid antenna; 3 power accessory outlets; instrumentation display includes water temperature gauge; seating capacity of 7, driver's and passenger's armrests; removable 40-60 folding 2nd row split-bench seat with reclining adjustable headrests; removable 50-50 folding 3rd row split-bench seat with reclining adjustable headrest; cloth seats, cloth door trim insert, full carpet floor covering with carpeted floor mats; interior lights include front and rear reading lights; front and rear cupholders, front underseat tray and carpeted cargo floor.

PLUS/PLUS EXTENDED (4A) (in addition to or instead of BASE (4A) equipment): 25 gal. capacity fuel tank (Extended), cruise control; power door locks with 2 stage unlock, remote keyless entry; ignition disable, panic alarm; deep tinted windows, power windows with driver's 1-touch down and interior lights include illuminated entry.

LS/LS EXTENDED (4A) (in addition to or instead of PLUS/PLUS EXTENDED (4A) equipment): Aluminum wheels, AM/FM stereo, clock, seek-scan, cassette, 4 performance speakers, auto equalizer, theft deterrent, and window grid antenna; instrumentation display includes compass, exterior temp, trip computer; power 1/4 vent windows and premium cloth seats.

LT EXTENDED (4A) (in addition to or instead of LS EXTENDED (4A) equipment): Traction control, touring ride suspension; roof rack; rear air conditioning with separate controls, rear heat ducts; power sliding passenger's side door, AM/FM stereo, clock, seek-scan, cassette, single CD, 4 performance speakers, auto equalizer, theft deterrent, and window grid antenna, rear audio controls; security system; driver's seat includes 4-way power seat, 8-way direction control and removable 2nd row captain's seat with reclining adjustable headrests.

WARNER BROS. EDITION EXTENDED (4A) (in addition to or instead of LS EXTENDED (4A) equipment): Auto-leveling suspension, front and rear body-colored bumpers with body-colored rub strip; body-colored bodyside molding; Warner Bros. badging; power sliding passenger's side door, AM/FM stereo, clock, seek-scan, cassette, single CD, 4 performance speakers, auto equalizer, theft deterrent, and window grid antenna, tri-mode rear audio controls, overhead flip-down LCD monitor, front console mounted stereo VCP with remote control, security system; manual 1/4 vent windows; removable 2nd row bucket seat with reclining adjustable headrests, 1 rear child seat; leather seats and body-colored door handles.

Base Prices

Code	Description	Invoice	MSRP
1UN16-1SV	Value (4A)	19101	20650
1UN16-1SA	Base Van (4A)	20227	22350
1UN16-1SB	Plus (4A)	21313	23550
1UM16-1SB	Plus Extended (4A)	22218	24550
1UN16-1SC	LS (4A)	22218	24550
1UM16-1SC	LS Extended (4A)	23123	25550
1UM16-1SD	LT Extended (4A)	25295	27950
1UM16-1SE	Warner Bros. Edition Extended (4A)	26240	28995
Destination Charge:		605	605

Accessories

Code	Description	Invoice	MSRP
—	Cloth Seat Trim (Base/Plus/Plus Ext.)	NC	NC
—	Custom Cloth Seat Trim (LS/LT) *Not available with Dark Teal interior color.*	NC	NC
—	Leather Seat Trim (LT) *Includes power driver's and passenger's seats and front underseat tray delete. NOT AVAILABLE ZP8.*	770	895
—	Leather and Cloth Seat Trim (WB)	NC	NC
1SA	Preferred Equipment Group 1SA (Base) *Includes vehicle with standard equipment.*	NC	NC
1SB	Preferred Equipment Group 1SB (Plus/Plus Extended) *Includes vehicle with standard equipment.*	NC	NC
1SC	Preferred Equipment Group 1SC (LS/LS Extended) *Includes vehicle with standard equipment.*	NC	NC
1SD	Preferred Equipment Group 1SD (LT) *Includes vehicle with standard equipment.*	NC	NC
1SE	Preferred Equipment Group 1SE (WB) *Includes vehicle with standard equipment.*	NC	NC
1SV	Preferred Equipment Group 1SV (Value) *Includes vehicle with standard equipment.*	NC	NC

CODE	DESCRIPTION	INVOICE	MSRP
ABB	7-Passenger Modular Bucket Seats (LS) *NOT AVAILABLE with ABD, ZP8.*	249	290
ABB	7-Passenger Seating with Rear Buckets (LS Extended) *NOT AVAILABLE with ABD, ZP8.*	249	290
ABD	7-Passenger Seating with 2nd Row Captain's Chairs (LS/LS Extended) *Includes 3rd row 50/50 split-bench seating. NOT AVAILABLE with AN2, AN5, ABB, ZP8.*	249	290
AG1	6-Way Power Driver's Seat (LS/LS Extended)	232	270
AN2	Integral Child Seat (Base/Plus/Plus Extended/LT) *NOT AVAILABLE with AN5.*	108	125
AN2	Integral Child Seat (LS/LS Extended/LT) *REQUIRES ZP8. NOT AVAILABLE with ABD, AN5.*	NC	NC
AN5	Dual Integrated Child Seats (Base/Plus/Plus Extended/LT) *NOT AVAILABLE with AN2.*	194	225
AN5	Dual Integrated Child Seats (LS/LS Extended/LT) *REQUIRES ZP8. NOT AVAILABLE with ABD, AN2.*	86	100
C34	Front and Rear Air Conditioning (Extended - Plus/LS)	408	475
C49	Rear Window Defogger (Value) *Includes rear window wiper/washer system.*	262	305
E58	Power Sliding Passenger's Side Door (LS/LS Extended)	387	450
E58	Power Sliding Passenger's Side Door (Plus/Plus Extended)	430	500
FE3	Touring Suspension Group (LS/LS Extended/WB) *Includes load leveling suspension with auxiliary air inflator. NOT AVAILABLE with P42, V92. INCLUDED in 1SD.*	310	360
FE3	Touring Suspension Group (LS/LS Extended/WB) *Includes load leveling suspension with auxiliary air inflator. REQUIRES P42. NOT AVAILABLE with V92. INCLUDED in 1SD.*	181	210
K05	Engine Block Heater	30	35
NW9	Traction Control (LS/LS Extended/WB) *INCLUDED in 1SD.*	168	195
P42	Self Sealing Tires (LS/LS Extended/WB) *Includes tires: P215/70R15 TOURING.*	258	300
P42	Self Sealing Tires (LT) *Includes P215/70R-15 touring tires.*	129	150
PH3	Wheels: 15" Cast Aluminum (Plus) *INCLUDED in 1SC, 1SD, 1SE.*	254	295
R6M	New Jersey Cost Surcharge	71	NC
UA6	Security System (Base/LS/LS Extended) *Interior content. INCLUDED in 1SD, 1SE.*	52	60
UK6	Rear Seat Audio Controls (LS/LS Extended) *Includes earphone jacks and headphones. INCLUDED in 1SD, 1SE.*	133	155
UL0	Radio: AM/FM Stereo with Cassette (Base/Plus/Plus Extended) *Includes digital clock, auto tone control, theft lock and premium front and rear coaxial speakers. NOT AVAILABLE with UN0, UP0. INCLUDED in 1SC.*	232	270
UN0	Radio: AM/FM Stereo with CD (Base/Plus/Plus Extended) *Includes digital clock, auto tone control, theft lock, speed compensated volume and premium front and rear coaxial speakers. NOT AVAILABLE with UP0.*	318	370

CODE	DESCRIPTION	INVOICE	MSRP
UNO	Radio: AM/FM Stereo with CD (LS/LS Extended) *Includes digital clock, auto tone control, theft lock, speed compensated volume and premium front and rear coaxial speakers. NOT AVAILABLE with UPO.*	86	100
UPO	Radio: AM/FM Stereo with CD and Cassette (Base/Plus/Plus Extended) *Includes auto reverse, auto tone control, digital clock, theft lock, speed compensated volume and premium front and rear coaxial speakers. NOT AVAILABLE with UNO. INCLUDED in 1SD, 1SE.*	404	470
UPO	Radio: AM/FM Stereo with CD and Cassette (LS/LS Extended) *Includes auto reverse, auto tone control, digital clock, theft lock, speed compensated volume and premium front and rear coaxial speakers. NOT AVAILABLE with UNO. INCLUDED in 1SD, 1SE.*	172	200
V54	Luggage Carrier (Plus/Plus Extended/LS/LS Extended) *INCLUDED in 1SD, 1SE.*	194	225
V92	Trailering Provisions (LS/LS Extended/WB) *Includes HD engine oil cooler, transmission oil cooler and touring suspension group. NOT AVAILABLE with P42.*	452	525
V92	Trailering Provisions (LS/LS Extended/WB) *Includes HD engine oil cooler, transmission oil cooler and touring suspension group. REQUIRES P42.*	322	375
V92	Trailering Provisions (LT) *Includes HD engine oil cooler and transmission oil cooler.*	142	165
XPU	Tires: P215/70R15 Touring (LS/LS Extended/WB) *REQUIRES P42.*	129	1500
ZP8	8-Passenger Seating (LS/LS Extended) *Includes 3 modular bucket seats in 2nd row and 3rd row 50/50 split bench seating. REQUIRES 1SC. NOT AVAILABLE with ABB, ABD.*	249	290
ZP8	8-Passenger Seating (LT) *Includes 3 bucket seats in 2nd row and 3rd row 50/50 split bench seating. NOT AVAILABLE with Cloth Seating.*	NC	NC

2000 TOWN AND COUNTRY

2000 Chrysler Town & Country

What's New?

The model lineup changes this year, and telling the difference between the LX and LXi will be easier to the untrained eye, thanks to distinctive exterior and interior modifications. New colors for 2000 are Shale Green, Bright White, Patriot Blue, Bright Silver and Inferno Red.

Review

Elegance and expressiveness. Grace and grandeur. Welcome to the Town & Country. Oh sure, you get the same fresh shape and interior space in a lower-priced Caravan or Voyager, the same carlike ride and handling qualities, the same practical virtues as a people and cargo hauler. What Chrysler adds to that mix is luxury, and plenty of it — and that's enough to attract a fair share of extra customers to the Chrysler end of the minivan spectrum.

In the past, Town & Country customers have had four distinct models to choose from: an LX model, an upscale LXi that promised features ordinarily found only on luxury cars, a super-luxury Limited and the short-wheelbase SX version. But this year, gone is the short-wheelbase offering, and the LX has been decontented. Both front-wheel or all-wheel drive return for 2000.

The LX is targeted for the $25,000-$30,000 range and still nets buyers quad seating, wood-grain trim, dual-zone air conditioning, quad headlamps and a monochromatic exterior. The Limited is still limited to those ready to cough up a heap to drive a minivan, but they get heated seats, distinctive badging, chrome 16-inch wheels, steering wheel-mounted stereo controls, logo'd floor mats, a rear bench seat with a center armrest, and suede accents and trim panels. But both of 'em get an integrated reclining child seat built into the mid-row Quad Command bucket seat.

What also sets them apart is what's under the hood. The LX and LXi front-wheel-drives come standard with a 3.3-liter V6, but the same LXi crowd can opt for a 3.8-liter V6, or they could just go ahead and buy the all-wheel-drive in order to get the 3.8-liter V6 as standard equipment. Limiteds score only the 3.8-liter. Still with us? All varieties are hooked to a four-speed automatic transaxle, but only the front-wheel-drives wear four-wheel ABS with discs and drums, while the all-wheel-drives have ABS and discs at all corners. The LXi has low-speed traction control, and the Limited gets it standard, but this is relevant only for the front-wheel-drives.

Want to just skip to the Reader's Digest version of the 2000 Chrysler Town & Country? It remains refined, luxurious and spacious with seating for seven. With all-wheel- and front-wheel-drive models available, plus three different trim levels for both, Chrysler has the minivan audience covered.

Standard Equipment

LX FWD (4A): 3.3L V6 OHV SMPI 12-valve engine, flexible fuel capable; 4-speed electronic OD auto transmission with lock-up; 500-amp battery; 125-amp HD alternator; front-wheel drive, 3.62 axle ratio; stainless steel exhaust; front independent strut suspension with anti-roll bar, front coil springs, rear non-independent suspension with rear leaf springs; power rack-and-pinion steering; front disc/rear drum brakes with 4-wheel antilock braking system; 20 gal. capacity fuel tank; rear lip spoiler, side impact bars; 4 doors with sliding left rear passenger's door, sliding right rear passenger's door, liftback rear cargo door; front and rear body-colored bumpers with chrome bumper insert, rear step; body-colored bodyside molding with chrome bodyside insert; monotone paint with bodyside accent stripe; aero-composite halogen headlamps; additional exterior lights include front fog/driving lights; driver's and passenger's power remote black heated folding outside mirrors; front and rear 15" x 6.5" steel wheels; P215/65SR15 A/S BSW front and rear tires; underbody mounted compact steel spare wheel; dual zone front air conditioning, rear heat ducts; AM/FM stereo, clock, seek-scan, cassette, 4 speakers, and fixed antenna; cruise control with steering wheel controls; power door locks, child safety rear door locks; 2 power accessory outlets, driver's foot rest; instrumentation display includes tachometer, water temperature gauge, compass, exterior temp, trip computer, trip odometer; warning indicators include oil pressure, water temp, battery, lights on, key in ignition, low fuel, low washer fluid, door ajar, trunk ajar; driver's and passenger's front airbags; deep tinted windows, power windows with driver's 1-touch down, power 1/4 vent windows; heated variable intermittent front windshield wipers, sun visor strip, variable intermittent rear wiper, rear window defroster; seating capacity of 7, front bucket seats, adjustable headrests, driver's and passenger's armrests, driver's seat includes 6-way power seat, lumbar support, passenger's seat includes 4-way direction control; removable 2nd row bucket seat with reclining adjustable headrests; removable full folding 3rd row bench seat with reclining adjustable headrest; front and rear height adjustable seatbelts; premium cloth seats, cloth door trim insert, full cloth headliner, full carpet floor covering with carpeted floor mats, deluxe sound insulation, simulated wood trim on instrument panel; interior lights include dome light with delay, front and rear reading lights, 2 door curb lights; steering wheel with tilt adjustment; dual illuminated vanity mirrors, dual auxiliary visors; day/night rearview mirror; full overhead console with storage, glove box with light, front and rear cupholders, 1 seat back storage pocket, driver's and passenger's door bins, front underseat tray; carpeted cargo floor, plastic trunk lid, cargo light; chrome grille, black side window moldings, black front windshield molding, black rear window molding and body-colored door handles.

LXi FWD (4A) (in addition to or instead of LX FWD (4A) equipment): Body-colored bodyside cladding; aero-composite halogen headlamps, delay-off feature; front and rear 16" x 6.5" steel wheels; P215/65SR16 touring A/S BSW front and rear tires; premium AM/FM stereo, clock, seek-scan, cassette, CD changer pre-wiring, in-dash CD pre-wiring, 10 premium speakers, amplifier, and fixed antenna; remote keyless entry; panic alarm; interior lights include illuminated entry; leather-wrapped steering wheel with tilt adjustment and instrument panel covered bin.

LIMITED FWD (4A) (in addition to or instead of LXi FWD (4A) equipment): 3.8L V6 OHV SMPI 12-valve engine; 600-amp battery, traction control, 3.43 axle ratio; auto-leveling suspension; roof rack; aero-composite halogen fully auto headlamps with delay-off feature; front and rear 16" x 6.5" chrome wheels; underbody mounted full-size steel spare wheel; rear air conditioning with separate controls; premium AM stereo/FM stereo, clock, seek-scan, cassette, single CD, 10 premium speakers, amplifier, graphic equalizer, and fixed antenna, radio steering wheel controls; garage door opener; security system; heated-cushion front bucket seats, passenger's seat includes 6-way power seat; leather seats, leatherette door trim insert; memory on driver's seat with 2 memory setting(s) includes settings for exterior mirrors; auto-dimming day/night rearview mirror and chrome door handles.

CODE	DESCRIPTION	INVOICE	MSRP

LX AWD (4A) (in addition to or instead of LX FWD (4A) equipment): 3.8L V6 OHV SMPI 12-valve engine; 600-amp battery; full-time all-wheel drive, 3.43 axle ratio; auto-leveling suspension and 4-wheel disc brakes with 4-wheel antilock braking system.

LXi AWD/LIMITED AWD (4A) (in addition to or instead of LXi FWD/LIMITED FWD (4A) equipment): 600-amp battery; full-time all-wheel drive, 3.43 axle ratio; auto-leveling suspension and 4-wheel disc brakes with 4-wheel antilock braking system.

Base Prices

CODE	DESCRIPTION	INVOICE	MSRP
NSYH53	LX FWD (4A)	24097	26525
NSCH53	LX AWD (4A)	26882	29690
NSYP53	LXi FWD (4A)	25905	28580
NSCP53	LXi AWD (4A)	28699	31755
NSYS53	Limited FWD (4A)	31053	34430
NSCS53	Limited AWD (4A)	33143	36805
Destination Charge:		590	590

Accessories

CODE	DESCRIPTION	INVOICE	MSRP
25N	Quick Order Package 25N (LX FWD) *Includes vehicle with standard equipment. REQUIRES EGM and DGB and 4XN. NOT AVAILABLE with EGA.*	NC	NC
25R	Quick Order Package 25R (LXi FWD) *Includes vehicle with standard equipment. REQUIRES EGM and DGB and (ALW or 4XN). NOT AVAILABLE with EGA, EGH, CMA, AHT.*	NC	NC
28N	Quick Order Package 28N (LX FWD) *Includes vehicle with standard equipment. REQUIRES EGA and DGB and 4XN. NOT AVAILABLE with EGM.*	NC	NC
28R	Quick Order Package 28R (LXi FWD) *Includes vehicle with standard equipment. REQUIRES EGA and DGB and (ALW or 4XN). NOT AVAILABLE with EGH, EGM, CMA, AHT.*	NC	NC
29N	Quick Order Package 29N (LX AWD) *Includes vehicle with standard equipment. REQUIRES EGH and DGB and 4XN.*	NC	NC
29R	Quick Order Package 29R (LXi) *Includes vehicle with standard equipment. REQUIRES EGH and DGB and (ALW or 4XN). NOT AVAILABLE with EGA, EGM, CMA, AHT.*	NC	NC
29Y	Quick Order Package 29Y (LXi AWD)	2797	3290
	Manufacturer Discount	(850)	(1000)
	Net Price *Includes steering wheel mounted audio controls, Climate Group III: rear air conditioning with heater; Convenience Group V: illuminated entry, headlamp off time delay, keyless entry with 2 transmitters; Convenience Group VI: security alarm, universal garage door opener; power heated exterior mirrors, AM/FM stereo with CD, cassette and equalizer; roof rack, leather low back bucket seats, 8-way power seats with driver's memory, tire: full size spare, underseat lockable storage compartment and wheels: 16" aluminum. REQUIRES EGH and DGB. NOT AVAILABLE with AA2, CYT, ALW.*	1947	2290

CODE	DESCRIPTION	INVOICE	MSRP
29Y	Quick Order Package 29Y (LXi FWD)	2945	3465
	Manufacturer Discount	(850)	(1000)
	Net Price	2095	2465
	Includes steering wheel mounted audio controls, Climate Group III: rear air conditioning with heater; universal garage door opener, power heated exterior mirrors, AM/FM stereo with CD, cassette and equalizer, roof rack, leather low back bucket seats, 8-way power seats with driver's memory, security alarm, tire: full size spare, underseat lockable storage compartment and wheels: 16" aluminum. REQUIRES DGB. NOT AVAILABLE with EGA, EGM, AA2, AAP, CYT, ALW, 4XN, AGA.		
29Z	Quick Order Package 29Z (Limited)	NC	NC
	Includes vehicle with standard equipment. REQUIRES EGH and DGB.		
3C4	California Bonus Discount (Limited)	(1275)	(1500)
	REQUIRES 29Z.		
3WL	Western Region Discount (Limited)	(850)	(1000)
	REQUIRES 29Z.		
3WT	Central Region Discount (Limited)	(850)	(1000)
	REQUIRES 29Z.		
3WX	Eastern Region Discount (Limited)	(850)	(1000)
	REQUIRES 29Z.		
4XN	Rear Air Conditioning Bypass (LX/LXi)	NC	NC
	NOT AVAILABLE with ALW, 29Y.		
AA2	Convenience Group VI (LXi)	204	240
	Includes universal garage door opener and security alarm. NOT AVAILABLE with 29Y.		
AAB	Climate Group III (LX)	383	450
	Includes rear air conditioning with heater. NOT AVAILABLE with 4XN. INCLUDED in 29Y.		
AAG	Convenience Group IV (LX)	204	240
	Includes headlight off time delay, remote keyless entry, security alarm and illuminated entry.		
AAH	Convenience Group V (LX)	332	390
	Includes headlight off time delay, remote keyless entry, illuminated entry and security alarm. INCLUDED in 29Y.		
AAP	Loading Group (FWD - LX/LXi)	153	180
	Includes tire: full size spare and HD suspension. NOT AVAILABLE with AHT, 29Y.		
AAP	Loading Group (FWD - LX/LXi)	94	110
	Includes tire: full size spare. REQUIRES AGA. NOT AVAILABLE with AHT, 29Y.		
AGA	Wheels/Handling Group (LX FWD)	306	360
	Includes front and rear stabilizer bars, HD suspension, tires: P215/65R16 A/S LBL touring and wheels: 16" aluminum.		
AGA	Wheels/Handling Group (LX FWD)	247	290
	Includes front and rear stabilizer bars, tires: P215/65R16 A/S LBL touring and wheels: 16" aluminum.		
AGA	Wheels/Handling Group (LXi FWD)	81	95
	Includes P215R65R16 LBL A/S touring tires, front and rear stabilizer bars and HD suspension. REQUIRES ALW.		

CODE	DESCRIPTION	INVOICE	MSRP
AGA	Wheels/Handling Group (LXi FWD) *Includes P215R65R16 LBL A/S touring tires, front and rear stabilizer bars and wheels: 16" aluminum. NOT AVAILABLE with 29Y.*	374	440
AGA	Wheels/Handling Group (LXi FWD) *Includes P215R65R16 LBL A/S touring tires, front and rear stabilizer bars, HD suspension and wheels: 16" aluminum. NOT AVAILABLE with 29Y.*	434	510
AGA	Wheels/Handling Group (LXi FWD) *Includes P215R65R16 LBL AS Touring tires and front and rear stabilizer bars. REQUIRES ALW.*	21	25
AHT	Trailer Tow Prep Group (AWD - LX/LXi) *Includes engine oil cooler, HD transmission oil cooler, HD radiator, tire: full size spare and trailer tow wiring harness. NOT AVAILABLE with 29Y.*	242	285
AHT	Trailer Tow Prep Group (AWD - LXi/Limited) *Includes engine oil cooler, HD transmission oil cooler, HD radiator and trailer tow wiring harness. NOT AVAILABLE with 29R.*	149	175
AHT	Trailer Tow Prep Group (FWD - LX/LXi) *Includes 600-amp maintenance free battery, engine oil cooler, HD transmission oil cooler, HD radiator, tire: full size spare, HD suspension and trailer tow wiring harness. NOT AVAILABLE with AAP, 29Y, AGA.*	302	355
AHT	Trailer Tow Prep Group (FWD - LX/LXi) *Includes engine oil cooler, HD transmission oil cooler, HD radiator, HD suspension and trailer tow wiring harness. NOT AVAILABLE with AAP, 25R, 28R, 29R, AGA.*	208	245
ALE	Value Plus Audio Group (LX)	612	720
	Manufacturer Discount	(383)	(450)
	Net Price *Includes AM/FM stereo with CD, cassette, equalizer, 200-watt amplifier and 10 Infinity speakers.*	229	270
ALW	Value Plus Popular Equipment Group (LXi)	999	1175
	Manufacturer Discount	(850)	(1000)
	Net Price *Includes rear air conditioning with heater, AM/FM stereo with CD, cassette and equalizer and wheels: 16" aluminum. NOT AVAILABLE with 29Y, 4XN.*	149	175
AWS	Smokers' Group *Includes front and rear ash receiver and cigar lighter.*	17	20
BNM	Traction Control (LXi)	149	175
CMA	Heated Front Seats (LXi) *REQUIRES 29Y. NOT AVAILABLE with 25R, 28R, 29R.*	213	250
CYT	7-Passenger Quad Buckets with Child Seat *NOT AVAILABLE with 29Y.*	106	125
DGB	Transmission: 4-Speed Automatic	NC	NC
EGA	Engine: 3.3L V6 MPI (FWD - LX/LXi) *NOT AVAILABLE with 25N, 29Y, 25R, 29R.*	NC	NC
EGH	Engine: 3.8L V6 MPI (LXi FWD)	434	510
	Manufacturer Discount	(43)	(50)
	Net Price *Includes traction control. REQUIRES 29R. NOT AVAILABLE with 25R, 28R.*	391	460

CODE	DESCRIPTION	INVOICE	MSRP
EGH	Engine: 3.8L V6 MPI (LXi FWD) *Includes traction control. REQUIRES 29Y.*	285	335
EGH	Engine: 3.8L V6 MPI (Limited/AWD - LX/LXi)	NC	NC
EGM	Engine: 3.3L V6 FFV (FWD - LX/LXi) *NOT AVAILABLE with 28N, 29Y, 28R, 29R.*	NC	NC
HL	Leather Low Back Bucket Seats (LXi) *REQUIRES 29Y.*	NC	NC
MWG	Roof Rack (LX/LXi) *INCLUDED in 29Y.*	166	195
NHK	Engine Block Heater	30	35
PEL	Inferno Red Tinted Pearl Coat	170	200
PWP	Golden White Pearl Tri-Coat (LXi/Limited)	170	200
SER	Load Leveling and Height Control (LX/LXi)	247	290
TBB	Tire: Full Size Spare (LX/LXi) *INCLUDED in 29Y.*	94	110
WNW	Wheels: 16" Aluminum (LX) *INCLUDED in 29Y.*	225	265

2000 CARAVAN / GRAND CARAVAN

2000 Dodge Grand Caravan

What's New?

New colors, more standard equipment, and an AWD Sport model keep Chrysler's best-selling minivans up to date until the redesigned 2001 model arrives.

Review

We used to call the Dodge Caravan, and its longer-wheelbase twin the Grand Caravan, the perfect family vehicles. That was before the substantially revised Ford Windstar and Honda's all-new Odyssey arrived in 1999 with top-notch crash-test scores and at least 200 horsepower under the hood. Those are our minivan recommendations for 2000. After all, what sense does it make to buy a family van that doesn't protect your family as well as other minivans on the market? But if you've gotta have a Chrysler and aren't much interested in having the safest van on the market, you could do worse than select either of these Dodges.

Buyers can select front-wheel-drive short-wheelbase Caravans in Base, SE, or Sport trim. All-wheel drive is available only on long-wheelbase Grand Caravan models, which can be purchased in the same trim levels as the stubby Caravan, with the addition of well-equipped LE and luxurious ES versions at the top of the food chain. In terms of size and features, Dodge has you covered with a wide variety of models.

The Caravan line offers several thoughtful details, but the most important are the easy-out rolling seats and the innovative driver's side sliding door. Optional on base Caravan and standard on everything else, the driver's side sliding door offers the convenience of loading kids and cargo from either side of the vehicle. But unlike competitors from Ford, General Motors and Honda, they aren't power-activated. Easy-out seats are a snap to release and remove, though lifting the seat from the rear of the van may still require two sets of biceps.

A 150-horsepower, 2.4-liter, dual-cam four (coupled with an archaic three-speed automatic) serves as the Caravan's base engine, but these sizeable vans benefit from a little extra oomph. A 3.0-liter V6 is standard on the Grand Caravan, and offers the same horsepower as the 2.4-liter but with added torque. A 3.3-liter V6, standard on SE and Sport trim, is a step in the right direction, but our favorite motor is the 3.8-liter unit, which outputs 180 horsepower and 240 foot-pounds of torque. The 3.8-liter engine (standard with all-wheel drive and ES trim; optional on LE), comes with a four-speed automatic transmission which provides shifts that are neat and smooth. ES models even have Dodge's AutoStick feature, which allows manual gear shifts for sportier driving.

Light steering response gives these minivans an undeniably carlike feel, with an exceptionally smooth ride. Highly maneuverable and easy to control, Caravans deliver exceptional handling. Sport models feature specially tuned shocks and springs for more capable canyon carving, and are genuinely fun to drive.

Due for a complete redesign in 2001, the Caravan and Grand Caravan can no longer be touted as the best-in-class minivans. The new models will need to match or beat Ford and Honda in terms of crashworthiness, features, and price to return the minivan-king crown to Chrysler's design. In the meantime, Dodge offers affordable transportation in just about any conceivable configuration.

Standard Equipment

CARAVAN BASE (3A): 2.4L I4 DOHC SMPI 16-valve engine; 3-speed auto transmission; 600-amp battery; 90-amp alternator; front-wheel drive, 3.61 axle ratio; stainless steel exhaust; front independent strut suspension with anti-roll bar, front coil springs, rear non-independent suspension with rear leaf springs; power rack-and-pinion steering; front disc/rear drum brakes; 20 gal. capacity fuel tank; front mud flaps, rear lip spoiler, side impact bars; 3 doors with sliding right rear passenger's door, liftback rear cargo door; front and rear colored bumpers with rear step; colored bodyside molding; monotone paint; aero-composite halogen headlamps; driver's and passenger's manual black folding outside mirrors; front and rear 14" x 6" steel wheels; P205/75SR14 A/S BSW front and rear tires; underbody mounted compact steel spare wheel; AM/FM stereo, clock, seek-scan, cassette, 4 speakers, and fixed antenna; child safety rear door locks; 2 power accessory outlets, driver's foot rest; instrumentation display includes water temperature gauge, trip odometer; warning indicators include oil pressure, water temp, battery, lights on, key in ignition, low fuel, low washer fluid, door ajar, trunk ajar; driver's and passenger's front airbags; tinted windows, fixed rear windows, manual 1/4 vent windows; variable intermittent front windshield wipers, sun visor strip, variable intermittent rear wiper; seating capacity of 5, front bucket seats, fixed headrests, driver's and passenger's armrests, driver's seat includes 4-way direction control, passenger's seat includes 4-way direction control; removable 2nd row bench seat with adjustable headrests; front and rear height adjustable seatbelts; cloth seats, full cloth headliner, full carpet floor covering; interior lights include dome light, front reading lights; vanity mirrors, dual auxiliary visors; day/night rearview mirror; glove box, front and rear cupholders, instrument panel bin, interior concealed storage; carpeted cargo floor, plastic trunk lid, cargo light; body-colored grille, black side window moldings, black front windshield molding, black rear window molding and black door handles.

GRAND CARAVAN BASE FWD (4A) (in addition to or instead of CARAVAN BASE (3A) equipment): 3.0L V6 SOHC SMPI 12-valve engine; 4-speed electronic OD auto transmission with lock-up; 500-amp battery; 3.45 axle ratio; sliding left rear passenger's door; air conditioning; seating capacity of 7 and removable full folding 3rd row bench seat with adjustable headrests.

SE FWD (4A) (in addition to or instead of CARAVAN BASE (3A)/GRAND CARAVAN BASE FWD (4A) equipment): 3.3L V6 OHV SMPI 12-valve engine, flexible fuel capable; 4-speed electronic OD auto transmission with lock-up (Caravan); 3.61 axle ratio; front disc/rear drum brakes with 4-wheel antilock braking system; driver's and passenger's power remote black heated folding outside mirrors; front and rear 15" x 6.5" steel wheels; P215/65SR15 A/S BSW front and rear tires; air conditioning (Caravan), rear heat ducts; cruise control with steering wheel controls; instrumentation display includes tachometer; power front windows with driver's 1-touch down, power 1/4 vent windows; heated variable intermittent front windshield wipers, rear window defroster; removable full folding 2nd row bench seat with reclining adjustable headrests; removable full folding 3rd row bench seat with reclining adjustable headrests (Caravan); cloth door trim insert, carpeted floor mats, deluxe sound insulation; steering wheel with tilt adjustment; dual illuminated vanity mirrors; glove box with light, driver's and passenger's door bins, front underseat tray and cargo net. NOTE: SPORT FWD REQUIRES contents of additional cost options 2*E or 2*N. Please see optional equipment list.

CODE	DESCRIPTION	INVOICE	MSRP

LE FWD (4A) (in addition to or instead of SE FWD (4A) equipment): Monotone paint with bodyside accent stripe; aero-composite halogen headlamps with delay-off feature; dual zone front air conditioning; premium AM/FM stereo, clock, seek-scan, cassette, CD changer pre-wiring, in-dash CD pre-wiring, 10 premium speakers, amplifier, graphic equalizer, and fixed antenna; power door locks, remote keyless entry; instrumentation display includes compass, exterior temp, trip computer; panic alarm; deep tinted windows; front bucket seats, adjustable headrests, driver's seat includes 6-way power seat, lumbar support; interior lights include rear reading lights, 2 door curb lights, illuminated entry; full overhead console with storage, instrument panel covered bin and 1 seat back storage pocket.

ES FWD (4A) (in addition to or instead of SPORT AWD PASSENGER VAN (4A) equipment): 3.8L V6 OHV SMPI 12-valve engine; automanual transmission; 600-amp battery; 125-amp alternator; traction control, 3.45 axle ratio; HD ride suspension, rear non-independent suspension with anti-roll bar; rear wing spoiler; monotone paint with bodyside accent stripe; aero-composite halogen fully auto headlamps with delay-off feature; additional exterior lights include front fog/driving lights; front and rear 17" x 6.5" silver alloy wheels; P215/60SR17 touring A/S BSW front and rear tires; underbody mounted full-size steel spare wheel; premium AM/FM stereo, clock, seek-scan, cassette, single CD, 10 premium speakers, amplifier, graphic equalizer, and fixed antenna, radio steering wheel controls; garage door opener; premium cloth seats; leather-wrapped steering wheel with tilt adjustment; auto-dimming day/night rearview mirror and driver's side exterior mirror.

AWD (4A) (in addition to or instead of FWD (4A) equipment): 3.8L V6 OHV SMPI 12-valve engine (SPORT/LE); Full-time 4-wheel drive, 3.61 axle ratio; auto-leveling suspension and 4-wheel disc brakes with 4-wheel antilock braking system.

Base Prices

CODE	DESCRIPTION	INVOICE	MSRP
NSKL52	Caravan Base (3A)	17123	18850
NSKH52	Caravan SE (4A)	20995	23250
NSKL53	Grand Caravan Base FWD (4A)	19910	21955
NSKH53	Grand Caravan SE FWD (4A)	21926	24245
NSKP53	Grand Caravan LE FWD (4A)	24667	27360
NSKX53	Grand Caravan ES FWD (4A)	26612	29570
NSDH53	Grand Caravan Sport AWD (4A)	25446	28245
NSDP53	Grand Caravan LE AWD (4A)	27461	30535
NSDX53	Grand Caravan ES AWD (4A)	28904	32175
Destination Charge:		590	590

Accessories

CODE	DESCRIPTION	INVOICE	MSRP
22S	Quick Order Package 22S (Caravan Base)	NC	NC
	Includes vehicle with standard equipment. REQUIRES (HAA or 4XA) and EDZ and DGA. NOT AVAILABLE with GKD, AAA, AAC, AAE, MWG, CYK, TBB, DGB, EFA, EGA, AAF, EGM, ALD, AAG.		
22T	Quick Order Package 22T (Caravan Base)	1084	1275
	Manufacturer Discount	(1084)	(1275)
	Net Price	NC	NC
	Includes air conditioning, front seat cargo net, 7-passenger seating, rear floor silencer and under seat lockable drawer. REQUIRES EDZ and DGA. NOT AVAILABLE with 4XA, AAC, DGB, EFA, EGA, EGM, ALD, AAG.		

CODE	DESCRIPTION	INVOICE	MSRP
25D	Quick Order Package 25D (SE)	NC	NC
	Includes vehicle with standard equipment. REQUIRES EGM and DGB and (4XN or AAB). NOT AVAILABLE with EGA, EFA.		
25E	Quick Order Package 25E Sport (SE)	1024	1205
	Manufacturer Discount	(234)	(275)
	Net Price	790	930
	Includes bright Sport badge, 125-amp alternator, fog lamps, sunscreen glass, body colored bodyside molding, rear fascia scuff pad, leather-wrapped steering wheel, body colored rear spoiler, 16" wheel covers and wheels/handling group: rear stabilizer bar, heavy duty suspension and tires: 215/65R16 A/S touring. REQUIRES EGM and DGB and 4XN. NOT AVAILABLE with E5, EGA, CYT, EFA.		
25K	Quick Order Package 25K (LE FWD)	NC	NC
	Includes vehicle with standard equipment. REQUIRES EGM and DGB. NOT AVAILABLE with EGA, EGH.		
25N	Quick Order Package 25N Sport (SE)	2253	2650
	Manufacturer Discount	(319)	(375)
	Net Price	1934	2275
	Includes bright Sport badge, 125-amp alternator, fog lamps, sunscreen glass, body colored bodyside molding, rear fascia scuff pad, leather-wrapped steering wheel, body colored rear spoiler, 16" wheel covers, wheels/handling group: rear stabilizer bar, heavy duty suspension and tires: 215/65R16 A/S touring; overhead console with trip computer, door courtesy lamps, second row reading lamps, power 8-way driver's seat with manual lumbar and 7-passenger seating with quad premium cloth lowback bucket seats. REQUIRES EGM and DGB and 4XN. NOT AVAILABLE with EGA, CYR, CYT, EFA.		
26T	Quick Order Package 26T (Caravan Base)	1084	1275
	Manufacturer Discount	(646)	(760)
	Net Price	438	515
	Includes air conditioning, front seat cargo net, 7-passenger seating, rear floor silencer and under seat lockable drawer. REQUIRES EFA and DGB. NOT AVAILABLE with 4XA, AAC, EDZ, EGA, DGA, EGM, AAE, AAF, AAG.		
26T	Quick Order Package 26T (Grand Caravan Base)	NC	NC
	Includes vehicle with standard equipment. REQUIRES EFA and DGB. NOT AVAILABLE with EGA.		
28D	Quick Order Package 28D (SE)	NC	NC
	Includes vehicle with standard equipment. REQUIRES EGA and DGB and (4XN or AAB). NOT AVAILABLE with EGM, EFA.		
28E	Quick Order Package 28E Sport (SE)	1024	1205
	Manufacturer Discount	(234)	(275)
	Net Price	790	930
	Includes bright Sport badge, 125-amp alternator, fog lamps, sunscreen glass, body colored bodyside molding, rear fascia scuff pad, leather-wrapped steering wheel, body colored rear spoiler, 16" wheel covers and wheels/handling group: rear stabilizer bar, heavy duty suspension and tires: 215/65R16 A/S touring. REQUIRES EGA and DGB and 4XN. NOT AVAILABLE with E5, EGM, CYT, EFA.		

CODE	DESCRIPTION	INVOICE	MSRP
28K	Quick Order Package 28K (LE FWD)	NC	NC
	Includes vehicle with standard equipment. REQUIRES EGA and DGB. NOT AVAILABLE with EGH, EGM.		
28N	Quick Order Package 28N Sport (SE)	2253	2650
	Manufacturer Discount	(319)	(375)
	Net Price	1934	2275
	Includes bright Sport badge, 125-amp alternator, fog lamps, sunscreen glass, body colored bodyside molding, rear fascia scuff pad, leather-wrapped steering wheel, body colored rear spoiler, 16" wheel covers, wheels/handling group: rear stabilizer bar, heavy duty suspension and tires: 215/65R16 A/S touring; overhead console with trip computer, door courtesy lamps, second row reading lamps, power 8-way driver's seat with manual lumbar and 7-passenger seating with quad premium cloth lowback bucket seats. REQUIRES EGA and DGB and 4XN. NOT AVAILABLE with EGM, CYR, CYT, EFA.		
28T	Quick Order Package 28T (Caravan Base)	1084	1275
	Manufacturer Discount	(646)	(760)
	Net Price	438	515
	Includes air conditioning, front seat cargo net, 7-passenger seating, rear floor silencer and under seat lockable drawer. REQUIRES EGA and DGB. NOT AVAILABLE with 4XA, AAC, EDZ, EFA, DGA, EGM, AAE, AAF, AAG.		
28T	Quick Order Package 28T (Grand Caravan Base)	NC	NC
	Includes vehicle with standard equipment. REQUIRES EGA and DGB. NOT AVAILABLE with EFA.		
29E	Quick Order Package 29E (Sport AWD)	NC	NC
	Includes vehicle with standard equipment. REQUIRES EGH and DGB. NOT AVAILABLE with E5.		
29K	Quick Order Package 29K (LE)	NC	NC
	Includes vehicle with standard equipment. REQUIRES EGH and DGB. NOT AVAILABLE with EGA, EGM.		
29M	Quick Order Package 29M (ES)	NC	NC
	Includes vehicle with standard equipment. REQUIRES EGH and DGB.		
29N	Quick Order Package 29N (Sport AWD)	1228	1445
	Manufacturer Discount	(85)	(100)
	Net Price	1143	1345
	Includes overhead console with trip computer, door courtesy lamps, second row reading lamps, 8-way power driver's seat with manual lumbar, 7-passenger quad premium cloth low back bucket seats. REQUIRES EGH and DGB. NOT AVAILABLE with CYR, CYT.		
3C4	California Bonus Discount (Grand Base FWD/Grand Sport)	(850)	(1000)
	REQUIRES 25N or 28N or 29N. NOT AVAILABLE with 25E, 28E, 29E.		
3C4	California Bonus Discount (Grand Caravan - LE/ES)	(425)	(500)
4XA	Air Conditioning Bypass (Caravan Base)	NC	NC
	NOT AVAILABLE with 22T, 26T, 28T, HAA.		
4XN	Rear Air Conditioning Bypass (Grand Caravan SE)	NC	NC
	NOT AVAILABLE with AAB.		

CODE	DESCRIPTION	INVOICE	MSRP
AAA	Climate Group II (Base)	383	450
	Includes sunscreen glass and windshield wiper de-icer. REQUIRES 22T or 26T or 28T. NOT AVAILABLE with 22S.		
AAB	Climate Group III (Grand Caravan - SE/Sport)	442	520
	*Includes air conditioning with dual temperature control, rear air conditioning and heater, 125-amp alternator, overhead console with trip computer, sunscreen glass and second row reading lamps. REQUIRES 2*E or 2*N (SE). NOT AVAILABLE with 4XN.*		
AAB	Climate Group III (Grand Caravan - SE/Sport)	608	715
	*Includes air conditioning with dual temperature control, rear air conditioning and heater, 125-amp alternator, overhead console with trip computer, sunscreen glass and second row reading lamps. REQUIRES 2*E or 2*N (SE). NOT AVAILABLE with 4XN.*		
AAB	Climate Group III (Grand Caravan SE)	991	1165
	Manufacturer Discount	(383)	(450)
	Net Price	608	715
	*Includes air conditioning with dual temperature control, rear air conditioning and heater, 125-amp alternator, overhead console with trip computer, sunscreen glass and second row reading lamps. REQUIRES AHT and 2*D. NOT AVAILABLE with 4XN, ALR.*		
AAB	Climate Group III (Grand Caravan SE)	1046	1230
	Manufacturer Discount	(383)	(450)
	Net Price	663	780
	Includes air conditioning with dual temperature control, rear air conditioning and heater, 125-amp alternator, overhead console with trip computer, sunscreen glass and second row reading lamps. NOT AVAILABLE with 4XN, ALR, AHT.		
AAC	Convenience Group I (Caravan Base)	370	435
	Includes exterior mirror heating element, power fold-away mirrors, speed control and tilt steering column. NOT AVAILABLE with 22S, 26T, 28T, AAG.		
AAE	Convenience Group II (Caravan Base)	638	750
	Includes speed sensitive power locks and Convenience Group I: exterior mirror heating element, power fold-away mirrors, speed control and tilt steering column. NOT AVAILABLE with 22S, AAC, 26T, 28T, AAG.		
AAF	Convenience Group III (Caravan Base)	952	1120
	Includes Convenience Group II: speed sensitive power locks and Convenience Group I: exterior mirror heating element, power fold-away mirrors, speed control and tilt steering column; power quarter vent windows and power windows with driver's 1 touch down. NOT AVAILABLE with 22S, 26T, 28T, AAG, AAC.		
AAG	Convenience Group IV (SE/Sport AWD)	204	240
	Includes headlamp off time delay, illuminated entry and keyless entry system with 2 transmitters.		
AAH	Convenience Group V (LE)	128	150
	Includes security alarm.		
AAH	Convenience Group V (SE/Sport AWD)	332	390
	Includes security alarm and Convenience Group IV: headlamp off time delay, illuminated entry and keyless entry system with 2 transmitters.		

CODE	DESCRIPTION	INVOICE	MSRP
AAP	Loading Group (LE FWD)	106	125
	REQUIRES AGA. NOT AVAILABLE with AHT.		
AAP	Loading Group (SE/LE FWD)	166	195
	*NOT AVAILABLE with AHT, 2*E, 2*N.*		
AGA	Wheels/Handling Group (LE FWD)	434	510
	Includes front and rear stabilizer bars, wheels: 16" aluminum (silver), tires: 215/ 65R16 A/S touring and HD suspension. INCLUDED in 25E, 28E, 25N, 28N.		
AHT	Trailer Tow Prep Group (ES)	149	175
	Includes power front disc/rear drum brakes, 600-amp maintenance free battery, HD transmission oil cooler, engine oil cooler, heavy duty radiator and trailer tow wiring harness.		
AHT	Trailer Tow Prep Group (Grand Caravan - SE/LE FWD)	370	435
	*Includes power front disc/rear drum brakes, 600-amp maintenance free battery, HD transmission oil cooler, engine oil cooler, heavy duty radiator, trailer tow wiring harness, 125-amp alternator, full size spare tire and heavy duty suspension. REQUIRES 2*D (SE) NOT AVAILABLE with AAP, AAB, ALK.*		
AHT	Trailer Tow Prep Group (Grand Caravan - SE/Sport)	255	300
	*Includes power front disc/rear drum brakes, 600-amp maintenance free battery, HD transmission oil cooler, engine oil cooler, heavy duty radiator, trailer tow wiring harness, 125-amp alternator, full size spare tire and heavy duty suspension. REQUIRES 2*E or 2*N (SE).*		
AHT	Trailer Tow Prep Group (LE AWD)	310	365
	Includes 125-amp alternator, 600-amp maintenance free battery, engine oil cooler, HD transmission oil cooler, HD radiator, full size spare tire and trailer tow wiring harness. NOT AVAILABLE with ALK.		
ALD	Value Plus V6 Group (Base)	995	1170
	Manufacturer Discount	(425)	(500)
	Net Price	570	670
	Includes deluxe door trim panel, speed sensitive power locks, heated exterior power fold-away mirrors, speed control, tilt steering column, power windows with driver's one-touch down and power quarter vent windows. NOT AVAILABLE with AAG, 22T, 22S, AAC.		
ALE	Value Plus Audio Group (SE/Sport AWD)	612	720
	Manufacturer Discount	(383)	(450)
	Net Price	229	270
	*Includes AM/FM stereo with cassette, CD, equalizer, 200-watt amplifier and 10 Infinity speakers. REQUIRES 2*E or 2*N (SE).*		
ALK	Value Plus LE Group (LE)	1050	1235
	Manufacturer Discount	(850)	(1000)
	Net Price	200	235
	Includes 125-amp alternator, rear air conditioning with heater and 7-passenger quad bucket seating. NOT AVAILABLE with AHT, CYT.		
ALK	Value Plus LE Group (LE)	995	1170
	Manufacturer Discount	(850)	(1000)
	Net Price	145	170
	Includes rear air conditioning with heater and 7-passenger quad bucket seating. REQUIRES AHT. NOT AVAILABLE with CYT.		

CODE	DESCRIPTION	INVOICE	MSRP
ALM	Value Plus ES Group (ES)	1122	1320
	Manufacturer Discount	(850)	(1000)
	Net Price	272	320
	Includes security alarm, rear air conditioinng with heater and 125-amp alternator. NOT AVAILABLE with CYT.		
ALR	Value Plus Climate Group (SE)	383	450
	Manufacturer Discount	(383)	(450)
	Net Price	NC	NC
	*Includes sunscreen glass. REQUIRES 2*D. NOT AVAILABLE with AAB.*		
ATB	Radio: AM/FM Stereo with Cassette and CD (SE)	612	720
	*Includes amplifier and 10 Infinity speakers. REQUIRES 2*D.*		
AWS	Smokers' Group	17	20
	Includes front and rear ash receivers and cigar lighter.		
BGF	Antilock Brakes (Base)	480	565
BNM	Traction Control (LE FWD)	149	175
CMA	Heated Front Seats (ES)	213	250
	REQUIRES HL. NOT AVAILABLE with CYT.		
CYE	7-Passenger Seating (Caravan Base)	319	375
	NOT AVAILABLE with CYK. INCLUDED in 22T, 26T, 28T.		
CYK	7-Passenger Seating with 2 Child Seats (Caravan Base)	200	235
	NOT AVAILABLE with 22S, CYE.		
CYK	7-Passenger Seating with 2 Child Seats (Grand Caravan Base)	200	235
CYR	7-Passenger Deluxe with 2 Child Seats (SE/Sport AWD)	191	225
	NOT AVAILABLE with CYS, CYT, 29N, E5, 25N, 28N.		
CYS	7-Passenger Quad Buckets (SE/Sport AWD)	591	695
	NOT AVAILABLE with CYR, CYT. INCLUDED in 29N, 25N, 28N.		
CYT	7 Passenger Quad Buckets with Child Seat (AWD)	697	820
	NOT AVAILABLE with CYR, CYS, 29N, HL, ALK, CMA, ALM.		
CYT	7-Passenger Quad Buckets with Child Seat (AWD)	106	125
	REQUIRES 29N (Sport), ALK (LE), ALM (ES). NOT AVAILABLE with CYR, CYS, 29E, HL, CMA.		
CYT	7-Passenger Quad Buckets with Child Seat (SE/LE FWD)	106	125
	*REQUIRES ALK (LE) or (2*E or 2*N) (SE). NOT AVAILABLE with CYR, CYS, HL, 25E, 28E.*		
CYT	7-Passenger Quad Buckets with Child Seat (SE/LE FWD/ES FWD)	697	820
	NOT AVAILABLE with CYR, CYS, HL, 25N, 28N.		
DGA	Transmission: 3-Speed Automatic (Caravan Base)	NC	NC
	NOT AVAILABLE with EGA, 28T, 26T, EFA, EGM.		
DGB	Transmission: 4-Speed Automatic (All Except Base Caravan)	NC	NC
DGB	Transmission: 4-Speed Automatic (Base Caravan)	170	200
	NOT AVAILABLE with EDZ, 22S, 22T.		
E5	Premium Cloth Low Back Bucket Seats (SE/Sport AWD)	NC	NC
	*REQUIRES 2*N (SE). NOT AVAILABLE with 25E, 28E, 29E, CYR.*		
EDZ	Engine: 2.4L 4 Cyl. DOHC 16V SMPI (Base Caravan)	NC	NC
	NOT AVAILABLE with DGB, 26T, 28T.		
EFA	Engine: 3.0L V6 MPI (Base Caravan)	680	800
	NOT AVAILABLE with DGA, 22S, 22T, 28T.		

CODE	DESCRIPTION	INVOICE	MSRP
EFA	Engine: 3.0L V6 MPI (Caravan SE)	(145)	(170)
	NOT AVAILABLE with 25D, 28D, 25E, 25N, 28E, 28N.		
EFA	Engine: 3.0L V6 MPI (Grand Caravan Base)	NC	NC
	NOT AVAILABLE with 28T.		
EGA	Engine: 3.3L V6 MPI (Base Caravan)	825	970
	NOT AVAILABLE with DGA, 22S, 22T, 26T.		
EGA	Engine: 3.3L V6 MPI (Grand Caravan Base)	145	170
	NOT AVAILABLE with 26T.		
EGA	Engine: 3.3L V6 MPI (SE/LE FWD)	NC	NC
	NOT AVAILABLE with 25K, 29K, 25D, 25E, 25N.		
EGH	Engine: 3.8L MPI V6 (AWD/ES FWD)	NC	NC
EGH	Engine: 3.8L MPI V6 (LE FWD)	434	510
	Manufacturer Discount	(43)	(50)
	Net Price	391	460
	Includes traction control. NOT AVAILABLE with 25K, 28K.		
EGM	Engine: 3.3L V6 FFV (Caravan Base)	825	970
	NOT AVAILABLE with 22S, 22T, 26T, 28T, DGA.		
EGM	Engine: 3.3L V6 FFV (SE/LE FWD)	NC	NC
	NOT AVAILABLE with 28D, 28E, 28N, 28K, 29K.		
GFA	Rear Window Defroster (Base)	166	195
	NOT AVAILABLE with ALD, AAC, AAE, AAF.		
GFA	Rear Window Defroster (Base)	196	230
GKD	Driver's Side Sliding Door (Caravan Base)	506	595
	NOT AVAILABLE with 22S.		
HAA	Air Conditioning (Caravan Base)	731	860
	NOT AVAILABLE with 4XA. INCLUDED in 22T, 26T, 28T.		
HL	Leather Low Back Bucket Seats (ES)	1058	1245
	REQUIRES ALM. NOT AVAILABLE with CYT.		
HL	Leather Low Back Bucket Seats (LE)	757	890
	NOT AVAILABLE with CYT.		
MWG	Roof Rack (All Except ES)	183	215
	NOT AVAILABLE with 22S.		
MWP	Body Colored Roof Rack (ES)	221	260
NHK	Engine Block Heater	30	35
PEL	Inferno Red Tinted Pearl Coat (SE/LE/ES)	170	200
	*REQUIRES 2*E or 2*N (SE).*		
PWP	Golden White Pearl Tri-Coat (ES)	170	200
RAZ	Radio: AM/FM Stereo with CD, Cassette and Equalizer (LE)	264	310
	Includes 4 speakers.		
RF8	Speaker Delete Credit (SE)	(251)	(295)
	*Deletes 10 Infinity speakers. REQUIRES ATB and 2*D. NOT AVAILABLE with 2*E or 2*N.*		
SER	Load Leveling and Height Control (Grand Caravan FWD)	247	290
TBB	Tire: Full Size Spare (All Except ES)	106	125
	REQUIRES 26T or 28T (Caravan). NOT AVAILABLE with 22S, AAP.		
WFX	Wheels: 17" Aluminum (Grand Caravan Base/Sport AWD)	404	475
	REQUIRES 25N or 28N or 29N. NOT AVAILABLE with WNG, 25E, 28E, 29E.		

CODE	DESCRIPTION	INVOICE	MSRP
WJB	Wheels: 15" Aluminum (SE) *REQUIRES 2*D.*	353	415
WNG	Wheels: 16" Aluminum (silver) (LE)	353	415
WNG	Wheels: 16" Aluminum (silver) (SE/Sport AWD) *REQUIRES 2*E or 2*N (SE).*	225	265

2000 DAKOTA

2000 Dodge Dakota

What's New?

The biggest change this year is design - the Dakota gets four full-size doors, and with that, a family name: Quad Cab. A 4.7-liter V8 has been added, but the 8-foot bed is gone. You can select from five more colors as well.

Review

Finally! We've been waiting with bated breath for this day, and now, a four-door Dodge Dakota has arrived. And even better, the engineers went above and beyond the call of duty and borrowed the Quad Cab concept from the Ram, thereby making the Dakota's new doors full-size, which means getting people and cargo in and out is a no-brainer. This did force the bed to be downsized, but the vehicle length remains virtually the same as the Club Cab, 215.1 inches.

There's another bonus for the 2000 Dakota - it brings the Jeep Grand Cherokee's next-generation 4.7-liter V8 to its Magnum-power lineup. The two-wheel-drive Regular and Club Cabs get a mini-Magnum 120-horsepower, 2.5-liter four-cylinder, but all Dakotas have access to a 3.9-liter that cranks out 175 horsepower, a 5.9-liter making 245 horses, and that 4.7-liter, which makes a whopping 235. Only the 5.9-liter cannot be mated to a manual transmission, and the 2.5-liter is without an automatic option. If you're worried about having to tow with a compact truck, keep in mind the Dakota's 6,200-pound towing capacity. In other words, no problem.

You'll likely have to keep reminding yourself that this is indeed a compact pickup - everything from its towing capacity and stance to its power and interior seems bigger than the norm. A 40/20/40 split seat is standard (but you can opt for high-back buckets), and rear passengers travel on a 60/40 split-folding bench seat, creating seating for six. The interior is quiet, and Dodge has improved the comfort level of the seats this year, none too soon.

Both two- and four-wheel drive are available, and on the four-bys, the independent front suspension was recently revised to improve an already solid ride quality. Steering was also switched to rack-and-pinion for better response. Underneath you'll find front disc brakes with optional ABS and rear drums with standard ABS (you can upgrade to slightly larger rear brakes with ABS). The transfer case remains in lever form, not a button, and is simple to engage.

Three body styles are available: Regular Cab, Club Cab, and Quad Cab. Want the ultimate attention-gettin' Dakota? The Regular and Club Cab two-wheel-drives can take advantage of the R/T Sport Group that includes a 250-horsepower 5.9-liter V8, a lowered suspension, and a high-performance tire-and-wheel combo.

The Dakota enters the new millennium with looks, power, and a much-desired configuration. It sure seems like it could be a very happy new year for Dodge.

Standard Equipment

BASE 2WD REGULAR CAB SB (5M): 2.5L I4 OHV SMPI 8-valve engine; 5-speed OD manual transmission; 600-amp battery; 117-amp alternator; rear-wheel drive, 3.55 axle ratio; stainless steel exhaust; HD ride suspension, front independent suspension with anti-roll bar, front coil springs, HD front shocks, rigid rear axle suspension with rear leaf springs, HD rear shocks; power rack-and-pinion steering; front disc/rear drum brakes with rear wheel antilock braking system; 22 gal. capacity fuel tank; side impact bars; front and rear argent bumpers with black rub strip, rear step; monotone paint; aero-composite halogen headlamps; driver's and passenger's manual black outside mirrors; front and rear 15" x 7" silver styled steel wheels; P215/75SR15 A/S BSW front and rear tires; underbody mounted full-size steel spare wheel with crankdown; AM/FM stereo, clock, seek-scan, cassette, 4 speakers, and fixed antenna; 1 power accessory outlet; instrumentation display includes tachometer, oil pressure gauge, water temperature gauge, volt gauge, trip odometer; warning indicators include battery, lights on, key in ignition, low fuel, low washer fluid; driver's front airbag, passenger's cancelable front airbag; ignition disable; tinted windows; variable intermittent front windshield wipers, sun visor strip; seating capacity of 3, bench front seat, fixed headrests, driver's seat includes 2-way direction control, passenger's seat includes 2-way direction control; front height adjustable seatbelts; vinyl seats, full cloth headliner, full vinyl floor covering, cabback insulator; interior lights include dome light with delay; sport steering wheel; passenger's side vanity mirror; day/night rearview mirror; glove box, front cupholder; argent grille, black side window moldings, black front windshield molding, black rear window molding and black door handles.

BASE 2WD CLUB CAB SB (5M) (in addition to or instead of BASE 2WD REGULAR CAB SB (5M) equipment): 3.92 axle ratio; deep tinted windows, vented rear windows; seating capacity of 6, 40-20-40 split-bench front seat, fixed headrests, center armrest with storage, driver's seat includes 4-way direction control, passenger's seat includes 4-way direction control; 40-60 folding rear split-bench seat; premium cloth seats and full carpet floor covering.

SPORT/SLT 2WD QUAD CAB (5M) (in addition to or instead of BASE 2WD CLUB CAB (5M) equipment): 3.9L V6 OHV SMPI 12-valve engine; 24 gal. capacity fuel tank; front and rear body-colored bumpers with black rub strip, rear step; alloy wheel on spare; additional exterior lights include pickup cargo box light, underhood light; child safety rear door locks; 2 power accessory outlets, front cigar lighter(s), smokers' package; manual front and rear windows; 40-60 folding rear split-bench seat with fixed headrests; interior lights include front and rear reading lights; mini overhead console glove box, front and rear cupholders, driver's and passenger's door bins and body-colored grille.

4WD (in addition to or instead of 2WD equipment): 3.9L V6 OHV SMPI 12-valve engine (Base); part-time 4-wheel drive and auto locking hub control and manual shift.

NOTE: All vehicles require selection of a Quick Order Package.

CODE	DESCRIPTION	INVOICE	MSRP

Base Prices

AN1L61	Base 2WD Regular Cab SB (5M)	12348	13555
AN1L31	Base 2WD Club Cab SB (5M)	15304	16880
AN1L84	Sport 2WD Quad Cab SB (5M)	17420	19250
AN1L84	SLT 2WD Quad Cab SB (5M)	17420	19250
AN5L61	Base 4WD Regular Cab SB (5M)	15436	17030
AN5L31	Base 4WD Club Cab SB (5M)	18155	20085
AN5L84	Sport 4WD Quad Cab SB (5M)	19768	21895
AN5L84	SLT 4WD Quad Cab SB (5M)	19768	21895
Destination Charge:		520	520

Accessories

21B	Quick Order Package 21B (2WD Club Cab)	833	980
	Manufacturer Discount	(833)	(980)
	Net Price	NC	NC
	Includes Sport appearance group: front door sport badge, cloth door trim panel with map pocket, body color fascias, body color grille, carpeted front seat area, wheels: 15" x 7" 5-spoke aluminum and tires: P215/75R15 RWL A/S. REQUIRES EPE and DDK and 4XA. NOT AVAILABLE with EHC, EML, EVA, DDC, DGB, Z1B, Z1D, ASU, NMC, DMC, ADJ.		
21B	Quick Order Package 21B (2WD Reg Cab)	1390	1635
	Manufacturer Discount	(553)	(650)
	Net Price	837	985
	Includes Sport appearance group: front door sport badge, cloth door trim panel with map pocket, body color fascias, body color grille, carpeted front seat area, wheels: 15" x 7" 5-spoke aluminum and tires: P215/75R15 RWL A/S and cloth 40/20/40 split bench seat. REQUIRES 4XA and EPE and DDK. NOT AVAILABLE with DGB, EHC, EML, EVA, AGU, NMC, ASU, ADJ, Z1K, AGB, DDC.		
21W	Quick Order Package 21W (2WD - Reg Cab/Club Cab)	NC	NC
	Includes vehicle with standard equipment. REQUIRES 4XA and EPE and DDK. NOT AVAILABLE with EHC, DGB, DDC, ADJ, NMC, Z1K, DMC, Z1B, Z1D.		
23B	Quick Order Package 23B (2WD Club Cab)	833	980
	Manufacturer Discount	(833)	(980)
	Net Price	NC	NC
	Includes Sport appearance group: front door sport badge, cloth door trim panel with map pocket, body color fascias, body color grille, carpeted front seat area, wheels: 15" x 7" 5-spoke aluminum and tires: P215/75R15 RWL A/S and 3.21 axle ratio. REQUIRES (Z1B or Z1D) and 4XA and EHC and DDC. NOT AVAILABLE with DGB, EVA, ADJ, NMC, ASU, EML.		
23B	Quick Order Package 23B (2WD Reg Cab)	1390	1635
	Manufacturer Discount	(553)	(650)
	Net Price	837	985
	Includes Sport appearance group: front door sport badge, cloth door trim panel with map pocket, body color fascias, body color grille, carpeted front seat area, wheels: 15" x 7" 5-spoke aluminum and tires: P215/75R15 RWL A/S and cloth 40/20/		

CODE	DESCRIPTION	INVOICE	MSRP
	40 split bench seat. REQUIRES 4XA and EHC and DDC. NOT AVAILABLE with DDK, EML, EPE, ASU, ADJ, DGB, EVA, NMC.		
23B	Quick Order Package 23B (4WD Club Cab)	973	1145
	Manufacturer Discount	(973)	(1145)
	Net Price	NC	NC
	Includes Sport appearance group: front door sport badge, cloth door trim panel with map pocket, body color fascias, body color grille, carpeted front seat area, wheels: 15" x 7" 5-spoke aluminum and tires: P235/75R15 RWL A/S. REQUIRES 4XA and EHC and DDC. NOT AVAILABLE with DGB, EVA, ADJ, DHC, NMC, AGU.		
23B	Quick Order Package 23B (4WD Reg Cab)	1543	1815
	Manufacturer Discount	(553)	(650)
	Net Price	990	1165
	Includes Sport appearance group: cloth 40/20/40 split bench seat, front door sport badge, cloth door trim panel with map pocket, body color fascias, body color grille, wheels: 15" x 7" 5-spoke aluminum, tires: P235/75R15XL A/S OWL and 3.55 axle ratio. REQUIRES 4XA and EHC and DDC. NOT AVAILABLE with DGB, EVA, ADJ, DHC, NMC.		
23B	Quick Order Package 23B (Sport Quad Cab)	NC	NC
	Includes vehicle with standard equipment. REQUIRES EHC and DDC and 4XA. NOT AVAILABLE with DGB, EML, EVA, DHC.		
23G	Quick Order Package 23G (2WD Club Cab)	1976	2325
	Manufacturer Discount	(1046)	(1230)
	Net Price	930	1095
	Includes SLT Decor group: SLT door and liftgate badging, front bright bumper, rear bright bumper with step pads, cloth door trim panel with map pocket, bright grille, hood insulation, light group: mini overhead console, cargo lamp, glove box lamp, underhood lamp, auxiliary 12V power outlet; deluxe convenience group: speed control and tilt steering column; wheels: 15" x 7" 5-spoke aluminum; air conditioning, front floor mats and 3.21 axle ratio. REQUIRES EHC and DDC. NOT AVAILABLE with DGB, EVA, ADJ, NMC, 4XA.		
23G	Quick Order Package 23G (2WD Reg Cab)	2559	3010
	Manufacturer Discount	(570)	(670)
	Net Price	1989	2340
	Includes SLT Decor group: SLT door and liftgate badging, front bright bumper, rear bright bumper with step pads, cloth door trim panel with map pocket, bright grille, hood insulation, light group: mini overhead console, cargo lamp, glove box lamp, underhood lamp, auxiliary 12V power outlet; deluxe convenience group: speed control and tilt steering column; wheels: 15" x 7" 5-spoke aluminum; air conditioning and front floor mats. REQUIRES EHC and DDC. NOT AVAILABLE with DGB, ADJ, EVA, NMC.		
23G	Quick Order Package 23G (4WD Club Cab)	2129	2505
	Manufacturer Discount	(1046)	(1230)
	Net Price	1083	1275
	Includes SLT Decor group: SLT door and liftgate badging, front bright bumper, rear bright bumper with step pads, cloth door trim panel with map pocket, bright grille, hood insulation, light group: mini overhead console, cargo lamp, glove box lamp, underhood lamp, auxiliary 12V power outlet; deluxe convenience group: speed		

CODE	DESCRIPTION	INVOICE	MSRP
	control and tilt steering column; wheels: 15" x 7" 5-spoke aluminum and tires: P235/75R15XL A/S OWL; air conditioning and front floor mats. REQUIRES EHC and DDC. NOT AVAILABLE with DGB, EVA, ADJ, DHC, NMC, ATK, 4XA.		
23G	**Quick Order Package 23G (4WD Reg Cab)**	2712	3190
	Manufacturer Discount	(570)	(670)
	Net Price	2142	2520
	Includes SLT Decor group: SLT door and liftgate badging, front bright bumper, rear bright bumper with step pads, cloth door trim panel with map pocket, bright grille, hood insulation, light group: mini overhead console, cargo lamp, glove box lamp, underhood lamp, auxiliary 12V power outlet; deluxe convenience group: speed control and tilt steering column; wheels: 15" x 7" 5-spoke aluminum and tires: P235/75R15XL A/S OWL; air conditioning and front floor mats. REQUIRES EHC and DDC. NOT AVAILABLE with DGB, EVA, ADJ, DHC, NMC.		
23G	**Quick Order Package 23G (SLT 2WD Quad Cab)**	1037	1220
	Manufacturer Discount	(225)	(265)
	Net Price	812	955
	Includes air conditioning, front bright bumper, rear bright bumper with step pads, deluxe convenience group: speed control, tilt steering column; front and rear floor mats and SLT Decor group: front bright bumper, rear bright bumper with step pads, bright grille and hood insulation. REQUIRES DDC and EHC. NOT AVAILABLE with DGB, EML, EVA.		
23G	**Quick Order Package 23G (SLT 4WD Quad Cab)**	1037	1220
	Manufacturer Discount	(85)	(100)
	Net Price	952	1120
	Includes air conditioning, front bright bumper, rear bright bumper with step pads, deluxe convenience group: speed control, tilt steering column; front and rear floor mats and SLT Decor group: front bright bumper, rear bright bumper with step pads, bright grille and hood insulation. REQUIRES DDC and EHC. NOT AVAILABLE with DGB, EML, EVA, DHC.		
23W	**Quick Order Package 23W (All Except Quad Cab)**	NC	NC
	Includes vehicle with standard equipment. REQUIRES 4XA and EHC and DDC or (Z1B or Z1D). NOT AVAILABLE with EPE, DDK, DGB, ADJ, NMC, DMH.		
24B	**Quick Order Package 24B (2WD Club Cab)**	833	980
	Manufacturer Discount	(833)	(980)
	Net Price	NC	NC
	Includes Sport appearance group: front door sport badge, cloth door trim panel with map pocket, body color fascias, body color grille, carpeted front seat area, wheels: 15" x 7" 5-spoke aluminum and tires: P215/75R15 RWL A/S and cloth 40/20/40 split bench seat. REQUIRES (Z1B or Z1D) and 4XA and EHC and DGB. NOT AVAILABLE with DDC, EVA, ASU, EML, DMC.		
24B	**Quick Order Package 24B (2WD Reg Cab)**	1390	1635
	Manufacturer Discount	(553)	(650)
	Net Price	837	985
	Includes Sport appearance group: front door sport badge, cloth door trim panel with map pocket, body color fascias, body color grille, carpeted front seat area, wheels: 15" x 7" 5-spoke aluminum and tires: P215/75R15 RWL A/S and cloth 40/20/		

CODE	DESCRIPTION	INVOICE	MSRP
	40 split bench seat. REQUIRES 4XA and EHC and DGB. NOT AVAILABLE with DDK, EML, EPE, ASU, DDC, EVA, DMC.		
24B	**Quick Order Package 24B (4WD Club Cab)**	973	1145
	Manufacturer Discount	(973)	(1145)
	Net Price	NC	NC
	Includes Sport appearance group: front door sport badge, cloth door trim panel with map pocket, body color fascias, body color grille, carpeted front seat area, wheels: 15" x 7" 5-spoke aluminum and tires: P235/75R15XL A/S OWL. REQUIRES 4XA and EHC and DGB. NOT AVAILABLE with DDC, EVA, DHC, AGU.		
24B	**Quick Order Package 24B (4WD Reg Cab)**	1543	1815
	Manufacturer Discount	(553)	(650)
	Net Price	990	1165
	Includes Sport appearance group: front door sport badge, cloth door trim panel with map pocket, body color fascias, body color grille, cloth 40/20/40 split bench seat, carpeted front seat area, wheels: 15" x 7" 5-spoke aluminum and tires: P235/75R15 RWL A/S. REQUIRES 4XA and EHC and DGB. NOT AVAILABLE with DDC, EVA, DHC.		
24B	**Quick Order Package 24B (Sport Quad Cab)**	NC	NC
	Includes vehicle with standard equipment. REQUIRES DGB and EHC and 4XA. NOT AVAILABLE with DDC, EML, EVA, DHC.		
24G	**Quick Order Package 24G (2WD Club Cab)**	1976	2325
	Manufacturer Discount	(1046)	(1230)
	Net Price	930	1095
	Includes SLT Decor group: SLT door and liftgate badging, front bright bumper, rear bright bumper with step pads, cloth door trim panel with map pocket, bright grille, hood insulation, light group: mini overhead console, cargo lamp, glove box lamp, underhood lamp, auxiliary 12V power outlet; deluxe convenience group: speed control and tilt steering column; wheels: 15" x 7" 5-spoke aluminum; air conditioning, and front floor mats. REQUIRES EHC and DGB. NOT AVAILABLE with DDC, EVA, DMC, 4XA.		
24G	**Quick Order Package 24G (2WD Reg Cab)**	2559	3010
	Manufacturer Discount	(570)	(670)
	Net Price	1989	2340
	Includes SLT Decor group: SLT door and liftgate badging, front bright bumper, rear bright bumper with step pads, cloth 40/20/40 split bench seat, cloth door trim panel with map pocket, bright grille, hood insulation, light group: mini overhead console, cargo lamp, glove box lamp, underhood lamp, auxiliary 12V power outlet; deluxe convenience group: speed control and tilt steering column; wheels: 15" x 7" 5-spoke aluminum; air conditioning and front floor mats. REQUIRES EHC and DGB. NOT AVAILABLE with DDC, EVA, DMC.		
24G	**Quick Order Package 24G (4WD Club Cab)**	2129	2505
	Manufacturer Discount	(1046)	(1230)
	Net Price	1083	1275
	Includes SLT Decor group: SLT door and liftgate badging, front bright bumper, rear bright bumper with step pads, cloth door trim panel with map pocket, bright grille, hood insulation, light group: mini overhead console, cargo lamp, glove box lamp, underhood lamp, auxiliary 12V power outlet; deluxe convenience group: speed		

CODE	DESCRIPTION	INVOICE	MSRP
	control and tilt steering column; wheels: 15" x 7" 5-spoke aluminum and tires: P235/75R15XL A/S OWL; air conditioning and front floor mats. REQUIRES EHC and DGB. NOT AVAILABLE with DDC, EVA, DHC, ATK, 4XA.		
24G	**Quick Order Package 24G (4WD Reg Cab)**	2712	3190
	Manufacturer Discount	(570)	(670)
	Net Price	2142	2520
	Includes SLT Decor group: SLT door and liftgate badging, front bright bumper, rear bright bumper with step pads, cloth door trim panel with map pocket, bright grille, hood insulation, light group: mini overhead console, cargo lamp, glove box lamp, underhood lamp, auxiliary 12V power outlet; deluxe convenience group: speed control and tilt steering column; wheels: 15" x 7" 5-spoke aluminum and tires: P235/75R15XL A/S OWL; air conditioning, cloth 40/20/40 split bench seat and front floor mats. REQUIRES EHC and DGB. NOT AVAILABLE with DDC, EVA, DHC.		
24G	**Quick Order Package 24G (SLT 2WD Quad Cab)**	1037	1220
	Manufacturer Discount	(225)	(265)
	Net Price	812	955
	Includes air conditioning, front bright bumper, rear bright bumper with step pads, deluxe convenience group: speed control, tilt steering column; front and rear floor mats and SLT Decor group: front bright bumper, rear bright bumper with step pads, bright grille and hood insulation. REQUIRES DGB and EHC. NOT AVAILABLE with DDC, EVA, EML.		
24G	**Quick Order Package 24G (SLT 4WD Quad Cab)**	1037	1220
	Manufacturer Discount	(85)	(100)
	Net Price	952	1120
	Includes air conditioning, front bright bumper, rear bright bumper with step pads, deluxe convenience group: speed control, tilt steering column; front and rear floor mats and SLT Decor group: front bright bumper, rear bright bumper with step pads, bright grille and hood insulation. REQUIRES DGB and EHC. NOT AVAILABLE with DDC, EVA, EML, DHC.		
24W	**Quick Order Package 24W (All Except Quad Cab)**	NC	NC
	Includes vehicle with standard equipment. REQUIRES 4XA and EHC and DGB or (Z1B or Z1D). NOT AVAILABLE with DDK, DDC, EPE, DMC.		
25B	**Quick Order Package 25B (2WD Club Cab)**	833	980
	Manufacturer Discount	(833)	(980)
	Net Price	NC	NC
	Includes Sport appearance group: front door sport badge, cloth door trim panel with map pocket, body color fascias, body color grille, carpeted front seat area, wheels: 15" x 7" 5-spoke aluminum and tires: P215/75R15 RWL A/S and cloth 40/20/40 split bench seat. REQUIRES (Z1B or Z1D) and 4XA and EVA and DDC. NOT AVAILABLE with EHC, DGB, ADJ, NMC, ASU, EML, DMC.		
25B	**Quick Order Package 25B (2WD Reg Cab)**	1390	1635
	Manufacturer Discount	(553)	(650)
	Net Price	837	985
	Includes Sport appearance group: front door sport badge, cloth door trim panel with map pocket, body color fascias, body color grille, carpeted front seat area, wheels: 15" x 7" 5-spoke aluminum and tires: P215/75R15 RWL A/S and cloth 40/20/		

CODE	DESCRIPTION	INVOICE	MSRP
	40 split bench seat. REQUIRES 4XA and EVA and DDC. NOT AVAILABLE with EPE, EHC, EML, DDK, ASU, DGB, DMC, NMC, ADJ.		
25B	**Quick Order Package 25B (4WD Club Cab)**	973	1145
	Manufacturer Discount	(973)	(1145)
	Net Price	NC	NC
	Includes Sport appearance group: front door sport badge, cloth door trim panel with map pocket, body color fascias, body color grille, carpeted front seat area, wheels: 15" x 7" 5-spoke aluminum and tires: P235/75R15XL A/S OWL. REQUIRES 4XA and EVA and DDC. NOT AVAILABLE with EHC, DGB, ADJ, DHC, NMC, AGU.		
25B	**Quick Order Package 25B (4WD Reg Cab)**	1543	1815
	Manufacturer Discount	(553)	(650)
	Net Price	990	1165
	Includes Sport appearance group: front door sport badge, cloth door trim panel with map pocket, body color fascias, body color grille, cloth 40/20/40 split bench seat, carpeted front seat area, wheels: 15" x 7" 5-spoke aluminum and tires: P235/75R15 RWL A/S. REQUIRES 4XA and EVA and DDC. NOT AVAILABLE with EHC, DGB, ADJ, DHC, NMC.		
25B	**Quick Order Package 25B (Sport Quad Cab)**	NC	NC
	Includes vehicle with standard equipment. REQUIRES DDC and EVA and 4XA. NOT AVAILABLE with DGB, EHC, EML, DHC.		
25G	**Quick Order Package 25G (2WD Club Cab)**	1976	2325
	Manufacturer Discount	(1046)	(1230)
	Net Price	930	1095
	Includes SLT Decor group: SLT door and liftgate badging, front bright bumper, rear bright bumper with step pads, cloth door trim panel with map pocket, bright grille, hood insulation, light group: mini overhead console, cargo lamp, glove box lamp, underhood lamp, auxiliary 12V power outlet; deluxe convenience group: speed control and tilt steering column; wheels: 15" x 7" 5-spoke aluminum; air conditioning and front floor mats. REQUIRES EVA and DDC. NOT AVAILABLE with ADJ, DGB, EHC, NMC, DMC, 4XA.		
25G	**Quick Order Package 25G (2WD Reg Cab)**	2559	3010
	Manufacturer Discount	(570)	(670)
	Net Price	1989	2340
	Includes SLT Decor group: SLT door and liftgate badging, front bright bumper, rear bright bumper with step pads, cloth door trim panel with map pocket, bright grille, hood insulation, light group: mini overhead console, cargo lamp, glove box lamp, underhood lamp, auxiliary 12V power outlet; deluxe convenience group: speed control and tilt steering column; wheels: 15" x 7" 5-spoke aluminum; air conditioning, front floor mats and cloth 40/20/40 split bench seat. REQUIRES EVA and DDC. NOT AVAILABLE with EHC, ADJ, DGB, DMC, NMC.		
25G	**Quick Order Package 25G (4WD Club Cab)**	2129	2505
	Manufacturer Discount	(1046)	(1230)
	Net Price	1083	1275
	Includes SLT Decor group: SLT door and liftgate badging, front bright bumper, rear bright bumper with step pads, cloth door trim panel with map pocket, bright grille, hood insulation, light group: mini overhead console, cargo lamp, glove box lamp, underhood lamp, auxiliary 12V power outlet; deluxe convenience group: speed		

CODE	DESCRIPTION	INVOICE	MSRP
	control and tilt steering column; wheels: 15" x 7" 5-spoke aluminum and tires: P235/75R15XL A/S OWL; air conditioning and front floor mats. REQUIRES EVA and DDC. NOT AVAILABLE with ADJ, DHC, DGB, EHC, NMC, ATK, 4XA.		
25G	**Quick Order Package 25G (4WD Reg Cab)**	2712	3190
	Manufacturer Discount	(570)	(670)
	Net Price	2142	2520
	Includes SLT Decor group: SLT door and liftgate badging, front bright bumper, rear bright bumper with step pads, cloth door trim panel with map pocket, bright grille, hood insulation, light group: mini overhead console, cargo lamp, glove box lamp, underhood lamp, auxiliary 12V power outlet; deluxe convenience group: speed control and tilt steering column; wheels: 15" x 7" 5-spoke aluminum and tires: P235/75R15XL A/S OWL; air conditioning, front floor mats and cloth 40/20/40 split bench seat. REQUIRES EVA and DDC. NOT AVAILABLE with ADJ, DHC, DGB, EHC, NMC.		
25G	**Quick Order Package 25G (SLT 2WD Quad Cab)**	1037	1220
	Manufacturer Discount	(225)	(265)
	Net Price	812	955
	Includes air conditioning, front bright bumper, rear bright bumper with step pads, deluxe convenience group: speed control, tilt steering column; front and rear floor mats and SLT Decor group: front bright bumper, rear bright bumper with step pads, bright grille and hood insulation. REQUIRES EVA and DDC. NOT AVAILABLE with DGB, EHC, EML.		
25G	**Quick Order Package 25G (SLT 4WD Quad Cab)**	1037	1220
	Manufacturer Discount	(85)	(100)
	Net Price	952	1120
	Includes air conditioning, front bright bumper, rear bright bumper with step pads, deluxe convenience group: speed control, tilt steering column; front and rear floor mats and SLT Decor group: front bright bumper, rear bright bumper with step pads, bright grille and hood insulation. REQUIRES EVA and DDC. NOT AVAILABLE with DGB, EHC, EML, DHC.		
26B	**Quick Order Package 26B (2WD Club Cab)**	833	980
	Manufacturer Discount	(833)	(980)
	Net Price	NC	NC
	Includes Sport appearance group: front door sport badge, cloth door trim panel with map pocket, body color fascias, body color grille, carpeted front seat area, wheels: 15" x 7" 5-spoke aluminum and tires: P215/75R15 RWL A/S and cloth 40/20/40 split bench seat. REQUIRES (Z1B or Z1D) and 4XA and EVA and DGB. NOT AVAILABLE with DDC, EHC, ASU, EML, DMC.		
26B	**Quick Order Package 26B (2WD Reg Cab)**	1390	1635
	Manufacturer Discount	(553)	(650)
	Net Price	837	985
	Includes Sport appearance group: front door sport badge, cloth door trim panel with map pocket, body color fascias, body color grille, carpeted front seat area, wheels: 15" x 7" 5-spoke aluminum and tires: P215/75R15 RWL A/S and cloth 40/20/40 split bench seat. REQUIRES 4XA and EVA and DGB. NOT AVAILABLE with EPE, EHC, EML, DDK, ASU, DDC, DMC.		

CODE	DESCRIPTION	INVOICE	MSRP
26B	**Quick Order Package 26B (4WD Club Cab)**	973	1145
	Manufacturer Discount	(973)	(1145)
	Net Price	NC	NC
	Includes Sport appearance group: front door sport badge, cloth door trim panel with map pocket, body color fascias, body color grille, carpeted front seat area, wheels: 15" x 7" 5-spoke aluminum and tires: P235/75R15XL A/S OWL. REQUIRES 4XA and EVA and DGB. NOT AVAILABLE with DDC, EHC, AGU.		
26B	**Quick Order Package 26B (4WD Reg Cab)**	1543	1815
	Manufacturer Discount	(553)	(650)
	Net Price	990	1165
	Includes Sport appearance group: front door sport badge, cloth door trim panel with map pocket, body color fascias, body color grille, cloth 40/20/40 split bench seat, carpeted front seat area, wheels: 15" x 7" 5-spoke aluminum and tires: P235/75R15 RWL A/S. REQUIRES 4XA and EVA and DGB. NOT AVAILABLE with DDC, EHC.		
26B	**Quick Order Package 26B (Sport Quad Cab)**	NC	NC
	Includes vehicle with standard equipment. REQUIRES DGB and EVA and 4XA. NOT AVAILABLE with DDC, EHC, EML.		
26G	**Quick Order Package 26G (2WD Club Cab)**	1976	2325
	Manufacturer Discount	(1046)	(1230)
	Net Price	930	1095
	Includes SLT Decor group: SLT door and liftgate badging, front bright bumper, rear bright bumper with step pads, cloth door trim panel with map pocket, bright grille, hood insulation, light group: mini overhead console, cargo lamp, glove box lamp, underhood lamp, auxiliary 12V power outlet; deluxe convenience group: speed control and tilt steering column; wheels: 15" x 7" 5-spoke aluminum; air conditioning and front floor mats.REQUIRES EVA and DGB. NOT AVAILABLE with EHC, DDC, DMC, 4XA.		
26G	**Quick Order Package 26G (2WD Reg Cab)**	2559	3010
	Manufacturer Discount	(570)	(670)
	Net Price	1989	2340
	Includes SLT Decor group: SLT door and liftgate badging, front bright bumper, rear bright bumper with step pads, cloth door trim panel with map pocket, bright grille, hood insulation, light group: mini overhead console, cargo lamp, glove box lamp, underhood lamp, auxiliary 12V power outlet; deluxe convenience group: speed control and tilt steering column; wheels: 15" x 7" 5-spoke aluminum; air conditioning, front floor mats and cloth 40/20/40 split bench seat. REQUIRES EVA and DGB. NOT AVAILABLE with EHC, DDC, DMC.		
26G	**Quick Order Package 26G (4WD Club Cab)**	2129	2505
	Manufacturer Discount	(1046)	(1230)
	Net Price	1083	1275
	Includes SLT Decor group: SLT door and liftgate badging, front bright bumper, rear bright bumper with step pads, cloth door trim panel with map pocket, bright grille, hood insulation, light group: mini overhead console, cargo lamp, glove box lamp, underhood lamp, auxiliary 12V power outlet; deluxe convenience group: speed control and tilt steering column; wheels: 15" x 7" 5-spoke aluminum and tires:		

CODE	DESCRIPTION	INVOICE	MSRP
	P235/75R15XL A/S OWL; air conditioning and front floor mats. REQUIRES EVA and DGB. NOT AVAILABLE with EHC, DDC, ATK, 4XA.		
26G	Quick Order Package 26G (4WD Reg Cab)	2712	3190
	Manufacturer Discount	(570)	(670)
	Net Price	2142	2520
	Includes SLT Decor group: SLT door and liftgate badging, front bright bumper, rear bright bumper with step pads, cloth door trim panel with map pocket, bright grille, hood insulation, light group: mini overhead console, cargo lamp, glove box lamp, underhood lamp, auxiliary 12V power outlet; deluxe convenience group: speed control and tilt steering column; wheels: 15" x 7" 5-spoke aluminum and tires: P235/75R15XL A/S OWL; air conditioning, cloth 40/20/40 split bench seat and front floor mats. REQUIRES EVA and DGB. NOT AVAILABLE with EHC, DDC.		
26G	Quick Order Package 26G (SLT 2WD Quad Cab)	1037	1220
	Manufacturer Discount	(225)	(265)
	Net Price	812	955
	Includes air conditioning, front bright bumper, rear bright bumper with step pads, deluxe convenience group: speed control, tilt steering column; front and rear floor mats and SLT Decor group: front bright bumper, rear bright bumper with step pads, bright grille and hood insulation. REQUIRES DGB and EVA. NOT AVAILABLE with DDC, EHC, EML.		
26G	Quick Order Package 26G (SLT 4WD Quad Cab)	1037	1220
	Manufacturer Discount	(85)	(100)
	Net Price	952	1120
	Includes air conditioning, front bright bumper, rear bright bumper with step pads, deluxe convenience group: speed control, tilt steering column; front and rear floor mats and SLT Decor group: front bright bumper, rear bright bumper with step pads, bright grille and hood insulation. REQUIRES DGB and EVA. NOT AVAILABLE with DDC, EHC, EML.		
28B	Quick Order Package 28B (2WD Club Cab)	833	980
	Manufacturer Discount	(833)	(980)
	Net Price	NC	NC
	Includes Sport appearance group: front door sport badge, cloth door trim panel with map pocket, body color fascias, body color grille, carpeted front seat area, wheels: 15" x 7" 5-spoke aluminum; cloth 40/20/40 split bench seat and 3.92 axle ratio. REQUIRES EML and DGB and 4XA and ASU. NOT AVAILABLE with AGU, Z1B, Z1D, DDC, DDK, EHC, EPE, EVA, DMC.		
28B	Quick Order Package 28B (2WD Reg Cab)	1390	1635
	Manufacturer Discount	(553)	(650)
	Net Price	837	985
	Includes Sport appearance group: front door sport badge, cloth door trim panel with map pocket, body color fascias, body color grille, carpeted front seat area, wheels: 15" x 7" 5-spoke aluminum; cloth 40/20/40 split bench seat and 3.92 axle ratio. REQUIRES 4XA and EML and DGB and ASU. NOT AVAILABLE with EPE, EHC, DDK, DDC, AGU, EVA, Z1K, DMC.		
28B	Quick Order Package 28B (Sport Quad Cab)	NC	NC
	Includes vehicle with standard equipment. REQUIRES DGB and EML and 4XA. NOT AVAILABLE with DDC, EHC, EVA, DHC.		

CODE	DESCRIPTION	INVOICE	MSRP
28G	Quick Order Package 28G (SLT 2WD Quad Cab)	1037	1220
	Manufacturer Discount	(225)	(265)
	Net Price	812	955
	Includes air conditioning, front bright bumper, rear bright bumper with step pads, deluxe convenience group: speed control, tilt steering column; front and rear floor mats and SLT Decor group: front bright bumper, rear bright bumper with step pads, bright grille and hood insulation. REQUIRES EML and DGB. NOT AVAILABLE with DDC, EHC, EVA.		
28G	Quick Order Package 28G (SLT 4WD Quad Cab)	1037	1220
	Manufacturer Discount	(85)	(100)
	Net Price	952	1120
	Includes air conditioning, front bright bumper, rear bright bumper with step pads, deluxe convenience group: speed control, tilt steering column; front and rear floor mats and SLT Decor group: front bright bumper, rear bright bumper with step pads, bright grille and hood insulation. REQUIRES EML and DGB. NOT AVAILABLE with DDC, EHC, EVA, DHC.		
4XA	Air Conditioning Bypass	NC	NC
	NOT AVAILABLE with AGU, 24G, 23G, 25G, 26G.		
ADA	Light Group (Club Cab)	132	155
	*Includes ash tray lamp, mini overhead console, cargo lamp, glove box lamp, underhood lamp, map/dome reading lamps and auxiliary 12V power outlet. REQUIRES 2*W or 2*B.*		
ADA	Light Group (Reg Cab)	123	145
	*Includes ash tray lamp, mini overhead console, cargo lamp, glove box lamp, underhood lamp and auxiliary 12V power outlet. REQUIRES 2*W or 2*B.*		
ADJ	HD Service Group	102	120
	Includes 136-amp alternator. REQUIRES 23B or 25B or 23G or 25G. NOT AVAILABLE with 24W, DGB, NMC, 24B, 26B, 28B, 24G, 26G.		
ADJ	HD Service Group	153	180
	Includes 136-amp alternator. REQUIRES 24B or 26B or 28B or 24G or 26G. NOT AVAILABLE with 23W, 21W, NMC, 21B, 23B, 25B, 23G, 25G.		
ADL	Skid Plate Group (4WD)	111	130
AGB	Tire and Handling Group (2WD - Club Cab/Quad Cab)	332	390
	Includes front and rear stabilizer bar, tires: P255/65R15 BSW and wheels: 15" x 8" aluminum. REQUIRES DMH or EVA. NOT AVAILABLE with ASU, TS1, EML.		
AGB	Tire and Handling Group (2WD Quad Cab)	276	325
	*Includes front and rear stabilizer bar, tires: P255/65R15 BSW and wheels: 15" x 8" aluminum. REQUIRES 2*B or 2*G. NOT AVAILABLE with EHC, EVA, TS1.*		
AGB	Tire and Handling Group (2WD Reg Cab)	310	365
	*Includes tires: P255/65R15 BSW and wheels: 15" x 8" aluminum. REQUIRES DMH and (2*B or 2*G). NOT AVAILABLE with ASU, EPE, 21B, DMC, TS1, Z1K.*		
AGB	Tire and Handling Group (4WD)	340	400
	*Includes front and rear stabilizer bar and wheels: 15" x 8" aluminum. NOT AVAILABLE with 2*W.*		

CODE	DESCRIPTION	INVOICE	MSRP
AGU	Sport Plus Group (2WD Club Cab)	1245	1465
	Manufacturer Discount	(298)	(350)
	Net Price	947	1115
	*Includes 136 -amp alternator, fog lamps, tire and handling group: front and rear stabilizer bar, tires: P255/65R15 BSW and wheels: 15" x 8" aluminum. REQUIRES 2*B. NOT AVAILABLE with 4XA, 28B, ASU, Z1D.*		
AGU	Sport Plus Group (2WD Reg Cab)	1216	1430
	Manufacturer Discount	(242)	(285)
	Net Price	974	1145
	Includes 136-amp alternator, fog lamps, tire and handling group: tires: P255/65R15 BSW and wheels: 15" x 8" aluminum. REQUIRES 25B or 26B or 23B or 24B. NOT AVAILABLE with ASU, EML, EPE, 21B, 28B, 4XA, Z1K, TS1.		
AGU	Sport Plus Group (4WD Club Cab)	1254	1475
	Manufacturer Discount	(502)	(590)
	Net Price	752	885
	*Includes 136-amp alternator, fog lamps, tire and handling group, front and rear stabilizer bar and wheels: 15" x 8" aluminum. REQUIRES 2*B and EVA. NOT AVAILABLE with 4XA, 23B, 24B, EHC.*		
AGU	Sport Plus Group (4WD Club Cab)	1254	1475
	Manufacturer Discount	(298)	(350)
	Net Price	956	1125
	*Includes 136-amp alternator, fog lamps, tire and handling group: front and rear stabilizer bar and wheels: 15" x 8" aluminum. REQUIRES 2*B. NOT AVAILABLE with 4XA, 25B, 26B, EVA.*		
AGU	Sport Plus Group (4WD Reg Cab)	1245	1465
	Manufacturer Discount	(242)	(285)
	Net Price	1003	1180
	*Includes 136-amp alternator, fog lamps, tire and handling group: front and rear stabilizer bar and wheels: 15" x 8" aluminum. REQUIRES 2*B. NOT AVAILABLE with 4XA.*		
AGU	Sport Plus Group (Sport 2WD Quad Cab)	1058	1245
	Manufacturer Discount	(298)	(350)
	Net Price	760	895
	*Includes air conditioning, fog lamps, tire and handling group: front and rear stabilizer bar, tires: P255/65R15 BSW and wheels: 15" x 8" aluminum. REQUIRES 2*B. NOT AVAILABLE with EHC, EVA, TS1, 4XA.*		
AGU	Sport Plus Group (Sport 2WD Quad Cab)	1114	1310
	Manufacturer Discount	(298)	(350)
	Net Price	816	960
	*Includes air conditioning, fog lamps, tire and handling group: front and rear stabilizer bar, tires: P255/65R15 BSW and wheels: 15" x 8" aluminum. REQUIRES EVA AND 2*B. NOT AVAILABLE with EML, TS1, 4XA.*		
AGU	Sport Plus Group (Sport 4WD Quad Cab)	1122	1320
	Manufacturer Discount	(298)	(350)
	Net Price	824	970
	*Includes air conditioning, fog lamps, tire and handling group: front and rear stabilizer bar and wheels: 15" x 8" aluminum. REQUIRES 2*B. NOT AVAILABLE with 4XA.*		

CODE	DESCRIPTION	INVOICE	MSRP
AHC	**Trailer Tow Group (Club Cab/Quad Cab/4WD Reg Cab)** *Includes Class IV platform hitch adaptor, wiring harness mounted on direct plug-in, 7/4 pin adaptor wiring, the hitch for direct plug-in and 7/4 pin pigtail. Must have heavy duty service package adaptor wiring pigtail, platform hitch receiver and 7-lead wiring harness. REQUIRES ADJ.*	234	275
AJB	**Security Alarm** *REQUIRES (2*B or 2*G) and (AJP or AJL or ATK).*	128	150
AJK	**Deluxe Convenience Group** *Includes speed control. REQUIRES 2*B. NOT AVAILABLE with 21B, EPE. INCLUDED in 23G, 24G, 25G, 26G, 28G.*	332	390
AJL	**Power Overhead Convenience Group (All Except Quad Cab)** *Includes auto day/night mirror, power convenience group, keyless entry, power locks and power windows with driver's one touch down. REQUIRES 2*B or 2*G. NOT AVAILABLE with ATK.*	642	755
AJL	**Power Overhead Convenience Group (Quad Cab)** *Includes overhead console, auto day/night mirror, power convenience group, keyless entry, power locks and power windows with driver's one touch down. NOT AVAILABLE with ATK.*	791	930
AJL	**Power Overhead Convenience Group** *Includes auto day/night mirror. REQUIRES 2*G.*	157	185
AJL	**Power Overhead Convenience Group** *Includes overhead console, auto day/night mirror, power convenience group: keyless entry, power locks and power windows with driver's one touch down. REQUIRES 2*B or 2*G. NOT AVAILABLE with ADA.*	667	785
AJP	**Power Convenience Group (All Except Quad Cab)** *Includes keyless entry, power locks and power windows with driver's one touch down. REQUIRES 2*B or 2*G.*	485	570
AJP	**Power Convenience Group (Quad Cab)** *Includes keyless entry, power locks and power windows with driver's one touch down.*	633	745
APD	**Two Tone Lower Paint** *REQUIRES 2*G. NOT AVAILABLE with PBT, PFA, PRV, PTL.*	166	195
ASU	**R/T Sport Group (2WD Club Cab)** *Includes 3.92 axle ratio, anti-spin differential, R/T badge, body colored front and rear bumpers, floor console, deluxe convenience group: speed control, tilt steering column; cloth door trim panel with map pocket, fog lamps, hood insulation, light group: mini overhead console, ash tray lamp, cargo lamp, glove box lamp, underhood lamp, overhead map/dome lamp and 12V auxiliary power outlet; cloth highback bucket seats, sport suspension: HD front and rear shock absorbers, rear HD stabilizer bar; leather-wrapped steering wheel, tires: P225/55R17 BSW, wheelflares and wheels: 17" x 9" aluminum. REQUIRES 28B and DGB. NOT AVAILABLE with AGU, AGB, TS1, PG8, 21B, 23B, 24B, 25B, 26B, EHC, EPE.*	2049	2410
ASU	**R/T Sport Group (2WD Reg Cab)** *Includes 3.92 axle ratio, anti-spin differential, R/T badge, body colored front and rear bumpers, floor console, deluxe convenience group: speed control, tilt steering column; cloth door trim panel with map pocket, fog lamps, hood insulation, light group: mini overhead console, ash tray lamp, cargo lamp, glove box lamp,*	2015	2370

CODE	DESCRIPTION	INVOICE	MSRP
	underhood lamp, overhead map/dome lamp and 12V auxiliary power outlet; cloth highback bucket seats, sport suspension: HD front and rear shock absorbers, rear HD stabilizer bar; leather-wrapped steering wheel, tires: P225/55R17 BSW, wheelflares and wheels: 17" x 9" aluminum. REQUIRES 28B. NOT AVAILABLE with AGU, AGB, TS1, PG8, 21B, 23B, 24B, 25B, 26B, EHC, EPE, Z1K.		
ATK	**SLT Plus Decor Group (2WD Club Cab)**	935	1100
	Manufacturer Discount	(383)	(450)
	Net Price	552	650
	*Includes power convenience group: keyless entry, power locks, power windows with driver's one touch down; power mirrors, tire and handling group: tires: P255/65R 15 BSW and wheels: 15" x 8" aluminum. REQUIRES 2*G and (DMD or DMH). NOT AVAILABLE with AJL, DMC, TS1, Z1D.*		
ATK	**SLT Plus Decor Group (2WD Reg Cab)**	914	1075
	Manufacturer Discount	(383)	(450)
	Net Price	531	625
	*Includes power convenience group: keyless entry, power locks, power windows with driver's one touch down; power mirrors, tire and handling group: tires: P255/65R 15 BSW and wheels: 15" x 8" aluminum. REQUIRES 2*G. NOT AVAILABLE with AJL, Z1K, TS1.*		
ATK	**SLT Plus Decor Group (4WD Club Cab)**	944	1110
	Manufacturer Discount	(502)	(590)
	Net Price	442	520
	*Includes power convenience group, keyless entry, power locks, power windows with driver's one touch down, power mirrors, tire and handling group, front and rear stabilizer bar and wheels: 15" x 8" aluminum. REQUIRES 2*G and EVA. NOT AVAILABLE with AJL, 23G, 24G.*		
ATK	**SLT Plus Decor Group (4WD Except Quad Cab)**	944	1110
	Manufacturer Discount	(213)	(250)
	Net Price	731	860
	*Includes power convenience group, keyless entry, power locks, power windows with driver's one touch down, power mirrors, tire and handling group, front and rear stabilizer bar and wheels: 15" x 8" aluminum. REQUIRES 2*G. NOT AVAILABLE with AJL, GT4, 25G, 26G, EVA.*		
ATK	**SLT Plus Decor Group (SLT 2WD Quad Cab)**	1029	1210
	Manufacturer Discount	(383)	(450)
	Net Price	646	760
	Includes power convenience group, keyless entry, power locks, power windows with driver's one touch down, power mirrors, tire and handling group, front and rear stabilizer bar and wheels: 15" x 8" aluminum. NOT AVAILABLE with EHC, EVA, GFA, AJL, TS1.		
ATK	**SLT Plus Decor Group (SLT 2WD Quad Cab)**	1084	1275
	Manufacturer Discount	(383)	(450)
	Net Price	701	825
	Includes power convenience group, keyless entry, power locks, power windows with driver's one touch down, power mirrors, tire and handling group, front and rear stabilizer bar and wheels: 15" x 8" aluminum. REQUIRES EVA. NOT AVAILABLE with EML, TS1, AJL, GFA.		

CODE	DESCRIPTION	INVOICE	MSRP
ATK	SLT Plus Decor Group (SLT 4WD Quad Cab)	1092	1285
	Manufacturer Discount	(213)	(250)
	Net Price	879	1035
	Includes power convenience group, keyless entry, power locks, power windows with driver's one touch down, power mirrors, tire and handling group, front and rear stabilizer bar and wheels: 15" x 8" aluminum. NOT AVAILABLE with AJL, GFA, GT4.		
BGK	4-Wheel Antilock Brakes	421	495
CLA	Front Floor Mats	26	30
	*REQUIRES 2*B or 2*G (Club Cab/Quad Cab). INCLUDED in 26G, 23G, 24G, 25G.*		
CLE	Front and Rear Floor Mats (Sport Quad Cab)	43	50
	INCLUDED in 23G, 24G, 25G, 26G, 28G.		
DDC	Transmission: HD 5-Speed Manual	NC	NC
	NOT AVAILABLE with 21W, 24W, EPE, 21B, 24B, 24G, 26B, 26G, 28B, EML, 28G, DHC.		
DDK	Transmission: HD 5-Speed Manual (2WD - Reg Cab/Club Cab)	(170)	(200)
	*REQUIRES 2*W or 2*B. NOT AVAILABLE with EHC, 23W, 24W, DMC, EML, 23B, 24B, 25B, 28B, 26B, EVA, Z1B.*		
DGB	Transmission: 4-Speed Automatic	829	975
	NOT AVAILABLE with EPE, 21B, 21W, 23W, 23B, 23G, 25B, 25G, DMC.		
DHC	Full Time Transfer Case	336	395
	REQUIRES 26B or 26G. NOT AVAILABLE with 23B, 24B, 25B, 23G, 24G, 25G, EHC, EML, DDC, 28B, 28G.		
DMC	3.21 Axle Ratio (2WD Except Quad Cab)	NC	NC
	REQUIRES 23W or 23B or 23G. NOT AVAILABLE with EPE, DDK, DGB, 21W, 24W, DSA, Z1K, EML, 24B, 25B, 26B, 28B, AGB, EVA, ASU, 24G, 25G, 26G, ATK, 21B, Z1D. INCLUDED in 23B, 23G.		
DMD	3.55 Axle Ratio (2WD Except Quad Cab)	34	40
	NOT AVAILABLE with 28B, 21B, 21W, Z1D. INCLUDED in 24B, 25B, 26B, 21B, 23B, 24G, 25G, 26G, 23G.		
DMH	3.92 Axle Ratio	34	40
	REQUIRES (25B and DSA) or ((DSA or DHC) and 26B) or 25B or 24B or 26G or 25G or 24G. NOT AVAILABLE with 23W, 21B, 28B.		
DSA	Anti-Spin Differential Axle	242	285
	NOT AVAILABLE with DMC. INCLUDED in 28B.		
EHC	Engine: 3.9L SMPI V6 Magnum (2WD Club Cab)	476	560
	Manufacturer Discount	(476)	(560)
	Net Price	NC	NC
	REQUIRES DGB or DDC. NOT AVAILABLE with DDK, 21W, 25B, 21B, 26B, 28B, ASU, 25G, 26G.		
EHC	Engine: 3.9L SMPI V6 Magnum (2WD Reg Cab)	476	560
	NOT AVAILABLE with DDK, 21W, 21B, 25B, 26B, 28B, ASU, 25G, 26G.		
EHC	Engine: 3.9L SMPI V6 Magnum (4WD/Quad Cab)	NC	NC
	REQUIRES (DGB and DMH) or DDC. NOT AVAILABLE with 25B, 26B, 25G, 26G, AGU, 28B, 28G, AGB, ATK, DHC.		
EML	Engine: 5.9L SMPI V8 Magnum (2WD Except Quad Cab)	1432	1685
	*REQUIRES DGB and 2*B. NOT AVAILABLE with DDK, 21B, 23B, 24B, 25B, 26B, AGU, DMC, Z1K.*		

CODE	DESCRIPTION	INVOICE	MSRP
EML	Engine: 5.9L SMPI V8 Magnum (2WD Quad Cab) *NOT AVAILABLE with DDC, 23B, 23G, 24B, 24G, 25B, 25G, 26B, 26G, AGU, ATK, TS1.*	1012	1190
EML	Engine: 5.9L SMPI V8 Magnum (4WD Quad Cab) *NOT AVAILABLE with DDC, 23B, 23G, 24B, 24G, 25B, 25G, 26B, 26G, DHC.*	956	1125
EPE	Engine: 2.5L SMPI I4 Magnum (2WD Club Cab) *REQUIRES DDK and (2*W or 2*B). NOT AVAILABLE with DDC, DGB, 28B, ASU, Z1D, DMC, Z1B.*	(170)	(200)
EPE	Engine: 2.5L SMPI I4 Magnum (2WD Reg Cab) *REQUIRES 2*W or 2*B. NOT AVAILABLE with DGB, DDC, 23W, 24W, NMC, DMC, 23B, 24B, 25B, 26B, 28B, AGU, AGB, ASU, SCG, RDZ.*	NC	NC
EVA	Engine: 4.7L V8 Next Generation Magnum (2WD Club Cab)	927	1090
	Manufacturer Discount	(476)	(560)
	Net Price *REQUIRES (DDC or DGB) and (2*B or 2*G). NOT AVAILABLE with 23B, 24B, 21B, 28B, 23G, 24G.*	451	530
EVA	Engine: 4.7L V8 Next Generation Magnum (2WD Reg Cab) *REQUIRES 2*B or 2*G. NOT AVAILABLE with DDK, 21B, 23B, 23G, 24B, 24G, 28B, DMC.*	927	1090
EVA	Engine: 4.7L V8 Next Generation Magnum (4WD/Quad Cab) *REQUIRES 2*B or 2*G. NOT AVAILABLE with 23B, 23G, 24B, 24G, AGU, ATK, 28B, 28G, AGB.*	502	590
G1	Cloth Bench Seat (Reg Cab) *REQUIRES 2*W.*	47	55
GFA	Rear Window Defroster (Quad Cab) *Includes power heated fold-away mirrors. NOT AVAILABLE with GFD, GUR, ATK.*	315	370
GFA	Rear Window Defroster (Quad Cab) *Includes power heated fold-away mirrors. REQUIRES ATK and 2*G. NOT AVAILABLE with GFD, GUR.*	196	230
GFD	Sliding Rear Window *NOT AVAILABLE with GFA.*	98	115
GT4	6" x 9" Power Fold-Away Mirrors (All Except 2WD Quad Cab) *REQUIRES 2*G. NOT AVAILABLE with GUR.*	17	20
GT4	6" x 9" Power Fold-Away Mirrors *NOT AVAILABLE with 2*W, GUR, ATK.*	136	160
GUR	Power Mirrors *NOT AVAILABLE with 2*W, GT4, GFA.*	119	140
HAA	Air Conditioning *NOT AVAILABLE with 4XA, 2*G (2WD Reg Cab/Quad Cab). INCLUDED in 23G, 24G, 25G, 26G, 28G.*	680	800
JPS	6-Way Power Driver's Seat (Club Cab/Quad Cab) *REQUIRES 2*B or 2*G.*	272	320
K17	Bodyside Molding *REQUIRES 2*G.*	64	75
K5	Cloth High-Back Bucket Seats *REQUIRES 2*B or 2*G. NOT AVAILABLE with 2*W.*	170	200

CODE	DESCRIPTION	INVOICE	MSRP
LNJ	Fog Lamps *REQUIRES ADA and (2*B or 2*G). NOT AVAILABLE with 2*W.*	102	120
NHK	Engine Block Heater	30	35
NMC	HD Engine Cooling *REQUIRES 23B or 25B or 23G or 25G. NOT AVAILABLE with 24W, DGB, 21W, EPE, ADJ, 24B, 26B, 28B, 21B, 24G, 26G.*	51	60
NMC	HD Engine Cooling *REQUIRES 24B or 26B or 28B or 24G or 26G. NOT AVAILABLE with 21W, 23W, EPE, ADJ, 21B, 23B, 25B, 23G, 25G.*	102	120
RAZ	Radio: AM/FM Stereo with Cassette, CD and Equalizer *Includes Infinity sound speakers. REQUIRES 2*B or 2*G. NOT AVAILABLE with RBN, RBR.*	561	660
RBN	Radio: AM/FM Stereo with Cassette and CD Changer Control *Includes Infinity sound speakers. REQUIRES 2*B or 2*G. NOT AVAILABLE with RAZ, RBR.*	255	300
RBR	Radio: AM/FM Stereo with CD *Includes Infinity sound speakers. REQUIRES 2*B or 2*G. NOT AVAILABLE with RBN, RAZ.*	408	480
RDZ	Steering Wheel Mounted Audio Controls *REQUIRES 2*B or 2*G and (SCG and RAZ or (AJL or AJP)). NOT AVAILABLE with EPE.*	64	75
SCG	Leather-Wrapped Steering Wheel *REQUIRES 2*B or 2*G. NOT AVAILABLE with EPE.*	43	50
SUA	Tilt Steering Column (2WD - Reg Cab/Club Cab) *NOT AVAILABLE with EHC, EVA, EML, 23B, 23W, 24B, 24W, 25B, 26B, 28B, 2*G. INCLUDED in 24G, 25G, 26G, 23G.*	119	140
TS1	Tires: P235/75R15XL AS BSW (2WD Reg Cab) *REQUIRES 2*B or 2*G. NOT AVAILABLE with ASU, AGB, AGU, ATK.*	55	65
TS1	Tires: P235/75R15XL AS BSW (2WD Reg Cab) *REQUIRES 2*W.*	162	190
TS1	Tires: P235/75R15XL BSW AS (2WD - Club Cab/Quad Cab) *REQUIRES 2*B or 2*G. NOT AVAILABLE with AGB, ASU, ATK, AGU, EML.*	55	65
TS1	Tires: P235/75R15XL BSW AS (2WD Club Cab) *REQUIRES 2*W.*	162	190
TS1	Tires: P235/75R15XL BSW AS (2WD Quad Cab) *REQUIRES 2*G. NOT AVAILABLE with ATK, AGB.*	NC	NC
Z1D	Payload: 2000 Lbs (2WD Club Cab) *Includes tires: P235/75R15XL BSW A/S. REQUIRES (23B and DSA) or (24B and DMH and DSA) or (26B and DSA and DMH) or 25B or 23G or 24G or 25G or 26G. NOT AVAILABLE with 21B, 28B, Z1B, DMC, EPE, AGU, ASU, ATK.*	157	185
Z1D	Payload: 2000 Lbs (2WD Club Cab) *Includes tires: P235/75R15XL BSW A/S. REQUIRES (23W and DSA) or (24W and DMH and DSA). NOT AVAILABLE with 21W, Z1B, DMC, EPE.*	264	310
Z1K	Payload: 2000 Lbs (2WD Reg Cab) *Includes 11" x 2" rear drum brakes and tires: P235/75R15XL A/S BSW. REQUIRES (23B and DSA) or (24B and DMH and DSA) or (26B and DSA and*	157	185

CODE	DESCRIPTION	INVOICE	MSRP
	DMH) or 25B or 23G or 24G or 25G or 26G. NOT AVAILABLE with 21B, 28B, DMC, AGU, AGB, ASU, EML, ATK.		
Z1K	**Payload: 2000 Lbs (2WD Reg Cab)** *Includes 11" x 2" rear drum brakes and tires: P235/75R15XL A/S BSW. REQUIRES (23W and DSA) or (24W and DMH and DSA). NOT AVAILABLE with 21W, DMC.*	264	310
Z5C	**Payload: 2000 Lbs (4WD Reg Cab)** *Includes 11" x 2" rear drum brakes and tires: P235/75R15XL A/S OWL. REQUIRES (24B and DMH) or (23B or 25B or 26B).*	47	55
Z5C	**Payload: 2000 Lbs (4WD Reg Cab)** *Includes 11" x 2" rear drum brakes and tires: P235/75R15XL A/S OWL. REQUIRES 23W or (24W and DMH). NOT AVAILABLE with TS1.*	306	360

2000 DURANGO

2000 Dodge Durango

What's New?

The next-generation 4.7-liter V8 is now available on four-wheel-drive models and is linked to an all-new automatic transmission. Rack-and-pinion steering becomes standard for both two- and four-wheel-drives. A Sport model with an appearance package has been added to the lineup that already includes the SLT and the decked-out SLT Plus models.

Review

The 2-year-old Durango is Dodge's fierce competitor in the sport-utility market. Eighty percent of its parts are shared with the Dakota, including the platform, but the Durango's frame is actually three times stiffer than the pickup's. Unfortunately, the rough ride doesn't let you forget its close relation to a truck platform. It's somewhat bouncy and you'll be aware of the stiffness, yet it's not miserable enough for it to lose its cushy-cruiser status.

The Durango may be compact on the outside, but once inside, you'll be shocked by the roominess. With a 7,600-pound towing capacity, it's an SUV that can be stuffed to the gills with family and friends, and still have the ability to haul your watercraft or other form of weekend fun. However, you'll have to make a choice: eight people, or useable cargo space, because you can't have the best of both worlds when there's a full house. The good news is that a roof rack is standard.

If you are taking advantage of the third row, you'll appreciate the ease of the fold-and-tumble second-row seating. Legroom is notable throughout, but larger folk may want to avoid the third row for anything other than short jaunts. Headroom shouldn't be an issue, thanks to the raised roof line. Overall, the interior is quite complacent, and instrumentation is simple and within reach, but expect wind noise and squeaking.

The 4x4s inherit the new 4.7-liter Magnum V8, a sprightly engine, requiring less-frequent fill-ups than with the other Magnums. The 5.2-liter Magnum V8 is standard on both the Sport and the SLT two-wheel-drives but the best choice for towing is the 5.9-liter V8.

Despite the 4x4 badging and rugged looks, don't kid yourself. Ground clearance is minimal and off-road ability is even less (the lack of tow hooks rests our case). The Durango really shines as a grocery-getter and soccer-team hauler. Emphasis for this vehicle is on utility.

The new Sport trim level joins the existing SLT and SLT Plus this year, which consists of an appearance package featuring two-tone paint, optional factory-installed running boards, five-spoke aluminum wheels, and Sierra Bronze Pearl Coat and Aquamarine Metallic exterior colors.

The Toyota 4Runner, Jeep Grand Cherokee and Ford Explorer are rivals, but none of them have bolted in a third row of seats yet, so the Durango has the advantage in terms of passenger capacity. Also, a fully equipped SLT Plus comes in under $35,000 (and remember, that's for a V8, four-wheel drive, and leather seats), making it a budget-conscious splurge.

Standard Equipment

BASE 2WD (4A): 5.2L V8 OHV SMPI 16-valve engine; 4-speed electronic OD auto transmission with lock-up; 600-amp battery; 136-amp alternator; rear-wheel drive, 3.55 axle ratio; stainless steel exhaust; front independent suspension with anti-roll bar, front coil springs, HD front shocks, rigid rear axle suspension with anti-roll bar, rear leaf springs, HD rear shocks; power rack-and-pinion steering; front disc/rear drum brakes with rear wheel antilock braking system; 25 gal. capacity fuel tank; rear lip spoiler, side impact bars; liftback rear cargo door; front and rear body-colored bumpers with rear step; monotone paint; aero-composite halogen headlamps; additional exterior lights include underhood light; driver's and passenger's power remote black outside mirrors; front and rear 15" x 7" silver alloy wheels; P235/75SR15 A/S BSW front and rear tires; underbody mounted full-size steel spare wheel with crankdown; air conditioning, rear heat ducts; AM/FM stereo, clock, seek-scan, cassette, 4 speakers, and fixed antenna; power door locks with 2 stage unlock, remote keyless entry, child safety rear door locks; 3 power accessory outlets, front cigar lighter(s); cruise control with steering wheel controls; smokers' package; instrumentation display includes tachometer, oil pressure gauge, water temperature gauge, volt gauge, trip odometer; warning indicators include oil pressure, battery, lights on, key in ignition, low fuel, low washer fluid, door ajar, trunk ajar; driver's and passenger's front airbags; panic alarm; deep tinted windows, power front and rear windows with driver's 1-touch down, fixed 1/4 vent windows; variable intermittent front windshield wipers, sun visor strip, fixed interval rear wiper, rear window defroster; seating capacity of 6, 40-20-40 split-bench front seat, fixed headrests, center armrest with storage, driver's seat includes 4-way direction control, passenger's seat includes 4-way direction control; 60-40 folding rear split-bench seat with adjustable headrests, center armrest; front and rear height adjustable seatbelts; cloth seats, vinyl door trim insert, full cloth headliner, full carpet floor covering, deluxe sound insulation; steering wheel with tilt adjustment; interior lights include dome light, front reading lights, illuminated entry; vanity mirrors; day/night rearview mirror; glove box with light, front and rear cupholders, 2 seat back storage pockets; carpeted cargo floor, carpeted trunk lid, cargo tie downs, cargo light, cargo concealed storage; body-colored grille, black side window moldings, black front windshield molding, black rear window molding and black door handles.

BASE 4WD (4A) (in addition to or instead of BASE 2WD (4A) equipment): 4.7L V8 SOHC SMPI 16-valve engine; part-time 4-wheel drive, auto locking hub control and manual shift, front torsion springs, front torsion bar; skid plate(s), side impact bars and plastic trunk lid.

CODE	DESCRIPTION	INVOICE	MSRP

Base Prices

CODE	DESCRIPTION	INVOICE	MSRP
DN1L74	Base 2WD (4A)	23635	26170
DN5L74	Base 4WD (4A)	25430	28170
Destination Charge:		535	535

Accessories

CODE	DESCRIPTION	INVOICE	MSRP
24B	**Quick Order Package 24B (2WD)**	NC	NC
	Includes vehicle with standard equipment. REQUIRES (HBA or 4XN) and ELF and DGB.		
24G	**Quick Order Package 24G (2WD)**	1046	1230
	Manufacturer Discount	(268)	(315)
	Net Price	778	915
	Includes SLT Decor group: SLT badging, front and rear body color bumpers, floor console, cloth door trim panel with map pocket, front and rear floor mats, fog lamps, body colored bodyside moldings, 6-way power driver's seat and cloth highback bucket seats; roof rack (150 lbs capacity) and tires: P235/75R15XL OWL A/S. REQUIRES (HBA or 4XN) and ELF and DGB. NOT AVAILABLE with EML.		
26B	**Quick Order Package 26B (4WD)**	NC	NC
	Includes vehicle with standard equipment. REQUIRES (HBA or 4XN) and EVA and DGB.		
26G	**Quick Order Package 26G (4WD)**	1046	1230
	Manufacturer Discount	(268)	(315)
	Net Price	778	915
	Includes SLT Decor group: SLT badging, front and rear body color bumpers, floor console, cloth door trim panel with map pocket, front and rear floor mats, fog lamps, body colored bodyside moldings, 6-way power driver's seat and cloth highback bucket seats; roof rack (150 lbs capacity) and tires: P235/75R15XL OWL A/S. REQUIRES (HBA or 4XN) and EVA. NOT AVAILABLE with EML.		
28G	**Quick Order Package 28G**	1046	1230
	Manufacturer Discount	(268)	(315)
	Net Price	778	915
	Includes SLT Decor group: SLT badging, front and rear body color bumpers, floor console, cloth door trim panel with map pocket, front and rear floor mats, fog lamps, body colored bodyside moldings, 6-way power driver's seat and cloth highback bucket seats; roof rack (150 lbs capacity) and tires: P235/75R15XL OWL A/S. REQUIRES (HBA or 4XN) and EML. NOT AVAILABLE with EVA, ELF.		
4XN	**Rear Air Conditioning Bypass**	NC	NC
	NOT AVAILABLE with HBA.		
ADJ	**HD Service Group**	204	240
	Includes 750-amp maintenance free battery and HD engine cooling.		
ADL	**Skid Plate Group (4WD)**	111	130
	Includes front suspension skid plate, fuel tank skid plate shield and transfer case skid plate shield.		
AFH	**Overhead Convenience Group**	349	410
	*Includes overhead console, auto day/night mirror and dual illuminated visor vanity mirrors. REQUIRES 2*G.*		

CODE	DESCRIPTION	INVOICE	MSRP
AHC	Trailer Tow Group *REQUIRES ADJ.*	234	275
AJB	Security Group *Includes security alarm. REQUIRES 2*G.*	128	150
ASU	R/T Sport Group (4WD SLT) *REQUIRES 26G or 28G.*	1398	1645
ATK	SLT Plus Decor Group (2WD)	2006	2360
	Manufacturer Discount	(255)	(300)
	Net Price *Includes steering wheel radio controls, premium door trim panel, woodgrain instrument panel, overhead convenience group: overhead console, auto day/night mirror, dual illuminated visor vanity mirrors; AM/FM stereo with CD, cassette and equalizer, 8 Infinity speakers, leather highback bucket seats, security group, tires: 31 x 10.5R15 A/S OWL and wheels: 15" x 8" aluminum. REQUIRES 2*G. NOT AVAILABLE with TSC, MRL.*	1751	2060
ATK	SLT Plus Decor Group (4WD)	2223	2615
	Manufacturer Discount	(255)	(300)
	Net Price *Includes steering wheel radio controls, premium door trim panel, woodgrain instrument panel, overhead convenience group: overhead console, auto day/night mirror, dual illuminated visor vanity mirrors; AM/FM stereo with CD, cassette and equalizer, 8 Infinity speakers, leather highback bucket seats, security group, tires: 31 x 10.5R15 A/S OWL, wheel flares and wheels: 15" x 8" aluminum. REQUIRES 2*G.*	1968	2315
BGK	4-Wheel Antilock Brakes	421	495
CFP	Third Row Seat *Includes rear 40/20/40 with fold and tumble capability. REQUIRES 26G or 28G or ATK.*	468	550
CLE	Front and Rear Floor Mats (4WD)	47	55
DGB	Transmission: 4-Speed Automatic *NOT AVAILABLE with EVA.*	NC	NC
DGB	Transmission: Multi-Speed Automatic (4WD) *NOT AVAILABLE with EML.*	NC	NC
DHC	Full Time Transfer Case (4WD) *REQUIRES 2*G.*	336	395
DMH	3.92 Axle Ratio	34	40
DSA	Anti-Spin Differential Axle	242	285
ELF	Engine: 5.2L SMPI V8 Magnum (2WD) *NOT AVAILABLE with 28G.*	NC	NC
EML	Engine: 5.9L SMPI V8 Magnum *REQUIRES 28G. NOT AVAILABLE with 26G, DGB, 24G.*	506	595
EVA	Engine: 4.7L V8 Next Generation Magnum (4WD) *NOT AVAILABLE with 28G, DGB.*	NC	NC
GTS	Power Heated Foldaway Mirrors *REQUIRES 2*G.*	64	75
HBA	Rear Air Conditioning W/O Heater *NOT AVAILABLE with 4XN.*	366	430

CODE	DESCRIPTION	INVOICE	MSRP
MRL	Body Color Running Boards *REQUIRES TSC and 2*G. NOT AVAILABLE with ATK.*	336	395
NHK	Engine Block Heater	30	35
RAZ	Radio: AM/FM Stereo with CD, Cassette and Equalizer	255	300
RCK	Infinity Speaker System *Includes 8 Infinity speakers in 6 locations.*	281	330
TSC	Tires: P235/75R15 AS BSW (2WD) *Includes wheel flares and wheels: 15" x 8" aluminum. REQUIRES 2*G. NOT AVAILABLE with ATK.*	213	250
TUT	Tires: 31 x 10.5R15 AS OWL (4WD) *Includes matching spare wheel, wheel flares and wheels: 15" x 8" aluminum. REQUIRES 2*G.*	395	465

2001 RAM PICKUP

2001 Dodge Ram 3500

What's New?

The 2001 Rams are identical to 2000 models in every way except their model-year classification. Is Chrysler trying to keep pace with Ford (who released 2001 and 2002 pricing on their F-Series before calendar year 1999 was even complete), or do they just want to avoid problems with federal standards for gas mileage by selling too many thirsty trucks in any given model year? You make the call.

Review

The Dodge boys must have known they had a winner on their hands the second they unveiled their bold Ram pickup in 1994. The risky love-it-or-hate-it styling turned nearly every head, and it takes two hands to count the number of lookalikes that have since debuted from other manufacturers.

The Ram comes in Regular, Club, and Quad Cab half-, three-quarter- and one-ton configurations, and all are equipped with Magnum power, be it modest or mammoth. There's a practical-and-it-feelsthat-way 3.9-liter V6 that makes 175 horsepower, and at the other extreme, heavy-duty 2500 and 3500 pickups can growl with a 8.0-liter V10, good for 310 horsepower (305 for California). Tucked in between for good measure is a 245-horse, 5.9-liter V8 and a 5.2-liter V8 worth 230 horsepower. A macho 5.9-liter, 24-valve inline-six turbodiesel is available if you like loads of torque (450 foot-pounds), low-maintenance, and the overly loud purr of a diesel, plus have about an extra five grand to spend. We've heard that 2002 will bring an aluminum-block 3.7-liter V6 based on the popular Grand Cherokee 4.7-liter V8, and there's also talk of 5.7-liter and 6.1-liter V8s.

The Regular Cab has bench seating for three, while the Club Cab can cram three both front and rear, although access to the rear for storage and seating is difficult. With the Quad Cab, rear-access doors on either side of the cab make that easier, yet they're not separate full-size doors like on the new Dakota Quad Cab. Inside, the Ram is fully modernized, with ergonomics that match the utility of the rest of the truck. The controls are properly placed and completely functional.

Automatic transmission shifts are firm, but not harsh, and the column-mounted shifter operates easily. The manual transmissions are simple to shift and the gates are perfectly spaced. The half-ton's manual tranny is a five-speed with overdrive, while the three-quarter and one-ton reap the rewards of a much beefier transmission that has a granny-low first gear for getting going while hauling a heavy load. Although it's a bulky vehicle, the Ram is surprisingly agile and reasonably surefooted, but think twice before making any quick maneuvers. Ride and handling are so competent you almost forget you're in a full-size pickup, except if you're in an unloaded three-quarter or one-ton, in which case you'll be reminded over every bump in the road.

Yes, it's a full-size truck, but it does extremely well on trails and other off-road excursions. Dodge is well aware of the Ram's capabilities and in 2000 they introduced the Ram Off-Road 4x4. Regular and Quad Cab short-bed 1500 four-wheel drives can take advantage of this off-road package that includes heavier-duty equipment, such as a limited slip, a recalibrated suspension for extra ground clearance, all-terrain tires, and steering gear designed for low speeds.

An all-new platform and redesign is likely for 2002, and Dodge is again hoping to build another talk of both the town and the competition.

2001 RAM 1500

Standard Equipment

WS 2WD REGULAR CAB SB/LB(5M): 3.9L V6 OHV SMPI 12-valve engine; 5-speed OD manual transmission; 600-amp battery; 117-amp alternator; rear-wheel drive, 3.21 axle ratio; stainless steel exhaust; front independent suspension with anti-roll bar, front coil springs, HD front shocks, rigid rear axle suspension with rear leaf springs, HD rear shocks; power re-circulating ball steering with vehicle speed-sensing assist; front disc/rear drum brakes with rear wheel antilock braking system; 26 gal. ? SB/35 gal. - LB capacity fuel tank; side impact bars; front argent bumper with black rub strip; monotone paint; aero-composite halogen headlamps; additional exterior lights include underhood light; driver's and passenger's manual black folding outside mirrors; front and rear 16" x 7" silver styled steel wheels; P225/75SR16 A/S BSW front and rear tires; underbody mounted full-size steel spare wheel with crankdown; 2 power accessory outlets, smokers' package; instrumentation display includes tachometer, oil pressure gauge, water temperature gauge, volt gauge, trip odometer; warning indicators include low oil level, lights on, key in ignition, low fuel; driver's front airbag, passenger's cancelable front airbag; tinted windows; variable intermittent front windshield wipers, sun visor strip; seating capacity of 3, bench front seat, fixed headrests, driver's seat includes 2-way direction control, passenger's seat includes 2-way direction control; front height adjustable seatbelts; vinyl seats, full cloth headliner, full vinyl floor covering, cabback insulator; interior lights include dome light; day/night rearview mirror; glove box, front cupholder, instrument panel bin, driver's and passenger's door bins; chrome grille, black side window moldings, black front windshield molding, black rear window molding and black door handles.

ST 2WD REGULAR CAB SB/LB(5M) (in addition to or instead of WS 2WD REGULAR CAB SB/LB (5M) equipment): Front and rear chrome bumpers with black rub strip, rear step; additional exterior lights include pickup cargo box light; AM/FM stereo, clock, seek-scan, cassette, 4 speakers, and fixed antenna; seating capacity of 3, 40-20-40 bench front seat, fixed headrests, center armrest with storage, driver's seat includes 4-way direction control, passenger's seat includes 4-way direction control and cargo concealed storage.

CLUB CAB SB/QUAD CAB SB/LB (5M) (in addition to or instead of REGULAR CAB SB/LB(5M) equipment): 5.2L V8 OHV SMPI 16-valve engine; warning indicators include low washer fluid; deep tinted windows, vented rear windows; seating capacity of 6, 40-20-40 split-bench front seat, fixed headrests, center armrest with storage, driver's seat includes 4-way direction control, easy entry, passenger's seat includes 4-way direction control, easy entry and full folding rear bench seat.

4WD (5M) (in addition to or instead of 2WD (5M) equipment): Part-time 4-wheel drive, auto locking hub control and manual shift, 3.55 axle ratio, front non-independent suspension with anti-roll bar and P245/75SR16 A/S BSW front and rear tires (Club Cab/Quad Cab).

Base Prices

Code	Description	Invoice	MSRP
BR1E61	WS 2WD Regular Cab SB (5M)	13613	14895
BR1E62	WS 2WD Regular Cab LB (5M)	13850	15165
BR1L61	ST 2WD Regular Cab SB (5M)	14679	16675
BR1L62	ST 2WD Regular Cab LB (5M)	14921	16960
BE1L31	ST 2WD Club Cab SB (5M)	17076	19460
BE1L33	ST 2WD Quad Cab SB (5M)	17827	20320
BE1L34	ST 2WD Quad Cab LB (5M)	18065	20600
BR6L61	ST 4WD Regular Cab SB (5M)	17925	20435
BR6L62	ST 4WD Regular Cab LB (5M)	18214	20775
BE6L31	ST 4WD Club Cab SB (5M)	19892	22720
BE6L33	ST 4WD Quad Cab SB (5M)	20572	23520
BE6L34	ST 4WD Quad Cab LB (5M)	20853	23850
Destination Charge:		650	650

Accessories

Code	Description	Invoice	MSRP
21A	Quick Order Package 21A (ST Reg Cab 2WD) *Includes 3.21 axle ratio. REQUIRES (HAA or 4XA) and EHC and DDC. NOT AVAILABLE with DMH, NMC, ELF, EML, DGB, GPC, AHC.*	NC	NC
21W	Quick Order Package 21W (WS) *Includes 3.21 axle ratio. REQUIRES (HAA or 4XA) and EHC and DDC. NOT AVAILABLE with DGB.*	NC	NC
22A	Quick Order Package 22A (ST 2WD Reg Cab) *Includes 3.55 axle ratio. REQUIRES (HAA or 4XA) and EHC and DGB. NOT AVAILABLE with DMH, NMC, ELF, EML, DDC, ADJ, GPC, AHC.*	NC	NC
22W	Quick Order Package 22W (ST) *Includes 3.55 axle ratio. REQUIRES (HAA or 4XA) and EHC and DGB. NOT AVAILABLE with DDC.*	NC	NC
23A	Quick Order Package 23A (ST) *Includes vehicle with standard equipment. REQUIRES (HAA or 4XA) and ELF and DDC. NOT AVAILABLE with DMH, EHC, EML, DGB.*	NC	NC

CODE	DESCRIPTION	INVOICE	MSRP
23G	**Quick Order Package 23G (ST 4WD Club/Quad Cab)**	2440	2870
	Manufacturer Discount	(595)	(700)
	Net Price	1845	2170
	Includes SLT Decor Group: black tailgate applique, carpeted floor covering, floor mats, hood insulation, passenger's side vanity mirror, power heated fold-away outside mirrors, body side molding, premium cloth 40/20/40 split bench seat, front bumper sight shields and leather-wrapped steering wheel; air conditioning, convenience group: tilt steering column, speed control; light group: mini overhead console, map/courtesy lamp; power windows with driver's one-touch down, tires: P245/75R16 BSW A/S and wheels: 16" x 7" cast aluminum. REQUIRES ELF and DDC. NOT AVAILABLE with DGB, AWL, EML, ATK, AGG.		
23G	**Quick Order Package 23G (ST Except 4WD Club/Quad Cab)**	2550	3000
	Manufacturer Discount	(595)	(700)
	Net Price	1955	2300
	Includes SLT Decor Group: black tailgate applique, carpeted floor covering, floor mats, hood insulation, passenger's side vanity mirror, power heated fold-away outside mirrors, body side molding, premium cloth 40/20/40 split bench seat, front bumper sight shields and leather-wrapped steering wheel; air conditioning, convenience group: tilt steering column, speed control; light group: mini overhead console, map/courtesy lamp; power windows with driver's one-touch down, tires: P245/75R16 BSW A/S and wheels: 16" x 7" cast aluminum. REQUIRES ELF and DDC. NOT AVAILABLE with DMH, DGB, EML, ATK, AGG, AWL.		
24A	**Quick Order Package 24A (ST)**	NC	NC
	Includes vehicle with standard equipment. REQUIRES (HAA or 4XA) and ELF and DGB. NOT AVAILABLE with ADJ, DDC, EML, EHC, NMC.		
24G	**Quick Order Package 24G (ST 4WD Club/Quad Cab)**	2440	2870
	Manufacturer Discount	(595)	(700)
	Net Price	1845	2170
	Includes SLT Decor Group: black tailgate applique, carpeted floor covering, floor mats, hood insulation, passenger's side vanity mirror, power heated fold-away outside mirrors, body side molding, premium cloth 40/20/40 split bench seat, front bumper sight shields and leather-wrapped steering wheel; air conditioning, convenience group: tilt steering column, speed control; light group: mini overhead console, map/courtesy lamp; power windows with driver's one-touch down, tires: P245/75R16 BSW A/S and wheels: 16" x 7" cast aluminum. REQUIRES ELF and DGB. NOT AVAILABLE with ADJ, DDC, NMC, EML, ATK, AGG.		
24G	**Quick Order Package 24G (ST Except 4WD Club/Quad Cab)**	2550	3000
	Manufacturer Discount	(595)	(700)
	Net Price	1955	2300
	Includes SLT Decor Group: black tailgate applique, carpeted floor covering, floor mats, hood insulation, passenger's side vanity mirror, power heated fold-away outside mirrors, body side molding, premium cloth 40/20/40 split bench seat, front bumper sight shields and leather-wrapped steering wheel; air conditioning, convenience group: tilt steering column, speed control; light group: mini overhead console, map/courtesy lamp; power windows with driver's one-touch down, tires: P245/75R16 BSW A/S and wheels: 16" x 7" cast aluminum. REQUIRES ELF and DGB. NOT AVAILABLE with ADJ, DDC, EML, NMC, ATK, AGG.		

CODE	DESCRIPTION	INVOICE	MSRP
26A	**Quick Order Package 26A (ST)**	NC	NC
	Includes vehicle with standard equipment. REQUIRES (HAA or 4XA) and EML and DGB. NOT AVAILABLE with ADJ, DDC, EHC, ELF, NMC, AYB.		
26G	**Quick Order Package 26G (ST 4WD Club/Quad Cab)**	2440	2870
	Manufacturer Discount	(595)	(700)
	Net Price	1845	2170
	Includes SLT Decor Group: black tailgate applique, carpeted floor covering, floor mats, hood insulation, passenger's side vanity mirror, power heated fold-away outside mirrors, body side molding, premium cloth 40/20/40 split bench seat, front bumper sight shields and leather-wrapped steering wheel; air conditioning, convenience group: tilt steering column, speed control; light group: mini overhead console, map/courtesy lamp; power windows with driver's one-touch down, tires: P245/75R16 BSW A/S and wheels: 16" x 7" cast aluminum. REQUIRES EML and DGB. NOT AVAILABLE with ADJ, ELF, DDC, NMC, ATK, AGG.		
26G	**Quick Order Package 26G (ST Except 4WD Club/Quad Cab)**	2550	3000
	Manufacturer Discount	(595)	(700)
	Net Price	1955	2300
	Includes SLT Decor Group: black tailgate applique, carpeted floor covering, floor mats, hood insulation, passenger's side vanity mirror, power heated fold-away outside mirrors, body side molding, premium cloth 40/20/40 split bench seat, front bumper sight shields and leather-wrapped steering wheel; air conditioning, convenience group: tilt steering column, speed control; light group: mini overhead console, map/courtesy lamp; power windows with driver's one-touch down, tires: P245/75R16 BSW A/S and wheels: 16" x 7" cast aluminum. REQUIRES EML and DGB. NOT AVAILABLE with ADJ, ELF, DDC, NMC, ATK, AGG.		
26H	**Quick Order Package 26H (ST 2WD Quad Cab)**	4127	4855
	Manufacturer Discount	(595)	(700)
	Net Price	3532	4155
	Includes SLT Decor Group: black tailgate applique, carpeted floor covering, floor mats, hood insulation, passenger's side vanity mirror, power heated fold-away outside mirrors, body side molding, heated leather 40/20/40 split bench power seat, front bumper sight shields and leather-wrapped steering wheel; air conditioning, convenience group: tilt steering column, speed control; light group: mini overhead console, map/courtesy lamp; power windows with driver's one-touch down, tires: P245/75R16 BSW A/S, wheels: 16" x 7" cast aluminum and woodgrain instrument panel bezel. REQUIRES EML and DGB and ATK. NOT AVAILABLE with DDC, ELF, CKJ, AJD, RBN, RBR, JPV, WDB, NMC, ADJ, RDZ, BGK, LNJ, GXM, RAZ, LSA, CUE, AWK, AGG.		
26H	**Quick Order Package 26H (ST 4WD Quad Cab)**	4016	4725
	Manufacturer Discount	(595)	(700)
	Net Price	3421	4025
	Includes SLT Decor Group: black tailgate applique, carpeted floor covering, floor mats, hood insulation, passenger's side vanity mirror, power heated fold-away outside mirrors, body side molding, heated leather 40/20/40 split bench power seat, front bumper sight shields and leather-wrapped steering wheel; air conditioning, convenience group: tilt steering column, speed control; light group: mini overhead console, map/courtesy lamp; power windows with driver's one-touch down, tires:		

CODE	DESCRIPTION	INVOICE	MSRP
	P245/75R16 BSW A/S, wheels: 16" x 7" cast aluminum and woodgrain instrument panel bezel. REQUIRES EML and DGB and ATK. NOT AVAILABLE with ELF, DDC, CKJ, AJD, AWL, RBN, RAZ, RBR, JPV, TYZ, TXW, WDB, ADJ, NMC, RDZ, LNJ, GXM, LSA, AGG, CUE, AWK, BGK, DMH.		
4XA	Air Conditioning Bypass *NOT AVAILABLE with HAA, AZB.*	NC	NC
4XM	No Rear Bumper (WS) *NOT AVAILABLE with MBD.*	NC	NC
ADA	Light Group (ST) *Includes glove box lamp, map/courtesy lamp, passenger's assist handles, deluxe headliner and mini overhead console. INCLUDED in 23G, 24G, 26G, 26H.*	77	90
ADJ	HD Service Group (4WD) *Includes 136-amp alternator, 750-amp maintenance free battery and HD engine cooling. NOT AVAILABLE with 23A, 23G, NMC, DDC.*	332	390
ADJ	HD Service Group (4WD) *Includes 136-amp alternator, 750-amp maintenance free battery, HD engine cooling and auxiliary transmission oil cooler. NOT AVAILABLE with 24A, 26A, 24G, 26G, NMC, DGB, 26H.*	221	260
ADJ	HD Service Group (ST) *Includes 750-amp maintenance free battery, HD engine cooling and auxiliary transmission oil cooler. NOT AVAILABLE with 21A, 23A, NMC, 23G, DDC.*	293	345
ADJ	HD Service Group *Includes 750-amp maintenance free battery. NOT AVAILABLE with 22A, 24A, 26A, NMC, 24G, 26G, DGB, 26H.*	183	215
AGG	Sport Appearance Group (ST 2WD) *Includes Sport badge and 16" x 7" cast aluminum wheels, front body color bumper, rear body color bumper, fog lamps, color keyed grille, quad halogen headlamps, tires: P245/75R16 OWL A/S and bodyside moldings delete. REQUIRES 2*G. NOT AVAILABLE with JPS, APD, WDB, 26H, ATK.*	429	505
AGG	Sport Appearance Group (ST 2WD Quad Cab) *Includes Sport badge and 16" x 7" cast aluminum wheels, front body color bumper, rear body color bumper, fog lamps, color keyed grille, quad halogen headlamps, tires: P245/75R16 OWL A/S and bodyside moldings delete. REQUIRES 2*G. NOT AVAILABLE with APD.*	310	365
AGG	Sport Appearance Group (ST 4WD) *Includes Sport badge and 16" x 7" cast aluminum wheels, front body color bumper, rear body color bumper, fog lamps, color keyed grille, quad halogen headlamps, tires: P245/75R16 OWL A/S and bodyside moldings delete. REQUIRES 26H. NOT AVAILABLE with TYZ, AHH, WDB, AWL, APD, ATK.*	672	790
AGG	Sport Appearance Group (ST 4WD Quad Cab) *Includes Sport badge and 16" x 7" cast aluminum wheels, front body color bumper, rear body color bumper, fog lamps, color keyed grille, quad halogen headlamps, tires: P245/75R16 OWL A/S and bodyside moldings delete. REQUIRES 2*G. NOT AVAILABLE with TYZ, AWL.*	553	650
AGG	Sport Appearance Group (ST 4WD SB) *Includes Sport badge and 16" x 7" cast aluminum wheels, front body color bumper, rear body color bumper, fog lamps, color keyed grille, quad halogen headlamps, tires:*	200	235

CODE	DESCRIPTION	INVOICE	MSRP
	*P245/75R16 OWL A/S and bodyside moldings delete. REQUIRES 2*G. NOT AVAILABLE with TYZ, AHH, WDB, APD, 26H, ATK.*		
AHC	Trailer Tow Group (ST)	234	275
	Includes HD flasher and 7-lead connector (on hitch). REQUIRES ADJ. NOT AVAILABLE with EHC, 21A, 22A.		
AHH	Light Duty Snow Plow Prep Group (ST 4WD Reg Cab SB)	72	85
	Manufacturer Discount	(72)	(85)
	Net Price	NC	NC
	Includes extra duty front suspension. Recommended front clearance lights, A/T tires and HD front springs. REQUIRES ADJ and AHC. NOT AVAILABLE with AGG.		
AJD	Leather Interior Group (ST Club/Quad Cab)	1352	1590
	*Includes woodgrain instrument panel bezel, 8-way power driver's seat, travel convenience group: overhead console with trip computer, auto dimming rear view mirror and illuminated visor vanity mirrors. REQUIRES 2*G. NOT AVAILABLE with 26H.*		
AJD	Leather Interior Group (ST Reg Cab)	1233	1450
	*Includes woodgrain instrument panel bezel, 6-way power driver's seat, travel convenience group: overhead console with trip computer, auto dimming rear view mirror and illuminated visor vanity mirrors. REQUIRES 2*G. NOT AVAILABLE with D3.*		
AJK	Convenience Group	332	390
	Includes speed control and tilt steering column. INCLUDED in 23G, 24G, 26G, 26H.		
AMR	Behind Seat Modular Storage Group (WS)	81	95
	Includes storage tray.		
APD	Lower Two-Tone Paint (ST)	191	225
	NOT AVAILABLE with AGG.		
APD	Two Tone Lower Paint (ST 2WD Reg Cab LB/4WD Club Cab)	191	225
	NOT AVAILABLE with AGG.		
ATK	SLT Plus Decor Group (ST Quad Cab)	1836	2160
	Includes steering wheel mounted audio controls, 4-wheel antilock brakes, fog lamps, travel convenience group: overhead console with trip computer, auto dimming rear view mirror, illuminated visor vanity mirrors; remote keyless entry, AM/FM stereo with CD, cassette, equalizer, 6 Infinity speakers, security alarm and rear underseat compartment storage. REQUIRES 26H. NOT AVAILABLE with 23G, 24G, 26G.		
AWK	Travel Convenience Group (ST)	293	345
	*Includes overhead console with trip computer, auto dimming rear view mirror, illuminated visor vanity mirrors. REQUIRES 2*G. NOT AVAILABLE with 26H.*		
AWL	Off-Road Group (ST 4WD SB)	1373	1615
	Includes transmission and fuel tank skid plate shields, off road badge, fog lamps, tires: LT275/70R17 on/off road and wheels: 17" x 8" aluminum. REQUIRES 23G. NOT AVAILABLE with BGK, TYZ, TXW, WDB, 24G, 26G, AGG, DGB, DMH, 26H.		
AWL	Off-Road Group (ST 4WD SB)	1483	1745
	Includes transmission and fuel tank skid plate shields, off road badge, fog lamps, tires: LT275/70R17 on/off road and wheels: 17" x 8" aluminum. REQUIRES 24G or 26G. NOT AVAILABLE with BGK, TXW, TYZ, WDB, 23G, AGG, DMH, DDC, 26H.		

CODE	DESCRIPTION	INVOICE	MSRP
AYB	Wheel Plus Group (ST 2WD)	633	745
	Manufacturer Discount	(340)	(400)
	Net Price	293	345
	*Includes wheels: 16" x 7" chrome and sliding rear window. REQUIRES EHC or ELF. NOT AVAILABLE with AZB, EML, 26A, 2*G or 26H.*		
AYB	Wheel Plus Group (ST 4WD Club/Quad Cab)	646	760
	Manufacturer Discount	(230)	(270)
	Net Price	416	490
	*Includes wheels: 16" x 7" chrome and sliding rear window. REQUIRES ELF. NOT AVAILABLE with TYX, EML, 26A, 2*G or 26H.*		
AYB	Wheel Plus Group (ST 4WD Reg Cab)	757	890
	Manufacturer Discount	(340)	(400)
	Net Price	417	490
	Includes wheels: 16" x 7" chrome and sliding rear window. REQUIRES 23A or 24A. NOT AVAILABLE with TYX, AZB.		
BGK	4-Wheel Antilock Brakes (2WD Club Cab/Quad Cab)	421	495
	NOT AVAILABLE with 26H, AWL.		
BGK	4-Wheel Antilock Brakes (Reg Cab/4WD Club Cab)	421	495
	NOT AVAILABLE with AWL.		
CF8	Rear Seat Delete (Quad Cab)	NC	NC
	*REQUIRES 2*A.*		
CKE	Carpet Floor Covering (ST)	94	110
	*REQUIRES 2*A. NOT AVAILABLE with D3.*		
CKJ	Black Vinyl Floor Covering (ST)	NC	NC
	*REQUIRES 2*G. NOT AVAILABLE with CUE, 26H.*		
CUE	Rear Underseat Compartment Storage (Quad Cab)	64	75
	*REQUIRES 2*G. NOT AVAILABLE with CKJ, 26H.*		
D3	Deluxe Cloth and Vinyl Bench Seat (WS)	94	110
DDC	Transmission: HD 5-Speed Manual	NC	NC
	NOT AVAILABLE with 22W, 22A, 26A, 24A, 24G, 26G, NMC, EML, DMH, 26H, AWL.		
DGB	Transmission: 4-Speed Automatic	829	975
	NOT AVAILABLE with 21W, 21A, 23A, 23G, NMC, ADJ.		
DMD	3.55 Axle Ratio (2WD)	43	50
	Recommended for high altitude. NOT AVAILABLE with DMH. INCLUDED in 22W, 22A.		
DMH	3.92 Axle Ratio (ST)	43	50
	REQUIRES DSA. NOT AVAILABLE with 21A, 22A, 23A, 23G, DMD, DDC, AWL, 26H.		
DSA	Anti-Spin Differential Axle	242	285
	REQUIRES DMD or DMH.		
EHC	Engine: 3.9L V6 SMPI Magnum (2WD Reg Cab)	NC	NC
	*NOT AVAILABLE with 23A, 24A, 26A, 2*G, 26H, AHC, GPC.*		
ELF	Engine: 5.2L SMPI V8 Magnum (2WD Club/Quad Cab/4WD)	NC	NC
	NOT AVAILABLE with 26A, 26G, 26H.		
ELF	Engine: 5.2L SMPI V8 Magnum (2WD Reg Cab)	502	590
	NOT AVAILABLE with 21A, 22A, 26A, 26G.		

CODE	DESCRIPTION	INVOICE	MSRP
EML	Engine: 5.9L SMPI V8 Magnum (All Except 2WD Reg Cab)	506	595
	Manufacturer Discount	(506)	(595)
	Net Price	NC	NC
	NOT AVAILABLE with 23A, 23G, 24G, 24A, DDC, AYB.		
EML	Engine: 5.9L SMPI V8 Magnum (ST 2WD Reg Cab)	1007	1185
	Manufacturer Discount	(506)	(595)
	Net Price	501	590
	NOT AVAILABLE with 21A, 22A, 23A, 23G, 24G, 24A, DDC, AYB.		
GFD	Sliding Rear Window	119	140
GPC	Dual 7" x 10" Bright Wide Mount Mirrors (4WD Quad Cab)	43	50
	*REQUIRES 2*A. NOT AVAILABLE with GPD.*		
GPC	Dual 7" x 10" Bright Wide Mount Mirrors (ST 4WD Quad Cab)	NC	NC
	*REQUIRES 2*G or 26H. NOT AVAILABLE with GPD.*		
GPC	Wide Mount 7"x10" Dual Bright Mirrors (ST Except 4WD Quad Cab)	43	50
	*NOT AVAILABLE with GPD, 21A, 22A, 2*G, 26H, EHC.*		
GPC	Wide Mount 7"x10" Dual Bright Mirrors (ST Except 4WD Quad Cab)	NC	NC
	*REQUIRES 2*G or 26H. NOT AVAILABLE with GPD.*		
GTS	Power Heated Foldaway Mirrors (Quad Cab)	123	145
	*REQUIRES HAA and 2*A. NOT AVAILABLE with GPC, GPD.*		
GTS	Power Heated Foldaway Mirrors (ST Except Quad Cab)	123	145
	*REQUIRES HAA and 2*A. NOT AVAILABLE with GPC, GPD, 4XA.*		
GXM	Remote Keyless Entry (ST)	162	190
	*NOT AVAILABLE with 26H or 2*A.*		
HAA	Air Conditioning	684	805
	*NOT AVAILABLE with 4XA. INCLUDED in 2*G, 26H.*		
JPS	6-Way Power Driver's Seat (ST Reg Cab)	272	320
	*REQUIRES 2*G or 26H. NOT AVAILABLE with AGG, D3.*		
JPV	8-Way Power Driver's Seat (Club/Quad Cab)	306	360
	*REQUIRES 2*G. NOT AVAILABLE with 26H.*		
K17	Stripe/Badge/Molding (ST)	89	105
	*REQUIRES 2*A.*		
LNJ	Fog Lamps (ST)	119	140
	*REQUIRES 2*G. NOT AVAILABLE with 26H.*		
LPE	Cargo Lamp (WS)	34	40
LSA	Security Alarm	128	150
	*REQUIRES 2*G, GXM and AWK. NOT AVAILABLE with 26H.*		
MBD	Rear Argent Bumper (WS)	115	135
	NOT AVAILABLE with 4XM.		
NHK	Engine Block Heater	77	90
NMC	HD Engine Cooling (ST)	111	130
	Includes auxiliary transmission oil cooler. NOT AVAILABLE with 23A, 21A, 22A, DDC, ADJ, 23G.		
NMC	HD Engine Cooling (ST)	60	70
	NOT AVAILABLE with 21A, 22A, 24A, 26A, DGB, ADJ, 24G, 26G, 26H.		
RAS	Radio: AM/FM Stereo with Cassette (WS)	340	400
RAZ	Radio: AM/FM Stereo with CD, Cassette and Equalizer (Quad Cab)	587	690
	*REQUIRES 2*G. NOT AVAILABLE with RBN, RBR, 26H.*		

CODE	DESCRIPTION	INVOICE	MSRP
RAZ	Radio: AM/FM Stereo w/CD, Cass. and EQ (ST Reg Cab/4WD Club Cab) *REQUIRES 2*G or 26H. NOT AVAILABLE with RBN, RBR.*	587	690
RAZ	Radio: AM/FM Stereo with Cassette, CD and Equalizer (2WD Club Cab) *REQUIRES 2*G or 26H. NOT AVAILABLE with RBN, RBR.*	587	690
RBN	Radio: AM/FM Stereo with Cassette and Changer Control (Quad Cab) *REQUIRES 2*G. NOT AVAILABLE with RAZ, RBR, RDZ, 26H.*	285	335
RBN	Radio: AM/FM Stereo with Cass. and Chgr. Control (ST 2WD Club Cab) *REQUIRES 2*G or 26H. NOT AVAILABLE with RAZ, RBR, RDZ.*	285	335
RBN	Radio: AM/FM Stereo with Cass. and Chgr. Control (ST Reg Cab/X-Cab) *REQUIRES 2*G or 26H. NOT AVAILABLE with RAZ, RBR, RDZ.*	285	335
RBR	Radio: AM/FM Stereo with CD (2WD Club Cab/4WD Quad Cab) *REQUIRES 2*G. NOT AVAILABLE with RBN, RAZ, RDZ, 26H.*	434	510
RBR	Radio: AM/FM Stereo with CD (2WD Quad Cab) *REQUIRES 2*G. NOT AVAILABLE with RBN, RAZ, RDZ, 26H.*	434	510
RBR	Radio: AM/FM Stereo with CD (ST Reg Cab/4WD Club Cab) *REQUIRES 2*G or 26H. NOT AVAILABLE with RBN, RAZ, RDZ.*	434	510
RDZ	Steering Wheel Mounted Audio Controls (ST) *REQUIRES 2*G, RAZ and GXM. NOT AVAILABLE with RBN, RBR, 26H.*	64	75
S9	Deluxe Cloth 40/20/40 Split Bench Seat (ST) *REQUIRES 2*A. NOT AVAILABLE with D3, TY.*	94	110
TXW	Tires: P265/75R16 OWL AT (ST 4WD Reg Cab SB) *REQUIRES 2*G or 26H. NOT AVAILABLE with TYZ, AWL.*	353	415
TXW	Tires: P265/75R16 OWL On/Off Road (ST 4WD - Reg Cab LB/X-Cab) *REQUIRES 2*G. NOT AVAILABLE with TYZ, AWL, 26H.*	353	415
TY	HD Vinyl 40/20/40 Front Bench Seat (Quad Cab) *NOT AVAILABLE with S9.*	NC	NC
TYU	Tires: P245/75R16 BSW AS (ST 2WD/4WD Except Quad Cab) *NOT AVAILABLE with AYB, TYX. INCLUDED in 23G, 24G, 26G, 26H.*	111	130
TYV	Tires: P245/75R16 AS OWL (ST 2WD Reg Cab) *REQUIRES 2*G or 26H.*	111	130
TYV	Tires: P245/75R16 OWL AS (ST 2WD Club/Quad Cab) *REQUIRES 2*G. NOT AVAILABLE with 26H.*	111	130
TYX	Tires: P245/75R16 BSW AT (ST 4WD Club Cab) *REQUIRES 2*A. NOT AVAILABLE with AYB.*	128	150
TYX	Tires: P245/75R16 BSW On/Off Road (4WD Quad Cab) *REQUIRES 2*A. NOT AVAILABLE with AYB.*	128	150
TYX	Tires: P245/75R16 BSW On/Off Road (4WD Reg Cab) *REQUIRES 2*A. NOT AVAILABLE with AYB.*	238	280
TYZ	Tires: P245/75R16 OWL AT (4WD - Reg Cab SB/Club Cab) *REQUIRES 2*G or 26H. NOT AVAILABLE with TXW, AGG, AWL.*	234	275
TYZ	Tires: P245/75R16 OWL On/Off Road (4WD - Reg Cab LB/X-Cab) *REQUIRES 2*G. NOT AVAILABLE with TXW, AGG, 26H, AWL.*	234	275
WDB	Wheels: 16" x 7" Chrome (ST) *REQUIRES 2*A.*	293	345
WDB	Wheels: 16" x 7" Chrome (ST) *REQUIRES 2*G. NOT AVAILABLE with AGG, 26H, AWL.*	NC	NC

2001 RAM 2500

Standard Equipment

ST 2WD REGULAR CAB LB (5M): 5.9L V8 OHV SMPI 16-valve engine; 5-speed OD manual transmission; 600-amp battery; 117-amp alternator; rear-wheel drive, power take-off provision, 3.54 axle ratio; stainless steel exhaust; front independent suspension with anti-roll bar, front coil springs, HD front shocks, rigid rear axle suspension with rear leaf springs, HD rear shocks; power re-circulating ball steering with vehicle speed-sensing assist; front disc/rear drum brakes with rear wheel antilock braking system; 35 gal. capacity fuel tank; side impact bars; front and rear chrome bumpers with black rub strip, rear step; monotone paint; aero-composite halogen headlamps; additional exterior lights include pickup cargo box light, underhood light; driver's and passenger's manual black folding outside mirrors; front and rear 16" x 7.5" silver styled steel wheels; LT245/75SR16 A/S BSW front and rear tires; underbody mounted full-size steel spare wheel with crankdown; AM/FM stereo, clock, seek-scan, cassette, 4 speakers, and fixed antenna; 2 power accessory outlets, smokers' package; instrumentation display includes tachometer, oil pressure gauge, water temperature gauge, volt gauge, trip odometer; warning indicators include low oil level, lights on, key in ignition, low fuel; driver's front airbag, passenger's cancelable front airbag; tinted windows; variable intermittent front windshield wipers, sun visor strip; seating capacity of 3, 40-20-40 split-bench front seat, fixed headrests, center armrest with storage, driver's seat includes 4-way direction control, passenger's seat includes 4-way direction control; front height adjustable seatbelts; vinyl seats, full cloth headliner, full vinyl floor covering, cabback insulator; interior lights include dome light; day/night rearview mirror; glove box, front cupholder, instrument panel bin; cargo concealed storage; chrome grille, black side window moldings, black front windshield molding, black rear window molding and black door handles.

ST 2WD QUAD CAB SB/LB (5M) (in addition to or instead of SL 2WD REGULAR CAB LB (5M) equipment): 34 gal. SB/35 gal. - LB capacity fuel tank; warning indicators include low washer fluid; deep tinted windows, vented rear windows; seating capacity of 6, driver's seat includes 4-way direction control, easy entry, passenger's seat includes 4-way direction control, easy entry and full folding rear bench seat.

4WD (5M) (in addition to or instead of 2WD (5M) equipment): Part-time 4-wheel drive, auto locking hub control and manual shift and front non-independent suspension with anti-roll bar.

Base Prices

BR2L62	ST 2WD Regular Cab LB (5M)	17709	20240
BE2L33	ST 2WD Quad Cab SB (5M)	19259	22005
BE2L34	ST 2WD Quad Cab LB (5M)	19421	22195
BR7L62	ST 4WD Regular Cab LB (5M)	20398	23345
BE7L33	ST 4WD Quad Cab SB (5M)	22043	25250
BE7L34	ST 4WD Quad Cab LB (5M)	22204	25440
Destination Charge:		650	650

Accessories

25A	Quick Order Package 25A *Includes 3.54 axle ratio. REQUIRES 4XA and EML and DDP. NOT AVAILABLE with DGB, DDX, EWA, ETC, DEE.*	NC	NC

CODE	DESCRIPTION	INVOICE	MSRP
25G	**Quick Order Package 25G**	2559	3010
	Manufacturer Discount	(595)	(700)
	Net Price	1964	2310
	Includes SLT Decor group: black tailgate applique, carpeted floor covering, floor mats, hood insulation, passenger's side vanity mirror, power heated fold-away outside mirrors, bodyside molding, premium cloth 40/20/40 front bench seat, front bumper sight shield and leather-wrapped steering wheel; air conditioning, woodgrain instrument panel bezel, convenience group: speed control, tilt steering column; light group: mini overhead console, glove box lamp, map/courtesy lamp; power door locks and power windows with driver's one touch down. REQUIRES EML and DDP. NOT AVAILABLE with EWA, ETC, DDX, DGB, DEE, ATK, AGG.		
25H	**Quick Order Package 25H (Quad Cab)**	4135	4865
	Manufacturer Discount	(595)	(700)
	Net Price	3540	4165
	Includes SLT Decor group: black tailgate applique, carpeted floor covering, floor mats, hood insulation, passenger's side vanity mirror, power heated fold-away outside mirrors, bodyside molding, leather 40/20/40 heated front bench seat with power adjustments, front bumper sight shield and leather-wrapped steering wheel; air conditioning, woodgrain instrument panel bezel, convenience group: speed control, tilt steering column; light group: mini overhead console, glove box lamp, map/courtesy lamp; power door locks and power windows with driver's one touch down. REQUIRES EML and DDP and ATK. NOT AVAILABLE with DGB, DDX, DEE, EWA, ETC, JPV, AJD, CKJ, RBR, RAZ, RBN, AGG, RDZ, BGK, LNJ, GXM, LSA, CUE, AWK, AHD.		
26A	**Quick Order Package 26A**	NC	NC
	Includes 3.54 axle ratio. REQUIRES 4XA and EML and DGB. NOT AVAILABLE with EWA, ETC, DDP, DDX, DEE.		
26G	**Quick Order Package 26G**	2559	3010
	Manufacturer Discount	(595)	(700)
	Net Price	1964	2310
	Includes SLT Decor group: black tailgate applique, carpeted floor covering, floor mats, hood insulation, passenger's side vanity mirror, power heated fold-away outside mirrors, bodyside molding, premium cloth 40/20/40 front bench seat, front bumper sight shield and leather-wrapped steering wheel; air conditioning, woodgrain instrument panel bezel, convenience group: speed control, tilt steering column; light group: mini overhead console, glove box lamp, map/courtesy lamp; power door locks and power windows with driver's one touch down. REQUIRES EML and DGB. NOT AVAILABLE with EWA, ETC, DDP, DDX, DEE, ATK, AGG.		
26H	**Quick Order Package 26H (Quad Cab)**	4135	4865
	Manufacturer Discount	(595)	(700)
	Net Price	3540	4165
	Includes SLT Decor group: black tailgate applique, carpeted floor covering, floor mats, hood insulation, passenger's side vanity mirror, power heated fold-away outside mirrors, bodyside molding, leather 40/20/40 heated front bench seat with power adjustments, front bumper sight shield and leather-wrapped steering wheel; air conditioning, woodgrain instrument panel bezel, convenience group: speed control, tilt steering column; light group: mini overhead console, glove box lamp, map/courtesy lamp; power door locks and power windows with driver's one touch down.		

CODE	DESCRIPTION	INVOICE	MSRP
	REQUIRES EML and DGB and ATK. NOT AVAILABLE with DDP, DDX, DEE, ETC, EWA, JPV, AJD, CKJ, RBR, RAZ, RBN, AGG, RDZ, BGK, LNJ, GXM, LSA, CUE, AWK, AHD.		
27A	Quick Order Package 27A	NC	NC
	Includes 3.54 axle ratio. REQUIRES 4XA and DDX. NOT AVAILABLE with EML, ETC, DDP, DGB, DEE.		
27G	Quick Order Package 27G	2559	3010
	Manufacturer Discount	(595)	(700)
	Net Price	1964	2310
	Includes SLT Decor group: black tailgate applique, carpeted floor covering, floor mats, hood insulation, passenger's side vanity mirror, power heated fold-away outside mirrors, bodyside molding, premium cloth 40/20/40 front bench seat, front bumper sight shield and leather-wrapped steering wheel; air conditioning, woodgrain instrument panel bezel, convenience group: speed control, tilt steering column; light group: mini overhead console, glove box lamp, map/courtesy lamp; power door locks and power windows with driver's one touch down. REQUIRES DDX. NOT AVAILABLE with EML, ETC, DDP, DGB, DEE, ATK, AGG.		
27H	Quick Order Package 27H (Quad Cab)	4135	4865
	Manufacturer Discount	(595)	(700)
	Net Price	3540	4165
	Includes SLT Decor group: black tailgate applique, carpeted floor covering, floor mats, hood insulation, passenger's side vanity mirror, power heated fold-away outside mirrors, bodyside molding, leather 40/20/40 heated front bench seat with power adjustments, front bumper sight shield and leather-wrapped steering wheel; air conditioning, woodgrain instrument panel bezel, convenience group: speed control, tilt steering column; light group: mini overhead console, glove box lamp, map/courtesy lamp; power door locks and power windows with driver's one touch down. REQUIRES DDX and ATK. NOT AVAILABLE with DDP, DGB, DEE, EML, ETC, JPV, AJD, CKJ, RBR, RAZ, RBN, AGG, RDZ, BGK, LNJ, GXM, LSA, CUE, AWK, AHD.		
28A	Quick Order Package 28A	NC	NC
	Includes 3.54 axle ratio. REQUIRES 4XA and DGB. NOT AVAILABLE with EML, ETC, DDP, DDX, DEE, DMF.		
28G	Quick Order Package 28G	2559	3010
	Manufacturer Discount	(595)	(700)
	Net Price	1964	2310
	Includes SLT Decor group: black tailgate applique, carpeted floor covering, floor mats, hood insulation, passenger's side vanity mirror, power heated fold-away outside mirrors, bodyside molding, premium cloth 40/20/40 front bench seat, front bumper sight shield and leather-wrapped steering wheel; air conditioning, woodgrain instrument panel bezel, convenience group: speed control, tilt steering column; light group: mini overhead console, glove box lamp, map/courtesy lamp; power door locks and power windows with driver's one touch down. REQUIRES DGB. NOT AVAILABLE with EML, ETC, DDP, DDX, DEE, DMF, ATK, AGG.		
28H	Quick Order Package 28H (Quad Cab)	4135	4865
	Manufacturer Discount	(595)	(700)
	Net Price	3540	4165
	Includes SLT Decor group: black tailgate applique, carpeted floor covering, floor mats, hood insulation, passenger's side vanity mirror, power heated fold-away outside		

CODE	DESCRIPTION	INVOICE	MSRP
	mirrors, bodyside molding, leather 40/20/40 heated front bench seat with power adjustments, front bumper sight shield and leather-wrapped steering wheel; air conditioning, woodgrain instrument panel bezel, convenience group: speed control, tilt steering column; light group: mini overhead console, glove box lamp, map/courtesy lamp; power door locks and power windows with driver's one touch down. REQUIRES DGB and ATK. NOT AVAILABLE with DDP, DDX, DEE, EML, ETC, JPV, AJD, CKJ, RBR, RAZ, RBN, AGG, RDZ, BGK, LNJ, GXM, LSA, CUE, AWK, AHD.		
2CA	**Quick Order Package 2CA**	NC	NC
	Includes 3.54 axle ratio. REQUIRES 4XA and DGB or AHC. NOT AVAILABLE with EML, EWA, DDP, DDX, DEE, AHD.		
2CG	**Quick Order Package 2CG**	2559	3010
	Manufacturer Discount	(595)	(700)
	Net Price	1964	2310
	Includes SLT Decor group: black tailgate applique, carpeted floor covering, floor mats, hood insulation, passenger's side vanity mirror, power heated fold-away outside mirrors, bodyside molding, premium cloth 40/20/40 front bench seat, front bumper sight shield and leather-wrapped steering wheel; air conditioning, woodgrain instrument panel bezel, convenience group: speed control, tilt steering column; light group: mini overhead console, glove box lamp, map/courtesy lamp; power door locks and power windows with driver's one touch down. REQUIRES DGB or AHC. NOT AVAILABLE with DDX, DDP, EML, EWA, DEE, ATK, AGG, AHD.		
2CH	**Quick Order Package 2CH (Quad Cab)**	4135	4865
	Manufacturer Discount	(595)	(700)
	Net Price	3540	4165
	Includes SLT Decor group: black tailgate applique, carpeted floor covering, floor mats, hood insulation, passenger's side vanity mirror, power heated fold-away outside mirrors, bodyside molding, leather 40/20/40 heated front bench seat with power adjustments, front bumper sight shield and leather-wrapped steering wheel; air conditioning, woodgrain instrument panel bezel, convenience group: speed control, tilt steering column; light group: mini overhead console, glove box lamp, map/courtesy lamp; power door locks and power windows with driver's one touch down. REQUIRES DGB and ATK or AHC. NOT AVAILABLE with DDP, DDX, DEE, EML, EWA, JPV, AJD, CKJ, RBR, RAZ, RBN, AGG, RDZ, BGK, LNJ, GXM, LSA, CUE, AWK, AHD.		
2GA	**Quick Order Package 2GA**	NC	NC
	Includes 3.54 axle ratio. REQUIRES 4XA and DDX or AHC. NOT AVAILABLE with EML, EWA, DDP, DGB, DEE, AHD.		
2GG	**Quick Order Package 2GG**	2559	3010
	Manufacturer Discount	(595)	(700)
	Net Price	1964	2310
	Includes SLT Decor group: black tailgate applique, carpeted floor covering, floor mats, hood insulation, passenger's side vanity mirror, power heated fold-away outside mirrors, bodyside molding, premium cloth 40/20/40 front bench seat, front bumper sight shield and leather-wrapped steering wheel; air conditioning, woodgrain instrument panel bezel, convenience group: speed control, tilt steering column; light group: mini overhead console, glove box lamp, map/courtesy lamp; power door locks and power windows with driver's one touch down. REQUIRES DDX or AHC. NOT AVAILABLE with EML, EWA, DDP, DGB, DEE, ATK, AGG, AHD.		

CODE	DESCRIPTION	INVOICE	MSRP
2GH	Quick Order Package 2GH (Quad Cab)	4135	4865
	Manufacturer Discount	(595)	(700)
	Net Price	3540	4165
	Includes SLT Decor group: black tailgate applique, carpeted floor covering, floor mats, hood insulation, passenger's side vanity mirror, power heated fold-away outside mirrors, bodyside molding, leather 40/20/40 heated front bench seat with power adjustments, front bumper sight shield and leather-wrapped steering wheel; air conditioning, woodgrain instrument panel bezel, convenience group: speed control, tilt steering column; light group: mini overhead console, glove box lamp, map/courtesy lamp; power door locks and power windows with driver's one touch down. REQUIRES DDX and ATK or AHC. NOT AVAILABLE with DDP, DEE, DGB, EML, EWA, JPV, AJD, CKJ, RBR, RAZ, RBN, AGG, RDZ, BGK, LNJ, GXM, LSA, CUE, AWK, AHD.		
2HA	Quick Order Package 2HA	NC	NC
	Includes 3.54 axle ratio. REQUIRES 4XA and DEE. NOT AVAILABLE with EML, EWA, DDP, DGB, DDX, AHD.		
2HG	Quick Order Package 2HG	2559	3010
	Manufacturer Discount	(595)	(700)
	Net Price	1964	2310
	Includes SLT Decor group: black tailgate applique, carpeted floor covering, floor mats, hood insulation, passenger's side vanity mirror, power heated fold-away outside mirrors, bodyside molding, premium cloth 40/20/40 front bench seat, front bumper sight shield and leather-wrapped steering wheel; air conditioning, woodgrain instrument panel bezel, convenience group: speed control, tilt steering column; light group: mini overhead console, glove box lamp, map/courtesy lamp; power door locks and power windows with driver's one touch down. REQUIRES DEE. NOT AVAILABLE with EML, EWA, DDP, DGB, DDX, ATK, AGG, AHD.		
2HH	Quick Order Package 2HH (Quad Cab)	4135	4865
	Manufacturer Discount	(595)	(700)
	Net Price	3540	4165
	Includes SLT Decor group: black tailgate applique, carpeted floor covering, floor mats, hood insulation, passenger's side vanity mirror, power heated fold-away outside mirrors, bodyside molding, leather 40/20/40 heated front bench seat with power adjustments, front bumper sight shield and leather-wrapped steering wheel; air conditioning, woodgrain instrument panel bezel, convenience group: speed control, tilt steering column; light group: mini overhead console, glove box lamp, map/courtesy lamp; power door locks and power windows with driver's one touch down. REQUIRES DEE and ATK. NOT AVAILABLE with DDP, DDX, DGB, EML, EWA, JPV, AJD, CKJ, RBR, RAZ, RBN, AGG, RDZ, BGK, LNJ, GXM, LSA, CUE, AWK, AHD.		
4XA	Air Conditioning Bypass	NC	NC
	*REQUIRES 2*A.*		
ADA	Light Group	77	90
	*Includes passenger assist handles, deluxe headliner, mini overhead console, glove box lamp and map/courtesy lamp. INCLUDED in 2*G, 2*H.*		
ADJ	HD Service Group (Reg Cab)	NC	NC
	Includes 136-amp alternator, dual 750-amp batteries and HD engine cooling. NOT AVAILABLE with 25A, 26A, 27A, 28A, NMC, EWA, ETC, EML, 25G, 26G, 27G, 28G.		

CODE	DESCRIPTION	INVOICE	MSRP
ADJ	**HD Service Group** *Includes 136-amp alternator, 750-amp maintenance free battery, HD engine cooling and transfer case skid plate shield. NOT AVAILABLE with 26A, 27A, 28A, 2GA, 2CA, ETC, EWA, 2HA, 26G, 27G, 28G, 2GG, 2CG, 2HG, NMC, DGB.*	281	330
ADJ	**HD Service Group** *Includes 136-amp alternator, 750-amp maintenance free battery, HD engine cooling, auxiliary transmission oil cooler and transfer case skid plate shield. NOT AVAILABLE with 25A, 27A, 28A, 2GA, 2CA, ETC, EWA, 2HA, 25G, 27G, 28G, 2GG, 2CG, 2HG, NMC, DDP, DDX, DEE.*	332	390
ADJ	**HD Service Group** *Includes 750-amp maintenance free battery and HD engine cooling. NOT AVAILABLE with 26A, 28A, 2CA, 2GA, 2HA, NMC, ETC; EWA, 26G, 28G, 2CG, 2GG, 2HG, DGB.*	242	285
ADJ	**HD Service Group** *Includes 750-amp maintenance free battery, HD engine cooling and auxiliary transmission oil cooler. NOT AVAILABLE with 25A, 27A, 2CA, 2GA, 2HA, NMC, ETC, EWA, 25G, 27G, 2CG, 2GG, 2HG, DDP, DDX, DEE.*	293	345
AGG	**Sport Appearance Group (Quad Cab)** *Includes sport badge, front body color bumper, rear body color bumper, body color grille, fog lamps, quad halogen headlamps, bodyside moldings delete, tires: LT265/75R16E BSW AS and wheels: 16" x 8" forged aluminum. REQUIRES 2*H. NOT AVAILABLE with APD, MXB, 2*A, 2*G, AHD.*	200	235
AGG	**Sport Appearance Group** *Includes sport badge, front body color bumper, rear body color bumper, body color grille, fog lamps, quad halogen headlamps, bodyside moldings delete, tires: LT265/75R16E BSW AS and wheels: 16" x 8" forged aluminum. REQUIRES 2*G. NOT AVAILABLE with APD, MXB, 2*A, 2*H, TXG, AHD, ATK.*	319	375
AHC	**Trailer Tow Group** *Includes HD flasher and platform hitch receiver (class IV). REQUIRES 27A or 28A or 2CA or 2GA or 2HA or 2GG or 27G or 28G or 2CG or 2HG.*	234	275
AHD	**HD Snow Plow Prep Group (4WD)**	157	185
	Manufacturer Discount	(72)	(85)
	Net Price *Includes computer selected springs and auto transmission oil overheat light. Front clearance lights (LNC) and I.D. lights are recommended. REQUIRES AHC. NOT AVAILABLE with 2GA, 2CA, 2HA, 2GG, 2CG, 2HG, AGG, 2CH, 25H, 26H, 27H, 28H, 2GH, 2HH.*	85	100
AHJ	**Camper Special Group** *Includes stabilizer bar and auxiliary springs. REQUIRES NMC.*	81	95
AJD	**Leather Interior Group (Quad Cab)** *Includes woodgrain instrument panel bezel, leather 40/20/40 split bench seat, power front seats, 8-way power driver's seat, travel convenience group: overhead console with trip computer, auto dimming rear view mirror and illuminated visor vanity mirrors. NOT AVAILABLE with 2*A, 2*H.*	1352	1590
AJD	**Leather Interior Group (Reg Cab)** *Includes woodgrain instrument panel bezel, leather 40/20/40 split bench seat, power front seats, 8-way power driver's seat, travel convenience group: overhead*	1233	1450

CODE	DESCRIPTION	INVOICE	MSRP
	*console with trip computer, auto dimming rear view mirror and illuminated visor vanity mirrors. REQUIRES 2*G.*		
AJK	Convenience Group	332	390
	*Includes speed control and tilt steering column. INCLUDED in 2*G, 2*H.*		
APD	Two Tone Lower Paint	191	225
	NOT AVAILABLE with AGG.		
ATK	SLT Plus Decor Group (Quad Cab)	1836	2160
	*Includes steering wheel mounted audio controls, 4-wheel antilock brakes, fog lamps, travel convenience group: overhead console with trip computer, illuminated visor vanity mirrors and auto dimming rearview mirror; remote keyless entry, AM/FM stereo with CD, cassette and equalizer, 6 Infinity speakers, security alarm and rear underseat compartment storage. REQUIRES 2*H. NOT AVAILABLE with 2*A or 2*G.*		
AWK	Travel Convenience Group	293	345
	*Includes overhead console with trip computer, auto dimming rearview mirror and illuminated visor vanity mirrors. REQUIRES 2*G. NOT AVAILABLE with 2*H.*		
BGK	4-Wheel Antilock Brakes	421	495
	*INCLUDED with 2*H.*		
CF8	Rear Seat Delete (Quad Cab)	NC	NC
	*REQUIRES 2*A.*		
CKE	Carpet Floor Covering	94	110
	*REQUIRES 2*A.*		
CKJ	Black Vinyl Floor Covering	NC	NC
	*REQUIRES 2*G. NOT AVAILABLE with CUE, 2*H.*		
CUE	Rear Underseat Compartment Storage (Quad Cab)	64	75
	*REQUIRES 2*G. NOT AVAILABLE with CKJ, 2*A. INCLUDED with 2*H.*		
DDP	Transmission: 5-Speed Manual	NC	NC
	NOT AVAILABLE with EWA, ETC, 26A, 27A, 28A, 2GA, 2CA, 26G, 27G, 28G, 2GG, 2CG, 2HA, 2HG, 26H, 27H, 28H, 2CH, 2GH, 2HH.		
DDX	Transmission: HD 5-Speed Manual	NC	NC
	NOT AVAILABLE with 25A, 26A, 28A, 2CA, 25G, 26G, 28G, 2CG, EML, 2HG, 2HA, 25H, 26H, 28H, 2HH, 2CH.		
DEE	Transmission: HD 6-Speed Manual	340	400
	NOT AVAILABLE with 25A, 25G, 26A, 26G, 27A, 27G, 28A, 28G, 2CA, 2CG, 2GA, 2GG, EWA, EML, 25H, 26H, 27H, 28H, 2GH, 2CH.		
DGB	Transmission: 4-Speed Automatic	829	975
	NOT AVAILABLE with 25A, 27A, 2GA, 25G, 27G, 2GG, 2HA, 2HG, NMC, 25H, 27H, 2GH, 2HH.		
DHG	Shift-On-The-Fly Transfer Case (4WD)	85	100
DMF	4.10 Axle Ratio	43	50
	REQUIRES DSA. NOT AVAILABLE with 28A, 28G.		
DSA	Anti-Spin Differential Axle	242	285
	REQUIRES ((25A or 26A) and DMF) or (27A or 28A or 2GA or 2CA or 2HA or 25G or 26G or 27G or 28G or 2GG or 2CG or 2HG).		
EML	Engine: 5.9L SMPI V8 Magnum	NC	NC
	NOT AVAILABLE with DDX, 27A, 28A, 2GA, 2CA, DEE, 2HA, 27G, 28G, 2GG, 2CG, 2HG, 27H, 28H, 2CH, 2GH, 2HH.		

CODE	DESCRIPTION	INVOICE	MSRP
ETC	Engine: 5.9L Cummins 24V Diesel *Includes EVAP control system delete, heavy duty insulation group with hood insulation and warning lights for low fuel, low oil, water in fuel, wait to start, brakes, antilock brakes and engine block heater. REQUIRES AHC. NOT AVAILABLE with 25A, 26A, 27A, 28A, DDP, NMC, 25G, 26G, 27G, 28G, 28H, 27H, 26H, 25H.*	3931	4625
EWA	Engine: 8.0L MPI V10 Magnum *Includes EVAP control system. NOT AVAILABLE with DDP, 25A, 26A, 2GA, 2CA, DEE, 2HA, NMC, 25G, 26G, 2GG, 2CG, 2HG, 25H, 26H, 2HH, 2GH, 2CH.*	400	470
GFD	Sliding Rear Window	119	140
GPC	Wide Mount 7" x 10" Dual Bright Mirrors *REQUIRES 2*A. NOT AVAILABLE with GPD, 2*G, 2*H.*	43	50
GPC	Wide Mount 7" x 10" Dual Bright Mirrors *REQUIRES 2*G or 2*H. NOT AVAILABLE with GPD, 2*A.*	NC	NC
GTS	Power Heated Fold-Away Mirrors (Quad Cab) *REQUIRES 2*A. NOT AVAILABLE with GPC, 4XA, GPD. INCLUDED in 2*G, 2*H.*	123	145
GTS	Power Heated Fold-Away Mirrors (Reg Cab) *REQUIRES 2*A. NOT AVAILABLE with GPC, GPD. INCLUDED in 2*G.*	123	145
GXM	Remote Keyless Entry *REQUIRES 2*G. NOT AVAILABLE with 2*A. INCLUDED in 2*H.*	162	190
HAA	Air Conditioning *REQUIRES 2*A. NOT AVAILABLE with 4XA. INCLUDED in 2*G, 2*H.*	684	805
JPS	6-Way Power Driver's Seat (Reg Cab) *REQUIRES 2*G. NOT AVAILABLE with 2*A.*	272	320
JPV	8-Way Power Driver's Seat (Quad Cab) *REQUIRES 2*G. NOT AVAILABLE with 2*A. INCLUDED in 2*H.*	306	360
K17	Stripe/Badge/Molding *REQUIRES 2*A. INCLUDED in 2*G, 2*H.*	89	105
LNC	Clearance Lamps	68	80
LNJ	Fog Lamps *REQUIRES 2*G. NOT AVAILABLE with 2*A. INCLUDED in 2*H.*	119	140
LSA	Security Alarm *REQUIRES 2*G, GXM and AWK. NOT AVAILABLE with 2*A. INCLUDED in 2*H.*	128	150
MXB	Front Air Dam *NOT AVAILABLE with AGG.*	21	25
NHK	Engine Block Heater	77	90
NMC	HD Engine Cooling *Includes auxiliary transmission oil cooler. NOT AVAILABLE with EWA, ETC, DDP, DDX, DEE.*	111	130
NMC	HD Engine Cooling *NOT AVAILABLE with DGB, EWA, ETC.*	60	70
RAZ	Radio: AM/FM Stereo with CD, Cassette and Equalizer (Quad Cab) *REQUIRES 2*G. NOT AVAILABLE with RBN, RBR, 2*A. INCLUDED in 2*H.*	587	690
RAZ	Radio: AM/FM Stereo with CD, Cassette and Equalizer (Reg Cab) *REQUIRES 2*G. NOT AVAILABLE with RBN, RBR, 2*A.*	587	690
RBN	Radio: AM/FM Stereo with Cassette and CD Changer Control (Quad Cab) *REQUIRES 2*G. NOT AVAILABLE with RAZ, RBR, RDZ, 2*A. INCLUDED in 2*H.*	285	335

CODE	DESCRIPTION	INVOICE	MSRP
RBN	Radio: AM/FM Stereo with Cassette and CD Changer Control (Reg Cab) *REQUIRES 2*G. NOT AVAILABLE with RAZ, RBR, RDZ, 2*A.*	285	335
RBR	Radio: AM/FM Stereo with CD (Quad Cab) *REQUIRES 2*G. NOT AVAILABLE with RBN, RAZ, RDZ, 2*H, 2*A.*	434	510
RBR	Radio: AM/FM Stereo with CD (Reg Cab) *REQUIRES 2*G. NOT AVAILABLE with RBN, RAZ, RDZ, 2*A.*	434	510
RDZ	Steering Wheel Mounted Audio Controls *REQUIRES 2*G, RAZ and GXM. NOT AVAILABLE with RBN, RBR, 2*A. INCLUDED in 2*H.*	64	75
S9	Deluxe Cloth 40/20/40 Split Bench Seat *REQUIRES 2*A. NOT AVAILABLE with TY, 2*H. INCLUDED in 2*G.*	94	110
TXF	Tires: LT265/75R16E AS BSW (4WD) *NOT AVAILABLE with TXG. INCLUDED in 2*G, 2*H.*	119	140
TXG	Tires: LT265/75R16E AT OWL (Quad Cab) *REQUIRES 2*G or 2*H. NOT AVAILABLE with 2*A.*	234	275
TXG	Tires: LT265/75R16E OWL On/Off Road (Reg Cab) *REQUIRES 2*G. NOT AVAILABLE with AGG 2*A.*	234	275
TXG	Tires: LT265/75R16E OWL On/Off Road (Reg Cab 4WD) *REQUIRES 2*A. NOT AVAILABLE with TXF, 2*G.*	353	415
TY	HD Vinyl 40/20/40 Front Bench Seat (Quad Cab) *REQUIRES 2*A. NOT AVAILABLE with S9, 2*G, 2*H.*	NC	NC

2001 RAM 3500

Standard Equipment

ST 2WD REGULAR CAB DRW LB (5M): 5.9L V8 OHV SMPI 16-valve engine; 5-speed OD manual transmission; 750-amp HD battery; HD radiator; 136-amp HD alternator; rear-wheel drive, power take-off provision, 3.54 axle ratio; stainless steel exhaust; front independent suspension with anti-roll bar, front coil springs, HD front shocks, rigid rear axle suspension with rear leaf springs, HD rear shocks; power re-circulating ball steering with vehicle speed-sensing assist; front disc/rear drum brakes with 4-wheel antilock braking system; 35 gal. capacity fuel tank; side impact bars; front and rear chrome bumpers with black rub strip, rear step; monotone paint; aero-composite halogen headlamps; additional exterior lights include cab clearance lights, pickup cargo box light; driver's and passenger's power remote black heated folding outside mirrors; front and rear 16" x 6" steel wheels; LT235/85SR16 A/S BSW front and rear tires; underbody mounted full-size steel spare wheel with crankdown; AM/FM stereo, clock, seek-scan, cassette, 4 speakers, and fixed antenna; 2 power accessory outlets; instrumentation display includes tachometer, oil pressure gauge, water temperature gauge, volt gauge, trip odometer; warning indicators include low oil level, lights on, key in ignition; driver's front airbag, passenger's cancelable front airbag; tinted windows; variable intermittent front windshield wipers, sun visor strip; seating capacity of 3, 40-20-40 split-bench front seat, fixed headrests, center armrest with storage, driver's seat includes 4-way direction control, passenger's seat includes 4-way direction control; front height adjustable seatbelts; vinyl seats, full cloth headliner, full vinyl floor covering, cabback insulator; interior lights include dome light; day/night rearview mirror; glove box, front cupholder, instrument panel bin, driver's and passenger's door bins; cargo concealed storage; chrome grille, black side window moldings, black front windshield molding, black rear window molding and black door handles.

ST 2WD QUAD CAB DRW LB (5M) (in addition to or instead of SLT 2WD REGULAR CAB DRW LB (5M) equipment): Additional exterior lights include underhood light; smokers' package; warning indicators include low washer fluid; deep tinted windows, vented rear windows; seating capacity of 6, driver's seat includes 4-way direction control, easy entry, passenger's seat includes 4-way direction control, easy entry and full folding rear bench seat.

4WD (5M) (in addition to or instead of 2WD (5M) equipment): Part-time 4- wheel drive, auto locking hub control and manual shift, power take-off provision; front non-independent suspension with anti-roll bar and skid plate(s)

Base Prices

Code	Description	Invoice	MSRP
BR3L62	ST 2WD Regular Cab DRW LB (5M)	19205	22000
BE3L34	ST 2WD Quad Cab DRW LB (5M)	21631	24795
BR8L62	ST 4WD Regular Cab DRW LB (5M)	21911	25125
BE8L34	ST 4WD Quad Cab DRW LB (5M)	24389	28010
Destination Charge:		650	650

Accessories

Code	Description	Invoice	MSRP
25A	Quick Order Package 25A	NC	NC
	Includes 3.54 axle ratio. REQUIRES EMM and DDP and (HAA or 4XA). NOT AVAILABLE with EML, ETC, EWA, DGB, DDX, DEE.		
25G	Quick Order Package 25G	2023	2380
	Manufacturer Discount	(595)	(700)
	Net Price	1428	1680
	Includes SLT Decor group: black tailgate applique, carpeted floor covering, floor mats, hood insulation, passenger's side vanity mirror, bodyside molding, premium cloth 40/20/40 front bench seat, front bumper sight shield and leather-wrapped steering wheel; air conditioning, woodgrain instrument panel bezel, convenience group: speed control, tilt steering column; light group: mini overhead console, glove box lamp, map/courtesy lamp; power door locks and power windows with driver's one touch down. REQUIRES EMM and DDP. NOT AVAILABLE with EML, ETC, EWA, DGB, DDX, DEE, ATK, AGG.		
25H	Quick Order Package 25H (Quad Cab)	3600	4235
	Manufacturer Discount	(595)	(700)
	Net Price	3005	3535
	Includes SLT Decor group: black tailgate applique, carpeted floor covering, floor mats, hood insulation, passenger's side vanity mirror, power heated fold-away outside mirrors, bodyside molding, leather 40/20/40 heated front bench seat with power adjustments, front bumper sight shield and leather-wrapped steering wheel; air conditioning, woodgrain instrument panel bezel, convenience group: speed control, tilt steering column; light group: mini overhead console, glove box lamp, map/courtesy lamp; power door locks and power windows with driver's one touch down. REQUIRES EMM and DDP and ATK. NOT AVAILABLE with DGB, DDX, DEE, EWA, ETC, JPV, AJD, CKJ, RBR, RAZ, LSA, RBN, EML, TST, RDZ, LNJ, GXM, AGG, CUE, AWK.		

CODE	DESCRIPTION	INVOICE	MSRP
26A	Quick Order Package 26A	NC	NC
	Includes 3.54 axle ratio. REQUIRES EMM and DGB and (HAA or 4XA). NOT AVAILABLE with EML, ETC, EWA, DDP, DDX, DEE.		
26G	Quick Order Package 26G	2023	2380
	Manufacturer Discount	(595)	(700)
	Net Price	1428	1680
	Includes SLT Decor group: black tailgate applique, carpeted floor covering, floor mats, hood insulation, passenger's side vanity mirror, bodyside molding, premium cloth 40/20/40 front bench seat, front bumper sight shield and leather-wrapped steering wheel; air conditioning, woodgrain instrument panel bezel, convenience group: speed control, tilt steering column; light group: mini overhead console, glove box lamp, map/courtesy lamp; power door locks and power windows with driver's one touch down. REQUIRES EMM and DGB. NOT AVAILABLE with EML, ETC, EWA, DDP, DDX, DEE, ATK, AGG.		
26H	Quick Order Package 26H (Quad Cab)	3600	4235
	Manufacturer Discount	(595)	(700)
	Net Price	3005	3535
	Includes SLT Decor group: black tailgate applique, carpeted floor covering, floor mats, hood insulation, passenger's side vanity mirror, power heated fold-away outside mirrors, bodyside molding, leather 40/20/40 heated front bench seat with power adjustments, front bumper sight shield and leather-wrapped steering wheel; air conditioning, woodgrain instrument panel bezel, convenience group: speed control, tilt steering column; light group: mini overhead console, glove box lamp, map/courtesy lamp; power door locks and power windows with driver's one touch down. REQUIRES EMM and DGB and ATK. NOT AVAILABLE with EWA, EML, ETC, DDP, DDX, DEE, JPV, AJD, CKJ, RBR, RBN, TST, RDZ, LNJ, GXM, RAZ, LSA, AGG, CUE, AWK.		
27A	Quick Order Package 27A	NC	NC
	Includes 3.54 axle ratio. REQUIRES EWA and DDX and (HAA or 4XA). NOT AVAILABLE with EMM, ETC, EML, DGB, DDP, DEE.		
27G	Quick Order Package 27G	2023	2380
	Manufacturer Discount	(595)	(700)
	Net Price	1428	1680
	Includes SLT Decor group: black tailgate applique, carpeted floor covering, floor mats, hood insulation, passenger's side vanity mirror, bodyside molding, premium cloth 40/20/40 front bench seat, front bumper sight shield and leather-wrapped steering wheel; air conditioning, woodgrain instrument panel bezel, convenience group: speed control, tilt steering column; light group: mini overhead console, glove box lamp, map/courtesy lamp; power door locks and power windows with driver's one touch down. REQUIRES EWA and DDX. NOT AVAILABLE with EMM, ETC, EML, DGB, DDP, DEE, ATK, AGG.		
27H	Quick Order Package 27H (Quad Cab)	3600	4235
	Manufacturer Discount	(595)	(700)
	Net Price	3005	3535
	Includes SLT Decor group: black tailgate applique, carpeted floor covering, floor mats, hood insulation, passenger's side vanity mirror, power heated fold-away outside mirrors, bodyside molding, leather 40/20/40 heated front bench seat with power		

CODE	DESCRIPTION	INVOICE	MSRP
	adjustments, front bumper sight shield and leather-wrapped steering wheel; air conditioning, woodgrain instrument panel bezel, convenience group: speed control, tilt steering column; light group: mini overhead console, glove box lamp, map/courtesy lamp; power door locks and power windows with driver's one touch down. REQUIRES EWA and DDX and ATK. NOT AVAILABLE with EML, EMM, ETC, DDP, DGB, DEE, JPV, AJD, CKJ, RBR, RAZ, RBN, TST, RDZ, LNJ, GXM, LSA, AGG, CUE, AWK.		
28A	**Quick Order Package 28A**	NC	NC
	Includes 3.54 axle ratio. REQUIRES EWA and DGB and (HAA or 4XA). NOT AVAILABLE with EMM, EML, ETC, DDP, DDX, DEE.		
28G	**Quick Order Package 28G**	2023	2380
	Manufacturer Discount	(595)	(700)
	Net Price	1428	1680
	Includes SLT Decor group: black tailgate applique, carpeted floor covering, floor mats, hood insulation, passenger's side vanity mirror, bodyside molding, premium cloth 40/20/40 front bench seat, front bumper sight shield and leather-wrapped steering wheel; air conditioning, woodgrain instrument panel bezel, convenience group: speed control, tilt steering column; light group: mini overhead console, glove box lamp, map/courtesy lamp; power door locks and power windows with driver's one touch down. REQUIRES EWA and DGB. NOT AVAILABLE with EMM, EML, ETC, DDP, DDX, DEE, ATK, AGG.		
28H	**Quick Order Package 28H (Quad Cab)**	3600	4235
	Manufacturer Discount	(595)	(700)
	Net Price	3005	3535
	Includes SLT Decor group: black tailgate applique, carpeted floor covering, floor mats, hood insulation, passenger's side vanity mirror, power heated fold-away outside mirrors, bodyside molding, leather 40/20/40 heated front bench seat with power adjustments, front bumper sight shield and leather-wrapped steering wheel; air conditioning, woodgrain instrument panel bezel, convenience group: speed control, tilt steering column; light group: mini overhead console, glove box lamp, map/courtesy lamp; power door locks and power windows with driver's one touch down. REQUIRES EWA and DGB and ATK. NOT AVAILABLE with EML, ETC, DDP, DDX, DEE, JPV, AJD, CKJ, RBR, RAZ, RBN, TST, RDZ, LNJ, GXM, LSA, AGG, CUE, AWK.		
2CA	**Quick Order Package 2CA**	NC	NC
	Includes 3.54 axle ratio. REQUIRES DGB and (HAA or 4XA). NOT AVAILABLE with EML, EMM, EWA, DDP, DDX, DEE, AHD.		
2CG	**Quick Order Package 2CG**	2023	2380
	Manufacturer Discount	(595)	(700)
	Net Price	1428	1680
	Includes SLT Decor group: black tailgate applique, carpeted floor covering, floor mats, hood insulation, passenger's side vanity mirror, bodyside molding, premium cloth 40/20/40 front bench seat, front bumper sight shield and leather-wrapped steering wheel; air conditioning, woodgrain instrument panel bezel, convenience group: speed control, tilt steering column; light group: mini overhead console, glove box lamp, map/courtesy lamp; power door locks and power windows with driver's one touch down. REQUIRES DGB. NOT AVAILABLE with EML, EMM, EWA, DDP, DDX, DEE, ATK, AGG, AHD.		

CODE	DESCRIPTION	INVOICE	MSRP
2CH	Quick Order Package 2CH (Quad Cab)	3600	4235
	Manufacturer Discount	(595)	(700)
	Net Price	3005	3535
	Includes SLT Decor group: black tailgate applique, carpeted floor covering, floor mats, hood insulation, passenger's side vanity mirror, power heated fold-away outside mirrors, bodyside molding, leather 40/20/40 heated front bench seat with power adjustments, front bumper sight shield and leather-wrapped steering wheel; air conditioning, woodgrain instrument panel bezel, convenience group: speed control, tilt steering column; light group: mini overhead console, glove box lamp, map/courtesy lamp; power door locks and power windows with driver's one touch down. REQUIRES ETC and DGB and ATK. NOT AVAILABLE with EML, EMM, EWA, DDP, DDX, DEE, CKJ, AJD, RBN, RAZ, RBR, TST, JPV, RDZ, LNJ, GXM, LSA, AGG, CUE, AWK, AHD.		
2EA	Quick Order Package 2EA	NC	NC
	Includes 3.54 axle ratio. REQUIRES EML and DDP and (HAA or 4XA). NOT AVAILABLE with EMM, ETC, EWA, DGB, DDX, DEE, AHD.		
2EG	Quick Order Package 2EG	2023	2380
	Manufacturer Discount	(595)	(700)
	Net Price	1428	1680
	Includes SLT Decor group: black tailgate applique, carpeted floor covering, floor mats, hood insulation, passenger's side vanity mirror, bodyside molding, premium cloth 40/20/40 front bench seat, front bumper sight shield and leather-wrapped steering wheel; air conditioning, woodgrain instrument panel bezel, convenience group: speed control, tilt steering column; light group: mini overhead console, glove box lamp, map/courtesy lamp; power door locks and power windows with driver's one touch down. REQUIRES EML and DDP. NOT AVAILABLE with EMM, ETC, EWA, DGB, DDX, DEE, AGG, ATK, AHD.		
2EH	Quick Order Package 2EH (Quad Cab)	3600	4235
	Manufacturer Discount	(595)	(700)
	Net Price	3005	3535
	Includes SLT Decor group: black tailgate applique, carpeted floor covering, floor mats, hood insulation, passenger's side vanity mirror, power heated fold-away outside mirrors, bodyside molding, leather 40/20/40 heated front bench seat with power adjustments, front bumper sight shield and leather-wrapped steering wheel; air conditioning, woodgrain instrument panel bezel, convenience group: speed control, tilt steering column; light group: mini overhead console, glove box lamp, map/courtesy lamp; power door locks and power windows with driver's one touch down. REQUIRES EML and DDP and ATK. NOT AVAILABLE with EMM, ETC, EWA, DGB, DDX, DEE, AJD, CKJ, JPV, RBN, RAZ, RBR, TST, RDZ, LNJ, GXM, LSA, AGG, CUE, AWK.		
2FA	Quick Order Package 2FA	NC	NC
	Includes 3.54 axle ratio. REQUIRES EML and DGB and (HAA or 4XA). NOT AVAILABLE with EMM, ETC, EWA, DDP, DDX, DEE, AHD.		

CODE	DESCRIPTION	INVOICE	MSRP
2FG	Quick Order Package 2FG	2023	2380
	Manufacturer Discount	(595)	(700)
	Net Price	1428	1680
	Includes SLT Decor group: black tailgate applique, carpeted floor covering, floor mats, hood insulation, passenger's side vanity mirror, bodyside molding, premium cloth 40/20/40 front bench seat, front bumper sight shield and leather-wrapped steering wheel; air conditioning, woodgrain instrument panel bezel, convenience group: speed control, tilt steering column; light group: mini overhead console, glove box lamp, map/courtesy lamp; power door locks and power windows with driver's one touch down. REQUIRES EML and DGB. NOT AVAILABLE with EMM, ETC, EWA, DDP, DDX, DEE, AGG, ATK, AHD.		
2FH	Quick Order Package 2FH (Quad Cab)	3600	4235
	Manufacturer Discount	(595)	(700)
	Net Price	3005	3535
	Includes SLT Decor group: black tailgate applique, carpeted floor covering, floor mats, hood insulation, passenger's side vanity mirror, power heated fold-away outside mirrors, bodyside molding, leather 40/20/40 heated front bench seat with power adjustments, front bumper sight shield and leather-wrapped steering wheel; air conditioning, woodgrain instrument panel bezel, convenience group: speed control, tilt steering column; light group: mini overhead console, glove box lamp, map/courtesy lamp; power door locks and power windows with driver's one touch down. REQUIRES EML and DGB and ATK. NOT AVAILABLE with EMM, ETC, EWA, DDP, DDX, DEE, AJD, CKJ, JPV, RBN, RAZ, RBR, TST, RDZ, LNJ, GXM, LSA, AGG, CUE, AWK.		
2GA	Quick Order Package 2GA	NC	NC
	Includes 3.54 axle ratio. REQUIRES DDX and (HAA or 4XA). NOT AVAILABLE with EMM, EML, EWA, DDP, DGB, DEE, AHD.		
2GG	Quick Order Package 2GG	2023	2380
	Manufacturer Discount	(595)	(700)
	Net Price	1428	1680
	Includes SLT Decor group: black tailgate applique, carpeted floor covering, floor mats, hood insulation, passenger's side vanity mirror, bodyside molding, premium cloth 40/20/40 front bench seat, front bumper sight shield and leather-wrapped steering wheel; air conditioning, woodgrain instrument panel bezel, convenience group: speed control, tilt steering column; light group: mini overhead console, glove box lamp, map/courtesy lamp; power door locks and power windows with driver's one touch down. REQUIRES DDX. NOT AVAILABLE with EMM, EML, EWA, DDP, DGB, DEE, ATK, AGG, AHD.		
2GH	Quick Order Package 2GH (Quad Cab)	3600	4235
	Manufacturer Discount	(595)	(700)
	Net Price	3005	3535
	Includes SLT Decor group: black tailgate applique, carpeted floor covering, floor mats, hood insulation, passenger's side vanity mirror, power heated fold-away outside mirrors, bodyside molding, leather 40/20/40 heated front bench seat with power adjustments, front bumper sight shield and leather-wrapped steering wheel; air conditioning, woodgrain instrument panel bezel, convenience group: speed control, tilt steering column; light group: mini overhead console, glove box lamp, map/		

CODE	DESCRIPTION	INVOICE	MSRP
	courtesy lamp; power door locks and power windows with driver's one touch down. REQUIRES ETC and DDX and ATK. NOT AVAILABLE with EML, EMM, EWA, DDP, DGB, DEE, JPV, AJD, CKJ, RBR, RAZ, RBN, TST, RDZ, LNJ, GXM, LSA, AGG, CUE, AWK, AHD.		
2HA	**Quick Order Package 2HA**	NC	NC
	Includes 3.54 axle ratio. REQUIRES DEE and (HAA or 4XA). NOT AVAILABLE with EMM, EML, EWA, DDP, DGB, DDX, AHD.		
2HG	**Quick Order Package 2HG**	2023	2380
	Manufacturer Discount	(595)	(700)
	Net Price	1428	1680
	Includes SLT Decor group: black tailgate applique, carpeted floor covering, floor mats, hood insulation, passenger's side vanity mirror, bodyside molding, premium cloth 40/20/40 front bench seat, front bumper sight shield and leather-wrapped steering wheel; air conditioning, woodgrain instrument panel bezel, convenience group: speed control, tilt steering column; light group: mini overhead console, glove box lamp, map/courtesy lamp; power door locks and power windows with driver's one touch down. REQUIRES DEE. NOT AVAILABLE with EMM, EML, EWA, DDP, DDX, DGB, ATK, AGG, AHD.		
2HH	**Quick Order Package 2HH (Quad Cab)**	3600	4235
	Manufacturer Discount	(595)	(700)
	Net Price	3005	3535
	Includes SLT Decor group: black tailgate applique, carpeted floor covering, floor mats, hood insulation, passenger's side vanity mirror, power heated fold-away outside mirrors, bodyside molding, leather 40/20/40 heated front bench seat with power adjustments, front bumper sight shield and leather-wrapped steering wheel; air conditioning, woodgrain instrument panel bezel, convenience group: speed control, tilt steering column; light group: mini overhead console, glove box lamp, map/courtesy lamp; power door locks and power windows with driver's one touch down. REQUIRES ETC and DEE and ATK. NOT AVAILABLE with EML, EMM, EWA, DDP, DGB, DDX, JPV, AJD, CKJ, RBR, RAZ, RBN, TST, RDZ, LNJ, GXM, LSA, AGG, CUE, AWK, AHD.		
4XA	**Air Conditioning Bypass**	NC	NC
	*NOT AVAILABLE with HAA 2*G, 2*H.*		
ADA	**Light Group**	77	90
	*Includes passenger's assist handles, deluxe headliner, mini overhead console, glove box lamp and map/courtesy lamp. INCLUDED in 2*G and 2*H.*		
AGG	**Sport Appearance Group (Quad Cab)**	200	235
	*Includes sport badge, front body color bumper, rear body color bumper, body color grille, fog lamps, quad halogen headlamps, bodyside moldings delete. REQUIRES 2*H. NOT AVAILABLE with MXB, 2*A, 2*G, AHD.*		
AGG	**Sport Appearance Group**	319	375
	*Includes sport badge, front body color bumper, rear body color bumper, body color grille, fog lamps, quad halogen headlamps, bodyside moldings delete. REQUIRES 2*G. NOT AVAILABLE with MXB, 2*A, 2*H, ATK, AHD.*		
AHC	**Trailer Tow Group**	234	275
	Includes HD flasher and platform hitch receiver (class IV).		

CODE	DESCRIPTION	INVOICE	MSRP
AHD	HD Snow Plow Prep Group (4WD Quad Cab)	72	85
	Manufacturer Discount	(72)	(85)
	Net Price	NC	NC
	Includes computer selected height adjustment springs, instrument panel transmission oil overheat warning light. Recommended items of equipment are front clearance lamps, I.D. lights and shift-on-the-fly transfer case. REQUIRES AHC and (EML or EMM or EWA). NOT AVAILABLE with AGG, 2GA, 2GG, 2GH, 2HA, 2HG, 2HH, 2CA, 2CG, 2CH.		
AHD	Snow Plow Prep Package (4WD Reg Cab)	72	85
	Manufacturer Discount	(72)	(85)
	Net Price	NC	NC
	Includes HD shift on-the-fly transfer case, computer selected springs and auto transmission oil overheat light. REQUIRES (EMM or EWA) and AHC. NOT AVAILABLE with 2EA, 2FA, 2EG, 2FG, 2GA, 2CA, 2GG, 2CG, 2HA, 2HG.		
AHJ	Camper Special Group	81	95
	Includes stabilizer bar and auxiliary springs.		
AJD	Leather Interior Group (Quad Cab)	1352	1590
	*Includes woodgrain instrument panel bezel, leather 40/20/40 front bench seat, 8-way power driver's seat, travel convenience group: overhead console with trip computer, illuminated visor vanity mirrors and auto dimming rearview mirror. REQUIRES 2*G. NOT AVAILABLE with 2*A, 2*H.*		
AJD	Leather Interior Group (Reg Cab)	1233	1450
	*Includes woodgrain instrument panel bezel, leather 40/20/40 front bench seat, 8-way power driver's seat, travel convenience group: overhead console with trip computer, illuminated visor vanity mirrors and auto dimming rearview mirror. REQUIRES 2*G. NOT AVAILABLE with 2*A.*		
AJK	Convenience Group	332	390
	*Includes speed control and tilt steering column. INCLUDED in 2*G, 2*H.*		
ATK	SLT Plus Decor Group (Quad Cab)	1415	1665
	*Includes steering wheel mounted audio controls, fog lamps, travel convenience group: overhead console with trip computer, illuminated visor vanity mirrors and auto dimming rearview mirror; remote keyless entry, AM/FM stereo with CD, cassette and equalizer, 6 Infinity speakers, security alarm and rear underseat compartment storage. REQUIRES 2*H. NOT AVAILABLE with 2*A, 2*G, TST, AGG.*		
AWK	Travel Convenience Group	293	345
	*Includes overhead console with trip computer, illuminated visor vanity mirrors and auto dimming rearview mirror. REQUIRES 2*G. NOT AVAILABLE with 2*A.*		
CF8	Rear Seat Delete (Quad Cab)	NC	NC
	*REQUIRES 2*A. NOT AVAILABLE with 2*G, 2*H.*		
CKE	Carpet Floor Covering	94	110
	*REQUIRES 2*A. NOT AVAILABLE with 2*G, 2*H.*		
CKJ	Black Vinyl Floor Covering	NC	NC
	*REQUIRES 2*G. NOT AVAILABLE with 2*A, 2*H, CUE.*		
CUE	Rear Underseat Compartment Storage (Quad Cab)	64	75
	*REQUIRES 2*G. NOT AVAILABLE with CKJ, 2*A.*		

CODE	DESCRIPTION	INVOICE	MSRP
DDP	Transmission: 5-Speed Manual *NOT AVAILABLE with DDX, DGB, EWA, ETC, 26A, 26G, 2FA, 2FG, 27A, 27G, 28A, 28G, 2CA, 2CG, 2GA, 2GG, 2HA, 2HG, 26H, 27H, 28H, 2FH, 2GH, 2HH, 2CH.*	NC	NC
DDX	Transmission: HD 5-Speed Manual *NOT AVAILABLE with DDP, DGB, EML, EMM, 25A, 25G, 26A, 26G, 2EA, 2EG, 2FA, 2FG, 28A, 28G, 2CA, 2CG, 2HA, 2HG, 25H, 26H, 2EH, 2FH, 28H, 2HH, 2CH.*	NC	NC
DEE	Transmission: HD 6-Speed Manual *NOT AVAILABLE with EMM, EML, EWA, 25A, 25G, 26A, 26G, 27A, 27G, 28A, 28G, 2CA, 2CG, 2EA, 2EG, 2FA, 2FG, 2GA, 2GG, 25H, 26H, 27H, 28H, 2GH, 2CH, 2EH, 2FH.*	340	400
DGB	Transmission: 4-Speed Automatic *NOT AVAILABLE with DDP, DDX, 25A, 25G, 2EA, 2EG, 27A, 27G, 2GA, 2GG, 2HA, 2HG, 25H, 2EH, 27H, 2GH, 2HH.*	829	975
DMF	4.10 Axle Ratio *REQUIRES DSA.*	43	50
DSA	Anti-Spin Differential Axle	242	285
EML	Engine: 5.9L SMPI V8 Magnum *NOT AVAILABLE with EMM, ETC, EWA, DDX, 25A, 25G, 26A, 26G, 27A, 27G, 28A, 28G, 2CA, 2CG, 2GA, 2GG, 2HA, 2HG, DEE, 25H, 26H, 27H, 28H, 2CH, 2GH, 2HH.*	NC	NC
EMM	Engine: 5.9L SMPI V8 Magnum *NOT AVAILABLE with EML, ETC, EWA, DDX, 2EA, 2EG, 2FA, 2FG, 27A, 27G, 28A, 28G, 2CA, 2CG, 2GA, 2GG, 2HA, 2HG, DEE, 2EH, 2FH, 2GH, 2HH, 2CH, 27H.*	NC	NC
ETC	Engine: 5.9L Cummins 24V Diesel *Includes evaporative control system delete, warning lights for low fuel, low oil, water in fuel, wait to start, brakes and antilock brakes and engine block heater. NOT AVAILABLE with EML, EMM, EWA, DDP, 25A, 26A, 27A, 28A, 2EA, 2FA, 25G, 26G, 27G, 28G, 2EG, 2FG, 25H, 26H, 27H, 28H, 2EH, 2FH.*	3931	4625
EWA	Engine: 8.0L MPI V10 Magnum *Includes evaporative control system and HD engine cooling. NOT AVAILABLE with EML, EMM, ETC, DDP, 25A, 25G, 26A, 26G, 2EA, 2EG, 2FA, 2FG, 2GA, 2GG, 2CA, 2CG, 2HA, 2HG, DEE, 25H, 26H, 2EH, 2FH, 2GH, 2HH, 2CH.*	400	470
GFD	Sliding Rear Window	119	140
GPC	Dual 7" x 10" Bright Wide Mount Mirrors (All Except 2WD Reg Cab) *NOT AVAILABLE with GPD.*	NC	NC
GXM	Remote Keyless Entry *REQUIRES 2*G. NOT AVAILABLE with 2*A.*	162	190
HAA	Air Conditioning *REQUIRES 2*A. NOT AVAILABLE with 4XA. INCLUDED in 2*G, 2*H.*	684	805
JPS	6-Way Power Driver's Seat (Reg Cab) *REQUIRES 2*G. NOT AVAILABLE with 2*A.*	272	320
JPV	8-Way Power Driver's Seat (Quad Cab) *REQUIRES 2*G. NOT AVAILABLE with 2*A.*	306	360
K17	Bodyside Molding *REQUIRES 2*A.*	89	105
LNJ	Fog Lamps *REQUIRES 2*G. NOT AVAILABLE with 2*A.*	119	140

CODE	DESCRIPTION	INVOICE	MSRP
LSA	Security Alarm *REQUIRES 2*G, GXM and AWK. NOT AVAILABLE with 2*A.*	128	150
MXB	Front Air Dam *NOT AVAILABLE with AGG.*	21	25
NHK	Engine Block Heater	77	90
RAZ	Radio: AM/FM Stereo with CD, Cassette and Equalizer *REQUIRES 2*G. NOT AVAILABLE with RBN; RBR, 2*A.*	587	690
RBN	Radio: AM/FM Stereo with Cassette and CD Changer Control *REQUIRES 2*G. NOT AVAILABLE with RAZ, RBR, RDZ, 2*A.*	285	335
RBR	Radio: AM/FM Stereo with CD *REQUIRES 2*G. NOT AVAILABLE with RBN, RAZ, RDZ, 2*A.*	434	510
RDZ	Steering Wheel Mounted Audio Controls *REQUIRES 2*G, RAZ and GXM. NOT AVAILABLE with RBN, RBR, 2*A.*	64	75
S9	Deluxe Cloth 40/20/40 Bench Seat *REQUIRES 2*A. NOT AVAILABLE with TY, 2*H. INCLUDED in 2*G.*	94	110
TST	Tires: LT235/85R16E BSW On/Off Road *On/off road. NOT AVAILABLE with ATK, 2*H.*	166	195
TY	HD Vinyl 40/20/40 Front Bench Seat (Quad Cab) *REQUIRES 2*A. NOT AVAILABLE with S9, 2*G, 2*H.*	NC	NC

2000 RAM WAGON

What's New?

Minor changes come with the 2000 model year, including hood-mounted windshield-washer nozzles and chrome-clad wheels. Sealing has been improved to reduce noise and keep out the weather, and Ram vans get a six-speaker audio system as standard equipment.

Review

Dodge's full-size vans and wagons haven't changed all that much despite nearly three decades of existence. Squint your eyes and the latest big Rams could almost be mistaken for the 1971 models. But this does not matter to Dodge fans. Chrysler hasn't yet found a need to change the brawny trucks in order to keep up with rivals from Ford and General Motors.

Despite the lack of a ground-up redesign, one-third of the components were all-new in 1998, including the instrument panel and brakes; in addition, the suspension was re-tuned and the body panels were transformed. So for 2000, only minor refinements were needed.

First, let's break down the Dodge lineup: There's a cargo van, a passenger wagon and a conversion van (built by factory-approved conversion specialists). The convert comes in three lengths and three load ranges, while the van and wagon are offered in four levels-a 1500, a 2500, a 3500 and a 3500 Maxi wagon. That last one has a payload of up to 4,245 pounds and standard seating for 15 passengers.

The base engine in the 1500 and 2500 series is a 3.9-liter V6, but most buyers would be better off with an optional V8, either a 5.2-liter or a 5.9-liter. With 295 foot-pounds of torque on tap, the 5.2-liter yields a rewarding combination of strength and economy, but no Ram vehicle ranks miserly at the gas pump. For demanding applications, your best bet might very well be the 5.9-liter, which packs 335 foot-pounds of twisting force. To compensate for thirsty engine choices, there's a 32-gallon gas tank on the 109-inch wheelbase vans and wagons, and a 35-gallon tank on all other models. The V6 is hooked to an automatic three-speed transmission, and both V8s are attached to an automatic four-speed. The van and the wagon have rear-wheel antilock braking, although four-wheel is optional on both.

Both also come with next-generation driver and front-passenger airbags, and if you opt for the power-convenience group, you can have the added security of an alarm system. If you want to fancy up your wagon, Dodge offers a premium-decor package that dresses up the trim panels, dashliner and side moldings. If towing is more your thing, there's a trailer-tow package that includes a 750-amp battery and a heavy-duty engine-cooling system.

The Dodge Ram Wagon has remained virtually the same for 30 years, as has its value, in-demand conveniences and practical price. As they say, if it ain't broke, don't fix it.

2000 Dodge Ram Wagon

Standard Equipment

1500 WAGON (3A): 3.9L V6 OHV SMPI 12-valve engine; 3-speed auto transmission; 600-amp battery; 136-amp alternator; rear-wheel drive, 3.55 axle ratio; stainless steel exhaust; front independent suspension with anti-roll bar, front coil springs, HD front shocks, rigid rear axle suspension with rear leaf springs, HD rear shocks; power rack-and-pinion steering; front disc/rear drum brakes with rear wheel antilock braking system; 32 gal. capacity fuel tank; side impact bars; 3 doors with split swing-out right rear passenger's door, conventional rear cargo door; front and rear chrome bumpers with black rub strip; monotone paint with bodyside accent stripe; aero-composite halogen headlamps; additional exterior lights include underhood light; driver's and passenger's manual black folding outside mirrors; front and rear 15" x 7" silver styled steel wheels; P235/75SR15 A/S BSW front and rear tires; underbody mounted full-size steel spare wheel; air conditioning; AM/FM stereo, clock, seek-scan, cassette, 6 speakers, and fixed antenna; 2 power accessory outlets, front cigar lighter(s), smokers' package; instrumentation display includes oil pressure gauge, water temperature gauge, volt gauge, trip odometer; warning indicators include oil pressure, battery, lights on, key in ignition, low washer fluid; driver's and passenger's front airbags; tinted windows, vented rear windows; variable intermittent front windshield wipers, vented rear window; seating capacity of 8, front bucket seats, fixed headrests, driver's and passenger's armrests, driver's seat includes 4-way direction control, passenger's seat includes 4-way direction control; removable 2nd row bench seat; removable 3rd row bench seat; front height adjustable seatbelts with front pretensioners; premium cloth seats, vinyl door trim insert, full cloth headliner, full carpet floor covering, deluxe sound insulation, plastic/rubber gear shift knob; interior lights include dome light, front reading lights; sport steering wheel with tilt adjustment; day/night rearview mirror; engine cover console with storage, locking glove box with light, front cupholder; carpeted cargo floor; chrome grille, black side window moldings, black front windshield molding, black rear window molding and black door handles.

2500 WAGON (4A) (in addition to or instead of 1500 WAGON (4A) equipment): 5.2L V8 OHV SMPI 16-valve engine; 4-speed electronic OD auto transmission with lock-up; 3.92 axle ratio; 35 gal. capacity fuel tank; front and rear 16" x 6.5" silver steel wheels; LT225/75SR16 A/S BSW front and rear tires and cargo light.

3500 MAXIWAGON (4A) (in addition to or instead of 2500 WAGON (4A) equipment): HD radiator; transmission oil cooler; LT245/75SR16 A/S BSW front and rear tires; seating capacity of 15 and vinyl cargo floor.

Base Prices

AB1L51	1500 Wagon (3A)	19259	21215
AB2L52	2500 Wagon (4A)	20336	23230
AB3L53	3500 Maxi-Wagon (4A)	22890	26235
Destination Charge:		630	630

Accessories

22C	**Quick Order Package 22C (1500)** *Includes vehicle with standard equipment. REQUIRES EHC and DGA. NOT AVAILABLE with AHC, ELF.*	NC	NC
26B	**Quick Order Package 26B (3500)** *Includes vehicle with standard equipment. REQUIRES ELF and DGB. NOT AVAILABLE with EML, ELN.*	NC	NC
26C	**Quick Order Package 26C (1500/2500)** *Includes vehicle with standard equipment. REQUIRES ELF and DGB. NOT AVAILABLE with EML, ELN, EHC.*	NC	NC
28B	**Quick Order Package 28B (3500)** *Includes vehicle with standard equipment. REQUIRES EML and DGB. NOT AVAILABLE with ELF, ELN.*	NC	NC
28C	**Quick Order Package 28C (2500)** *Includes vehicle with standard equipment. REQUIRES EML and DGB. NOT AVAILABLE with ELF, ELN.*	NC	NC
2XB	**Quick Order Package 2XB (3500)** *Includes vehicle with standard equipment. REQUIRES ELN and DGB. NOT AVAILABLE with ELF, EML, AHC.*	NC	NC
2XC	**Quick Order Package 2XC (2500)** *Includes vehicle with standard equipment. REQUIRES ELN and DGB. NOT AVAILABLE with EML, ELF, AHC, MBF.*	NC	NC
AHC	**Trailer Tow Prep Group (1500/2500)** *Includes 750-amp maintenance free battery, auxiliary transmission oil cooler and HD engine cooling. NOT AVAILABLE with ELN, 2XC, EHC, 22C, DGA.*	191	225
AHC	**Trailer Tow Prep Group (3500)** *Includes 750-amp maintenance free battery. NOT AVAILABLE with ELN, 2XB.*	81	95
AJP	**Power Convenience Group** *Includes illuminated entry, power door locks and power windows.*	608	715
ASP	**Premium Decor Group (1500/2500)** *Includes dashliner insulation, electric horns, lower bodyside and rear molding and power convenience group: illuminated entry, power door locks and power windows.*	1012	1190

CODE	DESCRIPTION	INVOICE	MSRP
ASP	Premium Decor Group (3500) *Includes dashliner insulation, carpeted cargo compartment, front seat area carpet, electric horns, front door installed premium door trim panel, illuminated passenger's visor mirror, power convenience group: illuminated entry, power door locks, power windows and lower bodyside and rear molding.*	1148	1350
BCQ	750-Amp Maintenance Free Battery	51	60
BGK	4-Wheel Antilock Brakes	421	495
CKE	Front Seat Area Carpet (3500) *REQUIRES ASP or CKN.*	51	60
CKN	Cargo Compartment Carpet (3500) *REQUIRES ASP or CKE.*	85	100
CKZ	Black Rubber Floor Covering (1500/2500)	NC	NC
CTJ	Premium Front Door Trim Panel (1500/3500) *REQUIRES AJP.*	43	50
CTJ	Premium Front Door Trim Panel (2500) *REQUIRES AJP.*	43	50
CYH	12-Passenger Seating (2500)	242	285
CYH	12-Passenger Seating (3500)	(242)	(285)
DGA	Transmission: 3-Speed Automatic (1500) *NOT AVAILABLE with ELF, AHC.*	NC	NC
DGB	Transmission: 4-Speed Automatic (1500) *NOT AVAILABLE with EHC.*	255	300
DGB	Transmission: 4-Speed Automatic (2500/3500)	NC	NC
DMH	3.92 Axle Ratio (1500) *NOT AVAILABLE with EHC, DSA. INCLUDED in 26B, 28B, 2XB, 28C, 2XC.*	34	40
DSA	Anti-Spin Differential Axle *NOT AVAILABLE with Z3F.*	242	285
EHC	Engine: 3.9L SMPI V6 Magnum (1500) *NOT AVAILABLE with DGB, AHC, 26C.*	NC	NC
ELF	Engine: 5.2L SMPI V8 Magnum (1500) *NOT AVAILABLE with DGA, 22C.*	502	590
ELF	Engine: 5.2L SMPI V8 Magnum (2500/3500) *NOT AVAILABLE with EML, Z3F, ELN, 28B, 2XB, 28C, 2XC.*	NC	NC
ELN	Engine: 5.2L V8 MPI CNG (2500/3500) *Includes compressed natural gas group: 16.3 gal. compressed natural gas (CNG) fuel tanks, CNG fuel system badge, tire: inside mounted spare and spare tire cover. NOT AVAILABLE with ELF, EML, 26B, 28B, HBB, Z3F, AHC, 26C, 28C, MBF.*	3668	4315
EML	Engine: 5.9L SMPI V8 Magnum (2500) *NOT AVAILABLE with 26C, 2XC.*	506	595
EML	Engine: 5.9L SMPI V8 Magnum (3500) *NOT AVAILABLE with ELF, ELN, 26B, 2XB.*	506	595
GAE	Sunscreen Glass (1500/3500)	366	430
GAE	Sunscreen Glass (2500)	366	430
GFA	Rear Window Defroster *NOT AVAILABLE with GLC.*	153	180
GKC	Right Sliding Door with Vented Glass (2500/3500)	NC	NC
GKC	Right Sliding Door with Vented Glass (1500)	NC	NC

CODE	DESCRIPTION	INVOICE	MSRP
GLC	Rear Hinged Doors with Vented Glass	NC	NC
	NOT AVAILABLE with GFA.		
GPA	Manual Delivery Mirrors	140	165
	NOT AVAILABLE with GPS.		
GPS	Dual 6" x 9" Black Power Mirrors (1500/3500)	136	160
	NOT AVAILABLE with GPA.		
GPS	Dual 6" x 9" Black Power Mirrors (2500)	136	160
	NOT AVAILABLE with GPA.		
HBB	Rear Air Conditioning and Heater (2500)	718	845
	Includes 750-amp maintenance free battery. REQUIRES ELF or EML. NOT AVAILABLE with ELN.		
HBB	Rear Air Conditioning and Heater (3500)	718	845
	Manufacturer Discount	(425)	(500)
	Net Price	293	345
	Includes 750-amp maintenance free battery. REQUIRES ELF or EML. NOT AVAILABLE with ELN.		
HD	HD Vinyl Bucket Seats	NC	NC
	NOT AVAILABLE with JPS.		
JPS	6-Way Power Driver's Seat	255	300
	NOT AVAILABLE with HD.		
LSA	Security Alarm	128	150
	REQUIRES AJP or ASP.		
MBF	Bright Rear Step Bumper	81	95
	NOT AVAILABLE with ELN, 2XC.		
NHB	Auxiliary Transmission Oil Cooler (1500/2500)	72	85
	REQUIRES NMC or AHC.		
NHK	Engine Block Heater	43	50
NHM	Speed Control	217	255
NMC	HD Engine Cooling (1500/2500)	72	85
	REQUIRES NHB.		
RAZ	Radio: AM/FM Stereo with Cassette, CD and Equalizer	191	225
	NOT AVAILABLE with RBN.		
RBN	Radio: AM/FM Stereo with Cassette and CD Changer Control	85	100
	NOT AVAILABLE with RAZ.		
RCE	Infinity Speaker System	387	455
TSF	Tires: P235/75R15 AS OWL (1500)	106	125
TWY	Tires: LT225/75R16D OWL AS (2500)	106	125
WDC	Wheels: 16" x 6.5" Chrome (2500/3500)	340	400
WJM	Wheels: 15" x 7" Chrome (1500)	128	150
Z3F	GVWR: 9,200 Lbs (3500)	221	260
	Includes 4.10 axle ratio and HD rear axle. REQUIRES EML. NOT AVAILABLE with DSA, ELF, ELN.		

2000 ECONOLINE WAGON

2000 Ford Econoline Wagon

What's New?

The 5.4-liter V8 and the 6.8-liter V10 gas engines generate more horsepower and torque. Four-wheel antilock brakes are now standard on all models. The Light Convenience Group, including courtesy lights, a rear cargo light, a chime warning module, a "headlamps on" alert, and illuminated courtesy door lights, is now standard on all models. The handling package has been made standard on all Econolines. The towing package is standard on all wagons. The instrument panel has been simplified. Remote keyless entry and power sail-mount mirrors are standard on recreational vans.

Review

Tough, roomy, rugged and reliable, Ford's Econoline full-size Wagons have a favorable, well-earned reputation. Since its introduction in 1960, Ford says it has sold more than 6 million Econolines.

The current lineup is quite extensive. The E-150 and E-350 Super Duty Wagons are the two Econolines designed to haul passengers. Econoline Wagons—all on a 138-inch wheelbase—accommodate seven or eight (E-150), 12 (E-350) or 15 (E-350 extended) passengers. Trailer ratings range from 4,700 pounds for an E-150 Wagon powered by a 4.2-liter V6, to 10,000 pounds for an E-350 Super Duty Extended Wagon with a 4.10 rear-axle ratio and either a 6.8-liter V10 or a 7.3-liter diesel.

The 5.4-liter Triton V8 and 6.8-liter V10 engines both serve up more power for 2000. The V8's horsepower increases from 235 to 255, and the V10 increases from 265 to 305. Torque increases from 335 foot-pounds to 350 for the V8 and from 410 to 420 for the V10. All engines are teamed with an automatic overdrive transmission, and all gasoline engines feature a fail-safe cooling system to help protect against engine damage in case of a coolant loss.

Driving a Econoline, despite its passenger seating, differs little from piloting a delivery vehicle, so it's not a logical choice for everyday motoring—though quite a few families happily employ their Wagons exactly that way. The virtues of sitting tall with a panoramic view of the road ahead can outweigh many a minor inconvenience—such as the difficulty of squeezing these biggies into urban parking spots and compact garages. Handling is light, seats are acceptably comfortable, and Wagons don't ride badly at all, considering the old-fashioned suspension configurations they employ.

If you want to purchase a new full-size wagon, you're going to end up with either the Econoline, the Chevrolet Express, the GMC Savana, or the Dodge Ram Wagon. No other manufacturer has deemed it worthy to bully its way into the full-size wagon market. All four vehicles have similar prices, wheelbases and maximum passenger capacities (15 people). The Express, Savana and Econoline have more powerful optional engines, however. Horsepower and torque output from the Ford V10 and the GM big-block V8 are very similar. For buyers in this market, it will most likely come down to pricing and getting the desired options.

Standard Equipment

E-150 XL WAGON (4A): 4.2L V6 OHV SMPI 12-valve engine; 4-speed electronic OD auto transmission with lock-up; 650-amp battery; 130-amp HD alternator; rear-wheel drive, 3.55 axle ratio; stainless steel exhaust; front independent suspension with anti-roll bar, front coil springs, HD front shocks, rigid rear axle suspension with rear leaf springs, HD rear shocks; power re-circulating ball steering; front disc/ rear drum brakes with 4-wheel antilock braking system; 35 gal. capacity fuel tank; side impact bars; 3 doors with split swing-out right rear passenger door, split swing-out rear cargo door; class I trailering, trailer harness; front and rear colored bumpers; monotone paint; sealed beam halogen headlamps; driver's and passenger's manual black folding outside mirrors; front and rear 15" x 6" steel wheels; P235/75SR15 A/S BSW front and rear tires; underbody mounted full-size steel spare wheel; air conditioning; AM/FM stereo, clock, seek-scan, 4 speakers, and fixed antenna; 2 power accessory outlets, smokers' package; instrumentation display includes oil pressure gauge, water temperature gauge, volt gauge, trip odometer; warning indicators include water temp, battery; driver's and passenger's front airbags; tinted windows, fixed 1/4 vent windows; variable intermittent front windshield wipers, sun visor strip; seating capacity of 8, front bucket seats, fixed headrests, driver's seat includes 2-way direction control, passenger's seat includes 2-way direction control; 2nd row bench seat; 3rd row bench seat; front height adjustable seatbelts with front pretensioners; vinyl seats, full cloth headliner, full vinyl floor covering; interior lights include dome light; passenger's side vanity mirror; day/night rearview mirror; engine cover console with storage, front cupholder, dashboard storage; vinyl cargo floor, fiberboard trunk lid, cargo light; colored grille, black side window moldings, black front windshield molding, black rear window molding and black door handles.

E-350 SUPER DUTY XL WAGON/ E-350 SUPER DUTY XL EXTENDED WAGON (4A) (in addition to or instead of E-150 XL WAGON (4A) equipment): 5.4L V8 SOHC SMPI 16-valve engine; 4-wheel disc brakes with 4-wheel antilock braking system; front and rear 16" x 7" steel wheels; LT225/ 75SR16 A/S BSW front and rear tires; warning indicators include oil pressure and seating capacity of 12 (15 - Extended).

XLT (in addition to or instead of XL equipment): Front and rear chrome bumpers; aero-composite halogen headlamps; driver's and passenger's power remote black folding outside mirrors; rear air conditioning and heater; AM/FM stereo, clock, seek-scan, cassette, 6 speakers, and fixed antenna; power windows with driver's 1-touch down; front captain's seats, fixed headrests, driver's and passenger's armrests, driver's seat includes 4-way direction control, passenger's seat includes 4-way direction control; cloth seats, full carpet floor covering, cruise control with steering wheel controls, steering wheel with tilt adjustment, deluxe sound insulation; interior lights include front reading lights, illuminated entry; driver's and passenger's door bins; carpeted cargo floor, plastic trunk lid and chrome grille.

Base Prices

E11	E-150 XL Wagon (4A)	19634	22540
E31	E-350 SD XL Wagon (4A)	22091	25430
S31	E-350 SD XL Extended Wagon (4A)	23468	27050
E11	E-150 XLT Wagon (4A)	22273	25645
E31	E-350 SD XLT Wagon (4A)	24704	28505
S31	E-350 SD XLT Extended Wagon (4A)	25015	28870
Destination Charge:		640	640

CODE	DESCRIPTION	INVOICE	MSRP

Accessories

CODE	DESCRIPTION	INVOICE	MSRP
166	Full Length Vinyl Floor Mat *REQUIRES 18G. INCLUDED in 710A, 700A, 721A.*	NC	NC
18A	Exterior Upgrade Package (XL) *Includes chrome bumpers, chrome grille and aerodynamic halogen headlamps. NOT AVAILABLE with 769.*	285	335
18G	Interior Upgrade Package (XL) *Includes dash absorber, warning chime, full length XLT carpeting, XLT side/rear cargo door trim panels, illuminated entry and headlights-on audible alert.*	522	615
216	8-Passenger Bucket Seating (E-350 XL) *Includes 2 standard buckets and two 3-passenger benches.*	(162)	(190)
218	12-Passenger Bucket Seating (E-350 XL Extended) *Available with Cloth Buckets - C2.*	(119)	(140)
21E	8-Passenger Captain's Chair Seating (E-350 XLT) *Includes dual captain's chairs and two 3-passenger benches.*	(162)	(190)
21M	12-Passenger Captain's Chair Seating (E-350 XLT Extended)	(118)	(140)
415	Deluxe Engine Console Cover (XL) *Includes dual stowage areas and 4 cupholders.*	51	60
419	Dual Illuminated Sun Visors (XLT)	43	50
41H	Engine Block Heater *Recommended when minimum temperature is -10F or below.*	30	35
428	High Altitude Principal Use *NOT AVAILABLE with 99S, XC9, 99M.*	NC	NC
429	Non-High Altitude Principal Use	NC	NC
449	Transmission: Electronic 4-Speed Automatic with OD (All Except E-150) *REQUIRES 99F. NOT AVAILABLE with 99M, 99S, 516.*	NC	NC
516	Spare Tire and Wheel Not Included (All Except E-150) *REQUIRES 99M. NOT AVAILABLE with 449, 99F, 99S.*	(204)	(240)
516	Spare Tire and Wheel Not Included (E-350) *REQUIRES 99M. NOT AVAILABLE with 449, 99S, 99F.*	(229)	(270)
52N	Speed Control/Tilt Steering Wheel (XL)	328	385
536	Trailer Towing Pkg (Class II/III/IV) (All Except E-150) *Includes frame mounted hitch, electric brake controller tap-in capability, trailer wiring harness (blade-style female connector) with bumper bracket and relay system for backup/B+/running lights. NOT AVAILABLE with 99M.*	221	260
548	Bright Swing-Out Recreational Mirrors *Deletes power mirrors when equipped.*	51	60
574	High Capacity Front and Rear Air Conditioning (XL) *Includes auxiliary heater and overhead ducts.*	702	825
588	Radio: Premium Electronic AM/FM Stereo with Cassette (XLT) *Includes clock and 6 speakers. NOT AVAILABLE with 58K.*	64	75
589	Radio: Electronic AM/FM Stereo with Cassette and Clock (XL) *Includes 4 speakers.*	132	155
58K	Radio: Electronic AM/FM Stereo with CD and Cassette (XLT) *Includes in-dash single disc CD player, cassette tape player, clock and 6 speakers. NOT AVAILABLE with 588.*	235	275

CODE	DESCRIPTION	INVOICE	MSRP
60S	Sliding Side Cargo Door	NC	NC
	Upgrade from standard 60/40 hinged door.		
632	Heavy Duty Battery	12	15
634	Battery: Heavy-Duty/Auxiliary (XLT)	123	145
	Includes 78 AH battery and 75 AH battery (deep-cycle non-starting). NOT AVAILABLE with 99F, 99M, 961.		
63A	Dual System Alternator (XLT Except E-150)	493	580
	Includes two 110-amp alternators. REQUIRES 99F. NOT AVAILABLE with 99M, 99S.		
644	16" Wheel Covers (XL Except E-150)	89	105
645	Wheels: 15" x 7" Bright Cast Aluminum (E-150 XLT)	263	310
	Includes 15" steel spare.		
65R	Extended Range NG Fuel Tank (E-350 Except Extended)	2593	3050
	Includes standard tank configuration plus 8.3 GGE @ 3,000 psi, 9.4 GGE @ 3,600 psi single interior tank mounted over rear axle (behind 3rd row seat) 24.5 GGE @ 3,000 psi total, 28.0 GGE @ 3,600 psi total and spare tire. REQUIRES 99M. NOT AVAILABLE with 99F, 99S.		
700A	Series Code 700A (E-150 XL)	NC	NC
	Includes vehicle with standard equipment.		
705A	Series Code 705A (E-150 XLT)	328	385
	Manufacturer Discount	(328)	(385)
	Net Price	NC	NC
	Includes vehicle with standard equipment.		
710A	Series Code 710A (E-350 XL Except Extended)	NC	NC
	Includes vehicle with standard equipment.		
713A	Series Code 713A (E-350 XLT Except Extended)	328	385
	Manufacturer Discount	(328)	(385)
	Net Price	NC	NC
	Includes vehicle with standard equipment.		
721A	Series Code 721A (E-350 XL Extended)	702	825
	Manufacturer Discount	(702)	(825)
	Net Price	NC	NC
	Includes vehicle with standard equipment.		
723A	Series Code 723A (E-350 XLT Extended)	702	825
	Manufacturer Discount	(702)	(825)
	Net Price	NC	NC
	Includes vehicle with standard equipment.		
768	Chrome Rear Step Bumper	119	140
	REQUIRES 18A. NOT AVAILABLE with 769.		
769	Light Charcoal Rear Step Bumper (XL)	102	120
	NOT AVAILABLE with 768, 18A.		
77C	Chateau Appearance Package (E-150 XLT)	876	1030
	Includes leather-wrapped steering wheel, wheels: 15" x 7" bright cast aluminum, lower accent two-tone paint, 7-passenger cloth quad captain's chairs and cloth seat trim. REQUIRES 924 or M77. NOT AVAILABLE with 933.		

CODE	DESCRIPTION	INVOICE	MSRP
77C	Chateau Appearance Package (E-350 XLT Except Extended) *Includes 16" full wheel covers, leather-wrapped steering wheel, lower accent two-tone paint, 7-passenger quad captain's chairs and cloth seat trim. REQUIRES 924 and M77. NOT AVAILABLE with 933.*	702	825
903	Power Door Locks/Windows (XL) *Includes memory lock module with sliding cargo door and XLT door trim panels.*	421	495
90P	Power Driver's Seat (XLT) *Includes manual lumbar.*	332	390
924	Privacy Glass	391	460
948	Remote Keyless Entry *Includes two transmitters and a passively activated system in combination with a remote entry transmitter that locks and unlock doors and activates interior lights and panic alarm. REQUIRES 18G (XL) and 903.*	170	200
961	Limited Function Auxiliary Control (All Except E-150) *REQUIRES 99F. NOT AVAILABLE with 99S, 99M, 634.*	170	200
99F	Engine: 7.3L DI Turbo Diesel V8 (All Except E-150) *Includes Power Stroke diesel and engine block heater. REQUIRES 449. NOT AVAILABLE with 634, XC4, 516, 65R.*	4242	4990
99L	Engine: 5.4L EFI V8 (E-150) *NOT AVAILABLE with 99W.*	1318	1550
99M	Engine: 5.4L EFI V8 Natural Gas (All Except E-150) *Includes 4.10 axle ratio, cloth seat trim, trailer tow package delete and interior mounted spare. NOT AVAILABLE with XC4, XC9, 536, 634, 63A, 961, 428, 449.*	5440	6400
99S	Engine: 6.8L EFI V10 (All Except E-150) *Includes 3.73 axle ratio. NOT AVAILABLE with XC9, 961, 428, 63A, 449, 516, 65R.*	595	700
99W	Engine: 4.6L EFI V8 (E-150)	638	750
M77	Chateau Appearance Package-Credit (E-150 XLT) *REQUIRES 77C.*	(876)	(1030)
M77	Chateau Appearance Package-Credit (E-350 XLT Except Extended) *REQUIRES 77C.*	(702)	(825)
T38	Tires: LT245/75Rx16E BSW AS (E-350 Except Extended) *NOT AVAILABLE with 516.*	NC	NC
X32	4.10 Axle Ratio (All Except E-150) *NOT AVAILABLE with XC4, XC9, XC2.*	38	45
XC2	Limited Slip with 4.10 Axle Ratio (All Except E-150) *NOT AVAILABLE with XC4, XC9, X32.*	267	315
XC4	Limited Slip with 3.73 Axle Ratio (All Except E-150) *REQUIRES 99S. NOT AVAILABLE with 99F, XC2, XC9, X32, 99M.*	267	315
XC9	Limited Slip with 3.55 Axle Ratio (All Except E-150) *NOT AVAILABLE with 99S, XC4, XC2, X32, 428, 99M.*	229	270
XH9	Limited Slip with 3.55 Axle Ratio (E-150)	229	270

2000 EXCURSION

2000 Ford Excursion

What's New?

The Excursion is an entirely new SUV based on Ford's F-250 Super Duty truck platform. It is the largest vehicle of its type, outgunning even the Chevy Suburban in terms of overall size and interior space.

Review

In a classic "bigger is better" move, Ford has decided to up the SUV ante by producing the largest soccer-mom mobile yet. The Excursion offers more interior room and cargo capacity than the previous heavy-weight title holder, the Chevrolet Suburban. At the same time, Ford is touting the Excursion's "earth-friendly" aspects like an engine lineup that meets LEV standards and the fact that 85 percent of the Excursion, by weight, is recyclable (never mind that the remaining 15 percent of an Excursion still equals about 2.5 Honda Civics).

The Excursion's base engine is a 5.4-liter V8 on two-wheel-drive models or a 6.8-liter V10 on models equipped with four-wheel drive. Optional with either drivetrain is a 7.3-liter V8 diesel that makes 235 horsepower and 500 foot-pounds of earth-shaking torque. All engines come with a four-speed automatic transmission as standard equipment; no manual transmission is offered in the Excursion.

Two trim levels are available. The base XLT model includes a three-piece rear door, running boards, remote keyless entry, driver and front-passenger airbags, four-wheel disc brakes with ABS, an AM/FM/cassette/CD stereo, six cupholders, power door locks, power windows, an overhead console, cloth seats, a 40/20/40 split-bench front seat and a third-row removable bench seat. Angle up to the Limited trim level and you get leather seating surfaces, front captain's chairs, woodgrain trim, rear-seat audio controls, a trip computer, power rear-quarter windows, 10 cupholders, aluminum wheels and illuminated running boards. Additional options like heated seats, heated exterior mirrors, a six-disc CD changer and a limited-slip axle can be ordered as well.

Since it's based off the F-250 Super Duty (the front doors, fenders, and hood will swap between them), Ford was able to develop the Excursion with a bare-minimum investment of company funds. This means a large profit margin for each Excursion sold, even by SUV standards. These same market forces were behind the Cadillac Escalade, Lincoln Navigator and Lexus LX470. We've begun to wonder how far this SUV thing can go, but if people keep buying them, automakers will keep building them.

Standard Equipment

XLT 2WD (4A): 5.4L V8 SOHC SMPI 16-valve engine; 4-speed electronic OD auto transmission with lock-up; 78-amp battery with run down protection; 130-amp alternator; rear-wheel drive, 3.73 axle ratio; stainless steel exhaust; firm ride suspension, front independent suspension with anti-roll bar, front coil springs, HD front shocks, rigid rear axle suspension with rear leaf springs, HD rear shocks; power re-circulating ball steering; 4-wheel disc brakes with 4-wheel antilock braking system; 44 gal. capacity fuel tank; running boards, side impact bars; dutch rear cargo door; HD trailering, trailer harness, trailer hitch; roof rack; front chrome bumper, front and rear black rub strip; rear tow hooks, rear step; body-colored bodyside molding; monotone paint; aero-composite halogen headlamps; additional exterior lights include cargo light, underhood light; driver's and passenger's power remote black heated folding outside mirrors; front and rear 16" x 7" steel wheels; LT265/75SR16 A/S BSW front and rear tires; inside mounted full-size steel spare wheel; air conditioning, rear air conditioning with separate controls, rear heat ducts; premium AM/FM stereo, clock, seek-scan, cassette, single CD, 4 speakers, and fixed antenna; cruise control with steering wheel controls; power door locks, keyless entry keypad, child safety rear door locks; 4 power accessory outlets, smokers' package; instrumentation display includes tachometer, oil pressure gauge, water temperature gauge, volt gauge, trip odometer; warning indicators include oil pressure, water temp, battery, key in ignition, low fuel, door ajar; driver's and passenger's front airbags; ignition disable; deep tinted windows, power front and rear windows with driver's 1-touch down, manual 1/4 vent windows; variable intermittent front windshield wipers, flip-up rear window, variable intermittent rear wiper, rear window defroster; seating capacity of 9, 40-20-40 split-bench front seat fixed headrests, center armrest with storage, driver's seat includes 4-way direction control, lumbar support, passenger's seat includes 4-way direction control; 60-40 folding rear split-bench reclining 2nd row seat with adjustable headrests, center armrest with storage; removable full folding 3rd row bench seat; front and rear height adjustable seatbelts; cloth seats, vinyl door trim insert, full cloth headliner, full carpet floor covering with carpeted floor mats; interior lights include dome light, front and rear reading lights, 2 door curb lights; leather-wrapped steering wheel with tilt adjustment; dual illuminated vanity mirrors, dual auxiliary visors; auto-dimming day/night rearview mirror; glove box with light, front and rear cupholders, instrument panel bin, dashboard storage, driver's and passenger's door bins; cargo net, cargo tie downs, cargo light; chrome grille, black side window moldings, black front windshield molding, black rear window molding and body-colored door handles.

LIMITED 2WD (4A) (in addition to or instead of XLT 2WD (4A) equipment): Illuminated running boards, front chrome bumper with front and rear colored rub strip; colored bodyside cladding, colored wheel well molding; monotone paint with bodyside accent stripe; premium AM/FM stereo, clock, seek-scan, cassette, single CD, 4 speakers, and fixed antenna; rear audio controls; 5 power accessory outlets, retained accessory power; instrumentation display includes compass; deep tinted windows, power 1/4 vent windows; seating capacity of 8, front captain's seats, fixed headrests, driver and passenger armrests, driver's seat includes 4-way power seat, 8-way direction control, lumbar support; leather seats; full floor console and full overhead console with storage.

XLT 4WD (4A) (in addition to or instead of XLT 2WD (4A) equipment): 6.8L V10 SOHC SMPI 20-valve engine; part-time 4 wheel drive, auto locking hub control and manual shift, 3.73 axle ratio; front non-independent suspension with anti-roll bar and front leaf springs.

LIMITED 4WD (4A) (in addition to or instead of LIMITED 2WD (4A) equipment): 6.8L V10 SOHC SMPI 20-valve engine; part-time 4 wheel drive, auto locking hub control and manual shift, 3.73 axle ratio; front non-independent suspension with anti-roll bar and front leaf springs.

CODE	DESCRIPTION	INVOICE	MSRP

Base Prices

CODE	DESCRIPTION	INVOICE	MSRP
U40	XLT 2WD (4A)	29286	33560
U41	XLT 4WD (4A)	32103	36875
U42	Limited 2WD (4A)	32473	37310
U43	Limited 4WD (4A)	35104	40405
Destination Charge:		700	700

Accessories

CODE	DESCRIPTION	INVOICE	MSRP
17J	**Comfort and Convenience Group (XLT)** *Includes trip computer, illuminated running boards, power driver's seat, cloth captain's chairs with console, floor console, rear radio controls, power rear quarter vent windows and paint stripe. NOT AVAILABLE with 17K, 574, 875.*	986	1160
17K	**Special Services Group (XLT)** *Includes front air conditioning, wheels: argent with black center, cloth full bench, manual black mirrors, standard rearview mirror, vinyl flooring, auxiliary air conditioning delete, 3rd row seat delete, bodyside molding delete, cargo net delete, floor mat delete, overhead console delete and roof rack cross members delete. NOT AVAILABLE with 17J, 64F, 91P, T48, T4T.*	(1696)	(1995)
4	**Leather Surface Captain's Chairs (XLT)** *NOT AVAILABLE with 17K, 574, 875.*	1105	1300
413	**Transfer Case Skid Plate (4WD)**	64	75
428	**High Altitude Principal Use**	NC	NC
429	**Non-High Altitude Principal Use**	NC	NC
54E	**Trailer Tow Manual Telescopic Mirror**	81	95
54Z	**Trailer Tow Power/Heated Mirror**	51	60
574	**Auxiliary Air Conditioning (XLT)** *REQUIRES 17K. NOT AVAILABLE with 17J, 64F, 91P.*	599	705
64F	**Wheels: Chrome Styled Aluminum (XLT)** *NOT AVAILABLE with 17K, 574, 875.*	263	310
76R	**Reverse Sensing System**	208	245
875	**3rd Row Seat (XLT)** *REQUIRES 17K. NOT AVAILABLE with 17J, 64F, 91P.*	544	640
90H	**Heated Seats (Limited)**	247	290
91P	**6-Disc CD Changer** *REQUIRES 17J. NOT AVAILABLE with 17K, 574, 875.*	421	495
99F	**Engine: 7.3L V8 Turbo Diesel (2WD)** *Includes engine block heater, 110-amp alternator and dual batteries. REQUIRES 449. NOT AVAILABLE with XC3.*	3910	4600
99F	**Engine: 7.3L V8 Turbo Diesel (4WD)** *Includes engine block heater, 110-amp alternator and dual batteries. REQUIRES 449. NOT AVAILABLE with XC3.*	3404	4005
99S	**Engine: 6.8L EFI V10 (2WD)** *NOT AVAILABLE with 449, XC1.*	506	595
T48	**Tires: LT265/75R16D OWL AS (XLT)** *REQUIRES 64F. NOT AVAILABLE with T4T, 17K.*	111	130

CODE	DESCRIPTION	INVOICE	MSRP
T4T	Tires: LT265/75R16D OWL AT (Limited)	111	130
T4T	Tires: LT265/75R16D OWL AT (XLT) *REQUIRES 64F. NOT AVAILABLE with T48, 17K.*	217	255
XC1	Limited Slip with 3.73 Axle Ratio *REQUIRES 99F and 449. NOT AVAILABLE with XC3, 99S.*	213	250
XC2	Limited Slip with 4.10 Axle Ratio (2WD) *NOT AVAILABLE with 99F, 99S, 449.*	213	250
XC3	Limited Slip with 4.30 Axle Ratio *REQUIRES 99S. NOT AVAILABLE with 99F, 449, XC1.*	213	250

2000 EXPEDITION

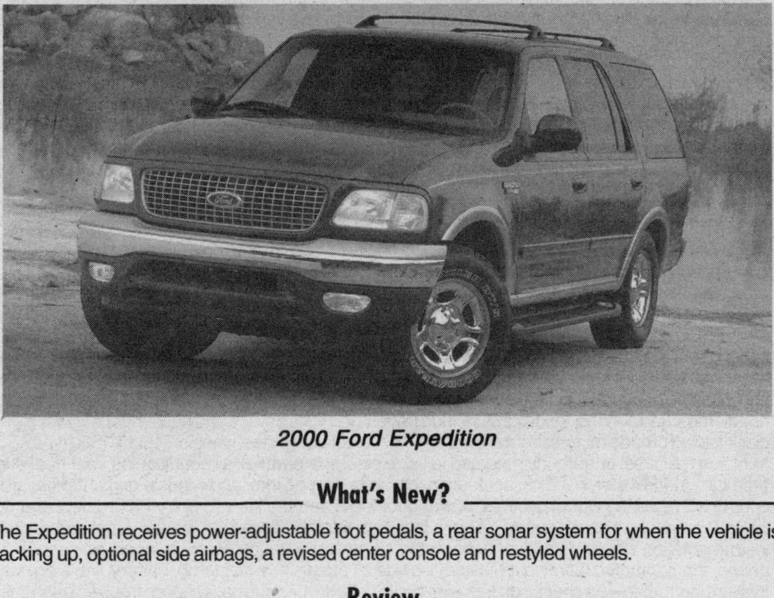

2000 Ford Expedition

What's New?

The Expedition receives power-adjustable foot pedals, a rear sonar system for when the vehicle is backing up, optional side airbags, a revised center console and restyled wheels.

Review

Which one do you think Goldilocks would pick? With the new Excursion on the breakfast table for 2000, it seems Ford has enough different-sized SUVs to satisfy everyone. And for those people who want something bigger than an Explorer, but smaller than an Excursion, the Expedition should be just right.

After allowing GM to dominate the full-size SUV arena for years, in 1997 Ford introduced the Expedition, which had its sights squarely aimed at the Chevy Tahoe and GMC Yukon. The Expedition can seat nine people with its optional third-row bench seat. The Expedition should also be easier to park and maneuver than a Suburban (or Excursion, for that matter). The vehicle has a solid payload and towing capacity: 2,000 lbs. and 8,000 lbs., respectively.

The sonar system and power-adjustable pedals (both which can also be found on a variety of other Ford products this year) are the two main upgrades for 2000. The Reverse Sensing System detects certain objects in the vehicle's path while backing up slowly. The system alerts drivers to objects behind the vehicle within 5.9 feet. Warning beeps are audible within the cabin and, as the vehicle approaches the object, the beeps sound more frequently, becoming a continuous tone when the object is within 10 inches of the vehicle. The power-adjustable pedals allow drivers of smaller stature to move the pedals toward their feet rather than moving the seat uncomfortably close to the steering wheel.

On the road the Expedition is well mannered. It's obviously not a car, but compared to the old Ford Bronco, the Expedition rides like a limousine. A revised center console, memory seats and an electrochromic rearview mirror (each of these is new for this year) should only add to the first-rate interior. Replacing the standard 60/40-split rear bench seat, Expedition buyers can now order the vehicle with two single seats instead of the standard 60/40-split rear bench seat. Like the second-row bench seating, the two individual seats can be stowed if extra cargo-carrying capacity is required.

Ford has put a lot of time and money into making this truck the next sales leader in their already dominant light-truck lineup. The Expedition comes standard with dual airbags, antilock brakes, and optional side airbags. Our biggest gripe stems from the powertrain. While Ford has boosted output for both the 4.6- and 5.4-liter engines, they still can seem less powerful when compared to the Vortec powerplants found in GM's full-size trucks. One option that we think everyone should investigate is the lighted running boards. The Expedition towers above the ground, and entering and exiting this truck will take its toll on most passengers after a few days

The Ford Expedition is a nice balance between comfort and function, and its ability to seat nine people makes it popular with large families and those who have to haul stuff around. Nevertheless, we can't overlook the Dodge Durango and the outstanding Chevrolet Tahoe and GMC Yukon when discussing big trucks. In the last few years, the mid- and full-size sport-ute market has gotten very competitive and the choices are much more difficult to make.

Standard Equipment

XLT 2WD (4A): 4.6L V8 SOHC SMPI 16-valve engine; 4-speed electronic OD auto transmission with lock-up; 650-amp battery with run down protection; 130-amp alternator; rear-wheel drive, 3.31 axle ratio; stainless steel exhaust; front independent suspension with anti-roll bar, front coil springs, rigid rear axle multi-link suspension with anti-roll bar, rear coil springs; power re-circulating ball steering with vehicle speed-sensing assist, power steering cooler; 4-wheel disc brakes with 4-wheel antilock braking system; 26 gal. capacity fuel tank; side impact bars; liftback rear cargo door; class II trailering, trailer harness; roof rack; front and rear chrome bumpers front with body-colored rub strip, rear step; body-colored bodyside molding with chrome bodyside insert; monotone paint; aero-composite halogen headlamps; additional exterior lights include underhood light; driver's and passenger's power remote black folding outside mirrors; front and rear 16" x 7" silver styled steel wheels; P255/70SR16 A/S BSW front and rear tires; underbody mounted full-size steel spare wheel; air conditioning, rear heat ducts; premium AM/FM stereo, clock, seek-scan, cassette, 4 speakers, and window grid antenna; cruise control with steering wheel controls; power door locks, remote keyless entry, child safety rear door locks; 2 power accessory outlets, driver's foot rest, retained accessory power, smokers' package; instrumentation display includes tachometer, oil pressure gauge, water temperature gauge, volt gauge, trip odometer; warning indicators include oil pressure, water temp, battery, lights on, key in ignition, low fuel, low washer fluid, door ajar, brake fluid; driver's and passenger's front airbags; ignition disable, panic alarm; tinted windows, power front and rear windows with driver's 1-touch down, fixed 1/4 vent windows; variable intermittent front windshield wipers, sun visor strip, flip-up rear window, fixed interval rear wiper, rear window defroster; seating capacity of 9, 40-60 split-bench front seat, fixed headrests, center armrest with storage, driver's seat includes 4-way power seat, 8-way direction control, lumbar support, power adjustable pedals; passenger's seat includes 4-way direction control; 60-40 folding rear split-bench 2nd row seat with reclining adjustable headrests, center armrest with storage; removable full folding 3rd row bench seat; front and rear height adjustable seatbelts; cloth seats, vinyl door trim insert, full cloth headliner, full carpet floor covering with carpeted floor mats; interior lights include dome light, front reading lights, 2 door curb lights, illuminated entry; steering wheel with tilt adjustment; dual auxiliary visors, passenger's side vanity mirror; day/night rearview mirror; glove box with light, front and rear cupholders, instrument panel bin, dashboard storage, driver's and passenger's door bins, rear door bins; carpeted cargo floor, plastic trunk lid, cargo tie

CODE	DESCRIPTION	INVOICE	MSRP

downs, cargo light, cargo concealed storage; chrome grille, black side window moldings, black front windshield molding, black rear window molding and body-colored door handles.

EDDIE BAUER 2WD (4A) (in addition to or instead of XLT 2WD (4A) equipment): Running boards; front and rear chrome bumpers with colored rub strip, body-colored bodyside molding, rocker panel extensions, colored wheel well molding; monotone paint with bodyside accent stripe; aero-composite halogen fully auto headlamps with delay-off feature; additional exterior lights include front fog/driving lights; driver's and passenger's power remote body-colored heated folding outside mirrors; front and rear 17" x 7" chrome styled steel wheels; P275/60SR17 A/S OWL front and rear tires; air conditioning with climate control, rear air conditioning with separate controls, rear heater; premium AM/FM stereo, clock, seek-scan, cassette, 4 premium speakers, auto equalizer, and window grid antenna, rear audio controls; 3 power accessory outlets; instrumentation display includes compass, trip computer; deep tinted windows, power 1/4 vent windows; seating capacity of 8, front captain's seats, fixed headrests, driver and passenger armrests, passenger's seat includes 4-way direction control, lumbar support; leather seats; memory on driver's seat with 2 memory setting(s) includes settings for exterior mirrors and power adjustable pedals; interior lights include front and rear reading lights; leather-wrapped steering wheel with tilt adjustment; dual illuminated vanity mirrors, dual auxiliary visors; auto-dimming day/night rearview mirror; full floor console, full overhead console with storage, 2 seat back storage pockets and body-colored grille.

XLT 4WD (4A) (in addition to or instead of XLT 2WD (4A) equipment): Part-time 4 wheel drive, auto locking hub control and electronic shift, front torsion springs, front torsion bar; 30 gal. capacity fuel tank; front tow hooks and P275/60SR17 AT BSW front tires.

EDDIE BAUER 4WD (4A) (in addition to or instead of EDDIE BAUER 2WD (4A) equipment): 5.4L V8 SOHC SMPI 16-valve engine; HD radiator; part-time 4 wheel drive, auto locking hub control and electronic shift, limited slip differential, 3.55 axle ratio; front torsion springs, front torsion bar; 30 gal. capacity fuel tank; front tow hooks and P265/70SR17 AT OWL front and rear tires.

Base Prices

CODE	DESCRIPTION	INVOICE	MSRP
U15	XLT 2WD (4A)	25998	29750
U16	XLT 4WD (4A)	28438	32620
U17	Eddie Bauer 2WD (4A)	31344	36040
U18	Eddie Bauer 4WD (4A)	34532	39790
Destination Charge:		640	640

Accessories

CODE	DESCRIPTION	INVOICE	MSRP
1	Leather Captain's Chairs (XLT) *Includes vinyl 3rd row seating, 6-way power driver seat and floor console. REQUIRES 66A.*	1156	1360
162	Reverse Sensing System *REQUIRES 67A.*	206	245
21B	2nd Row Leather Captain's Chairs (Eddie Bauer) *Includes fold flat feature with carpet on backside.*	676	795
413	Skid Plate Package (4WD) *Includes front differential/suspension, fuel tank and transfer case.*	89	105
428	High Altitude Principal Use *REQUIRES XH6.*	NC	NC
429	Non-High Altitude Principal Use	NC	NC

CODE	DESCRIPTION	INVOICE	MSRP
43M	Power Moon Roof *Includes sunshade. REQUIRES 552.*	680	800
44E	Transmission: 4-Speed Automatic with OD *REQUIRES 99L. NOT AVAILABLE with XH7.*	NC	NC
535	Trailer Towing Group (Class III) (2WD) *Includes 7-pin trailer wiring harness, frame mounted trailer hitch (Class III), super engine cooling, auxiliary transmission oil cooler, rear load leveling and 30 gallon fuel tank. See salesperson for specific trailer towing limits and corresponding required equipment.*	748	880
535	Trailer Towing Group (Class III) (4WD) *Includes 7-pin trailer wiring harness, frame mounted trailer hitch (Class III), super engine cooling and auxiliary transmission oil cooler. See salesperson for specific trailer towing limits and corresponding required equipment.*	332	390
54H	Heated Mirrors (XLT)	43	50
552	Premium Sport Appearance Group (XLT 2WD) *Includes sport woven cloth captain's chairs, accent color rear bumper, fog lamps, step bar, wheel lip moldings, wheels: 17" chrome styled steel and tires: P275/60R17 A/S OWL. REQUIRES 66A.*	1101	1295
552	Premium Sport Appearance Group (XLT 4WD) *Includes sport woven cloth captain's chairs, accent color rear bumper, fog lamps, skid plate package, step bar, wheels: 17" chrome styled steel and tires: P265/70R17 AT OWL. REQUIRES 66A.*	1186	1395
585	Radio: AM/FM Stereo with Single CD *NOT AVAILABLE with 91P.*	85	100
646	Wheels: 16" Cast Aluminum (XLT) *REQUIRES T65.*	213	250
66A	Comfort/Convenience Group (XLT) *Includes cloth captain's chairs, floor console, auxiliary heater/air conditioner (rear), dual illuminated visor vanity mirrors, privacy glass, electrochromic mirror, illuminated running boards and overhead console. NOT AVAILABLE with 87D.*	1870	2200
67A	Side Air Bags *REQUIRES 66A (XLT).*	335	395
68P	Four Corner Load Leveling Suspension (4WD) *REQUIRES 535.*	692	815
87D	3rd Row Bench Seat Delete (XLT) *REQUIRES S. NOT AVAILABLE with 66A.*	(544)	(640)
90H	Driver's and Passenger's Heated Front Seats (Eddie Bauer)	251	295
91P	6-Disc CD Changer (XLT) *REQUIRES 66A. NOT AVAILABLE with 585.*	421	495
99L	Engine: 5.4L SOHC (XLT/Eddie Bauer 2WD) *Includes super engine cooling. REQUIRES 44E. NOT AVAILABLE with XH7.*	591	695
M	Cloth Captain's Chairs Delete (XLT) *REQUIRES 66A. NOT AVAILABLE with S, 1, 87D, 552, 162, 67A.*	(328)	(385)
R91	6-Disc CD Changer (Eddie Bauer) *REQUIRES U91.*	421	495
T65	Tires: P255/70R16 AT OWL (XLT) *REQUIRES 646.*	196	230

CODE	DESCRIPTION	INVOICE	MSRP
U57	Auxiliary Heater/AC-Discount (XLT) *REQUIRES 66A.*	(599)	(705)
U91	6-Disc CD Changer Discount (Eddie Bauer) *REQUIRES R91.*	(421)	(495)
XH6	Limited Slip with 3.73 Axle Ratio *REQUIRES 99L. NOT AVAILABLE with XH7, XH9.*	217	255
XH7	Limited Slip with 3.31 Axle Ratio (2WD) *NOT AVAILABLE with 99L, 44E, XH9, XH6.*	217	255
XH9	Limited Slip with 3.55 Axle Ratio (All Except Eddie Bauer 4WD) *REQUIRES 99L. NOT AVAILABLE with XH6, XH7.*	217	255

2000 EXPLORER

2000 Ford Explorer

What's New?

The recently introduced Reverse Sensing System continues to be an option. A color-keyed, two-spoke leather-wrapped steering wheel (with auxiliary audio, climate and speed control) is now standard on Eddie Bauer models. XLT Sport/Eddie Bauer/Limited models with 5.0-liter V8s receive a trailer-towing package as standard equipment. The XL is available only for fleet sales, and the XLS replaces the XL Appearance as base retail model.

Review

Since its introduction in 1991, the Ford Explorer has resided at the top of the sport-utility sales heap. This is totally understandable, as the Explorer combines style, comfort and room in a go-anywhere package. The modern-day Country Squire, some have called it, after the segment-leading station wagon of the 1960s.

The Explorer's sales success is, of course, do to with America's big appetite for SUVs. But it's also a compliment to Ford, as the Explorer gets just about everything right. The interior instills a feeling of quality that is missing from the Chevrolet Blazer. An organically sweeping dashboard houses radio controls that can be operated without a magnifying glass. Materials in the Explorer look and feel rich. Rear-seat comfort surpasses Chevy, and entry/exit is easier than the Jeep Cherokee. Explorers offer more cargo capacity than most rivals do, and five passengers can ride with ease.

The Explorer's standard 4.0-liter V6 is the smallest engine found in a domestic sport-ute. Acceleration is fine from a standstill, but step on the gas at 50 mph and not much happens. That's not good news when there's a need to pass or merge. To compensate, Ford also offers an OHV 5.0-liter V8 engine that used to power the old Mustang GT. While the acceleration with the 5.0-liter motor is improved over the base V6, it gives up a lot in fuel consumption. Fortunately, Ford introduced an optional SOHC V6 in 1997 that offers nearly as much power as the V8. In addition, this engine costs less and offers greater fuel efficiency. We recommend this engine over the other two motor choices due to its great power and affordable price.

Explorers retain a distinctly trucklike character, which could be a bonus or a demerit. They're tough and solid, though steering is a little slow and ponderous and the body leans through tight corners. Braking is excellent and the suspension has a compliant attitude, but Ford's Explorer can bounce around over rough pavement, making occupants regret the Denver omelet they had for breakfast.

Ford has a philosophy of building vehicles that everyone can be happy with. Sure, the Jeep Grand Cherokee feels sportier, and the Chevrolet Blazer looks cooler, but the Explorer has just the right amount of class and ruggedness to make it America's best-selling off-roader. If you are thinking about buying a sport-ute, chances are you've already checked out the Explorer. If you haven't, do yourself a favor and find out why there are so many of these trucks on the road.

Standard Equipment

SPORT 2WD (5M): 4.0L V6 OHV SMPI 12-valve engine; 5-speed OD manual transmission; 650-amp battery with run down protection; HD radiator; 95-amp alternator; rear-wheel drive, 3.27 axle ratio; steel exhaust; front independent suspension with anti-roll bar, front torsion springs, front torsion bar, HD front shocks, rigid rear axle suspension with anti-roll bar, rear leaf springs, HD rear shocks; power rack-and-pinion steering, power steering cooler; 4-wheel disc brakes with 4-wheel antilock braking system; 17.5 gal. capacity fuel tank; liftback rear cargo door; roof rack; front and rear argent bumpers with black rub strip, rear step; body-colored bodyside molding, rocker panel extensions, black fender flares; monotone clearcoat paint; aero-composite halogen headlamps; driver's and passenger's power remote black folding outside mirrors; front and rear 15" x 7" silver alloy wheels; P235/75SR15 AT OWL front and rear tires; underbody mounted full-size steel spare wheel with crankdown; air conditioning, rear heat ducts; AM/FM stereo, clock, seek-scan, cassette, 4 speakers, and fixed antenna; automatic power door locks with 2 stage unlock, power remote hatch/trunk release; 2 power accessory outlets, retained accessory power; instrumentation display includes tachometer, oil pressure gauge, water temperature gauge, volt gauge, trip odometer; warning indicators include oil pressure, battery, lights on, key in ignition, door ajar; driver's and passenger's front airbags; ignition disable; deep tinted windows, power windows with driver's 1-touch down, fixed 1/4 vent windows; variable intermittent front windshield wipers, sun visor strip, flip-up rear window, fixed interval rear wiper, rear window defroster; seating capacity of 4, front captain's seats, fixed headrests, driver's seat includes 4-way direction control, passenger's seat includes 4-way direction control; 50-50 folding rear bench seat with tilt headrests; front height adjustable seatbelts; cloth seats, vinyl door trim insert, full cloth headliner, full color-keyed carpet floor covering, deluxe sound insulation; interior lights include dome light with fade, front reading lights, illuminated entry; dual auxiliary visors, passenger's side vanity mirror; day/night rearview mirror; partial floor console, glove box with light, driver's and passenger's door bins; carpeted cargo floor, vinyl trunk lid, cargo tie downs, cargo light; body-colored grille, black side window moldings, black front windshield molding, black rear window molding and body-colored door handles.

XLS 2WD (5M) (in addition to or instead of SPORT 2WD (5M) equipment): 21 gal. capacity fuel tank; body-colored bodyside molding with chrome bodyside insert; power door locks with 2 stage unlock, child safety rear door locks; tinted windows, power front and rear windows with driver's 1-touch down, fixed 1/4 vent windows; seating capacity of 5, center armrest with storage and 60-40 folding rear bench seat with tilt headrests.

XLT 2WD (5A) (in addition to or instead of XLS 2WD (5A) equipment): 5-speed electronic OD auto transmission; 3.55 axle ratio; front and rear chrome bumpers with black rub strip; monotone paint with bodyside accent stripe; additional exterior lights include front fog/driving lights; rear air conditioning ducts and controls, AM/FM stereo, clock, seek-scan, single CD, 4 speakers, and fixed antenna, rear audio controls; cruise control with steering wheel controls; power door locks with 2 stage unlock, remote keyless entry, keyless entry keypad, smokers' package; instrumentation display includes compass, exterior temp; panic alarm, security system; deep tinted windows; front sports seats, fixed headrests, center armrest with storage, driver's seat includes 4-way power seat, 8-way direction control, lumbar support, passenger's seat includes 4-way direction control, lumbar support; premium cloth seats, carpeted floor mats; interior lights include front and rear reading lights; leather-wrapped steering wheel with tilt adjustment; dual illuminated vanity mirrors; full floor console, full overhead console with storage, front cupholder; cargo cover and chrome grille.

EDDIE BAUER 2WD (5A) (in addition to or instead of XLT 2WD (5A) equipment): 4.0L V6 SOHC SMPI 12-valve engine; transmission oil cooler; running boards; front and rear body-colored rub strip, front chrome bumper, rear body-colored bumper; body-colored bodyside molding with chrome bodyside insert, body-colored fender flares; lower accent two-tone paint; aero-composite halogen fully auto headlamps with delay-off feature; front and rear 16" x 7" polished alloy wheels; P255/70SR16 AT OWL front and rear tires; air conditioning with climate control and rear ducts; MACH AM/FM stereo, clock, seek-scan, single CD, 4 speakers, amplifier, sub-woofer and fixed antenna (No Cost Option 916), radio steering wheel controls; garage door opener; instrumentation display includes systems monitor, trip computer; warning indicators include low fuel, low washer fluid, trunk ajar, service interval and auto-dimming day/night rearview mirror and leather seating surfaces (No Cost Option F).

LIMITED 2WD (5A) (in addition to or instead of EDDIE BAUER 2WD SPORT UTILITY (5A) equipment): Front and rear body-colored bumpers with body-colored rub strip; additional exterior lights include underhood light; driver's and passenger's power remote black heated folding outside mirrors; driver's seat includes 4-way power seat, 8-way direction control, power lumbar support, passenger's seat includes 4-way power seat, 8-way direction control, power lumbar support (No Cost Option 1); 3-position memory on driver's seat, leather door trim insert, simulated wood trim on instrument panel and body-colored grille.

4WD (in addition to or instead of 2WD equipment): Part-time 4 wheel drive, auto ride control/auto-leveling suspension (Limited), auto locking hub control and electronic shift, front torsion springs, front torsion bar, 3.27 (Sport)/3.55 (XLS)/3.73 (XLT)/4.1 (Eddie Bauer/Limited) axle ratio and skid plate(s).

AWD (in addition to or instead of 4WD equipment): Full-time 4 wheel drive, limited slip differential, auto ride control/auto-leveling suspension (Limited) and 3.73 axle ratio.

Base Prices

U60	Sport 2WD (5M)	18153	19970
U70	Sport 4WD (5M)	20881	23070
U62	XLS 2WD (5M)	21159	23385
U72	XLS 4WD (5M)	22813	25265
U63	XLT 2WD (5A)	24586	27280
U73	XLT 4WD (5A)	26316	29245
U83	XLT AWD (5A)	26976	29995
U64	Eddie Bauer 2WD (5A)	28595	31835
U74	Eddie Bauer 4WD (5A)	30324	33800
U84	Eddie Bauer AWD (5A)	30689	34215

CODE	DESCRIPTION	INVOICE	MSRP
U65	Limited 2WD (5A)	28820	32090
U75	Limited 4WD (5A)	30549	34055
U85	Limited AWD (5A)	30914	34470
Destination Charge:		550	550

Accessories

CODE	DESCRIPTION	INVOICE	MSRP
1	Luxury Leather Bucket Seats (Limited)	808	950
	Manufacturer Discount	(808)	(950)
	Net Price	NC	NC
	Includes 6-way power driver's/passenger's seats, power driver's/passenger's lumbar support and 3-position driver's memory seat.		
182	Side Step Bar (Sport)	251	295
	In medium platinum.		
186	Running Boards (XLT)	336	395
	Deletes rocker moldings.		
21A	Front Side Airbags	336	395
	REQUIRES F (4-Door) or 94A (Sport).		
21H	Heated Front Seats (Eddie Bauer)	217	255
21H	Heated Front Seats (Limited)	217	255
	Manufacturer Discount	(217)	(255)
	Net Price	NC	NC
41H	Engine Block Heater	30	35
	Includes 400-watt single element.		
428	High Altitude Principal Use	NC	NC
	REQUIRES 44U. NOT AVAILABLE with 99P.		
429	Non-High Altitude Principal Use	NC	NC
439	Power Moonroof (Sport)	680	800
	Includes overhead console. REQUIRES 94A and 47P.		
439	Power Moonroof with Shade (XLT/Eddie Bauer/Limited)	680	800
	Includes front overhead console.		
44D	Transmission: 5-Speed Automatic with OD (Sport/XLS)	931	1095
	REQUIRES 94A.		
44D	Transmission: 5-Speed Automatic with OD (XLT Except AWD)	931	1095
	Manufacturer Discount	(931)	(1095)
	Net Price	NC	NC
	NOT AVAILABLE with 99P.		
44U	Transmission: 4-Speed Auto. with OD (Eddie Bauer/Limited Except 4WD)	NC	NC
	REQUIRES 99P.		
44U	Transmission: 4-Speed Automatic with OD (XLT 2WD)	931	1095
	REQUIRES 99P. NOT AVAILABLE with 99E.		
44U	Transmission: 4-Speed Automatic with OD (XLT AWD)	NC	NC

CODE	DESCRIPTION	INVOICE	MSRP
47E	XLT Sport Group (XLT)	931	1095
	Manufacturer Discount	(255)	(300)
	Net Price	676	795
	Includes color-keyed bodyside molding/grille, XLT badging, front and rear bumpers, side step bar, wheel lip molding system and wheels: 16" machined aluminum. REQUIRES 99P.		
47E	XLT Sport Group (XLT - 4WD/AWD)	931	1095
	Includes color-keyed bodyside molding/grille, XLT badging, front and rear bumpers, side step bars, wheel lip molding system and wheels: 16" machined aluminum.		
47P	Premium Sport Group (Sport 2WD)	1360	1600
	Manufacturer Discount	(425)	(500)
	Net Price	935	1100
	Includes fog lamps, front and rear bumpers in medium platinum, side step bar, tires: P235/75R15SL AT OWL, wheels: 15" chrome steel, 3.73 axle ratio, wheel lip molding system and tow hooks (front). REQUIRES 55T.		
47P	Premium Sport Group (Sport 2WD)	1360	1600
	Manufacturer Discount	(425)	(500)
	Net Price	935	1100
	Includes fog lamps, front and rear bumpers in medium platinum, side step bar, tires: P235/75R15SL AT OWL, wheels: 15" chrome steel, wheel lip molding system and tow hooks (front). REQUIRES 55T and 44D.		
47P	Premium Sport Package (Sport 4WD)	1360	1600
	Manufacturer Discount	(425)	(500)
	Net Price	935	1100
	Includes fog lamps, front and rear bumpers in medium platinum, side step bar, tires: P255/70R16SL AT OWL, wheels: 16" machined aluminum, wheel lip molding system, tow hooks (front) and 4.10 axle ratio. REQUIRES 55T. NOT AVAILABLE with 44D.		
534	Trailer Towing Prep Package	302	355
	Includes wiring harness and heavy duty flasher. Recommended for towing trailers.		
55G	Convenience Group (XLS)	638	750
	Includes cargo cover, privacy glass, remote keyless entry, panic alarm, speed control and tilt steering wheel.		
55T	Convenience Group (Sport)	638	750
	Includes cargo cover, floor mats, remote keyless entry, panic alarm, speed control and leather-wrapped tilt steering wheel. U5T is recommended.		
58K	Radio: AM/FM Stereo with CD and Cassette (Sport)	196	230
	Includes 80-watt amp, in-dash CD, clock and 4 speakers. NOT AVAILABLE with 916, 58Z, 94A.		
58K	Radio: AM/FM Stereo with CD and Cassette (Sport)	111	130
	Includes 80-watt amp, in-dash CD, clock and 4 speakers. NOT AVAILABLE with 916, 58Z.		
58K	Radio: AM/FM Stereo with CD and Cassette (XLS)	196	230
	Includes 80-watt amp, in-dash CD, clock and 4 speakers. NOT AVAILABLE with 58Z, 66S.		

CODE	DESCRIPTION	INVOICE	MSRP
58K	Radio: AM/FM Stereo with CD and Cassette (XLS/XLT)	111	130
	Includes 80-watt amp, in-dash CD, clock and 4 speakers. NOT AVAILABLE with 58Z, 916.		
58Z	Radio: AM/FM Stereo, Clock and CD (Sport/XLS)	85	100
	Includes 24-watt amp, in-dash CD and 4 speakers. NOT AVAILABLE with 58K, 916.		
59B	Electrochromic Mirror (XLT)	158	185
	Includes auto day/night mirror and auto headlamps.		
66S	XLS Sport Group (XLS)	1275	1500
	Manufacturer Discount	(425)	(500)
	Net Price	850	1000
	Includes wheels: 15" chrome steel, AM/FM stereo with clock and CD, fog lamps, removable storage bag, side step bar, unique cloth captain's chairs, door mounted XLS badge and wheel lip molding system.		
67H	Homelink with Travelnote (XLT)	182	215
68L	Rear Load Leveling (4WD - XLT/Eddie Bauer/Limited)	298	350
	REQUIRES F.		
76R	Reverse Sensing System (XLT/Eddie Bauer/Limited)	217	255
87K	Skid Plates (4WD/AWD)	106	125
916	Radio: Ford MACH Audio System (Eddie Bauer/Limited)	565	665
	Manufacturer Discount	(565)	(665)
	Net Price	NC	NC
	Includes cassette, CD, 290-watt (peak power) amp, clock, sub-woofer and digital signal processor.		
916	Radio: Ford MACH Audio System (Sport/XLT)	565	665
	Includes cassette, CD, 290-watt (peak power) amp, clock, sub-woofer and digital signal processor. REQUIRES 94A and 44D. NOT AVAILABLE with 58K, 58Z.		
91P	6-Disc CD Changer	336	395
	REQUIRES 94A and 44D.		
94A	Comfort Group (Sport)	2503	2945
	Manufacturer Discount	(931)	(1095)
	Net Price	1572	1850
	Includes keypad/autolock, puddle lamps located on outside rearview mirrors, cloth sport bucket seats, AM/FM stereo with clock and CD, electrochromic mirror, autolamp, high-series floor console, dual illuminated visor vanity mirrors and overhead console. REQUIRES 55T and 44D. NOT AVAILABLE with 58K.		
954	Two-Tone Rocker Paint (XLT)	102	120
99E	Engine: 4.0L SOHC V6 (Sport/XLS/XLT Except AWD)	459	540
	NOT AVAILABLE with 44U.		
99P	Engine: 5.0L EFI V8 (2WD - Eddie Bauer/Limited)	358	421
	Includes trailer towing prep package. REQUIRES 44U. NOT AVAILABLE with 534.		
99P	Engine: 5.0L EFI V8 (AWD)	NC	NC
	REQUIRES 58K or 916.		
99P	Engine: 5.0L EFI V8 (XLT 2WD)	659	775
	REQUIRES 44U. NOT AVAILABLE with 44D, 534, 428.		

CODE	DESCRIPTION	INVOICE	MSRP
F	Leather Sport Bucket Seats (Eddie Bauer)	808	950
	Manufacturer Discount	(808)	(950)
	Net Price	NC	NC
	Includes 6-way power driver's/passenger's and manual driver's/passenger's lumbar support.		
F	Leather Sport Bucket Seats (Sport)	557	655
	Includes 6-way power driver's/passenger's and manual driver's/passenger's lumbar support. REQUIRES 94A.		
F	Leather Sport Bucket Seats (XLT)	808	950
	Includes 6-way power driver/passenger and manual driver/passenger lumbar support.		
G	Cloth Sport Bucket Seats (XLS)	238	280
	REQUIRES 21A.		
PWF	Pearlescent Paint (Limited)	170	200
U5T	Convenience Group Discount (Sport)	(302)	(355)
	REQUIRES 55T.		

2001 EXPLORER SPORT

2001 Ford Explorer Sport

What's New?

The 2001 Ford Explorer Sport receives styling changes as well as minor mechanical and interior improvements.

Review

For the 2001 model year, Ford has updated the two-door Ford Explorer Sport. Primarily, these changes are aimed at making the Sport model more distinctive within the Explorer lineup. But there are also some mechanical changes that should address some of the problems we had with the previous model.

Though the 2001 Sport still lacks the versatility of a four-door Explorer, it does offer even sportier looks. Every outer body panel except the liftgate has been updated. Styling cues from the 2000 model's Premium Sport Group — an optional package that included side and wheel-lip moldings — are now integrated into the sheetmetal of all 2001 models. The new Explorer Sport also features a more distinctive hood, grille and bumpers. There are also three new exterior colors: Mandarin Gold, Estate Green and Island Blue. Both two-wheel and four-wheel drive models are available.

Inside, the Explorer Sport's front seats feature a more durable fabric and new dual-density foam. Seat travel for the driver has been increased by 1 inch. Three seat choices are available in the Explorer Sport: standard cloth captain's chairs, power-adjustable cloth sport-bucket seats, or power-adjustable leather sport-bucket seats. The sport-bucket seats are exclusive to the Explorer Sport model. The 50/50-split rear bench seat can be folded flat to allow more space for cargo. Maximum cargo capacity is 71.4 cubic feet.

There are other improvements to the interior, including new trim, a standard CD player, deeper and larger cupholders, and a freshened instrument panel. The instrument panel features a new gauge cluster with white dial faces. There's also an optional Pioneer six-disc in-dash CD player and an optional overhead console.

One complaint we had with the previous Explorer Sport was the choppy ride. Hopefully, Ford has improved things with new two-stage variable-rate taper leaf springs for the rear suspension. The Explorer's shocks are also changed to better match the new spring rates. Ford says the end result is improved handling and ride quality. There are also new urethane body mounts and new sound-deadening material for a reduction in noise, vibration and harshness.

The 2001 Explorer Sport features a 4.0-liter SOHC V6 as standard equipment. The engine produces 205 horsepower at 5,250 rpm and 240 foot-pounds of torque at 3,750 rpm. It's mated to a five-speed automatic transmission. Ford says a five-speed manual transmission will be offered on Sport models beginning in fall 2000.

For safety, the Sport comes equipped with front airbags, optional seat-mounted side airbags, and child safety seat-anchor brackets. The 2001 Sport also features bigger front brakes than the previous model for improved performance and durability.

While not a complete redesign, Ford's changes to the Explorer Sport are significant enough to make it worth a look. If the improvements to the suspension and interior work as advertised, this could be one of the better two-door SUVs available.

Standard Equipment

BASE 2WD (5A): 4.0L V6 SOHC SMPI 12-valve engine; 5-speed electronic OD auto transmission; 650-amp battery with run down protection; 130-amp alternator; rear-wheel drive, 3.73 axle ratio; steel exhaust; front independent suspension with anti-roll bar, front torsion springs, front torsion bar, gas-pressurized front shocks, rigid rear axle suspension with anti-roll bar, HD rear leaf springs, gas-pressurized rear shocks; power rack-and-pinion steering, power steering cooler; 4-wheel disc brakes with 4-wheel antilock braking system; 17.5 gal. capacity fuel tank; side impact bars; liftback rear cargo door; trailer harness; roof rack; front and rear argent bumpers with black rub strip, rear step; body-colored bodyside molding; rocker panel extensions, body-colored fender flares; clearcoat monotone paint; aero-composite halogen headlamps; driver's and passenger's power remote black folding outside mirrors; front and rear 15" x 7" silver alloy wheels; P235/75SR15 A/S OWL front and rear tires; underbody mounted full-size steel spare wheel; air conditioning, rear heat ducts; premium AM/FM stereo, clock, seek-scan, single CD, 4 speakers, and fixed antenna; power door locks with 2 stage unlock; 2 power accessory outlets, retained accessory power, smokers' package; instrumentation display includes tachometer, oil pressure gauge, water temperature gauge, volt gauge, trip odometer; warning indicators include oil pressure, water temp, battery, lights on, key in ignition, low fuel, door ajar; driver's and passenger's front airbags; ignition disable; deep tinted windows, power windows with driver's 1-touch down, fixed 1/4 vent windows; variable intermittent front windshield wipers, sun visor strip, flip-up rear window, fixed interval rear wiper, rear window defroster; seating capacity of 4, front captain's seats, fixed headrests, center armrest with storage, driver's seat includes 4-way direction control, easy entry, passenger's seat includes 4-way direction control, easy entry; 50-50 folding rear

CODE	DESCRIPTION	INVOICE	MSRP

bench seat with tilt headrests; front height adjustable seatbelts; cloth seats, vinyl door trim insert, full cloth headliner, full color-keyed carpet floor covering with carpeted floor mats; interior lights include dome light with fade, front and rear reading lights, illuminated entry; passenger's side vanity mirror, driver's side auxiliary visor; day/night rearview mirror; partial floor console, glove box with light, front and rear cupholders, driver's and passenger's door bins; carpeted cargo floor, plastic trunk lid, cargo tie downs, cargo light; body-colored grille, black side window moldings, black front windshield molding, black rear window molding and body-colored door handles.

BASE 4WD (5A) (in addition to or instead of BASE 2WD (5A) equipment): Four-wheel drive and auto locking hub control and electronic shift.

Base Prices

CODE	DESCRIPTION	INVOICE	MSRP
U60	Base 2WD (5A)	19604	21675
U70	Base 4WD (5A)	22262	24695
Destination Charge:		550	550

Accessories

CODE	DESCRIPTION	INVOICE	MSRP
21A	Front Side Airbags *REQUIRES 553 and 47P.*	332	390
41H	Engine Block Heater	30	35
428	High Altitude Principal Use	NC	NC
429	Non-High Altitude Principal Use	NC	NC
439	Power Moonroof *REQUIRES (60A or 60B) and 553.*	680	800
47P	Premium Sport Group (2WD) *Includes fog lamps, front tow hooks, tires: P235/75R15 AT OWL and side step bar. REQUIRES 553.*	468	550
47P	Premium Sport Group (4WD) *Includes fog lamps, front tow hooks, wheels: 16" bright cast aluminum, tires: P255/70R16 AT OWL, side step bar and 4.10 axle ratio. REQUIRES 553. NOT AVAILABLE with XD4.*	595	700
553	Convenience Group *Includes autolock/relock, remote keyless entry, speed control, leather-wrapped tilt steering wheel and puddle lamps.*	638	750
60A	Cloth Comfort Group *Includes high series floor console and overhead console. REQUIRES 553. NOT AVAILABLE with 60B.*	795	935
60B	Leather Comfort Group *Includes high series floor console and overhead console. REQUIRES 553. NOT AVAILABLE with 60A.*	1271	1495
87K	Skid Plates (4WD) *Includes fuel tank and transfer case shields.*	106	125
916	Radio: AM/FM Stereo with 6-Disc CD *Includes clock, 6-disc in-dash CD, Pioneer Audiophile System, 290-watts (peak power), 6 speakers and sub-woofer.*	433	510

CODE	DESCRIPTION	INVOICE	MSRP
XD2	Limited Slip Rear Axle with 4.10 (4WD) *REQUIRES 47P. NOT AVAILABLE with XD4.*	302	355
XD4	Limited Slip Rear Axle with 3.73 *NOT AVAILABLE with XD2, 47P.*	302	355

2001 EXPLORER SPORT TRAC

2001 Ford Explorer Sport Trac

What's New?

The Sport Trac is an offshoot of the SUV. Basically, Ford has grafted a small cargo bed to the back of a redesigned Ford Explorer.

Review

Just when you thought the SUV market couldn't get any bigger, along comes the Ford Explorer Sport Trac. Not quite a pickup truck, not quite an SUV, the Sport Trac takes elements from both to create a whole new type of Ford vehicle.

Marketed as a vehicle for people with active lifestyles, the 2001 Explorer Sport Trac is based on the Explorer platform. From the C-pillar forward, the Sport Trac is a five-passenger SUV. Rearward of the C-pillar, there's a one-piece, all-composite cargo area. Made of durable sheet-molding composite, it has molded-in texture and a mar-resistant low-gloss coating. The cargo area is normally 4 feet in length, but an optional cargo keeper also extends the utility of the cargo area. This U-shaped tubular device hinges on the interior sides of the cargo area and rests on the cargo floor. When flipped out over Explorer Sport Trac's tailgate, it extends the cargo area length to almost 6 feet.

There's also an optional two-piece foldable and lockable hard tonneau cover to provide protection for items contained in the cargo area. It comes with a removable divider that increases storage flexibility for the cargo area.

All Explorer Sport Trac models are equipped with Ford's proven 4.0-liter V6 engine. This single-overhead cam engine, which produces 206 horsepower at 5,000 rpm and 238 foot-pounds of torque at 4,000 rpm, is linked to an electronically controlled five-speed automatic transmission. Four-wheel drive is optional. All models can tow up to 5,300 pounds.

Explorer Sport Trac shares its basic front and rear suspension geometry with the current four-door Ford Explorer. However, Ford says the Sport Trac's bushings, spring rates, shock valving and stabilizer bars have been modified for improved ride, handling and noise/vibration/harshness performance.

All Explorer Sport Trac models come with a standard four-wheel antilock braking system. The system controls the front wheels independently and the rear wheels in tandem to improve vehicle control under heavy braking in most operating conditions. The system includes dynamic rear proportioning to help optimize stopping performance under varying vehicle load conditions.

While you can look forward to more manufacturers entering this SUV niche, the Sport Trac's main competitors at this point are the Nissan Frontier Crew Cab and Dodge Dakota Quad Cab. The Nissan and Dodge vehicles are based off pickup trucks, but both are similar in that they compromise between the true truck and SUV abilities. What does this mean? If you want to haul stuff around, buy a Ford F-150 with a full-size bed. It works better. If you want to haul a family around, buy an Explorer. It works better. But if you need both, the Sport Trac compromise between pickup and sport-ute might suit you.

Standard Equipment

BASE 2WD (5A): 4.0L V6 SOHC SMPI 12-valve engine; 5-speed electronic OD auto transmission; 650-amp battery with run down protection; 130-amp alternator; rear-wheel drive, 3.73 axle ratio; steel exhaust; front independent suspension with anti-roll bar, front torsion springs, front torsion bar, gas-pressurized front shocks, rigid rear axle suspension with anti-roll bar, HD rear leaf springs, gas-pressurized rear shocks; power rack-and-pinion steering; power steering cooler; 4-wheel disc brakes with 4-wheel antilock braking system; 20.5 gal. capacity fuel tank; side impact bars; tailgate rear cargo door; trailer harness; roof rack; front and rear argent bumpers with black rub strip, rear step; body-colored bodyside molding, rocker panel extensions, body-colored fender flares; monotone paint; aero-composite halogen headlamps; additional exterior lights include pickup cargo box light; driver's and passenger's power remote black folding outside mirrors; front and rear 15" x 7" silver styled steel wheels; P235/75SR15 A/S OWL front and rear tires; underbody mounted full-size steel spare wheel; air conditioning, rear heat ducts; premium AM/FM stereo, clock, seek-scan, single CD, 4 speakers, and fixed antenna; power door locks with 2 stage unlock, child safety rear door locks; 3 power accessory outlets, retained accessory power, smokers' package; instrumentation display includes tachometer, oil pressure gauge, water temperature gauge, volt gauge, trip odometer; warning indicators include oil pressure, water temp, battery, lights on, key in ignition, door ajar; driver's and passenger's front airbags; ignition disable; deep tinted windows, power front and rear windows with driver's 1-touch down; variable intermittent front windshield wipers, sun visor strip, power rear window; seating capacity of 5, front captain's seats, fixed headrests, center armrest with storage, driver's seat includes 4-way direction control, passenger's seat includes 4-way direction control; 60-40 folding rear bench seat with tilt headrests; front height adjustable seatbelts; cloth seats, vinyl door trim insert, full cloth headliner, full vinyl floor covering with carpeted floor mats; interior lights include dome light with fade, front and rear reading lights, illuminated entry; passenger's side vanity mirror; day/night rearview mirror; partial floor console, glove box with light, front and rear cupholders; carpeted cargo floor, plastic trunk lid; body-colored grille, black side window moldings, black front windshield molding, black rear window molding and body-colored door handles.

BASE 4WD (5A) (in addition to or instead of BASE 2WD (5A) equipment): Auto full-time 4-wheel drive, auto locking hub control and electronic shift and front tow hooks.

Base Prices

U67	Base 2WD (5A)	20330	22500
U77	Base 4WD (5A)	22768	25270
Destination Charge:		550	550

CODE	DESCRIPTION	INVOICE	MSRP
	Accessories		
20T	Payload Package #2 (4WD) *Includes 1460 lbs maximum payload and 5880 lbs GVWR.*	85	100
20W	Payload Package #2 (2WD) *Includes 1500 lbs maximum payload and 5700 lbs GVWR.*	85	100
41H	Engine Block Heater	30	35
428	High Altitude Principal Use	NC	NC
429	Non-High Altitude Principal Use	NC	NC
439	Power Moonroof *REQUIRES (60A or 60B) and 553.*	680	800
47P	Premium Sport Group *Includes fog lamps, tires: P255/70R16 AT OWL, wheels: 16" bright cast aluminum, side step bar and 4.10 axle ratio. NOT AVAILABLE with XD4.*	595	700
553	Convenience Group *Includes autolock/relock, remote keyless entry, speed control and leather-wrapped tilt steering wheel.*	638	750
581	Radio: AM/FM Stereo with CD *Includes 6-disc in-dash CD, clock, 4 speakers and 80-watts continuous power.*	229	270
60A	Cloth Comfort Group *Includes low back cloth bucket seats and overhead console. REQUIRES 553. NOT AVAILABLE with 60B.*	795	935
60B	Leather Comfort Group *Includes leather low-back bucket seats, high series floor console and overhead console. REQUIRES 553. NOT AVAILABLE with 60A.*	1271	1495
63E	Cargo Cage	166	195
86T	Hard Tonneau Cover *2-piece folding and lockable.*	502	590
87K	Skid Plates (4WD) *Includes fuel tank and transfer case.*	106	125
XD2	Limited Slip Rear Axle with 4.10 *REQUIRES 47P. NOT AVAILABLE with XD4.*	302	355
XD4	Limited Slip Rear Axle with 3.73 *NOT AVAILABLE with XD2, 47P.*	302	355

2000 SVT F-150 LIGHTNING

What's New?

Completely new in 1999, the 2000 Lightning is the same, except for a new Silver Clearcoat exterior color.

Review

Take Ford's latest F-150 truck in shortbed, flareside form, add in a healthy mix of SVT philosophy and components, and Lightning will strike.

In this case, the spark is supplied by a reworked 5.4-liter Triton V8 engine with forged pistons, reduced compression, and a Roots-type supercharger from Eaton. Complete with an intercooler and a two-channel throttle body, this engine belts out 360 horsepower (100 more than a standard 5.4-liter Triton) and a massive 440 foot-pounds of torque. Aided by a beefed-up automatic transmission, 9.75-inch rear axle and 12.1-inch front-disc brakes, the Lightning guarantees a thrill ride with the first turn of the key.

SVT didn't stop with the drivetrain. To keep all those extra horses from getting out of sorts, a unique suspension setup was created for the Lightning. This includes a lower front and rear ride height, specially calibrated shock absorbers, and two antiroll bars. These components ride on 18 x 9.5-inch five-spoke wheels with 295/45-18 Z-rated Goodyear tires for extra stick during acceleration and handling maneuvers.

The standard cab holds a radically non-standard interior featuring black-on-white SVT instrumentation (complete with boost gauge) and black-and-white leather seats. The driver's seat is power-adjustable and an optional six-CD changer can be ordered to beef up the standard, premium sound system.

Exterior enhancements are limited to a special front air dam with twin driving lights, a black grille, custom rocker panels, the aforementioned 18-inch wheels, and twin ceramic exhaust pipes. Color choices are limited to black, silver, red or white. A soft bed cover, as well as a Class III tow hitch, can be added to accent the truck's looks and utility.

If you're looking for a serious high-performance truck, you can stop your search right here. Nothing else comes close. A lot of "sporting" cars don't even match the Lightning's performance numbers. But the biggest question is why SVT offers the Lightning only as a regular-cab model when the world has clearly been moving toward more room and more doors each year. Dodge, with its Dakota R/T, is the only manufacturer smart enough to realize that performance and utility are not mutually exclusive. That said, the new Lightning is no toy, as its payload and towing capacity is only slightly diminished over the standard F-Series pickup. SVT is obviously betting that the old standard of a full-size, standard-cab performance truck will sell, if executed well. And this new truck is certainly well-executed.

2000 Ford SVT F-150 Lightning Pickup

Standard Equipment

SVT LIGHTNING (4A): 5.4L V8 SOHC SMPI intercooled supercharged 16-valve engine; 4-speed electronic OD auto transmission with lock-up; 540-amp HD battery with run down protection; engine oil cooler, HD radiator; 120-amp alternator; transmission, oil cooler; rear-wheel drive, limited slip differential, 3.55 axle ratio; dual stainless steel exhaust; sport ride suspension, front independent

CODE	DESCRIPTION	INVOICE	MSRP

suspension with anti-roll bar, front coil springs, gas-pressurized front shocks, rigid rear axle suspension with anti-roll bar, rear leaf springs, gas-pressurized rear shocks; power re-circulating ball steering, power steering cooler; 4-wheel disc brakes with 4-wheel antilock braking system; 25 gal. capacity fuel tank; side impact bars; flare pickup box; front and rear body-colored bumpers with black rub strip, rear step; rocker panel extensions; clearcoat monotone paint; aero-composite halogen fully auto headlamps; additional exterior lights include front fog/driving lights, pickup cargo box light, underhood light; driver's and passenger's power remote body-colored folding outside mirrors; front and rear 18" x 9.5" painted alloy wheels; P295/45ZR18 performance BSW front and rear tires; underbody mounted compact steel spare wheel; air conditioning; premium AM/FM stereo, clock, seek-scan, 6-disc CD changer, 4 speakers, auto equalizer, and fixed antenna; cruise control with steering wheel controls; power door locks, remote keyless entry; 2 power accessory outlets, driver's foot rest, retained accessory power, smokers' package; instrumentation display includes tachometer, oil pressure gauge, water temperature gauge, compass, exterior temp, trip odometer; warning indicators include oil pressure, water temp, battery, key in ignition, low fuel, low washer fluid, door ajar, brake fluid; driver's front airbag, passenger's cancelable front airbag; ignition disable; tinted windows, power windows with driver's 1-touch down; variable intermittent front windshield wipers, sun visor strip, sliding rear window; seating capacity of 3, 60-40 split-bench front seat, fixed headrests, center armrest with storage, driver's seat includes 4-way power seat, 8-way direction control, lumbar support, passenger's seat includes 4-way direction control; front height adjustable seatbelts; cloth-leather seats, leather door trim insert, full cloth headliner, full color-keyed carpet floor covering with floor mats, plastic/rubber gear shift knob, cabback insulator; interior lights include dome light, front reading lights, 2 door curb lights, illuminated entry; leather-wrapped steering wheel with tilt adjustment; passenger's side vanity mirror; day/night rearview mirror; mini overhead console locking glove box, front cupholder, instrument panel bin, driver's and passenger's door bins; body-colored grille, black side window moldings, black front windshield molding, black rear window molding and body-colored door handles.

Base Prices

CODE	DESCRIPTION	INVOICE	MSRP
F07-1	F-150 SVT Lightning (4A)	26568	30710
Destination Charge:		665	665

Accessories

CODE	DESCRIPTION	INVOICE	MSRP
428	High Altitude Principal Use	NC	NC
429	Non-High Altitude Principal Use	NC	NC
520A	Series Code 520A *Includes vehicle with standard equipment.*	NC	NC
535	Class III Trailer Towing Group *Includes trailer towing preparation, 7-pin trailer wiring harness and Class III frame mounted hitch.*	208	245
86T	Tonneau Cover	128	150
91P	Premium AM/FM Stereo with Cassette *Includes 6-disc CD changer.*	178	210

2000 F-SERIES PICKUP

What's New?

A limited-edition Harley-Davidson F-150 is available for 2000. The under 8,500-pound GVW F-250 has been discontinued and replaced by the F-150 7700 Payload Group. A new overhead console and left- and right-side visor vanity mirrors are optional on XL models and standard on XLT and Lariat F-150 pickups. A driver's-side keypad entry system is available on Lariat models. Chromed steel wheels and 17-inch tires are now available on 2WD models. A comfort-enhancing flip-up 40/60 rear seat has been added to the F-150 SuperCab.

2000 Ford F-150 Pickup

Review

When Ford introduced the new family of F-Series trucks in 1996 as 1997 models, there was uproar among old-school Blue Oval fans. Gone were the Twin-I-Beam suspension, pushrod engine, and traditional box-like styling. The new model appeared with a short- and long-arm front suspension, a range of overhead-cam engines, and more swoops than a Dairy Queen sundae.

The past few years have quelled the whining, however. In fact, the F-Series continues to be the top-selling truck in America. Chevy's new Silverado is picking up steam, but the F-150 continues to have many positive attributes.

The SLA suspension provides excellent on- and off-road articulation, giving the most demanding drivers a quality ride. Open-road driving in the F-Series trucks is equally pleasant due to their precise steering, competent braking and forgiving suspension. A certain amount of "truck-like" handling is unavoidable when discussing a...well, truck, but, for something designed to carry cargo and not carve canyons, Ford has created an extremely user-friendly rig. An unexpected bonus is the solid, rattle-free ride.

Power choices for the F-Series range consist of a standard 4.2-liter V6, an optional 4.6-liter Triton V8, or the even-larger optional 5.4-liter Triton V8. The V6 and 4.6-liter V8 can be ordered with a manual transmission, while the 5.4-liter comes only with an automatic. Power is acceptable with all of the engines, but the 260-horsepower, 5.4-liter Triton V8 can't match the top V8 engine offered in the Silverado. If you're looking for maximum stoplight acceleration from an F-150, you'll need to opt for the SVT F-150 Lightning.

Back in 1997, the F-150's interior was a vast improvement over its predecessor. And as a whole, the F-150 interior is a good one. But as trucks are becoming more mainstream, we find ourselves becoming less forgiving about idiosyncrasies. Our gripes center on a number of ergonomic mishaps, as well as the overall look which tries to be progressive but ends up looking goofy. The round, "aero" styling, small radio controls, and overall gauge placement just doesn't work, especially in a truck. We're also not very impressed with the F-150's seat comfort.

Where the F-150 excels is its functionality. If you are looking to haul or tow, it doesn't get much better than this. The SuperCab version, with its four doors, offers increased utility. Arriving about the time you read this is a 2001 model called the SuperCrew. The SuperCrew's cab is 12 inches longer than the SuperCab's to provide even more room. The doors are also larger, to aid entry and egress. To improve passenger comfort, the SuperCrew will offer an Expedition-like 60/40 rear seat

If you're looking for more style than a regular F-150 can provide, check out the limited-edition 2000 Harley-Davidson F-150. The new Harley-Davidson F-150 is a black monochromatic 2WD SuperCab pickup with a flareside box topped by a hard-shell tonneau cover. It comes equipped with a 5.4-liter V8, special exhaust, and 20-inch, five-spoke cast aluminum wheels wrapped with 275/45R20 Goodyear Eagle GTII tires. Inside, the limited-edition Harley-Davidson F-150 features the famous look of Harley-Davidson accessories, including a dash ornament, black leather seats and trim, a black leather accessory pouch on the center console, and a unique "spun metal" instrument cluster.

2000 F-150 PICKUP

Standard Equipment

WORK SERIES 2WD REGULAR CAB SB/LB (5M): 4.2L V6 OHV SMPI 12-valve engine; 5-speed OD manual transmission; 540-amp battery with run down protection; 95-amp alternator; rear-wheel drive, 3.55 axle ratio; stainless steel exhaust; front independent suspension with anti-roll bar, front coil springs, rigid rear axle suspension with rear leaf springs; power re-circulating ball steering; front disc/rear drum brakes with rear wheel antilock braking system; 30 gal. capacity fuel tank; side impact bars; trailer harness; front and rear argent bumpers with rear step; monotone paint; aero-composite halogen headlamps; additional exterior lights include pickup cargo box light; driver's and passenger's manual black folding outside mirrors; front and rear 16" x 7" silver steel wheels; P235/70SR16 A/S BSW front and rear tires; underbody mounted full-size steel spare wheel with crankdown; AM/FM stereo, clock, seek-scan, 2 speakers, and fixed antenna; 2 power accessory outlets, driver's foot rest; instrumentation display includes oil pressure gauge, water temperature gauge, volt gauge, trip odometer; warning indicators include oil pressure, water temp, battery, key in ignition, low fuel, door ajar, brake fluid; driver's front airbag, passenger's cancelable front airbag; ignition disable; tinted windows; variable intermittent front windshield wipers, sun visor strip; seating capacity of 3, bench front seat, fixed headrests, driver's seat includes 2-way direction control, passenger's seat includes 2-way direction control; front height adjustable seatbelts; vinyl seats, vinyl door trim insert, full cloth headliner, full vinyl floor covering, cabback insulator; interior lights include dome light; day/night rearview mirror; glove box, front cupholder, instrument panel bin; vinyl cargo floor; argent grille, black side window moldings, black front windshield molding, black rear window molding and black door handles.

XL (in addition to or instead of WORK SERIES equipment): Front and rear chrome bumpers with front black rub strip; additional exterior lights include underhood light; cloth seats; interior lights include front reading lights; passenger's side vanity mirror; driver's and passenger's door bins and chrome grille.

XLT (in addition to or instead of XL equipment): Front and rear chrome bumpers with front body-colored rub strip, body-colored bodyside molding with chrome bodyside insert; driver's and passenger's power remote chrome folding outside mirrors; AM/FM stereo, clock, seek-scan, cassette, 4 speakers, and fixed antenna; cruise control with steering wheel controls; retained accessory power; instrumentation display includes tachometer; warning indicators include low washer fluid; power door locks, power windows with driver's 1-touch down; 40-60 split-bench front seat, fixed headrests, center armrest with storage, driver's seat includes 4-way direction control, lumbar support, passenger's seat includes 4-way direction control; cloth seats, full color-keyed carpet floor covering with carpeted floor mats; interior lights include 2 door curb lights; steering wheel with tilt adjustment; vanity mirrors; carpeted cargo floor, cargo concealed storage and body-colored door handles.

SUPERCAB 2WD WS/XL/XLT SB/LB (5M) (in addition to or instead REGULAR CAB 2WD SB/LB (5M) equipment): 115-amp alternator; 3.08 axle ratio; seating capacity of 6 and 40-60 folding rear bench seat.

LARIAT (5M) (in addition to or instead of XLT equipment): 4.6L V8 SOHC SMPI 16-valve engine; 110-amp alternator, body-colored wheel well molding; aero-composite halogen fully auto headlamps; driver's and passenger's power remote body-colored folding outside mirrors; front and rear 17" x 7" chrome steel wheels; P275/60SR17 A/S OWL front and rear tires; air conditioning, premium AM/FM stereo, clock, seek-scan, single CD, 4 speakers, and fixed antenna; remote keyless entry, driver's side keypad entry; deep tinted windows; fixed headrests, center armrest with storage, driver's seat includes 4-way power seat, 8-way direction control, lumbar support; leather seats; interior lights include illuminated entry; leather-wrapped steering wheel with tilt adjustment and body-colored grille.

4WD REGULAR CAB SB/LB (in addition to or instead of 2WD REGULAR CAB SB/LB equipment): Part-time 4 wheel drive, auto locking hub control with manual shift, 3.31 axle ratio; front torsion springs, front torsion bar, 24.5 gal. (SB) 30 gal. (LB) capacity fuel tank; colored wheel well molding.

4WD SUPERCAB SB/LB (in addition to or instead of 4WD REGULAR CAB SB/LB equipment): 4.6L V8 SOHC SMPI 16-valve engine; 110-amp alternator; seating capacity of 6, 40-60 folding rear bench seat.

Base Prices

F17	Work Series 2WD Reg Cab SB (5M)	13999	15380
F17-8	Work Series 2WD Reg Cab LB (5M)	14255	15670
F17	XL 2WD Regular Cab Styleside SB (5M)	14332	16315
F17-8	XL 2WD Regular Cab Styleside LB (5M)	14587	16615
F07	XL 2WD Regular Cab Flareside SB (5M)	15192	17325
X17	Work Series 2WD SuperCab SB (5M)	16279	17970
X17-8	Work Series 2WD SuperCab LB (5M)	16534	18260
F18	Work Series 4WD Regular Cab SB (5M)	16833	18600
F18-8	Work Series 4WD Regular Cab LB (5M)	17089	18890
X17	XL 2WD SuperCab Styleside SB (5M)	16615	19000
F17	XLT 2WD Regular Cab Styleside SB (5M)	16844	19270
X17-8	XL 2WD SuperCab Styleside LB (5M)	16870	19300
F17-8	XLT 2WD Regular Cab Styleside LB (5M)	17095	19565
F18	XL 4WD Regular Cab Styleside SB (5M)	17172	19655
F18-8	XL 4WD Regular Cab Styleside LB (5M)	17427	19955
X07	XL 2WD SuperCab Flareside SB (5M)	17473	20010
F07	XLT 2WD Regular Cab Flareside SB (5M)	17703	20280
F08	XL 4WD Regular Cab Flareside SB (5M)	18030	20665
X18	Work Series 4WD SuperCab SB (5M)	19561	21700
X18-8	Work Series 4WD SuperCab LB (5M)	19817	21990
X17	XLT 2WD SuperCab Styleside SB (5M)	19165	22000
X17-8	XLT 2WD SuperCab Styleside LB (5M)	19420	22300
F18	XLT 4WD Regular Cab Styleside SB (5M)	19748	22685
X18	XL 4WD SuperCab Styleside SB (5M)	19900	22865
F18-8	XLT 4WD Regular Cab Styleside LB (5M)	20011	22995
X07	XLT 2WD SuperCab Flareside SB (5M)	20023	23010
X18-8	XL 4WD SuperCab Styleside LB (5M)	20155	23165
F08	XLT 4WD Regular Cab Flareside SB (5M)	20606	23695
X08	XL 4WD SuperCab Flareside SB (5M)	20759	23875

CODE	DESCRIPTION	INVOICE	MSRP
X17	Lariat 2WD SuperCab Styleside SB (4A)	22383	25785
X18	XLT 4WD SuperCab Styleside SB (5M)	22403	25810
X17-8	Lariat 2WD SuperCab Styleside LB (4A)	22638	26085
X18-8	XLT 4WD SuperCab Styleside LB (5M)	22658	26110
X07	Lariat 2WD SuperCab Flareside Flareside SB (4A)	23241	26795
X08	XLT 4WD SuperCab Flareside SB (5M)	23267	26825
X18	Lariat 4WD SuperCab Styleside SB (4A)	25183	29080
X18-8	Lariat 4WD SuperCab Styleside LB (4A)	25438	29380
X08	Lariat 4WD SuperCab Flareside SB (4A)	26042	30090
Destination Charge:		665	665

Accessories

CODE	DESCRIPTION	INVOICE	MSRP
—	Bonus Discount with 4.2L Engine (992) (WS Except 4WD X-Cab) *NOT AVAILABLE with 99W, 44E, 99L, 99Z, 627, XB6, 99M.*	(425)	(500)
—	Rear Storage Bin Delete (XLT 2WD) *NOT AVAILABLE with 91P.*	(51)	(60)
—	Special Discount (4WD Reg Cab Flareside - XL/XLT) *REQUIRES 992 and 44M. NOT AVAILABLE with 44E, 99L, 99W.*	(858)	(1010)
—	Special Discount with Manual Transmission and A/C (WS/XL) *NOT AVAILABLE with 99L, 44E, 531, 535, 99Z, 627, XB6.*	(425)	(500)
—	Special Discount with Manual Transmission and A/C (XLT) *NOT AVAILABLE with 99L, 44E, 531, 535, 99Z, 627, XB6.*	(425)	(500)
167	Carpeted Color-Keyed Floor Mats (XL Reg Cab) *REQUIRES 168.*	26	30
167	Carpeted Color-Keyed Floor Mats (XL X-Cab) *REQUIRES 168.*	43	50
167	Carpeted Color-Keyed Floor Mats (XLT Reg Cab)	26	30
167	Carpeted Color-Keyed Floor Mats (XLT X-Cab)	43	50
168	Color-Keyed Carpeting (XL)	85	100
16G	Carpet/Floor Mat Delete (XLT) *Replace with black vinyl mat. NOT AVAILABLE with 167.*	(43)	(50)
17P	Power Adjustable Driver's Pedals	102	120
18E	Black Cab Steps (2WD Styleside Except WS) *Includes black platform type.*	213	250
18E	Black Cab Steps (WD Styleside/Flareside - Except WS) *Includes black tubular type and deletes front fender flaps. NOT AVAILABLE with 99Z, 66N, 66P, 653.*	298	350
215	4x4 Electric Shift-On-The-Fly (4WD - XLT/Lariat) *REQUIRES (99L and 44E) or 99W or 99Z.*	136	160
413	Skid Plates (4WD Except Reg Cab SB) *Includes transfer case and fuel tank skid plates.*	136	160
413	Skid Plates (Reg Cab 4WD SB) *Includes transfer case and fuel tank skid plates.*	68	80
41H	Engine Block Heater *Includes 600-watt element and 72-amp HD battery. Recommended when minimum temperature is -10 degrees F or below. NOT AVAILABLE with 535.*	77	90

CODE	DESCRIPTION	INVOICE	MSRP
428	High Altitude Principal Use	NC	NC
	NOT AVAILABLE with 429, 93N, X27.		
429	Non-High Altitude Principal Use	NC	NC
	NOT AVAILABLE with 428.		
433	Sliding Rear Window	107	125
44E	Transmission: Electric 4-Speed Automatic with OD (All Except Lariat)	931	1095
	REQUIRES 99L or 99Z or 99M. NOT AVAILABLE with 99W, special discount with manual transmission and A/C, (ITP) bonus discount with 4.2L engine (992), 531, 535, 622, 94S, B3A, B3E, B3N, B3G, (PAYLD4) payload package, B3B, special discount, X27, B3S.		
44E	Transmission: Electric 4-Speed Automatic with OD (Lariat)	NC	NC
44U	Transmission: 4-Speed Automatic with OD (WS/XL/XLT)	931	1095
	NOT AVAILABLE with special discount with manual transmission and AC, 622, 531, (ITP) bonus discount with 4.2L engine (992), B3A, B3E, B3G, B3N, (PAYLD4) payload package, B3B, 94T, special discount, 99Z, XB6, 627, 99M, 66N, 66P. INCLUDED in 508A.		
473	Top 3 Accessories Package	638	750
	Includes bedliner, styled molded running boards and wrap-around hood deflector. Available only in the following cities/regions: California, Memphis, Atlanta and Denver. NOT AVAILABLE with 18E, 47D.		
500A	Series Code 500A (WS)	NC	NC
	Includes vehicle with standard equipment.		
502A	Series Code 502A (XL)	NC	NC
	Includes vehicle with standard equipment.		
507A	Series Code 507A (XLT)	1003	1180
	Manufacturer Discount	(1003)	(1180)
	Net Price	NC	NC
	Includes air conditioning and 4-wheel antilock brakes.		
508A	Series Code 508A (Lariat)	1250	1470
	Manufacturer Discount	(1250)	(1470)
	Net Price	NC	NC
	Includes transmission: 4-speed auto with overdrive and 4-wheel antilock brakes.		
52N	Speed Control/Tilt Steering Wheel (WS)	328	385
531	HD Electrical/Cooling Package	178	210
	Manufacturer Discount	(51)	(60)
	Net Price	127	150
	This package required to tow over 4000 lbs. Includes 72-amp HD battery, transmission oil cooler (with 44U or 44E) and super engine cooling. NOT AVAILABLE with special discount with manual transmission and A/C, 535, 41H, payload package.		
531	HD Electrical/Cooling Package	178	210
	Manufacturer Discount	(98)	(115)
	Net Price	80	95
	This package required to tow over 4000 lbs. Includes 72-amp HD battery, transmission oil cooler (with 44U or 44E) and super engine cooling. NOT AVAILABLE with special discount with manual transmission and A/C, 535, payload package.		

CODE	DESCRIPTION	INVOICE	MSRP
531	HD Electrical/Cooling Package	178	210
	Manufacturer Discount	(157)	(185)
	Net Price	21	25
	This package required to tow over 4000 lbs. Includes 72-amp HD battery, transmission oil cooler (with 44U) and super engine cooling. NOT AVAILABLE with 535, 99L, 44E, payload package, 99Z, 99M.		
531	HD Electrical/Cooling Package	178	210
	This package required to tow over 4000 lbs. Includes 72-amp HD battery, transmission oil cooler (with 44U) and super engine cooling. NOT AVAILABLE with 99W, 99L, 44E, special discount with manual transmission and A/C, 41H, 535, 99Z, 99M.		
531	HD Electrical/Cooling Package	178	210
	Manufacturer Discount	(110)	(130)
	Net Price	68	80
	This package required to tow over 4000 lbs. Includes 72-amp HD battery, transmission oil cooler (with 44U) and super engine cooling. NOT AVAILABLE with 41H, 535, 99L, 44E, payload package, 99Z, 99M.		
531	HD Electrical/Cooling Package	178	210
	Manufacturer Discount	(59)	(70)
	Net Price	119	140
	This package required to tow over 4000 lbs. Includes 72-amp HD battery, transmission oil cooler (with 44U) and super engine cooling. NOT AVAILABLE with 99W, 99L, 41H, 535, 44E, 99Z, 99M.		
531	HD Electrical/Cooling Package	178	210
	Manufacturer Discount	(106)	(125)
	Net Price	72	85
	This package required to tow over 4000 lbs. Includes 72-amp HD battery, transmission oil cooler (with 44U) and super engine cooling. NOT AVAILABLE with 99W, 99L, 535, 44E, 99Z, 99M.		
531	HD Electrical/Cooling Package	178	210
	Manufacturer Discount	(47)	(55)
	Net Price	131	155
	This package required to tow over 4000 lbs. Includes 72-amp HD battery, transmission oil cooler (with 44U) and super engine cooling. NOT AVAILABLE with 99W, 99L, special discount with manual transmission and A/C, 535, 44E, 99Z, 99M.		
535	Trailer Towing Group	340	400
	Manufacturer Discount	(51)	(60)
	Net Price	289	340
	Includes 7-pin trailer wiring harness, Class III frame mounted hitch, HD electrical/ cooling pkg, 72-amp HD battery, super engine cooling and HD shock absorbers. NOT AVAILABLE with 41H, special discount with manual transmission and AC, 531, payload package.		

CODE	DESCRIPTION	INVOICE	MSRP
535	Trailer Towing Group	340	400
	Manufacturer Discount	(110)	(130)
	Net Price	230	270
	Includes 7-pin trailer wiring harness, Class III frame mounted hitch, HD electrical/ cooling pkg, 72-amp HD battery, super engine cooling and HD shock absorbers. NOT AVAILABLE with 99L, 41H, 531, 44E, payload package, 99Z, 99M.		
535	Trailer Towing Group	340	400
	Manufacturer Discount	(157)	(185)
	Net Price	183	215
	Includes 7-pin trailer wiring harness, Class III frame mounted hitch, HD electrical/ cooling pkg, 72-amp HD battery, super engine cooling and HD shock absorbers. NOT AVAILABLE with 99L, 531, 44E, payload package, 99Z, 99M.		
535	Trailer Towing Group	340	400
	Manufacturer Discount	(59)	(70)
	Net Price	281	330
	Includes 7-pin trailer wiring harness, Class III frame mounted hitch, HD electrical/ cooling pkg, 72-amp HD battery, super engine cooling and HD shock absorbers. NOT AVAILABLE with 99W, 99L, 41H, 531, 44E, 99Z, 99M.		
535	Trailer Towing Group	340	400
	Manufacturer Discount	(106)	(125)
	Net Price	234	275
	Includes 7-pin trailer wiring harness, Class III frame mounted hitch, HD electrical/ cooling pkg, 72-amp HD battery, super engine cooling and HD shock absorbers. NOT AVAILABLE with 99W, 99L, 531, 44E, 99Z, 99M.		
535	Trailer Towing Group	340	400
	Manufacturer Discount	(47)	(55)
	Net Price	293	345
	Includes 7-pin trailer wiring harness, Class III frame mounted hitch, HD electrical/ cooling pkg, 72-amp HD battery, super engine cooling and HD shock absorbers. NOT AVAILABLE with 99W, 99L, special discount with manual transmission and A/C, 531, 44E, 99Z, 99M.		
535	Trailer Towing Group	340	400
	Manufacturer Discount	(98)	(115)
	Net Price	242	285
	Includes 7-pin trailer wiring harness, Class III frame mounted hitch, HD electrical/ cooling pkg, 72-amp HD battery, super engine cooling and HD shock absorbers. NOT AVAILABLE with special discount with manual transmission and A/C, 531, Payload Package.		
535	Trailer Towing Group	340	400
	Includes 7-pin trailer wiring harness, Class III frame mounted hitch, HD electrical/ cooling pkg, 72-amp HD battery, super engine cooling and HD shock absorbers. NOT AVAILABLE with special discount with manual transmission and A/C, 99W, 44E, 99L, 41H, 531, 99Z, 99M.		
53T	Tow Hooks (4WD - WS/XL)	34	40
	Includes 2 cast iron front tow hooks.		

CODE	DESCRIPTION	INVOICE	MSRP
55R	**Off-Road Equipment Group (Lariat 4WD)** *Includes 4x4 off-road decal, front frame crossmember, wheels: 17" cast aluminum, skid plates and HD shock absorbers. NOT AVAILABLE with 627, T65.*	383	450
55R	**Off-Road Equipment Group (XLT 4WD)** *Includes 4x4 off-road decal, front frame crossmember, wheels: 17" cast aluminum, skid plates and HD shock absorbers. REQUIRES 99L or 99W or 99Z. NOT AVAILABLE with T3P, T53, T65, 627.*	846	995
55R	**Regional Off-Road Equipment Group (Lariat 4WD)** *Includes 4x4 off-road decal, front frame crossmember, wheels: 17" cast aluminum, skid plates and HD shock absorbers. NOT AVAILABLE with 627, T65.*	383	450
55R	**Regional Off-Road Equipment Group (XLT 4WD X-Cab)** *Includes 4x4 off-road decal, front frame crossmember, wheels: 17" cast aluminum, skid plates and HD shock absorbers. NOT AVAILABLE with 627, T3P, T53, T65.*	846	995
572	**Air Conditioning (WS/XL)**	684	805
585	**Radio: AM/FM Stereo with CD (XL)** *Includes premium sound, 4 speakers, clock and speed compensated volume control. REQUIRES 60B. NOT AVAILABLE with 589, B3E, B3N.*	273	320
585	**Radio: AM/FM Stereo with CD (XLT)** *Includes premium sound, 4 speakers, clock and speed compensated volume control. NOT AVAILABLE with 589, 91P.*	162	190
589	**Radio: AM/FM Stereo with Cassette and Clock (Lariat)** *Includes 4 speakers. NOT AVAILABLE with 91P, H. INCLUDED in 507A.*	(162)	(190)
589	**Radio: AM/FM Stereo with Cassette and Clock (XL)** *Includes 4 speakers. NOT AVAILABLE with 585.*	111	130
595	**Fog Lamps (XL 4WD)**	119	140
60B	**Convenience Group (XL)** *Includes speed control, tilt steering wheel, tailgate lock and overhead console.*	357	420
60C	**Remote Keyless Entry (XLT)** *Includes 2 key fobs and illuminated entry.*	128	150
622	**Optional Payload Package #2 (2WD Reg Cab Styleside SB)** *Includes GVWR of 6050 lbs and maximum payload of 2020 lbs, 3.55 axle ratio, tires: P255/70R16SL A/S BSW, HD shocks and springs. NOT AVAILABLE with 99L, 99W, 44E.*	229	270
622	**Payload Group #2 (2WD Reg Cab Styleside LB)** *Includes GVWR of 6000 lbs and maximum payload of 1885 lbs, tires: P255/70R16SL A/S BSW, HD shocks and springs. NOT AVAILABLE with 623, 627, 44E, 99L, 99M, 99Z, 99W, X27, XB6, 66N, 66P.*	229	270
622	**Payload Group #2 (WS 2WD Reg Cab LB)** *Includes GVWR of 6000 lbs, maximum payload of 1885 lbs, tires: P255/70R16SL A/S BSW, HD shocks and springs and wheels: 16" styled steel. NOT AVAILABLE with 623, 627, 99L, 99M, 99W, 99Z, 44E, X27, XB6, 66N, 66P.*	399	470
622	**Payload Group #2 (WS 2WD Reg Cab SB)** *Includes GVWR of 6050 lbs, maximum payload of 2020 lbs, 3.55 axle ratio, tires: P255/70R16SL A/S BSW, HD shocks and springs and wheels: 16" styled steel. NOT AVAILABLE with 99W, 99L.*	399	470

CODE	DESCRIPTION	INVOICE	MSRP
623	**Payload Group #3 (2WD Reg Cab Styleside LB)** *Includes GVWR of 6600 lbs and maximum payload of 2385 lbs, tires: P255/70R16SL A/S BSW, HD shocks and springs. REQUIRES (99L and 44E) or 99W. NOT AVAILABLE with 622, 627, X27, XB6, 66N, 66P.*	229	270
623	**Payload Group #3 (WS 2WD Reg Cab Styleside)** *Includes GVWR of 6600 lbs and maximum payload of 2385 lbs, tires: P255/70R16SL A/S BSW, HD shocks and springs and wheels: 16" styled steel. REQUIRES (99L and 44E) or 99W. NOT AVAILABLE with 622, 627, X27, XB6, 66N, 66P.*	399	470
627	**7700 Payload Group (X-Cab Styleside SB/Reg Cab Styleside LB)** *NOTE: This package replaces the F-250 LD line. Includes GVWR of 7700 lbs and maximum payload of 1830 lbs. Includes heavy duty components, larger brakes, higher capacity 7-lug wheels, heavy duty frame, HD shocks and springs, HD electrical/cooling pkg, 72-amp HD battery, super engine cooling and auxiliary transmission oil cooler. REQUIRES 99L or 99M. NOT AVAILABLE with 99W, X27, XH9, X19, bonus discount with 4.2L engine (992), special discount with manual transmission and A/C, 94S, 94T, T65, T53, 55R, 622, 623.*	1101	1295
63L	**Lariat Upgrade Package (Lariat)** *Includes color-keyed running boards, power sliding rear window, simulated wood grain trim and electrochromic interior mirror. NOT AVAILABLE with 433, 18E, 99Z.*	846	995
641	**Wheels: 16" Polished Aluminum (XL)** *REQUIRES 94S.*	170	200
653	**Optional Tank Configuration (Reg Cab)** *REQUIRES 99M or 66P. NOT AVAILABLE with 66N, 86T, 99L, 99W, 18E.*	115	135
66N	**Natural Gas Fuel System (Reg Cab Styleside LB/X-cab Styleside SB)** *Includes CNG: 12.5 GGE (gasoline gallon equivalent) @ 3,600 psi and single in-bed fuel tank. REQUIRES 627 and 99Z. NOT AVAILABLE with 66P, 86T, 99L, 99W, 18E, 99M, 622, 623, 653.*	5041	5930
66P	**Propane Fuel System (Reg Cab Styleside LB/X-cab Styleside SB)** *LPG: 26.2 GGE (gasoline gallon equivalent) and single in-bed fuel tank. REQUIRES 627 and 99Z. NOT AVAILABLE with 66N, 86T, 99L, 99W, 18E, 99M, 622, 623.*	4416	5195
67B	**4-Wheel Antilock Brakes (WS/XL - Reg Cab SB/4WD Reg Cab LB)** *Includes 4-wheel disc brakes.*	319	375
67B	**4-Wheel Antilock Brakes (WS/XL Except Reg Cab SB/4WD Reg Cab LB)** *Includes 4-wheel disc brakes.*	319	375
86T	**Soft Tonneau Cover (Styleside)** *NOT AVAILABLE with 66N, 66P, 99Z, 653.*	128	150
90P	**Power Driver's Seat (XLT)** *Includes autolamp. REQUIRES 44E or 507A.*	306	360
91P	**Radio: Premium AM/FM Stereo with CD Changer and Cassette (Lariat)** *Includes premium sound, 4 speakers, speed compensated volume control and 6-disc CD changer and behind seat storage delete. REQUIRES H.*	178	210
91P	**Radio: Premium AM/FM Stereo with CD Changer and Cassette (XLT)** *Includes premium sound, 4 speakers, speed compensated volume control and 6-disc CD changer. REQUIRES F. NOT AVAILABLE with 585, Rear Bin Delete.*	340	400

CODE	DESCRIPTION	INVOICE	MSRP
94S	**XL Sport Group (XL 2WD SB)** .... *Includes Sport decals, color-keyed front and rear bumpers, color-keyed mirrors, leather-wrapped steering wheel, tires: P255/70R16SL A/S OWL, 3.55 axle ratio, fog lamps, tachometer, color-keyed grille and 40/60 unique cloth split bench seat. NOT AVAILABLE with 99L, 99W, 44E, T53, M, 627, X27.*	421	495
94S	**XL Sport Group (XL 4WD SB)** .... *Includes 4x4 Sport decals, color-keyed front and rear bumpers, color-keyed mirrors, leather-wrapped steering wheel, tires: P255/70R16SL A/S OWL, 3.55 axle ratio, fog lamps, tachometer, color-keyed grille and 40/60 unique cloth split bench seat. NOT AVAILABLE with 99L, 99W, 44E, T53, T65, M, 627, X27.*	506	595
94T	**XLT Sport Group (XLT)** .... *Includes Sport decal, color-keyed front and rear bumpers, color-keyed power mirrors, leather-wrapped steering wheel, wheels: 17" cast aluminum, argent grille insert and 40/60 unique cloth split bench seat. REQUIRES 99L or 99W. NOT AVAILABLE with 954, T53, F, T3P, T65, T5E, 627, X27, B3S.*	506	595
954	**Two Tone Lower Paint (XLT/Lariat)**	192	225
99L	**Engine: 5.4L EFI V8 (4WD X-Cab and Lariat)** .... *Includes payload package. REQUIRES 44E or 67B or ((T3P or T65)). NOT AVAILABLE with 66N, 66P, special discount with manual transmission and A/C, 531, 535, 94S.*	680	800
99L	**Engine: 5.4L EFI V8 (All Except 4WD X-Cab and Lariat)** .... *Includes payload package. REQUIRES 44E or 67B. NOT AVAILABLE with 622, special discount with manual transmission and A/C, bonus discount with 4.2L engine (992), 531, 535, 94S, B3A, B3E, B3N, B3G, payload package, B3B, special discount, 66N, 66P, B3S, 653.*	1318	1550
99M	**Engine: 5.4L Natural Gas (WS/XL - 2WD Reg Cab Styleside LB)** .... *Standard tank configuration: 18.2 GGE (gasoline gallon equivalent) @ 3,600 psi (single in-bed tank plus single underbody midship tank). Optional tank configuration: 21.6 GGE @ 3,600 psi (dual in-bed tanks plus single underbody midship tank) and 3.73 axle ratio. REQUIRES 627 and 44E. NOT AVAILABLE with 622, XH9, bonus discount with 4.2L engine (992), X19, X27, 66N, 66P, 531, 535, B3A, B3N.*	5622	6615
99W	**Engine: 4.6L EFI V8 (All Except 4WD X-Cab and Lariat)** .... *Includes payload package. NOT AVAILABLE with 44E, 535, bonus discount with 4.2L engine (992), 94S, 622, B3A, B3E, B3G, B3N, payload package, B3B, special discount, 627, XB6, 66N, 66P, B3S, 653.*	638	750
99Z	**Engine: 5.4L Bi-Fuel Prep (X-Cab Styleside SB/Reg Cab Styleside LB)** .... *REQUIRES (66N or 66P) and 44E or (T65 or T3P). NOT AVAILABLE with bonus discount with 4.2L engine (992), special discount with manual transmission and A/C, 535, 531, 86T, X27, B3A, B3E, B3N, B3G, B3S, 18E, XB6, 622, X19.*	1330	1565
B3A	**No Charge V6 Package (XL/XLT Except 4WD X-Cab)** .... *REQUIRES B3E or B3N or B3G or B3B or B3S. NOT AVAILABLE with 99L, 99W, 44E, 99Z, 99M.*	NC	NC
B3B	**No Charge V6 Package (XL - Reg Cab Flareside/2WD X-Cab Flareside)** .... *Includes tires: P255/70R16SL A/S OWL, black cab steps and 3.55 axle ratio. NOT AVAILABLE with 44E, 99L, 99W, B3E, B3N, T53, T3P, T65.*	NC	NC

CODE	DESCRIPTION	INVOICE	MSRP
B3E	No Charge Sport Package (XL SB) *Includes AM/FM stereo with cassette and clock radio. NOT AVAILABLE with 44E, 99L, 99W, 585, B3N, B3B, T53, T65, 99Z.*	NC	NC
B3G	No Charge V6 Package with 60C (XLT - SB/Reg Cab LB/2WD X-Cab LB) *Includes remote keyless entry, illuminated entry and 3.55 axle ratio. NOT AVAILABLE with 44E, 99L, 99W, T53, T3P, T5E, 99Z, B3S.*	NC	NC
B3G	No Charge V6 Package with F (XLT - SB/Reg Cab LB/2WD X-Cab LB) *Includes cloth captain's seats, center console and 3.55 axle ratio. NOT AVAILABLE with 44E, 99L, 99W, T53, T3P, T5E, 99Z, B3S.*	NC	NC
B3N	No Charge V6 Package (XL - SB/Reg Cab LB/2WD X-Cab LB) *Includes AM/FM stereo with cassette, clock radio and 3.55 axle ratio. NOT AVAILABLE with 44E, 99L, 99W, 585, B3E, T53, B3B, T3P, T65, 99Z, 99M.*	NC	NC
B3S	No Charge Oklahoma Sport Package (XLT 2WD X-Cab SB) *Includes XLT sport group, color-keyed front and rear bumpers, color-keyed power mirrors, leather-wrapped steering wheel, tires: P275/60R17 A/S OWL, wheels: 17" cast aluminum, argent grille insert and 40/60 unique cloth split bench seat. NOT AVAILABLE with 94T, 44E, 99L, 99W, 99Z, B3G, T53.*	NC	NC
B3S	No Charge Sport Package (XLT 2WD X-Cab SB) *Includes XLT sport group, color-keyed front and rear bumpers, color-keyed power mirrors, leather-wrapped steering wheel, tires: P275/60R17 A/S OWL, wheels: 17" cast aluminum, argent grille insert and 40/60 unique cloth split bench seat. NOT AVAILABLE with 44E, 99L, 99W, 99Z, B3G, T53.*	NC	NC
B3S	No Charge Texas Sport Package (XLT 2WD X-Cab SB) *Includes XLT sport group, color-keyed front and rear bumpers, color-keyed power mirrors, leather-wrapped steering wheel, tires: P275/60R17 A/S OWL, wheels: 17" cast aluminum, argent grille insert and 40/60 unique cloth split bench seat. NOT AVAILABLE with 94T, 44E, 99L, 99W, 99Z, B3G, T53.*	NC	NC
C	Cloth Bench Seat (WS)	213	250
F	Cloth Captain's Seats (XLT) *Includes driver's lumbar and center console. REQUIRES 44E or 507A. NOT AVAILABLE with 94T.*	417	490
H	Leather Captain's Seats (Lariat) *Includes driver's lumbar, vinyl rear seat and center console.*	417	490
M	40/60 Split Bench with Driver's Lumbar (XL) *NOT AVAILABLE with 94S.*	221	260
T3P	Tires: LT245/75R16D AT OWL (4WD) *REQUIRES (99L or 99W) or X19 or 99Z. NOT AVAILABLE with T53, T65, B3N, 94T, 55R, T5E, B3G, B3B.*	591	695
T53	Tires: P235/70R16SL AS OWL (XL/XLT) *Includes BSW AS spare. NOT AVAILABLE with 94S, 94T, B3N, B3G, B3B, B3E, T3P, T65, 55R, T5E, B3S, 627.*	107	125
T55	Tires: P255/70R16SL AS OWL (XLT 2WD) *Includes BSW AS spare. REQUIRES (99W or 99L) or X19 or 99Z. NOT AVAILABLE with T53, 94T, B3S.*	251	295
T5E	Tires: LT265/70R17 OWL AT (4WD - XLT/Lariat) *Includes spare tire and 3.55 axle ratio. REQUIRES 55R. NOT AVAILABLE with T3P, T53, T65, 94T, B3G.*	255	300

CODE	DESCRIPTION	INVOICE	MSRP
T65	Tires: P255/70R16SL AT OWL (4WD Except Lariat) *REQUIRES (99L or 99W) or X19 or 99Z. NOT AVAILABLE with T3P, 94S, T53, B3E, B3N, 94T, 55R, T5E, B3B, 627.*	340	400
T65	Tires: P255/70R16SL AT OWL (XL 4WD SB) *REQUIRES 94S. NOT AVAILABLE with T3P, T53, B3E, B3N, B3B, 627.*	107	125
X19	3.55 Axle Ratio *NOT AVAILABLE with XH9, XB6, 627, 99M, 99Z.*	43	50
X27	3.31 Axle Ratio (2WD) *REQUIRES 99L or 99W. NOT AVAILABLE with XH9, 428, 44E, XB6, 99Z, 627, 94S, 94T, 622, 623, 99M.*	43	50
XH9	Limited Slip with 3.55 Axle Ratio *NOT AVAILABLE with X19, X27, XB6, 627, 99M.*	243	285

2001 F-SERIES PICKUP

2001 Ford F-150 SuperCrew

What's New?

The SuperCrew is an F-150 with four real doors separated by a B-pillar. It gains extra rear-seat room in exchange for a smaller cargo bed.

Review

Offered in both XLT and Lariat trim levels, the 2001 F-150 SuperCrew has been designed for consumers who want more interior space without compromising the functional capability and versatility of a full-size pickup.

Unlike the SuperCab, which has smaller hinged doors that swing out from the C-pillar, the SuperCrew actually mates an Expedition cabin with a shortened cargo bed. It has four full-size doors separated by a B-pillar on each side, with inside and outside handles on each door. Despite the larger cabin, the

F-150 SuperCrew is still the same overall length as the SuperCab model (Though this doesn't mean that the F-150 is as easy to park as an Escort, mind you.).

The SuperCrew boasts 12 inches more cab length than the 2000 SuperCab model. A front 40/60 bench seat, which seats up to three people, is standard. Captain's chairs with a floor-mounted center console are optional. A full-size 60/40 split-fold rear seat is standard, increasing interior space versatility. It can accommodate passengers, bulky loads or a combination of both. The rear seating area also features a power point, reading lamps and cupholders.

The F-150 SuperCrew's interior also includes standard power adjustable pedals. The brake and accelerator pedals can be adjusted up to 3 inches forward in a horizontal plane from their standard location. This provides greater comfort for a wider range of drivers, as well as moving shorter stature drivers further away from the front airbag.

The side effect of the increased interior space is a reduction in bed length. The pickup box measures 5.5 feet long, about a foot shorter than the normal F-150 bed. Width is the same as all other F-150 trucks. Ford believes the increased versatility of four doors will outweigh the loss of maximum cargo space.

Larger items (such as 4x8 sheets of plywood) will fit between the wheel humps and can be carried with the tailgate lowered. An optional bed extender allows more flexibility when transporting large items such as lumber, cinder blocks or firewood. The tubular steel bed extender is a curved cage unit attaching to the rear of the pickup bed. With the tailgate lowered, the unit pivots from its stowed position within the box and locks into place extending the load floor to 7 feet. With the tailgate closed the stowed bed extender provides a convenient storage area, keeping smaller items from sliding around the bed while the truck is in motion. The bed extender can also be removed, allowing full, unobstructed use of the cargo box. Standard payload of 1,765 pounds is the same as the F-150 SuperCab.

The F-150 SuperCrew offers a choice of two V8 engines, each with a four-speed automatic transmission. The two-valve, 4.6-liter SOHC V8 delivers 220 horsepower at 4,500 rpm. Peak torque is 290 foot-pounds at 3,250 rpm. The two-valve, 5.4-liter SOHC V8 delivers a maximum power output of 260 horsepower at 4,500 rpm with torque of 350 foot-pounds at 2,500 rpm. Both engines meet federal low-emission vehicle (LEV) standards.

The Ford F-150 is the top-selling vehicle in America, so there's no reason to doubt that the SuperCrew will be a success. The smaller bed will certainly make some people dismiss the SuperCrew, but the advantage of four real doors shouldn't be ignored.

2001 F-150 PICKUP

Standard Equipment

XLT 2WD SUPERCREW STYLESIDE SB (4A): 4.6L V8 SOHC SMPI 16-valve engine; 4-speed electronic OD auto transmission with lock-up; 540-amp battery with run down protection; 110-amp alternator; rear-wheel drive, 3.55 axle ratio; stainless steel exhaust; front independent suspension with anti-roll bar, front coil springs, gas-pressurized front shocks, rigid rear axle suspension with rear leaf springs, gas-pressurized rear shocks; power re-circulating ball steering; 4-wheel disc brakes with 4-wheel antilock braking system; 25.1 gal. capacity fuel tank; side impact bars; trailer harness; front and rear chrome bumpers, front body-colored rub strip, rear step; body-colored bodyside molding with chrome bodyside insert; monotone paint; aero-composite halogen headlamps; additional exterior lights include pickup cargo box light, underhood light; driver's and passenger's power remote chrome folding outside mirrors; front and rear 16" x 7" polished alloy wheels; P255/70SR16 A/S OWL front and rear tires; underbody mounted full-size steel spare wheel with crankdown; air conditioning; premium AM/FM stereo, clock, seek-scan, single CD, 4 speakers, auto equalizer, and fixed antenna; cruise control with steering wheel controls; power door locks; 3 power accessory outlets, driver's foot rest, retained accessory power; instrumentation display includes tachometer, oil pressure gauge, water temperature gauge, volt gauge, compass, exterior temp, trip odometer; warning indicators include oil pressure, water temp, battery, key in ignition, low fuel, low washer fluid, door ajar, brake fluid; driver's front airbag, passenger's cancelable front airbag; ignition disable; deep tinted windows, power front and rear windows with driver's 1-touch down; variable intermittent front windshield wipers, sun visor strip; seating capacity of 6, 40-60 split-bench front seat, fixed headrests, center armrest with storage, driver's seat includes 4-way direction control, lumbar support, passenger's seat includes 4-way direction control; 60-40 folding rear split-bench seat; front and rear height adjustable seatbelts; cloth seats, vinyl door trim insert, full cloth headliner, full color-keyed carpet floor covering with carpeted floor mats, cabback insulator; interior lights include dome light, front and rear reading lights, 4 door curb lights; steering wheel with tilt adjustment; vanity mirrors; day/night rearview mirror; full overhead console with storage, glove box, front and rear cupholders, instrument panel bin, interior concealed storage, driver's and passenger's door bins, rear door bins; chrome grille, black side window moldings, black front windshield molding, black rear window molding and body-colored door handles.

LARIAT 2WD SUPERCREW STYLESIDE SB (4A) (in addition to or instead of XLT 2WD SUPERCREW STYLESIDE SB (4A) equipment): Body-colored wheel well molding; aero-composite halogen fully auto headlamps; driver's and passenger's power remote body-colored folding outside mirrors; front and rear 17" x 7" chrome steel wheels; P275/60SR17 A/S OWL front and rear tires; remote keyless entry; driver's seat includes 4-way power seat, 8-way direction control, lumbar support; leather seats; interior lights include 4 door curb lights, illuminated entry; leather-wrapped steering wheel with tilt adjustment and body-colored grille.

4WD (4A) (in addition to or instead of 2WD (4A) equipment): Part-time 4-wheel drive, auto locking hub control and electronic shift, front torsion springs, front torsion bar; front tow hooks; additional exterior lights include front fog/driving lights.

Base Prices

CODE	DESCRIPTION	INVOICE	MSRP
W07	XLT 2WD SuperCrew Styleside (4A)	22752	26090
W07	Lariat 2WD SuperCrew Styleside (4A)	24094	27670
W08	XLT 4WD SuperCrew Styleside (4A)	25488	29310
W08	Lariat 4WD SuperCrew Styleside (4A)	27031	31125
Destination Charge:		665	665

Accessories

CODE	DESCRIPTION	INVOICE	MSRP
18E	Black Platform Type Cab Steps	213	250
413	Skid Plates (4WD) *Includes transfer case, fuel tank and cross member skid plates.*	136	160
41H	Engine Block Heater *Includes heavy duty battery. Recommended when minimum temperature is -10 degrees F or below. NOT AVAILABLE with 535.*	77	90
428	High Altitude Principal Use *Required for areas over 4,000 feet elevation.*	NC	NC
433	Manual Sliding Rear Window	107	125
43M	Power Moonroof *NOT AVAILABLE with 91E.*	688	810
47F	XLT Appearance Package (XLT 2WD) *Includes mesh grille insert, color-keyed grille surround and color-keyed mirrors.*	NC	NC
507A	Series Code 507A (XLT) *Includes vehicle with standard equipment.*	NC	NC
508A	Series Code 508A (4WD) *Includes vehicle with standard equipment.*	NC	NC

CODE	DESCRIPTION	INVOICE	MSRP
535	Class III Trailer Towing Group	289	340
	Manufacturer Discount	(47)	(55)
	Net Price	242	285
	Includes class III frame mounted hitch, 7-pin trailer wiring harness, HD electrical/ cooling package and HD shock absorbers. Note: this package required to tow over 4000 lbs. See salesperson for specific trailer towing limits and corresponding required equipment.		
535	Class III Trailer Towing Group	289	340
	Includes class III frame mounted hitch, 7-pin trailer wiring harness, HD electrical/ cooling package and HD shock absorbers. Note: this package required to tow over 4000 lbs. See salesperson for specific trailer towing limits and corresponding required equipment. NOT AVAILABLE with 41H.		
60C	Remote Keyless Entry (XLT)	128	150
	Includes 2 key fobs and illuminated entry. INCLUDED in 508A.		
63E	Pickup Bed Extender	166	195
	Stainless cage which folds onto tailgate to effectively extend length of pickup box.		
646	Wheels: 16" 5-Spoke Cast Aluminum (Four) (XLT)	NC	NC
	NOT AVAILABLE with 64Z.		
64Z	Wheels: 17" 10-Spoke Cast Aluminum (XLT 4WD)	NC	NC
	NOT AVAILABLE with 646, T3P, T65.		
90P	Power Driver's Seat (XLT)	306	360
	Includes Autolamp. INCLUDED in 508A.		
91E	Rear Seat Audio/Video (VHS) System	1101	1295
	NOT AVAILABLE with 43M.		
91P	Radio: Premium AM/FM Stereo with Cassette and 6-Disc CD	178	210
	Includes premium sound, 4 speakers and speed compensated volume control.		
954	Two-Tone Lower Paint	192	225
99L	Engine: 5.4L EFI V8	680	800
	Includes payload package.		
F	Cloth Captain's Chairs (XLT)	417	490
	Includes driver's lumbar and center console.		
H	Leather Captain's Chairs (Lariat)	417	490
	Includes driver's lumbar and premium leather seating surfaces in front and rear and center console.		
T34	Tires: LT245/75R16D AS BSW (XLT 2WD)	132	155
T3P	Tires: LT245/75R16D OWL AT (Five) (XLT 4WD)	340	400
	NOT AVAILABLE with T65, 64Z.		
T5N	Tires: P265/70R17 OWL AT (Five) (XLT 4WD)	289	340
	REQUIRES 64Z. NOT AVAILABLE with T3P, T65, 646.		
T65	Tires: P255/70R16SL OWL AT (Five) (XLT 4WD)	107	125
	NOT AVAILABLE with T3P, 64Z.		
XH9	Limited Slip with 3.55 Axle Ratio	243	285

2000 F-SERIES SUPER DUTY PICKUP

2000 Ford F-250 Super Duty

What's New?

Four-wheel antilock brakes are now standard on F-250 and F-350 trucks with Lariat trim levels. XL trim level trucks now have optional bucket seats. Clean fuel (LEV) gasoline engines are standard on all Super Duty trucks. Power windows and locks are now standard on XLT trim levels. The trailer/tow mirrors now telescope manually. Rear bumpers are standard on all F-250 and F-350 pickups. All Super Duty trucks get new interior and exterior colors.

Review

Commercial/small business demand is one of the fastest growing segments in the expanding truck market. With its F-Super Duty trucks, Ford is aiming squarely at fulfilling this segment.

The Super Duty trucks are built on a separate platform than the smaller F-150. The line of trucks comes in 44 different configurations, many of which are unique to the truck market. Ford Super Duty trucks are powered by a Triton 5.4-liter V8 or a 6.8-liter V10. The V8 generates 260 horsepower at 4,500 rpm and 350 foot-pounds of torque at 2,500 rpm. The V10 generates 275 horsepower at 4,250 rpm and 410 foot-pounds of torque at 2,650 rpm. A 7.3-liter diesel V8 is also available, and it makes 235 horsepower at 2,700 rpm and 500 foot-pounds of torque at 1,600 rpm.

Ford F-Super Duty models are available in Regular Cab, four-door SuperCab, and Crew Cab. The overall look is much more aggressive than the standard F-150, and its bigger dimensions allow Ford to use larger cabs without compromising load space. Given their size, the F-250 and F-350 Super Duty trucks maintain a confident on- and off-road feel. They feature updated power steering systems and enhanced suspension components to improve vehicle ride, handling, responsiveness, and maneuverability. Just don't mistake them for a car. Unlike the F-150, Dodge Ram and Chevy Silverado (all of which have become much more comfortable and user-friendly these past few years), the Super Duty vehicles are true trucks. They ride harshly when unloaded and 4x4 trucks come only with manually locking hubs. These manual hubs (along with the solid front and rear axles) do give the Super Duty trucks improved off-road capabilities, however.

Inside, the roomy cabs have larger, more comfortable seats and greater seat-track travel. In addition, there are many interior convenience features designed for today's stylish business owners. For example, a fold-down armrest and utility bin is designed to house a portable fax machine or laptop computer. In the Crew Cab XLT and Lariat models, a new rear bench seat incorporates a fold-down armrest and a cupholder. For truck owners who don't want to skimp on luxury, leather seating, a leather-wrapped steering wheel, air conditioning and power windows are just some of the many options available.

The F-Super Duty series isn't for everyone. However, if you need more truck than the regular F-Series can provide, Ford has quite an impressive lineup to peruse.

2000 F-250 SUPER DUTY PICKUP

Standard Equipment

XL 2WD SD REGULAR CAB LB (5M): 5.4L V8 SOHC SMPI 16-valve engine; 5-speed OD manual transmission; 750-amp HD battery with run down protection; 95-amp alternator; rear-wheel drive, power take-off provision, 4.1 axle ratio; stainless steel exhaust; firm ride suspension, front independent suspension front coil springs, HD front shocks, rigid rear axle suspension with rear leaf springs, HD rear shocks; power re-circulating ball steering; 4-wheel disc brakes with rear wheel antilock braking system; 38 gal. capacity fuel tank; trailer harness; front and rear argent bumpers with front tow hooks, rear step; monotone paint; sealed beam halogen headlamps; additional exterior lights include pickup cargo box light; driver's and passenger's manual black folding outside mirrors; front and rear 16" x 7" silver steel wheels; LT235/85SR16 A/S BSW front and rear tires; underbody mounted full-size steel spare wheel with crankdown; AM/FM stereo, clock, seek-scan, 2 speakers, and fixed antenna; 2 power accessory outlets, smokers' package; instrumentation display includes tachometer, oil pressure gauge, water temperature gauge, volt gauge, trip odometer; warning indicators include oil pressure, water temp, battery, key in ignition, low fuel, door ajar; driver's front airbag, passenger's cancelable front airbag; tinted windows; fixed interval front windshield wipers, sun visor strip; seating capacity of 3, bench front seat, fixed headrests, driver's seat includes 2-way direction control, passenger's seat includes 2-way direction control; front height adjustable seatbelts; vinyl seats, full cloth headliner, full vinyl floor covering, cabback insulator; interior lights include dome light with delay; day/night rearview mirror; glove box, front cupholder, instrument panel bin, dashboard storage; argent grille, black side window moldings, black front windshield molding, black rear window molding and black door handles.

XL 2WD SD SUPERCAB/CREW CAB SB/LB (5M) (in addition to or instead of XL 2WD SD REGULAR CAB LB (5M) equipment): 29 gal. capacity fuel tank (SB); flip-out rear/quarter glass (SuperCab), manual rear windows (Crew Cab), seating capacity of 6, full folding rear bench seat and rear seat grab handles (Crew Cab).

XLT (in addition to or instead of XL equipment): Black bodyside molding with chrome bodyside insert; aero-composite halogen headlamps; additional exterior lights include underhood light; air conditioning; AM/FM stereo, clock, seek-scan, cassette, 4 speakers, and fixed antenna; cruise control with steering wheel controls; retained accessory power; tinted windows, power windows with driver's 1-touch down; 40-20-40 split-bench front seat, fixed headrests, center armrest with storage, driver's seat includes 4-way direction control, passenger's seat includes 4-way direction control; rear seat center armrest with storage (Crew Cab), cloth seats, full color-keyed carpet floor covering with floor mats; interior lights include front reading lights; steering wheel with tilt adjustment; passenger's side vanity mirror; driver's and passenger's door bins; cargo concealed storage and chrome grille.

LARIAT (in addition to or instead of XLT equipment): Four-wheel disc brakes with 4-wheel antilock braking system; running boards; front and rear chrome bumpers with rear tow hooks; driver's and passenger's power remote black folding outside mirrors; power door locks with 2 stage unlock, remote keyless entry; instrumentation display includes compass, trip computer; driver's seat includes 4-way power seat, 8-way direction control; leather seats; interior lights include 2 door curb lights; leather-wrapped steering wheel with tilt adjustment; dual auxiliary visors and full overhead console with storage.

CODE	DESCRIPTION	INVOICE	MSRP

4WD (in addition to or instead of 2WD equipment): Part-time 4 wheel drive, manual locking hub control and manual shift, front non-independent suspension with anti-roll bar and front leaf springs.

Base Prices

CODE	DESCRIPTION	INVOICE	MSRP
F20	XL 2WD SD Regular Cab LB (5M)	17698	20110
X20	XL 2WD SD SuperCab SB (5M)	19543	22280
X20-8	XL 2WD SD SuperCab LB (5M)	19713	22480
F20	XLT 2WD SD Regular Cab LB (5M)	19896	22695
F21	XL 4WD SD Regular Cab LB (5M)	20317	23190
W20	XL 2WD SD Crew Cab SB (5M)	20657	23590
W20-8	XL 2WD SD Crew Cab LB (5M)	20827	23790
F20	Lariat 2WD SD Regular Cab LB (5M)	21371	24430
X20	XLT 2WD SD SuperCab SB (5M)	21404	24470
X20-8	XLT 2WD SD SuperCab LB (5M)	21574	24670
X21	XL 4WD SD SuperCab SB (5M)	22161	25360
X21-8	XL 4WD SD SuperCab LB (5M)	22331	25560
F21	XLT 4WD SD Regular Cab LB (5M)	22509	25770
X20	Lariat 2WD SD SuperCab SB (5M)	22867	26190
W20	XLT 2WD SD Crew Cab SB (5M)	23007	26355
X20-8	Lariat 2WD SD SuperCab LB (5M)	23037	26390
W20-8	XLT 2WD SD Crew Cab LB (5M)	23177	26555
W21	XL 4WD SD Crew Cab SB (5M)	23270	26665
W21-8	XL 4WD SD Crew Cab LB (5M)	23444	26870
F21	Lariat 4WD SD Regular Cab LB (5M)	23988	27510
X21	XLT 4WD SD SuperCab SB (5M)	24018	27545
X21-8	XLT 4WD SD SuperCab LB (5M)	24188	27745
W20	Lariat 2WD SD Crew Cab SB (5M)	24482	28090
W20-8	Lariat 2WD SD Crew Cab LB (5M)	24652	28290
X21	Lariat 4WD SD SuperCab SB (5M)	25476	29260
W21	XLT 4WD SD Crew Cab SB (5M)	25625	29435
X21-8	Lariat 4WD SD SuperCab LB (5M)	25646	29460
W21-8	XLT 4WD SD Crew Cab LB (5M)	25795	29635
W21	Lariat 4WD SD Crew Cab SB (5M)	27095	31165
W21-8	Lariat 4WD SD Crew Cab LB (5M)	27269	31370
Destination Charge:		665	665

Accessories

CODE	DESCRIPTION	INVOICE	MSRP
166	Carpet Delete (XLT/Lariat) *Replaced with black floor mat. NOT AVAILABLE with 66D.*	(43)	(50)
17F	XL Decor Group (XL) *Includes locking tailgate, chrome front bumper with lower valance, aero halogen headlights and wheels: steel with full wheel covers.*	149	175

CODE	DESCRIPTION	INVOICE	MSRP
18L	Cab Steps (Reg Cab - XL/XLT) *Integrated and molded black.*	272	320
18L	Cab Steps (X-Cab/Crew Cab - XL/XLT) *Integrated and molded black.*	314	370
2	Cloth Luxury Captain's Chairs (XLT) *Includes floor console.*	NC	NC
213	4x4 Electric Shift-On-The-Fly (4WD) *Includes auto-manual locking hubs.*	136	160
4	Leather Luxury Captain's Chairs (Lariat) *Includes floor console.*	NC	NC
41H	Engine Block Heater *Recommended when minimum temperature is -10 degrees F or below.*	30	35
428	High Altitude Principal Use	NC	NC
429	Non-High Altitude Principal Use	NC	NC
433	Sliding Rear Window	107	125
446	Transmission: HD 6-Speed Manual with Overdrive *Includes transmission power take-off provision. REQUIRES 99F. NOT AVAILABLE with 99S, X32, XC2, XC3, 62R, 531, 532.*	NC	NC
449	Transmission: 4-Speed Automatic *REQUIRES 99F. NOT AVAILABLE with 99S, X32, XC2, XC3.*	931	1095
44E	Transmission: 4-Speed Automatic *Deletes provisions for a power take-off (PTO). REQUIRES 99S. NOT AVAILABLE with 99F, XC3.*	931	1095
44E	Transmission: 4-Speed Automatic with 5.4L *Required in California. Deletes provisions for a power take-off (PTO). REQUIRES 99L or 99S. NOT AVAILABLE with 99F, XC3, 66D (in California).*	931	1095
52N	Speed Control/Tilt Steering Wheel (XL) *INCLUDED in 607A, 608A.*	328	385
531	Trailer Towing Package *Includes 7-wire harness, trailer brake wiring kit, front stabilizer bar, 130-amp alternator and Trailer Tow Guide. NOTE: Consult with salesperson for specific trailer towing or camper limits and corresponding required equipment, axle ratios and model availability. NOT AVAILABLE with 532, 99F, 446, 86M.*	132	155
531	Trailer Towing Package *Includes 7-wire harness, trailer brake wiring kit, front stabilizer bar, 130-amp alternator and Trailer Tow Guide. NOTE: Consult with salesperson for specific trailer towing or camper limits and corresponding required equipment, axle ratios and model availability. REQUIRES 532. NOT AVAILABLE with 446, 99S, 86M.*	59	70
531	Trailer Towing Package *Includes 7-wire harness, trailer brake wiring kit, front stabilizer bar, 130-amp alternator and Trailer Tow Guide. NOTE: Consult with salesperson for specific trailer towing or camper limits and corresponding required equipment, axle ratios and model availability. REQUIRES 86M. NOT AVAILABLE with 446, 532, 99S.*	77	90

CODE	DESCRIPTION	INVOICE	MSRP
531	Trailer Towing Package	132	155
	Manufacturer Discount	(51)	(60)
	Net Price	81	95
	Includes 7-wire harness, trailer brake wiring kit, front stabilizer bar, 130-amp alternator and trailer tow guide. NOTE: Consult with salesperson for specific trailer towing or camper limits and corresponding required equipment, axle ratios and model availability. REQUIRES 99F. NOT AVAILABLE with 532, 99S, 86M.		
532	Camper Package	251	295
	Includes slide-in camper certification, front stabilizer bar, rear stabilizer bar, auxiliary rear springs and 130-amp altemator. NOTE: Consult salesperson for specific trailer towing or camper limits and corresponding required equipment, axle ratios and model availability. NOT AVAILABLE with 674, 99F, 446, 66D, 86M.		
532	Camper Package	251	295
	Manufacturer Discount	(51)	(60)
	Net Price	200	235
	Includes slide-in camper certification, front stabilizer bar, rear stabilizer bar, auxiliary rear springs and 130-amp altemator. NOTE: Consult salesperson for specific trailer towing or camper limits and corresponding required equipment, axle ratios and model availability. REQUIRES 99F. NOT AVAILABLE with 99S, 674, 66D, 86M.		
54Q	Power Mirrors (XLT)	85	100
	NOT AVAILABLE with 54U, 54Y. INCLUDED in Lariat.		
54U	Manual Trailer Tow Mirrors (XL/XLT)	47	55
	NOT AVAILABLE with 54Q, 54Y.		
54Y	Power Trailer Tow Mirrors (Lariat)	47	55
54Y	Power Trailer Tow Mirrors (XLT)	132	155
	NOT AVAILABLE with 54U, 54Q.		
552	Passenger's Air Bag (LB)	255	300
	REQUIRES 66D.		
55R	Off-Road Package (4WD)	107	125
	Includes off-road 4x4 decal and fuel tank and transfer case skid plates.		
572	Air Conditioning (XL)	684	805
589	Radio: AM/FM Stereo with Cassette (XL)	115	135
	Includes clock and 4 speakers. NOT AVAILABLE with 58K.		
58K	Radio: AM/FM Stereo with CD and Cassette (XL)	277	325
	Includes clock, premium sound with amplifier and 4 speakers. NOT AVAILABLE with 589.		
58K	Radio: AM/FM Stereo with CD and Cassette (XLT/Lariat)	162	190
	Includes clock, premium sound with amplifier and 4 speakers.		
592	Roof Clearance Lights	47	55
60D	XLT Upgrade Package (XLT)	427	500
	Includes premium AM/FM stereo with CD, cab steps, sliding rear window, privacy glass and tires: LT 265/75R16E A/S OWL. REQUIRES 99F and 446. NOT AVAILABLE WITH T3N, T3R, T43, T4B, T4R, 99S, 44E, 449.		
62R	Transmission Power Take-Off Provision	213	250
	Provision only. Requires aftermarket power take-off. REQUIRES (99S and 44E) or (99F and 449). NOT AVAILABLE with 446.		

CODE	DESCRIPTION	INVOICE	MSRP
63T	Dual Alternator *REQUIRES 99F. NOT AVAILABLE with 99S.*	285	335
64F	Wheels: Forged Deluxe Aluminum (4) (XL) *NOT AVAILABLE with 17F. INCLUDED in XLT.*	323	380
64F	Wheels: Forged Deluxe Aluminum (4) (XL) *REQUIRES 17F.*	272	320
66D	Pickup Box Delete (LB) *Deletes passenger side air bag, pickup box and tailgate. NOTE: Incomplete vehicle package - requires further manufacture and certification by a final stage manufacturer. NOT AVAILABLE with 768, 532, 954.*	(510)	(600)
674	Heavy Service Suspension Package *Includes front stabilizer bar, heavy service front springs and auxiliary rear springs. NOTE: Recommended only on vehicles which will permanently utilize aftermarket equipment such as heavy-duty winches, brush guards or other apparatus which loads the front axle to the specified gross axle weight rating (GAWR). REQUIRES 531. NOT AVAILABLE with 532, 86M.*	149	175
67B	4-Wheel Antilock Brakes (XL/XLT)	319	375
86M	Snow Plow Package (4WD) *Includes highest front gawr springs (5200 lbs), auxiliary rear springs and 130-amp alternator. NOT AVAILABLE with 99F, 674, 531, 532.*	158	185
86M	Snow Plow Package (4WD Reg Cab)	158	185
	Manufacturer Discount	(51)	(60)
	Net Price *Includes highest front gawr springs (5200 lbs) and auxiliary rear springs. REQUIRES 99F. NOT AVAILABLE with 674, 531, 532, 99S.*	107	125
86R	Trailer Hitch Receiver (Class IV) *REQUIRES 532 or 531.*	128	150
87D	Rear Seat Delete (XL X-Cab)	(352)	(415)
90P	6-Way Power's Driver Seat (XLT) *REQUIRES 948. INCLUDED in 608A.*	247	290
924	Privacy Glass (XLT/Lariat) *Includes side quarter on X-Cab and rear doors on Crew Cab. REQUIRES 433.*	85	100
948	Remote Keyless Entry (XLT) *Includes two step unlock system and door courtesy lights.*	144	170
954	Lower Accent Two-Tone Paint (XLT/Lariat) *Includes unique accent color (Lariat). NOT AVAILABLE with 66D.*	192	225
96P	Auxiliary Idle Control Kit (LPO) *APC Module functions: battery charge protection, high idle control, LCD RPM/voltage readout. Kit includes: auxiliary idle control module, mounting bracket, hardware, wiring harness and instruction booklet. Stationary use only. REQUIRES 99F. NOT AVAILABLE with 99S.*	178	210
99F	Engine: 7.3L DI Turbo Diesel V8 *Includes 3.73 axle ratio, dual 78-ah batteries, engine block heater and 130-amp alternator. REQUIRES 446 or 449. NOT AVAILABLE with XC2, XC3, 532, X32, 44E, 86M.*	3910	4600
99S	Engine: 6.8L EFI V10 *NOT AVAILABLE with 446, XC2, 532, 531, X32, 96P, 449, 63T, X31, 86M.*	510	600

CODE	DESCRIPTION	INVOICE	MSRP
C	HD Cloth Full Bench Seat (XL - X-Cab/Crew Cab) *NOT AVAILABLE with K, G, H, J.*	221	260
C	HD Cloth Full Bench Seat (XL Reg Cab) *NOT AVAILABLE with K, G, H, J.*	136	160
G	HD Cloth Bucket Seats (XL - X-Cab/Crew Cab) *NOT AVAILABLE with H, J, K, C.*	391	460
G	HD Cloth Bucket Seats (XL Reg Cab) *NOT AVAILABLE with C, H, J, K.*	306	360
H	HD Knitted Vinyl Bucket Seats (XL - X-Cab/Crew Cab) *NOT AVAILABLE with G, J, K, C.*	298	350
H	HD Knitted Vinyl Bucket Seats (XL Reg Cab) *NOT AVAILABLE with C, G, J, K.*	255	300
J	HD Vinyl Full Bucket Seats (XL) *NOT AVAILABLE with C, G, H, K.*	170	200
K	HD Knitted Vinyl Full Bench Seat (XL Reg Cab) *NOT AVAILABLE with C, G, H, J.*	85	100
K	HD Knitted Vinyl Full Bench Seat (XL X-Cab) *NOT AVAILABLE with C, G, H, J.*	128	150
M76	Rear Bumper Delete	(85)	(100)
T3N	Tires: LT235/85R16E AT BSW *NOT AVAILABLE with T3R, T43, T4B, T46, T4R.*	107	125
T3R	Tires: LT235/85R16E AT OWL *NOT AVAILABLE with T3N, T43, T4B, T46, T4R.*	217	255
T43	Tires: LT265/75Rx16E AS BSW (XL/XLT) *NOT AVAILABLE with T3N, T3R, T4B, T46, T4R.*	166	195
T46	Tires: LT265/75R16E AS OWL *NOT AVAILABLE with T3N, T3R, T43, T4B, T4R.*	267	315
T4B	Tires: LT265/75R16E AT BSW (XL/XLT) *NOT AVAILABLE with T3N, T3R, T43, T46, T4R.*	267	315
T4R	Tires: LT265/75R16E AT OWL (XLT) *REQUIRES 60D. NOT AVAILABLE with T3N, T3R, T43, T4B, T46.*	107	125
T4R	Tires: LT265/75R16E AT OWL (XLT/Lariat) *NOT AVAILABLE with 60D, T3N, T3R, T43, T4B, T46.*	370	435
X31	3.73 Axle Ratio *NOT AVAILABLE with XC2, 99S, XC3, XC1, X32.*	NC	NC
X32	4.10 Axle Ratio *NOT AVAILABLE with 99S, 99F, 446, XC1, XC2, XC3, 449, X31.*	43	50
XC1	Limited Slip with 3.73 Axle Ratio *REQUIRES 99F or 99S. NOT AVAILABLE with X32, X31, XC2, XC3.*	243	285
XC2	Limited Slip with 4.10 Axle Ratio *NOT AVAILABLE with 99S, 99F, 446, X31, X32, XC3, 449, XC1.*	243	285
XC3	Limited Slip with 4.30 Axle Ratio *NOT AVAILABLE with 99F, X31, X32, 446, 44E, XC1, XC2, 449.*	NC	NC
XC3	Limited Slip with 4.30 Axle Ratio *REQUIRES 99S. NOT AVAILABLE with 99F, 446, X32, XC2, X31, 44E, XC1, 449.*	285	335

2000 F-350 SUPER DUTY PICKUP

Standard Equipment

XL 2WD SD REGULAR CAB SRW (5M): 5.4L V8 SOHC SMPI 16-valve engine; 5-speed OD manual transmission; 750-amp HD battery with run down protection; 95-amp alternator; rear-wheel drive, power take-off provision, 3.73 axle ratio; stainless steel exhaust; firm ride suspension, front independent suspension, front coil springs, HD front shocks, rigid rear axle suspension with rear leaf springs, HD rear shocks; power re-circulating ball steering; 4-wheel disc brakes with rear wheel antilock braking system; 38 gal. capacity fuel tank; trailer harness; front and rear argent bumpers with front tow hooks, rear step; monotone paint; sealed beam halogen headlamps; additional exterior lights include pickup cargo box light; driver's and passenger's manual black folding outside mirrors; front and rear 16" x 7" silver steel wheels; LT265/75SR16 A/S BSW front and rear tires; underbody mounted full-size steel spare wheel with crankdown; AM/FM stereo, clock, seek-scan, 2 speakers, and fixed antenna; 2 power accessory outlets, smokers' package; instrumentation display includes tachometer, oil pressure gauge, water temperature gauge, volt gauge, trip odometer; warning indicators include oil pressure, water temp, battery, key in ignition, low fuel, door ajar; driver's front airbag, passenger's cancelable front airbag; tinted windows; fixed interval front windshield wipers, sun visor strip; seating capacity of 3, bench front, seat fixed headrests, driver's seat includes 2-way direction control, passenger's seat includes 2-way direction control; front height adjustable seatbelts; vinyl seats, full cloth headliner, full vinyl floor covering, cabback insulator; interior lights include dome light with delay; day/night rearview mirror; glove box, front cupholder, instrument panel bin, dashboard storage; argent grille, black side window moldings, black front windshield molding, black rear window molding and black door handles.

XL 2WD SD REGULAR CAB DRW (5M) (in addition to or instead of XL 2WD SD REGULAR CAB SRW (5M) equipment): 4-wheel disc brakes with 4-wheel antilock braking system; additional exterior lights include cab clearance lights; front and rear 16" x 6" silver steel wheels and LT215/85SR16 A/S BSW front and rear tires.

XL 2WD SD SUPER CAB SRW/DRW SB/LB (5M) (in addition to or instead of XL 2WD SD REGULAR CAB SRW/DRW (5M) equipment): 29 gal. (38 gal. - LB) capacity fuel tank; seating capacity of 6 and full folding rear bench seat.

XL 2WD SD CREW CAB SRW SB/LB (5M) (in addition to or instead of XL 2WD SD SUPER CAB SRW/DRW HD (5M) equipment): Passenger's non-deactivating front airbag and manual rear windows.

XL 2WD SD CREW CAB DRW SB/LB (5M) (in addition to or instead of XL 2WD SD CREW CAB SRW SB/LB (5M) equipment): 6.8L V10 SOHC SMPI 20-valve engine.

XLT (in addition to or instead of XL equipment): Front and rear chrome bumpers with front tow hooks; black bodyside molding with chrome bodyside insert; aero-composite halogen headlamps; additional exterior lights include underhood light; aluminum wheels, air conditioning; AM/FM stereo, clock, seek-scan, cassette, 4 speakers, and fixed antenna; cruise control with steering wheel controls; retained accessory power, power windows with driver's 1-touch down; 40-20-40 split-bench front seat, fixed headrests, center armrest with storage, driver's seat includes 4-way direction control, passenger's seat includes 4-way direction control; cloth seats, vinyl door trim insert, full color-keyed carpet floor covering with floor mats; interior lights include dome light (two sets - Crew Cab) with delay, front (and rear - Crew Cab) reading lights; steering wheel with tilt adjustment; passenger's side vanity mirror; driver's and passenger's door bins; cargo concealed storage and chrome grille.

LARIAT (in addition to or instead of XLT equipment): Driver's and passenger's power remote black folding outside mirrors; power door locks with 2 stage unlock, remote keyless entry; 2 power accessory outlets; instrumentation display includes compass, trip computer, driver's seat includes 4-way power seat, 8-way direction control; leather seats; interior lights include 2 door curb lights; leather-wrapped steering wheel with tilt adjustment; dual auxiliary visors and full overhead console with storage.

4WD (in addition to or instead of 2WD equipment): Part-time 4 wheel drive, manual locking hub control and manual shift and front non-independent suspension with anti-roll bar.

Base Prices

Code	Description	Invoice	MSRP
F30	XL 2WD SD Regular Cab SRW LB (5M)	18085	20565
F32	XL 2WD SD Regular Cab DRW LB (5M)	18906	21530
X30	XL 2WD SD SuperCab SRW SB (5M)	20214	23070
X30-8	XL 2WD SD SuperCab SRW LB (5M)	20384	23270
F30	XLT 2WD SD Regular Cab SRW LB (5M)	20580	23500
F31	XL 4WD SD Regular Cab SRW LB (5M)	20699	23640
X32	XL 2WD SD SuperCab DRW LB (5M)	21201	24230
W30	XL 2WD SD Crew Cab SRW SB (5M)	21388	24450
W30-8	XL 2WD SD Crew Cab SRW LB (5M)	21218	24250
F32	XLT 2WD SD Regular Cab DRW LB (5M)	21541	24630
F33	XL 4WD SD Regular Cab DRW LB (5M)	21612	24715
F30	Lariat 2WD SD Regular Cab SRW LB (5	22059	25240
W32	XL 2WD SD Crew Cab DRW SB (5M)	22246	25460
X30	XLT 2WD SD SuperCab SRW SB (5M)	22547	25815
W32-8	XL 2WD SD Crew Cab DRW LB (5M)	22416	25660
X30-8	XLT 2WD SD SuperCab SRW LB (5M)	22377	25615
F32	Lariat 2WD SD Regular Cab DRW LB (5	22816	26130
X31	XL 4WD SD SuperCab SRW SB (5M)	22833	26150
X31-8	XL 4WD SD SuperCab SRW LB (5M)	23003	26350
F31	XLT 4WD SD Regular Cab SRW LB (5M)	23203	26585
X32	XLT 2WD SD SuperCab DRW LB (5M)	23500	26935
W31	XL 4WD SD Crew Cab SRW SB (5M)	24006	27530
X30	Lariat 2WD SD SuperCab SRW SB (5M)	23844	27340
W30	XLT 2WD SD Crew Cab SRW SB (5M)	23865	27365
X33	XL 4WD SD SuperCab DRW LB (5M)	23912	27420
W31-8	XL 4WD SD Crew Cab SRW LB (5M)	23836	27330
X30-8	Lariat 2WD SD SuperCab SRW LB (5M)	23014	27540
W30-8	XLT 2WD SD Crew Cab SRW LB (5M)	24035	27665
F33	XLT 4WD SD Regular Cab DRW LB (5M)	24243	27810
F31	Lariat 4WD SD Regular Cab SRW LB (5	24677	28320
X32	Lariat 2WD SD SuperCab DRW LB (5M)	24757	28415
W33	XL 4WD SD Crew Cab DRW SB (5M)	25128	28850
X31	XLT 4WD SD SuperCab SRW SB (5M)	24996	28695
W32	XLT 2WD SD Crew Cab DRW SB (5M)	25038	28745
W33-8	XL 4WD SD Crew Cab DRW LB (5M)	24958	28650
X31-8	XLT 4WD SD SuperCab SRW LB (5M)	25166	28895

CODE	DESCRIPTION	INVOICE	MSRP
W32-8	XLT 2WD SD Crew Cab DRW LB (5M)	25208	28945
W30	Lariat 2WD SD Crew Cab SRW SB (5M)	25344	29105
W30-8	Lariat 2WD SD Crew Cab SRW LB (5M)	25514	29305
F33	Lariat 4WD SD Regular Cab DRW LB (5	25518	29310
X33	XLT 4WD SD SuperCab DRW LB (5M)	26207	30120
W31	XLT 4WD SD Crew Cab SRW SB (5M)	26279	30205
W32	Lariat 2WD SD Crew Cab DRW SB (5M)	26479	30440
W31-8	XLT 4WD SD Crew Cab SRW LB (5M)	26449	30405
X31	Lariat 4WD SD SuperCab SRW SB (5M)	26627	30615
W32-8	Lariat 2WD SD Crew Cab DRW LB (5M)	26309	30240
X31-8	Lariat 4WD SD SuperCab SRW LB (5M)	26457	30415
X33	Lariat 4WD SD SuperCab DRW LB (5M)	27465	31600
W33	XLT 4WD SD Crew Cab DRW SB (5M)	27538	31685
W33-8	XLT 4WD SD Crew Cab DRW LB (5M)	27708	31885
W31	Lariat 4WD SD Crew Cab SRW SB (5M)	27754	31940
W31-8	Lariat 4WD SD Crew Cab SRW LB (5M)	27924	32140
W33	Lariat 4WD SD Crew Cab DRW SB (5M)	28813	33185
W33-8	Lariat 4WD SD Crew Cab DRW LB (5M)	28983	33385
Destination Charge:		665	665

Accessories

CODE	DESCRIPTION	INVOICE	MSRP
13C001	Special Paint: Cramer Brown Tan/Copper *REQUIRES SP101.*	NC	NC
166	Carpet Delete (XLT/Lariat) *Replaced with black floor mat. INCLUDED in 610A, 620A.*	(43)	(50)
17F	XL Decor Group (XL) *Includes locking tailgate, chrome front bumper with lower valance and aero halogen headlights.*	100	115
17F	XL Decor Group (XL) *Includes locking tailgate, chrome front bumper with lower valance, aero halogen headlamps and wheels: steel with full wheel covers.*	150	175
18L	Cab Steps (Reg Cab - XL/XLT) *Integrated and molded black. INCLUDED in 618A, 628A.*	272	320
18L	Cab Steps (X-Cab - XL/XLT) *Integrated and molded black. INCLUDED in 618A, 628A.*	314	370
2	Cloth Luxury Captain's Chairs (XLT)	NC	NC
213	4x4 Electric Shift-On-The-Fly (4WD) *Includes auto-manual locking hubs.*	136	160
4	Leather Luxury Captain's Chairs (Lariat)	NC	NC
41H	Engine Block Heater *Recommended when minimum temperature is -10 degrees F or below. INCLUDED in 99F.*	30	35
428	High Altitude Principal Use *NOT AVAILABLE with 429, 93N.*	NC	NC

CODE	DESCRIPTION	INVOICE	MSRP
429	Non-High Altitude Principal Use *NOT AVAILABLE with 428.*	NC	NC
433	Sliding Rear Window	107	125
446	Transmission: HD 6-Speed Manual with Overdrive *Includes transmission power take-off provision. REQUIRES 99F. NOT AVAILABLE with XD2, XD3, 532, 531, 62R, 86M, XF3, 17S.*	NC	NC
449	Transmission: Electronic 4-Speed Automatic *REQUIRES 99F. NOT AVAILABLE with XD2, XD3, 532, 531, 86M, XF3.*	931	1095
44E	Transmission: Electronic 4-Speed Auto (All Except Crew Cab DRW) *NOT AVAILABLE with 99F, 531, 532, 86M, 63T.*	931	1095
52N	Speed Control/Tilt Steering Wheel (XL) *INCLUDED in 617A, 618A, 627A, 628A.*	328	385
531	Trailer Towing Package *Includes 7-wire harness, trailer brake wiring kit, trailer tow guide and front stabilizer bar. NOTE: Salesperson should be consulted for specific trailer towing or camper limits and corresponding required equipment, axle ratios, model availability and vehicle height consideration. NOT AVAILABLE with 532, 449, 99F, 446, 96P, 86M.*	132	155
531	Trailer Towing Package *Includes 7-wire harness, trailer brake wiring kit, trailer tow guide and front stabilizer bar. NOTE: Salesperson should be consulted for specific trailer towing or camper limits and corresponding required equipment, axle ratios, model availability and vehicle height consideration. REQUIRES 532. NOT AVAILABLE with 449, 446, 96P, 44E, XD2, XD3, 86M.*	59	70
531	Trailer Towing Package	132	155
	Manufacturer Discount	(51)	(60)
	Net Price *Includes 7-wire harness, trailer brake wiring kit, trailer tow guide and front stabilizer bar. NOTE: Salesperson should be consulted for specific trailer towing or camper limits and corresponding required equipment, axle ratios, model availability and vehicle height consideration. REQUIRES 99F. NOT AVAILABLE with 532, 44E, XD2, XD3, 86M.*	81	95
532	Camper Package *Includes auxiliary rear springs, slide-in camper certification, front stabilizer bar and rear stabilizer bar. NOTE: Salesperson should be consulted for specific trailer towing or camper limits and corresponding required equipment, axle ratios and model availability. NOT AVAILABLE with 99F, 446, 449, 674, 531, 96P, 86M, 66D, 552.*	251	295
532	Camper Package	251	295
	Manufacturer Discount	(51)	(60)
	Net Price *Includes auxiliary rear springs, slide-in camper certification, front stabilizer bar and rear stabilizer bar. NOTE: Salesperson should be consulted for specific trailer towing or camper limits and corresponding required equipment, axle ratios and model availability. REQUIRES 99F. NOT AVAILABLE with 674, 531, 44E, XD2, XD3, 86M, 66D, 552.*	200	235
54Q	Power Mirrors (XLT) *NOT AVAILABLE with 54U, 54Y. INCLUDED in 618A, 628A.*	85	100

CODE	DESCRIPTION	INVOICE	MSRP
54U	Manual Trailer Tow Mirrors (XL/XLT) *NOT AVAILABLE with 54Q, 54Y.*	47	55
54Y	Power Trailer Tow Mirrors (Lariat)	47	55
54Y	Power Trailer Tow Mirrors (XLT) *NOT AVAILABLE with 54U, 54Q.*	132	155
55R	Off-Road Package (4WD) *Includes fuel tank and transfer case skid plates and off-road 4x4 decal.*	107	125
572	Air Conditioning (XL) *INCLUDED in 617A, 618A, 627A, 628A.*	684	805
589	Radio: AM/FM Stereo with Cassette and Clock (XL) *Includes 4 speakers. NOT AVAILABLE with 58K. INCLUDED in 617A, 618A, 627A, 628A.*	115	135
58K	Radio: Premium AM/FM Stereo with Cassette and CD (XL) *Includes premium sound with amplifier, 4 speakers and clock.*	277	325
58K	Radio: Premium AM/FM Stereo with Cassette and CD (XLT/Lariat) *Includes premium sound with amplifier, 4 speakers and clock.*	162	190
592	Roof Clearance Lights (SRW)	47	55
60D	XLT Upgrade Package (XLT) *Includes premium AM/FM stereo with cassette and CD, cab steps, sliding rear window, privacy glass and tires: LT265/75R16E A/S OWL (SRW)/LT235/85R16E A/S OWL (DRW). REQUIRES 99F and 446. NOT AVAILABLE with 99S, 449, 44E, 531, 532, T4B, T4R.*	NC	NC
610A	Series Code 610A (XL SRW) *Includes vehicle with standard equipment. REQUIRES 47Z.*	NC	NC
617A	Series Code 617A (XLT SRW) *Includes vehicle with standard equipment. REQUIRES 47Z.*	NC	NC
618A	Series Code 618A (Lariat SRW) *Includes vehicle with standard equipment. REQUIRES 47Z.*	NC	NC
620A	Series Code 620A (XL DRW) *Includes vehicle with standard equipment. REQUIRES 47Z.*	NC	NC
627A	Series Code 627A (XLT DRW) *Includes vehicle with standard equipment. REQUIRES 47Z.*	NC	NC
628A	Series Code 628A (Lariat DRW) *Includes vehicle with standard equipment. REQUIRES 47Z.*	NC	NC
62R	Transmission Power Take-Off Provision *Provision only. Requires aftermarket PTO. REQUIRES 44E or (99F and 449). NOT AVAILABLE with 446.*	213	250
63T	Dual Alternators *REQUIRES 99F. NOT AVAILABLE with 44E.*	285	335
649	Wheels: Polished Aluminum (4) (XL DRW) *INCLUDED in 627A, 628A.*	493	580
64F	Wheels: Forged Deluxe Aluminum (4) (XL SRW) *NOT AVAILABLE with 17F. INCLUDED in 617A.*	323	380
64F	Wheels: Forged Deluxe Aluminum (4) (XL SRW) *REQUIRES 17F. INCLUDED in 617A.*	272	320

CODE	DESCRIPTION	INVOICE	MSRP
66D	Pickup Box Delete (LB) *Includes spare tire delete, passenger's side air bag delete. Deletes pickup box and tailgate. NOTE: Incomplete vehicle package - requires further manufacture and certification by a final stage manufacturer. REQUIRES 620A or 446 or 449 or 627A or (54Y and 628A) or 54Y or 44E. NOT AVAILABLE with 768, 769, 532.*	(510)	(600)
674	Heavy Service Suspension Package *Includes heavy service front springs and auxiliary rear springs. NOTE: recommended only on vehicles which will permanently utilize aftermarket equipment such as heavy-duty winches and brush guards or other apparatus which loads the front axle to the specified gross axle weight rating (GAWR). NOT AVAILABLE with 532, 86M.*	149	175
67B	4-Wheel Antilock Brakes (SRW - XL/XLT) *INCLUDED in 618A.*	319	375
768	Chrome Rear Step Bumper Delete (XLT/Lariat) *NOT AVAILABLE with 66D.*	(85)	(100)
769	Argent Rear Step Bumper Delete (XL)	(85)	(100)
86M	Snow Plow Package (4WD LB)	158	185
	Manufacturer Discount	(51)	(60)
	Net Price *Includes auxiliary rear springs. REQUIRES 99F. NOT AVAILABLE with 674, 532, 531, 44E, XD2, XD3.*	107	125
86M	Snow Plow Package (4WD LB) *Includes auxiliary rear springs and highest front gawr springs (5200 lbs). NOT AVAILABLE with 446, 449, 99F, 674, 532, 531, 96P.*	158	185
86R	Trailer Hitch Receiver (Class IV) *REQUIRES 532 or 531.*	128	150
87D	Rear Seat Delete (XL X-Cab)	(352)	(415)
90P	6-Way Power Driver's Seat (XLT) *REQUIRES 948. INCLUDED in 618A, 628A.*	247	290
924	Privacy Glass (XLT/Lariat) *REQUIRES 433.*	85	100
948	Remote Keyless Entry (XLT) *Includes 2-step unlock system and door courtesy lights. INCLUDED in 618A, 628A.*	144	170
954	Lower Accent Two-Tone Paint (XLT/Lariat) *Includes unique accent color (Lariat).*	192	225
96P	Auxiliary Idle Control Kit *APC module function includes battery charge protection, high idle control and LCD RPM/voltage readout. Kit includes auxiliary idle control module, mounting bracket/hardware, wiring harness and instruction booklet. NOTE: stationary use only and kit is shipped in box to vehicle operations for "in cab" shipment. REQUIRES (99F and 449 and 62R) or (99F and 446). NOT AVAILABLE with 532, 531, 86M.*	178	210
99F	Engine: 7.3L DI Turbo Diesel V8 (All Except Crew Cab SRW) *Power stroke diesel. Includes dual 78-ah batteries, 130-amp HD alternator and engine block heater. REQUIRES 446 or 449. NOT AVAILABLE with 44E, XD2, XD3, 532, XF3.*	3910	4600
99F	Engine: 7.3L DI Turbo Diesel V8 (Crew Cab SRW) *Power stroke diesel. Includes dual 78-ah batteries, 130-amp HD alternator and engine block heater. REQUIRES 446 or 449. NOT AVAILABLE with 532, XF3, 44E.*	3613	4250

CODE	DESCRIPTION	INVOICE	MSRP
99S	Engine: 6.8L EFI V10 *NOT AVAILABLE with 446, 449, XD2, 531, 532, 96P, 86M, XF2, 63T.*	510	600
C	HD Cloth Full Bench Seat (XL - X-Cab/Crew Cab) *NOT AVAILABLE with K, G, H, J.*	221	260
C	HD Cloth Full Bench Seat (XL Reg Cab) *NOT AVAILABLE with K, G, H, J.*	136	160
G	HD Cloth Bucket Seats (XL - X-Cab/Crew Cab) *NOT AVAILABLE with K, C, H, J.*	391	460
G	HD Cloth Bucket Seats (XL Reg Cab) *NOT AVAILABLE with K, C, H, J.*	306	360
H	HD Knitted Vinyl Bucket Seats (XL - X-Cab/Crew Cab) *NOT AVAILABLE with K, C, G, J.*	298	350
H	HD Knitted Vinyl Bucket Seats (XL Reg Cab) *NOT AVAILABLE with K, C, G, J.*	255	300
J	HD Vinyl Full Bucket Seats (XL) *NOT AVAILABLE with K, C, G, H.*	170	200
K	HD Knitted Vinyl Full Bench Seat (XL - X-Cab/Crew Cab) *NOT AVAILABLE with C, G, H, J.*	128	150
K	HD Knitted Vinyl Full Bench Seat (XL Reg Cab) *NOT AVAILABLE with C, G, H, J.*	85	100
M76	Rear Bumper Delete *REQUIRES 769.*	(85)	(100)
SP101	Paint Scheme	NC	NC
T35	Tires: LT235/85R16E AS BSW (2WD DRW) *NOT AVAILABLE with T3N, T36, T3R, 515.*	144	170
T36	Tires: LT235/85R16E AS OWL (2WD DRW) *NOT AVAILABLE with T35, T3N, T3R, 515.*	251	295
T36	Tires: LT235/85R16E AS OWL (4WD DRW) *NOT AVAILABLE with T3N, T3R, 515.*	128	150
T3N	Tires: LT235/85R16E AT BSW (2WD DRW) *NOT AVAILABLE with T35, T36, T3R, 512.*	251	295
T3N	Tires: LT235/85R16E AT BSW (4WD DRW) *NOT AVAILABLE with T36, T3R, 512.*	128	150
T3R	Tires: LT235/85R16E AT OWL (2WD DRW) *NOT AVAILABLE with T35, T3N, T36, 512.*	357	420
T3R	Tires: LT235/85R16E AT OWL (4WD DRW) *NOT AVAILABLE with T3N, T36, 512.*	357	420
T3R	Tires: LT235/85R16E AT OWL (DRW) *REQUIRES 60D. NOT AVAILABLE with T35, T3N, T36.*	128	150
T46	Tires: LT265/75R16E AS OWL (SRW) *NOT AVAILABLE with T4B, T4R.*	107	125
T4B	Tires: LT265/75R16E AT BSW (SRW) *NOT AVAILABLE with T46, T4R.*	107	125
T4R	Tires: LT265/75R16E AT OWL (SRW) *NOT AVAILABLE with T4B, T46.*	213	250
T4R	Tires: LT265/75R16E AT OWL (SRW) *REQUIRES 60D. NOT AVAILABLE with T4B, T46.*	107	125

CODE	DESCRIPTION	INVOICE	MSRP
XD1	Limited Slip with 3.73 Axle Ratio (SRW) *REQUIRES 44E or 99F. NOT AVAILABLE with XD2, XD3.*	243	285
XD2	Limited Slip with 4.10 Axle Ratio (SRW) *REQUIRES 44E. NOT AVAILABLE with 449, 99F, 446, XD1, XD3, 531, 532, 86M.*	243	285
XD3	Limited Slip with 4.30 Axle Ratio (SRW) *NOT AVAILABLE with 99F, 449, 446, XD1, XD2, 531, 532, 86M.*	285	335
XF2	Limited Slip with 4.10 Axle Ratio (DRW) *REQUIRES 99F. NOT AVAILABLE with XF3.*	243	285
XF3	Limited Slip with 4.30 Axle Ratio (DRW) *REQUIRES 99S. NOT AVAILABLE with XF2, 99F, 446, 449.*	243	285

2000 RANGER

2000 Ford Ranger

What's New?

For 2000, the 4x2 can be had with a torsion-bar suspension and a larger tire/wheel package, giving it the tough look of its 4x4 cousin. All Ranger models have new wheel designs, and the XLT 4x4 Off-Road Group receives a stainless steel front-suspension skid plate.

Review

Whether it's image or utility that attracts you to a compact truck, Ford stands ready to seduce you into its strong-selling Ranger. The standard engine on 4x2 models is Ford's 2.5-liter four-cylinder engine. A 3.0-liter flexible-fuel V6 is standard on 4x4 models, and a 4.0-liter V6 is available on all models. With the larger V6, acceleration is impressively brisk, especially from a standstill or when merging and passing. This engine is available with a five-speed automatic transmission. Its upshifts are crisp and barely noticed, with just a slight jolt under hard throttle, and downshifts deliver only slightly more harshness. Push-button four-wheel drive, if installed, is a snap to use.

Well-controlled overall, with good steering feedback, Rangers handle easily, corner capably, maneuver neatly, and stay reasonably stable on curves. Occupants aren't likely to complain about the ride, either, though it can grow bouncy around town. Gas mileage isn't the greatest with the big engine and automatic.

The four-door SuperCab—available in two- and four-wheel drive—makes it easy to access the storage compartment from either side of the truck, a big assist when loading cargo and gear. The optional rear doors hinge off the corner pillars of the cab and swing out 90 degrees from the doorsill. There are no B-pillars to obstruct loading. Completing the Ford Ranger pickup line are regular cab, short- and long-wheelbase 4x2 and 4x4 models.

The Ranger is equipped with dual airbags and side-impact protection beams. The rear doors for 4x2 and 4x4 SuperCab models also have side-door intrusion beams for extra safety protection. ABS is optional.

The optional suspension package for 2000 4x2 Rangers is called the XL Stance package. It includes the 3.0-liter flexible-fuel V6 engine, and Ford hopes to attract Ranger buyers who want that 4x4 look, but don't need the off-road capabilities.

The 3.0-liter flexible-fuel V6 can burn 100 percent unleaded gasoline, E-85 (ethanol) or any combination of the two, meaning owners can fuel up on E-85 whenever it's available. When E-85 is unavailable, regular unleaded gasoline can be used with no detriment to performance. Ford's Ranger continues to be available as an Electric Vehicle (EV). Qualifying as a Zero-Emissions Vehicle (ZEV), Ranger EV is based on the regular cab, 112-inch wheelbase model.

Ford has had the best-selling small trucks in the country for years. Fun to drive, sharp looking and well built, the Ranger delivers a solid compact-pickup experience. Its most serious competition comes from the Dodge Dakota, which is slightly larger and offers V8 power.

Standard Equipment

XL 2WD REGULAR CAB SB/LB (5M): 2.5L I4 SOHC SMPI 8-valve engine; 5-speed OD manual transmission; 540-amp battery with run down protection; 95-amp alternator; rear-wheel drive, 3.73 axle ratio; partial stainless steel exhaust; front independent suspension with anti-roll bar, front coil springs, gas-pressurized front shocks, rigid rear axle suspension with rear leaf springs, gas-pressurized rear shocks; power rack-and-pinion steering; front disc/rear drum brakes with rear wheel antilock braking system; 16.5 gal. (20 gal. - LB) capacity fuel tank; front and rear mud flaps, side impact bars; trailer harness; front and rear black bumpers with rear step; monotone paint; aero-composite halogen headlamps; driver's and passenger's manual black folding outside mirrors; front and rear 15" x 6" argent steel wheels with chrome hub covers; P225/70SR15 A/S BSW front and rear tires; underbody mounted full-size steel spare wheel with crankdown; AM/FM stereo, clock, seek-scan, 2 speakers, and fixed antenna; 2 power accessory outlets, smokers' package; instrumentation display includes oil pressure gauge, water temperature gauge, volt gauge, trip odometer; warning indicators include battery, lights on, key in ignition, door ajar; driver's front airbag, passenger's cancelable front airbag; tinted windows; speed sensitive variable intermittent front windshield wipers, sun visor strip; seating capacity of 3, 60-40 split-bench front seat, fixed headrests, driver's seat includes 2-way direction control, passenger's seat includes 2-way direction control; front height adjustable seatbelts; vinyl seats, full cloth headliner, full vinyl floor covering; interior lights include dome light; day/night rearview mirror; glove box, front cupholder; black grille, black side window moldings, black front windshield molding, black rear window molding and black door handles.

XLT 2WD REGULAR CAB SB/LB (5M) (in addition to or instead of XL 2WD REGULAR CAB SB/LB (5M) equipment): Front and rear chrome bumpers with rear step; additional exterior lights include pickup cargo box light; front and rear 15" x 6" silver steel wheels; spare tire lock; AM/FM stereo, clock, seek-scan, single CD, 4 speakers, and fixed antenna; center armrest with storage, driver's seat includes 4-way direction control, passenger's seat includes 4-way direction control; cloth seats, vinyl door trim insert, full color-keyed carpet floor covering; interior lights include front reading lights; passenger's side vanity mirror; passenger's side grab handle, driver's and passenger's door bins; cargo concealed storage; chrome grille.

SUPERCAB SB (5M) (in addition to or instead of REGULAR CAB SB (5M) equipment): 4.1 axle ratio; 19.5 gal. capacity fuel tank; seating capacity of 5, center armrest with storage, driver's seat includes 4-

CODE	DESCRIPTION	INVOICE	MSRP

way direction control, passenger's seat includes 4-way direction control; 50-50 side-facing folding rear jump seats and cloth seats.

XL 4WD (5M) (in addition to or instead of XL 2WD (5M) equipment): 3.0L V6 OHV SMPI 12-valve engine, flexible fuel capable; part-time 4 wheel drive, auto locking hub control and electronic shift, 3.73 axle ratio; front torsion springs, front torsion bar, HD front shocks, HD rear shocks; front tow hooks; black fender flares; P215/75SR15 AT OWL front and rear tires; instrumentation display includes tachometer and ignition disable.

XLT 4WD (5M) (in addition to or instead of XLT 2WD (5M) equipment): 3.0L V6 OHV SMPI 12-valve engine, flexible fuel capable; part-time 4 wheel drive, auto locking hub control and electronic shift, 3.73 axle ratio; front torsion springs, front torsion bar, HD front shocks, HD rear shocks; front tow hooks; black fender flares; P215/75SR15 AT OWL front and rear tires; front disc/rear drum brakes with 4-wheel antilock braking system; additional exterior lights include front fog/driving lights, pickup cargo box light; front and rear 15" x 7" silver alloy wheels; P235/75SR15 AT OWL front and rear tires; instrumentation display includes tachometer, ignition disable.

Base Prices

R10	XL 2WD Regular Cab SB (5M)	10912	11485
R10-7	XL 2WD Regular Cab LB (5M)	11345	11955
R10	XLT 2WD Regular Cab SB (5M)	12278	13560
R10-7	XLT 2WD Regular Cab LB (5M)	12761	14110
R14	XL 2WD SuperCab SB (5M)	13672	15145
R14	XLT 2WD SuperCab SB (5M)	14244	15795
R11	XL 4WD Regular Cab SB (5M)	14904	15825
R11-7	XL 4WD Regular Cab LB (5M)	15337	16295
R15	XL 4WD SuperCab SB (5M)	15688	17435
R11	XLT 4WD Regular Cab SB (5M)	16163	17975
R11-7	XLT 4WD Regular Cab LB (5M)	16664	18545
R15	XLT 4WD Super Cab SB (5M)	17672	19690
Destination Charge:		535	535

Accessories

173	Flareside Box (All Except XL 4WD Reg Cab) *NOT AVAILABLE with 91S, 99V, 95P.*	421	495
173	Flareside Box (XLT SuperCab)	421	495
	Manufacturer Discount	(421)	(495)
	Net Price *NOT AVAILABLE with 99X, 95P.*	NC	NC
18P	Step Bar (XL 2WD Reg Cab SB/XLT) *REQUIRES 91S or 95P.*	250	295
202	Optional Payload Package #2 (2WD Reg Cab SB) *Maximum payload 1660 lbs with GVWR 4760 lbs. NOT AVAILABLE with 91S.*	64	75
205	Optional Payload Package #2 (2WD Reg Cab LB) *Maximum payload 1660 lbs with GVWR 4800 lbs.*	64	75
20B	Optional Payload Package #2 (2WD SuperCab) *Maximum payload 1620 lbs with GVWR 4960 lbs.*	64	75

CODE	DESCRIPTION	INVOICE	MSRP
20G	Optional Payload Package #2 (4WD Reg Cab LB) *Maximum payload 1540 lbs with GVWR 5020 lbs.*	64	75
20T	Optional Payload Package #2 (4WD SuperCab) *Maximum payload 1540 lbs with GVWR 5140 lbs.*	64	75
20W	Optional Payload Package #2 (4WD Reg Cab SB) *Maximum payload 1540 lbs with GVWR 4980 lbs.*	64	75
41H	Cold Weather Package (LPO) *Includes battery blanket. Recommended when minimum temperature is -10 F or below and engine block immersion heater. REQUIRES 99X. NOT AVAILABLE with 99V.*	26	30
428	High Altitude Principal Use *NOT AVAILABLE with X87.*	NC	NC
429	Non-High Altitude Principal Use	NC	NC
433	Sliding Rear Window *Includes privacy glass.*	107	125
44D	Transmission: 5-Speed Automatic with Overdrive *REQUIRES 99X. NOT AVAILABLE with 99V, XF6, X87.*	973	1145
44T	Transmission: 4-Speed Auto with Overdrive *REQUIRES 99V. NOT AVAILABLE with 99X, XR5, XR6.*	931	1095
47F	Power Equipment Group (XLT) *Includes power door locks, power windows with driver's one-touch down, remote keyless entry and panic alarm.*	455	535
47P	Convenience Group (XLT) *Includes leather-wrapped steering wheel and speed control/tilt steering wheel.*	336	395
52N	Speed Control/Tilt Steering Wheel (XL)	336	395
53L	Class III Trailer Tow Hitch Receiver (All Except XL 2WD Reg Cab) *REQUIRES 99V or 99X.*	182	215
572	Air Conditioning (XL) *INCLUDED in 864A.*	684	805
589	Radio: AM/FM Stereo with Cassette and Clock (XL) *Includes 4 speakers.*	119	140
58K	Radio: AM/FM Stereo Dual Media (XLT) *Includes CD and cassette player with 80-watt amplifier and clock.*	111	130
58Z	Radio: AM/FM Stereo with Clock and CD (XL) *Includes 4 speakers. NOT AVAILABLE with 589. INCLUDED in 864A.*	204	240
63B	4-Door Supercab (XL SuperCab) *Includes pivoting rear quarter window delete, jump seats delete, and carpet. REQUIRES 99V or 99X.*	488	575
63B	4-Door Supercab (XLT SuperCab) *Includes pivoting rear quarter window delete. REQUIRES 99V or 99X.*	591	695
64G	Wheel and Tire Group (XLT 2WD) *Includes wheels: 15" chrome styled steel and tires: P225/70R15 A/S OWL.*	277	325
64G	Wheel and Tire Group (XLT 2WD)	277	325
	Manufacturer Discount	(277)	(325)
	Net Price *Includes wheels: 15" chrome styled steel and tires: P225/70R15 A/S OWL. NOT AVAILABLE with 173.*	NC	NC

CODE	DESCRIPTION	INVOICE	MSRP
67B	4-Wheel ABS Brakes (XL/XLT 2WD)	255	300
861A	Series Code 861A (XL) *Includes vehicle with standard equipment. REQUIRES 20B or 99X or 99V.*	NC	NC
864A	Series Code 864A (XLT)	684	805
	Manufacturer Discount	(684)	(805)
	Net Price *Includes vehicle with standard equipment. REQUIRES 20B or 99X or 99V.*	NC	NC
91R	Off-Road Package (XLT 4WD) *Includes bulge body shocks, styled manual mirrors and off-road decal. NOT AVAILABLE with 95P, XF6, XR6, X87.*	336	395
91S	Trailhead Group (XL 2WD Reg Cab SB) *Includes valance, styled manual mirrors, wheels: 16" 5-spoke cast aluminum, tires: P245/75RX16AL OWL AT, standard torsion bar suspension, argent grille, argent front and rear bumpers, fog lamps, front tow hooks, payload package #2, tachometer and 4.10 axle ratio. REQUIRES 99V. NOT AVAILABLE with 95S, 173, XF6, 202.*	1356	1595
95P	XLT Sport Appearance Group (XLT 2WD) *Includes styled manual mirrors, color-keyed front and rear bumpers, color-keyed grille, tachometer, Sport decal and fog lamps. NOT AVAILABLE with 99V, 99X, 173.*	370	435
95P	XLT Sport Appearance Group (XLT 2WD) *Includes styled manual mirrors, color-keyed front and rear bumpers, color-keyed grille, tachometer, Sport decal and fog lamps. REQUIRES 99X.*	421	495
95P	XLT Sport Appearance Group (XLT 4WD) *Includes fog lamps, styled manual mirrors, color-keyed front and rear bumpers, color-keyed grille and Sport decal. NOT AVAILABLE with 91R.*	336	395
95S	XL Sport Appearance Package (XL 2WD) *Includes wheels: 15" silver styled steel, Sport decal, spare tire lock, color-keyed front and rear bumpers and color-keyed grille. NOT AVAILABLE with 91S, 99V, 99X.*	336	395
99V	Engine: 3.0L FFV V6 (2WD) *Flexible fuel capable. Includes Securilock. NOT AVAILABLE with X87, 44D, XR5, 95S, 95P, 41H.*	336	395
99X	Engine: 4.0L EFI V6 (XLT 2WD) *Includes 3.55 axle ratio and Securilock. NOT AVAILABLE with 44T, X87, XF6, 95P, 173.*	1101	1295
99X	Engine: 4.0L EFI V6 (XLT 4WD) *Includes 3.73 axle ratio. NOT AVAILABLE with 44T, XF6, X87, 173.*	592	695
E	60/40 Split Cloth Bench Seat (XL Reg Cab) *Includes floor consolette and integrated center arm rest. INCLUDED in 864A.*	251	295
G	Cloth Sport Bucket Seats (XLT) *Includes driver's side manual lumbar support and floor console.*	306	360
X87	4.10 Axle Ratio (All Except XL 4WD) *NOT AVAILABLE with 428, 99V, 99X, XF6, XR5, 44D, XR6, XR7, 91R.*	NC	NC
X97	4.10 Axle Ratio (XLT 4WD) *REQUIRES 99V.*	43	50
XF6	Limited Slip with 3.73 Axle Ratio *REQUIRES 99V and 202 or 205 or 20W or 20G. NOT AVAILABLE with 99X, X87, 44D, 91S, 91R, XR7.*	251	295

CODE	DESCRIPTION	INVOICE	MSRP
XR5	Limited Slip with 3.55 Axle Ratio (2WD) *REQUIRES 99X and 202 or 205. NOT AVAILABLE with 99V, 44T, X87.*	251	295
XR6	Limited Slip with 3.73 Axle Ratio (4WD SuperCab) *REQUIRES 99X and 20W or 20G. NOT AVAILABLE with 44T, XR7, 91R, X87.*	251	295
XR7	Limited Slip with 4.10 Axle Ratio (4WD Reg Cab) *REQUIRES 20W or 20G. NOT AVAILABLE with XR6, XF6, 91R, 99X.*	293	345
XR7	Limited Slip with 4.10 Axle Ratio (XL 2WD Reg Cab SB/XLT 4WD) *REQUIRES 91S or 20W or 20G. NOT AVAILABLE with 99X, X87.*	251	295

2000 WINDSTAR

2000 Ford Windstar

What's New?

The 2000 Windstar Wagon is essentially a carryover from the 1999 model year. The two main additions are power-adjustable pedals and a rear-seat entertainment center. A child seat-anchor system is now standard.

Review

Much of the Ford Windstar's reputation is based on safety. And in the highly contested minivan market, that's a pretty good piece of turf to stake a claim on. In the five straight years it has been tested, the Windstar has earned the U.S. government's highest frontal crash-test rating for both the driver and front passenger. Additionally, the Windstar can be equipped with optional side-impact airbags that give the minivan top government marks on side-impact crash safety.

In 1999, the Windstar gained dual-power sliding doors, head-and-chest side airbags and a sonar-based reverse sensing system. For 2000, new power-adjustable pedals enable the driver to move the gas and brake pedals up to 4 inches toward the seat while maintaining a safe operating distance from the steering wheel. Adding to the safety of the vehicle is a standard child seat-anchor system that meets new U.S. government requirements. The anchors provide a more secure attachment point for the child safety seat.

A rear-seat entertainment system, also new for 2000, helps back-seat passengers enjoy the ride. The system features a video cassette player and a video monitor with a 6.4-inch LCD screen that flips down from the center console for viewing. The console also contains RCA jacks for video game use. In addition, Windstar's Personal Audio System, introduced in 1999, allows front-seat passengers to listen to one media, such as radio or tape, while rear-seat passengers can listen to a separate media (such as a CD) through headphones. An innovative seating design allows the second-row bench seat to be positioned on either the right or left side of the vehicle, meaning the aisle to the third-row seat can be set up based on owner preference.

The 3.8-liter V6 (the only engine offered on four-door models) generates a robust, although somewhat noisy, 200 horsepower. Ford says the engine meets current ultra-low-emission vehicle (ULEV) standards.

The Windstar is a strong competitor within the minivan market. It suffers a bit because of the goofy front-end styling and a wallowing ride that can sometimes be unnerving on twisty mountain roads. But if you are making a minivan purchase, the Windstar's versatility and safety should not be overlooked.

Standard Equipment

BASE (4A): 3.0L V6 OHV SMPI 12-valve engine; 4-speed electronic OD auto transmission with lock-up; 540-amp battery with rundown protection; 130-amp alternator; front-wheel drive, 3.98 axle ratio; stainless steel exhaust; front independent strut suspension with anti-roll bar, front coil springs, rear non-independent suspension with rear coil springs; power rack-and-pinion steering; front disc/rear drum brakes with 4-wheel antilock braking system; 26 gal. capacity fuel tank; side impact bars; 3 doors with sliding right rear passenger's door, liftback rear cargo door; front and rear argent bumpers with rear step; black bodyside molding, rocker panel extensions; monotone paint; aero-composite halogen headlamps; driver's and passenger's power remote black folding outside mirrors; front and rear 15" x 6" steel wheels; P205/70SR15 A/S BSW front and rear tires; underbody mounted compact steel spare wheel; air conditioning; AM/FM stereo, clock, seek-scan, 4 speakers, and window grid antenna; power door locks, child safety rear door locks; 3 power accessory outlets, smokers' package; instrumentation display includes tachometer, water temperature gauge, trip odometer; warning indicators include oil pressure, battery, low oil level, lights on, key in ignition, low fuel, low washer fluid, bulb failure, door ajar; driver's and passenger's front airbags; ignition disable; tinted windows; variable intermittent front windshield wipers, sun visor strip, fixed interval rear wiper, rear window defroster; seating capacity of 7, front bucket seats, fixed headrests, driver's seat includes 4-way direction control, passenger's seat includes 4-way direction control; front height adjustable seatbelts; cloth seats, vinyl door trim insert, front cloth headliner, front carpet floor covering; interior lights include dome light with fade; vanity mirrors; day/night rearview mirror; locking glove box, front cupholder, instrument panel bin, driver's and passenger's door bins; vinyl cargo floor, cargo light; body-colored grille, black side window moldings, black front windshield molding, black rear window molding and black door handles; cabin air filter; retained accessory power; driver's and passenger's armrests, removable 2nd row full folding bench seat with adjustable headrests; removable 3rd row full folding bench seat with adjustable headrest; front and rear height adjustable seatbelts; deluxe sound insulation; carpeted cargo floor and plastic trunk lid.

LX (4A) (in addition to or instead of BASE (4A) equipment): Front and rear colored; colored bodyside molding; AM/FM stereo, clock, seek-scan, cassette, 4 speakers, and window grid antenna; cruise control with steering wheel controls; power windows with driver's 1-touch down, power 1/4 vent windows; remote keyless entry; removable 2nd row full folding bench seat with reclining adjustable headrests; removable 3rd row full folding bench seat with reclining adjustable headrest; cloth door trim insert; interior lights include rear reading lights, illuminated entry; steering wheel with tilt adjustment; locking glove box with light, rear cupholders and 2 seat back storage pockets.

SE (4A) (in addition to or instead of LX (4A) equipment): 3.8L V6 OHV SMPI 12-valve engine; 650-amp battery with run down protection; 3.56 axle ratio; roof rack; front and rear body-colored bumpers with chrome bumper insert; body-colored bodyside molding with chrome bodyside insert; 4 doors with sliding right and left rear passenger's doors, additional exterior lights include cornering lights; P215/70SR15 A/S BSW front and rear tires; rear air conditioning with separate controls, rear heater; panic alarm; audio includes auto-reverse cassette; deep tinted windows; driver's seat includes 4-way power seat, 8-way direction control, power 2-way lumbar support; interior lights include front and rear reading lights, 2 door curb lights; carpeted floor mats, leather-wrapped steering wheel with tilt adjustment; dual illuminated vanity mirrors; full overhead console with storage, front underseat tray; cargo net; chrome grille and body-colored door handles.

SEL (4A) (in addition to or instead of SE (4A) equipment): 750-amp battery with run down protection; front and rear colored bumpers with chrome bumper insert, colored bodyside cladding; lower accent two-tone paint; aero-composite halogen fully auto headlamps; 4 doors with power sliding right and left rear passenger's doors, additional exterior lights include front fog/driving lights; front and rear 16" x 6" machined alloy wheels; P225/60SR16 A/S BSW front and rear tires; premium AM/FM stereo, clock, seek-scan, auto-reverse cassette, single CD, 4 speakers, and window grid antenna, rear audio controls; garage door opener; instrumentation display includes compass, exterior temp; warning indicators include service interval; simulated wood trim on instrument panel; passenger's seat includes 4-way power seat, 8-way direction control, power 2-way lumbar support; leather seats, vinyl door trim insert and auto-dimming day/night rearview mirror.

Base Prices

Code	Description	Invoice	MSRP
A50	Base (4A)	19798	21415
A51	LX (4A)	21658	24015
A52	SE (4A)	24826	27615
A53	SEL (4A)	27462	30610
Destination Charge:		605	605

Accessories

Code	Description	Invoice	MSRP
152	Electronics Group (SE)	455	535
	Includes electrochromic lighting package, message center and trainable transmitter.		
167	Floor Mats (Base/LX)	77	90
184	LH Manual Sliding Door (4th Door) (Base/LX)	425	500
	Includes tires: P215/70R15 BSW. NOT AVAILABLE with 86C, 18E.		
18D	RH/LH Power Sliding Doors (2) (SE)	765	900
	Includes side-to-side indexing of 2nd row. NOT AVAILABLE with 18E, B3N.		
18E	RH Power Door/LH Manual Door (LX)	850	1000
	REQUIRES 86C and 41N. NOT AVAILABLE with 184.		
18E	RH Power Door/LH Manual Door (SE)	425	500
	NOT AVAILABLE with 18D.		
2	Low Back Leather Seating Surface (SE)	735	865
	Includes driver's and passenger's power seats and 2nd/3rd row leather seating surfaces.		
21L	Quad Buckets with Power Driver's Seat (LX)	910	1070
	Includes high back front seats and low back 2nd row seats. REQUIRES 86C. NOT AVAILABLE with 21P, 21Q.		
21L	Quad Buckets with Power Driver's Seat (SE/SEL)	910	1070
	Manufacturer Discount	(910)	(1070)
	Net Price	NC	NC
	Includes low back front and low back 2nd row.		
21P	High Back Buckets with Power Driver's Seat (LX)	277	325
	REQUIRES 86C. NOT AVAILABLE with 21Q, 21L.		

CODE	DESCRIPTION	INVOICE	MSRP
21Q	Quad Buckets (LX) *Includes 1st row high back buckets, 2nd row low back buckets, 3rd row bench and dump/slide adjustable tracks on 2nd row. REQUIRES 86C and (64F or 184 or 539). NOT AVAILABLE with 21L, 21P, 68P.*	633	745
414	Floor Console (LX/SE/SEL) *NOT AVAILABLE with 91E.*	132	155
41N	Full Overhead Console (LX) *Includes conversation mirror, coin holder, sunglasses holder, garage door opener holder, dome lamp, provision for rear audio controls for personal audio system, provision for power sliding door switch and reading lamp. REQUIRES 184 or 18E. NOT AVAILABLE with 64F.*	85	100
428	High Altitude Principal Use *NOT AVAILABLE with 93N.*	NC	NC
429	Non-High Altitude Principal Use	NC	NC
43B	Reverse Sensing System (LX/SE/SEL) *REQUIRES 184 or 18E.*	208	245
52N	Speed Control/Tilt Steering Wheel (Base)	319	375
539	Trailer Towing Package (Class II) (LX/SE/SEL) *Includes HD halfshafts, high speed ambient temperature package (Class II), 78-a.h. battery, tire: full size spare, auxiliary transmission oil cooler and trailer tow electrical package (Class I).*	400	470
589	Radio: AM/FM Stereo with Cassette (Base)	144	170
58K	Personal Audio System (LX/SE) *Includes mini overhead console, premium AM/FM stereo/cassette/in-dash single CD (dual media), 4 speakers and rear seat audio controls.*	255	300
60S	Family Security Package (LX) *Includes tires: P215/70R15 BSW self-sealing, traction control, perimeter anti-theft, remote keyless entry, light/visibility group and heated mirrors.*	408	480
60S	Family Security Package (SE) *Includes tires: P215/70R15 BSW self-sealing, traction control, perimeter anti-theft system, remote keyless entry, light/visibility group and heated mirrors. NOT AVAILABLE with 64T.*	370	435
60S	Family Security Package (SEL) *Includes traction control, perimeter anti-theft system, remote keyless entry, light/visibility group and heated mirrors.*	234	275
615	Roof Rack (LX)	149	175
64F	Wheels: 15" Aluminum (LX) *Includes tires: P215/70R15 BSW. REQUIRES 18E. NOT AVAILABLE with 86C, 41N.*	352	415
64T	Wheels: 16" Machined (SE) *Includes tires: P225/60R16 BSW. NOT AVAILABLE with 60S.*	192	225
65T	Trailer Tow Electical Package Class I *Includes module, wiring and jumper for trailering light hook up. Required for all class I towing applications.*	30	35
67E	Enhanced Seating Group (Base) *Includes adjustable rear seat tracks, reclining rear seat backs, rear bench seat rollers, 2nd row seat mounted cupholders and map pocket.*	348	410

CODE	DESCRIPTION	INVOICE	MSRP
68P	Adjustable Accelerator/Brake Pedals (LX/SE/SEL) *REQUIRES 21L or 21P. NOT AVAILABLE with 21Q.*	102	120
86C	Comfort Group (Base/LX) *Includes provision for rear radio controls, auxiliary climate control system, privacy glass, roof rack (LX) and mini overhead console. REQUIRES 67E. NOT AVAILABLE with 184.*	820	965
86C	Comfort Group (LX) *Includes provision for rear radio controls, auxiliary climate control system, privacy glass, roof rack and mini overhead console. NOT AVAILABLE with 64F.*	820	965
91E	Rear Seat Entertainment System *Includes unique console. NOT AVAILABLE with 91P, 414.*	1101	1295
91P	CD Changer Prep (LX/SE/SEL) *REQUIRES 414. NOT AVAILABLE with 91E.*	34	40
924	Privacy Glass (LX)	352	415
948	Remote Keyless Entry (Base)	213	250
994	Engine: 3.8L SPI V6 (Base/LX)	583	685
	Manufacturer Discount	(583)	(685)
	Net Price *Includes 72-a.h. battery and 3.56 axle ratio.*	NC	NC
A3D	Side Air Bags *REQUIRES 67E (Base).*	332	390

2000 ENVOY

2000 GMC Envoy

What's New?

Upgraded seats and V6 engine improvements headline changes to GM's high-end compact SUV. There's also a new metallic exterior paint color, and a heavy-duty battery is now standard.

Review

GMC jumped on the luxury compact SUV bandwagon in 1998, dolling up a four-door, four-wheel-drive Jimmy, packing it full of fancy touches and calling it the Envoy. For the past two years, Envoy has received minor feature enhancements to its staggering list of standard equipment.

Motivated by the same 190-horse, Vortec 4.3-liter V6 and four-speed automatic transmission that's found in the Jimmy, the Envoy disguises its rugged underpinnings with full-wrap body cladding, molded wheel flares and a monochrome paint scheme. Envoy also has a unique body-colored front bumper/fascia with upper and lower grilles, chrome accents, round fog lamps and integrated tow hooks. Out back there's a step bumper with integrated trailer hitch, as well as a rear spoiler whose rearward edge incorporates a neon Center High Mounted Stop Lamp (CHMSL), though rear styling is hardly distinctive enough to tell it apart from GM stablemates.

Envoy features high-intensity discharge headlamps. These lamps offer more than two-and-a-half times the light emitted by halogen bulbs and provide a longer, wider beam. Other standard equipment on the Envoy includes depowered airbags, the PassLock theft-deterrent system, remote entry, electronic climate control, retained accessory power, self-dimming outside heated mirrors and tinted glass behind the B-pillars. There's even a built-in air compressor as part of the standard Premium Luxury Ride suspension that includes an automatic load-leveling system.

Inside you'll find a variety of luxury touches, including Zebrano wood trim and heated Nuance leather power seating with the "Envoy" badge stitched into the headrests. Designers sought a cockpit theme by putting the gauges on a semicircular cluster and angling the instrument panel 15 degrees toward the driver. The center console can hold a cell phone, while the overhead unit includes a three-button HomeLink transmitter. The standard sound system is none other than GM's Premium Bose unit, with CD player and high-tech Bose Nd speakers for deep bass tones.

Envoy's four-wheel-drive system employs GM's AutoTrac two-speed active transfer case, which allows for automatic shifting from all-wheel drive to four-wheel drive when road conditions warrant. Plus, there's a "tow/haul" button on the transmission shift lever that adjusts the shift points in the electronically controlled automatic when the vehicle is heavily loaded or towing a trailer. GMC packs tons of standard equipment on this sport-ute (among the rare options are a power sunroof and GM's dealer-installed OnStar mobile communications system) and wraps it with a cleanly upscale look. Priced competitively in this segment, the Envoy is one to look at if you are thinking along the lines of a Ford Explorer Limited, or perhaps the Infiniti QX4.

Standard Equipment

ENVOY (4A): 4.3L V6 OHV SMPI 12-valve engine; 4-speed electronic OD auto transmission with lock-up; 690-amp battery with run down protection; engine oil cooler; 100-amp alternator; transmission oil cooler; part-time 4-wheel drive, auto locking hub control and electronic shift, 3.42 axle ratio; stainless steel exhaust; comfort ride suspension, auto-leveling suspension, front independent suspension with anti-roll bar, front torsion springs, front torsion bar, premium front shocks, rigid rear axle suspension with anti-roll bar, rear leaf springs, premium rear shocks; power re-circulating ball steering; 4-wheel disc brakes with 4-wheel antilock braking system; 18 gal. capacity fuel tank; rear wing spoiler, side impact bars; tailgate rear cargo door; HD trailering, trailer harness, trailer hitch; roof rack; front and rear body-colored bumpers with chrome bumper insert, front tow hooks, rear step; chrome bodyside insert, body-colored bodyside cladding; monotone paint; aero-composite halogen fully auto headlamps; additional exterior lights include front fog/driving lights, underhood light; driver's and passenger's power remote body-colored heated electric folding outside mirrors; front and rear 15" x 7" polished alloy wheels; P235/70SR15 A/S BSW front and rear tires; underbody mounted full-size steel spare wheel with crankdown; air conditioning with climate control, rear heat ducts; premium AM/FM stereo, clock, seek-scan, cassette 6-disc CD changer, 6 premium speakers, premium amplifier, auto equalizer, theft deterrent, and fixed antenna, radio steering wheel controls, rear controls; cruise control; power door locks, remote keyless entry, child safety rear door locks, power remote hatch/trunk release, keyfob rear window remote release; cell phone pre-wiring, 5 power accessory outlets, retained accessory power, garage door opener; instrumentation display includes tachometer, oil pressure gauge, water temperature gauge, volt gauge, compass, exterior temp, trip computer, trip odometer; warning indicators include battery, lights on, key in ignition, trunk ajar; driver's and passenger's front airbags; ignition disable, panic alarm, security system; deep tinted windows, power front and rear windows with driver's 1-touch down, fixed 1/4 vent windows; variable intermittent front windshield wipers, sun visor strip, flip-up rear window, fixed interval rear wiper, rear window defroster; seating capacity of 5, heated-cushion front bucket seats, adjustable tilt headrests, center armrest with storage, driver's seat includes 6-way power seat, power 2-way lumbar support, passenger's seat includes 4-way power seat, 8-way direction control, power 2-way lumbar support; 60-40 folding rear bench seat with adjustable headrests; leather seats, leather door trim insert, full cloth headliner, full color-keyed carpet floor covering with carpeted floor mats; memory on driver's seat with 2 memory setting(s); interior lights include dome light, front and rear reading lights, illuminated entry; leather-wrapped steering wheel with tilt adjustment; dual illuminated vanity mirrors, dual auxiliary visors; auto-dimming day/night rearview mirror; full floor console, full overhead console with storage, glove box with light, front and rear cupholders, instrument panel bin, 1 seat back storage pocket, driver's and passenger's door bins, rear door bins; carpeted cargo floor, carpeted trunk lid, cargo cover, cargo net, cargo tie downs, cargo light; body-colored grille, black side window moldings, black front windshield molding, black rear window molding and body-colored door handles.

Base Prices

TT10506-YC7 Envoy (4A)	31014	34270
Destination Charge:	550	550

Accessories

1SG	Marketing Option Package 1SG *Includes vehicle with standard equipment.*	NC	NC

CODE	DESCRIPTION	INVOICE	MSRP
CF5	Electric Sliding Glass Sunroof *Includes express open and wind deflector.*	645	750
G80	Locking Rear Differential *REQUIRES GT4.*	232	270
GT4	3.73 Axle Ratio *REQUIRES G80.*	NC	NC
K05	Engine Block Heater	17	20
R6M	New Jersey Cost Surcharge	70	NC

2000 JIMMY

2000 GMC Jimmy

What's New?

For 2000, GMC is celebrating the 30th anniversary of its Jimmy nameplate with a dolled-up Diamond Edition model. Other changes center on new equipment and suspension packaging. A heavy-duty battery is now standard, and Jimmy's V6 has been upgraded with a roller timing chain, sprocket and rocker arms for improved durability and reduced noise. There are also two new exterior colors, while the SLE gets a revised cloth interior.

Review

GMC is positioning the Jimmy as a luxury SUV, more upscale than its platform pals, the Chevy Blazer and Olds Bravada. But there's not a whole lot to set these three apart. Like its stablemates, Jimmy received minor styling tweaks for 1998. The result was a clean-looking four-door version, but we like the profile of the two-door with its distinctive C-pillar treatment. In an effort to separate GMC's compact SUV from the pack this year, there's a 2000 Jimmy Diamond Edition model to mark the nameplate's 30th anniversary.

The Diamond Edition boasts two-tone paint and a slew of aftermarket-style add-ons, such as a prominent grille guard with integrated fog lamps, aluminum side-step tubes, bodyside cladding and special badging. Should you desire, you can opt for high-intensity discharge headlamps borrowed from Jimmy's snooty sister, the GMC Envoy. Inside, the Diamond Edition earns its moniker with diamond-quilted perforated leather.

If the idea of a high-profile, limited-edition sport utility goes beyond your needs, the regular Jimmy lineup can be tailored to suit any driving requirement. The only difficulty is deciding what to include. Despite GMC dropping the old base SL model for retail customers, there are three different trim levels. SLS (sport) trim is now standard on two-door Jimmys and SLE (comfort) trim is now the standard for four-doors. If you need all the bells and whistles, opt for SLT (luxury/touring) equipment. Two-wheel-drive models can be had with Euro- or Luxury-Ride suspensions in either two- or four-door versions, while four-wheel-drive Jimmys add the choice of off-road underpinnings on two-doors.

Jimmy features strong acceleration from its Vortec 4300 V6 and smooth four-speed automatic. A "tow/haul" mode button helps optimize shifts when pulling a load, and the available AutoTrac automatic two-speed transfer case makes four-wheel traction a snap. Four-wheel antilock braking with four-wheel discs is standard. Inside, there's plenty of elbow room, and headroom is immense. There's space for three in back, but restrict it to two unless you enjoy hearing comfort complaints. The short rear seat feels hard and there's no foot room under front seats, meaning the back seat is not an enjoyable place.

Overall, Jimmy is easy to handle and fun to drive, and uplevel versions can be downright luxurious. You've also got a huge options list to help you customize your Jimmy to your tastes. Just be careful not to overdo it, because the price tag can zip skyward in a hurry.

Standard Equipment

SLS BASE 2WD 2-DOOR (5M): 4.3L V6 OHV SMPI 12-valve engine; 5-speed OD manual transmission; 690-amp HD battery with run down protection; 100-amp alternator; rear-wheel drive, 3.42 axle ratio; stainless steel exhaust; touring ride suspension, front independent suspension with anti-roll bar, HD front coil springs, premium front shocks, rigid rear axle suspension with anti-roll bar, HD rear leaf springs, premium rear shocks; power re-circulating ball steering; 4-wheel disc brakes with 4-wheel antilock braking system; 19 gal. capacity fuel tank; front license plate bracket, side impact bars; tailgate rear cargo door; roof rack; front and rear body-colored bumpers with rear step; monotone paint; aero-composite halogen fully auto headlamps with daytime running lights; additional exterior lights include underhood light; driver's and passenger's manual black folding outside mirrors; front and rear 15" x 7" silver alloy wheels; P235/70SR15 A/S BSW front and rear tires; inside mounted full-size steel spare wheel; air conditioning, rear heat ducts; AM/FM stereo, clock, seek-scan, cassette, 4 speakers, and fixed antenna; 1 power accessory outlet, retained accessory power, smokers' package; instrumentation display includes tachometer, oil pressure gauge, water temperature gauge, volt gauge, trip odometer; warning indicators include battery, lights on, key in ignition, trunk ajar; driver's and passenger's front airbags; ignition disable, security system; deep tinted windows, vented rear windows, fixed 1/4 vent windows; variable intermittent front windshield wipers, sun visor strip, flip-up rear window; seating capacity of 5, front bucket seats, fixed headrests, center armrest with storage, driver's seat includes 4-way direction control, lumbar support, passenger's seat includes 4-way direction control, lumbar support, easy entry; 60-40 folding rear bench seat with adjustable headrests; cloth seats, cloth door trim insert, full cloth headliner, full color-keyed carpet floor covering with carpeted floor mats; interior lights include dome light, illuminated entry; passenger's side vanity mirror; day/night rearview mirror; full floor console, glove box with light, front and rear cupholders, instrument panel bin, dashboard storage, driver's and passenger's door bins; carpeted cargo floor, carpeted trunk lid, cargo tie downs, cargo light; body-colored grille, black side window moldings, black front windshield molding, black rear window molding and black door handles.

SLS CONVENIENCE 2WD 2-DOOR (4A) (in addition to or instead of SLS BASE 2-DOOR (4A) equipment): 4-speed electronic OD auto transmission with lock-up; engine oil cooler; transmission oil cooler; 3.08 axle ratio; driver's and passenger's power remote black heated folding outside mirrors; AM/FM stereo, clock, seek-scan, single CD, 6 performance speakers, auto equalizer, theft deterrent, and fixed antenna; cruise control; power door locks with 2 stage unlock, remote keyless entry, power remote hatch/trunk release; 3 power accessory outlets; instrumentation display includes compass, exterior temp; panic alarm; power windows with driver's 1-touch down; fixed interval rear wiper, rear window defroster; interior lights include front and rear reading lights; leather-wrapped steering wheel with tilt adjustment; dual illuminated vanity mirrors, dual auxiliary visors; full overhead console with storage and cargo net.

SLE 2WD 4-DOOR (4A) (in addition to or instead of SLS CONVENIENCE 2WD 2-DOOR (4A) equipment): Driver's selectable multi-mode transmission; luxury ride suspension; 18 gal. capacity fuel tank; chrome bodyside insert, body-colored bodyside cladding; additional exterior lights include front fog/driving lights; underbody mounted full-size steel spare wheel with crankdown; child safety rear door locks; 2 power accessory outlets, power front and rear windows with driver's 1-touch down; front bucket seats, adjustable tilt headrests, driver's seat includes 6-way power seat, power 2-way lumbar support, passenger's seat includes 4-way direction control, power 2-way lumbar support; 2 seat back storage pockets and chrome grille.

SLT 2WD 4-DOOR (4A) (in addition to or instead of SLE 2WD 4-DOOR (4A) equipment): Leather seats, leatherette door trim insert and interior lights include illuminated entry.

DIAMOND EDITION 2WD 4-DOOR (4A) (in addition to or instead of SLT 2WD 4-DOOR (4A) equipment): Diamond silver metallic bodyside insert; 7-pronged universal trailering connector with 4-pronged adapter, 2" trailer ball, hitch tube and full color-keyed carpet floor covering with carpeted floor mats and reversible rear compartment covering.

SLS 4WD (5M)/SLE 4WD (4A) (in addition to or instead of SLS 2WD (5M)/SLE 2WD (4A) equipment): Part-time 4-wheel drive, auto locking hub control and electronic shift; front independent torsion suspension with anti-roll bar, HD front torsion springs, HD front torsion bar and front tow hooks.

SLT 4WD (4A)/DIAMOND EDITION 4WD (4A) (in addition to or instead of SLT 2WD (4A)/DIAMOND EDITION 2WD (4A) equipment): Autotrac full-time 4-wheel drive, auto locking hub control and electronic shift, 3.42 axle ratio; front independent torsion suspension with anti-roll bar, front torsion springs, front torsion bar and front tow hooks.

DIAMOND EDITION 4WD With 1SK (4A) (in addition to or instead of DIAMOND EDITION 4WD (4A) equipment): Electronic climate control, Bose AM/FM stereo, clock, seek-scan, cassette, 6 premium speakers, CD changer controls, auto equalizer, theft deterrent, and fixed antenna; deluxe overhead console: outside temperature gauge, compass, trip computer; heated-cushion front bucket seats, passenger's seat includes 6-way power seat, power 2-way lumbar support; memory on driver's seat with 2 memory setting(s) and auto-dimming day/night rearview mirror and exterior mirrors.

Base Prices

TS10516	SLS Base 2WD 2-Door (5M)	17258	19070
TS10516	SLS Convenience 2WD 2-Door (4A)	19883	21970
TT10516	SLS Base 4WD 2-Door (5M)	19973	22070
TT10516	SLS Convenience 4WD 2-Door (4A)	22598	24970
TS10506	SLE 2WD 4-Door(4A)	23955	26470
TS10506	SLT 2WD 4-Door (4A)	25132	27770
TT10506	SLE 4WD 4-Door (4A)	25765	28470
TT10506	SLT 4WD 4-Door (4A)	26942	29770
TS10506	Diamond Edition 2WD 4-Door (4A)	26670	29470
TT10506	Diamond Edition 4WD 4-Door (4A)	28480	31470
TT10506	Diamond Edition w/1SK 4WD (4A)	30109	33270
Destination Charge:		525	525

CODE	DESCRIPTION	INVOICE	MSRP
	Accessories		
1SA	**Marketing Option Package 1SA (SLS Base)** *Includes vehicle with standard equipment.*	NC	NC
1SB	**Marketing Option Package 1SB (SLS Convenience)** *Includes vehicle with standard equipment.*	NC	NC
1SC	**Marketing Option Package 1SC (SLE)** *Includes vehicle with standard equipment.*	NC	NC
1SD	**Marketing Option Package 1SD (SLE)** *Includes SLE Luxury Decor: steering wheel radio controls, Bose premium sound system, deluxe overhead console: outside temperature gauge, compass, trip computer; 8-way power passenger's seat and inside light sensitive rearview mirror.*	1075	1250
1SE	**Marketing Option Package 1SE (SLT)** *Includes vehicle with standard equipment.*	NC	NC
1SF	**Marketing Option Package 1SF (SLT)** *Includes SLT Luxury Decor: electronic climate control, steering wheel radio controls, Bose premium sound system, deluxe overhead console: outside temperature gauge, compass, trip computer; 8-way power passenger's seat, 2 position memory driver's seat, driver's and passenger's heated seats and inside light sensitive rearview mirror.*	1548	1800
1SH	**Marketing Option Package 1SH (Diamond Edition)** *Includes vehicle with standard equipment.*	NC	NC
1SJ	**Marketing Option Package 1SJ (Diamond Edition)** *Includes Diamond Edition Luxury Decor: electronic climate control, steering wheel radio controls, Bose premium sound system, deluxe overhead console: outside temperature gauge, compass, trip computer; 8-way power passenger's seat, 2 position memory driver's seat, driver's and passenger's heated seats and inside light sensitive rearview mirror.*	1548	1800
1SK	**Marketing Option Pkg 1SK (Diamond Edition 4WD)** *Includes Diamond Edition Special Decor: rear load leveling suspension; high-intensity headlamps; air conditioning with climate control; Bose AM/FM stereo, clock, seek-scan, cassette, 6 premium speakers, CD changer controls, auto equalizer, theft deterrent, and fixed antenna; remote 6-disc CD changer, radio steering wheel controls, rear audio controls; instrumentation display trip computer, trip odometer; heated-cushion front bucket seats, passenger's seat includes 6-way power seat, power 2-way lumbar support; memory on driver's seat with 2 memory setting(s) and auto-dimming day/night rearview mirror and exterior mirrors.*	1075	1250
AG1	**6-Way Power Driver's Seat (SLS)**	206	240
AJ1	**Deep Tinted Glass (SLS Base)** *Excludes tinted glass on windshield, driver and passenger windows. INCLUDED in 1SB.*	99	115
ANL	**Fog Lamps (SLS Convenience 2WD)**	99	115
CF5	**Sliding Electric Glass Sunroof (All Except SLS Base)** *Includes express open feature and wind deflector.*	645	750
DK8	**Deluxe Overhead Console (SLS Convenience)** *Includes outside temperature gauge, compass, trip computer and universal garage door opener.*	112	130

CODE	DESCRIPTION	INVOICE	MSRP
G80	Locking Rear Differential *NOT AVAILABLE with GU4.*	232	270
GT4	3.73 Axle Ratio (4WD) *NOT AVAILABLE with M50.*	NC	NC
GU4	3.08 Axle Ratio (2WD) *NOT AVAILABLE with M50.*	NC	NC
K05	Engine Block Heater	28	33
M30	Transmission: 4-Speed Automatic with Overdrive (SLS Base) *Includes engine oil cooler and transmission oil cooler. INCLUDED in 1SB.*	860	1000
M50	Transmission: 5-Speed Manual with Overdrive (SLS Convenience) *Includes engine oil cooler delete and transmission oil cooler delete. NOT AVAILABLE with U1Z, UQ3, UPO, GT4. INCLUDED in 1SA.*	(860)	(1000)
NP8	Autotrac Active Transfer Case (4WD - SLS Convenience/SLE) *Includes 2-speed transfer case with automatic 4-wheel drive and neutral modes.*	194	225
P16	Spare Wheel and Tire Carrier (SLS 4WD) *Includes gray cover with GMC lettering. Exterior tailgate mounted.*	137	159
QBG	Tires: P235/70R15 AS WOL SBR (SLS/SLE/SLT) *Includes front and rear tires. NOT AVAILABLE with QEB, ZM6.*	114	133
QEB	Tires: P235/75R15 AT WOL SBR (4WD - SLS/SLE/SLT) *Includes front, rear tires and tire: spare P235/75R15 AT WOL SBR. REQUIRES P16. NOT AVAILABLE with QBG.*	144	168
R6M	New Jersey Cost Surcharge	70	NC
RYJ	Retractable Cargo Cover (SLS Convenience 4WD) *REQUIRES P16.*	59	69
U1Z	6-Disc CD Changer (All Except Diamond Edition w/1SK) *REQUIRES ULO. NOT AVAILABLE with UPO, M50. INCLUDED in 1SK.*	340	395
UK3	Steering Wheel Radio Controls (SLS Convenience) *REQUIRES ULO. NOT AVAILABLE with M50.*	108	125
ULO	Radio: AM/FM Stereo w/ Cass (SLS Convenience) *Includes electronically tuned FM stereo, speed sensitive volume, theft lock, auto tone control, auto reverse, music search cassette player, enhanced performance 6-speaker system and clock. NOT AVAILABLE with UPO.*	(86)	(100)
ULO	Radio: AM/FM Stereo with Cassette (All Except SLS) *Includes electronically tuned FM stereo, speed sensitive volume, theft lock, auto tone control, auto reverse, music search cassette player, enhanced performance 6-speaker system and clock. INCLUDED in 1SK.*	NC	NC
ULO	Radio: AM/FM Stereo with Cassette (SLS Base) *Includes electronically tuned FM stereo, speed sensitive volume, theft lock, auto tone control, auto reverse, music search cassette player, enhanced performance 6-speaker system and clock. NOT AVAILABLE with UPO.*	69	80
UNO	Radio: AM/FM Stereo with CD (SLS Base) *Includes electronically tuned FM stereo, speed sensitive volume, theft lock, auto tone control, enhanced performance 6-speaker system and clock. NOT AVAILABLE with ULO, UPO. INCLUDED in 1SB.*	155	180

CODE	DESCRIPTION	INVOICE	MSRP
UP0	Radio: AM/FM Stereo w/ CD and Remote Cass (SLS Base) *Includes electronically tuned FM stereo, speed sensitive volume, theft lock, seek-scan, auto tone control, auto reverse, remote music search cassette player, enhanced performance 6-speaker system and clock. NOT AVAILABLE with UL0, U1Z, UQ3.*	241	280
UP0	Radio: AM/FM Stereo w/ CD and Remote Cass (SLS Convenience) *Includes electronically tuned FM stereo, speed sensitive volume, theft lock, seek-scan, auto tone control, auto reverse, remote music search cassette player, enhanced performance 6-speaker system and clock. NOT AVAILABLE with U1Z, UQ3, M50, UL0.*	86	100
UQ3	Bose Premium Sound System (SLS) *NOT AVAILABLE with UP0, M50.*	426	495
Z82	Heavy Duty Trailering Equipment (SLS) *Includes 8-wire harness (7-wire with CHMSL wire), trailering hitch platform and heavy duty flasher. INCLUDED in 1SH, 1SK, 1SJ. NOT AVAILABLE with M50 or GT4.*	181	210
Z82	Heavy-Duty Trailering Equipment (SLE/SLT) *Includes 8-wire harness (7-wire with CHMSL wire), trailering hitch platform and heavy duty flasher. INCLUDED in 1SH, 1SK, 1SJ. NOT AVAILABLE with M50 or GT4.*	181	210
ZAA	Tire: Compact Spare (2-Door)	(65)	(75)
ZM5	Underbody Shield Package (4WD) *Includes transfer case shield, front differential skid plates, steering linkage shield and fuel tank shield.*	108	126
ZM6	Off-Road Suspension Package (SLS 4WD) *Includes 46mm high-pressure monotube gas Bilstein shocks, upsized torsion bars, front and rear urethane jounce bumpers, front and rear stabilizer bar and larger body mounts. REQUIRES QEB. NOT AVAILABLE with QBG, ZAA.*	211	245
ZM8	Rear Window Convenience Package (SLS Base) *Includes electric tailgate release, rear window defogger and rear wiper/washer. INCLUDED in 1SB.*	277	322
ZQ3	Convenience Group (SLS Base) *Includes tilt wheel and speed control. INCLUDED in 1SB.*	340	395
ZQ6	Power Convenience Group (SLS Base) *Includes power door locks, power windows and dual heated power exterior mirrors. INCLUDED in 1SB.*	460	535
ZY2	Two-Tone Paint (SLE/SLT)	194	225

2000 SAFARI

What's New?

The 2000 Safari gets engineering enhancements for its 4.3-liter V6 and ABS components, a tow/haul mode for its four-speed automatic transmission, revised lighting and power locking functions, a larger (27-gallon) composite fuel tank, and a third-row seat as standard equipment.

2000 GMC Safari

Review

Choosing between a Chevrolet Astro and a GMC Safari is more a matter of image than necessity. Tangible differences between the two are modest, a fact that's true of most Chevrolet and GMC cousins. Once you've decided that a rear-drive (or all-wheel-drive) General Motors midsize van is the rational choice, you'll likely be satisfied with either one.

Because of their traditional-type full-frame construction and standard rear-drive layout, Safaris are most adept at heavy hauling and burly trailer towing. This is one of the very few minivans (GMC calls it a midsize) on the market that can combine up to 6,000 pounds of trailering capacity with room for eight people. Not everyone will relish the truck-like ride over harsh road surfaces, but it's not bad when the highway smoothes out. Don't expect top-notch fuel mileage, though.

GM's 4300 Vortec V6 is standard, sporting a new roller timing chain and rocker arms for improved durability and reduced noise. It sends 190 horsepower and a healthy 250 foot-pounds of torque to an electronically controlled, four-speed automatic overdrive transmission, equipped this year with a tow/haul mode for improved performance under loads. Long-life engine coolant and spark plugs help keep maintenance costs to a minimum. All-wheel-drive models have GM's AutoTrac transfer case, which automatically transfers power to the front axle when rear-wheel slippage is detected.

Safaris come in three trim levels, a base SL, midlevel SLE and top-of-the line SLT, with a third-row bench and eight-passenger seating standard on all three (though opting for center-row buckets cuts seating to seven). Instead of the typical minivan lift-up rear door, GMC offers right- and left-hand rear load doors, and gives you the option of choosing "dutch" doors (standard on SLT), which feature a liftglass with a split tailgate. GM's PassLock theft-deterrent system is also standard, and the OnStar mobile communications system is available as a dealer-installed option.

Dual airbags are housed in an artfully styled dashboard, and four-wheel disc/drum antilock brakes are standard. So are features such as speed-sensitive power steering, delayed interior lighting, twin under-seat rear-passenger heating ducts, overhead reading lamps, various built-in cupholders and storage bins and three power outlets (in addition to the cigarette lighter). New this year are auto-on headlamps, retained accessory power and expanded power locking functions.

Whether your choice is simple rear-drive or full-time all-wheel drive, Safaris enjoy the rare ability to handle the kinds of towing/hauling tasks that pose problems for most front-drive minivans. And when transporting people dictates that eight is just enough, Safari is packaged to be just right.

Standard Equipment

SL RWD PASSENGER (4A): 4.3L V6 OHV SMPI 12-valve engine; 4-speed electronic OD auto transmission with lock-up; 600-amp battery with run down protection; engine oil cooler, HD radiator; 100-amp alternator; driver's selectable multi-mode transmission, transmission oil cooler; rear-wheel drive, 3.23 axle ratio; partial stainless steel exhaust; front independent suspension with anti-roll bar, front coil springs, rigid rear axle suspension with rear leaf springs; power re-circulating ball steering with vehicle speed-sensing assist; front disc/rear drum brakes with 4-wheel antilock braking system; 27 gal. capacity fuel tank; front license plate bracket, side impact bars; 3 doors with sliding right rear passenger's door, split swing-out rear cargo door; trailer harness; front and rear body-colored bumpers with rear step; monotone paint; sealed beam halogen headlamps with daytime running lights; driver's and passenger's manual black folding outside mirrors; front and rear 15" x 6" painted steel wheels; P215/75SR15 A/S BSW front and rear tires; underbody mounted compact steel spare wheel with crankdown; air conditioning, rear heat ducts; AM/FM stereo, clock, seek-scan, 6 speakers, and fixed antenna; child safety rear door locks; 3 power accessory outlets, retained accessory power, smokers' package; instrumentation display includes oil pressure gauge, water temperature gauge, volt gauge, trip odometer; warning indicators include oil pressure, battery, lights on, key in ignition, low fuel; driver's and passenger's front airbags; ignition disable; tinted windows, fixed 1/4 vent windows; variable intermittent front windshield wipers, sun visor strip; seating capacity of 8, front bucket seats, fixed headrests, driver's and passenger's armrests, driver's seat includes 4-way direction control, lumbar support, passenger's seat includes 4-way direction control, lumbar support; removable 2nd row bench seat with adjustable headrests; removable full folding 3rd row bench seat with adjustable headrest; front height adjustable seatbelts; cloth seats, cloth door trim insert, full cloth headliner, full color-keyed carpet floor covering; interior lights include dome light with delay; vanity mirrors, dual auxiliary visors; day/night rearview mirror; engine cover console with storage, locking glove box with light, front and rear cupholders, 2 seat back storage pockets, driver's and passenger's door bins; carpeted cargo floor, plastic trunk lid, cargo light; argent grille, black side window moldings, black front windshield molding, black rear window molding and black door handles.

SL AWD PASSENGER (4A) (in addition to or instead of SL RWD PASSENGER (4A) equipment): Full-time 4 wheel drive, 3.42 axle ratio; front torsion springs and front torsion bar.

Base Prices

CODE	DESCRIPTION	INVOICE	MSRP
TM11006	SL RWD Passenger (4A)	19594	21651
TL11006	SL AWD Passenger (4A)	21676	23951
Destination Charge:		620	620

Accessories

CODE	DESCRIPTION	INVOICE	MSRP
—	Leather Seat Trim *REQUIRES 1SE.*	817	950
1SA	Marketing Option Package 1SA *Includes vehicle with standard equipment.*	NC	NC
1SE	Marketing Option Package 1SE	5722	6653
	Manufacturer Discount	(688)	(800)
	Net Price *Includes SLT Decor Package: front and rear air conditioning, rear heat, power 6-way driver's seat, dutch doors, wheels: 15" x 6.5" brushed aluminum, cargo convenience net, power convenience group: power windows, power door locks; convenience group: tilt steering column, cruise control; color-keyed rubber floor mats, overhead console with electronics, four map reading lamps, dome lamp, dual illuminated visor vanity mirrors, compass and outside temperature display, uplevel grille with chrome*	5034	5853

CODE	DESCRIPTION	INVOICE	MSRP
	accents, composite headlamps, remote keyless entry system, remote panic alarm, roof mounted black luggage carrier, dual electric control exterior mirrors, deep tinted glass and AM/FM stereo with cassette, CD and seek/scan.		
1SE	**Marketing Option Package 1SE**	5747	6683
	Manufacturer Discount	(688)	(800)
	Net Price	5059	5883
	Includes SLT Decor Package: front and rear air conditioning, rear heat, power 6-way driver's seat, dutch doors, wheels: 15" x 6.5" brushed aluminum, cargo convenience net, power convenience group: power windows, power door locks; convenience group: tilt steering column, cruise control; color-keyed rubber floor mats, overhead console with electronics, four map reading lamps, dome lamp, dual illuminated visor vanity mirrors, compass and outside temperature display, uplevel grille with chrome accents, composite headlamps, remote keyless entry system, remote panic alarm, roof mounted black luggage carrier, dual electric control exterior mirrors, deep tinted glass and AM/FM stereo with cassette, CD and seek/scan. NOT AVAILABLE with AG2.		
1SV	**Marketing Option Package 1SV (AWD)**	2860	3326
	Manufacturer Discount	(2302)	(2677)
	Net Price	558	649
	Includes SLE Decor Package: panel doors, wheels: 15" x 6.5" chrome appearance, AM/FM stereo with cassette and seek/scan, cargo convenience net, power convenience group: power windows, power door locks; convenience group: tilt steering column, cruise control; color-keyed rubber floor mats, overhead console with electronics, four map reading lamps, dome lamp, dual illuminated visor vanity mirrors, compass and outside temperature display, uplevel grille with chrome accents, composite headlamps, remote keyless entry system, remote panic alarm, roof mounted black luggage carrier, dual electric control exterior mirrors and deep tinted glass.		
1SV	**Marketing Option Package 1SV (AWD)**	2886	3356
	Manufacturer Discount	(2302)	(2677)
	Net Price	584	679
	Includes SLE Decor Package: panel doors, wheels: 15" x 6.5" chrome appearance, AM/FM stereo with cassette and seek/scan, cargo convenience net, power convenience group: power windows, power door locks; convenience group: tilt steering column, cruise control; color-keyed rubber floor mats, overhead console with electronics, four map reading lamps, dome lamp, dual illuminated visor vanity mirrors, compass and outside temperature display, uplevel grille with chrome accents, composite headlamps, remote keyless entry system, remote panic alarm, roof mounted black luggage carrier, dual electric control exterior mirrors and deep tinted glass. NOT AVAILABLE with AG2.		
1SV	**Marketing Option Package 1SV (RWD)**	2860	3326
	Manufacturer Discount	(1872)	(2177)
	Net Price	988	1149
	Includes SLE Decor Package: panel doors, wheels: 15" x 6.5" chrome appearance, AM/FM stereo with cassette and seek/scan, cargo convenience net, power convenience group: power windows, power door locks; convenience group: tilt steering column, cruise control; color-keyed rubber floor mats, overhead console with		

CODE	DESCRIPTION	INVOICE	MSRP
	electronics, four map reading lamps, dome lamp, dual illuminated visor vanity mirrors, compass and outside temperature display, uplevel grille with chrome accents, composite headlamps, remote keyless entry system, remote panic alarm, roof mounted black luggage carrier, dual electric control exterior mirrors and deep tinted glass.		
1SV	Marketing Option Package 1SV (RWD)	2886	3356
	Manufacturer Discount	(1872)	(2177)
	Net Price	1014	1179
	Includes SLE Decor Package: panel doors, wheels: 15" x 6.5" chrome appearance, AM/FM stereo with cassette and seek/scan, cargo convenience net, power convenience group: power windows, power door locks; convenience group: tilt steering column, cruise control; color-keyed rubber floor mats, overhead console with electronics, four map reading lamps, dome lamp, dual illuminated visor vanity mirrors, compass and outside temperature display, uplevel grille with chrome accents, composite headlamps, remote keyless entry system, remote panic alarm, roof mounted black luggage carrier, dual electric control exterior mirrors and deep tinted glass. NOT AVAILABLE with AG2.		
AG1	Power Driver's Seat	206	240
	REQUIRES 1SV. INCLUDED in 1SE.		
AG2	Power Passenger's Seat	206	240
	NOT AVAILABLE with 1SA. REQUIRES AG1.		
AJ1	Deep Tinted Glass	249	290
	Includes all windows except windshield, passenger's and driver's doors. INCLUDED in 1SV, 1SE.		
AN0	Seat Package	144	168
	Includes inboard/outboard armrests, map pockets and manually adjustable lumbar support on driver's seat.		
AP9	Cargo Convenience Net	26	30
	INCLUDED in 1SV, 1SE.		
AU0	Remote Keyless Entry System	146	170
	Includes 2 transmitters and remote panic alarm. INCLUDED in 1SV, 1SE.		
AU3	Power Door Locks	192	223
	INCLUDED in 1SV, 1SE.		
B37	Color-Keyed Rubber Floor Mats	59	69
	Includes front and rear seating areas. INCLUDED in 1SV, 1SE.		
B88	Bodyside Moldings with Bright Insert	104	121
BVE	Running Boards	344	400
C36	Auxiliary Rear Heater	176	205
	INCLUDED in 1SE.		
C69	Front and Rear Air Conditioning	450	523
	Includes 105-amp generator. INCLUDED in 1SE.		
C95	Reading Lamps	28	33
	NOT AVAILABLE with DK8. INCLUDED in 1SE.		
D48	Dual Electric Control Exterior Mirrors	84	98
	Black below-eye-line type. REQUIRES ZQ2. INCLUDED in 1SV, 1SE.		

CODE	DESCRIPTION	INVOICE	MSRP
DK8	**Overhead Console with Electronics (RWD)** *Includes 2 storage compartments, garage door opener compartment, four map reading lamps, dome lamp, dual illuminated visor vanity mirrors, compass and outside temperature display. REQUIRES 1SV or 1SE.*	55	64
DK8	**Overhead Console with Electronics** *Includes 2 storage compartments, garage door opener compartment, four map reading lamps, dome lamp, dual illuminated visor vanity mirrors, compass and outside temperature display. NOT AVAILABLE with C95. INCLUDED in 1SV, 1SE.*	192	223
E54	**Dutch Doors** *Includes lower swing-out with liftgate and intermittent rear window wiper/washer. INCLUDED in 1SE.*	445	518
E54	**Dutch Doors** *Includes lower swing-out with liftgate and intermittent rear window wiper/washer. REQUIRES 1SV. INCLUDED in 1SE.*	395	459
G80	**Locking Rear Differential**	217	252
GT4	**3.73 Axle Ratio**	NC	NC
GU6	**3.42 Axle Ratio**	NC	NC
NC7	**Federal Emission Override**	NC	NC
NP5	**Leather-Wrapped Steering Wheel** *REQUIRES 1SV.*	46	54
PA6	**Wheels: 15" x 6.5" Painted Styled Steel** *Includes 4 silver only wheels. NOT AVAILABLE with PF3. REQUIRES 1SA.*	79	92
PC2	**Wheels: 15" x 6.5" Chrome Appearance** *Includes 4 styled wheels. NOT AVAILABLE with PA6, PF3. REQUIRES 1SA. INCLUDED in 1SV.*	292	340
PC2	**Wheels: 15" x 6.5" Chrome Appearance** *Includes 4 styled wheels. NOT AVAILABLE with PF3. REQUIRES 1SE. INCLUDED in 1SV.*	(22)	(25)
PF3	**Wheels: 15" x 6.5" Brushed Aluminum (AWD)** *Includes 4 wheels. REQUIRES 1SV. INCLUDED in 1SE.*	235	273
PF3	**Wheels: 15" x 6.5" Brushed Aluminum (FWD)** *Includes 4 wheels. REQUIRES 1SV. INCLUDED in 1SE.*	22	25
PF3	**Wheels: 15" x 6.5" Brushed Aluminum** *Includes 4 wheels. NOT AVAILABLE with PA6. REQUIRES 1SA. INCLUDED in 1SE.*	314	365
QCM	**Tires: P215/75R15 AS WOL SBR** *Includes front, rear and compact spare.*	76	88
R6M	**New Jersey Cost Surcharge**	64	NC
TL1	**Uplevel Grille with Chrome Accents** *Includes body colored painted bumpers and composite headlamps. REQUIRES 1SA. INCLUDED in 1SV, 1SE.*	189	220
UG1	**Garage Door Opener** *Includes 3-channel universal Homelink transmitter. REQUIRES DK8.*	99	115
UK6	**Rear Seat Audio Controls with Jacks** *Does not include headphones. REQUIRES 1SV and (UL0 or UP0). NOT AVAILABLE with UN0.*	108	125

CODE	DESCRIPTION	INVOICE	MSRP
ULO	**Radio: AM/FM Stereo with Cassette and Automatic Tone Control** *Includes clock, electronically tuned AM/FM stereo, 4 coaxial front speakers, 4 extended range rear speakers, theft lock feature, speed volume control and auto tone controls. REQUIRES 1SV. NOT AVAILABLE with UPO, UNO.*	264	307
UM6	**Radio: AM/FM Stereo with Cassette** *Includes clock, electronically tuned AM/FM stereo, 4 coaxial front speakers and 4 extended range rear speakers. REQUIRES 1SA. INCLUDED in 1SV.*	126	147
UNO	**Radio: AM/FM Stereo with CD and Automatic Tone Control** *Includes clock, electronically tuned AM/FM stereo, 4 coaxial front speakers, 4 extended range rear speakers, theft lock feature, speed volume control and auto tone controls. REQUIRES 1SV. NOT AVAILABLE with UK6, ULO, UPO.*	350	407
UPO	**Radio: AM/FM Stereo with CD and Cassette** *Includes clock, electronically tuned AM/FM stereo, 4 coaxial front speakers, 4 extended range rear speakers, theft lock feature, speed volume control and auto tone controls. REQUIRES 1SV. NOT AVAILABLE with ULO, UNO. INCLUDED in 1SE.*	436	507
V10	**Cold Climate Package** *Includes extra coolant protection and engine block heater.*	40	46
V54	**Roof Mounted Black Luggage Carrier** *REQUIRES 1SA. INCLUDED in 1SV, 1SE.*	108	126
Z82	**HD Trailering Equipment** *Includes trailering hitch platform and 8-wire harness.*	266	309
ZP7	**7-Passenger Seating (AWD)** *Includes driver's and passenger's front reclining buckets with adjustable up and down headrests, 2 middle reclining bucket seats, removable split-back reclining rear passengers' bench with fold-down center console, convenience tray with 2 cup holders and seat package. REQUIRES 1SE.*	494	574
ZP7	**7-Passenger Seating (RWD)** *Includes driver's and passenger's front reclining buckets with adjustable up and down headrests, 2 middle reclining bucket seats, removable split-back reclining rear passengers' bench with fold-down center console, convenience tray with 2 cup holders and seat package. REQUIRES 1SE.*	NC	NC
ZP7	**7-Passenger Seating** *Includes 4 high-back buckets with integral headrests, dual armrests, removable rear passenger bench and seat package. REQUIRES 1SV.*	273	318
ZQ2	**Power Convenience Group** *Includes power windows and power door locks. REQUIRES 1SA. INCLUDED in 1SV, 1SE.*	408	474
ZQ3	**Convenience Group** *Includes tilt steering column and cruise control. REQUIRES 1SA. INCLUDED in 1SV, 1SE.*	329	383
ZY2	**Two-Tone Paint with Lower Cladding** *NOT AVAILABLE with 1SA.*	NC	NC

2000 SAVANA

2000 GMC Savana

What's New?

GMC's full-size passenger van gets improved powertrains, increased trailer ratings, seat-mounted tether anchors for installing child safety seats and an optional rear-window defogger.

Review

When the then-new Savana arrived in small numbers for 1996, it had been 25 years since GM redesigned its full-size van. The GMC Rally Van and Vandura were introduced way back in 1971 (when vans were groovy), and sold steadily until they were discontinued. Competition and safety regulations had forced GM to redo the big vans for '96, but by then Ford had already re-engineered the Econoline twice! To help distinguish the all-new design, GMC rebadged its new van Savana.

Savana features flush glass and door handles, hidden door hinges, standard four-wheel antilock brakes and dual airbags. Front foot- and legroom is adequate, and front seats offer a wide range of travel. Front air conditioning and rear heat ducts are standard, but for better warming (and cooling), an optional rear heating and air-conditioning unit is available. The center console contains two cupholders, an auxiliary power outlet and storage for items like CDs and cassettes. Savana is available in 135- and 155-inch wheelbases, three weight series (1500, 2500 or 3500) and two (base SL and luxury SLE) trim levels. There is a choice of side-entry doors as well: a sliding door or a pair of 60/40 hinged doors.

Inside the short-wheelbase Savana, you'll find 267 cubic feet of cargo area, while the extended version provides a whopping 317 cubic feet of volume with the rear seats removed. Up to 15 passengers can be seated within the longer van on as many as five bench seats. Rear hinged doors open a full 180 degrees for easy loading and do not conceal high-mounted taillights when opened. Gross vehicle weight ratings of up to 9,500 pounds are available on either wheelbase.

The base engine is a 200-horsepower Vortec 4300 V6 that is quieter and more durable this year, thanks to a new roller timing chain and rocker arms. Optional motors include the GM family of V8s, from the popular Vortec 5000, to the venerable 5700, to the monster Vortec 7400. Also available is a robust 6.5-liter turbodiesel V8 good for 195 horsepower and 430 stump-pulling foot-pounds of torque. A new exhaust system with specially designed catalytic converters help all but the biggest engines meet California low-emission vehicle (LEV) standards. GM's heavy-duty 4L80-E transmission handles all the shifting chores, featuring a more efficient torque converter.

Savana's styling is rounded and bulbous, with a front end that mimics GM's truck family and a high-arched rear with D-pillar mounted taillights. Easily as odd-looking as the old Lumina minivan's high-mounted rear lamps, the round-topped rear and sheer size of this van make it seem as if you were looking at the rear of a commuter train car. Like it or not, this design is different enough to wear well into the next century.

Standard Equipment

G1500 PASSENGER VAN LD (4A): 4.3L V6 OHV SMPI 12-valve engine; 4-speed electronic OD auto transmission with lock-up; 600-amp HD battery; 100-amp alternator; rear-wheel drive, 3.42 axle ratio; stainless steel exhaust; front independent suspension with anti-roll bar, HD front coil springs, rigid rear axle suspension with HD rear leaf springs; power re-circulating ball steering with vehicle speed-sensing assist; front disc/rear drum brakes with 4-wheel antilock braking system; 31 gal. capacity fuel tank; 3 doors with split swing-out right rear passenger's door, split swing-out rear cargo door; front and rear argent bumpers with rear step; monotone paint; sealed beam halogen headlamps with daytime running lights; additional exterior lights include underhood light; driver's and passenger's manual remote black folding outside mirrors; front and rear 15" x 7" silver styled steel wheels; P235/75SR15 A/S BSW front and rear tires; underbody mounted full-size steel spare wheel; air conditioning, rear heat ducts; AM/FM stereo, clock, seek-scan, 4 speakers, and fixed antenna; child safety rear door locks; 2 power accessory outlets; instrumentation display includes oil pressure gauge, water temperature gauge, volt gauge, trip odometer; warning indicators include battery, lights on, key in ignition; driver's and passenger's front airbags; ignition disable; tinted windows, fixed 1/4 vent windows; variable intermittent front windshield wipers, vented rear windows; seating capacity of 8, front bucket seats, fixed headrests, driver's seat includes 4-way direction control, passenger's seat includes 4-way direction control; removable 2nd row bench seat; removable 3rd row bench seat; front height adjustable seatbelts; vinyl seats, full cloth headliner, full vinyl floor covering; interior lights include dome light; day/night rearview mirror; engine cover console with storage, glove box, front cupholder, instrument panel covered bin, 2 seat back storage pockets, driver's and passenger's door bins; vinyl cargo floor, plastic trunk lid, cargo light; argent grille, black side window moldings, black front windshield molding, black rear window molding and black door handles.

G2500 PASSENGER VAN HD (4A)/G2500 EXT. PASSENGER VAN HD (4A) (in addition to or instead of STANDARD G1500 PASSENGER VAN LD (4A) equipment): 5.7L V8 OHV SMPI 16-valve engine; 124-amp alternator; 3.73 axle ratio; front and rear 16" x 6.5" silver styled steel wheels; LT225/75SR16 A/S BSW front and rear tires and seating capacity of 12.

G3500 PASSENGER VAN HD (4A)/G3500 EXT. PASSENGER VAN HD (4A) (in addition to or instead of SLE G2500 PASSENGER VAN HD (4A) equipment): LT245/75SR16 A/S BSW front and rear tires.

Base Prices

TG11406	Standard G1500 Pass Van LD (4A)	20417	23334
TG21406	Standard G2500 Pass Van HD (4A)	22605	25834
TG31406	Standard G3500 Pass Van HD (4A)	22854	26123
TG21706	Standard G2500 Ext Pass Van (4A)	23392	26734
TG31706	Standard G3500 Ext Pass Van (4A)	23681	27068
Destination Charge:		640	640

Accessories

—	Custom Cloth Seat Trim	NC	NC
1SA	Marketing Option Package 1SA *Includes vehicle with standard equipment.*	NC	NC

CODE	DESCRIPTION	INVOICE	MSRP
1SB	Marketing Option Package 1SB *Includes power convenience group: power door locks, power windows; convenience group: tilt steering and speed control.*	739	859
AG1	6-Way Power Driver's Seat	206	240
AG2	6-Way Power Passenger's Seat *REQUIRES AG1.*	206	240
AJ1	Deep Tinted Glass *Excludes windshield, driver's and front passenger's windows. INCLUDED in 1SD.*	335	390
B30	Full Floor Carpeting *Includes front and rear mats.*	126	147
C36	Rear Heater	206	240
C49	Electric Rear Window Defogger *REQUIRES AJ1.*	132	154
C69	Front and Rear Air Conditioning (1500) *Includes rear heater and 124-amp generator. INCLUDED in 1SD.*	740	860
C69	Front and Rear Air Conditioning (Regular - 2500/3500) *Includes 124-amp generator and rear heater. INCLUDED in 1SD.*	691	804
C69	Front and Rear Air Conditioning *Includes 124-amp generator and rear heater. REQUIRES 1SD (Standard - 1500/2500/3500).*	NC	NC
DE5	RH/LH Electric Control Mirrors *Includes electric defoggers and right hand convex mirror. REQUIRES ZQ2. INCLUDED in 1SD.*	97	113
G80	Locking Rear Differential	217	252
GT4	3.73 Axle Ratio *NOT AVAILABLE with L30.*	NC	NC
GT5	4.10 Axle Ratio (All Except 1500)	NC	NC
KL5	Conversion Ready Engine (All Except 1500) *Includes internal modifications for operation of natural or propane gas. NOT AVAILABLE with L65, L29.*	108	125
KW2	124-Amp Generator (1500)	52	60
L29	Engine: Vortec 7400 V8 SFI (3500) *NOT AVAILABLE with KL5.*	516	600
L30	Engine: Vortec 5000 SFI V8 (1500) *NOT AVAILABLE with GT4.*	426	495
L31	Engine: Vortec 5700 SFI V8 (1500)	1028	1195
L65	Engine: 6.5L V8 Turbo Diesel (2500 Regular/3500) *Includes glow plugs, integral 2 stage fuel filter, fuel/water separator, instrument panel warning light, dual batteries, internal and external engine oil cooler, HD radiator, extra sound insulation, block heater and fuel filter change signal. NOT AVAILABLE with KL5, V10.*	2460	2860
N90	Wheels: Cast Aluminum (4) (1500) *NOT AVAILABLE with P06.*	267	310
NP5	Leather-Wrapped Steering Wheel	52	60
P06	Four Stainless Steel Trim Rings *Includes chrome center caps. NOT AVAILABLE with N90. INCLUDED in 1SC, 1SD.*	52	60
R6M	New Jersey Cost Surcharge	64	NC

CODE	DESCRIPTION	INVOICE	MSRP
TR9	Auxiliary Lamps *Includes dome lamps, override switch, stepwell lamps, underhood lamp and reading lamps. INCLUDED in 1SC, 1SD.*	138	160
U75	Power Radio Antenna	73	85
ULO	Radio: AM/FM Stereo with Cassette *Includes clock, auto reverse cassette player with music search, auto tone control, 4 front speakers, 4 rear speakers and power radio antenna. REQUIRES ZQ2. NOT AVAILABLE with UM6, UNO, UPO.*	380	442
UM6	Radio: AM/FM Stereo with Cassette *Includes clock, 2 front speakers and 2 extended range rear speakers. NOT AVAILABLE with ULO, UNO, UPO.*	126	147
UNO	Radio: AM/FM Stereo with CD *Includes clock, auto tone control, 4 front speakers, 4 rear speakers and power radio antenna. REQUIRES ZQ2. NOT AVAILABLE with UM6, ULO, UPO.*	466	542
UPO	Radio: AM/FM Stereo with CD and Cassette *Includes clock, auto tone control and 4 front speakers, 4 rear speakers and power radio antenna. REQUIRES ZQ2. NOT AVAILABLE with UM6, ULO, UNO.*	552	642
V10	Cold Climate Package *Includes block heater. NOT AVAILABLE with L65.*	41	48
XHB	Tires: Front P235/75R15 WSW SBR (1500) *REQUIRES YHB and ZHB. NOT AVAILABLE with XHM, YHM, ZHM.*	34	40
XHM	Tires: Front P235/75R15 OWL SBR (1500) *REQUIRES YHM and ZHM. NOT AVAILABLE with XHB, YHB, ZHB.*	43	50
YA2	Sliding Side Door	NC	NC
YHB	Tires: Rear P235/75R15 WSW SBR (1500) *REQUIRES XHB and ZHB. NOT AVAILABLE with XHM, YHM, ZHM.*	34	40
YHM	Tires: Rear P235/75R15 OWL SBR (1500) *REQUIRES XHM and ZHM. NOT AVAILABLE with XHB, YHB, ZHB.*	43	50
Z82	HD Trailering Equipment *Includes trailering hitch platform and 8-wire harness.*	267	310
ZHB	Tires: Spare P235/75R15 WSW SBR (1500) *REQUIRES XHB and YHB. NOT AVAILABLE with XHM, YHM, ZHM.*	17	20
ZHM	Tires: Spare P235/75R15 OWL SBR (1500) *REQUIRES XHM and YHM. NOT AVAILABLE with XHB, YHB, ZHB.*	22	25
ZP3	15-Passenger Seating (3500 Regular) *Includes 2 front high back buckets, three 3-passenger bench seats, and one 4-passenger bench seat.*	319	371
ZP5	5 Passenger Seating (1500) *Includes 2 front high back bucket seats and 1 3-passenger bench seat.*	(319)	(371)
ZP8	8 Passenger Seating (2500) *Includes 2 high back bucket seats and two 3-passenger bench seats.*	(319)	(371)
ZQ2	Power Convenience Group *Includes power door locks and power windows. INCLUDED in 1SB, 1SC, 1SD.*	408	474
ZQ3	Convenience Group *Includes tilt steering and speed control. INCLUDED in 1SB, 1SC, 1SD.*	331	385

2000 SIERRA PICKUP

2000 GMC Sierra

What's New?

After a complete redesign last year, GMC's Silverado-based pickup finally gets a fourth door on the extended cab. There's also more power on tap in the 4.8- and 5.3-liter engines, increased trailer ratings and standard programmable automatic door locks. New factory appearance items, such as wheel-lip flares and a soft tonneau cover, are now available on some models.

Review

Thanks to the myriad of improvements that came with the introduction of the '99 Sierra, GMC's full-size pickup now moves to the refinement stage for 2000. Employing unique, three-piece frame construction, Sierras come in either 1500 (half-ton) or 2500 (three-quarter-ton) series.

Perhaps the biggest draw for GMC's big pickup is a first-class engine lineup. The base Vortec 4.3-liter V6 has been upgraded this year to improve durability, emissions and fuel economy. It now features a roller timing chain and rocker arms, extended-life spark plugs and coolant and a new oil-level sensor. But more impressive are the three V8s, two of which tout power increases this year thanks to new camshafts. The Vortec 4800 V8 (standard on 1500 Series extended-cab models) makes 270 horsepower (up from last year's 255). And the 5.3-liter V8 gains 15 horses (now at 285) and 10 more foot-pounds of torque (to 325). Both engines enjoy a long, flat torque curve for sustained hauling performance. You can also opt for a 6.0-liter V8 with 300 horsepower.

Each truck is available with a five-speed manual or four-speed automatic transmission. As usual, there is a variety of configurations to choose from, including the regular or extended cabs, short or long beds, Wideside or Sportside box designs, two- or four-wheel-drive versions, three trim levels (SL, SLE or SLT) and a dizzying array of options. As a premium truck brand, GMC says it is designing vehicles geared more toward on-road purposes. In other words, if you want a dirt-crunching, rock-hopping vehicle made by GM, Chevy would be the place to shop.

For 2000, the roomy extended cabs get a fourth-door for better rear-seat access, and with improved V8 power and a new rating system methodology, all Sierras enjoy higher trailer-towing ratings than last year. Inside, you'll find ample storage areas, including a center armrest that is large enough for a laptop computer or a six-pack of soda, depending on your priorities. Reduced-force airbags (with passenger-side on/off switch) are standard, plus several safety and convenience features have been revamped, including locking and illuminated entry functions.

The Sierra boasts far too many features to list here, but suffice it to say that GMC has a very competitive product compared to its Ford and Dodge rivals. But because GMC is set on segmenting itself as the premium truck division that caters to upscale truck buyers, prepare yourself for price creep to start forcing less-affluent young cowboy types to shop elsewhere.

2000 SIERRA 1500

Standard Equipment

SL 2WD REGULAR CAB SB/LB (5M): 4.3L V6 OHV SMPI 12-valve engine; 5-speed OD manual transmission; 600-amp HD battery with run down protection; engine oil cooler; 105-amp alternator; rear-wheel drive, 3.08 axle ratio; stainless steel exhaust; front independent suspension with anti-roll bar, front coil springs, rigid rear axle suspension with rear leaf springs; power rack-and-pinion steering with vehicle speed-sensing assist; 4-wheel disc brakes with 4-wheel antilock braking system; 26 gal. (34 gal. - LB) capacity fuel tank; side impact bars; trailer harness; front chrome bumper, rear argent bumper, front and rear black rub strip, rear tow hooks, rear step; monotone paint; aero-composite halogen auto on headlamps with daytime running lights; additional exterior lights include pickup cargo box light, underhood light; driver's and passenger's manual black folding outside mirrors; front and rear 16" x 6.5" silver styled steel wheels; P235/75SR16 A/S BSW front and rear tires; underbody mounted full-size steel spare wheel with crankdown; AM/FM stereo, clock, seek-scan, 2 speakers, and fixed antenna; 3 power accessory outlets, retained accessory power; instrumentation display includes tachometer, oil pressure gauge, water temperature gauge, volt gauge, trip odometer; warning indicators include oil pressure, water temp, battery, low oil level, low coolant, lights on, key in ignition, low fuel, low washer fluid, door ajar, service interval; driver's front airbag, passenger's cancelable front airbag; ignition disable; tinted windows; variable intermittent front windshield wipers; seating capacity of 3, 40-20-40 split-bench front seat, adjustable headrests, center armrest with storage, driver's seat includes 4-way direction control, lumbar support, passenger's seat includes 4-way direction control lumbar support; premium cloth seats, full cloth headliner, full carpet floor covering with floor mats, cabback insulator; interior lights include dome light, front reading lights, illuminated entry; sport steering wheel with tilt adjustment; passenger's side vanity mirror; day/night rearview mirror; glove box with light, front cupholder, 2 seat back storage pockets, driver's and passenger's door bins; argent grille, black side window moldings, black front windshield molding, black rear window molding and black door handles.

SL 2WD EXTENDED CAB SB/LB (4A) (in addition to or instead of SL 2WD REGULAR CAB SB/LB (4A) equipment): 4.8L V8 OHV SMPI 16-valve engine; 4-speed electronic OD auto transmission with lock-up; driver's selectable multi-mode transmission, HD transmission oil cooler; 3.42 axle ratio; rear heat ducts; AM/FM stereo, clock, seek-scan, 4 speakers, and fixed antenna; seating capacity of 6, passenger's seat includes 4-way direction control, lumbar support, easy entry; full folding rear bench seat with adjustable headrests and rear floor mats.

4WD (in addition to or instead of 2WD equipment): Part-time 4 wheel drive, auto locking hub control and manual shift, 3.73 axle ratio; front independent torsion suspension with anti-roll bar, front torsion springs, front torsion bar; power re-circulating ball steering with vehicle speed-sensing assist and P245/75SR16 A/S BSW front and rear tires.

SLE DECOR (in addition to or instead of SL DECOR equipment): Front and rear chrome bumpers, front body-colored rub strip, rear black rub strip; chrome bodyside molding; driver's and passenger's power remote chrome folding outside mirrors; air conditioning, air filter; AM/FM stereo, clock, seek-scan, single CD, 6 performance speakers, auto equalizer, theft deterrent, and fixed antenna; cruise control; power door locks with 2 stage unlock, remote keyless entry; ignition disable, panic alarm, security system; power windows with driver's 1-touch down; interior lights include 2 door curb lights; leather-wrapped sport steering wheel with tilt adjustment and chrome grille.

CODE	DESCRIPTION	INVOICE	MSRP

Base Prices

TC15703	SL 2WD Regular Cab SB (5M)	14752	16300
TC15903	SL 2WD Regular Cab LB (5M)	15023	16600
TC15753	SL 2WD Extended Cab SB (4A)	19477	22259
TC15953	SL 2WD Extended Cab LB (4A)	19739	22559
TC15703	SLE 2WD Regular Cab SB (5M)	17512	20014
TC15903	SLE 2WD Regular Cab LB (5M)	17775	20314
TC15753	SLE 2WD Extended Cab SB (4A)	21568	24649
TC15953	SLE 2WD Extended Cab LB (4A)	21830	24949
TK15703	SL 4WD Regular Cab SB (5M)	17536	19377
TK15903	SL 4WD Regular Cab LB (5M)	17808	19677
TK15753	SL 4WD Extended Cab SB (4A)	22156	25321
TK15953	SL 4WD Extended Cab LB (4A)	22418	25621
TK15703	SLE 4WD Regular Cab SB (5M)	20192	23076
TK15903	SLE 4WD Regular Cab LB (5M)	20454	23376
TK15753	SLE 4WD Extended Cab SB (4A)	24247	27711
TK15953	SLE 4WD Extended Cab LB (4A)	24510	28011
Destination Charge:		665	665

Accessories

—	4th Door (X-Cab)	289	330
—	Vinyl Seat Trim (SL) *Includes fixed center section and deletes the following: manual lumbars, reclining seat, adjustable outboard head restraints, center fold down armrests and storage pocket behind seats. NOT AVAILABLE with A95.*	NC	NC
1SA	Marketing Option Package 1SA (SL) *Includes vehicle with standard equipment. NOT AVAILABLE with PY2, R6S.*	NC	NC
1SB	Marketing Option Package 1SB (SL) *Includes wheels: 16" x 7" aluminum painted argent, spare wheel not matching, chrome grille surround, chrome rear bumper and exterior black body moldings.*	538	625
1SC	Marketing Option Package 1SC (SLE) *Includes vehicle with standard equipment.*	NC	NC
1SD	Marketing Option Package 1SD (SLE 2WD X-Cab) *Includes SLT Decor package: wheels: 16" x 6.5" chrome plated steel, handling/trailering suspension package, electrochromic inside mirror with compass/temperature display and leather 6-way power driver's and passenger's seats.*	1505	1750
1SD	Marketing Option Package 1SD (SLE 4WD X-Cab) *Includes SLT Decor package: wheels: 16" x 6.5" chrome plated steel, firm/HD suspension, high pressure gas shock absorbers, Autotrac active transfer case, electrochromic inside mirror with compass/temperature display and leather 6-way power driver's and passenger's seats.*	1828	2125
A28	Sliding Rear Window *NOT AVAILABLE with C49.*	108	125

CODE	DESCRIPTION	INVOICE	MSRP
A95	Reclining Front Bucket Seats (SLE) *Includes inboard armrests, dual adjustable headrests, manual lumbar, storage pockets behind seats and overhead console.*	366	425
AG2	6-Way Power Driver's and Passenger's Seat Adjuster (SLE) *Included in 1SD.*	413	480
AJ1	Deep Tinted Glass (Reg Cab) *Includes rear window. REQUIRES A28 or C49.*	43	50
AJ1	Deep Tinted Glass (X-Cab) *Includes rear and rear quarter windows.*	92	107
AU3	Power Door Locks (SL)	139	162
B71	Front and Rear Wheel Flares (4WD)	155	180
C49	Electric Rear Window Defogger *REQUIRES C60. NOT AVAILABLE with A28.*	150	175
C60	Air Conditioning (SL) *Includes micron air filtration.*	710	825
DF2	Exterior High Visibility Extendable Mirrors (SL) *7.5"H x 10.5"W. Manually controlled. Black with adjustable arm feature to provide field of vision for vehicles to 96" wide. Dual segment mirror on driver's side provides enhanced wide angle capacity.*	52	60
DF2	Exterior High Visibility Extendable Mirrors (SLE) *7.5"H x 10.5"W. Manually controlled. Black with adjustable arm feature to provide field of vision for vehicles to 96" wide. Dual segment mirror on driver's side provides enhanced wide angle capacity. NOT AVAILABLE with DL8.*	(33)	(38)
DF5	Electrochromic Inside Mirror (SLE) *Includes auto-dimming rear view mirror with compass/temperature display. INCLUDED in 1SD.*	150	175
DL8	Power Heated Exterior Mirrors with Chrome Cap (SLE) *Electronically controlled. REQUIRES C49. NOT AVAILABLE with DF2.*	36	42
E62	Sportside Body (SL SB) *NOT AVAILABLE with L35 or MG5*	770	895
E62	Sportside Body (SLE SB) *NOT AVAILABLE with L35 or MG5*	684	795
E95	Soft Black Tonneau Cover	206	240
G80	Locking Rear Differential *Includes premium carbon fiber friction plates. REQUIRES GT4 or GU6.*	245	285
GT4	3.73 Axle Ratio *NOT AVAILABLE with GT5.*	NC	NC
GT5	4.10 Axle Ratio (4WD) *REQUIRES LM7 or LR4.*	NC	NC
GU6	3.42 Axle Ratio (2WD Reg Cab)	NC	NC
K05	Engine Block Heater	30	35
K34	Cruise Control (SL)	206	240
K47	High Capacity Air Cleaner	22	25
KNP	HD Auxiliary Transmission Cooling *Includes external air to oil cooling. REQUIRES M30.*	82	95
L35	Engine: Vortec 4300 V6 (2WD X-Cab) *NOT AVAILABLE with Z82, UY2.*	(512)	(595)

CODE	DESCRIPTION	INVOICE	MSRP
LM7	Engine: Vortec 5300 SFI V8 (Reg Cab) *REQUIRES M30 and (GT4 or GU6). NOT AVAILABLE with VYU.*	1286	1495
LM7	Engine: Vortec 5300 SFI V8 (X-Cab)	688	800
LR4	Engine: Vortec 4800 SFI V8 (Reg Cab) *REQUIRES GT4 or GU6.*	598	695
M30	Transmission: 4-Speed Automatic with Overdrive (Reg Cab) *Includes electronic control and internal water to oil cooling. NOT AVAILABLE with VYU.*	942	1095
MG5	Transmission: 5-Speed Manual with Overdrive (X-Cab) *NOT AVAILABLE with KNP, LM7, Z82, UY2.*	(856)	(995)
NC7	Federal Emission Override	NC	NC
NP8	Autotrac Active Transfer Case (4WD) *REQUIRES M30. INCLUDED in 1SD.*	322	375
NZZ	Off-Road Skid Plates (4WD) *Inlcudes plastic front underbody shield starting behind front bumper and running to 1st cross member protecting front underbody, oil pan, front differential case and steel transfer case. INCLUDED in Z71.*	82	95
PF4	Wheels: 16" x 7" Bright Cast Aluminum (4) (SLE) *REQUIRES A95 . NOT AVAILABLE with QC3. INCLUDED in 1SD.*	95	110
PF9	Wheels: 16" x 7" Aluminum Painted Argent (4) (SL) *NOT AVAILABLE with PY2. INCLUDED in 1SB.*	267	310
PY2	Wheels: 16" x 6.5" Chrome Plated Steel (SL) *Includes 4 wheels, chrome center cap and 6 lugs. REQUIRES 1SB. NOT AVAILABLE with PF9, 1SA, QGC, QGD. INCLUDED in 1SC, 1SD.*	267	310
QBN	Tires: LT245/75R16C On/Off Road BSW (SLE 4WD) *REQUIRES Z71 or 1SD. NOT AVAILABLE with QBX, QGA, QGB, QNL, QGC, QGD, Z83.*	138	161
QBX	Tires: LT245/75R16C On/Off Road OWL (SLE 4WD) *REQUIRES Z71 or 1SD. NOT AVAILABLE with QBN, QGA, QGB, QNL, QGC, QGD, Z83.*	245	286
QC3	Wheels: 16" x 7" Cast Aluminum (4) (SLE) *REQUIRES A95 or AN3. NOT AVAILABLE with PF4.*	95	110
QCC	Tires: P255/70R16 AS BSW (2WD) *REQUIRES ZX3 or Z85. NOT AVAILABLE with QCJ, QNG.*	146	170
QCJ	Tires: P255/70R16 AS WOL (2WD) *REQUIRES ZX3 or Z85. NOT AVAILABLE with QNG, QCC.*	254	295
QGA	Tires: P245/75R16 BSW AT (4WD SL) *NOT AVAILABLE with QBN, QBX, QGB, QGC, QGD, QNL, Z71.*	90	105
QGB	Tires: P245/75R16 AT WOL (4WD) *NOT AVAILABLE with QBN, QBX, QGA, QGC, QGD, QNL, Z71.*	198	230
QGC	Tires: P265/75R16 AT BSW (4WD) *REQUIRES PF4, PF9 or QC3. NOT AVAILABLE with QBN, QBX, QGA, QGB, QGD, QNL, PY2, Z83.*	206	240
QGD	Tires: P265/75R16 AT WOL (4WD) *REQUIRES PF4, PF9 or QC3. NOT AVAILABLE with QBN, QBX, QGA, QGB, QGD, QNL, PY2, Z83.*	314	365

CODE	DESCRIPTION	INVOICE	MSRP
QNG	Tires: P235/75R16 AS WOL (2WD) *REQUIRES Z83. NOT AVAILABLE with QCC, QCJ, Z82, ZX3.*	108	125
QNL	Tires: P245/75R16 AS OWL (4WD) *NOT AVAILABLE with QBN, QBX, QGA, QGB, QGC, QGD, Z71.*	108	125
R6M	New Jersey Cost Surcharge	74	NC
R6R	Commercial Group (SL X-Cab) *Includes transmission: 4-speed automatic with overdrive, 40/20/40 split bench seat without: manual lumbar, reclining seats, adjustable head restraints, center fold down console or storage pocket behind seats and custom cloth seat trim. NOT AVAILABLE with cloth seat trim.*	(329)	(382)
R6R	Commercial Group (SL X-Cab) *Includes transmission: 4-speed automatic with overdrive, 40/20/40 split bench seat without: manual lumbar, reclining seats, adjustable head restraints, center fold down console or storage pocket behind seats and custom cloth seat trim. REQUIRES 1SA or 1SB. NOT AVAILABLE with vinyl seat trim.*	(86)	(100)
R6R	Commercial Group 1 (SL Reg Cab) *Includes transmission: 4-speed automatic with overdrive, 40/20/40 split bench seat without: manual lumbar, reclining seats, adjustable head restraints, center fold down console or storage pocket behind seats and custom cloth seat trim. NOT AVAILABLE with vinyl seat trim.*	856	995
R6R	Commercial Group 1 (SL Reg Cab) *Includes transmission: 4-speed automatic with overdrive, 40/20/40 split bench seat without: manual lumbar, reclining seats, adjustable head restraints, center fold down console or storage pocket behind seats and custom cloth seat trim. REQUIRES 1SA or 1SB. NOT AVAILABLE with cloth seat trim.*	613	713
R6S	Convenience Group (SL Reg Cab) *Includes cruise control, air conditioning, AM/FM stereo with cassette and seek/scan and power door locks. REQUIRES 1SB. NOT AVAILABLE with 1SA.*	1201	1397
R6S	Convenience Group (SL X-Cab) *Includes cruise control, air conditioning, AM/FM stereo with cassette and seek/scan and power door locks. REQUIRES 1SB. NOT AVAILABLE with 1SA.*	1184	1377
R6T	Convenience Plus Group (SLE 2WD) *Includes 6-way power driver's and passenger's seat, electrochromic inside mirror and compass/temperature display. REQUIRES 1SC.*	563	655
R6T	Convenience Plus Group (SLE 4WD) *Includes 6-way power driver's and passenger's seat, electrochromic inside mirror and compass/temperature display. REQUIRES 1SC.*	886	1030
T96	Front Fog Lamps (SLE) *REQUIRES LM7 or LR4.*	120	140
UL5	Radio Delete (SL) *Includes instrument panel storage bin, antenna and base 2 speaker system. NOT AVAILABLE with UM6.*	(215)	(250)
UM6	Radio: AM/FM Stereo with Cassette (SL Reg Cab) *Includes electronically tuned FM stereo, clock and 4 speakers. NOT AVAILABLE with UL5.*	146	170

CODE	DESCRIPTION	INVOICE	MSRP
UM6	**Radio: AM/FM Stereo with Cassette (SL X-Cab)** *Includes electronically tuned FM stereo, clock and 4 speakers. NOT AVAILABLE with UL5.*	129	150
UP0	**Radio: AM/FM Stereo with CD and Cassette (SLE X-Cab)** *Includes clock, electronically tuned FM stereo, speed sensitive volume, theft lock, seek/scan, selective tone control, auto reverse and music search cassette player with enhanced performance 6 speaker system. REQUIRES A95 or NP8 (4WD). NOT AVAILABLE with AE7. INCLUDED in R6U.*	86	100
UV8	**Cellular Phone Provisions** *For permanent installation of cellular phone. Includes wiring for remote microphone jumper harness and cellular phone jumper harness. Wiring includes 6 leads - 2 for microphone, 1 for battery feed, 1 for ground, 1 for ignition and 1 for Class II Communications.*	43	50
UY2	**Camper and Fifth Wheel Wiring Provisions (All Except SLE 4WD X-Cab)** *Includes gooseneck trailer provision. Provides an additional 8-wire independently fused wiring harness routed to the front of the pickup box and an additional 7-way sealed connector which mates to the trailer harness. REQUIRES (LR4 and M30 and Z82) or (LM7 and Z82). NOT AVAILABLE with L35.*	22	25
V76	**Tow Hooks (2WD)**	33	38
VB3	**Chrome Rear Bumper (SL)** *Includes black step pad and rub strip. NOT AVAILABLE with VF7. INCLUDED in 1SB.*	86	100
VF7	**Rear Bumper Delete (SL)** *NOT AVAILABLE with Z82, VB3.*	(86)	(100)
VF7	**Rear Bumper Delete (SLE)** *NOT AVAILABLE with Z82.*	(172)	(200)
VYU	**Snow Plow Prep Package (4WD Reg Cab SB)** *Provides additional front spring capacity to accomomodate the extra weight of a snowplow. Also, provides body equipment to prepare for typical snowplow equipment installation. Includes increased front torsion spring rate with greater load carrying capacity, 10-amp power for each rear backup light and roof mounted emergency light, high airflow front bumper, forward lamp wiring harness with in-line connector, 42mm diameter access hole with grommet in front of dash panel, mounting location for snowplow controls, HD front torsion bars, 130-amp generator and HD auxiliary transmission cooling. REQUIRES LR4, M30. NOT AVAILABLE with ZX3, Z82.*	245	285
VYU	**Snow Plow Prep Package (4WD Reg Cab SB)** *Provides additional front spring capacity to accomomodate the extra weight of a snowplow. Also, provides body equipment to prepare for typical snowplow equipment installation. Includes increased front torsion spring rate with greater load carrying capacity, 10-amp power for each rear backup light and roof mounted emergency light, high airflow front bumper, forward lamp wiring harness with in-line connector, 42mm diameter access hole with grommet in front of dash panel, mounting location for snowplow controls, HD front torsion bars, 130-amp generator and HD auxiliary transmission cooling. REQUIRES Z82, LR4. NOT AVAILABLE with M30, LM7, ZX3.*	163	190

CODE	DESCRIPTION	INVOICE	MSRP
Z71	**Off-Road Chassis Equipment Package (4WD SLE)** *Provides for the rigors of off-highway driving. Designed to accommodate large suspension inputs with minimal impact to highway ride and handling. Also provides chassis component shields. Includes same load carrying capacity spring as Z83, increased rate springs, jounce bumpers, stabilizer bar, Z71 decal on side of cargo box, special removeable front air dam, wider aspect and aggressive tread tires for maximum traction in loose soil, off-road skid plates, high capacity air cleaner and high pressure gas shock absorbers. REQUIRES (QBN or QBX or QGC or QGD) or (GT5 and (QBN or QBX or QGC or QGD)). NOT AVAILABLE with QGA, QNL, ZX3.*	258	300
Z82	**HD Trailering Equipment** *Includes electric trailer brake wire harness with mounting provisions, 8-wire harness with fully independent fused trailering circuits with 7-way sealed connector, an instrument panel jumper wiring harness for electric trailer brake controller, a 1-way sealed connector for the CHMSL, tow/haul mode selector, trailer hitch platform and HD auxiliary transmission cooling. REQUIRES (LM7 or LR4) and (GU6 or GT4) and M30. NOT AVAILABLE with VF7, QNG, L35, VYU.*	245	285
Z85	**Handling/Trailering Suspension Package** *Provides increased damping for firmer highway ride and improved handling while trailering. Includes same load carrying capacity springs as Z83, heavy-duty engine/transmission oil cooling capability is provided with internal cooler and wider aspect ratio tires with greater load carrying capacity than Z83 and high pressure gas shock absorbers. NOT AVAILABLE with Z71, ZX3. INCLUDED in 1SD.*	82	95
ZX3	**Ride Control Suspension (SLE)** *Provides driver with ability to select either a solid/smooth ride or a handling/trailering ride. For suspensions, the purpose is similar to the auto tow/haul mode. Includes instrument panel switch for driver's suspension setting control, same load carrying capacity springs as Z83, provides tow/haul like performance choice for suspensions and wider aspect ratio tires with greater load carrying capacity than standard and high pressure gas shock absorbers. REQUIRES LM7 or LR4. NOT AVAILABLE with QNG, VYU, Z71, 1SD.*	361	420
ZX3	**Ride Control Suspension (SLE X-Cab)** *Provides driver with ability to select either a solid/smooth ride or a handling/trailering ride. For suspensions, the purpose is similar to the auto tow/haul mode. Includes instrument panel switch for driver's suspension setting control, same load carrying capacity springs as Z83, provides tow/haul like performance choice for suspensions and wider aspect ratio tires with greater load carrying capacity than standard and high pressure gas shock absorbers. REQUIRES 1SD.*	280	325
ZY2	**Two-Tone Paint (SLE)** *NOT AVAILABLE with E62.*	215	250

2000 SIERRA 2500

Standard Equipment

SL 2WD REGULAR CAB HD LB (5M): 6.0L V8 OHV SMPI 16-valve engine; 5-speed OD manual transmission; 600-amp HD battery with run down protection; HD engine oil cooler; 105-amp alternator; rear-wheel drive, power take-off provision, 3.73 axle ratio; stainless steel exhaust; front independent suspension with anti-roll bar, front coil springs, rigid rear axle suspension with rear leaf springs; power re-circulating ball steering with vehicle speed-sensing assist; 4-wheel disc brakes with 4-wheel antilock braking system; 34 gal. capacity fuel tank; side impact bars; trailer harness; front and rear black rub strip, front chrome bumper, rear argent bumper, front tow hooks, rear step; monotone paint; aero-composite halogen auto on headlamps with daytime running lights; additional exterior lights include pickup cargo box light, underhood light; driver's and passenger's manual black folding outside mirrors; front and rear 16" x 6.5" silver styled steel wheels; LT245/75SR16 A/S BSW front and rear tires; underbody mounted full-size steel spare wheel with crankdown; AM/FM stereo, clock, seek-scan, 2 speakers, and fixed antenna; 3 power accessory outlets, retained accessory power, smokers' package; instrumentation display includes tachometer, oil pressure gauge, water temperature gauge, volt gauge, trip odometer; warning indicators include oil pressure, water temp, battery, low oil level, low coolant, lights on, key in ignition, low fuel, low washer fluid, door ajar, service interval; driver's front airbag, passenger's cancelable front airbag; ignition disable; tinted windows; variable intermittent front windshield wipers, sun visor strip; seating capacity of 3, 40-20-40 split-bench front seat, adjustable headrests, center armrest with storage, driver's seat includes 4-way direction control, lumbar support, passenger's seat includes 4-way direction control, lumbar support; premium cloth seats, full cloth headliner, full color-keyed carpet floor covering with floor mats, plastic/rubber gear shift knob, cabback insulator; interior lights include dome light, front reading lights; sport steering wheel with tilt adjustment; passenger's side vanity mirror; day/night rearview mirror; glove box with light, front cupholder, 2 seat back storage pockets, driver's and passenger's door bins; argent grille, black side window moldings, black front windshield molding, black rear window molding and black door handles.

SL 2WD REGULAR CAB LB (4A) (in addition to or instead of SL 2WD REGULAR CAB LB HD (4A) equipment): 5.3L V8 OHV SMPI 16-valve engine; 4-speed electronic OD auto transmission with lock-up; driver's selectable multi-mode transmission, HD transmission oil cooler; LT225/75SR16 A/S BSW front and rear tires.

SL 2WD EXTENDED CAB SB (4A) (in addition to or instead of SL 2WD REGULAR CAB LB (4A) equipment): 3.42 axle ratio; 26 gal. capacity fuel tank; rear heat ducts; AM/FM stereo, clock, seek-scan, 4 speakers, and fixed antenna; vented rear windows; seating capacity of 6; full folding rear bench seat with adjustable headrests and full color-keyed carpet floor covering with rubber front and rear floor mats.

SL 2WD EXTENDED CAB HD LB (4A) (in addition to or instead of SL 2WD REGULAR CAB HD LB (5M) equipment): 4-speed electronic OD auto transmission with lock-up; driver's selectable multi-mode transmission, HD transmission oil cooler; chrome bodyside molding; rear heat ducts; AM/FM stereo, clock, seek-scan, 4 speakers, and fixed antenna; vented rear windows; seating capacity of 6; full folding rear bench seat with adjustable headrests and full color-keyed carpet floor covering with rubber front and rear floor mats.

SLE (in addition to or instead of SL equipment): Front and rear chrome bumpers, front body-colored rub strip, black rear rub strip; chrome bodyside molding; driver's and passenger's power remote black folding outside mirrors; front and rear 16" x 6.5" chrome styled steel wheels; air conditioning; AM/FM stereo, clock, seek-scan, single CD, 6 performance speakers, auto equalizer, theft deterrent, and fixed antenna; cruise control; power door locks with 2 stage unlock, remote keyless entry; ignition disable, panic alarm, security system; power windows with driver's 1-touch down; interior lights include 2 door curb lights, illuminated entry; leather-wrapped sport steering wheel with tilt adjustment and chrome grille.

4WD REGULAR CAB LB HD (in addition to or instead of SL 2WD REGULAR CAB LB HD equipment): Part-time 4-wheel drive, auto locking hub control and manual shift, power take-off provision; front independent torsion suspension with anti-roll bar, front torsion springs, front torsion bar and black fender flares.

Base Prices

Code	Description	Invoice	MSRP
TC25903-C6P	SL 2WD Regular Cab HD LB	18492	21134
TC25903	SL 2WD Regular Cab LB (4A)	18839	21530
TC25903-C6P	SLE 2WD Regular Cab HD LB (5M)	20584	23524
TC25903	SLE 2WD Regular Cab LB (4A)	20930	23920
TC25753	SL 2WD Extended Cab SB 3-Door (4A)	20803	23775
TC25753-1	SL 2WD Extended Cab SB 4-Door (4A)	21004	24005
TC25753	SLE 2WD Extended Cab SB 3-Door (4A)	22894	26165
TC25753-1	SLE 2WD Extended Cab SB 4-Door (4A)	22964	26245
TC25953	SL 2WD Extended Cab HD LB (4A)	21677	24774
TC25953	SLE 2WD Extended Cab HD LB (4A)	23769	27164
TK25903	SL 4WD Regular Cab HD LB (5M)	21172	24196
TK25903	SLE 4WD Regular Cab HD LB (5M)	23263	26586
TK25753	SL 4WD Extended Cab SB (4A)	24094	27536
TK25753	SLE 4WD Extended Cab SB (4A)	26185	29926
TK25953	SL 4WD Extended Cab HD LB (4A)	24357	27836
TK25953	SLE 4WD Extended Cab HD LB (4A)	26448	30226
Destination Charge:		665	665

Accessories

Code	Description	Invoice	MSRP
1SA	Marketing Option Package 1SA (SL) *Includes vehicle with standard equipment. NOT AVAILABLE with R6S.*	NC	NC
1SB	Marketing Option Package 1SB (SL) *Includes chrome grille surround, chromed rear step bumper with step pad, black exterior moldings and chrome center caps.*	322	375
1SC	Marketing Option Package 1SC (SLE) *Includes vehicle with standard equipment. NOT AVAILABLE with PYO.*	NC	NC
1SD	Marketing Option Package 1SD (SLE X-Cab 2WD) *Includes SLT Decor package: 6-way power leather reclining split bench front seat, manual lumbar support, fold down center armrest, rear seat storage pockets; handling/trailering suspension package, electrochromic inside mirror and compass/temperature display.*	1505	1750
1SD	Marketing Option Package 1SD (SLE X-Cab 4WD) *Includes SLT Decor package: 6-way power leather reclining split bench front seat, manual lumbar support, fold down center armrest, rear seat storage pockets; handling/trailering suspension package, electrochromic inside mirror, compass/temperature display and Autotrac active transfer case.*	1828	2125
A28	Sliding Rear Window *NOT AVAILABLE with C49.*	108	125

CODE	DESCRIPTION	INVOICE	MSRP
A95	Front Reclining Bucket Seats (SLE) *Includes inboard armrests, dual adjustable headrests, seatback storage pockets, manual lumbar, floor console and overhead console. NOT AVAILABLE with R6U.*	366	425
AG2	6-Way Power Driver's and Passenger's Seat Adjuster (SLE) *REQUIRES 1SC. INCLUDED with 1SD.*	413	480
AJ1	Deep Tinted Glass (Reg Cab) *Includes light tinted rear window with C49. REQUIRES A28 or C49.*	43	50
AJ1	Deep Tinted Glass (X-Cab) *Includes light tinted rear window with C49.*	92	107
AU3	Power Door Locks (SL) *REQUIRES R6R.*	139	162
BG9	Rubber Floor Covering (Reg Cab LD/2WD X-Cab) *NOT AVAILABLE with 1SD.*	(86)	(100)
C49	Electric Rear Window Defogger *REQUIRES C60. NOT AVAILABLE with A28.*	150	175
C60	Air Conditioning (SL) *Includes micron air filtration.*	710	825
C6P	GVWR: 8,600 Lbs (Reg Cab HD/4WD X-Cab SB/X-Cab LB) *NOT AVAILABLE with MT1.*	NC	NC
DF2	High Visibility Extendable Mirrors (SL) *Manually controlled 7.5"H x 10.5"W. Black with adjustable arm feature to provide field of vision for vehicles to 96" wide. Dual segment mirror on driver's side provides enhanced wide angle capacity. NOT AVAILABLE with DL8.*	(33)	(38)
DF2	High Visibility Extendable Mirrors (SLE) *Manually controlled 7.5"H x 10.5"W. Black with adjustable arm feature to provide field of vision for vehicles to 96" wide. Dual segment mirror on driver's side provides enhanced wide angle capacity.*	52	60
DF5	Electrochromic Inside Mirror (SLE) *Includes auto-dimming rear view mirror and compass/temperature display. INCLUDED in 1SD.*	150	175
DL8	Power Heated Exterior Mirrors with Chrome Cap (SLE) *Electronically controlled. REQUIRES C49. NOT AVAILABLE with DF2.*	36	42
E95	Soft Black Tonneau Cover	206	240
G80	Locking Rear Differential *Includes premium carbon fiber friction plates. REQUIRES GT5.*	245	285
GT5	4.10 Axle Ratio	NC	NC
K05	Engine Block Heater	30	35
K34	Cruise Control (SL)	206	240
K47	High Capacity Air Cleaner	22	25
KC4	Engine Oil Cooler *REQUIRES LQ4.*	116	135
KNP	HD Auxiliary Transmission Cooler *REQUIRES MT1. NOT AVAILABLE with MW3.*	82	95
LQ4	Engine: Vortec 6000 V8 SFI (Reg Cab HD/2WD X-Cab LB/4WD) *Includes high capacity air cleaner. REQUIRES GT5.*	305	355
MT1	Transmission: 4-Speed Automatic with Overdrive (All Except Reg Cab HD) *NOT AVAILABLE with C6P, VYU.*	NC	NC

CODE	DESCRIPTION	INVOICE	MSRP
MT1	Transmission: 4-Speed Automatic with Overdrive (Reg Cab HD) *Includes HD auxiliary transmission cooler. NOT AVAILABLE with VYU.*	942	1095
MW3	Transmission: 5-Speed Manual with OD (2WD X-Cab SB/Reg Cab LD) *NOT AVAILABLE with C6P, VYU.*	(942)	(1095)
MW3	Transmission: 5-Spd. Manual w/OD (All Except 2WD X-Cab SB/Reg Cab LD) *NOT AVAILABLE with NP8.*	NC	NC
NP8	Autotrac Active Transfer Case (SLE 4WD) *REQUIRES MT1. INCLUDED in 1SD.*	322	375
NZZ	Off-Road Skid Plates (4WD) *Includes aluminum front underbody shield starting behind front bumper and running to 1st cross member protecting front underbody, oil pan, differential case and steel transfer case frame mounted shields.*	82	95
P03	Chrome Center Caps (SL) *INCLUDED in 1SB.*	52	60
P03	Chrome Center Caps (SL) *REQUIRES PY2. INCLUDED in 1SB.*	NC	NC
PY0	Wheels: 16" x 6.5" Forged Aluminum (SLE X-Cab) *Includes 4 polished wheels and chrome center caps. NOT AVAILABLE with 1SC.*	95	110
PY2	Wheels: 16" x 6.5" Chrome Plated Steel (SL) *Includes 4 wheels. REQUIRES 1SB. NOT AVAILABLE with 1SA. INCLUDED in 1SC, 1SD.*	267	310
QIW	Tires: LT245/75R16E AT BSW SBR (All Except X-Cab SB) *NOT AVAILABLE with QIZ.*	47	55
QIW	Tires: LT245/75R16E AT BSW SBR (Reg Cab LD/2WD X-Cab SB) *NOT AVAILABLE with QIZ, C6P.*	241	280
QIZ	Tires: LT245/75R16E AS BSW SBR (All Except X-Cab SB) *NOT AVAILABLE with QIW.*	NC	NC
QIZ	Tires: LT245/75R16E AS BSW SBR (Reg Cab LD/2WD X-Cab SB) *NOT AVAILABLE with QIW, C6P.*	194	225
R6M	New Jersey Cost Surcharge	74	NC
R6R	Commercial Group (SL) *Includes 40/20/40 reclining split bench seat and vinyl floor covering. NOT AVAILABLE with A95.*	(329)	(382)
R6R	Commercial Group (SL) *Includes 40/20/40 reclining split bench seat and vinyl floor covering. NOT AVAILABLE with ~~V, A95.*	(86)	(100)
R6S	Convenience Group (SL Reg Cab) *Includes cruise control, AM/FM stereo with seek, scan and cassette, air conditioning and power door locks. REQUIRES 1SB. NOT AVAILABLE with 1SA.*	1201	1397
R6S	Convenience Group (SL X-Cab) *Includes cruise control, AM/FM stereo with seek, scan and cassette, air conditioning and power door locks. REQUIRES 1SB. NOT AVAILABLE with 1SA.*	1184	1377
R6T	Convenience Plus Group (SLE 2WD) *Includes electrochromic inside mirror, compass/temperature display and 6-way power driver's and passenger's seat adjuster.*	563	655

CODE	DESCRIPTION	INVOICE	MSRP
R6T	**Convenience Plus Group (SLE 4WD)** *Includes Autotrac active transfer case, electrochromic inside mirror, compass/ temperature display and 6-way power driver's and passenger's seat adjuster.*	886	1030
R6U	**Comfort Group (SLE)** *Includes full feature high back bucket seats, overhead console and floor console. REQUIRES 1SD. NOT AVAILABLE with A95.*	666	775
T96	**Front Fog Lamps (SLE)**	120	140
TP2	**600 CCA Auxiliary HD Battery**	116	135
UL5	**Radio Delete (SL)** *Includes front fender hole plugs and instrument panel storage bin. NOT AVAILABLE with UM6.*	(215)	(250)
UM6	**Radio: AM/FM Stereo with Cassette (SL Reg Cab)** *Includes clock and electronically tuned FM stereo with 4 speakers. NOT AVAILABLE with UL5.*	146	170
UM6	**Radio: AM/FM Stereo with Cassette (SL X-Cab)** *Includes clock and electronically tuned FM stereo with 4 speakers. NOT AVAILABLE with UL5.*	129	150
UP0	**Radio: AM/FM Stereo with CD and Cassette (SLE X-Cab)** *Includes electronically tuned FM stereo, clock, speed sensitive volume, theft lock, selective tone control, auto reverse and music search cassette player and enhanced performance 6-speaker system. REQUIRES A95 or NP8 or R6U.*	86	100
UV8	**Cellular Phone Provisions** *Includes wiring for remote microphone jumper harness and cellular phone jumper harness. Wiring includes 6 leads - 2 for microphone, 1 for battery feed, 1 for ground, 1 for ignition and 1 for Class II Communications. For permanent installation of celullar phone.*	43	50
UY2	**Camper and Fifth Wheel Wiring Provisions** *Provides an additional 8-wire independently fused wiring harness routed to the front of the pickup box and an additional 7-way sealed connector which mates to the trailer harness. REQUIRES Z82. NOT AVAILABLE with VYU.*	22	25
VB3	**Chromed Rear Step Bumper with Step Pad (SL)** *Includes rub strip. NOT AVAILABLE with VF7. INCLUDED in 1SB.*	86	100
VF7	**Rear Bumper Delete (SL)** *NOT AVAILABLE with Z82, VB3, VYU.*	(86)	(100)
VF7	**Rear Bumper Delete (SLE)** *NOT AVAILABLE with Z82.*	(172)	(200)
VYU	**Snow Plow Prep Package (4WD)** *Includes increased front spring rate/load (torsion bars), 10-amp power for rear backup light and roof mounted emergency light, high airflow bumpers, forward lamp wiring harness with in-line connector, 42mm diameter access hole with grommet, mounting location for snow plow controls and 130-amp generator. NOT AVAILABLE with VF7.*	163	190
VYU	**Snow Plow Prep Package (4WD)** *Includes increased front spring rate/load (torsion bars), 10-amp power for rear backup light and roof mounted emergency light, high airflow bumpers, forward lamp wiring harness with in-line connector, 42mm diameter access hole with grommet,*	280	325

CODE	DESCRIPTION	INVOICE	MSRP
	mounting location for snow plow controls, 130-amp generator and engine oil cooler. NOT AVAILABLE with Z82, UY2, MW3.		
VYU	Snow Plow Prep Package *Includes increased front spring rate/load (torsion bars), 10-amp power for rear backup light and roof mounted emergency light, high airflow bumpers, forward lamp wiring harness with in-line connector, 42mm diameter access hole with grommet, mounting location for snow plow controls, 130-amp generator, engine oil cooler and HD auxiliary transmission cooler. REQUIRES MW3. NOT AVAILABLE with Z82, UY2, MT1, 1SD.*	245	285
Z82	HD Trailering Equipment *Includes electric trailer brake wire harness with mounting provisions, an 8-wire harness with fully independent fused trailering circuits with 7-way sealed connector, an IP jumper wiring harness for electric trailer brake controller and a 1-way sealed connector for the CHMSL and trailer hitch platform. NOT AVAILABLE with VF7, LM7.*	280	325
Z82	HD Trailering Equipment *Includes electric trailer brake wire harness with mounting provisions, an 8-wire harness with fully independent fused trailering circuits with 7-way sealed connector, an IP jumper wiring harness for electric trailer brake controller, a 1-way sealed connector for the CHMSL, trailer hitch platform and HD auxiliary transmission cooler. REQUIRES LM7. NOT AVAILABLE with VF7.*	245	285
Z85	Handling/Trailering Suspension Package *Includes same load carrying capacity springs as Z83, black color shock absorber tubes (low pressure gas charged with 35mm piston diameter, heavy duty engine and transmission oil cooling capability is provided with internal cooling and wider aspect ratio tires with greater load carrying capacity than standard. REQUIRES QIW or QIZ. INCLUDED in 1SD.*	82	95
ZY2	Two Tone Paint Application (SLE)	215	250
~~V	Vinyl Seat Trim (SL) *Includes fixed center section without manual lumbars, with out reclining seat, without adjustable outboard head restraints, without center fold down amrest and seatback storage pockets delete. NOT AVAILABLE with R6R, A95.*	NC	NC

2000 SIERRA CLASSIC

What's New?

GM has refined the Sierra Classic lineup, dropping all 1500 series (half-ton) trucks in favor of workhorse 2500 (three-quarter-ton) and 3500 (one-ton) series models. The only other news is the addition of a new exterior paint color, as this old truck platform (based on the previous-generation C/K pickup) soldiers on into its second decade.

Review

The GMC Sierra became the "Sierra Classic" to distinguish the old C/K-derived version from the all-new Silverado-based Sierra that arrived in showrooms for 1999. To help bolster stocks of work-oriented pickups until heavy-duty derivatives of the new Sierra can be built, this previous-generation model continues to be offered, albeit now only in 2500 or 3500 series form. In other words, if you want a traditional half-ton pickup, you've got to buy the new Sierra.

Like last year, changes are limited to some mechanical upgrades and a new exterior paint color, Emerald Green. After the all-new Sierra hit the showrooms, it made no sense for further revisions to this stopgap version whose days were numbered. So why bother even considering a brand-new copy of the old model? Simple: It's all a matter of availability, and cost. Available as a regular cab, extended cab, four-door crew cab and even as a bare-bones chassis cab in either two- or four-wheel drive, these trucks are both plentiful and competitively priced. Besides, some truck traditionalists actually prefer the Classic's squared-off look over the new Sierra's sculpted lines.

Despite the aging design of the Sierra Classic's underpinnings, both of its gasoline engines benefit from the very latest Vortec GM technology, which means healthy power and torque ratings. The standard 5700 Vortec V8 makes 255 horsepower, and is a much more satisfying powerplant underfoot than Ford's overhead-cam truck engines. For even more power you can opt for the 7400 V8 with 290 horses and some 410 foot-pounds of torque. If you need true stump-pulling muscle, there's also a 6.5-liter turbodiesel, which cranks out a whopping 430 foot-pounds of torque when mated to an electronically controlled four-speed automatic transmission with overdrive. A rugged five-speed manual is also available.

Just because these are previous-design vehicles, creature comforts aren't totally forgotten. The Sierra Classic was part of the 1990's truck revolution that saw manufacturers strive to make their trucks more carlike. Consequently, seats in the Classic are sturdy and comfortable, shoulder belts are height-adjustable to fit a variety of physiques, and upholstery choices include leather.

Power speaks volumes in the truck market, and having competitive horsepower numbers goes a long way toward selling the consumer on these older designs. The burly, workhorse nature of these pickups gives both Chevrolet and GMC's Ford/Dodge rivals a "Classic" run for their money.

2000 GMC Sierra Classic

2000 SIERRA CLASSIC 2500

Standard Equipment

SL 2WD REGULAR CAB HD LB (5M): 5.7L V8 OHV SMPI 16-valve engine; 5-speed OD manual transmission; 600-amp HD battery; engine oil cooler; 100-amp alternator; rear-wheel drive, power take-off provision, 3.73 axle ratio; stainless steel exhaust; front independent suspension with anti-roll bar, front coil springs, rigid rear axle suspension with rear leaf springs; power re-circulating ball

CODE	DESCRIPTION	INVOICE	MSRP

steering with vehicle speed-sensing assist; front disc/rear drum brakes with 4-wheel antilock braking system; 34 gal. capacity fuel tank; side impact bars; trailer harness; front chrome bumper, rear black bumper, rear step; monotone paint; sealed beam halogen headlamps with daytime running lights; additional exterior lights include pickup cargo box light, underhood light; driver's and passenger's manual black folding outside mirrors; front and rear 16" x 6.5" painted styled steel wheels; LT245/75SR16 A/S BSW front and rear tires; underbody mounted full-size steel spare wheel with crankdown; AM/FM stereo, clock, seek-scan, 4 speakers, and fixed antenna; 3 power accessory outlets, smokers' package; instrumentation display includes tachometer, oil pressure gauge, water temperature gauge, volt gauge, trip odometer; warning indicators include battery, lights on, key in ignition, door ajar; ignition disable; tinted windows; variable intermittent front windshield wipers, sun visor strip; seating capacity of 3, bench front seat, adjustable headrests, driver's seat includes 2-way direction control, passenger's seat includes 2-way direction control; front height adjustable seatbelts; vinyl seats, full cloth headliner, full vinyl floor covering, plastic/rubber gear shift knob, cabback insulator; interior lights include dome light, front reading lights; sport steering wheel; passenger's side vanity mirror; day/night rearview mirror; glove box with light, front cupholder, dashboard storage, driver's and passenger's door bins; argent grille, black side window moldings, black front windshield molding, black rear window molding and black door handles.

SL 2WD EXTENDED CAB HD LB (5M) (in addition to or instead of SL 2WD REGULAR CAB HD LB (5M) equipment): Rear heat ducts; vented rear windows; seating capacity of 6, 60-40 split-bench front seat, adjustable headrests, driver's seat includes 4-way direction control, easy entry, passenger's seat includes 4-way direction control, easy entry and full folding rear bench seat with adjustable headrests.

SL 2WD CREW CAB HD SB (4A) (in addition to or instead of SL 2WD EXTENDED CAB HD LB (4A) equipment): 4-speed electronic OD auto transmission with lock-up; transmission oil cooler; 26 gal. capacity fuel tank; front chrome bumper with black rub strip, chrome bumper insert; black bodyside molding with chrome bodyside insert; manual front and rear windows; child safety rear door locks; bench front seat, adjustable headrests, driver's seat includes 2-way direction control, passenger's seat includes 2-way direction control; full folding rear bench seat with reclining adjustable headrests and rear door bins.

4WD (in addition to or instead of 2WD equipment): Part-time 4-wheel drive, auto locking hub control and manual shift; front independent torsion suspension with anti-roll bar, front torsion springs, front torsion bar; front tow hooks and black fender flares.

Base Prices

TC20903	SL 2WD Regular Cab HD LB (5M)	17120	19567
TC20953	SL 2WD Extended Cab HD LB (5M)	18611	21271
TC20743	SL 2WD Crew Cab HD SB	20869	23851
TK20903	SL 4WD Regular Cab HD LB (5M)	19531	22322
TK20753	SL 4WD Extended Cab HD SB (5M)	21329	24377
TK20953	SL 4WD Extended Cab HD LB	21440	24504
TK20743	SL 4WD Crew Cab HD SB (4A)	23646	27025
Destination Charge:		665	665

Accessories

—	Cloth Seat Trim (Reg Cab/X-Cab) *REQUIRES 1SA. NOT AVAILABLE with ~~D, A95.*	NC	NC
1SA	Marketing Option Package 1SA *Includes vehicle with standard equipment. REQUIRES YG6 or C60.*	NC	NC

CODE	DESCRIPTION	INVOICE	MSRP
1SB	**Marketing Option Package 1SB (Crew Cab)**	692	805
	Includes vehicle with standard equipment. NOT AVAILABLE with YG6.		
1SB	**Marketing Option Package 1SB (Reg Cab/X-Cab)**	1150	1337
	Manufacturer Discount	(430)	(500)
	Net Price	720	837
	Includes air conditioning, AM/FM stereo with seek, scan and cassette and convenience package: tilt steering and speed control. NOT AVAILABLE with YG6, UL5.		
1SC	**Marketing Option Package 1SC (Crew Cab)**	3156	3670
	Includes air conditioning, AM/FM stereo with seek, scan and cassette, convenience package: tilt steering, speed control; SLE Decor package: power door locks, power windows with driver's side express down, leather-wrapped steering wheel, chrome rear step bumper with rub strip, remote power exterior mirrors, bright trim rings and hub caps and deluxe front appearance package: color-keyed grille and composite halogen headlamps.		
1SC	**Marketing Option Package 1SC (Reg Cab/X-Cab)**	2611	3036
	Manufacturer Discount	(645)	(750)
	Net Price	1966	2286
	Includes air conditioning, AM/FM stereo with seek, scan and cassette, convenience package: tilt steering, speed control; SLE Decor package: power door locks, power windows with driver's side express down, leather-wrapped steering wheel, chrome rear step bumper with rub strip, remote power exterior mirrors, bright trim rings and hub caps and deluxe front appearance package: color-keyed grille and composite halogen headlamps.		
1SD	**Marketing Option Package 1SD (Crew Cab)**	4601	5350
	Includes air conditioning, convenience package: tilt wheel, speed control; SLT Decor package: power door locks, power windows with driver's side express down, leather-wrapped steering wheel, chrome rear step bumper with rub strip, remote power exterior mirrors, bright trim rings and hub caps and deluxe front appearance package: color-keyed grille and composite halogen headlamps; ultrasoft leather seat trim, leather-wrapped steering wheel, chromed rear step bumper with step pad, AM/FM stereo with seek, scan, cassette and 6 speakers, 60/40 reclining split-bench seat, 6-way power driver's seat adjuster and remote keyless entry system.		
1SD	**Marketing Option Package 1SD (Reg Cab)**	3827	4450
	Manufacturer Discount	(645)	(750)
	Net Price	3182	3700
	Includes air conditioning, convenience package: tilt wheel, speed control; SLT Decor package: power door locks, power windows with driver's side express down, leather-wrapped steering wheel, chrome rear step bumper with rub strip, remote power exterior mirrors, bright trim rings and hub caps and deluxe front appearance package: color-keyed grille and composite halogen headlamps; ultrasoft leather seat trim, leather-wrapped steering wheel, chromed rear step bumper with step pad, AM/FM stereo with seek, scan, cassette and 6 speakers, 60/40 reclining split-bench seat, 6-way power driver's seat adjuster and remote keyless entry system. REQUIRES MT1.		

CODE	DESCRIPTION	INVOICE	MSRP
1SD	**Marketing Option Package 1SD (X-Cab)**	3884	4516
	Manufacturer Discount	(645)	(750)
	Net Price	3239	3766
	Includes air conditioning, convenience package: tilt wheel, speed control; SLT Decor package: power door locks, power windows with driver's side express down, leather-wrapped steering wheel, chrome rear step bumper with rub strip, remote power exterior mirrors, bright trim rings and hub caps and deluxe front appearance package: color-keyed grille and composite halogen headlamps; ultrasoft leather seat trim, leather-wrapped steering wheel, chromed rear step bumper with step pad, AM/FM stereo with seek, scan, cassette and 6 speakers, 60/40 reclining split-bench seat, 6-way power driver's seat adjuster and remote keyless entry system. REQUIRES MT1.		
1SH	**Marketing Option Package 1SH (X-Cab)**	5341	6211
	Manufacturer Discount	(645)	(750)
	Net Price	4696	5461
	Includes engine: Vortec 7400 V8 SFI, transmission: 4-speed automatic with overdrive, HD auxiliary transmission cooling, air conditioning, convenience package: tilt wheel, speed control; SLT Decor package: power door locks, power windows with driver's side express down, leather-wrapped steering wheel, chrome rear step bumper with rub strip, remote power exterior mirrors, bright trim rings and hub caps and deluxe front appearance package: color-keyed grille and composite halogen headlamps; ultrasoft leather seat trim, leather-wrapped steering wheel, chromed rear step bumper with step pad, AM/FM stereo with seek, scan, cassette and 6 speakers, 60/40 reclining split-bench seat, 6-way power driver's seat adjuster and remote keyless entry system.		
1SH	**Marketing Option Package 1SH (X-Cab)**	4069	4731
	Manufacturer Discount	(645)	(750)
	Net Price	3424	3981
	Includes engine: Vortec 7400 V8 SFI, transmission: 4-speed automatic with overdrive, HD auxiliary transmission cooling, air conditioning, AM/FM stereo with seek, scan and cassette, 60/40 reclining split-bench seat, convenience package: tilt steering, speed control; SLE Decor package: power door locks, power windows with driver's side express down, leather-wrapped steering wheel, chrome rear step bumper with rub strip, remote power exterior mirrors, bright trim rings and hub caps and deluxe front appearance package: color-keyed grille and composite halogen headlamps.		
1SR	**Marketing Option Package 1SR "Performax" (Reg Cab 2WD)**	2507	2315
	Manufacturer Discount	(602)	(700)
	Net Price	1905	1615
	Includes engine: Vortec 5700 V8 SFI, transmission: 4-speed automatic with overdrive, HD auxiliary transmission cooling, air conditioning, convenience package: tilt steering, speed control; AM/FM stereo with seek, scan and cassette, bright appearance group: deluxe front appearance package: color-keyed grille, composite halogen headlamps; chrome front bumper with rub strip, chrome rear step bumper with rub strip, bright exterior moldings, bright trim rings and hub caps. NOT AVAILABLE with UL5, YG6, L65.		

CODE	DESCRIPTION	INVOICE	MSRP
1SR	Marketing Option Package 1SR "Performax" (Reg Cab 4WD)	2480	2884
	Manufacturer Discount	(602)	(700)
	Net Price	1878	2184
	Includes engine: Vortec 5700 V8 SFI, transmission: 4-speed automatic with overdrive, HD auxiliary transmission cooling, air conditioning, convenience package: tilt steering, speed control; AM/FM stereo with seek, scan and cassette, bright appearance group: deluxe front appearance package: color-keyed grille, composite halogen headlamps; chrome front bumper with rub strip, chrome rear step bumper with rub strip, bright exterior moldings, bright trim rings and hub caps. NOT AVAILABLE with UL5, YG6, L65.		
A28	Sliding Rear Window	99	115
	NOT AVAILABLE with C49, AJ1.		
A95	Front Reclining Bucket Seats (Crew Cab)	364	423
	Includes 3-passenger adjustable split back rear bench seat, inboard armrests, dual adjustable headrests, left hand power lumbar and storage pockets behind seats, roof console and floor console. NOT AVAILABLE with 1SA, 1SB, 1SR.		
A95	Front Reclining Bucket Seats (Reg Cab)	332	386
	Includes inboard armrests, dual adjustable headrests, left hand power lumbar and easy entry feature. NOT AVAILABLE with 1SA, 1SB, 1SR.		
A95	Front Reclining Bucket Seats (X-Cab)	232	270
	Includes inboard armrests, dual adjustable headrests, left hand power lumbar, easy entry feature and overhead console. NOT AVAILABLE with 1SA, 1SB, 1SR.		
AE7	60/40 Reclining Split-Bench Seat (Crew Cab)	86	100
	Includes 3-passenger adjustable split back rear bench seat. REQUIRES 1SC. NOT AVAILABLE with A95, 1SA, 1SB. INCLUDED in 1SD, 1SH.		
AE7	60/40 Reclining Split-Bench Seat (Reg Cab)	150	174
	REQUIRES 1SC. NOT AVAILABLE with A95, 1SA, 1SB. INCLUDED in 1SD, 1SH.		
AG9	6-Way Power Driver's Seat Adjuster (Crew Cab)	206	240
	REQUIRES A95, 1SC. INCLUDED in 1SD, 1SH.		
AG9	6-Way Power Driver's Seat Adjuster (Reg Cab/X-Cab)	206	240
	REQUIRES 1SC and (~~D or A95). INCLUDED in 1SD, 1SH.		
AJ1	Deep Tinted Glass (Crew Cab)	185	215
	Excludes tinted glass on windshield, driver's and front passenger's windows. NOT AVAILABLE with A28.		
AJ1	Deep Tinted Glass (Crew Cab)	155	180
	Excludes tinted glass on windshield, driver's and front passenger's windows. Includes light tinted rear window.		
AJ1	Deep Tinted Glass (Reg Cab)	30	35
	Excludes tinted glass on windshield, driver's and front passenger's windows.		
AJ1	Deep Tinted Glass (X-Cab)	92	107
	Excludes tinted glass on windshield, driver's and front passenger's windows. NOT AVAILABLE with C49.		
AJ1	Deep Tinted Glass (X-Cab)	62	72
	Includes light tinted rear window and excludes tinted glass on windshield and driver's and front passenger's windows. REQUIRES 1SC or 1SD or 1SH.		
AU0	Remote Keyless Entry System	129	150
	Includes 2 transmitters. REQUIRES 1SC. INCLUDED in 1SD, 1SH.		

CODE	DESCRIPTION	INVOICE	MSRP
AU3	Power Door Locks (Crew Cab) *REQUIRES 1SA or 1SB or 1SR.*	192	223
AU3	Power Door Locks (Reg Cab/X-Cab) *REQUIRES 1SA or 1SB or 1SR.*	134	156
B30	Full Floor Color-Keyed Carpeting (Reg Cab) *Includes vinyl floor mats. REQUIRES 1SA or 1SB or 1SR.*	47	55
B30	Full Floor Color-Keyed Carpeting (X-Cab) *Includes front mats only. REQUIRES 1SA or 1SB or 1SR.*	61	71
B30	Full Floor Color-Keyed Carpeting (X-Cab) *Includes vinyl floor mats. REQUIRES 1SA or 1SB or 1SR. NOT AVAILABLE with YG4.*	75	87
B85	Bright Exterior Moldings (2WD - Reg Cab/X-Cab) *Includes wheel opening and body side moldings. REQUIRES 1SA or 1SB or 1SR.*	92	107
B85	Bright Exterior Moldings (4WD - Reg Cab/X-Cab) *Includes wheel opening and body side moldings. REQUIRES 1SA or 1SB or 1SR.*	65	76
BG9	Color-Keyed Rubber Floor Covering (Reg Cab) *Replaces carpet and floor mats. REQUIRES 1SC or 1SD or 1SH.*	(30)	(35)
BG9	Color-Keyed Rubber Floor Covering (X-Cab) *Replaces carpet and floor mats. REQUIRES 1SC or 1SD or 1SH.*	(44)	(51)
BZY	Black Bedliner Insert (Crew Cab)	194	225
BZY	Black Bedliner Insert (Reg Cab/X-Cab) *NOT AVAILABLE with KL6.*	194	225
C49	Electric Rear Window Defogger (X-Cab/Crew Cab) *REQUIRES 1SC or 1SD or 1SH. NOT AVAILABLE with A28.*	150	175
C60	Air Conditioning *REQUIRES 1SA. NOT AVAILABLE with YG6. INCLUDED in 1SB, 1SR, 1SC, 1SD, 1SH.*	692	805
DD7	Electrochromic Inside Mirror *Includes light-sensitive rear view mirror. REQUIRES 1SC or 1SD or 1SH.*	125	145
DF2	Camper Type Exterior Mirrors *7.5"W x 10.5"H stainless steel. Adjustable arm feature to provide field of vision for vehicles to 96" wide. REQUIRES 1SC or 1SD or 1SH.*	(39)	(45)
DF2	Camper Type Exterior Mirrors *7.5"W x 10.5"H stainless steel. Adjustable arm feature to provide field of vision for vehicles to 96" wide. Shipped loose for dealer installation. NOT AVAILABLE with 1SC, 1SD, 1SH.*	46	53
EF1	Rear Bumper Delete (Reg Cab/X-Cab) *Vehicles registered in certain states must have a rear bumper to be operated on their roads. Consult your local laws. NOT AVAILABLE with 1SC, 1SD, 1SH, Z82, VB3.*	(112)	(130)
EF1	Rear Bumper Delete (Reg Cab/X-Cab) *Vehicles registered in certain states must have a rear bumper to be operated on their roads. Consult your local laws. REQUIRES 1SC or 1SD or 1SH. NOT AVAILABLE with Z82.*	(172)	(200)
F60	HD Front Springs (4WD - Reg Cab/X-Cab)	54	63
G80	Locking Rear Differential	245	285
GT5	4.10 Axle Ratio *NOT AVAILABLE with KL6.*	NC	NC

CODE	DESCRIPTION	INVOICE	MSRP
K47	High Capacity Air Cleaner	22	25
KL5	Conversion Ready Engine (Reg Cab/X-Cab) *Includes internal modifications for operation of natural or propane gas. REQUIRES MT1. NOT AVAILABLE with Z81, L29, L65.*	108	125
KL6	Natural Gas Fuel System (Bi-Fuel) (Reg Cab) *Natural gas and gasoline capable. REQUIRES MT1. NOT AVAILABLE with L29, L65, GT5, Z81, BZY.*	4988	5800
L29	Engine: Vortec 7400 V8 SFI *NOT AVAILABLE with Z81, KL5, L65, KL6, VYU. INCLUDED in 1SH.*	516	600
L65	Engine: 6.5L V8 Turbo Diesel (Reg Cab/X-Cab) *Includes hydraulic brakes, extra sound insulation, glow plugs, integral two stage fuel filter, fuel and water separator with instrument panel warning light and fuel filter change signal, dual batteries, HD radiator, engine oil cooler and engine block heater. NOT AVAILABLE with Z81, KL5, TP2, V10, L29, KL6, 1SR, VYU.*	2460	2860
MT1	Transmission: 4-Speed Automatic with Overdrive (Reg Cab/X-Cab) *Includes HD auxiliary transmission cooling. INCLUDED in 1SR, 1SH.*	942	1095
MW3	Transmission: 5-Speed Manual with Overdrive (Crew Cab) *Includes auxiliary transmission cooler delete. REQUIRES L29. NOT AVAILABLE with UP0, NP1.*	(942)	(1095)
NP1	Electronic Shift Transfer Case (4WD) *REQUIRES MT1. NOT AVAILABLE with MW3.*	129	150
NZZ	Off-Road Skid Plates (4WD) *Includes differential and transfer case shields.*	82	95
P06	Bright Trim Rings and Hub Caps *REQUIRES 1SA or 1SB.*	52	60
R6M	New Jersey Cost Surcharge	74	NC
R9Q	Bright Appearance Group (2WD - Reg Cab/X-Cab) *Includes deluxe front appearance package: color-keyed grille, composite halogen headlamps, chrome front bumper with rub strip; chrome rear step bumper with rub strip, bright exterior moldings, bright trim rings and hub caps. REQUIRES 1SA or 1SB. INCLUDED in 1SR.*	415	483
R9Q	Bright Appearance Group (4WD - Reg Cab/X-Cab) *Includes deluxe front appearance package: color-keyed grille, composite halogen headlamps, chrome front bumper with rub strip; chrome rear step bumper with rub strip, bright exterior moldings, bright trim rings and hub caps. REQUIRES 1SA or 1SB. INCLUDED in 1SR.*	389	452
R9R	Bright Appearance Group Discount (Reg Cab/X-Cab) *REQUIRES R9Q. NOT AVAILABLE with 1SR.*	(172)	(200)
TP2	HD 600-CCA Auxiliary Battery *NOT AVAILABLE with L65, Z81.*	115	134
U01	Roof Marker Lamps (5)	47	55
UL0	Radio: AM/FM Stereo with Cassette *Includes clock, ETR AM/ FM stereo, speed sensitive volume, theft lock, auto tone control, auto reverse, music search and an enhanced performance 6-speaker system. REQUIRES 1SC. NOT AVAILABLE with UN0, UP0. INCLUDED in 1SD, 1SH.*	77	90

CODE	DESCRIPTION	INVOICE	MSRP
UL5	Radio Delete *Includes front fender hole plugs and instrument panel storage bin. REQUIRES 1SA. NOT AVAILABLE with 1SB, 1SR.*	(247)	(287)
UM6	Radio: AM/FM Stereo with Cassette *Includes clock and ETR AM/FM stereo with 4 speakers. REQUIRES 1SA. NOT AVAILABLE with UL5. INCLUDED in 1SB, 1SR, 1SC, 1SH.*	126	147
UN0	Radio: AM/FM Stereo with CD *Includes ETR AM/FM stereo, clock, speed sensitive volume, theft lock, auto tone control and enhanced performance 6-speaker system. REQUIRES 1SC or 1SD or 1SH. NOT AVAILABLE with UL0, UP0.*	163	190
UP0	Radio: AM/FM Stereo with CD and Cassette (Crew Cab) *Includes ETR AM/FM stereo, clock, speed sensitive volume, theft lock, auto tone control, auto reverse/music search cassette and enhanced performance 6-speaker system. REQUIRES 1SC or 1SD or 1SH. NOT AVAILABLE with UL0, UN0, MW3.*	249	290
UP0	Radio: AM/FM Stereo with CD and Cassette (Reg Cab/X-Cab) *Includes ETR AM/FM stereo, clock, speed sensitive volume, theft lock, auto tone control, auto reverse/music search cassette and enhanced performance 6-speaker system. REQUIRES MT1 and (1SC or 1SD) or 1SH. NOT AVAILABLE with UN0, UL0.*	249	290
V10	Cold Climate Package *Includes special insulation and engine block heater. NOT AVAILABLE with L65, Z81.*	28	33
V22	Deluxe Front Appearance Package *Includes dual horns, color-keyed grille and composite halogen headlamps. REQUIRES 1SA or 1SB.*	164	191
V76	Tow Hooks (2WD)	33	38
VB3	Chrome Rear Step Bumper with Rub Strip (Reg Cab/X-Cab) *Includes step pad. REQUIRES VG3 and (1SA or 1SB). NOT AVAILABLE with EF1.*	85	99
VB3	Chromed Rear Step Bumper with Step Pad (Crew Cab) *REQUIRES 1SA or 1SB.*	85	99
VG3	Chrome Front Bumper with Rub Strip (Reg Cab/X-Cab) *Includes black bumper guards with diesel engines. REQUIRES 1SA or 1SB.*	22	26
VYU	Snow Plow Prep Package *Includes HD front springs and HD power steering cooler. NOT AVAILABLE with L29, L65.*	101	118
XGK	Tires: Front LT245/75R16E On-Off Road (4WD - Reg Cab/X-Cab) *REQUIRES YGK.*	19	23
YG4	Rear Seat Delete (X-Cab) *REQUIRES 1SA or 1SB. NOT AVAILABLE with B30, A95, ~~D.*	(374)	(435)
YG6	Air Conditioning Not Desired *REQUIRES 1SA. NOT AVAILABLE with C60, 1SR.*	NC	NC
YGK	Tires: Rear LT245/75R16E AT BSW *REQUIRES ZGK.*	19	23
Z81	Camper Equipment Package (Reg Cab/X-Cab) *Includes wiring harness and camper type exterior mirrors. REQUIRES 1SA or 1SB. NOT AVAILABLE with L29, KL5, TP2, V10, KL6.*	85	99

CODE	DESCRIPTION	INVOICE	MSRP
Z81	Camper Equipment Package (Reg Cab/X-Cab) *Includes wiring harness and camper type exterior mirrors. REQUIRES 1SC or 1SD or 1SH. NOT AVAILABLE with L29, KL5, V10, TP2, KL6.*	NC	NC
Z81	Camper Equipment Package *Includes wiring harness, HD auxiliary battery and camper type exterior mirrors. REQUIRES 1SA or 1SB. NOT AVAILABLE with L65, KL6.*	200	233
Z81	Camper Equipment Package *Includes wiring harness, HD auxiliary battery and camper type exterior mirrors. REQUIRES 1SC or 1SD or 1SH. NOT AVAILABLE with L65, KL6.*	116	135
Z82	HD Trailering Equipment *NOT AVAILABLE with EF1.*	141	164
ZGK	Tire: Spare LT245/75R16E AT BSW *REQUIRES XGK and YGK.*	9	11
ZQ3	Convenience Package *Includes speed control and tilt steering wheel. REQUIRES 1SA. INCLUDED in 1SB, 1SR, 1SC, 1SD, 1SH.*	331	385
~~D	Custom Cloth Seat Trim (Reg Cab/X-Cab) *REQUIRES A95 and 1SC.*	NC	NC
~~D	Custom Cloth Seat Trim *Includes center fold down storage armrest with coin holder, map strap, writing board and LH power lumbar. REQUIRES 1SC. NOT AVAILABLE with A95.*	NC	NC

2000 SIERRA CLASSIC 3500

Standard Equipment

SL 2WD REGULAR CAB SRW LB (5M): 5.7L V8 OHV SMPI 16-valve engine; 5-speed OD manual transmission; 600-amp HD battery; engine oil cooler; 100-amp alternator; rear-wheel drive, power take-off provision, 4.1 axle ratio; stainless steel exhaust; front independent suspension with anti-roll bar, front coil springs, rigid rear axle suspension with rear leaf springs; power re-circulating ball steering with vehicle speed-sensing assist; front disc/rear drum brakes with 4-wheel antilock braking system; 34 gal. capacity fuel tank; side impact bars; trailer harness; front chrome bumper, rear black bumper, rear step; monotone paint; sealed beam halogen headlamps with daytime running lights; additional exterior lights include pickup cargo box light, underhood light; driver's and passenger's manual black folding outside mirrors; front and rear 16" x 6.5" painted styled steel wheels; LT245/75SR16 A/S BSW front and rear tires; underbody mounted full-size steel spare wheel with crankdown; AM/FM stereo, clock, seek-scan, 4 speakers, and fixed antenna; 3 power accessory outlets; instrumentation display includes tachometer, oil pressure gauge, water temperature gauge, volt gauge, trip odometer; warning indicators include battery, lights on, key in ignition, door ajar; ignition disable; tinted windows; variable intermittent front windshield wipers, sun visor strip; seating capacity of 3, bench front seat, adjustable headrests, driver's seat includes 2-way direction control, passenger's seat includes 2-way direction control; front height adjustable seatbelts; vinyl seats, full cloth headliner, full vinyl floor covering, plastic/rubber gear shift knob, cabback insulator; interior lights include dome light, front reading lights; sport steering wheel; passenger's side vanity mirror; day/night rearview mirror; glove box with light, front cupholder, dashboard storage, driver's and passenger's door bins; argent grille, black side window moldings, black front windshield molding, black rear window molding and black door handles.

CODE	DESCRIPTION	INVOICE	MSRP

SL 2WD EXTENDED CAB DRW LB (5M) (in addition to or instead of CLASSIC SL 2WD REGULAR CAB SRW LB (5M) equipment): Additional exterior lights include cab clearance lights; front and rear 16" x 6" painted steel wheels; LT225/75SR16 A/S BSW front and rear tires; rear heat ducts; vented rear windows; seating capacity of 6, 60-40 split-bench front seat, adjustable headrests, driver's seat includes 4-way direction control, easy entry, passenger's seat includes 4-way direction control, easy entry and full folding rear bench seat with adjustable headrests.

SL 2WD CREW CAB DRW SB (5M) (in addition to or instead of SL 2WD EXTENDED CAB DRW LB (5M) equipment): 7.4L V8 OHV SMPI 16-valve engine; 26 gal. capacity fuel tank; chrome bumper insert; manual front and rear windows; child safety rear door locks, bench front seat, adjustable headrests, driver's seat includes 2-way direction control, passenger's seat includes 2-way direction control; full folding rear bench seat with reclining adjustable headrests and rear door bins.

SL 2WD CREW CAB SRW LB (5M) (in addition to or instead of SL 2WD CREW CAB DRW SB (5M) equipment): 5.7L V8 OHV SMPI 16-valve engine; chrome wheel well molding; front and rear 16" x 6.5" painted styled steel wheels; LT245/75SR16 A/S BSW front and rear tires; rear heat ducts; manual front and rear windows; seating capacity of 6; full folding rear bench seat with reclining adjustable headrests and rear door bins.

4WD (in addition to or instead of 2WD equipment): Part-time 4-wheel drive, auto locking hub control and manual shift; front independent torsion suspension with HD anti-roll bar, front torsion springs, front torsion bar, front tow hooks and black fender flares.

Base Prices

TC30903-E63	SL 2WD Regular Cab SRW LB (5M)	17556	20065
TC30953-E63	SL 2WD Extended Cab DRW LB (5M)	20642	23591
TC30743	SL 2WD Crew Cab DRW SB (5M)	21766	24875
TC30943-E63	SL 2WD Crew Cab SRW LB (5M)	20470	23395
TK30903-E63	SL 4WD Regular Cab SRW LB (5M)	20181	23065
TK30953-E63	SL 4WD Extended Cab DRW LB (5M)	23014	26302
TK30743	SL 4WD Crew Cab DRW SB (5M)	24543	28049
TK30943-E63	SL 4WD Crew Cab SRW LB (5M)	23247	26569
Destination Charge:		665	665

Accessories

—	Cloth Seat Trim (Reg Cab/X-Cab) *REQUIRES 1SA or 1SB. NOT AVAILABLE with A95.*	NC	NC
—	Custom Cloth Seat Trim (Reg Cab/X-Cab) *Includes dual adjustable headrests, inboard armrests, driver's power lumbar and storage pocket behind seats. REQUIRES 1SC. NOT AVAILABLE with AE7.*	NC	NC
—	Custom Cloth Seat Trim *Includes center fold down storage armrest, driver's power lumbar and storage pocket behind seats. REQUIRES 1SC. NOT AVAILABLE with A95.*	NC	NC
1SA	Marketing Option Package 1SA *Includes vehicle with standard equipment. REQUIRES YG6.*	NC	NC
1SB	Marketing Option Package 1SB (Crew Cab) *Includes air conditioning, AM/FM stereo with cassette and seek/scan, tilt wheel and speed control. NOT AVAILABLE with YG6.*	692	805

CODE	DESCRIPTION	INVOICE	MSRP
1SB	**Marketing Option Package 1SB (Reg Cab/X-Cab)**	1150	1337
	Manufacturer Discount	(430)	(500)
	Net Price	720	837
	Includes air conditioning, AM/FM stereo with cassette and seek/scan, tilt wheel and speed control. NOT AVAILABLE with YG6.		
1SC	**Marketing Option Package 1SC (Crew Cab)**	3156	3670
	Includes SLE Decor package: air conditioning, bright appearance package: color-keyed grille, composite halogen headlamps, dual horns, front and rear chrome bumpers, bright exterior moldings, bright wheel trim; tilt wheel, speed control, AM/FM stereo with cassette, power door locks, power windows, leather-wrappped steering wheel, color keyed carpet, composite halogen headlamps, power remote folding mirrors and bright trim rings and hub caps.		
1SC	**Marketing Option Package 1SC (Reg Cab/X-Cab)**	2611	3036
	Manufacturer Discount	(645)	(750)
	Net Price	1966	2286
	Includes SLE Decor package: air conditioning, bright appearance package: color-keyed grille, composite halogen headlamps, dual horns, front and rear chrome bumpers, bright exterior moldings, bright wheel trim; tilt wheel, speed control, AM/FM stereo with cassette, power door locks, power windows, leather-wrappped steering wheel, color keyed carpet, composite halogen headlamps, power remote folding mirrors and bright trim rings and hub caps.		
1SD	**Marketing Option Package 1SD (Crew Cab)**	4601	5350
	Includes SLT Decor package: air conditioning, bright appearance package: color-keyed grille, composite halogen headlamps, dual horns, front and rear chrome bumpers, bright exterior moldings, bright wheel trim; tilt wheel, speed control, AM/FM stereo with cassette, seek/scan and 6 speakers, power door locks, power windows, leather-wrappped steering wheel, color keyed carpet, composite halogen headlamps, power remote folding mirrors, bright trim rings and hub caps, front 60/40 reclining split bench seat, ultra soft leather seat trim, center fold down storage armrest, driver's power lumbar, storage pocket behind seats and remote keyless entry system. REQUIRES L29 or L65 or MT1.		
1SD	**Marketing Option Package 1SD (Reg Cab)**	3827	4450
	Manufacturer Discount	(645)	(750)
	Net Price	3182	3700
	Includes SLT Decor package: air conditioning, bright appearance package: color-keyed grille, composite halogen headlamps, dual horns, front and rear chrome bumpers, bright exterior moldings, bright wheel trim; tilt wheel, speed control, AM/FM stereo with cassette, seek/scan and 6 speakers, power door locks, power windows, leather-wrappped steering wheel, color keyed carpet, composite halogen headlamps, power remote folding mirrors, bright trim rings and hub caps, front 60/40 reclining split bench seat, ultra soft leather seat trim, center fold down storage armrest, driver's power lumbar, storage pocket behind seats and remote keyless entry system. REQUIRES MT1 or L29 or L65.		

CODE	DESCRIPTION	INVOICE	MSRP
1SD	Marketing Option Package 1SD (X-Cab)	3884	4516
	Manufacturer Discount	(645)	(750)
	Net Price	3239	3766
	Includes SLT Decor package: air conditioning, bright appearance package: color-keyed grille, composite halogen headlamps, dual horns, front and rear chrome bumpers, bright exterior moldings, bright wheel trim; tilt wheel, speed control, AM/FM stereo with cassette, seek/scan and 6 speakers, power door locks, power windows, leather-wrappped steering wheel, color keyed carpet, composite halogen headlamps, power remote folding mirrors, bright trim rings and hub caps, front 60/40 reclining split bench seat, ultra soft leather seat trim, center fold down storage armrest, driver's power lumbar, storage pocket behind seats and remote keyless entry system. REQUIRES MT1 or L29 or L65.		
1SK	Marketing Option Package 1SK Turbomax (X-Cab)	6012	6991
	Manufacturer Discount	(645)	(750)
	Net Price	5367	6241
	Includes SLE Decor package: air conditioning, bright appearance package: color-keyed grille, composite halogen headlamps, dual horns, front and rear chrome bumpers, bright exterior moldings, bright wheel trim; tilt wheel, speed control, AM/FM stereo with cassette, power door locks, power windows, leather-wrappped steering wheel, color keyed carpet, composite halogen headlamps, power remote folding mirrors, bright trim rings and hub caps, gvwr: 10,000 lbs, dual rear wheels, engine: 6.5L V8 turbo diesel, dual batteries, HD radiator, engine oil cooler, extra sound insulation, engine block heater, transmission: 4-speed automatic with overdrive and external transmission cooling. NOT AVAILABLE with KL5, V10.		
1SK	Marketing Option Package 1SK Turbomax (X-Cab)	7285	8471
	Manufacturer Discount	(645)	(750)
	Net Price	6640	7721
	Includes SLT Decor package: air conditioning, bright appearance package: color-keyed grille, composite halogen headlamps, dual horns, front and rear chrome bumpers, bright exterior moldings, bright wheel trim; tilt wheel, speed control, AM/FM stereo with cassette, seek/scan and 6 speakers, power door locks, power windows, leather-wrappped steering wheel, color keyed carpet, composite halogen headlamps, power remote folding mirrors, bright trim rings and hub caps, front 60/40 reclining split bench seat, ultra soft leather seat trim, center fold down storage armrest, driver's power lumbar, storage pocket behind seats, remote keyless entry system; gvwr: 10,000 lbs, dual rear wheels, engine: 6.5L V8 turbo diesel, dual batteries, transmission: 4-speed automatic with overdrive, HD radiator, engine oil cooler, extra sound insulation and engine block heater. NOT AVAILABLE with KL5, V10.		
A28	Sliding Rear Window	99	115
	NOT AVAILABLE with C49.		
A95	Front Reclining Bucket Seats (Crew Cab)	364	423
	Includes 3-passenger adjustable split back rear bench seats. NOT-AVAILABLE with AE7, 1SA, 1SB.		
A95	Front Reclining Bucket Seats (Reg Cab)	332	386
	Includes floor console. REQUIRES 1SC. NOT AVAILABLE with AE7.		
A95	Front Reclining Bucket Seats (X-Cab)	232	270
	Includes overhead console. NOT AVAILABLE with 1SA or 1SB.		

CODE	DESCRIPTION	INVOICE	MSRP
AE7	**Front 60/40 Reclining Split Bench Seat (2WD Reg Cab)** *NOT AVAILABLE with A95, L65. REQUIRES 1SC. INCLUDED in 1SD, 1SK.*	150	174
AE7	**Front 60/40 Reclining Split Bench Seat (Crew Cab)** *Includes 3-passenger adjustable split back rear bench seat. REQUIRES 1SC. NOT AVAILABLE with A95. INCLUDED in 1SD, 1SK.*	86	100
AG9	**6-Way Power Seat Adjuster (X-Cab/Crew Cab)** *Driver's side only. REQUIRES 1SC and (A95 or AE7). INCLUDED in 1SD, 1SK.*	206	240
AJ1	**Deep Tinted Glass (Crew Cab)** *Excludes tinted glass on windshield, driver's and passenger's windows. NOT AVAILABLE with A28.*	185	215
AJ1	**Deep Tinted Glass (Crew Cab)** *Excludes tinted glass on windshield, driver's and passenger's windows. Includes light tinted rear window.*	155	180
AJ1	**Deep Tinted Glass (Reg Cab)** *Excludes tinted glass on windshield, driver's and passenger's windows.*	30	35
AJ1	**Deep Tinted Glass (X-Cab)** *Excludes tinted glass on windshield, driver's and passenger's windows. NOT AVAILABLE with C49.*	92	107
AJ1	**Deep Tinted Glass (X-Cab)** *Excludes tinted glass on windshield, driver's and passenger's windows. Includes light tinted rear window. NOT AVAILABLE with 1SA or 1SB.*	62	72
AU0	**Remote Keyless Entry System** *Includes 2 transmitters. REQUIRES 1SC. INCLUDED in 1SD, 1SK.*	129	150
AU3	**Power Door Locks (Crew Cab)** *REQUIRES 1SA or 1SB.*	192	223
AU3	**Power Door Locks (Reg Cab/X-Cab)** *REQUIRES 1SA or 1SB.*	134	156
B30	**Full Floor Color-Keyed Carpeting (Reg Cab)** *Includes vinyl floor mats. REQUIRES 1SA or 1SB.*	47	55
B30	**Full Floor Color-Keyed Carpeting (X-Cab)** *Includes front vinyl floor mats only. REQUIRES 1SA or 1SB.*	61	71
B30	**Full Floor Color-Keyed Carpeting (X-Cab)** *Includes vinyl floor mats. REQUIRES 1SA or 1SB. NOT AVAILABLE with YG4.*	75	87
B85	**Bright Exterior Moldings (2WD Reg Cab)** *Includes body side moldings and wheel opening moldings. REQUIRES 1SA or 1SB. NOT AVAILABLE with R05.*	92	107
B85	**Bright Exterior Moldings (4WD Reg Cab)** *Includes body side moldings. REQUIRES 1SA or 1SB. NOT AVAILABLE with R05.*	65	76
BG9	**Color-Keyed Rubber Floor Covering (Reg Cab)** *Replaces carpet and floor mats. NOT AVAILABLE with 1SA or 1SB.*	(30)	(35)
BG9	**Color-Keyed Rubber Floor Covering (X-Cab)** *Replaces carpet and floor mats. NOT AVAILABLE with 1SA or 1SB.*	(44)	(51)
BZY	**Black Insert Bedliner** *NOT AVAILABLE with ZW9.*	194	225
C49	**Electric Rear Window Defogger** *NOT AVAILABLE with A28, AJ1.*	150	175

CODE	DESCRIPTION	INVOICE	MSRP
C60	Air Conditioning *NOT AVAILABLE with YG6. REQUIRES 1SA. INCLUDED in 1SB, 1SC, 1SD, 1SK.*	692	805
C6Y	GVWR: 9,600 Lbs (2WD Crew Cab LB) *Includes 4100 lbs front and 6084 lbs rear GAWR. REQUIRES Z81. NOT AVAILABLE with HC4, C7A, R05, ZW9.*	NC	NC
C7A	GVWR: 10,000 Lbs (All Except Crew Cab SB) *Includes 3600 lbs front and 7500 lbs rear GAWR. REQUIRES R05. NOT AVAILABLE with C6Y, Z81. INCLUDED in 1SK.*	NC	NC
DD7	Electrochromic Inside Mirror (Reg Cab/X-Cab) *Includes light-sensitive rear view mirror and 8-point compass. NOT AVAILABLE with 1SA or 1SB.*	125	145
DF2	Camper Type Exterior Mirrors *7.5" W x 10.5" H stainless steel. Adjustable arm feature to provide field of vision for vehicles to 96" wide. NOT AVAILABLE with 1SA or 1SB.*	(39)	(45)
DF2	Camper Type Exterior Mirrors *7.5" W x 10.5" H stainless steel. Adjustable arm feature to provide field of vision for vehicles to 96" wide. REQUIRES 1SA or 1SB.*	46	53
EF1	Rear Bumper Delete (Reg Cab/X-Cab) *Vehicles registered in certain states MUST have a rear bumper to be operated on their roads. Consult your local laws. REQUIRES 1SA or 1SB. NOT AVAILABLE with Z82, R9Q.*	(112)	(130)
EF1	Rear Bumper Delete *Vehicles registered in certain states MUST have a rear bumper to be operated on their roads. Consult your local laws. NOT AVAILABLE with 1SA, 1SB, Z82, ZW9.*	(172)	(200)
F60	HD Front Springs (4WD)	54	63
G80	Locking Rear Differential	245	285
HC4	4.56 Rear Axle Ratio *REQUIRES (MT1 and G80 and C7A) or (L29 and G80 and C7A). NOT AVAILABLE with L65, C6Y.*	NC	NC
K47	High Capacity Air Cleaner	22	25
KL5	Conversion Ready Engine (Reg Cab/X-Cab) *Internal modifications for operation of natural or propane gas. REQUIRES MT1. NOT AVAILABLE with L29, L65, 1SK.*	108	125
KL6	Natural Gas Fuel System (Bi-Fuel) (4WD Crew Cab SRW LB) *Includes CNG horsepower of 215 @ 4800 rpm and torque of 285 @ 2800 rpm, maximum trailer weight: 8,300 lbs, 13 gallon cng fuel tank, payload: 2695 lbs. REQUIRES MT1. NOT AVAILABLE with L29, L65, BZY, HC4.*	4988	5800
L29	Engine: Vortec 7400 V8 SFI (All Except Crew Cab SB) *NOT AVAILABLE with KL5, Z81, VYU.*	516	600
L65	Engine: 6.5L V8 Turbo Diesel (All Except Crew Cab SB) *Includes hydraulic brakes, glow plugs, integral two stage fuel filter, fuel and water separator with instrument panel warning light and fuel filter change signal, dual batteries, HD radiator, engine oil cooler, extra sound insulation and engine block heater. NOT AVAILABLE with HC4, KL5, TP2, V10, AE7, VYU. INCLUDED in 1SK.*	2460	2860
MT1	Transmission: 4-Speed Automatic with Overdrive *Includes external transmission cooling. INCLUDED in 1SK.*	942	1095

CODE	DESCRIPTION	INVOICE	MSRP
NZZ	**Off-Road Skid Plates (4WD)** *Includes differential and transfer case shields.*	82	95
P06	**Four Trim Rings and Hub Caps** *Bright metal. REQUIRES 1SA or 1SB.*	52	60
R05	**Dual Rear Wheels (Crew Cab LB)** *REQUIRES C7A. NOT AVAILABLE with C6Y, YGK, ZGK, U01, XGK. INCLUDED in 1SK.*	737	857
R05	**Dual Rear Wheels (Reg Cab)** *REQUIRES (C7A and XHP and (YHP or YHR) and (ZHP or ZHR)) or (C7A and XYK and YYK and ZYK) or XHR or (XYL and YYL and ZYL). NOT AVAILABLE with YGK, ZGK, B85, R9Q, U01, XGK. INCLUDED in 1SK.*	821	955
R6M	**New Jersey Cost Surcharge (Crew Cab)**	127	NC
R6M	**New Jersey Cost Surcharge**	74	NC
R9Q	**Bright Appearance Group (2WD Reg Cab)** *Includes deluxe front appearance package: color-keyed grille, composite halogen headlamps, chromed front bumper with rub strip; chromed rear bumper with step pad, bright exterior moldings and four trim rings and hub caps. REQUIRES 1SA or 1SB. NOT AVAILABLE with R05, EF1.*	415	483
R9Q	**Bright Appearance Group (Reg Cab 4WD)** *Includes deluxe front appearance package: color-keyed grille, composite halogen headlamps, chromed front bumper with rub strip; chromed rear bumper with step pad, bright exterior moldings and four trim rings and hub caps. REQUIRES 1SA or 1SB. NOT AVAILABLE with R05, EF1.*	389	452
R9Q	**Bright Appearance Group (Reg Cab/X-Cab)** *Includes deluxe front appearance package: color-keyed grille, composite halogen headlamps, chromed front bumper with rub strip; chromed rear bumper with step pad and four trim rings and hub caps. REQUIRES R05 and (1SA or 1SB). NOT AVAILABLE with EF1.*	323	376
R9R	**Bright Appearance Group Discount (Reg Cab/X-Cab)** *REQUIRES R9Q.*	(172)	(200)
TP2	**600 CCA Auxiliary HD Battery** *NOT AVAILABLE with L65.*	115	134
U01	**Five Roof Marker Lamps (Reg Cab/Crew Cab LB)** *NOT AVAILABLE with R05.*	47	55
UL0	**Radio: AM/FM Stereo with Cassette** *Includes clock, speed sensitive volume, theft lock, auto tone control, auto reverse and music search cassette player and enhanced performance 6-speaker system. REQUIRES 1SC. NOT AVAILABLE with UN0, UP0. INCLUDED in 1SD, 1SK.*	77	90
UL5	**Radio Delete** *Includes front fender hole plugs and instrument panel storage bin. REQUIRES 1SA. NOT AVAILABLE with UM6.*	(247)	(287)
UM6	**Radio: AM/FM Stereo with Cassette (All Except Crew Cab LB)** *Includes clock and 4 speakers. NOT AVAILABLE with UL5. REQUIRES 1SA. INCLUDED in 1SB, 1SC, 1SK.*	126	147
UM6	**Radio: AM/FM Stereo with Cassette (Crew Cab LB)** *Includes clock and 4 speakers. NOT AVAILABLE with UL5. REQUIRES 1SA. INCLUDED in 1SB, 1SC, 1SK.*	126	147

CODE	DESCRIPTION	INVOICE	MSRP
UN0	Radio: AM/FM Stereo with CD (All Except Crew Cab LB) *Includes clock, speed sensitive volume, theft lock, auto tone control and enhanced performance 6-speaker system. NOT AVAILABLE with UP0.*	163	190
UN0	Radio: AM/FM Stereo with CD (Crew Cab LB) *Includes clock, speed sensitive volume, theft lock, auto tone control and enhanced performance 6-speaker system. NOT AVAILABLE with UP0, 1SA, 1SB.*	163	190
UP0	Radio: AM/FM Stereo with CD and Cassette (All Except Crew Cab LB) *Includes clock, speed sensitive volume, theft lock, seek-scan, auto tone control, auto reverse and music search cassette player and enhanced performance 6-speaker system. REQUIRES MT1. NOT AVAILABLE with UN0, 1SA, 1SB.*	249	290
UP0	Radio: AM/FM Stereo with CD and Cassette (Crew Cab LB) *Includes clock, speed sensitive volume, theft lock, auto tone control, auto reverse and music search cassette player and enhanced performance 6-speaker system. REQUIRES MT1. NOT AVAILABLE with UN0, 1SA or 1SB.*	249	290
V10	Cold Climate Package *Includes special insulation and engine block heater. NOT AVAILABLE with L65, 1SK.*	28	33
V22	Deluxe Front Appearance Package *Includes dual horns, color-keyed grille and composite halogen headlamps. REQUIRES 1SA or 1SB.*	164	191
V76	Tow Hooks (2WD)	33	38
VB3	Chromed Rear Bumper with Step Pad *Includes rub strip. REQUIRES 1SA or 1SB. NOT AVAILABLE with EF1, ZW9.*	85	99
VG3	Chromed Front Bumper with Rub Strip (Reg Cab/X-Cab) *Includes black bumper guards with diesel engine. REQUIRES 1SA or 1SB.*	22	26
VYU	Snow Plow Prep Package (4WD - Reg Cab/X-Cab) *Includes HD front springs and heavy-duty power steering cooler. NOT AVAILABLE with L29, L65.*	101	118
XGK	Tires: Front LT245/75R16E AT BSW (4WD Crew Cab LB) *REQUIRES YGK and ZGK. NOT AVAILABLE with YHP, ZHP, YHR, ZHR, YYK, ZYK, YYL, ZYL, XHP, XHR, XYK, XYL, R05.*	19	23
XGK	Tires: Front LT245/75R16E SBR On-Off Road (4WD Reg Cab) *REQUIRES YGK and ZGK. NOT AVAILABLE with YHP, ZHP, YHR, ZHR, YYK, ZYK, YYL, ZYL, XHP, XHR, XYK, XYL, R05.*	19	23
XHP	Tires: Front LT225/75R16D AS BSW (Crew Cab LB) *REQUIRES R05. NOT AVAILABLE with YGK, ZGK, XYK, YYK, ZYK, YYL, ZYL, XGK, XHR, XYL.*	(58)	(68)
XHP	Tires: Front LT225/75R16D AS BSW SBR (Reg Cab) *REQUIRES R05. NOT AVAILABLE with YYK, YGK, ZGK, ZYK, XYK, XGK, XHR, XYL, YYL, ZYL.*	(58)	(68)
XHR	Tires: Front LT225/75R16D AT BSW (4WD Crew Cab LB) *REQUIRES YHR and ZHR and R05. NOT AVAILABLE with YHP, ZHP, YGK, ZGK, YYK, ZYK, YYL, ZYL, XGK, XHP, XYK, XYL.*	(40)	(46)
XHR	Tires: Front LT225/75R16D SBR On-Off Road (4WD - X-Cab/Crew Cab SB) *REQUIRES YHR and ZHR. NOT AVAILABLE with XYK, XYL, YYK, YYL, ZYK, ZYL.*	19	22
XHR	Tires: Front LT225/75R16D SBR On-Off Road (4WD Reg Cab) *REQUIRES YHR and ZHR and R05. NOT AVAILABLE with YHP, ZHP, YGK, ZGK, YYK, ZYK, YYL, ZYL, XGK, XHP, XYK, XYL.*	(40)	(46)

CODE	DESCRIPTION	INVOICE	MSRP
XYK	Tires: Front LT215/85R16D Highway BSW (Reg Cab/Crew Cab LB) *REQUIRES YYK and ZYK and R05. NOT AVAILABLE with ZHR, XHP, YHP, ZHP, YGK, YHR, ZGK, YYL, ZYL, XGK, XHR, XYL.*	64	74
XYK	Tires: Front LT215/85R16D Highway BSW (X-Cab/Crew Cab SB) *REQUIRES YYK and ZYK. NOT AVAILABLE with YHR, ZHR, XHR, XYL, YYL, ZYL.*	122	142
XYL	Tires: Front LT215/85R16D AT BSW (4WD Crew Cab LB) *REQUIRES YYL and F60 and ZYL and R05. NOT AVAILABLE with XGK, XHP, XHR, XYK, YGK, YHP, YHR, YYK, ZGK, ZHP, ZHR, ZYK.*	112	130
XYL	Tires: Front LT215/85R16D On-Off Road BSW (4WD - X-Cab/Crew Cab SB) *REQUIRES YYL and ZYL and F60. NOT AVAILABLE with XHR, XYK, YHR, YYK, ZHR, ZYK.*	170	198
XYL	Tires: Front LT215/85R16D On-Off Road BSW (4WD Reg Cab) *REQUIRES YYL and ZYL and F60 and R05. NOT AVAILABLE with XGK, XHP, XHR, XYK, YGK, YHP, YHR, YYK, ZGK, ZHP, ZHR, ZYK.*	112	130
YG4	Rear Seat Delete (X-Cab) *REQUIRES 1SA or 1SB. NOT AVAILABLE with A95.*	(374)	(435)
YG6	Air Conditioning Not Desired *REQUIRES 1SA.*	NC	NC
YGK	Tires: Rear LT245/75R16E SBR On-Off Road (Reg Cab/Crew Cab LB) *REQUIRES ZGK or XGK. NOT AVAILABLE with XHP, XYK, YHP, YHR, YYK, ZHR, ZHP, ZYK, R05, XHR, XYL, YYL, ZYL.*	19	23
YHP	Tires: Rear LT225/75R16D AS BSW (Crew Cab LB) *REQUIRES XHP and R05 and ZHP. NOT AVAILABLE with YGK, ZGK, YHR, ZHR, XYK, YYK, ZYK, YYL, ZYL, XGK, XHR, XYL.*	370	430
YHP	Tires: Rear LT225/75R16D AS BSW SBR (Reg Cab) *REQUIRES XHP and ZHP and R05. NOT AVAILABLE with YHR, YGK, YYK, ZHR, ZGK, XYK, ZYK, YYL, ZYL, XGK, XHR, XYL.*	370	430
YHR	Tires: Rear LT225/75R16D SBR On-Off Road (Reg Cab/Crew Cab LB) *REQUIRES ZHR and R05 or XHR. NOT AVAILABLE with YHP, YGK, YYK, ZHP, XYK, ZGK, ZYK, YYL, XGK, XYL, ZYL.*	408	474
YHR	Tires: Rear LT225/75R16D SBR On-Off Road (X-Cab/Crew Cab SB) *REQUIRES ZHR or XHR. NOT AVAILABLE with YYK, XYK, ZYK, XYL, YYL, ZYL.*	38	44
YYK	Tires: Rear LT215/85R16/D BSW Highway (2WD X-Cab) *REQUIRES ZYK and XYK. NOT AVAILABLE with YHR, ZHR.*	244	284
YYK	Tires: Rear LT215/85R16/D BSW Highway (Reg Cab/Crew Cab LB) *REQUIRES XYK and ZYK and R05. NOT AVAILABLE with XHP, YHP, YHR, YGK, ZHR, ZHP, ZGK, YYL, ZYL, XGK, XHR, XYL.*	614	714
YYK	Tires: Rear LT215/85R16D Highway BSW (4WD Reg Cab) *REQUIRES XYK and ZYK and R05. NOT AVAILABLE with YHP, YHR, YGK, YYL, ZHR, ZHP, ZGK, ZYL, XGK, XHP, XHR, XYL.*	614	714
YYK	Tires: Rear LT215/85R16D Highway BSW (4WD X-Cab/Crew Cab SB) *REQUIRES XYK and ZYK. NOT AVAILABLE with XHR, XYL, YHR, YYL, ZHR, ZYL.*	244	284
YYL	Tires: Rear LT215/85R16D AT BSW (4WD Crew Cab LB) *REQUIRES XYL and R05 and ZYL. NOT AVAILABLE with XGK, XHP, XHR, XYK, YGK, YHP, YHR, YYK, ZGK, ZHP, ZHR, ZYK.*	710	826

CODE	DESCRIPTION	INVOICE	MSRP
YYL	Tires: Rear LT215/85R16D On-Off Road BSW (4WD - X-Cab/Crew Cab SB) *REQUIRES F60 and XYL and ZYL. NOT AVAILABLE with XHR, XYK, YHR, YYK, ZHR, ZYK.*	341	396
YYL	Tires: Rear LT215/85R16D On-Off Road BSW (4WD Reg Cab) *REQUIRES XYL and F60 and ZYL and R05. NOT AVAILABLE with XGK, XHP, XHR, XYK, YGK, YHP, YHR, YYK, ZGK, ZHP, ZHR, ZYK.*	710	826
Z81	Camper Equipment Package *Includes wiring harness and camper type exterior mirrors. REQUIRES C6Y and (1SA or 1SB). NOT AVAILABLE with C7A, ZW9, L29.*	85	99
Z81	Camper Equipment Package *Includes wiring harness and camper type exterior mirrors. REQUIRES C6Y. NOT AVAILABLE with 1SA, 1SB, C7A, ZW9, L29.*	NC	NC
Z81	Camper Equipment Package *Includes wiring harness, camper type exterior mirrors and 600-CCA auxiliary HD battery. REQUIRES C6Y and (1SA or 1SB). NOT AVAILABLE with L65, C7A, ZW9.*	200	233
Z81	Camper Equipment Package *Includes wiring harness, camper type exterior mirrors and 600-CCA auxiliary HD battery. REQUIRES C6Y. NOT AVAILABLE with 1SA, 1SB, L65, C7A, ZW9.*	116	135
Z82	Heavy Duty Trailering Equipment (Crew Cab) *Includes HD hazard flasher and trailer hitch platform. NOT AVAILABLE with EF1, ZW9.*	141	164
Z82	Heavy Duty Trailering Equipment (Reg Cab/X-Cab) *Includes trailer hitch platform. NOT AVAILABLE with EF1.*	141	164
ZGK	Tire: Spare LT245/75R16E SBR On-Off Road (Reg Cab/Crew Cab LB) *REQUIRES YGK or XGK. NOT AVAILABLE with XHP, XYK, YHP, YHR, YYK, ZHR, ZHP, ZYK, R05, XHR, XYL, YYL, ZYL.*	9	11
ZHP	Tire: Spare LT225/75R16D AS BSW SBR (Reg Cab) *REQUIRES XHP and YHP and R05. NOT AVAILABLE with YHR, ZHR, YGK, YYK, ZGK, ZYK, XYK, YYL, ZYL, XGK, XHR, XYL.*	(29)	(34)
ZHP	Tire: Spare LT225/75R16D BSW AS (Crew Cab LB) *REQUIRES XHP and YHP and R05. NOT AVAILABLE with YGK, ZGK, YHR, ZHR, XYK, YYK, ZYK, YYL, ZYL, XGK, XHR, XYL.*	(29)	(34)
ZHR	Tire: Spare LT225/75R16D SBR On-Off Road (Reg Cab/Crew Cab LB) *REQUIRES YHR and R05 or XHR. NOT AVAILABLE with XYK, YHP, YGK, YYK, ZHP, ZGK, ZYK, YYL, ZYL, XGK, XYL.*	(20)	(23)
ZHR	Tire: Spare LT225/75R16D SBR On-Off Road (X-Cab/Crew Cab SB) *REQUIRES YHR or XHR. NOT AVAILABLE with XYK, YYK, ZYK, XYL, YYL, ZYL.*	9	11
ZQ3	Tilt Wheel and Speed Control *REQUIRES 1SA. INCLUDED in 1SB, 1SC, 1SD, 1SK.*	331	385
ZYK	Tire: Spare LT215/85R16D Highway BSW (Reg Cab/Crew Cab LB) *REQUIRES XYK and YYK and R05. NOT AVAILABLE with XHP, YHP, YHR, YGK, ZHR, ZGK, ZHP, YYL, ZYL, XGK, XHR, XYL.*	32	37
ZYK	Tire: Spare LT215/85R16D Highway BSW (X-Cab/Crew Cab SB) *REQUIRES XYK and YYK. NOT AVAILABLE with YHR, ZHR, XHR, XYL, YYL, ZYL.*	61	71
ZYL	Tire: Spare LT215/85R16D AT BSW (4WD Crew Cab LB) *REQUIRES F60 and XYL and YYL and R05. NOT AVAILABLE with XGK, XHP, XHR, XYK, YGK, YHP, YHR, YYK, ZGK, ZHP, ZHR, ZYK.*	56	65

CODE	DESCRIPTION	INVOICE	MSRP
ZYL	Tire: Spare LT215/85R16D On-Off Road BSW (4WD - X-Cab/Crew Cab SB) . *REQUIRES F60 and XYL and YYL. NOT AVAILABLE with XHR, XYK, YHR, YYK, ZHR, ZYK.*	85	99
ZYL	Tire: Spare LT215/85R16D On-Off Road BSW (4WD Reg Cab) .... *REQUIRES XYL and YYL and F60 and R05. NOT AVAILABLE with XGK, XHP, XHR, XYK, YGK, YHP, YHR, YYK, ZGK, ZHP, ZHR, ZYK.*	56	65

2000 SONOMA

2000 GMC Sonoma

What's New?

Four-wheel-drive Sonomas get a higher-output V6 and a handling/trailering suspension standard. GMC drops the 4WD long-bed and High-Rider regular-cab models and adds a new, lower-priced base-trim extended-cab package. All versions get a boost in trailer ratings and a new paint color.

Review

With an aggressive look, available sport suspension, a third-door extended cab, snazzy Sportside bed and a strong 4.3-liter V6 under the hood, GMC's Sonoma is being positioned as a more versatile alternative to the traditional sporty coupe. But pitchmen aside, Sonomas can actually be fitted to suit just about any requirement, from utility hauler to off-road bruiser. You can choose from three wheelbases, three cabs, a short box or long box in Wideside or Sportside configuration and two- or four-wheel drive. Then, you still have to consider three trim levels (SL, SLS and SLE), two engines (a four-cylinder or V6), a manual or automatic transmission, and no less than five different suspension systems (three for 2WD and two for 4WD models). Whew!

Four-wheel-drive models, which already have four-wheel disc brakes and GM's electronic InstaTrac transfer case standard, find more power from the Vortec 4300 V6, and a standard handling/trailering suspension that was optional last year. The high-output V6 now makes 190 horsepower (up 10 from '99) and is standard on all 4WD trucks. Opt for the 4.3 in a 2WD Sonoma, and it will deliver 180 horsepower. The base powertrain is a 120-horsepower 2.2-liter four-cylinder mated to a five-speed manual gearbox. A four-speed automatic is optional.

Two-wheel-drive buyers can choose from an all-purpose "smooth-ride" suspension, a firmer "heavy-duty" setup for work, and a handling-oriented ZQ8 "sport" suspension tuned for optimum cornering. With the "high-payload" suspension standard on 4WD trucks, you'll want to order the High-Rider package if serious off-roading will be part of your driving mix. Tagged the ZR2 option, High-Riders boast a bigger, reinforced frame, beefy shocks and three-ply all-terrain tires.

Inside, Sonomas and Chevrolet S-Series pickups are virtually identical, with a roomy cab and modern dash layout. Center stack controls are canted toward the driver for easy access. Unfortunately, the cloth trim and carpeting feel thin, and plastic used for dash panels and switchgear still looks as though it was sourced from a toy company. On extended-cab trucks, an optional left-side access panel makes loading passengers or cargo into the rear of the cab much easier, but choosing the three-door cab eliminates one of the rear foldout jump seats.

Outfit a Sonoma with the 180-horse V6 and five-speed stick and add the ZQ8 sport suspension, and this little truck performs as energetically as some sports cars did a decade or so ago. The curvy Sportside box and sharp, five-spoke alloys nicely complement the package, turning the Sonoma into a true factory sport truck.

Sure, competitors from Ford and Toyota come across as more refined vehicles than Sonoma, and the one from Dodge feels large enough to be in a class by itself. But if you're looking for a sporty hauler at a value-packed price, Sonoma is the hot ticket.

Standard Equipment

SL 2WD REGULAR CAB SB (5M): 2.2L I4 OHV SMPI 8-valve engine; 5-speed OD manual transmission; 525-amp battery with run down protection; 100-amp alternator; rear-wheel drive, 3.73 axle ratio; stainless steel exhaust; comfort ride suspension, front independent suspension with anti-roll bar, front coil springs, rigid rear axle suspension with rear leaf springs; power re-circulating ball steering; front disc/rear drum brakes with 4-wheel antilock braking system; 19 gal. capacity fuel tank; front license plate bracket, side impact bars; front and rear body-colored bumpers with rear step; monotone paint; aero-composite halogen fully auto headlamps with daytime running lights, delay-off feature; additional exterior lights include underhood light; driver's and passenger's manual black folding outside mirrors; front and rear 15" x 7" painted styled steel wheels; P205/75SR15 A/S BSW front and rear tires; underbody mounted compact steel spare wheel with crankdown; AM/FM stereo, clock, seek-scan, 4 speakers, and fixed antenna; 1 power accessory outlet, retained accessory power; instrumentation display includes oil pressure gauge, water temperature gauge, volt gauge, trip odometer; warning indicators include battery, lights on, key in ignition; driver's front airbag, passenger's cancelable front airbag; ignition disable; tinted windows; variable intermittent front windshield wipers, sun visor strip; seating capacity of 3, bench front seat, fixed headrests, driver's seat includes 2-way direction control, passenger's seat includes 2-way direction control; full cloth headliner, full vinyl floor covering, cabback insulator; interior lights include dome light with fade; day/night rearview mirror; glove box with light, front cupholder, driver's and passenger's door bins; cargo concealed storage; argent grille, black side window moldings, black front windshield molding, black rear window molding and black door handles.

SL 2WD REGULAR CAB LB (5M) (in addition to or instead of SL 2WD REGULAR CAB SB(5M) equipment): HD ride suspension, HD front shocks, rigid rear axle suspension with HD rear leaf springs and HD rear shocks.

SL 2WD EXTENDED CAB SB (5M) (in addition to or instead of SLS 2WD REGULAR CAB SB (5M) equipment): 4.1 axle ratio; vented rear windows; seating capacity of 5, 60-40 split-bench front seat, fixed headrests, center armrest with storage, driver's seat includes 4-way direction control, passenger's seat includes 4-way direction control, easy entry; 50-50 folding side facing rear jump seat; premium cloth seats; rear console with storage, front and rear cupholders and 2 seat back storage pockets.

SLS (in addition to or instead of SL equipment): Monotone paint with bodyside accent stripe; 3 power accessory outlets, 60-40 split-bench front seat, fixed headrests, center armrest with storage, driver's seat includes 4-way direction control, passenger's seat includes 4-way direction control; premium cloth seats, cloth door trim insert, full carpet floor covering with floor mats; interior lights include illuminated entry and body-colored grille.

4WD (in addition to or instead of 2WD equipment): 4.3L V6 OHV SMPI 12-valve engine; part-time 4 wheel drive, auto locking hub control with electronic shift, 3.42 axle ratio; HD ride suspension, front independent torsion suspension with anti-roll bar, front torsion springs, front torsion bar, HD front shocks, rigid rear axle suspension with HD rear leaf springs, HD rear shocks; 4-wheel disc brakes with 4-wheel antilock braking system; front and rear body-colored bumpers with front tow hooks; P235/70SR15 A/S BSW front and rear tires and instrumentation display includes tachometer.

Base Prices

Code	Description	Invoice	MSRP
TS10603	SL 2WD Regular Cab SB (5M)	11911	12604
TS10803	SL 2WD Regular Cab LB (5M)	12242	12955
TS10603	SLS 2WD Regular Cab SB (5M)	12455	13762
TS10803	SLS 2WD Regular Cab LB (5M)	12772	14113
TS10653	SL 2WD Extended Cab SB(5M)	13990	14804
TS10653	SLS 2WD Extended Cab SB (5M)	14537	16063
TT10603	SL 4WD Regular Cab SB (5M)	15912	16838
TT10603	SLS 4WD Regular Cab SB (5M)	16440	18166
TT10653	SL 4WD Extended Cab SB (5M)	17730	18762
TT10653	SLS 4WD Extended Cab SB (5M)	18295	20216
Destination Charge:		520	520

Accessories

Code	Description	Invoice	MSRP
—	Custom Cloth Seat Trim (SL Reg Cab) *NOT AVAILABLE with AV5.*	NC	NC
—	Custom Vinyl Seat Trim (SL Reg Cab) *NOT AVAILABLE with AV5.*	NC	NC
1SA	Marketing Option Package 1SA (SL) *Includes SL Decor package. REQUIRES C60 or R6G.*	(387)	(450)
1SC	Marketing Option Package 1SC (SLS) *Includes SLS Sport Decor package. REQUIRES C60 or R6G.*	(387)	(450)
1SD	Marketing Option Package 1SD (SLS) *Includes SLE Comfort Decor. REQUIRES (C60 or R6G) and YC5.*	NC	NC
1SE	Marketing Option Package 1SE (SLS 2WD Reg Cab SB)	1583	1841
	Manufacturer Discount	(860)	(1000)
	Net Price *Includes SLS Sport Decor package, gvwr: 4,200 lbs, wheels: 15" x 7" aluminum (4), tires: P205/75R15 A/S BSW SBR, air conditioning, AM/FM stereo with CD, seek and scan; tilt wheel and cruise control. NOT AVAILABLE with M30, UM6, UL0.*	723	841
1SE	Marketing Option Package 1SE (SLS 2WD Reg Cab SB)	1583	1841
	Manufacturer Discount	(1140)	(1325)
	Net Price *Includes SLS Sport Decor package, gvwr: 4,200 lbs, wheels: 15" x 7" aluminum (4), tires: P205/75R15 A/S BSW SBR, air conditioning, AM/FM stereo with CD, seek and scan; tilt wheel and cruise control. NOT AVAILABLE with UM6, UL0.*	443	516

CODE	DESCRIPTION	INVOICE	MSRP
1SF	Super Spec Package 1SF (SLS 2WD X-Cab SB)	1837	2136
	Includes SLS Sport Decor package, wheels: 15" x 7" aluminum (4), tilt wheel, cruise control, tachometer, gvwr: 4,600 lbs, heavy duty suspension package, 4.10 axle ratio, third door and driver's side jump seat delete. NOT AVAILABLE with ULO, UM6, M50.		
1SF	Super Spec Package 1SF (SLS 2WD X-Cab SB)	1837	2136
	Manufacturer Discount	(1140)	(1325)
	Net Price	697	811
	Includes SLS Sport Decor package, wheels: 15" x 7" aluminum (4), tilt wheel, cruise control, tachometer, gvwr: 4,600 lbs, heavy duty suspension package, 4.10 axle ratio, third door and driver's side jump seat delete. NOT AVAILABLE with ULO, UM6, M50.		
1SF	Super Spec Package 1SF (SLS 2WD X-Cab SB)	1837	2136
	Manufacturer Discount	(860)	(1000)
	Net Price	977	1136
	Includes SLS Sport Decor package, wheels: 15" x 7" aluminum (4), tilt wheel, cruise control, tachometer, gvwr: 4,600 lbs, heavy duty suspension package, 4.10 axle ratio, third door and driver's side jump seat delete. NOT AVAILABLE with ULO, UM6.		
1SG	Super Spec Package 1SG (SLS 2WD X-Cab SB)	3855	4482
	Manufacturer Discount	(1140)	(1325)
	Net Price	2715	3157
	Includes SLS Sport Decor package, gvwr: 4,600 lbs, heavy duty suspension package, wheels: 15" x 7" aluminum (4), tilt wheel, cruise control, tachometer, third door, driver's side jump seat delete and deep tinted glass. NOT AVAILABLE with ULO, UM6, M50.		
1SG	Super Spec Package 1SG (SLS 2WD X-Cab SB)	3855	4482
	Includes SLS Sport Decor package, gvwr: 4,600 lbs, heavy duty suspension package, wheels: 15" x 7" aluminum (4), tilt wheel, cruise control, tachometer, third door, driver's side jump seat delete and deep tinted glass. NOT AVAILABLE with ULO, UM6.		
1SH	Super Spec Package 1SH (SLS 4WD X-Cab SB)	2612	3037
	Includes SLS Sport Decor package, heavy duty suspension package, tilt wheel, cruise control, third door, driver's side jump seat delete, gvwr: 5,150 lbs and wheels: 15" x 7" aluminum (4). NOT AVAILABLE with UM6, ULO, M30.		
1SH	Super Spec Package 1SH (SLS 4WD X-Cab SB)	2612	3037
	Manufacturer Discount	(1140)	(1325)
	Net Price	1472	1712
	Includes SLS Sport Decor package, heavy duty suspension package, tilt wheel, cruise control, third door, driver's side jump seat delete, gvwr: 5,150 lbs and wheels: 15" x 7" aluminum (4). NOT AVAILABLE with UM6, ULO.		
1SJ	Super Spec Package 1SJ (SLS 4WD X-Cab SB)	5419	6301
	Manufacturer Discount	(1140)	(1325)
	Net Price	4279	4976
	Includes SLS Sport Decor package, gvwr: 4,900 lbs, Highrider suspension package, front and rear wheel opening flares, tires: 31 x 10.5R15 A/T BSW, tire: spare 31x10.5R15 A/T BSW, composite underbody shield package, locking rear		

CODE	DESCRIPTION	INVOICE	MSRP
	differential, wheels: 15" x 7" aluminum (4), AM/FM stereo with CD and cassette, power convenience package: power locks, power windows; dual electric outside rearview mirrors, remote keyless entry, tilt wheel, cruise control, leather-wrapped steering wheel, third door and driver's side jump seat delete. NOT AVAILABLE with UM6, ULO.		
1SJ	**Super Spec Package 1SJ (SLS 4WD X-Cab SB)**	5419	6301
	Includes SLS Sport Decor package, gvwr: 4,900 lbs, Highrider suspension package, front and rear wheel opening flares, tires: 31 x 10.5R15 A/T BSW, tire: spare 31x10.5R15 A/T BSW, composite underbody shield package, locking rear differential, wheels: 15" x 7" aluminum (4), AM/FM stereo with CD and cassette, power convenience package: power locks, power windows; dual electric outside rearview mirrors, remote keyless entry, tilt wheel, cruise control, leather-wrapped steering wheel, third door and driver's side jump seat delete. NOT AVAILABLE with UM6, ULO, M30.		
1SR	**Marketing Option Package 1SR "Hot Looks" (SLS 2WD Reg Cab SB)**	2686	3018
	Manufacturer Discount	(1185)	(1331)
	Net Price	1501	1687
	Includes sport suspension package, wheels: 16" x 8" aluminum (4), tires: P235/55R16 A/S BSW SBR, air conditioning, AM/FM stereo with CD, seek and scan, tilt wheel, cruise control, front 60/40 reclining split bench seat, deep tinted glass and tachometer. NOT AVAILABLE with M50, GU4, GU6, C5D, QCA, ZCE, V10, R6G, UM6, UPO, AV5, ZQ6, A28, ZCA, Z85, ULO, M30.		
1SR	**Marketing Option Package 1SR "Hot Looks" (SLS 2WD Reg Cab SB)**	2686	3018
	Manufacturer Discount	(1474)	(1656)
	Net Price	1212	1362
	Includes sport suspension package, wheels: 16" x 8" aluminum (4), tires: P235/55R16 A/S BSW SBR, air conditioning, AM/FM stereo with CD, seek and scan, tilt wheel, cruise control, front 60/40 reclining split bench seat, deep tinted glass and tachometer. NOT AVAILABLE with M50, GU4, GU6, C5D, QCA, ZCE, V10, R6G, UM6, UPO, AV5, ZQ6, A28, ZCA, Z85, ULO.		
1SR	**Marketing Option Package 1SR "Hot Looks" (SLS 2WD X-Cab)**	3002	3373
	Manufacturer Discount	(1474)	(1656)
	Net Price	1528	1717
	Includes sport suspension package, wheels: 16" x 8" aluminum (4), tires: P235/55R16 A/S BSW SBR, air conditioning, tilt wheel, cruise control, front 60/40 reclining split bench seat, deep tinted glass, tachometer, third door and driver's side jump seat delete. NOT AVAILABLE with C5D, Z85, M50, GU4, GU6, V10, QCA, ZCE, ZCA, R6G, UM6, ZQ6, A28.		
1SR	**Marketing Option Package 1SR "Hot Looks" (SLS 2WD X-Cab)**	3002	3373
	Manufacturer Discount	(1185)	(1331)
	Net Price	1817	2042
	Includes sport suspension package, wheels: 16" x 8" aluminum (4), tires: P235/55R16 A/S BSW SBR, air conditioning, tilt wheel, cruise control, front 60/40 reclining split bench seat, deep tinted glass, tachometer, third door and driver's side jump seat delete. NOT AVAILABLE with C5D, Z85, M50, GU4, GU6, V10, QCA, ZCE, ZCA, R6G, UM6, ZQ6, A28, M30.		

CODE	DESCRIPTION	INVOICE	MSRP
1ST	Marketing Option Package 1ST "Towing" (SLS 4WD X-Cab)	3019	3392
	Manufacturer Discount	(1480)	(1663)
	Net Price	1539	1729
	Includes air conditioning, tilt wheel, cruise control, third door, driver's side jump seat delete, tachometer and electronic shift 2-speed transfer case. NOT AVAILABLE with C5A, ZR2, M50, V10, R6G, UM6, UP0, A28, ZBF, UL0.		
A28	Sliding Rear Window	103	120
AJ1	Deep Tinted Glass (Reg Cab)	64	75
	Includes rear window only. INCLUDED in 1SH, 1SG, 1SJ.		
AJ1	Deep Tinted Glass (X-Cab)	99	115
	Includes rear window and rear quarter glass. INCLUDED in 1SH, 1SG, 1SJ.		
AM6	Front 60/40 Reclining Split Bench Seat (SLS 4WD Reg Cab/4WD X-Cab)	(215)	(250)
	Includes folding back, recliner, folding center armrest with storage and 2 cupholders. REQUIRES M30. NOT AVAILABLE with AV5, UP0, ZR2. INCLUDED in 1SE, 1SF, 1SG.		
ANL	Fog Lamps (SLS)	99	115
	Includes air deflector. NOT AVAILABLE with ZR2.		
AV5	Front Reclining Bucket Seats (All Except 2WD SL)	NC	NC
	Includes folding seat backs, driver manual lumbar adjuster and floor console. NOT AVAILABLE with Custom Cloth Seat Trim, Custom Vinyl Seat Trim, AM6. INCLUDED in 1SH, 1SJ.		
B30	Full Floor Color Keyed Carpeting (SL)	60	70
C3A	GVWR: 4,400 Lbs (SLS 2WD X-Cab SB)	NC	NC
	Includes 2500 lbs. front and 2700 lbs. rear GAWR. REQUIRES ZQ8. NOT AVAILABLE with QCA, ZCA, ZCE.		
C5A	GVWR: 4,900 Lbs (2WD Reg Cab LB/SLS 4WD X-Cab SB)	NC	NC
	REQUIRES (M50 and GU4) or (M30 and GU4) or ZR2. NOT AVAILABLE with GT5, Z85, ZBF, QEB. INCLUDED in 1SJ.		
C5D	GVWR: 4,600 Lbs (2WD)	NC	NC
	REQUIRES Z85. NOT AVAILABLE with M50, GU4, GU6, C5A, C3A. INCLUDED in 1SF, 1SG.		
C60	Air Conditioning	692	805
	NOT AVAILABLE with R6G. INCLUDED in 1SE, 1SF, 1SH, 1SG, 1SJ.		
E24	Third Door (X-Cab)	254	295
	Hinged door to rear of cab - Located on driver's side of vehicle. Includes passenger's side jump seat only. Rear speakers repositioned to doors. INCLUDED in 1SF, 1SH, 1SG, 1SJ.		
G80	Locking Rear Differential	232	270
	REQUIRES (M50 and GU4) or (M30 and GU6). NOT AVAILABLE with GT5. INCLUDED in 1SJ.		
GT5	4.10 Axle Ratio (2WD)	NC	NC
	REQUIRES M30. NOT AVAILABLE with M50, GU4, GU6, G80, C5A, 1SG. INCLUDED in 1SF.		
GU4	3.08 Axle Ratio (2WD)	NC	NC
	REQUIRES M50 or M30 or C5A. NOT AVAILABLE with GT5, GU6.		

CODE	DESCRIPTION	INVOICE	MSRP
GU6	3.42 Axle Ratio *REQUIRES M30. NOT AVAILABLE with GT5, GU4, M50, ZR2. INCLUDED in 1SH, 1SG.*	NC	NC
L35	Engine: Vortec 4300 (262 CID) V6 SFI (2WD) *Includes tachometer. REQUIRES GU4 or C5A. NOT AVAILABLE with GT5, 1SE.*	1028	1195
M30	Transmission: 4-Speed Electronic Automatic with Overdrive *Includes brake/transmission shift interlock. REQUIRES GU6 or GU4 or GT5 or C5A or (1SA and N60) or (1SC and ZQ8) or 1SD. NOT AVAILABLE with M50.*	942	1095
M50	Transmission: 5-Speed Manual with Overdrive *REQUIRES GU4 or C5A. NOT AVAILABLE with GT5, M30, GU6, UP0, AM6.*	NC	NC
N60	Wheels: 15" x 7" Aluminum (4) (SL 2WD) *INCLUDED in 1SE, 1SF, 1SG.*	320	372
N60	Wheels: 15" x 7" Aluminum (4) (SLS 2WD) *NOT AVAILABLE with ZQ8. INCLUDED in 1SE, 1SF, 1SG.*	241	280
N90	Wheels: 15" x 7" Aluminum (4) (SL 4WD) *INCLUDED in 1SH, 1SJ.*	320	372
N90	Wheels: 15" x 7" Aluminum (4) (SLS 4WD) *NOT AVAILABLE with ZR2. INCLUDED in 1SH, 1SJ.*	241	280
NP5	Leather-Wrapped Steering Wheel (SLS) *INCLUDED in 1SJ.*	46	54
QCA	Tires: P205/75R15 AS WOL SBR (2WD) *Includes front and rear. NOT AVAILABLE with ZQ8, ZCE, C3A.*	104	121
QEB	Tires: P235/75R15 On/Off Road WOL SBR (4WD) *NOT AVAILABLE with ZBF, ZR2, C5A.*	187	218
R6G	Air Conditioning Not Desired (Reg Cab) *NOT AVAILABLE with C60.*	NC	NC
R6M	New Jersey Cost Surcharge	46	NC
U16	Tachometer (2WD) *INCLUDED in 1SE, 1SF, 1SH, 1SG, 1SJ.*	51	59
UA1	Heavy Duty Battery	48	56
UL0	Radio: AM/FM Stereo with Cassette (SLS) *Includes clock. REQUIRES 1SC. NOT AVAILABLE with UM6, 1SE, UN0, UP0, 1SF, 1SG, 1SH, 1SJ.*	174	202
UL5	Radio Delete (SL) *NOT AVAILABLE with UM6.*	(194)	(226)
UM6	Radio: AM/FM Stereo with Cassette (All Except 4WD X-Cab) *Includes clock and 4 speakers. REQUIRES 1SC. NOT AVAILABLE with UL5, UN0, UP0, 1SE, UL0, 1SF, 1SG, 1SH, 1SJ.*	105	122
UN0	Radio: AM/FM Stereo with CD (SLS) *Includes clock, speed sensitive volume, theft lock and auto tone control and 4 speakers. NOT AVAILABLE with UP0, UM6, UL0. INCLUDED in 1SE, 1SF, 1SH, 1SG.*	260	302
UP0	Radio: AM/FM Stereo with CD and Cassette (4WD X-Cab) *Includes clock, speed sensitive volume, theft lock, seek-scan, auto tone control, music search cassette player and 4 speakers. REQUIRES (1SH or 1SJ) and M30. NOT AVAILABLE with AM6, UM6, UN0, UL0.*	86	100

CODE	DESCRIPTION	INVOICE	MSRP
UP0	Radio: AM/FM Stereo with CD and Cassette (SLS Except 4WD X-Cab) *Includes clock, electronically tuned FM stereo, speed sensitive volume, theft lock, seek-scan, auto tone control, auto reverse and music search cassette player with 4 speakers. REQUIRES M30 and AV5. NOT AVAILABLE with UM6, UN0, UL0, AM6. INCLUDED in 1SJ.*	346	402
V10	Cold Climate Package *Includes heavy duty battery and engine block heater.*	77	89
VF7	Rear Bumper Delete	NC	NC
Z85	Heavy Duty Suspension Package (Reg Cab SB) *Includes heavy duty rear springs and heavy duty front/rear shocks. REQUIRES C5D. NOT AVAILABLE with ZQ8. INCLUDED in 1SF, 1SH, 1SG.*	220	256
ZBF	Tire: Spare P235/70R15 AS BSW SBR (4WD) *NOT AVAILABLE with QEB, ZR2, C5A.*	82	95
ZCA	Tire: Spare P205/75R15 AS WOL SBR (2WD) *REQUIRES QCA. NOT AVAILABLE with ZQ8, ZCE, C3A.*	82	95
ZCE	Tire: Spare P205/75R15 AS BSW SBR (2WD) *NOT AVAILABLE with ZQ8, QCA, ZCA, C3A.*	82	95
ZM5	Composite Underbody Shield Package (4WD Except SL X-Cab) *Includes transfer case shield, front differential skid plates, fuel tank shield and steering linkage shields. INCLUDED in 1SJ.*	108	126
ZQ3	Tilt Wheel and Cruise Control *INCLUDED in 1SE, 1SF, 1SH, 1SG, 1SJ.*	340	395
ZQ6	Power Convenience Package (SLE) *Includes power locks, power windows, dual electric outside rearview mirrors and remote keyless entry. REQUIRES C60. INCLUDED in 1SJ.*	684	795
ZQ8	Sport Suspension Package (SLS SB) *Includes special coil springs for reduced trim height, heavy duty front/rear stabilizer bars, 46mm DeCarbon front/rear shocks, urethane jounce bumpers, wheels: 16" x 8" aluminum (4) and tires: P235/55R16 A/S BSW SBR. REQUIRES U16 or C3A. NOT AVAILABLE with N60, Z85, ZCE, QCA, ZCA.*	632	735
ZR2	Highrider Suspension Package (SLS 4WD X-Cab SB) *Includes 46mm Bilstein shocks, heavy-duty springs, additional chassis enhancements for increased width/height, front and rear wheel opening flares, tires: 31 x 10.5R15 A/T BSW, tire: spare 31x10.5R15 A/T BSW and composite underbody shield package. REQUIRES G80 and C5A. NOT AVAILABLE with GU6, Z85, ZBF, QEB, AM6, ANL. INCLUDED in 1SJ.*	1544	1795

2000 YUKON

What's New?

Completely redesigned, Yukon is based on the new Sierra pickup platform with zippy V8 engines and a stouter chassis for a better, more isolated ride.

2000 GMC Yukon

Review

Yukons are popular SUVs, and rightly so. Featuring room for the family and plenty of gear in one of two well-appointed trim levels in either two- or four-wheel drive with four doors, the Yukon is versatile enough for any task thrown its way. For 2000, GMC has redesigned the truck from top to bottom, providing buyers with stronger engines, a more robust foundation, more seats inside, and nicely updated sheetmetal that, if not ground-breaking, is at least attractive.

Starting with the stiff new Sierra pickup platform, engineers ladled a number of luxury goodies atop a slightly larger four-door cabin. In keeping with its rugged luxo-truck image, even basic Yukon SLEs are well-equipped with a 275-horsepower, 4.8-liter Vortec V8 engine, aluminum alloy wheels, deep tinted glass, and front and rear air conditioning. Other standards include power windows, locks and doors, a CD player pumping out the jams through nine premium quality speakers, and an electrochromic rearview mirror with compass.

Step up to SLT trim and you'll be rewarded with leather upholstery. All Yukons come with four-wheel disc ABS for short stopping distances and a five-link, semi-floating coil-spring rear suspension for improved ride characteristics. An optional Autoride suspension system can vary shock dampening automatically as needed, and 4WD models can be equipped with a stout Z71 off-road suspension package. Front and side airbags are standard, and an optional traction-control system keeps the 2WD Yukon's tail planted in the slippery stuff.

An automatic transmission is the only way you can go in the new Yukon, but an optional 5.3-liter V8 engine is available if you need the extra torque for towing. Also extra cost is a power sunroof, automatic climate control, rear-seat audio controls, a luxury package that adds heated power front seats and a HomeLink transmitter, and, for the first time, a third-row seat that expands seating to a maximum of nine passengers, albeit at the expense of valuable cargo space.

One of the great things about the Yukon is that it gives you plenty of interior room and luggage capacity in a garageable, daily-driver package. Despite its full-size SUV status, it's manageable in tight quarters and quite responsive, particularly the 2WD model, which is equipped with a carlike rack-and-pinion steering system. And now, with third-row seating, you can have the practicality of a minivan and the go-anywhere capability of an SUV, in one easy-to-live-with package. And no, GM is NOT paying us to say this.

Despite cheap interior plastics, the Yukon is undoubtedly one of the best big SUVs you can buy. Perfect for a family and able to tote the in-laws in a pinch, the ruggedly stylish and easy to drive Yukon should prove to be a big hit. Get down to the local GMC dealer before the crush of consumers drives demand far above supply.

Standard Equipment

SLE 2WD (4A): 4.8L V8 OHV SMPI 16-valve engine; 4-speed electronic OD auto transmission with lock-up; 600-amp battery with run down protection; 130-amp alternator; driver's selectable multi-mode transmission; rear-wheel drive, 3.42 axle ratio; stainless steel exhaust; auto-leveling suspension, front independent suspension with anti-roll bar, front torsion springs, front torsion bar, rigid rear axle multi-link suspension with rear coil springs; power rack-and-pinion steering; 4-wheel disc brakes with 4-wheel antilock braking system; 26 gal. capacity fuel tank; side impact bars; split liftback rear cargo door; trailer harness; roof rack; front and rear chrome bumpers front with body-colored bumper insert, rear bumper black rub strip, front tow hooks, rear step; body-colored bodyside molding with chrome bodyside insert, chrome wheel well molding; monotone paint; aero-composite halogen fully auto headlamps with daytime running lights; additional exterior lights include front fog/driving lights, underhood light; driver's and passenger's power remote body-colored heated folding outside mirrors; front and rear 16" x 7" silver alloy wheels; P245/75SR16 touring A/S BSW front and rear tires; underbody mounted full-size alloy spare wheel with crankdown; air conditioning, air filter, rear heat ducts; AM/FM stereo, clock, seek-scan, single CD, 9 performance speakers, amplifier, auto equalizer, theft deterrent, and fixed antenna; cruise control; power door locks with 2 stage unlock, remote keyless entry, child safety rear door locks; 3 power accessory outlets, front cigar lighter(s), retained accessory power, smokers' package; instrumentation display includes tachometer, oil pressure gauge, water temperature gauge, volt gauge, compass, exterior temp, trip odometer; warning indicators include oil pressure, water temp, battery, low oil level, low coolant, lights on, key in ignition, low fuel, low washer fluid, door ajar, trunk ajar, service interval; driver's and passenger's front airbags, driver's and front passenger's seat mounted side airbags; ignition disable, panic alarm; deep tinted windows, power front and rear windows with driver's 1-touch down, flip-up 1/4 vent windows; variable intermittent front windshield wipers, sun visor strip, rear window defroster and windshield wiper; seating capacity of 6, 40-20-40 split-bench front seat, fixed headrests, center armrest with storage, driver's seat includes 4-way power seat, 8-way direction control, lumbar support, passenger's seat includes 4-way power seat, 8-way direction control, lumbar support; 60-40 folding rear split-bench seat with adjustable headrests, center armrest with storage; front and rear height adjustable seatbelts; premium cloth seats, cloth door trim insert, full cloth headliner, full color-keyed carpet floor covering with carpeted floor mats, plastic/rubber gear shift knob; interior lights include dome light with delay, front reading lights, 4 door curb lights, illuminated entry; leather-wrapped sport steering wheel with tilt adjustment; dual illuminated vanity mirrors, dual auxiliary visors; auto-dimming day/night rearview mirror; mini overhead console, glove box with light, front and rear cupholders, instrument panel bin, 2 seat back storage pockets, driver's and passenger's door bins; carpeted cargo floor, plastic trunk lid, cargo cover, cargo net, cargo light; chrome grille, black side window moldings, black front windshield molding, black rear window molding and body-colored door handles.

SLE 4WD (4A) (in addition to or instead of SLE 2WD (4A) equipment): Part-time 4-wheel drive, auto locking hub control and electronic shift, front independent torsion suspension with anti-roll bar, front torsion springs, front torsion bar and power re-circulating ball steering with engine speed-sensing assist.

Base Prices

TC15706	SLE 2WD (4A)	27761	31727
TK15706	SLE 4WD (4A)	30279	34605
Destination Charge:		675	675

CODE	DESCRIPTION	INVOICE	MSRP

Accessories

CODE	DESCRIPTION	INVOICE	MSRP
1SB	**Marketing Option Package 1SB** *Includes vehicle with standard equipment.*	NC	NC
1SC	**Marketing Option Package 1SC** *Includes SLT Decor package: premium smooth ride suspension package, liftgate with liftglass rear door system, rear wiper/washer, front recovery hooks, carpeted floor mats, cargo floor mats, 6-way power's driver seat adjuster, 6-way power passenger's seat adjuster, rear wiper/washer, front fog lamps, electronic cruise control, front air conditioning, rear air conditioning, remote keyless entry system, roof luggage carrier, electric rear window defogger, deep tinted glass, wheels: 16" x 7" bright cast aluminum (4), AM/FM stereo with CD, cassette, seek and scan, front reclining 40-20-40 split-bench seats and ultrasoft premium cloth trim.*	1320	1535
1SD	**Marketing Option Package 1SD** *Includes SLT Decor package: premium smooth ride suspension package, liftgate with liftglass rear door system, rear wiper/washer, front recovery hooks, carpeted floor mats, cargo floor mats, 6-way power's driver seat adjuster, 6-way power passenger's seat adjuster, rear wiper/washer, front fog lamps, electronic cruise control, front air conditioning, rear air conditioning, remote keyless entry system, roof luggage carrier, electric rear window defogger, deep tinted glass, wheels: 16" x 7" bright cast aluminum (4), AM/FM stereo with CD, cassette, seek and scan, front reclining bucket seats, ultrasoft leather seat trim, OnStar communications system, front full feature bucket seats, floor console, power lumbar, power seat back recliner, dual inboard armrests, heated driver's and passenger's seat, 2 position driver's memory seats, storage pockets behind both seats, luxury convenience package, heated driver and passenger seat, power passenger seat, heated electrochromic exterior mirror, Homelink transmitter, gas preloaded shock absorbers, driver's side electrochromic mirror and Homelink garage door opener. NOT AVAILABLE with AE7, UV8, A95.*	2590	3012
A95	**Front Reclining Bucket Seats** *Includes inboard armrests, floor console, dual adjustable headrests, driver's and passenger's 6-way power seats and storage pocket behind seats. NOT AVAILABLE with AE7. REQUIRES 1SB. INCLUDED in 1SC.*	322	375
AE7	**Front 40/20/40 Split Bench Seat** *Includes driver's and passenger's reclining seats, manual lumbars, driver's 6-way power adjustable seat, center fold down armrest, storage pockets behind seats and adjustable outboard head restraints. NOT AVAILABLE with 1SD, UK6, A95. REQUIRES 1SC. INCLUDED in 1SB.*	(430)	(500)
AS3	**Third Row 50/50 Split Seat** *Includes forward folding back with release latch and single handle release mechanism accessible from the rear of the vehicle, seat articulates forward (without removal) and seat halves are removable on rollers without tools. REQUIRES C5H and 1SB. NOT AVAILABLE with C7K, ZW9, Z71.*	477	555
BVE	**Side Step Running Boards** *Running boards mount between front wheels and rear wheels at bottom of rocker panel.*	280	325
C36	**Rear Heat**	176	205

CODE	DESCRIPTION	INVOICE	MSRP
C5H	GVWR: 6900 Lbs (4WD) *Includes 3800 lbs. front and 4000 lbs. rear GAWR. REQUIRES AS3. NOT AVAILABLE with C5U.*	NC	NC
C5U	GVWR: 6,800 Lbs *Includes 3150 lbs. front and 4000 lbs. rear GAWR. NOT AVAILABLE with C7K, C5H.*	NC	NC
C68	Electronic Climate Control *NOT AVAILABLE with CF5.*	108	125
C7K	GVWR: 6,500 Lbs (2WD) *Includes 3150 lbs. front and 3750 lbs. rear GAWR. NOT AVAILABLE with AS3, C5U.*	NC	NC
CF5	Electric Sliding Sunroof *Includes Homelink garage door opener. REQUIRES 1SB or 1SC. NOT AVAILABLE with C68, V53.*	856	995
CF5	Electric Sliding Sunroof *Includes Homelink garage door opener. REQUIRES 1SD. NOT AVAILABLE with C68, V53, 1SC.*	748	870
DF2	Camper Type Exterior Mirrors	43	50
G80	Locking Rear Differential	217	252
GT4	3.73 Axle Ratio *NOT AVAILABLE with GT5.*	NC	NC
GT5	4.10 Axle Ratio (4WD) *NOT AVAILABLE with GT4.*	NC	NC
K05	Engine Block Heater (Cold Weather)	28	33
K47	High Capacity Air Cleaner	22	25
KNP	HD Auxilliary Transmission Cooling System	83	96
LM7	Engine: Vortec 5300 V8 SFI	602	700
NC7	Federal Emission Override *Must be ordered for units shipped to federal areas.*	NC	NC
NW7	Electronic Traction Control (2WD) *REQUIRES G80.*	168	195
NZZ	Off-Road Skid Plates (4WD) *Includes aluminum front underbody shield starting behind front bumper and running to 1st cross-member and steel transfer case frame mounted shields, protecting front underbody, oil pan and differential case.*	82	95
PF4	Wheels: 16" x 7" Bright Cast Aluminum (4) *Machined. INCLUDED in 1SC, 1SD.*	95	110
QBN	Tires: LT245/75R16C On/Off Road BSW SBR (4WD) *Includes 2020 lbs front and rear tire capacity. REQUIRES Z71. NOT AVAILABLE with QGC, QGD, QIX, QMJ, QMK, QBX.*	114	133
QBX	Tires: LT245/75R16C On/Off Road WOL SBR (4WD) *Includes 2020 lbs front and rear tire capacity. REQUIRES Z71. NOT AVAILABLE with QGC, QGD, QIX, QMJ, QMK, QBN.*	222	258
QC3	Wheels: 16" x 7" Polished Cast Aluminum (4) *REQUIRES 1SC or 1SD.*	95	110
QGC	Tires: P265/75R16 BW SBR AT (4WD) *Includes 2364 lbs front and rear tire capacity. REQUIRES Z71. NOT AVAILABLE with QBN, QBX, QGD, QIX, QMJ, QMK.*	90	105

CODE	DESCRIPTION	INVOICE	MSRP
QGD	**Tires: P265/75R16 AT WOL SBR (4WD)** *Includes 2364 lbs front and rear tire capacity. REQUIRES Z71. NOT AVAILABLE with QBN, QBX, QGC, QIX, QMJ, QMK.*	198	230
QIX	**Tires: LT265/75R16C On-Off Road BSW SBR (4WD)** *Includes 2100 lbs front and rear tire capacity. REQUIRES Z71. NOT AVAILABLE with QBN, QBX, QGC, QGD, QMJ, QMK.*	214	249
QMJ	**Tires: P265/70R16 AT BW SBR** *Includes 2184 lbs front and rear tire capacity. NOT AVAILABLE with QMK, QBN, QBX, QGC, QGD, QIX.*	NC	NC
QMK	**Tires: P265/70R16 WOL SBR AT** *Includes 2184 lbs front and rear tire capacity. NOT AVAILABLE with QMJ, QBN, QBX, QGC, QGD, QIX.*	108	125
R6M	**New Jersey Cost Surcharge**	83	NC
UK6	**Rear Seat Audio Radio Control** *Includes rear seat audio system with dual headphone jacks, controls for volume, station, selection and media. REQUIRES A95. NOT AVAILABLE with AE7. INCLUDED in 1SD.*	142	165
UP0	**Radio: AM/FM Stereo with CD and Cassette** *Includes clock, speed sensitive volume, theft lock, auto tone control, auto reverse and music search cassette player with enhanced performance 8-speaker system and subwoofer. REQUIRES A95 and 1SB. INCLUDED in 1SC, 1SD.*	108	125
UV8	**Cellular Phone Provision** *Includes wiring for remote microphone jumper harness and cellular phone jumper harness. Wiring includes 6 leads - 2 for microphone, 1 for battery feed, 1 for ground, 1 for ignition and 1 for Class II communications. NOT AVAILABLE with 1SD.*	43	50
V53	**Roof Luggage Carrier Delete** *NOT AVAILABLE with CF5.*	NC	NC
Z55	**Autoride** *Automatically changes the shock dampening for driving conditions and/or transient suspension inputs to optimize ride control. Includes orange color DeCarbon shock absorbers (high pressure gas charged with 46mm piston diameter). Biases suspension dampening toward firm setting when tow/haul mode selected. Includes wider aspect ratio tires with greater load carrying capacity than standard. NOT AVAILABLE with Z71.*	602	700
Z71	**Off-Road Chassis Equipment Package (4WD)** *Includes increased rate springs, shock absorbers, jounce bumpers, stabilizer bar, red color Monroe shock absorber tubes (high pressure gas charged with 46mm piston diameter), special removable front air dam and wider aspect, aggressive tread tires for maximum traction in loose soil; off-road skid plates, high capacity air cleaner and gas shocks. REQUIRES C5U. NOT AVAILABLE with AS3, Z55.*	168	195
Z82	**HD Trailering Equipment (2WD)** *Includes trailering hitch platform, electric trailer brake wire harness with mounting provisions, a 7-wire harness with fully independent fused trailering circuits with 7-way sealed connector and IP jumper wiring harness for electric trailer brake controller and electronic traction control. REQUIRES (KNP and K47 and G80 and LM7) or (KNP and K47 and G80 and GT4).*	141	126

CODE	DESCRIPTION	INVOICE	MSRP
Z82	HD Trailering Equipment (4WD) *Includes trailering hitch platform, electric trailer brake wire harness with mounting provisions, a 7-wire harness with fully independent fused trailering circuits with 7-way sealed connector and IP jumper wiring harness for electric trailer brake controller. REQUIRES KNP.*	141	164
ZW9	Panel Doors *NOT AVAILABLE with AS3.*	NC	NC
ZY2	Conventional Two-Tone Paint	172	200

2000 YUKON DENALI

2000 GMC Yukon Denali

What's New?

For the 2000 model year, GMC's Yukon Denali gets a new exterior color and adds GM's OnStar communications system to its already impressive factory-installed standard equipment list.

Review

America seems to have an insatiable appetite for upscale SUVs right now, and big, gussied-up utes derived from a full-size pickup turn out to be the most profitable automotive product on the planet. So what's more logical than taking the old Chevy Tahoe/GMC Yukon, bolting on a new face, tossing in luxury features and marketing it as a four-wheel-drive limo for the well-heeled?

Enter the GMC Yukon Denali (and its dolled-up sister, the Cadillac Escalade). Exterior styling differs from the donor previous-generation Yukon by the use of more distinct sheetmetal from the hoodline forward, plus a bold rectangular center-port grille. Reflector-optic halogen headlamps and recessed projector-beam fog lamps reside in a smoothed-out front fascia. Body-color cladding and integrated running boards spruce up the flanks, with textured body-color door handles, outside rearview mirrors and color-keyed rails on the flush roof rack completing the monotone look. Out back, a functional step bumper conceals a standard trailer hitch.

The Denali's interior boasts upper and lower consoles packed with storage cubbies and features such as reading lamps, cupholders, a rear power point and audio controls. Instrumentation is backlit in blue with white pointers and includes a tachometer. Luxury touches abound, with Zebrano wood trim, leather front and rear heated seats, and a premium Bose sound system. GM's factory-installed OnStar mobile communications system is now standard equipment.

Powering all this opulence is a 5.7-liter pushrod V8 packing 255 horsepower. The Vortec 5700 puts its 330 foot-pounds of torque to the ground via a four-speed automatic transmission and the Auto Trac full-time four-wheel-drive system. When activated, the AutoTrac transfer case will automatically shift from two-wheel drive to 4WD when it senses wheel slippage. Denali rides on unique six-spoke chromed aluminum wheels wearing Firestone 265/70R-16 touring tires designed especially for sport-utility applications on- and off-road in both wet and dry conditions.

Available in an array of exterior colors, the Denali provides a "look-at-me" driving experience around town and a king-of-the-road feel out on the highway. Frankly, you expect a lot from a truck with a $40K-plus price tag. But understand that it is all riding atop a pickup platform that is more than a decade old. That means this truck has all the flaws inherent to its humble underpinnings, such as sloppy steering, numb brakes and unrefined ride. What's worse is the use of GM's previous-generation interior plastics, which simply aren't in keeping with Denali's price.

For our money, the Denali lost much of its luster when Cadillac literally thieved the whole vehicle from GMC to offer the Escalade. Add in its dated mechanicals, and Denali becomes a tough sell.

Standard Equipment

DENALI (4A): 5.7L V8 OHV SMPI 16-valve engine; 4-speed electronic OD auto transmission with lock-up; 600-amp battery with run down protection; engine oil cooler; 140-amp alternator; transmission oil cooler; auto full-time 4 wheel drive, auto locking hub control and electronic shift, limited slip differential, 3.73 axle ratio; stainless steel exhaust; front independent suspension with anti-roll bar, front torsion springs, front torsion bar, premium front shocks, rigid rear axle suspension with rear leaf springs, premium rear shocks; power re-circulating ball steering with vehicle speed-sensing assist; front disc/rear drum brakes with 4-wheel antilock braking system; 29.5 gal. capacity fuel tank; front license plate bracket, running boards, side impact bars; split swing-out rear cargo door; HD trailering, trailer harness, trailer hitch; roof rack; front and rear body-colored bumpers with front tow hooks, rear step; body-colored bodyside cladding, body-colored fender flares; monotone paint; aero-composite halogen fully auto headlamps with daytime running lights; additional exterior lights include front fog/ driving lights, underhood light; driver's and passenger's power remote body-colored heated folding outside mirrors; front and rear 16" x 7" chrome alloy wheels; P265/70SR16 AT BSW front and rear tires; underbody mounted full-size steel spare wheel with crankdown; air conditioning, rear air conditioning with separate controls, rear heat ducts; AM/FM stereo, clock, seek-scan, cassette, 6-disc CD changer, 7 premium speakers, amplifier, auto equalizer, theft deterrent, and fixed antenna, rear audio controls; cruise control; power door locks, remote keyless entry, child safety rear door locks, power remote hatch/trunk release; 4 power accessory outlets, retained accessory power, garage door opener, emergency "S.O.S"; instrumentation display includes tachometer, oil pressure gauge, water temperature gauge, volt gauge, compass, exterior temp, trip odometer; warning indicators include battery, lights on, key in ignition, door ajar; driver's and passenger's front airbags; ignition disable, panic alarm, security system; deep tinted windows, power front and rear windows with driver's 1-touch down, fixed 1/4 vent windows; variable intermittent front windshield wipers, rear window defroster; seating capacity of 5, heated-cushion front bucket seats, adjustable tilt headrests, driver's and passenger's armrests, driver's seat includes 4-way power seat, 8-way direction control, power 2-way lumbar support, passenger's seat includes 4-way power seat, 8-way direction control, power 2-way lumbar support; heated 60-40 folding rear split-bench seat with tilt headrests, center armrest with storage; front and rear height adjustable seatbelts; leather seats, cloth door trim insert, full cloth headliner, full color-keyed carpet floor covering with carpeted floor mats, deluxe sound insulation, genuine wood trim on instrument panel; interior lights include dome light with fade, front and rear reading lights, 4 door curb lights, illuminated entry; leather-wrapped sport steering wheel with tilt adjustment; dual illuminated vanity mirrors, dual auxiliary visors; auto-dimming day/night rearview mirror; full floor console, full overhead console with storage, glove box with light, front and rear cupholders, 2 seat back storage pockets, driver's and passenger's door bins; carpeted cargo floor, carpeted trunk lid, cargo cover, cargo net, cargo light; chrome grille, black side window moldings, black front windshield molding, black rear window molding and body-colored door handles.

Base Prices

TK10706-Y91	Yukon Denali (4A)	38093	43535
Destination Charge:		675	675

Accessories

1SF	Denali Marketing Option Package 1 *Includes vehicle with standard equipment.*	NC	NC
R6M	New Jersey Cost Surcharge	83	NC

2000 YUKON XL

2000 Yukon XL

What's New?

The 2000 GMC Yukon XL is a complete redesign of last year's Suburban model, adding a little bit of body size but a whole lot of mechanical and comfort upgrades.

Review

The 2000 Yukon XL continues to build on GMC's desire to compete in the luxury SUV market. Just a few inches longer than its brother, the non-XL Yukon, this former Suburban — based on a new GM platform first seen as the foundation of the Chevy Silverado and GMC Sierra pickups — has the power, handling and indulgences to appeal to upscale SUV buyers. This is a complete overhaul, with the Yukon XL leaving its Chevy roots behind and stepping forward as a full GMC nameplate.

Available in a light-duty 1500 model and a heavy-duty 2500, the 2000 Yukon XL's contours have been reshaped to appear more muscular, foreshadowing the upgrades under the hood. The standard engine on all 1500 series models is the 4.8-liter Vortec V8, with 275 horsepower at 5200 rpm. Optional on the 1500 and standard on 2500s is a 5.3-liter Vortec V8 engine, offering 285 horsepower at 5200 rpm, 30 more horsepower than the larger 5700 Vortec it replaces. The standard engine on 2500s with a Gross Vehicle Weight rating over 7,200 lbs is the 6.0-liter Vortec V8, offering 300 horsepower at 4800 rpm. All engines drive a four-speed automatic transmission, improved to increase oil life and to operate at lower temperatures than previous transmissions.

The towing capabilities of this GMC have been increased as well. The 5.3-liter and 6.0-liter engines show maximum trailer capacities of 9,000 and 10,500 pounds, respectively. A 23 percent stiffer body and chassis, independent front torsion bar suspension and rear self-leveling, five-link coil-spring underpinnings make for fewer squeaks and rattles and better handling. The three-quarter ton suspension uses multileaf springs and a semifloating rear axle.

The overall driving experience has been heightened with the aid of a wider track and shorter turning diameters on both the two- and four-wheel-drive versions and standard variable-effort power steering system. This last feature adapts the required steering effort to the vehicle speed, providing more responsive feel at highway speeds, but reduced effort for parking maneuvers.

Interior space has been increased, with more room all around. With three rows of seats, the XL can carry nine passengers. Either of the halves of the third-row seat can be folded or removed for greater cargo capacity. With the second and third-row seats removed, you can drop a 4x8 sheet of plywood on the floor with the rear doors closed, due in part to the spare being moved under the cargo body. However, the base models aren't as nicely equipped on the inside, with plenty of plastic molding. To get the nice stuff, you have to upgrade to SLT trim.

The Yukon XL still carries much of its former Suburban self, but this redesign has made it a better vehicle. There are still a few shortcomings, but with the optional upgrades, the powerful engine choices and a better driving feel it's worth a look-see.

Standard Equipment

1500 SLE 2WD (4A): 5.3L V8 OHV SMPI 16-valve engine; 4-speed electronic OD auto transmission with lock-up; 600-amp HD battery with run down protection; 130-amp alternator; driver's selectable multi-mode transmission; rear-wheel drive, 3.73 axle ratio; stainless steel exhaust; front independent torsion suspension with HD anti-roll bar, front torsion springs, front torsion bar, rigid rear axle multi-link suspension with anti-roll bar, rear coil springs; power re-circulating ball steering; 4-wheel disc brakes with 4-wheel antilock braking system; 32.5 gal. capacity fuel tank; side impact bars; split swing-out rear cargo door; trailer harness; roof rack; front and rear chrome bumpers, front body-colored rub strip, rear colored rub strip, front tow hooks, rear step; body-colored bodyside molding with chrome bodyside insert, chrome wheel well molding; monotone paint; aero-composite halogen fully auto headlamps with daytime running lights; additional exterior lights include front fog/driving lights, underhood light; driver's and passenger's power remote body-colored heated folding outside mirrors; front and rear 16" x 7" silver alloy wheels; P265/70SR16 A/S BSW front and rear tires; underbody mounted full-size steel spare wheel with crankdown; air conditioning, rear air conditioning with separate controls, air filter, rear heat ducts, rear heater; AM/FM stereo, clock, seek-scan, single CD, 9 performance speakers, amplifier, auto equalizer, theft deterrent, and fixed antenna; cruise control; power door locks with 2 stage unlock, remote keyless entry, child safety rear door locks; 3 power accessory outlets, front cigar lighter(s), retained accessory power, smokers' package; instrumentation display includes tachometer, oil pressure gauge, water temperature gauge, volt gauge, compass, exterior temp, trip odometer; warning indicators include oil pressure, water temp, battery, low oil level, low coolant, lights on, key in ignition, low fuel, low washer fluid, door ajar, trunk ajar, service interval; driver's and passenger's front airbags, driver's and front passenger's seat mounted side airbags; ignition disable, panic alarm, security system; deep tinted windows, power front and rear windows with driver's 1-touch down, fixed 1/4 vent windows; variable intermittent front windshield wipers, sun visor strip, rear window defroster; seating capacity of 9, 40-20-40 bench front seat, adjustable tilt headrests, center armrest with storage, driver's seat includes 4-way power seat, 8-way direction control, lumbar support, passenger's seat includes 4-way direction control, lumbar support; 60-40 folding rear split-bench 2nd row seat with adjustable headrests, center armrest with storage; removable full folding 3rd row bench seat with fixed headrest; front height adjustable seatbelts; cloth seats, cloth door trim insert, full cloth headliner, full color-keyed carpet floor covering with carpeted floor mats; interior lights include dome light with delay, front reading lights, 4 door curb lights, illuminated entry; leather-wrapped sport steering wheel with tilt adjustment; dual illuminated vanity mirrors, dual auxiliary visors; auto-dimming day/night rearview mirror; mini overhead console, glove box with light, front and rear cupholders, instrument panel bin, interior concealed storage, 2 seat back storage pockets, driver's and passenger's door bins; carpeted cargo floor, plastic trunk lid, cargo cover, cargo net, cargo tie downs, cargo light; chrome grille, black side window moldings, black front windshield molding, black rear window molding and body-colored door handles.

2500 SLE 2WD (4A) (in addition to or instead of 1500 SLE 2WD (4A) equipment): 6.0L V8 OHV SMPI 16-valve engine; transmission oil cooler; 4.1 axle ratio; firm ride suspension, front independent suspension with HD anti-roll bar, front coil springs, rigid rear axle suspension with anti-roll bar, HD rear leaf springs; 38 gal. capacity fuel tank; front and rear 16" x 6.5" chrome styled steel wheels and LT245/75SR16 A/S BSW front and rear tires.

1500 SLE 4WD (4A) (in addition to or instead of 1500 SLE 2WD (4A) equipment): Part-time 4-wheel drive, auto locking hub control and electronic shift and power re-circulating ball steering with vehicle speed-sensing assist.

2500 SLE 4WD (4A) (in addition to or instead of 2500 SLE 2WD (4A) equipment): Part-time 4 wheel drive, auto locking hub control and electronic shift, front independent torsion suspension with HD anti-roll bar, front torsion springs and front torsion bar.

Base Prices

Code	Description	Invoice	MSRP
TC15906	1500 SLE 2WD (4A)	30160	34468
TC25906	2500 SLE 2WD (4A)	31488	35986
TK15906	1500 SLE 4WD (4A)	32678	37346
TK25906	2500 SLE 4WD (4A)	34080	38948
Destination Charge:		710	710

Accessories

Code	Description	Invoice	MSRP
1SB	**Marketing Option Package 1SB** *Includes vehicle with standard equipment.*	NC	NC
1SC	**Marketing Option Package 1SC** *Includes SLT Decor package: liftgate with liftglass rear door system, rear wiper/washer, front recovery hooks, front carpeted mats, intermediate carpeted mats, rear carpeted mats, load floor mats, front fog lamps, auxiliary rear heater, rear wiper/washer, 6-way power driver's side seat adjuster, 6-way power passenger's side seat adjuster, electronic cruise control, front air conditioning, rear air conditioning, folding rear seats, third seat floor mats, folding center seat, center fold down armrest with cupholders, remote keyless entry system, roof luggage carrier, electric rear window defogger, deep tinted glass, AM/FM stereo with CD, cassette, seek and scan, front reclining bucket seats and ultrasoft leather seat trim. NOT AVAILABLE with CF5.*	1879	2185
1SD	**Marketing Option Package 1SD** *Includes SLT Decor package: liftgate with liftglass rear door system, rear wiper/washer, front recovery hooks, front carpeted mats, intermediate carpeted mats, rear carpeted mats, load floor mats, front fog lamps, auxiliary rear heater, rear wiper/washer, front full feature bucket seats, floor console, power lumbar, 6-way power adjustable seat, power seat back recliner, dual inboard armrests, 2 position driver's memory seats, storage pockets behind both seats, electronic cruise control, front air conditioning, rear air conditioning, folding rear seats, third seat floor mats, folding*	2285	2657

CODE	DESCRIPTION	INVOICE	MSRP
	center seat, center fold down armrest with cupholders, remote keyless entry system, roof luggage carrier, electric rear window defogger, deep tinted glass, AM/FM stereo with CD, cassette, seek and scan, ultrasoft leather seat trim, electronic climate control, OnStar communications system, luxury convenience package: heated driver's and passenger's seat, power passenger's seat, heated electrochromic exterior mirror; gas preloaded shock absorbers, driver's side electrochromic mirror and Homelink garage door opener. NOT AVAILABLE with AE7, DF2, UV8, A95.		
A95	**Front Reclining Bucket Seats**	322	375
	Includes manual lumbars, inboard armrests, roof console, floor console, dual adjustable headrests, driver's and passenger's 6-way power seats and storage pocket behind seats. REQUIRES 1SB. NOT AVAILABLE with AE7. INCLUDED in 1SC.		
AE7	**Front 40/20/40 Split Bench Seat**	(430)	(500)
	Includes center fold down storage armrest with coin holder, map strap and writing board, manual lumbars, driver's and front passenger's 6-way power adjustable seats and storage pockets behind seats. REQUIRES 1SC. NOT AVAILABLE with UK6, 1SD, AL4, A95. INCLUDED in 1SB.		
AL4	**Center Bucket Seats**	249	290
	Includes 2 reclining buckets mounted in the second row. REQUIRES 1SC or 1SD. NOT AVAILABLE with AE7.		
BVE	**Side Step Running Boards**	280	325
	Running boards mount between front wheels and rear wheels at bottom of rocker panel.		
C68	**Electronic Climate Control**	108	125
	NOT AVAILABLE with CF5. INCLUDED in 1SD.		
CF5	**Electric Sliding Sunroof**	748	870
	Includes Homelink garage door opener and electronic climate control delete. REQUIRES 1SD. NOT AVAILABLE with C68, V53, U01, 1SC.		
CF5	**Electric Sliding Sunroof**	856	995
	Includes Homelink garage door opener. NOT AVAILABLE with C68, V53, U01, 1SD.		
DF2	**Camper Type Exterior Mirrors**	43	50
	Adjustable arm feature to provide field of vision for vehicles to 96" wide. NOT AVAILABLE with 1SD.		
G80	**Locking Rear Differential**	217	252
GT5	**4.10 Axle Ratio**	NC	NC
K05	**Engine Block Heater (Cold Weather)**	28	33
K47	**High Capacity Air Cleaner**	22	25
	REQUIRES 1SB.		
KC4	**Engine Oil Cooler (2500)**	116	135
KNP	**HD Auxiliary Transmission Cooling System (1500)**	83	96
NC7	**Federal Emission Override**	NC	NC
	Must be ordered for units shipped to federal areas.		
NW7	**Electronic Traction Control (2WD)**	168	195
	REQUIRES G80.		
NZZ	**Off-Road Skid Plates (4WD)**	82	95
	Includes aluminum front underbody shield starting behind front bumper and running to 1st cross member and steel transfer case frame mounted shields. Protects front underbody, oil pan and differential case .		

CODE	DESCRIPTION	INVOICE	MSRP
PF4	Wheels: 16" x 7" Bright Cast Aluminum (4) (1500) *REQUIRES 1SB.*	95	110
PY0	Wheels: 16" x 6.5" Polished Forged Aluminum (2500) *REQUIRES 1SB.*	95	110
QC3	Wheels: 16" x 7" Polished Cast Aluminum (4) (1500) *Same style as PF9. REQUIRES 1SC or 1SD. NOT AVAILABLE with PF4.*	95	110
QIW	Tires: LT245/75R16E On/Off Road BW SBR (2500 4WD) *Includes 2205 lbs front and 3042 lbs rear tire capacity.*	124	144
QMJ	Tires: P265/70R16 AT BW SBR (1500) *Includes 2184 lbs front and rear tire capacity. NOT AVAILABLE with QMK.*	NC	NC
QMK	Tires: P265/70R16 WOL SBR AT (1500) *Includes 2184 lbs front and rear tire capacity. NOT AVAILABLE with QMJ.*	108	125
R6M	New Jersey Cost Surcharge	94	NC
U01	Five Roof Marker Lamps *NOT AVAILABLE with CF5.*	47	55
UK6	Rear Seat Audio Radio Control *Includes rear seat audio system with dual headphone jacks, controls for volume, station, selection and media. REQUIRES A95. NOT AVAILABLE with AE7. INCLUDED in 1SD.*	142	165
UP0	Radio: AM/FM Stereo with CD and Cassette *Includes clock, speed sensitive volume, theft lock, auto tone control, auto reverse and music search cassette player with enhanced performance 8-speaker system and subwoofer. REQUIRES A95 and 1SB. INCLUDED in 1SC, 1SD.*	108	125
UV8	Cellular Phone Provision *Includes wiring for remote microphone jumper harness and cellular phone jumper harness. Wiring includes 6 leads - 2 for microphone, 1 for battery feed, 1 for ground, 1 for ignition and 1 for Class II communications. NOT AVAILABLE with 1SD.*	43	50
V53	Roof Luggage Carrier Delete *NOT AVAILABLE with CF5.*	NC	NC
YG4	Rear Seat Not Desired	NC	NC
Z55	Autoride (1500) *Includes wider aspect ratio tires with greater load carrying capacity than standard. Automatically changes the shock dampening for driving conditions and/or transient suspension inputs to optimize control. Includes orange color DeCarbon shock absorbers (high pressure gas charged with 46mm piston diameter). Biases suspension dampening toward firm setting when tow/haul mode selected.*	602	700
Z55	Autoride (2500) *Includes wider aspect ratio tires with greater load carrying capacity than standard. Automatically changes the shock dampening for driving conditions and/or transient suspension inputs to optimize control. Includes orange color DeCarbon shock absorbers (high pressure gas charged with 46mm piston diameter). Biases suspension dampening toward firm setting when tow/haul mode selected. NOT AVAILABLE with Z85.*	679	790
Z82	HD Trailering Equipment (2WD) *Includes trailering hitch platform, electric trailer brake wire harness with mounting provisions, a 7-wire harness with fully independent fused trailering circuits with*	309	359

CODE	DESCRIPTION	INVOICE	MSRP
	7-way sealed connector, IP jumper wiring harness for electric trailer brake controller and transmission fluid temperature gauge. and electronic traction control. REQUIRES G80 and KC4 or KNP.		
Z82	HD Trailering Equipment (4WD)	141	164
	Includes trailering hitch platform, electric trailer brake wire harness with mounting provisions, a 7-wire harness with fully independent fused trailering circuits with 7-way sealed connector, IP jumper wiring harness for electric trailer brake controller and transmission fluid temperature gauge. REQUIRES KC4 or KNP.		
Z85	Handling/Trailering Suspension Package (2500)	34	40
	Includes wider aspect ratio tires with greater load carrying capacity than Z83. Same load carrying capacity springs as Z83. Blue color Monroe shock absorber tubes (high pressure gas charged with 36mm piston diameter on 1500 series). Heavy duty engine and transmission oil cooling capability is provided with internal cooling. NOT AVAILABLE with Z55.		
ZW9	Panel Doors	NC	NC
ZY2	Conventional Two-Tone Paint	172	200

2000 CR-V

2000 Honda CR-V

What's New?

The 2000 Honda CR-V gets no changes this year.

Review

If sport-utilities were driven the way they were originally intended, you'd have a hard time convincing yourself that the 2000 Honda CR-V is the vehicle of choice. However, since most of the SUVs on the road these days spend all of their time on the road, the CR-V is a great combination of a car-like ride and interior with truck-like visibility and ground clearance.

Built on the Civic platform, the CR-V successfully integrates familiar Honda components into a visually pleasing design. The 2.0-liter DOHC inline four-cylinder engine is back again, making 146 horsepower and 133 foot-pounds of torque. Honda's familiar four-speed automatic transmission, with an overdrive on/off switch, puts that power to the wheels and a four-wheel double-wishbone suspension gives this vehicle its nice ride.

The CR-V's Real Time four-wheel-drive system is a derivative of the unit that Honda initially offered on their Civic wagon. All 4WD models come with a five-speed manual transmission, while the four-speed automatic is optional. A front-wheel-drive model is offered, but it comes only with the automatic transmission. The result of using all of these car components is not surprising: the CR-V looks and feels like a car.

The CR-V's interior is instantly recognizable to anyone who has spent time in Honda's passenger cars. Functionality takes precedence over style in the CR-V's cabin, and the result is easy-to-read gauges, well-placed controls (except for dash-mounted electric window switches), and high-quality, if somewhat uninspired, interior materials. Cargo capacity is an impressive 67.2 cubic feet when the rear seats are folded. The CR-V offers comfortable chairs for its occupants, each of which provides excellent visibility and the ability to recline when the trip grows long. The front passenger benefits from a left-side armrest and rear passengers will enjoy the door-mounted cupholders.

Available in either LX or EX trim levels, the CR-V is surprisingly well-equipped even in base LX form. Air conditioning with a filtration system is standard, as are power windows, power door locks, rear window wiper and defogger, AM/FM stereo with cassette, cruise control and a folding picnic table that doubles as a cargo area cover. Antilock brakes are available only on the EX model, which also comes with a CD player, remote entry system and alloy wheels.

The CR-V is not meant to replace hard-core recreational vehicles like the Jeep Wrangler or Toyota 4Runner. Instead, it is meant for the person who wants the look and feel of a sport utility without having to pay an exorbitant sticker price and huge gas bills. The CR-V will get people to work and back in all but the worst weather, and to their favorite picnic area, assuming it's not on the Rubicon Trail.

Standard Equipment

LX FWD (4A): 2.0L I4 DOHC MPI 16-valve engine; 4-speed electronic OD auto transmission; front-wheel drive, 4.36 axle ratio; steel exhaust; front independent double wishbone suspension with anti-roll bar, front coil springs, rear independent double wishbone suspension with anti-roll bar, rear coil springs; power rack-and-pinion steering with engine speed-sensing assist; front disc/rear drum brakes; 15.3 gal. capacity fuel tank; rear mud flaps, side impact bars; conventional rear cargo door; front and rear black bumpers with rear step; black bodyside molding, rocker panel extensions, black wheel well molding; monotone paint; aero-composite halogen headlamps; driver's and passenger's power remote black folding outside mirrors; front and rear 15" x 6" silver styled steel wheels; P205/70SR15 M&S BSW front and rear tires; outside rear mounted full-size steel spare wheel; air conditioning, air filter, rear heat ducts; AM/FM stereo, seek-scan, auto-reverse cassette, 4 speakers, and manual retractable antenna; cruise control with steering wheel controls; power door locks, child safety rear door locks, remote fuel release, power rear window remote release; 2 power accessory outlets, driver's foot rest; instrumentation display includes tachometer, water temperature gauge, in-dash clock, trip odometer; warning indicators include oil pressure, battery, lights on, key in ignition, low fuel, trunk ajar; driver's and passenger's front airbags; tinted windows, power front and rear windows with driver's 1-touch down, fixed 1/4 vent windows; fixed interval front windshield wipers, flip-up rear window, fixed interval rear wiper, rear window defroster; seating capacity of 5, front bucket seats, adjustable headrests, driver armrest, driver's seat includes 6-way direction control, passenger's seat includes 4-way direction control; 50-50 folding rear split-bench seat with reclining adjustable headrests, center armrest; front height adjustable seatbelts with front pretensioners; cloth seats, vinyl door trim insert, full cloth headliner, full carpet floor covering, plastic/rubber gear shift knob; interior lights include dome light, front reading lights; steering wheel with tilt adjustment; vanity mirrors; day/night rearview mirror; partial floor console, locking glove box, front and rear cupholders, instrument panel bin, 2 seat back storage pockets, driver's and passenger's door bins, rear door bins, front underseat tray; carpeted cargo floor, plastic trunk lid, cargo tie downs, cargo light, cargo concealed storage; black grille, black side window moldings, black front windshield molding, black rear window molding and black door handles.

LX AWD (5M) (in addition to or instead of LX FWD (4A) equipment): 5-speed OD manual transmission; full-time 4- wheel drive and 4.56 axle ratio.

EX AWD (5M) (in addition to or instead of LX AWD (5M) equipment): Front disc/rear drum brakes with 4-wheel antilock braking system; driver's and passenger's power remote body-colored folding outside mirrors; front and rear 15" x 6" alloy wheels; outside rear mounted full-size alloy spare wheel; AM/FM stereo, seek-scan, single CD, 4 speakers, and manual retractable antenna; remote keyless entry; panic alarm and body-colored door handles.

Base Prices

Code	Description	Invoice	MSRP
RD284YPBW	LX FWD (4A)	17036	18650
RD174YPBW	LX AWD (5M)	17401	19050
RD176YEW	EX AWD (5M)	18770	20550
Destination Charge:		415	415

Accessories

Code	Description	Invoice	MSRP
—	Transmission: 4-Speed Automatic (AWD) *Includes 4.36 axle ratio.*	730	800

2000 ODYSSEY

2000 Honda Odyssey

What's New?

Since it was redesigned last year, the only new feature is an optional navigation system on the EX.

Review

The second-generation Honda Odyssey is only a year old, and already it is recognized as the new minivan benchmark. It's powered by a 3.5-liter 24-valve VTEC V6 that produces up to 210 horsepower and 229 foot-pounds of torque, according to Honda. It requires 91-octane, but when we filled a test Odyssey with 87-octane fuel, it made 205 horses and 217 foot-pounds of torque. The V6 is based on the Accord's 3.0-liter engine but it offers substantially more power, since the Odyssey's got a bit of extra girth.

The base model LX includes such standard fare as dual sliding doors, power windows (including power rear-vent windows), power locks, power mirrors, cruise control, a theft-deterrent system, two 12-volt power outlets, front and rear air conditioning, antilock brakes, and, of course, the 3.5-liter V6 engine. The EX features such niceties as dual power sliding doors, body-colored door handles, a roof rack, keyless remote, an eight-way power driver's seat, alloy wheels, traction control, a CD player and steering-wheel-mounted radio controls.

Sitting on a four-wheel independent suspension, a first in the minivan segment, the Odyssey is supported comfortably and keeps the driver in touch with the road. Combined with the Odyssey's wide track, the suspension adds a nimble feel. Body roll around corners is well-damped for a vehicle of this height.

The most unique Odyssey feature continues to be its hideaway, or "magic" seat. With a minimum of effort and the use of one set of hands only, the rear seat can be folded out of sight and be flush with the floor in a matter of seconds. The second-row seats are convertible and can be used as separate captain's chairs or as a bench.

A minivan would not be complete without safety features, and the Odyssey comes with its share. All seven seats have headrests and three-point seatbelts, both firsts in the minivan market. ABS and an Electronic Brake Distribution system (EBD) are also standard. EBD senses the placement and amount of cargo, then compensates for it during hard braking to avoid rear-wheel lockup.

Terrific safety record, kid-friendly features, and nice power to boot—the Honda Odyssey might just be the ultimate family vehicle.

Standard Equipment

LX (4A): 3.5L V6 SOHC SMPI with variable valve timing 24-valve engine; 4-speed electronic OD auto transmission with lock-up; 130-amp alternator; front-wheel drive, 3.94 axle ratio; steel exhaust; front independent strut suspension with anti-roll bar, front coil springs, rear independent double wishbone suspension with anti-roll bar, rear coil springs; power rack-and-pinion steering; front disc/rear drum brakes with 4-wheel antilock braking system; 20 gal. capacity fuel tank; side impact bars; 4 doors with sliding left rear passenger's door, sliding right rear passenger's door, liftback rear cargo door; front and rear body-colored bumpers with rear step; black bodyside molding; clearcoat monotone paint; aero-composite halogen headlamps; driver's and passenger's power remote black folding outside mirrors; front and rear 16" x 6.5" steel wheels; P215/65TR16 A/S BSW front and rear tires; inside mounted compact steel spare wheel; air conditioning, air filter, rear heat ducts; AM/FM stereo, seek-scan, cassette, 4 speakers, and fixed antenna; cruise control with steering wheel controls; power door locks with 2 stage unlock, child safety rear door locks, remote fuel release; 2 power accessory outlets, driver's foot rest, retained accessory power; instrumentation display includes tachometer, water temperature gauge, in-dash clock, trip odometer; warning indicators include oil pressure, battery, low oil level, lights on, key in ignition, low fuel, bulb failure, door ajar, trunk ajar, service interval; driver's and passenger's front airbags; ignition disable; deep tinted windows with driver's 1-touch down, power 1/4 vent windows; variable intermittent front windshield wipers, sun visor strip, rear window wiper, rear window defroster; seating capacity of 7, front captain's seats, adjustable headrests, driver and passenger armrests, driver's seat includes 4-way direction control, passenger's seat includes, 4-way direction control; removable 50-50 folding 2nd row bench seat with reclining adjustable headrests; full folding 3rd row bench seat with adjustable headrest; front and rear height adjustable seatbelts with front pretensioners; cloth seats, cloth door trim insert, full cloth headliner, full carpet floor covering, plastic/rubber gear shift knob; interior lights include dome light, front and rear reading lights, 2 door curb lights; steering wheel with tilt adjustment; dual illuminated vanity mirrors, dual auxiliary visors; day/night rearview mirror; partial floor console, mini overhead console with storage, glove box, front and rear cupholders, instrument panel bin, 1 seat back storage pocket; carpeted cargo floor, plastic trunk lid, cargo light, cargo concealed storage; chrome grille, black side window moldings, black front windshield molding, black rear window molding and black door handles.

EX (4A) (in addition to or instead of LX (4A) equipment): Traction control; roof rack; body-colored bodyside molding; aero-composite halogen auto off headlamps; driver's and passenger's power remote body-colored folding outside mirrors; front and rear 16" x 6.5" alloy wheels; air conditioning with climate control; AM/FM stereo, seek-scan, single CD, 6 speakers, and fixed antenna, radio steering wheel controls; remote keyless entry, garage door opener; panic alarm; driver's seat includes 6-way power seat, lumbar support; removable 50-50 folding 2nd row captain's seat with reclining adjustable headrests; auto-dimming day/night rearview mirror; 2 seat back storage pockets, front underseat tray; cargo net and body-colored door handles.

Base Prices

RL185YEW	LX (4A)	20767	23400
RL186YPKW	EX (4A)	23417	26000
Destination Charge:		415	415

Accessories

—	Navigation System (EX)	1778	2000

2000 PASSPORT

2000 Honda Passport

What's New?

The Passport receives fresh front and rear fascias, a modified grille, redesigned front combination lamps and a host of new features for a new, top-of-the-line EX-L trim level.

Review

Honda's Passport competes well against midsized SUVs and has grown into a powerful, attractive alternative to the market leaders. Offering one of the stronger engines in its class, Passport changes little for 2000. Bolder exterior features, a few new standards and a new, upscale EX-L model are the main differences from the 1999 model.

Honda has added aggressive-looking front and rear fascias, a modified grille, and redesigned front combination lamps to the attractive Passport. Four-wheel-drive models also get a standard limited-slip rear differential, providing greater traction to the rear wheels. All models come standard with 16-inch alloy wheels and tires. Last year's arguably useful hatchgate is now an option, as all spares can be stored underneath. The interior provides user-friendly ergonomics, but plastic trim feels somewhat cheap. Clamber aboard and head for the hills - it's easy with push-button 4WD and standard antilock brakes that thwart nature's attempts to impede your progress.

All trim levels are offered with two- or four-wheel drive and come with a powerful 3.2-liter six-cylinder engine, with 205 horsepower to whisk you along with verve. The new EX-L (luxury package) model distinguishes itself with eye-catching two-tone paint, color-keyed body-side moldings, fender flares, and leather-trimmed seats and interior door panels. An AM/FM stereo system with in-dash, six-CD changer is standard, and available only on the EX-L. Finishing touches on their top model include a leather-wrapped steering wheel, wood-grain interior trim and, for when you're hopelessly lost on the off-road highway after dark, map lighting to find your way back to civilization and a safe covered parking spot.

Problems with the Passport are minimal. The location of the push-button 4WD switch is absurd, located directly next to the cruise-control button where it could be activated accidentally. Removable headrests, in lieu of the manual or auto-folding ones offered on competing models, don't have a place to go and could be a nuisance when you drop the back seats down for storage. Off-road, the Passport feels somewhat undersprung, but takes bumps and dips easily if speeds are kept down. Our final complaint is that the front seats are uncomfortable for larger, heavier folk. But, you were thinking about joining a gym anyway. So, it shouldn't be an issue, right?

The new Passport is a good blend of old-fashioned truck toughness and modern-day car-like convenience. While pleasant to look at already, the new aggressive features should make it stand out more from the crowd. If you prefer the strong engine or the fancy EX-L, perhaps you'll even open your wallet for one. However, there are plenty of quality vehicles in this class. If you're shopping for a new SUV, look at the Passport, but we recommend that you check out others as well.

Standard Equipment

LX 2WD (5M): 3.2L V6 DOHC SMPI 24-valve engine; 5-speed OD manual transmission; rear-wheel drive, 4.3 axle ratio; steel exhaust; front independent double wishbone suspension with anti-roll bar, front torsion springs, rigid rear axle multi-link suspension with anti-roll bar, rear coil springs; power rack-and-pinion steering with engine speed-sensing assist; front disc/rear drum brakes with 4-wheel antilock braking system; 21.1 gal. capacity fuel tank; front and rear mud flaps, skid plate(s), side impact bars; conventional rear cargo door; roof rack; front and rear body-colored bumpers with rear step; monotone paint; aero-composite halogen headlamps; driver's and passenger's power remote black folding outside mirrors; front and rear 16" x 7" painted styled steel wheels; P225/75SR16 M&S BSW front and rear tires; outside rear mounted full-size steel spare wheel; air conditioning; AM/FM stereo, seek-scan, cassette, 6 speakers, and fixed antenna; cruise control; power door locks, child safety rear door locks, power remote hatch/trunk release, power rear window remote release; 1 power accessory outlet; instrumentation display includes tachometer, water temperature gauge, in-dash clock, trip odometer; warning indicators include water temp, battery, lights on, key in ignition, low fuel, trunk ajar; driver's and passenger's front airbags; tinted windows, power front and rear windows with driver's 1-touch down, fixed 1/4 vent windows; variable intermittent front windshield wipers, sun visor strip, rear window wiper, rear window defroster; seating capacity of 5, front bucket seats, adjustable headrests, center armrest with storage, driver's seat includes 4-way direction control, passenger's seat includes 4-way direction control; 60-40 folding rear bench seat with reclining adjustable headrests; front and rear height adjustable seatbelts; cloth seats, cloth door trim insert, full cloth headliner, full carpet floor covering, plastic/rubber gear shift knob; interior lights include dome light, front reading lights, 4 door curb lights; steering wheel with tilt adjustment; vanity mirrors; day/night rearview mirror; full floor console, locking glove box with light, front and rear cupholders, 1 seat back storage pocket, driver's and passenger's door bins; carpeted cargo floor, plastic trunk lid, cargo cover, cargo net, cargo tie downs, cargo light; black grille, black side window moldings, black front windshield molding, black rear window molding and black door handles.

EX 2WD (4A) (in addition to or instead of LX 2WD (5M) equipment): Four-speed electronic OD auto transmission with lock-up; driver's selectable multi-mode transmission; 4.1 axle ratio; front express open sliding and tilting glass sunroof with sunshade; additional exterior lights include front fog/driving lights; driver's and passenger's power remote body-colored heated folding outside mirrors; P245/70SR16 M&S BSW front and rear tires; inside under cargo mounted full-size steel spare wheel; remote keyless entry; panic alarm, security system; deep tinted windows; simulated wood trim on instrument panel; leather-wrapped steering wheel with tilt adjustment; dual illuminated vanity mirrors; 2 seat back storage pockets and body-colored door handles.

4WD (in addition to or instead of 2WD equipment): Part-time 4-wheel drive, auto locking hub control and electronic shift, viscous limited slip differential; 4-wheel disc brakes with 4-wheel antilock braking system and P245/70SR16 M&S BSW front and rear tires (LX).

CODE	DESCRIPTION	INVOICE	MSRP
	Base Prices		
9B214Y2B1	LX 2WD (5M)	20358	22800
9B315Y4B1	LX 4WD (5M)	23167	25950
9B226Y2EA	EX 2WD (4A)	23747	26600
9B326Y4EA	EX 4WD (4A)	25933	29050
Destination Charge:		415	415
	Accessories		
—	Luxury Package (EX) *Includes two-tone paint, fender flares, body side molding, leather seat trim, leather door trim panels and AM/FM stereo with cassette.*	981	1100
4AT	Transmission: 4-Speed Automatic (LX 2WD) *Includes 4.10 axle ratio.*	1025	1150
4AT	Transmission: 4-Speed Automatic (LX 4WD) *Includes 4.10 axle ratio.*	1025	1150

2000 QX4

2000 Infiniti QX4

What's New?

Infiniti's luxury SUV gets minor improvements to its emissions system but is otherwise a carryover from the 1999 model year. Early reports indicate a more powerful QX4 will be available in mid-2000 as a 2001 model.

Review

In 1997, Infiniti released a luxury sport-utility vehicle based on the then-new Nissan Pathfinder. With little to differentiate the QX4 from the Pathfinder, other than a $10,000 price increase and a fancy-shmancy four-wheel-drive system, many critics unleashed a torrent of criticism at the vehicle. The problem was not that people disliked the mechanics, driving style or appearance of this truck; they just couldn't get around the fact that the QX4 offered little, other than full-time 4WD and an impressive Infiniti warranty, to distinguish itself from the already-capable Pathfinder.

The critics might have cried foul, but the buying public seemed not to notice. The QX4 has been a strong seller for Infiniti, outpacing the optimistic projections that Infiniti had for this sport-ute. In its first year out, the QX4 received an award from J. D. Power & Associates in their initial quality study, ranking the QX4 the best compact sport-utility vehicle. Seems that those who did buy this truck were pretty darned happy with the purchase.

So what is it that people like about the QX4? Well, there is the full-time 4WD system that offers drivers the security of having maximum traction without having to change gear levers or control knobs. Called All-Mode 4WD, the system employs a wet multi-plate clutch in the center differential that shifts power between the front and rear wheels depending on road surface conditions. It does this by monitoring power distribution and wheel slippage via electronic sensors in the front and rear differentials, a throttle position sensor, and a transfer unit sensor in the antilock braking system. The unit ensures that the tires have traction by shifting up to 50 percent of the power to the front wheels if the rear wheels start to slip.

Last year, Infiniti added side airbags with head protection, UV cut glass, new halogen headlights with a multi-parabola reflector, black rear privacy glass which replaced the previous bronze, automatic cut-off headlights, an Infiniti Immobilizer System, five new paint colors and the company retained the accessory power for the sunroof and windows. This year, only the emissions system has been improved.

CODE	DESCRIPTION	INVOICE	MSRP

Despite these upgrades, the similarities between the QX4 and the Pathfinder keep us from highly recommending the Infiniti, especially with a more powerful version of the Pathfinder due to arrive soon. The QX4's price premium offers a better warranty and dealer experience, but for our money we'd stick with the Nissan.

Standard Equipment

QX4 (4A): 3.3L V6 SOHC SMPI 12-valve engine; 4-speed electronic OD auto transmission with lock-up; 90-amp alternator; transmission, oil cooler; auto full-time 4 wheel drive, auto locking hub control and electronic shift, 4.64 axle ratio; stainless steel exhaust; front independent strut suspension with anti-roll bar, front coil springs, rigid rear axle multi-link suspension with anti-roll bar, rear coil springs; power rack-and-pinion steering with engine speed-sensing assist; front disc/rear drum brakes with 4-wheel antilock braking system; 21.1 gal. capacity fuel tank; front license plate bracket, front and rear mud flaps, running boards, skid plate(s), side impact bars; liftback rear cargo door; roof rack; front and rear body-colored bumpers with front and rear tow hooks, rear step; body-colored bodyside cladding, body-colored fender flares; monotone paint; aero-composite halogen auto off headlamps; additional exterior lights include front fog/driving lights; driver's and passenger's power remote body-colored heated folding outside mirrors; front and rear 16" x 7" silver alloy wheels; P255/65HR16 A/S BSW front and rear tires; underbody mounted full-size alloy spare wheel; air conditioning with climate control, air filter, rear heat ducts; premium AM/FM stereo, clock, seek-scan, cassette, single CD, 6 premium speakers, theft deterrent, and power retractable diversity antenna; cruise control with steering wheel controls; power door locks with 2 stage unlock, remote keyless entry, child safety rear door locks, power remote hatch/trunk release, power remote fuel release, power rear window remote release; 3 power accessory outlets, driver's foot rest, retained accessory power, garage door opener; instrumentation display includes tachometer, water temperature gauge, compass, exterior temp, trip odometer; warning indicators include oil pressure, water temp, battery, lights on, key in ignition, low fuel, low washer fluid, bulb failure, door ajar; driver's and passenger's front airbags, driver's and front passenger's seat mounted side airbags; ignition disable, panic alarm, security system; deep tinted windows, power front and rear windows with driver's 1-touch down, fixed 1/4 vent windows; variable intermittent front windshield wipers, flip-up rear window, fixed interval rear wiper, rear window defroster; seating capacity of 5, front bucket seats, adjustable headrests, center armrest with storage, driver's seat includes 6-way power seat, lumbar support, passenger's seat includes 4-way power seat; 60-40 folding rear bench seat with reclining adjustable headrests, center armrest; front height adjustable seatbelts with front pretensioners; leather seats, leatherette door trim insert, full cloth headliner, full carpet floor covering with carpeted floor mats, simulated wood trim on instrument panel, leather-wrapped gear shift knob; interior lights include dome light with fade, front and rear reading lights, illuminated entry; leather-wrapped steering wheel with tilt adjustment; dual illuminated vanity mirrors, dual auxiliary visors; day/night rearview mirror; full floor console, mini overhead console with storage, locking glove box, front and rear cupholders, 2 seat back storage pockets, driver's and passenger's door bins, rear door bins; carpeted cargo floor, plastic trunk lid, cargo cover, cargo net, cargo tie downs, cargo light, cargo concealed storage; body-colored grille, black side window moldings, black front windshield molding, black rear window molding and body-colored door handles.

Base Prices

CODE	DESCRIPTION	INVOICE	MSRP
71010	QX4 (4A)	32153	35550
Destination Charge:		525	525

Accessories

CODE	DESCRIPTION	INVOICE	MSRP
E10	Two-Tone Paint	263	500
F01	Infiniti Communicator *Includes 4-year Infiniti response center fee and 4-year cellular service fee.*	1378	1599

CODE	DESCRIPTION	INVOICE	MSRP
H17	Sunroof Preferred Package *Includes power sliding sunroof with sunshade, 6-disc CD changer and rear window wind deflector. NOT AVAILABLE with S02, H18, H19.*	1129	1250
H18	Sunroof Preferred Package *Includes power sliding sunroof with sunshade, 6-disc CD changer and rear window wind deflector. REQUIRES S02. NOT AVAILABLE with H17, H19.*	1129	1250
H19	Power Sliding Sunroof *Includes rear tilt feature and sliding sunshade. NOT AVAILABLE with H17, H18, S02.*	858	950
S02	Premium Sport Package *Includes heated driver's and front passenger's seats, HD battery and limited slip rear differential. REQUIRES H18. NOT AVAILABLE with H17, X03, H19.*	632	700
W17	Towing Package	294	390
X03	Heated Seats Package *Includes heated driver's and front passenger's seats and HD battery. NOT AVAILABLE with S02.*	361	400

2000 HOMBRE

2000 Isuzu Hombre

What's New?

Hombres receive an upgraded standard suspension package and V6 engines get a horsepower boost. The three-door spacecab gets an additional S trim model.

Review

Isuzu's entry in the compact-pickup market, the Hombre, is built using sheetmetal stamped by General Motors with basic mechanical and structural components donated from the Chevrolet S-10/GMC Sonoma twins. When it debuted in 1996, the Hombre came with two-wheel drive, a regular cab and a weak, 2.2-liter four-cylinder engine — not exactly the tough stuff truck buyers craved.

Built in the United States, Hombres are currently available in a variety of cab and powertrain configurations, ranging from a standard-cab, 2WD model with a 2.2-liter four-cylinder engine to a 4WD, 4.3-liter V6 Spacecab model featuring an optional third door.

Isuzu introduced the Spacecab extended-cab model, a 4.3-liter V6 engine and a four-speed automatic transmission in 1997, adding four-wheel drive in 1998. Last year, Hombres received a new bumper design and a third-door option. For 2000, Isuzu ups the ante, making the heavy-duty suspension standard, bumping the 4WD V6 horsepower by 10 (2WD models get five) and the 2.2 four cylinder becomes a dual fuel engine, burning E85 alcohol and gasoline.

The regular-cab versions are available in S and XS trim levels, and options are few. S models are the workhorses, with vinyl floor covering and limited options that include air conditioning, stereo and rear step bumper. Hombre XS models are better equipped, offering custom cloth upholstery, carpeted floors and a tachometer.

Extended-cab models are now offered in S and XS trim, providing vinyl folding jump seats in the rear and easy-entry seats in the front. If ordered with the optional third door, the truck comes equipped with only one jump seat.

Four-wheel antilock brakes, battery-rundown protection, auto on/off headlamps and a theft-deterrent system are standard on all models. As before, 4WD Hombre buyers will enjoy standard alloy wheels and will benefit from a midyear tire upgrade to an aggressive 235/75R15 size.

Isuzu hasn't been selling many pickups in the past several years. As personal-use pickup sales skyrocketed, the company stuck with basic trucks more suited for work than play. Indications are that Hombre can't change Isuzu's bleak forecast in this segment.

Standard Equipment

S 2WD REGULAR CAB (5M): 2.2L I4 OHV SMPI 8-valve engine; 5-speed OD manual transmission; 690-amp battery with run down protection; 100-amp alternator; rear-wheel drive, 3.73 axle ratio; stainless steel exhaust; HD ride suspension, front independent double wishbone suspension with anti-roll bar, front coil springs, rigid rear axle suspension with HD rear leaf springs; power re-circulating ball steering; front disc/rear drum brakes with 4-wheel antilock braking system; 18.5 gal. capacity fuel tank; side impact bars; front black bumper; clearcoat monotone paint; aero-composite halogen fully auto headlamps with daytime running lights; driver's and passenger's manual black folding outside mirrors; front and rear 15" x 7" steel wheels; P205/75SR15 A/S BSW front and rear tires; underbody mounted compact steel spare wheel; radio prep and fixed antenna; 1 power accessory outlet, front lighter element(s), retained accessory power, smokers' package; instrumentation display includes oil pressure gauge, water temperature gauge, volt gauge, trip odometer; warning indicators include battery, lights on, key in ignition, low fuel; driver's front airbag, passenger's cancelable front airbag; tinted windows; variable intermittent front windshield wipers, sun visor strip; seating capacity of 3, bench front seat, fixed headrests, driver's seat includes 2-way direction control, passenger's seat includes 2-way direction control; cloth seats, vinyl door trim insert, full cloth headliner, full vinyl floor covering, plastic/rubber gear shift knob, cabback insulator; interior lights include dome light with delay; day/night rearview mirror; glove box with light, front cupholder, driver's and passenger's door bins; cargo concealed storage; black grille, black side window moldings, black front windshield molding, black rear window molding and black door handles.

S 2.2L 2WD SPACE CAB (5M) (in addition to or instead of S 2WD REGULAR CAB (5M) equipment): 4.1 axle ratio; ignition disable; vented rear windows; seating capacity of 5; 50-50 folding side facing rear jump seats; interior lights include front reading lights; dual illuminated vanity mirrors, dual auxiliary visors and carpeted cargo floor.

S 4.3L 2WD SPACE CAB (4A) (in addition to or instead of S 2.2L 2WD SPACE CAB (5M) equipment): 4.3L V6 OHV SMPI 12-valve engine; 4-speed electronic OD auto transmission with lock-up.

XS 2WD REGULAR CAB (5M) (in addition to or instead of S 2WD REGULAR CAB (5M) equipment): Rear black bumpers with rear step; air conditioning; instrumentation display includes tachometer; 60-40 split-bench front seat, fixed headrests, center armrest with storage, driver's seat includes 4-way direction control, passenger's seat includes 4-way direction control; premium cloth seats, cloth door trim insert and full carpet floor covering.

XS 2.2L 2WD SPACE CAB (5M) (in addition to or instead of S 2.2L 2WD SPACE CAB (5M) equipment): 3.42 axle ratio; air conditioning; instrumentation display includes tachometer; variable intermittent front windshield wipers; sliding rear window; 60-40 split-bench front seat, fixed headrests; driver's seat includes 4-way direction control, passenger's seat includes 4-way direction control, easy entry; premium cloth seats, cloth door trim insert and full carpet floor covering with carpeted floor mats.

XS 4.3L 2WD SPACE CAB (4A) (in addition to or instead of S 4.3L 2WD SPACE CAB (4A) equipment): Air conditioning; 3 power accessory outlets, retained accessory power; instrumentation display includes tachometer; variable intermittent front windshield wipers, sliding rear window; 60-40 split-bench front seat fixed headrests, center armrest with storage, driver's seat includes 4-way direction control, passenger's seat includes 4-way direction control, easy entry; premium cloth seats, cloth door trim insert and full carpet floor covering with carpeted floor mats.

S 4WD REGULAR CAB (5M) (in addition to or instead of S 2WD REGULAR CAB (5M) equipment): 4.3L V6 OHV SMPI 12-valve engine; part-time 4-wheel drive, auto locking hub control and electronic shift, 3.42 axle ratio; front torsion springs, front torsion bar; 4-wheel disc brakes with 4-wheel antilock braking system; front and rear black bumpers with front tow hooks, rear step; P235/70SR15 A/S BSW front and rear tires; underbody mounted full-size steel spare wheel; air conditioning; AM/FM stereo, clock, seek-scan, 4 speakers, and fixed antenna; instrumentation display includes tachometer and ignition disable.

CODE	DESCRIPTION	INVOICE	MSRP

S 4WD SPACE CAB (5M) (in addition to or instead of S 4WD REGULAR CAB (5M) equipment): Radio prep and fixed antenna; vented rear windows; seating capacity of 5; 50-50 folding rear side facing jump seats; interior lights include front reading lights and carpeted cargo floor.

XS 4WD SPACE CAB (5M) (in addition to or instead of S 4WD SPACE CAB (5M) equipment): AM/FM stereo, clock, seek-scan, cassette, 4 speakers, and fixed antenna; 3 power accessory outlets, retained accessory power; variable intermittent front windshield wipers, sliding rear window; 60-40 split-bench front seat, fixed headrests, center armrest with storage, driver's seat includes 4-way direction control, passenger's seat includes 4-way direction control, easy entry; premium cloth seats, cloth door trim insert, full carpet floor covering with carpeted floor mats; dual illuminated vanity mirrors and dual auxiliary visors.

Base Prices

CODE	DESCRIPTION	INVOICE	MSRP
P15	S 2WD Regular Cab SB (5M)	11021	11360
P25	XS 2WD Regular Cab SB (5M)	11962	12860
P05	S 2.2L 2WD Space Cab SB (5M)	12908	13450
P55	XS 2.2L 2WD Space Cab SB (5M)	14425	15510
P74	S 4.3L 2WD Space Cab SB (4A)	14885	15670
P64	XS 4.3L 2WD Space Cab SB (4A)	16329	17560
T35	S 4WD Regular Cab SB (5M)	16923	17815
T75	S 4WD Space Cab SB (5M)	17873	18820
T65	XS 4WD Space Cab SB (5M)	18694	20100
Destination Charge:		495	495

Accessories

CODE	DESCRIPTION	INVOICE	MSRP
4AT	Transmission: 4-Speed Automatic (S 2.2L 2WD X-Cab)	951	985
4AT	Transmission: 4-Speed Automatic (S 2WD Reg Cab)	1016	1050
4AT	Transmission: 4-Speed Automatic (S 4WD X-Cab)	1473	1545
4AT	Transmission: 4-Speed Automatic (XS 2.2L 2WD X-Cab)	1187	1280
4AT	Transmission: 4-Speed Automatic (XS 2WD Reg Cab)	995	1075
4AT	Transmission: 4-Speed Automatic (XS 4WD X-Cab)	1962	2110
A1	Air Conditioning (S)	735	835
C1	Convenience Package (XS V6 2WD X-Cab) *Includes tilt wheel and cruise control.*	400	425
CPT	Floor Carpeting (S X-Cab)	70	80
F2	Radio: AM/FM Stereo with Clock and 4 Speakers (S)	207	235
I2	Rear Step Bumper (S 2WD Reg Cab)	53	60
JHG	Floor Mats (S X-Cab) *INCLUDED in P2.*	26	30
M1	Wheels: Alloy (2WD X-Cab Except S V6)	246	280
P2	Preferred Equipment Package (XS 2WD Reg Cab) *Includes sliding rear window, AM/FM stereo with cassette and 4 speakers, tachometer and floor mats.*	443	471
P6	Power Package (XS V6 X-Cab) *Includes power windows, power door locks and power outside mirrors.*	612	650
TDR	Driver's Side Third Door (X-Cab) *Deletes 1 rear jumpseat.*	329	375

2000 RODEO

2000 Isuzu Rodeo

What's New?

The Rodeo marches into the 2000 model year with an aggressive exterior restyle, a collection of ergonomic and quality improvements, and interior upgrades.

Review

When it comes to figuring out which truck best meets your needs, it almost always requires a compromise of some sort or another. The closest thing to perfect in this price range has been the lower trim levels of the Ford Explorer, and spectacular sales of this popular SUV prove that buyers find its combination of room, style and power the best in the segment.

The Explorer is a fine sport-ute, but there's another face in this neighborhood that deserves consideration. Enter the restyled Isuzu Rodeo with over 200 changes, including an aggressive new appearance, updated seating, 16-inch wheels and an optional Intelligent Suspension Control system.

The Rodeo's interior provides cupholders, excellent ergonomics, and plastic trim/switchgear that looks and feels somewhat cheap. Clamber aboard and head for the hills; it's easy to thwart nature's obstacles with push-button 4WD and standard antilock brakes.

Buyers can also select the new Ironman LS package, which includes V6, air conditioning, power moonroof, alloy wheels and Intelligent Suspension Control, which automatically adjusts to one of 17 shock rebound and compression rates, depending on road conditions.

Three trim levels are available: S, LS and LSE. The basic Rodeo has two-wheel drive and a weak 2.2-liter four-cylinder engine. Step up to the S V6 and a 205-horsepower, 3.2-liter unit whisks you along with verve.

At the top of the complaint list about the truck is the ridiculous location of the push-button 4WD switch, located directly next to the cruise-control button, where it could be activated accidentally. Off-road, the new Isuzu feels somewhat undersprung, but takes bumps and dips easily if speeds are kept to a minimum. Front bucket seats are vastly improved this year and rear-seat riders enjoy a supportive bench seat and plenty of legroom.

For 2000, Isuzu also added a transferable 10-year/120,000-mile powertrain warranty for all of its SUVs, making it the longest powertrain warranty offered by any automaker in the United States.

The Rodeo is an excellent blend of old-fashioned truck toughness and modern-day car-like convenience. If you're looking for a new $30,000 SUV, this one should be on your shopping list.

Standard Equipment

S 2.2L 2WD (5M): 2.2L I4 DOHC SMPI 16-valve engine; 5-speed OD manual transmission; 600-amp battery; 100-amp alternator; rear-wheel drive, 4.3 axle ratio; stainless steel exhaust; front independent double wishbone suspension with anti-roll bar, front torsion springs, front torsion bar, gas-pressurized front shocks, rigid rear axle multi-link suspension with anti-roll bar, rear coil springs, gas-pressurized rear shocks; power rack-and-pinion steering with engine speed-sensing assist; front disc/rear drum brakes with 4-wheel antilock braking system; 21.1 gal. capacity fuel tank; front and rear mud flaps, skid plate(s), side impact bars; conventional rear cargo door; trailer harness; front and rear black bumpers with front and rear tow hooks, rear step; clearcoat monotone paint; aero-composite halogen headlamps; driver's and passenger's manual black folding outside mirrors; front and rear 16" x 7" silver styled steel wheels; P225/75SR16 M&S BSW front and rear tires; underbody mounted full-size steel spare wheel; rear heat ducts; AM/FM stereo, seek-scan, cassette, 4 speakers, and fixed antenna; child safety rear door locks; 2 power accessory outlets, driver's foot rest; instrumentation display includes tachometer, water temperature gauge, in-dash clock, trip odometer; warning indicators include oil pressure, battery, lights on, key in ignition, low fuel, door ajar, trunk ajar; driver's and passenger's front airbags; tinted windows, manual front and rear windows; fixed interval front windshield wipers, flip-up rear window, rear window defroster; seating capacity of 5, front bucket seats, adjustable headrests, driver's seat includes 4-way direction control, passenger's seat includes 4-way direction control; 60-40 folding rear split-bench seat with reclining adjustable headrests; front and rear height adjustable seatbelts; cloth seats, cloth door trim insert, full cloth headliner, full carpet floor covering, plastic/rubber gear shift knob; interior lights include dome light, front reading lights; dual illuminated vanity mirrors; day/night rearview mirror; full floor console, locking glove box, front and rear cupholders, 1 seat back storage pocket, driver's and passenger's door bins; carpeted cargo floor, plastic trunk lid, cargo tie downs, cargo light; body-colored grille, black side window moldings, black front windshield molding, black rear window molding and black door handles.

S 3.2L 2WD (5M) (in addition to or instead of S 2.2L 2WD (5M) equipment): 3.2L V6 DOHC SMPI 24-valve engine; 90-amp alternator; P245/70SR16 M&S BSW front and rear tires; cruise control and steering wheel with tilt adjustment.

LS 2WD (5M) (in addition to or instead of S 3.2L 2WD (5M) equipment): Roof rack; front and rear body-colored bumpers with front and rear tow hooks; driver's and passenger's power remote black heated folding outside mirrors; air conditioning, rear heat ducts; AM/FM stereo, seek-scan, cassette, CD changer pre-wiring, in-dash CD pre-wiring, 6 speakers, and fixed antenna; power door locks with 2 stage unlock, remote keyless entry; 3 power accessory outlets; panic alarm; power front and rear windows with driver's 1-touch down; variable intermittent front windshield wipers, fixed interval rear wiper; carpeted floor mats; interior lights include 2 door curb lights; 2 seat back storage pockets; cargo cover and cargo net.

LSE 2WD (4A) (in addition to or instead of LS 2WD (5M) equipment): Four-speed electronic OD auto transmission with lock-up; driver's selectable multi-mode transmission; auto ride control; front power sliding and tilting glass sunroof with sunshade; body-colored bodyside molding; additional exterior lights include front fog/driving lights; driver's and passenger's power remote body-colored heated folding outside mirrors; front and rear 16" x 7" silver alloy wheels; AM/FM stereo, seek-scan, cassette, 6-disc CD changer, 6 speakers, and fixed antenna; deep tinted windows; leather seats, leather door trim insert; simulated wood trim on instrument panel; leather-wrapped steering wheel with tilt adjustment and body-colored door handles.

4WD (in addition to or instead of 2WD (equipment): Part-time 4-wheel drive, auto locking hub control and electronic shift, limited slip differential (LS/LSE), 4.3 axle ratio; 4-wheel disc brakes with 4-wheel antilock braking system and outside rear mounted full-size steel (S/LS)/alloy (LSE) spare wheel.

CODE	DESCRIPTION	INVOICE	MSRP

Base Prices

P45	S 2.2L 2WD (5M)	16995	18080
R45	S 3.2L 2WD (5M)	19097	20985
R55	LS 2WD (5M)	21091	23435
V45	S 4WD (5M)	21330	23440
V55	LS 4WD (5M)	23508	26120
R64	LSE 2WD (4A)	25767	28790
V64	LSE 4WD (4A)	27982	31265
Destination Charge:		495	495

Accessories

AQR	Air Conditioning (S 2.2L) *NOT AVAILABLE with P21.*	836	950
ARR	Air Conditioning (S 3.2L) *NOT AVAILABLE with P21.*	836	950
BSB	Tube Side Step (4WD) *REQUIRES RMQ. NOT AVAILABLE with BSU.*	278	355
BSS	Tube Side Step (2WD Except S 2.2L) *REQUIRES RMQ.*	278	355
BSU	Tube Side Step (4WD - S 3.2L/LS) *NOT AVAILABLE with BSB.*	278	355
CMC	Gray Cargo Mat	47	60
E5	Intermittent Rear Wiper/Washer (S)	41	47
ENN	Cargo Convenience Net (S)	20	25
FDX	Radio: AM/FM Stereo with Cassette and 6-CD Changer (LS)	311	353
FDY	In-Dash 6-Disc CD Changer (LS)	508	650
FLZ	In-Dash CD Player (LS)	428	550
GPG	Gold Package (LSE) *Includes gold badging, tires: P245/70R16 and wheels: 16" 6-spoke gold accent alloy.*	312	400
GRG	Brush Guard	233	298
H2	Power Moonroof (LS) *REQUIRES RMQ.*	616	700
IPR	Ironman Package (LS) *Includes intelligent suspension control, titan gray front and rear bumpers, titan gray face hybrid spare tire cover, aero roof rack crossbars, Ironman triathalon graphics and Ironman heathered floor mats. NOT AVAILABLE with RBS, OMG, OMI, OMK, OMV, OMZ.*	926	1052
JAH	Gray Carpeted Floor Mats (S 2.2L)	43	55
JBG	Gray Carpeted Floor Mats (S 3.2L)	43	55
M2	Wheels: 16" Aluminum (LS) *Includes tires: P245/70R16.*	352	400
OFT	Titan Gray Overfenders (S 3.2L 2WD) *REQUIRES RMQ. NOT AVAILABLE with RBS.*	228	259
OM	Titan Gray Body Side Moldings (S)	81	104

CODE	DESCRIPTION	INVOICE	MSRP
OME	Titan Gray Body Side Moldings (LS) *NOT AVAILABLE with OMG, OMI, OMK, OMV, OMZ, IPR.*	81	104
OMG	Palazzo Red Body Side Moldings (LS) *NOT AVAILABLE with OMI, OMK, OMV, OMZ, IPR.*	81	104
OMI	Garden Green Body Side Moldings (LS) *NOT AVAILABLE with OMG, OMK, OMV, OMZ, IPR.*	81	104
OMK	Silver Body Side Moldings (LS) *NOT AVAILABLE with OMG, OMI, OMV, OMZ, IPR.*	81	104
OMV	Alpine White Body Side Moldings (LS) *NOT AVAILABLE with OMG, OMI, OMK, OMZ, IPR.*	81	104
OMZ	Roman Bronze Body Side Moldings (LS) *NOT AVAILABLE with OMG, OMI, OMK, OMV, IPR.*	81	104
P21	Preferred Equipment Package #1 (S) *Includes aero roof rails. NOT AVAILABLE with AQR, ARR.*	889	1010
R1	Outside Spare Mount and Cover (4WD/LS 2WD) *NOT AVAILABLE with TRV.*	NC	NC
RBS	Running Board *NOT AVAILABLE with IPR.*	280	360
RMQ	Transmission: 4-Speed Automatic with Overdrive (LS) *Includes power/winter mode and shift lock, black resin shift knob with black bezel and shift position indicator. NOT AVAILABLE with BSU.*	900	1000
RMQ	Transmission: 4-Speed Automatic with Overdrive (S 3.2L) *Includes power/winter mode and shift lock, black resin shift knob with black bezel and shift position indicator. NOT AVAILABLE with BSU.*	910	1000
RSP	Rear Roof Spoiler	77	98
SCO	Center Armrest Pad (Gray) (S)	31	40
TLG	Tail Lamp Guards (4WD)	66	84
TLG	Tail Lamp Trim (2WD)	66	84
TRP	Trailer Hitch *NOTE: with outside spare tire mount. NOT AVAILABLE with TRV.*	198	253
TRV	Trailer Hitch *NOTE: with spare tire mounted under vehicle. NOT AVAILABLE with R1, TRP.*	198	253
UCC	Retractable Gray Cargo Cover (S)	70	90

2000 CHEROKEE

2000 Jeep Cherokee

What's New?

The 2000 compact Cherokee scores the '99 Grand Cherokee's redesigned 4.0-liter PowerTech inline six in addition to a new five-speed manual transmission. The Limited model sports bright chrome accents, including the front grille, the headlamp surrounds, the side graphics, the rear license-plate brow, and the 16-inch wheels.

Review

Some things never change and the Jeep Cherokee is one of those mainstays. Unlike its posh and bigger Grand Cherokee sibling, which keeps adding comforts and graceful touches, the ever-practical Cherokee simply keeps on rolling, looking little different now from when it was first introduced in 1984. But that's all going to change with the 2001 model, when it gets its first serious redesign, lifting some styling cues from the Jeep Dakar concept, which sort of looks like a squashed Jeep Wrangler. Not that we fear change—we fear aerodynamic-based change. Watch for the hip-to-be-square Cherokee to go rounded, seriously rounded, next year.

However, this year, the Cherokee nabs the optional redesigned 4.0-liter PowerTech inline six-cylinder, which is said to be quieter, cleaner, and more refined than the previous version it has had since 1987—the new powerplant makes 190 horsepower at 4,600 rpm and 225 foot-pounds of torque at 3,000 rpm. It also complies with the U.S. low-emission vehicle (LEV) requirements. The standard engine is the wimpier 2.5-liter PowerTech inline four-cylinder, and either engine can be mated to the five-speed manual or the optional three-speed automatic transmission.

The Cherokee is one of the few SUVs that can actually balance on- and off-road duties. The coil-front/rear-leaf suspension continues to provide a smooth ride, while the Command-Trac (part-time) and Select-Trac (full-time) transfer cases are still around to help buyers escape far beyond where some of the more luxurious SUVs wimp out. Although if you tend to be city folk, two-wheel drive is still available for 2000.

Two- and four-door configurations remain, and four trim levels are at your disposal—Limited, Sport, Classic, and SE. New exterior colors are Patriot Blue, Sienna, Silverstone, and Medium Fern Green. A radio/cassette combo is standard, and both the Classic and Limited versions have cast aluminum wheels.

If you're a fan of this body style, you might want to scoop up this collector's item while you can. After all, you can't go wrong with an SUV that in 16 years hasn't needed to out-trick itself to become more competitive.

Standard Equipment

SE 2WD 2-DOOR (5M): 2.5L I4 OHV SPI 8-valve engine; 5-speed OD manual transmission; 500-amp battery; 124-amp alternator; rear-wheel drive, 4.1 axle ratio; stainless steel exhaust; front non-independent suspension with anti-roll bar, front coil springs, rigid rear axle suspension with anti-roll bar, rear leaf springs; power re-circulating ball steering; front disc/rear drum brakes; 20 gal. capacity fuel tank; side impact bars; liftback rear cargo door; front and rear black bumpers with front black rub strip, rear step; black fender flares; monotone paint; sealed beam halogen headlamps; driver's and passenger's manual black folding outside mirrors; front and rear 15" x 7" silver styled steel wheels; P215/75SR15 A/S BSW front and rear tires; inside mounted compact steel spare wheel; rear heat ducts; AM/FM stereo, clock, seek-scan, cassette, 4 speakers, and fixed antenna; 1 power accessory outlet; instrumentation display trip odometer; warning indicators include oil pressure, water temp, battery, lights on, key in ignition, trunk ajar; driver's and passenger's front airbags; tinted windows, fixed rear windows; variable intermittent front windshield wipers, sun visor strip, rear window defroster; seating capacity of 5, front bucket seats, fixed headrests, center armrest with storage, driver's seat includes 4-way direction control, passenger's seat includes 4-way direction control; removable full folding rear bench seat; vinyl seats, vinyl door trim insert, full cloth headliner, full carpet floor covering, deluxe sound insulation, plastic/rubber gear shift knob; interior lights include dome light; day/night rearview mirror; full floor console, locking glove box with light, front cupholder, instrument panel bin; carpeted cargo floor, plastic trunk lid, cargo tie downs, cargo light; black grille, black side window moldings, black front windshield molding, black rear window molding and black door handles.

SE 2WD 4-DOOR (5M) (in addition to or instead of SE 2WD 2-DOOR (5M) equipment): Child safety rear door locks; manual front and rear windows and fixed 1/4 vent windows.

SPORT 2WD (5M) (in addition to or instead of SE 2WD (5M) equipment): 4.0L I6 OHV SMPI 12-valve engine; 3.07 axle ratio; black bodyside molding, black fender flares; monotone paint with badging; front and rear 15" x 7" full-face steel wheels; P225/75SR15 A/T BSW front and rear tires; instrumentation display includes tachometer, oil pressure gauge, water temperature gauge, volt gauge; warning indicators include low fuel and premium cloth seats.

CLASSIC 2WD (4A) (in addition to or instead of SPORT 2WD (4A) equipment): 4-speed electronic OD auto transmission with lock-up; 3.55 axle ratio; roof rack; front and rear body-colored bumpers front with body-colored rub strip, rear step; body-colored bodyside molding, body-colored fender flares; driver's and passenger's power remote black folding outside mirrors; front and rear 16" x 7" silver alloy wheels; P225/70SR16 A/S BSW front and rear tires; fixed interval rear wiper; front bucket seats, adjustable headrests, carpeted floor mats; leather-wrapped steering wheel and body-colored grille.

LIMITED 2WD (4A) (in addition to or instead of CLASSIC 2WD (4A) equipment): Air conditioning; deep tinted windows; leather seats; full overhead console with storage and cargo cover.

SE 4WD/SPORT 4WD/CLASSIC 4WD (in addition to or instead of SE 2WD/SPORT 2WD/CLASSIC 2WD equipment): Part-time 4-wheel drive, auto locking hub control and manual shift.

LIMITED 4WD (4A) (in addition to or instead of LIMITED 2WD (4A) equipment): Auto full-time 4-wheel drive, auto locking hub control and manual shift and inside mounted full-size alloy spare wheel.

CODE	DESCRIPTION	INVOICE	MSRP

Base Prices

CODE	DESCRIPTION	INVOICE	MSRP
XJTL72	SE 2WD 2-Door (5M)	15455	16445
XJTL74	SE 2WD 4-Door (5M)	16421	17485
XJJL72	SE 4WD 2-Door (5M)	16854	17960
XJJL74	SE 4WD 4-Door (5M)	17815	18995
XJTH72	Sport 2WD 2-Door (5M)	17096	18870
XJTH74	Sport 2WD 4-Door (5M)	18026	19905
XJJH72	Sport 4WD 2-Door (5M)	18444	20380
XJJH74	Sport 4WD 4-Door (5M)	19375	21415
XJTP74	Classic 2WD 4-Door (4A)	19316	21370
XJJP74	Classic 4WD 4-Door (4A)	20669	22885
XJTS74	Limited 2WD 4-Door (4A)	20829	23090
XJJS74	Limited 4WD 4-Door (4A)	22715	25210
Destination Charge:		535	535

Accessories

CODE	DESCRIPTION	INVOICE	MSRP
22A	**Quick Order Package 22A (SE 2WD)** *Includes vehicle with standard equipment. REQUIRES EPE and DGA and 4XA. NOT AVAILABLE with DDQ, DGB, DDD, ERH, DSA, BGK, AJK, NHK, CLE, AA3, GXX, AWS, TBB, CSA, AHT, AYB, GAF, M5.*	NC	NC
22B	**Quick Order Package 22B (SE 2WD)** *Includes vehicle with standard equipment. REQUIRES EPE and DGA and AA3. NOT AVAILABLE with DDQ, DDD, DGB, ERH, 4XA, AHT.*	NC	NC
23A	**Quick Order Package 23A (SE)** *Includes vehicle with standard equipment. REQUIRES EPE and DDQ and 4XA. NOT AVAILABLE with DGA, ERH, DDD, DGB, DSA, BGK, AJK, NHK, CLE, AA3, GXX, AWS, TBB, CSA, AHT, AYB, GAF, M5.*	NC	NC
23B	**Quick Order Package 23B (SE)** *Includes vehicle with standard equipment. REQUIRES EPE and DDQ and AA3. NOT AVAILABLE with DGA, ERH, DDD, DGB, 4XA, AHT.*	NC	NC
25A	**Quick Order Package 25A (SE)** *Includes vehicle with standard equipment. REQUIRES ERH and DDD and 4XA. NOT AVAILABLE with EPE, DGA, DDQ, DGB, DSA, BGK, AJK, NHK, CLE, AA3, GXX, AWS, TBB, CSA, AHT, AYB, GAF, M5.*	NC	NC
25B	**Quick Order Package 25B (SE)** *Includes vehicle with standard equipment. REQUIRES ERH and DDD and AA3. NOT AVAILABLE with EPE, DGA, DDQ, DGB, 4XA, AHT.*	NC	NC
25J	**Quick Order Package 25J (Sport)** *Includes vehicle with standard equipment. REQUIRES ERH and DDD and AA4. NOT AVAILABLE with AHT, DGB, DHP.*	NC	NC
26A	**Quick Order Package 26A (SE)** *Includes vehicle with standard equipment. REQUIRES ERH and DGB and 4XA. NOT AVAILABLE with DDD, DDQ, DGA, EPE, DSA, BGK, AJK, NHK, CLE, AA3, GXX, AWS, TBB, CSA, AHT, AYB, GAF, M5.*	NC	NC

CODE	DESCRIPTION	INVOICE	MSRP
26B	Quick Order Package 26B (SE)	NC	NC
	Includes vehicle with standard equipment. REQUIRES ERH and DGB and AA3. NOT AVAILABLE with EPE, DGA, DDQ, DDD, 4XA.		
26H	Quick Order Package 26H Limited (Limited)	NC	NC
	Includes vehicle with standard equipment. REQUIRES ERH and DGB and AA6.		
26J	Quick Order Package 26J (Sport)	NC	NC
	Includes vehicle with standard equipment. REQUIRES ERH and DGB and AA4. NOT AVAILABLE with DDD.		
26S	Quick Order Package 26S (Classic)	NC	NC
	Includes vehicle with standard equipment. REQUIRES ERH and DGB and AA5.		
4XA	Air Conditioning Bypass (SE)	NC	NC
	NOT AVAILABLE with 22B, 23B, 25B, 26B.		
AA3	SE Special Value Group (SE)	1084	1275
	Manufacturer Discount	(1084)	(1275)
	Net Price	NC	NC
	Includes air conditioning, power fold-away mirrors, premium cloth hi-back bucket seats and rear window wiper/washer. NOT AVAILABLE with 22A, 23A, 25A, 26A.		
AA4	Sport Value Group (Sport 2-Door)	1845	2170
	Manufacturer Discount	(1845)	(2170)
	Net Price	NC	NC
	Includes Sport Value Group discount, air conditioning, front and rear floor mats, remote keyless entry, light group, headlight off time delay, underhood light, front map/dome lights, illuminated visor vanity mirrors, power door locks, power fold-away mirrors, roof rack, tilt steering column, leather-wrapped steering wheel, power windows and rear window wiper/washer.		
AA4	Sport Value Group (Sport 4-Door)	1993	2345
	Manufacturer Discount	(1993)	(2345)
	Net Price	NC	NC
	Includes Sport Value Group discount, air conditioning, front and rear floor mats, remote keyless entry, light group, headlight off time delay, underhood light, front map/dome lights, illuminated visor vanity mirrors, power door locks, power fold-away mirrors, roof rack, tilt steering column, leather-wrapped steering wheel, power windows and rear window wiper/washer.		
AA5	Classic Value Group (Classic)	1551	1825
	Manufacturer Discount	(1551)	(1825)
	Net Price	NC	NC
	Includes air conditioning, remote keyless entry, light group: headlight off time delay, underhood light, front map/dome lights, illuminated visor vanity mirrors; power door locks, tilt steering column and power windows.		
AA6	Limited Value Group (Limited)	1751	2060
	Manufacturer Discount	(1751)	(2060)
	Net Price	NC	NC
	Includes remote keyless entry, light group: headlight off time delay, underhood light, front map/dome lights, illuminated visor vanity mirrors; power door locks, 6-way power driver's seat, premium leather low back buckets, speed control, tilt steering column and power windows.		

CODE	DESCRIPTION	INVOICE	MSRP
AHT	Trailer Tow Group (4WD Except SE) *Includes equalizer hitch, 7-wire receptacle and 4-wire trailer adapter and auxiliary transmission oil cooler. REQUIRES 26J (Sport) and TBB. NOT AVAILABLE with 25J.*	208	245
AHT	Trailer Tow Group *Includes equalizer hitch, 7-wire receptacle and 4-wire trailer adapter and auxiliary transmission oil cooler. REQUIRES 26B (SE) and (TBB or AY) or 26J (Sport). NOT AVAILABLE with 22A, 23A, 25A, 26A, 22B, 23B, 25B, 25J, AWE.*	310	365
AJK	Convenience Group (SE) *Includes speed control, tilt steering column and leather-wrapped steering wheel. NOT AVAILABLE with 22A, 23A, 25A, 26A.*	374	440
AWE	Up Country Suspension Package (4WD - Classic/Limited) *Includes Trac-Lok differential axle, skid plate group, delete rear stabilizer bar and tow hooks.*	616	725
AWE	Up Country Suspension Package (Sport 4WD) *Includes Trac-Lok differential axle, skid plate group, tire: full size spare, delete rear stabilizer bar and tow hooks. REQUIRES AA4.*	663	780
AWE	Up Country Suspension Package (Sport 4WD) *Includes Trac-Lok differential axle, skid plate group, tire: full size spare, delete rear stabilizer bar and tow hooks. REQUIRES AA4.*	718	845
AWS	Smokers' Group *Includes front/rear ash receiver and cigar lighter. NOT AVAILABLE with 22A, 23A, 25A, 26A.*	17	20
AYB	Wheel Plus Group (SE) *Includes tire: full size spare, tires: P225/75R15 Wrangler RT/S A/T and wheels: 15" x 7" aluminum Ecco. NOT AVAILABLE with 22A, 23A, 25A, 26A.*	744	875
BGK	4-Wheel Antilock Brakes *REQUIRES ERH and (22B or 25B or 26B) (SE). NOT AVAILABLE with 22A, 23A, 25A, 26A, EPE.*	510	600
CLE	Front and Rear Floor Mats (SE) *NOT AVAILABLE with 22A, 23A, 25A, 26A.*	43	50
CSA	Spare Tire Cover (SE) *NOT AVAILABLE with 22A, 23A, 25A, 26A.*	43	50
CSC	Cargo Compartment Cover (Sport/Classic)	64	75
CUN	Overhead Console (Classic)	200	235
DDD	Transmission: 5-Speed HD Manual (SE/Sport) *Includes 3.07 axle ratio. NOT AVAILABLE with 22A, 22B, 23A, 23B, 26A, 26B, EPE, 26J.*	NC	NC
DDQ	Transmission: 5-Speed Manual (SE) *Includes 4.10 axle ratio. NOT AVAILABLE with 25A, 22A, 22B, 26A, 25B, 26B, ERH.*	NC	NC
DGA	Transmission: 3-Speed Automatic (SE 2WD) *Includes 3.55 axle ratio. NOT AVAILABLE with 23A, 25A, 26A, 23B, 25B, 26B, ERH.*	531	625
DGB	Transmission: 4-Speed Automatic (Classic/Limited)	NC	NC
DGB	Transmission: 4-Speed Automatic (SE/Sport) *NOT AVAILABLE with 22A, 23A, 25A, 22B, 23B, 25B, EPE, 25J.*	803	945

CODE	DESCRIPTION	INVOICE	MSRP
DHP	Selec-Trac Full Time 4WD System (4WD - Sport/Classic) *REQUIRES AA4 and AWE. NOT AVAILABLE with 25J.*	336	395
DHP	Selec-Trac Full Time 4WD System (4WD - Sport/Classic) *REQUIRES AA4. NOT AVAILABLE with 25J.*	459	540
DHP	Selec-Trac Full Time 4WD System (Sport) *Includes tire: full size spare. REQUIRES AA4. NOT AVAILABLE with 25J.*	514	605
DSA	Trac-Lok Differential Axle (SE/Sport) *REQUIRES TBB or AYB. NOT AVAILABLE with 22A, 23A, 25A, 26A.*	242	285
EPE	Engine: 2.5L Power Tech I4 (SE) *NOT AVAILABLE with DGB, DDD, BGK, 25A, 25B, 26A, 26B.*	NC	NC
ERH	Engine: 4.0L Power-Tech I6 (SE) *NOT AVAILABLE with 22A, 23A, 22B, 23B, DDQ, DGA.*	846	995
ERH	Engine: 4.0L Power-Tech I6 (Sport/Classic/Limited)	NC	NC
GAF	Deep Tint Sunscreen Glass (Sport 2-Door)	319	375
GAL	Deep Tint Sunscreen Glass (Sport 4-Door/Classic)	230	270
GTS	Power Heated Fold-Away Mirrors (Sport/Classic/Limited) *REQUIRES AA4.*	38	45
GXX	Sentry Key Theft Deterrent System *NOT AVAILABLE with 22A, 23A, 25A, 26A.*	64	75
HAA	Air Conditioning (SE) *NOT AVAILABLE with 4XA, 22B, 23B, 25B, 26B, ERH.*	723	850
JPM	Heated Front Seats (Limited)	468	550
JPS	6-Way Power Driver's Seat (Classic)	255	300
LNJ	Fog Lamps (Sport/Classic/Limited)	94	110
M5	Premium Cloth Hi-Back Bucket Seats (SE/Sport) *REQUIRES AA3. NOT AVAILABLE with 22A, 23A, 25A, 26A.*	NC	NC
MWG	Roof Rack (SE) *NOT AVAILABLE with 22A, 23A, 25A, 26A.*	119	140
NHK	Engine Block Heater *NOT AVAILABLE with 22A, 23A, 25A, 26A.*	34	40
NHM	Speed Control (Sport/Classic)	213	250
RAZ	Radio: AM/FM Stereo with CD, Cass. and Equalizer (Sport/Classic/Limited) *Includes 4 speakers.*	349	410
RCG	6 Premium Infinity Speakers (Classic/Limited) *REQUIRES RAZ.*	298	350
TBB	Tire: Full Size Spare (Classic 4WD) *Includes matching spare wheel.*	170	210
TBB	Tire: Full Size Spare (SE) *Includes matching spare wheel. NOT AVAILABLE with 22A, 23A, 25A, 26A.*	64	75
TBB	Tire: Full Size Spare (Sport) *Includes matching spare wheel. REQUIRES AA4.*	123	145
TBB	Tire: Full Size Spare (Sport/2WD - Classic/Limited) *Includes matching spare wheel. REQUIRES AA4 and WJU or AA5 or AA6.*	179	210
WJU	Wheels: Body Color 15" x 7" Aluminum Ecco (Sport)	208	245
WJW	Wheels: 15" x 7" Aluminum Ecco (Sport) *NOT AVAILABLE with WJU.*	208	245

2000 GRAND CHEROKEE

2000 Jeep Grand Cherokee

What's New?

New exterior cladding has been slapped onto the Laredo, and both models have received interior touch-ups. Two-wheel drive is available with the 4.7-liter V8. Shale Green and Silverstone are the new skin tones.

Review

The designers of the Jeep Grand Cherokee are taking some much needed R&R following last year's introduction of the second-generation Grand, so there have been no significant mechanical or appearance changes. It was the first redesign since its 1992 introduction (as a '93 model), and the public basically gained an all-new best-of-the-best Jeep. Signature items like the vertical slot grille and trapezoidal wheel openings remained but were altered just enough to distance it from the previous generation. It was also made 4 inches longer and outfitted with redesigned recirculating-ball steering, a fresh three-link rear suspension, and front Quadra Link coil suspension that make it stable and carlike, and handle like a pro. Another notable improvement was the new automatic transmission, which increases initial acceleration and provides smoother shifting between gears.

The Grand's standard engine is a 4.0-liter inline six, and the next step up is the optional 4.7-liter V8. In fact, this potent power-maker has been such a hit that Chrysler is morphing from it a version for the 2000 Durango, as well as a 3.7-liter V6 engine in the future for the Town & Country and Dodge Ram, and a variant for the next-generation Chrysler 300 and upcoming Dodge Charger.

You'll find cloth surroundings standard inside the Laredo, while the Limited lets you slide behind the wheel in leather-trimmed comfort (optional on the Laredo); the leather front seats feature 10-way power-seating choices, but you'll likely find your comfort level short of that. We're huge fans of the behind-the-wheel stereo controls (standard on Limited, optional on Laredo), the Infinity sound system and the Infrared Dual Zone Climate Control System that allows the driver and passenger to have separate control settings.

Also new to the '99 Grand was the Quadra-Drive four-wheel-drive system that keeps things moving even if only one tire has traction, and its reaction time is faster than you can say "stuck." The Laredo's standard transfer case is the full-time Selec-Trac, while the Limited's is the on-demand Quadra-Trac II. While going off-road may not be something you've considered doing with your just-purchased luxury vehicle, remember that this is a Jeep, the original 4x4, and it hasn't lost any of its go-anywhere war heritage. It makes itself at home on the asphalt or in the boonies, and the 4x4 systems make it a walk in the park - even if it's a rocky one.

Standard Equipment

LAREDO 2WD (4A): 4.0L I6 OHV SMPI 12-valve engine; 4-speed electronic OD auto transmission with lock-up; 625-amp battery with run down protection; 136-amp alternator; rear-wheel drive, 3.55 axle ratio; stainless steel exhaust; front non-independent suspension with anti-roll bar, front coil springs, rigid rear axle suspension with anti-roll bar, rear coil springs; power re-circulating ball steering; 4-wheel disc brakes with 4-wheel antilock braking system; 20.5 gal. capacity fuel tank; side impact bars; liftback rear cargo door; roof rack; front and rear black bumpers with rear step; black bodyside cladding; monotone paint; aero-composite halogen headlamps, delay-off feature; additional exterior lights include underhood light; driver's and passenger's power remote black folding outside mirrors; front and rear 16" x 7" silver alloy wheels; P225/75SR16 A/S BSW front and rear tires; inside under cargo mounted compact steel spare wheel; air conditioning, rear heat ducts; AM/FM stereo, clock, seek-scan, cassette, 6 speakers, and fixed antenna; cruise control with steering wheel controls; power door locks, child safety rear door locks; 2 power accessory outlets, front cigar lighter(s), driver's foot rest, retained accessory power, smokers' package; instrumentation display includes tachometer, oil pressure gauge, water temperature gauge, volt gauge, compass, exterior temp, systems monitor, trip computer, trip odometer; warning indicators include oil pressure, water temp, battery, lights on, key in ignition, low fuel; driver's and passenger's front airbags; ignition disable, panic alarm; deep tinted windows, power front and rear windows with driver's 1-touch down, fixed 1/4 vent windows; variable intermittent front windshield wipers, sun visor strip, flip-up rear window, fixed interval rear wiper, rear window defroster; seating capacity of 5, front bucket seats, adjustable headrests, center armrest with storage, driver's seat includes 4-way direction control, passenger's seat includes 4-way direction control; removable 60-40 folding rear bench seat with adjustable headrests; front and rear height adjustable seatbelts; cloth seats, vinyl door trim insert, full cloth headliner, full carpet floor covering, deluxe sound insulation, simulated wood trim on instrument panel, plastic/rubber gear shift knob; interior lights include dome light with fade, front and rear reading lights, illuminated entry; steering wheel with tilt adjustment; vanity mirrors, passenger's side auxiliary visor; day/night rearview mirror; full floor console, mini overhead console, locking glove box with light, front and rear cupholders, driver's and passenger's door bins; carpeted cargo floor, carpeted trunk lid, cargo tie downs, cargo light; chrome grille, black side window moldings, black front windshield molding, black rear window molding and black door handles.

LIMITED 2WD (4A) (in addition to or instead of LAREDO 2WD (4A) equipment): Front and rear body-colored bumpers with rear step; body-colored bodyside cladding; monotone paint with bodyside accent stripe; aero-composite halogen fully auto headlamps, delay-off feature; additional exterior lights include front fog/driving lights; driver's and passenger's power remote black heated folding outside mirrors; P245/70SR16 performance A/S BSW front and rear tires; dual zone front air conditioning with climate control; AM stereo/FM stereo, clock, seek-scan, cassette, single CD, 6 premium speakers, amplifier, graphic equalizer, and fixed antenna, radio steering wheel controls; remote keyless entry; 3 power accessory outlets, garage door opener; warning indicators include low oil level, low coolant, low washer fluid, bulb failure, door ajar, trunk ajar, service interval; security system; driver's seat includes 6-way power seat, power 2-way lumbar support, passenger's seat includes 6-way power seat, power 2-way lumbar support; leather seats, full carpet floor covering with carpeted floor mats; memory on driver's seat with 2 memory setting(s) includes settings for exterior mirrors; interior lights include 2 door curb lights; leather-wrapped steering wheel with tilt adjustment; dual illuminated vanity mirrors; auto-dimming day/night rearview mirror; 2 seat back storage pockets; cargo cover, cargo net and body-colored grille.

LAREDO 4WD (4A) (in addition to or instead of LAREDO 2WD (4A) equipment): Part-time 4-wheel drive, auto locking hub control and manual shift.

LIMITED 4WD (4A) (in addition to or instead of LIMITED 2WD (4A) equipment): Quadra-Trac II on demand 4-wheel drive.

Base Prices

Code	Description	Invoice	MSRP
WJTH74	Laredo 2WD (4A)	24258	26765
WJJH74	Laredo 4WD (4A)	26027	28735
WJTP74	Limited 2WD (4A)	28962	32110
WJJP74	Limited 4WD (4A)	31135	34540
Destination Charge:		535	535

Accessories

26E Quick Order Package 26E (Laredo) ..... NC NC
Includes vehicle with standard equipment. REQUIRES ERH. NOT AVAILABLE with ATA, ADE, EVA, AHX, TTB.

26F Quick Order Package 26F (Laredo) 2474 2910
Manufacturer Discount ..... (680) (800)
Net Price 1794 2110
Includes fog lamps, universal garage door opener, remote keyless entry, luxury group: auto headlamps, front power seats, auto dimming rearview mirror; illuminated visor vanity mirrors, power heated fold-away mirrors, AM/FM stereo with CD, cassette and equalizer, security alarm, Infinity 6-speaker sound system and tires: P225/75R16 OWL A/S. REQUIRES ERH. NOT AVAILABLE with EVA, ADC, AHX, TTB.

26G Quick Order Package 26G (Limited) ..... NC NC
Includes vehicle with standard equipment. REQUIRES ERH. NOT AVAILABLE with EVA, AHX.

26K Quick Order Package 26K (Limited) 893 1050
Includes power sunroof and cold weather group: power heated fold-away mirrors, heated seats and 10-way power driver's seat. REQUIRES ERH. NOT AVAILABLE with EVA, AHX.

28E Quick Order Package 28E (Laredo) ..... NC NC
Includes vehicle with standard equipment. REQUIRES EVA. NOT AVAILABLE with ERH, ATA, AHT, AHC, ADE, TTB, AWB.

28F Quick Order Package 28F (Laredo) 2474 2910
Manufacturer Discount ..... (680) (800)
Net Price 1794 2110
Includes fog lamps, universal garage door opener, remote keyless entry, luxury group: auto headlamps, front power seats, auto dimming rearview mirror; illuminated visor vanity mirrors, power heated fold-away mirrors, AM/FM stereo with CD, cassette and equalizer, security alarm, Infinity 6-speaker sound system and tires: P225/75R16 OWL A/S. REQUIRES EVA. NOT AVAILABLE with ERH, ADC, AHT, AHC, TTB, AWB.

28G Quick Order Package 28G (Limited) ..... NC NC
Includes vehicle with standard equipment. REQUIRES EVA. NOT AVAILABLE with ERH, AHT, AHC.

CODE	DESCRIPTION	INVOICE	MSRP
28K	Quick Order Package 28K (Limited)	893	1050
	Includes power sunroof and cold weather group: power heated fold-away mirrors, heated seats and 10-way power driver's seat. REQUIRES EVA. NOT AVAILABLE with ERH, AHT, AHC.		
ADC	Convenience Group (Laredo)	544	640
	Manufacturer Discount	(425)	(500)
	Net Price	119	140
	Includes cargo net, cargo compartment cover, front and rear floor mats, remote keyless entry and tires: P225/75R16 OWL A/S. REQUIRES 26E or 28E. NOT AVAILABLE with 26F, 28F, TTB, AWE.		
ADC	Convenience Group with AWE (Laredo 4WD)	701	825
	Manufacturer Discount	(425)	(500)
	Net Price	276	325
	Includes cargo net, cargo compartment cover, front and rear floor mats, remote keyless entry and tires: P225/75R16 OWL A/S. REQUIRES 26E or 28E. NOT AVAILABLE with 26F, 28F, TTB.		
ADE	Cold Weather Group (Laredo)	255	300
	Includes power heated fold-away mirrors and power heated seats. REQUIRES FL and AFF. NOT AVAILABLE with 26F, 28F. INCLUDED in 26K, 28K.		
ADE	Cold Weather Group	213	250
	Includes power heated fold-away mirrors, heated seats and 10-way power driver's seat. REQUIRES FL. NOT AVAILABLE with 26E, 28E. INCLUDED in 26K, 28K.		
ADL	Skid Plate Group (4WD)	170	200
	Includes skid plate package and tow hooks.		
AFF	Luxury Group (Laredo)	638	750
	Includes auto headlamps and front power seats. REQUIRES ATA or RCE. INCLUDED in 26F, 28F.		
AHC	Trailer Tow Prep Group	89	105
	Includes Class III for 4.0L I6, mechanical cooling fan, trailer tow wiring assembly and 3.73 axle ratio. REQUIRES 26. NOT AVAILABLE with AHT, 28E, 28F, 28G, 28K.*		
AHT	Trailer Tow Group	306	360
	Includes 5000 lb maximum loaded trailer weight, 750 lb maximum tongue weight, 64 square foot maximum trailer frontal area, 25 foot maximum trailer length, frame mounted receiver hitch (equalizer type), 7-way round wiring adapter, plastic receiver cover, wiring connector, 7-way round to 4-way flat plug receiver cover and 3.73 axle ratio. REQUIRES TBW and (26E or 26F) (Laredo) or (26G or 26K) (Limited) or AWE. NOT AVAILABLE with AHC, 28E, 28F, 28G, 28K, AHX.		
AHX	Trailer Tow Group IV	217	255
	Includes 64 square foot maximum trailer frontal area and 30 foot maximum trailer length, frame mounted receiver hitch (equalizer type), 7-way round wiring connector, 7-way round to 4-way flat plug adapter, plastic receiver cover and maximum trailer weight (6500 lb). REQUIRES TBW and (28E or 28F) (Laredo) or (28G or 28K) (Limited) or AWE. NOT AVAILABLE with 26E, 26F, 26G, 26K, AHT.		
ATA	Radio: Infinity AM/FM Stereo with Cassette (Laredo)	888	1045
	Includes remote 10-disc CD changer, covered cargo storage, 12V rear power outlet and Infinity 6-speaker sound system. NOT AVAILABLE with 26F, RAZ, 28F.		

CODE	DESCRIPTION	INVOICE	MSRP
ATA	Radio: Infinity AM/FM Stereo with Cassette *Includes remote 10-disc CD changer, covered cargo storage, 12V rear power outlet and Infinity 6-speaker sound system. NOT AVAILABLE with 26E, RAZ, 28E.*	255	300
AWB	Quadra Drive 4WD System (Laredo 4WD) *Includes Quadra Trac II on demand 4WD system, vari-lock progressive axles, Quadra Drive badge, Dana rear axle and 3.73 axle ratio. NOT AVAILABLE with 26E, 26F, DSA, DHP.*	468	550
AWB	Quadra Drive 4WD System (Laredo 4WD) *Includes Quadra Trac II on demand 4WD system, vari-lock progressive axles, Quadra Drive badge, Dana rear axle and 3.73 axle ratio. NOT AVAILABLE with 28E, 28F, DSA, DHP.*	846	995
AWE	Up Country Suspension Group (Laredo 4WD) *Includes unique front and rear springs, jounce bumpers/rear spacers and rear sway bar and bushings; skid plate group, tow hooks, tire: full-size spare, wheel: spare matching 5th wheel and HD suspension. REQUIRES 26E or 28E. NOT AVAILABLE with ADC.*	489	575
AWE	Up Country Suspension Group (Limited 4WD) *Includes unique front and rear springs, jounce bumpers/rear spacers and rear sway bar and bushings; skid plate group, tow hooks, tire: full-size spare, wheel: spare matching 5th wheel and HD suspension.*	332	390
AWE	Up Country Suspension Group with ADC (Laredo 4WD) *Includes unique front and rear springs, jounce bumpers/rear spacers and rear sway bar and bushings; skid plate group, tow hooks, tire: full-size spare, wheel: spare matching 5th wheel and HD suspension. REQUIRES (26E or 28E) and ADC. NOT AVAILABLE with 26F, 28F.*	332	390
DGB	Transmission: 4-Speed Automatic *NOT AVAILABLE with EVA, Z1B, Z6B.*	NC	NC
DGB	Transmission: Multi-Speed Automatic *NOT AVAILABLE with ERH.*	NC	NC
DHF	Quadra Trac II On Demand 4WD System (Laredo 4WD)	378	445
DHP	Selec-Trac Full Time 4WD System (4WD) *REQUIRES 28E or 28F (Laredo). NOT AVAILABLE with AWB.*	NC	NC
DSA	Trac-Lok Differential Axle *REQUIRES DHP. NOT AVAILABLE with AWB.*	242	285
ERH	Engine: 4.0L Power-Tech I6 *NOT AVAILABLE with 28E, 28F, 28G, 28K, Z1B, Z6B.*	NC	NC
EVA	Engine: 4.7L Power Tech V8 (Laredo 2WD/Limited) *Includes 3.73 axle ratio. NOT AVAILABLE with DGB, 26E, 26F, 26G, 26K.*	910	1070
EVA	Engine: 4.7L Power Tech V8 (Laredo 4WD) *Includes 3.73 axle ratio and Quadra Trac II on demand 4WD system. NOT AVAILABLE with 26E, 26F, DGB.*	990	1165
FL	Leather Low Back Bucket Seats (Laredo) *REQUIRES AFF.*	591	695
GTM	Power Heated Fold-Away Mirrors (Laredo) *INCLUDED in 26F, 28F.*	43	50
GWA	Power Sunroof *INCLUDED in 26K, 28K.*	680	800

CODE	DESCRIPTION	INVOICE	MSRP
LNJ	Fog Lamps (Laredo) *INCLUDED in 26F, 28F.*	102	120
LSA	Security Alarm (Laredo) *INCLUDED in 26F, 28F.*	128	150
NHK	Engine Block Heater	34	40
PUL	Sienna Tinted Pearl Coat	170	200
RAZ	Radio: AM/FM Stereo with CD, Cassette and EQ (Laredo) *NOT AVAILABLE with ATA. INCLUDED in 26F, 28F.*	285	335
RCE	Infinity 6-Speaker Sound System (Laredo) *REQUIRES ATA or RAZ. INCLUDED in 26F, 28F.*	349	410
TBW	Tire: Full Size Spare *Includes wheel: spare matching 5th wheel.*	136	160
TTB	Tires: P245/70R16 OWL AT (Laredo) *NOT AVAILABLE with 26F, 28F, ADC.*	370	435
TTB	Tires: P245/70R16 OWL AT (Laredo)	157	185
TTB	Tires: P245/70R16 OWL AT (Limited)	NC	NC

2000 WRANGLER

2000 Jeep Wrangler

What's New?

A reengineered 4.0-liter PowerTech inline six-cylinder that is more refined and quiet, with reduced emissions, is standard for Sport and Sahara for 2000. Shift quality kicks up a notch, thanks to an all-new five-speed manual transmission. A radio/cassette combo with four speakers is now standard for the Sport, and the Sahara gains a radio/CD. Solar Yellow, Patriot Blue and Silverstone are additional exterior colors.

Review

The Wrangler continues to be the off-road icon, even unmodified. The Jeep began as a vehicle for military use and has retained its Spartan utility while slowly evolving into a practical and popular means of transportation. The Wrangler has never lost its drive-me-hard-through-the-slop origins, despite its improvements for enjoyable daily commuting. And it's one of the cheapest convertibles around.

Available in SE, Sport and Sahara trim levels, the Wrangler fits into several budgets. Our favorite model is the Sport, with a gutsy 4.0-liter inline six engine that has been cured this year of one of our chief complaints, its noise. It can be hooked to either the standard five-speed manual or a three-speed automatic transmission. The SE is for people who don't mind a lack of power (a 2.5-liter is all she wrote at this level) and four-wheel ABS. The Sahara is the priciest of the batch, and while it gets you the same 4.0-liter offering as the Sport, a leather-wrapped steering wheel, front and rear tow hooks, the Convenience Group (with lockable storage and dual cupholders), and the Heavy-Duty Electrical Group are among its as official features.

Nobody, however, will mistake the Wrangler for a smooth-running family sedan; it's very much a truck, thanks to its high step-in height and abundant wind and road noise, particularly with the soft top. On the street, its petite size and tight turning radius make it a blast to maneuver, but it can get a little scary to drive and control at freeway speeds in severely high winds.

Its performance off-road is unmatchable. The Wrangler's Quadra-Coil suspension allows an additional 7 inches of articulation over the old leaf-spring setup, thus resulting in increased approach and departure angles. And the abundance of aftermarket parts to modify the Wrangler make it enormously popular with the rock-crawling crowd.

The Wrangler does have its quirks—rear visibility can be a challenge, and taking off and putting on the soft top aren't exactly going to be quick. And once it's on, be prepared for the flapping. Yet we're willing to look away from those flaws since it's fun to drive, cheap, and a terrific multipurpose tool.

The year 2002 has been targeted for a Wrangler redesign, which will likely incorporate the looks and maybe even mechanicals from two concept vehicles, the Jeep Icon and the Jeepster. Food for thought: The Icon has four-wheel independent suspension (diehard Jeep fans will tell you its not a real Jeep without those solid axles), 19-inch wheels, and a front transaxle.

Standard Equipment

SE (5M): 2.5L I4 OHV SPI 8-valve engine; 5-speed OD manual transmission; 500-amp battery; 81-amp alternator; part-time 4-wheel drive, auto locking hub control and manual shift, 4.11 axle ratio; stainless steel exhaust; front non-independent suspension with anti-roll bar, front coil springs, gas-pressurized front shocks, rear non-independent suspension with anti-roll bar, rear coil springs, gas-pressurized rear shocks; power rack-and-pinion steering; front disc/rear drum brakes; 19 gal. capacity fuel tank; skid plate(s); tailgate rear cargo door; manual convertible roof with roll-over protection; front and rear black bumpers; black fender flares; clearcoat monotone paint with bodyside accent stripe; sealed beam halogen headlamps; driver's and passenger's manual black folding outside mirrors; front and rear 15" x 6" silver styled steel wheels; P205/75SR15 AT BSW front and rear tires; outside rear mounted full-size steel spare wheel; fixed antenna; 1 power accessory outlet, front cigar lighter(s), smokers' package; instrumentation display includes tachometer, oil pressure gauge, water temperature gauge, volt gauge, trip odometer; warning indicators include battery, key in ignition, low fuel; driver's front airbag, passenger's cancelable front airbag; tinted windows, manual front windows; fixed interval front windshield wipers; seating capacity of 2, front bucket seats, fixed headrests, driver's seat includes 4-way direction control, passenger's seat includes 4-way direction control, easy entry; front height adjustable seatbelts; vinyl seats, front carpet floor covering, plastic/rubber gear shift knob; day/night rearview mirror; partial floor console, locking glove box, front cupholder, dashboard storage, driver's and passenger's door bins; cargo tie downs; body-colored grille, black front windshield molding and black door handles.

SPORT (5M) (in addition to or instead of SE (5M) equipment): 4.0L I6 OHV SMPI 12-valve engine; 3.07 axle ratio; front and rear 15" x 7" silver steel wheels; P215/75SR15 AT RBL front and rear tires; AM/

FM stereo, clock, seek-scan, cassette, 4 speakers, and fixed antenna; seating capacity of 4; removable full folding rear bench seat and full carpet floor covering.

SAHARA (5M) (in addition to or instead of SPORT (5M) equipment): 600-amp HD battery; 117-amp HD alternator; running boards, skid plate(s); front and rear tow hooks; body-colored fender flares; additional exterior lights include front fog/driving lights, underhood light; front and rear 16" x 7" silver alloy wheels; P225/70SR16 AT BSW front and rear tires; AM/FM stereo, clock, seek-scan, single CD, 4 speakers, and fixed antenna; variable intermittent front windshield wipers; premium cloth seats, full carpet floor covering with floor mats; interior lights include dome light; leather-wrapped steering wheel with tilt adjustment; full floor console and 2 seat back storage pockets.

Base Prices

Code	Description	Invoice	MSRP
TJJL77	SE (5M)	13868	14460
TJJH77	Sport (5M)	16665	18460
TJJP77	Sahara (5M)	18363	20390
Destination Charge:		535	535

Accessories

Code	Description	Invoice	MSRP
22A	**Quick Order Package 22A (SE)** *Includes vehicle with standard equipment. REQUIRES (HAA or 4XA) and EPE and DGA. NOT AVAILABLE with DSA, DDQ, ADH, CSA, GCD, JKC, NHM, AEM, J6.*	NC	NC
22N	**Quick Order Package 22N (SE)** *Includes rear seat/wheelhouse/cargo carpet, AM/FM stereo with cassette and 4 speakers with sound bar, rear folding seat and vinyl highback bucket seats. REQUIRES (HAA or 4XA) and EPE and DGA. NOT AVAILABLE with DSA, DDQ, RBR, K5.*	1114	1310
23A	**Quick Order Package 23A (SE)** *Includes vehicle with standard equipment. REQUIRES (HAA or 4XA) and EPE and DDQ. NOT AVAILABLE with DGA, ADH, CSA, GCD, JKC, NHM, AEM, J6.*	NC	NC
23N	**Quick Order Package 23N (SE)** *Includes rear seat/wheelhouse/cargo carpet, AM/FM stereo with cassette and 4 speakers with sound bar, rear folding seat and vinyl highback bucket seats. REQUIRES (HAA or 4XA) and EPE and DDQ. NOT AVAILABLE with DGA, RBR, K5.*	1114	1310
24C	**Quick Order Package 24C (Sport)** *Includes vehicle with standard equipment. REQUIRES (HAA or 4XA) and ERH and DGA. NOT AVAILABLE with AAS, TRN, DDD.*	NC	NC
24D	**Quick Order Package 24D (Sport)** *Includes full length floor console, underhood lamp, courtesy lamps, tilt steering column, leather-wrapped steering wheel, wheel: matching spare and variable intermittent windshield wipers. REQUIRES (HAA or 4XA) and ERH and DGA. NOT AVAILABLE with TRN, DDD, AAC, ADC, NHM.*	446	525
24G	**Quick Order Package 24G (Sahara)** *Includes vehicle with standard equipment. REQUIRES (HAA or 4XA) and ERH and DGA. NOT AVAILABLE with DDD.*	NC	NC
25C	**Quick Order Package 25C (Sport)** *Includes vehicle with standard equipment. REQUIRES (HAA or 4XA) and ERH and DDD. NOT AVAILABLE with DGA, AAS, TRN.*	NC	NC

CODE	DESCRIPTION	INVOICE	MSRP
25D	**Quick Order Package 25D (Sport)** *Includes full length floor console, underhood lamp, courtesy lamps, tilt steering column, leather-wrapped steering wheel, matching spare wheel and variable intermittent windshield wipers. REQUIRES (HAA or 4XA) and ERH and DDD. NOT AVAILABLE with DGA, TRN, AAC, ADC, NHM.*	446	525
25G	**Quick Order Package 25G (Sahara)** *Includes vehicle with standard equipment. REQUIRES (HAA or 4XA) and ERH and DDD. NOT AVAILABLE with DGA.*	NC	NC
4XA	**Air Conditioning Bypass** *NOT AVAILABLE with HAA.*	NC	NC
6**	**Hardtop (SE/Sport)** *Includes tinted glass on rear doors/quarter windows/liftgate, rear cargo lamp and rear window wiper/washer. REQUIRES 22A or 23A or 22N or 23N or 24C or 25C or 24D or 25D.*	642	755
6**	**Hardtop (Sahara)** *Includes deep tinted glass, rear cargo lamp, rear window wiper/washer. REQUIRES 24G or 25G.*	986	1160
AAC	**Convenience Group I (SE/Sport)** *Includes tilt steering column and leather-wrapped steering wheel. NOT AVAILABLE with 24D, 25D, NHM.*	208	245
AAS	**30" Tire and Wheel Group (Sahara)** *Includes full size spare tire, high pressure gas charged shocks, tires: 30 x 9.5R15 Wrangler AT OWL and wheels: 15" x 8" aluminum.*	306	360
AAS	**30" Tire and Wheel Group (Sport)** *Includes full size spare tire, high pressure gas charged shocks, tires: 30 x 9.5R15 Wrangler AT OWL and wheels: 15" x 8" aluminum. NOT AVAILABLE with TRN, CSA, WJ1, 24C, 25C.*	570	670
AAS	**30" Tire and Wheel Group (Sport)** *Includes full size spare tire, high pressure gas charged shocks, tires: 30 x 9.5R15 Wrangler AT OWL and wheels: 15" x 8" aluminum. REQUIRES BGK, DDD and DSA. NOT AVAILABLE with TRN, CSA, WJ1, 24D, 25D.*	667	785
ADC	**Convenience Group (SE/Sport)** *Includes full length floor console, underhood lamp and courtesy lamps. NOT AVAILABLE with 24D, 25D.*	140	165
ADH	**HD Electrical Group (SE/Sport)** *Includes 117-amp alternator and 600-amp maintenance free battery. NOT AVAILABLE with 22A, 23A.*	115	135
AEM	**Dual Top Group with Matching Colors (SE/Sport)** *Includes hard top and easy folding soft top and full metal doors with roll-up windows. REQUIRES VK.*	1186	1395
AEM	**Dual Top Group with Matching Colors (Sahara)** *Includes hard top, easy folding soft top and full metal doors with roll-up windows. REQUIRES VK.*	1530	1800
BGK	**4-Wheel Antilock Brakes (Sport/Sahara)** *REQUIRES DSA. NOT AVAILABLE with DRK.*	510	600
CLC	**Front Floor Mats (SE/Sport)**	26	30

CODE	DESCRIPTION	INVOICE	MSRP
CSA	Spare Tire Cover (SE/Sport) *NOT AVAILABLE with 22A, 23A, AAS.*	43	50
DDD	Transmission: 5-Speed HD Manual (Sport/Sahara) *Includes 3.07 axle ratio. NOT AVAILABLE with 24C, 24D, 24G.*	NC	NC
DDQ	Transmission: 5-Speed Manual (SE) *Includes 4.11 axle ratio. NOT AVAILABLE with 22A, 22N.*	NC	NC
DGA	Transmission: 3-Speed Automatic *NOT AVAILABLE with 23A, 23N, DSA, 25C, 25D, 25G.*	531	625
DRK	Dana 44 Rear Axle (Sport/Sahara) *NOT AVAILABLE with BGK.*	506	595
DSA	Trac-Lok Differential Axle *REQUIRES (23A or 23N) (SE) and (TBB or TRN). NOT AVAILABLE with 22A, 22N, DGA.*	242	285
EPE	Engine: 2.5L Power-Tech I4 (SE)	NC	NC
ERH	Engine: 4.0L Power-Tech I6 (Sport/Sahara)	NC	NC
GCD	Hard Top Deep Tint Sunscreen Glass (SE/Sport) *Includes rear window defroster. REQUIRES VK.*	344	405
GCF	Full Metal Doors with Roll-Up Windows	106	125
GFA	Rear Window Defroster (SE/Sport) *REQUIRES (ADH or HAA) and (VK or AEM).*	140	165
GXX	Sentry Key Theft Deterrent System	64	75
HAA	Air Conditioning *NOT AVAILABLE with 4XA.*	761	895
J6	Vinyl High-Back Bucket Seats (SE/Sport) *REQUIRES 22N or 23N. NOT AVAILABLE with K5, 22A, 23A.*	NC	NC
JKC	Add-A-Trunk with Lockable Storage *NOT AVAILABLE with 22A, 23A.*	106	125
K5	Cloth High-Back Bucket Seats (SE) *NOT AVAILABLE with J6, 22N, 23N.*	633	745
K5	Cloth High-Back Bucket Seats (SE/Sport) *NOT AVAILABLE with J6, 22A, 23A.*	128	150
LNJ	Fog Lamps (Sport) *REQUIRES ADH or HAA.*	102	120
MRJ	Bodyside Steps (SE/Sport)	64	75
NHK	Engine Block Heater	30	35
NHM	Speed Control (SE/Sport) *Includes leather-wrapped steering wheel. REQUIRES 22N or 23N (SE). NOT AVAILABLE with 22A, 23A, AAC, 24D, 25D.*	255	300
NHM	Speed Control *REQUIRES 22N or 23N (SE). NOT AVAILABLE with 22A, 23A.*	213	250
RAS	Radio: AM/FM Stereo with Cassette (SE) *Includes fixed antenna, rear sport bar with full padding and 4 speakers with sound bar. NOT AVAILABLE with RBR. INCLUDED in 22N, 23N.*	608	715
RBR	Radio: AM/FM Stereo with CD (SE) *Includes fixed antenna, rear sport bar with full padding and 4 speakers with sound bar. NOT AVAILABLE with 22N, 23N, RAS.*	714	840

CODE	DESCRIPTION	INVOICE	MSRP
RBR	Radio: AM/FM Stereo with CD (SE/Sport) *Includes fixed antenna, rear sport bar with full padding and 4 speakers with sound bar. NOT AVAILABLE with 22A, 23A, RAS.*	106	125
SDU	High Pressure Gas Charged Shocks (Sport/Sahara)	77	90
TBB	Tire: Full Size Spare (SE/Sport) *Includes matching spare wheel. INCLUDED in 24D, 25D.*	98	115
TBB	Tire: Full Size Spare (Sahara) *Includes matching spare wheel.*	183	215
TRN	Tires: P225/75R15 Wrangler AT OWL (SE) *Includes tire: full size spare*	400	470
TRN	Tires: P225/75R15 Wrangler AT OWL (Sport) *Includes full size spare tire and matching spare wheel. NOT AVAILABLE with AAS, 24C, 25C.*	264	310
TRN	Tires: P225/75R15 Wrangler AT OWL (Sport) *NOT AVAILABLE with AAS, 24D, 25D.*	361	425
VK	Hard Top *Includes full metal door with roll-up windows, rear cargo lamp and rear window wiper/washer. REQUIRES AEM.*	NC	NC
WJ1	Wheels: 15" x 7" Grizzly Aluminum (SE) *NOT AVAILABLE with WJ5.*	421	495
WJ1	Wheels: 15" x 7" Grizzly Aluminum (Sport) *NOT AVAILABLE with AAS.*	225	265
WJ5	Wheels: 15" x 7" Full-Face Steel (SE) *NOT AVAILABLE with WJ1.*	196	230
XEW	Tow Hooks (2 Front/1 Rear) (SE/Sport)	51	60

2000 SPORTAGE

2000 Kia Sportage

What's New?

Kia ushers in 2000 with a new sound system, dual airbags, new colors and some additional equipment, but keeps last year's MSRP.

Review

Part owned by Ford and Mazda before Hyundai acquired the company, Kia relies heavily on resources from all three companies as it treads water in a tough marketplace. The Sportage is the product of collaboration between Kia, Ford, Mazda and suspension-tuning guru Lotus. Designed from the start as a sport utility, the Sportage sports tough ladder-frame construction, shift-on-the-fly four-wheel drive, and a Mazda-based 2.0-liter, 16-valve engine that makes 130 horsepower and 127 foot-pounds of torque.

Two trim levels are available: base and EX. Sportage is well-trimmed, including power windows, split folding rear seats, a remote fuel door release, power mirrors, dual airbags, a rear defroster and air conditioning. Optional equipment includes four-wheel antilock brakes, leather interior, cruise control and an automatic transmission. Interior materials are not the Sportage's strong suit with headliner, dash panel, and seat fabric quality well below that of the more expensive CR-V's or RAV4's materials.

A wide variety of colors are available on the Sportage models, a few of which appear to have originated from the minds of the folks currently in charge of painting Hot Wheels cars. The look is rugged yet cute; perfect for family duty in the 'burbs. On-road driving offers a blend of controlled body roll, adequate steering feedback and limited acceleration. On freeway expansion joints the Sportage can feel choppy but not overly harsh or jarring.

On the pavement, we found the Sportage confidence inspiring and fun to drive. The Lotus engineers worked wonders here, and the Sportage is stable and comfortable. In the four-door model, the seating position is high and upright, visibility is outstanding, and the layout of the dashboard and controls makes the Sportage easy to manipulate. Rear seat riders get minimal legroom, but the "stadium style" elevated seating offers a clear view of the outside world. The convertible model offers an easy-folding soft top and a full-size spare tire mounted in an outside carrier. From the driver's seat, the Sportage looks and feels much more substantial than its low price would lead you to believe.

A more powerful engine, along with higher-grade interior materials, would do wonders for this Kia's overall desirability. Still, you can't deny its substantial price advantage over the competition. It's not as roomy as the CR-V and it may not have the attitude (or V6) that's found in Nissan's new Xterra, but the Sportage will serve your SUV needs in both on-road function and off-road fun. For young families and active singles looking to get into a sport-ute without getting into financial servitude, the Sportage is worth a look.

Standard Equipment

BASE 2WD CONVERTIBLE (4A): 2.0L I4 DOHC MPI 16-valve engine; 4-speed electronic OD auto transmission with lock-up; 48-amp battery; 70-amp alternator; rear-wheel drive, 4.78 axle ratio; partial stainless steel exhaust; front independent double wishbone suspension, front coil springs, rigid rear axle multi-link suspension with anti-roll bar, rear coil springs; power re-circulating ball steering with engine speed-sensing assist; front disc/rear drum brakes; 14 gal. capacity fuel tank; side impact bars; conventional rear cargo door; manual convertible roof with roll-over protection; front and rear body-colored bumpers with front tow hooks; monotone paint; aero-composite halogen headlamps; driver's and passenger's power remote black folding outside mirrors; front and rear 15" x 6" silver styled steel wheels; P205/75SR15 A/S BSW front and rear tires; outside rear mounted full-size steel spare wheel; radio prep, 6 speakers; power door locks, remote fuel release; 1 power accessory outlet; instrumentation display includes tachometer, water temperature gauge, in-dash clock, trip odometer; warning indicators include oil pressure, battery, key in ignition, low fuel; driver's and passenger's front airbags; security system; tinted windows, fixed 1/4 vent windows; fixed interval front windshield wipers; seating capacity of 5, front bucket seats, adjustable headrests, center armrest with storage, driver's seat includes 4-way direction control, lumbar support, passenger's seat includes 4-way direction control; full folding rear bench seat; front height adjustable seatbelts; cloth seats, cloth door trim insert, full cloth headliner, full carpet floor covering, plastic/rubber gear shift knob; interior lights include dome light; steering wheel with tilt adjustment; day/night rearview mirror; full floor console, glove box, front cupholder, instrument panel bin, driver's and passenger's door bins; carpeted cargo floor, plastic trunk lid; body-colored grille, chrome side window moldings, black front windshield molding and black door handles.

BASE 2WD 4-DOOR (5M) (in addition to or instead of BASE 2WD CONVERTIBLE (5M) equipment): 15.8 gal. capacity fuel tank; liftback rear cargo door; power front and rear windows; rear window defroster and 50-50 folding rear bench seat with fixed headrests.

EX 2WD 4-DOOR (5M) (in addition to or instead of BASE 2WD 4-DOOR (5M) equipment): Roof rack; front and rear colored bumpers with front tow hooks; colored bodyside cladding, rocker panel extensions, colored fender flares; lower accent two-tone paint with bodyside accent stripe; driver's and passenger's power remote body-colored folding outside mirrors; front and rear 15" x 6" silver styled alloy wheels; air conditioning; AM/FM stereo, seek-scan, single CD, 6 speakers, and fixed antenna; cruise control; deep tinted windows; variable intermittent front windshield wipers, rear window wiper; simulated wood trim on instrument panel and passenger's side vanity mirror.

BASE 4WD CONVERTIBLE (5M) (in addition to or instead of BASE 2WD CONVERTIBLE (5M) equipment): 5-speed OD manual transmission; part-time 4 wheel drive, auto locking hub control and manual shift and 4.78 axle ratio.

BASE 4WD 4-DOOR (5M) (in addition to or instead of BASE 2WD 4-DOOR (5M) equipment): Part-time 4 wheel drive, auto locking hub control and manual shift, 4.78 axle ratio; front and rear 15" x 6" silver styled alloy wheels and outside rear mounted full-size alloy spare wheel.

EX 4WD 4-DOOR (5M) (in addition to or instead of EX 2WD 4-DOOR (5M) equipment): Part-time 4 wheel drive, auto locking hub control and manual shift, 4.78 axle ratio and warning indicators include oil pressure, battery, key in ignition and low fuel.

CODE	DESCRIPTION	INVOICE	MSRP
	Base Prices		
42212	Base 2WD Convertible (4A)	13144	13995
42411	Base 4WD Convertible (5M)	13493	14495
42221	Base 2WD 4-Door (5M)	13885	14795
42421	Base 4WD 4-Door (5M)	15159	16295
42241	EX 2WD 4-Door (5M)	16202	17395
42441	EX 4WD 4-Door (5M)	17158	18595
Destination Charge:		450	450
	Accessories		
AB	4-Wheel Antilock Brakes	425	490
AC	Air Conditioning (Base)	772	900
AT	Transmission: 4-Speed Automatic (4-Door)	940	1000
AW	Alloy Wheels (Convertible/Base 2WD 4-Door)	284	340
CD	Radio: AM/FM Stereo with CD (Base) *NOT AVAILABLE with RM.*	389	475
CF	Carpeted Floor Mats (4) *NOT AVAILABLE with CM.*	50	69
CM	Carpeted Mat Set (5) (4-Door) *NOT AVAILABLE with CF.*	87	119
CP	Cruise Control (Convertible)	208	250
CT	Cargo Tray (4-Door)	42	67
GP	Graphics Package (Convertible)	64	92
LE	Leather Package (EX) *Includes full leather seats and leather door panel insert.*	787	900
RK	Remote Keyless Entry	147	225
RM	Radio: AM/FM with Cassette Deck (Base) *NOT AVAILABLE with CD.*	250	320
RR	Roof Rack (Base 4-Door)	156	195
RW	Rear Window Wiper (Base 4-Door)	104	125
SG	Sport Appearance Graphic (Base 4-Door)	63	95
SP	Rear Spoiler (4-Door)	149	189

2000 DISCOVERY SERIES II

2000 Land Rover Discovery Series II

What's New?

The Discovery was completely redesigned last year and sees only minor interior trim revisions for the 2000 model year.

Review

Like the Land Rovers of yesteryear, the current Discovery Series II exhibits excellent off-road prowess and distinctive, hardy styling. But it also utilizes advanced performance features that promise a more capable on-road driving experience. The success of Lincoln's Navigator and Lexus' LX 470 has convinced Land Rover to create a kinder, gentler SUV.

With 85 percent of the truck's parts replaced in 1999, the Discovery Series II is 6.5 inches longer and 3.8 inches wider than the first Discovery. Furthermore, this is the first sport-utility vehicle to be equipped with Active Cornering Enhancement (ACE), which uses a hydraulic system to control body roll on turns, and Hill Descent Control (HDC), a driver-activated feature which supplements traditional braking when descending steep, slippery slopes in extreme conditions. Other features include a self-leveling suspension, traction control, forward-facing rear jump seats and Optikool glass that reduces ultraviolet rays by 31 percent and heat transmission by 76 percent.

Just one body style is available: a five-door wagon with permanent four-wheel drive and a standard adaptive automatic transmission that adjusts to different driving styles. Beneath the vehicle's hood is a modern version of the 4.0-liter, V8 engine that powered the previous Discovery. This V8 makes 188 horsepower and 18 foot-pounds more torque than the engine in the 1998 version, at a lower rpm. This powerplant is rated for only 13 mpg in the city and 16 mpg for highway driving, though, and that's with a light foot. The previous model exhibited gear noise and other aural annoyances, but Land Rover has dramatically reduced noise, vibration and harshness (NVH) levels in the current truck. The Series II's stance was widened last year by 2.1 inches at the front and 2.9 inches at the rear, making for a smoother on-road feel, and the self-leveling suspension benefits off-roaders by allowing the driver to raise or lower the rear of the truck by 1.6 inches.

Inside the Series II, both front and backseat passengers sit high for a superior view. Seating can be expanded to seven, in the form of forward-facing, storable rear jump seats. The driver and front passenger receive adjustable lumbar support and enjoy the benefits of dual temperature control air conditioning as well as a full-size glove box and four cupholders.

Legendary off-road capabilities help make the aluminum-bodied Discovery Series II an attractive choice in this segment, augmented by safety equipment like ABS and traction control. With competitors releasing new hybrid sport-utes faster than horses can race the Kentucky Derby, Land Rover remains true to its original industry mission – building a go-anywhere, do-anything vehicle. The Series II will undoubtedly live up to that reputation, but with the advanced suspension, powertrain and handling features available on the truck, urban driving has become a bit more enjoyable as well.

Standard Equipment

CLOTH (4A): 4.0L V8 OHV SMPI 16-valve engine, requires premium unleaded fuel; 4-speed electronic OD auto transmission with lock-up; 590-amp battery; engine oil cooler, HD radiator, HD starter; 130-amp alternator; driver's selectable multi-mode transmission, transmission oil cooler; full-time 4-wheel drive, traction control, 3.54 axle ratio; steel exhaust; HD ride suspension, front non-independent suspension with anti-roll bar, front coil springs, rigid rear axle multi-link suspension with anti-roll bar, rear coil springs; power re-circulating ball steering; 4-wheel disc brakes with 4-wheel antilock braking system; 24.6 gal. capacity fuel tank; rear mud flaps, side impact bars; conventional rear cargo door; class III trailering, trailer harness, trailer hitch; roof rack; front body-colored bumper with black rub strip, rear black bumper, front and rear tow hooks, rear step; rocker panel extensions, black fender flares; monotone paint; aero-composite halogen headlamps with washer, delay-off feature; additional exterior lights include front fog/driving lights; driver's and passenger's power remote body-colored heated folding outside mirrors; front and rear 16" x 8" silver alloy wheels; P255/65HR16 M&S BSW front and rear tires; outside rear mounted full-size alloy spare wheel; dual zone front air conditioning with climate control, rear heat ducts; premium AM/FM stereo, seek-scan, cassette, 6 premium speakers, amplifier, and window grid diversity antenna, radio steering wheel controls; cruise control with steering wheel controls; power door locks with 2 stage unlock, remote keyless entry, child safety rear door locks, remote fuel release; 1 power accessory outlet, driver's foot rest, retained accessory power, garage door opener, smokers' package; instrumentation display includes tachometer, water temperature gauge, in-dash clock, compass, exterior temp, trip odometer; warning indicators include oil pressure, water temp, battery, low oil level, low coolant, lights on, key in ignition, low fuel; driver's and passenger's front airbags; ignition disable, security system; deep tinted windows, power front and rear windows with driver's and passenger's 1-touch down, fixed 1/4 vent windows; variable intermittent front windshield wipers, variable intermittent rear wiper, rear window defroster; seating capacity of 5, front bucket seats, adjustable headrests, center armrest with storage, driver's seat includes 4-way direction control, lumbar support, passenger's seat includes 4-way direction control, lumbar support; 60-40 folding rear split-bench seat with adjustable headrests, center armrest; seatbelts with front pretensioners; cloth seats, cloth door trim insert, full cloth headliner, full color-keyed carpet floor covering, plastic/rubber gear shift knob; interior lights include dome light with fade, front reading lights, 4 door curb lights; leather-wrapped steering wheel with tilt adjustment; dual illuminated vanity mirrors; auto-dimming day/night rearview mirror; full floor console, mini overhead console, glove box, front and rear cupholders, 2 seat back storage pockets, driver's and passenger's door bins; carpeted cargo floor, plastic trunk lid, cargo cover, cargo net, cargo light; black grille, black side window moldings, black front windshield molding, black rear window molding and black door handles.

LEATHER (4A) (in addition to or instead of CLOTH (4A) equipment): Stainless steel exhaust; premium AM/FM stereo, seek-scan, cassette, 12 premium speakers, premium amplifier, and window grid diversity antenna; driver's seat includes 6-way power seat, power 2-way lumbar support, passenger's seat includes 6-way power seat, power 2-way lumbar support; leather seats, leather door trim insert and genuine wood trim on instrument panel.

Base Prices

SDVC	Cloth (4A)	30394	34150
SDVL	Leather (4A)	32129	36100
Destination Charge:		625	625

CODE	DESCRIPTION	INVOICE	MSRP
	Accessories		
—	6-Disc CD Changer	556	625
697	Java Black Paint	267	300
C01	Cloth Group 1 (Cloth) *Includes dual sunroofs.*	1335	1500
CCP	Cold Climate Package *Includes heated front seats and heated front windshield.*	445	500
CRS	Cloth Rear Seat Package (Cloth) *Includes forward facing rear seat, rear step and self leveling rear suspension (SLS).*	1558	1750
L01	Leather Group 1 (Leather) *Includes dual sunroofs. NOT AVAILABLE with L02, L03.*	1335	1500
L02	Leather Group 2 (Leather) *Includes dual sunroofs, rear seat package: forward facing rear seat, rear step, self leveling rear suspension (SLS) and remote ice controls. NOT AVAILABLE with L01, L03.*	2893	3250
L03	Leather Group 3 (Leather) *Includes dual sunroofs, rear seat package: forward facing rear seat, rear step, self leveling rear suspension (SLS), remote ice controls and rear air conditioning. NOT AVAILABLE with L01, L02.*	3561	4000
LJ	Lightstone Leather Interior (Leather)	445	500
PPK	Performance Package *Includes active cornering enhancement (ACE), wheels: 18" Proline alloy and tires: P255/55HR18.*	2581	2900
RAC	Rear Air Conditioning	668	750
RSP	Rear Seat Package (Leather) *Includes forward facing rear seat, rear step, self leveling rear suspension (SLS) and remote ice controls.*	1588	1750
SLS	Self Leveling Rear Suspension (SLS)	668	750
SUN	Dual Sunroofs	1335	1500

2000 RX 300

2000 Lexus RX 300

What's New?

The RX 300 remains mechanically unchanged. A Mineral Green Opalescent paint replaces Desert Bronze Metallic on the order sheet.

Review

Lexus, like many manufacturers these days, has jumped on the sedan/sport-utility hybrid bandwagon with the RX 300. Touted as a "new breed of SUV," the RX 300 is supposed to offer the style, versatility, and poor-weather traction of an all-wheel-drive SUV without negatively affecting ride, fuel economy, or ease of entry/exit.

Rather than a conventional body-on-frame design, the RX 300 is built on a unibody platform. It is a mid-sized SUV, with dimensions similar to those of the Jeep Grand Cherokee. Powering the RX 300 is a 3.0-liter V6 producing 220 horsepower and 222 foot-pounds of torque. A continuously variable valve timing (VVT-i) system allows the Lexus engine to generate more low-end torque for more pulling power and standing-start response. Eighty percent of peak torque is available as low as 1,600 rpm.

Now in its second year of production, the RX 300 can be had in front-wheel drive, which improves both performance and gas mileage. To add to the front-wheel-drive model's capability in less than perfect weather, electronic traction control is optional. Full-time four-wheel drive is also available with a viscous center coupling that directs torque to the wheels with the most traction whenever slippage occurs.

The RX 300 tackles urban pavement quite well. Body roll isn't excessive and the brakes are strong. City driving is made easy thanks to a smooth four-speed automatic transmission. The RX 300 gets a bit chicken when it comes to the serious stuff, however. It lacks a low-range transfer case, and maximum towing capacity is 3,500 pounds, which is 3,000 pounds less than a 4x4 Jeep Grand Cherokee V8's maximum towing capacity.

Sitting inside the RX 300 is like sitting in a sedan with excellent road visibility. It's spacious and comfortable in the front seats or the rear bench. The optional leather package includes leather trim on the seating surfaces and headrests, and the surfaces actually feel like leather instead of vinyl. The seats, both front and back, offer plenty of thigh support for a variety of leg sizes. Dashboard material and instruments feel substantial, though the center-console display screen can wash out in sunlight.

With its long list of luxury and safety features (side airbags are standard in the RX 300) Lexus is able to offer a lot of car (in the guise of a truck) for not a lot of money. While we wouldn't recommend the RX to anyone with serious off-road aspirations, it fulfills its intended mission of giving semi-affluent buyers an SUV that won't offend the other country club members.

Standard Equipment

FWD (4A): 3.0L V6 DOHC SMPI with variable valve timing 24-valve engine; 4-speed electronic auto transmission with lock-up; 80-amp alternator; driver's selectable multi-mode transmission; front-wheel drive, 3.08 axle ratio; stainless steel exhaust; front independent strut suspension with anti-roll bar, front coil springs, gas-pressurized front shocks, rear independent strut suspension with anti-roll bar, rear coil springs, gas-pressurized rear shocks; power rack-and-pinion steering with engine speed-sensing assist; 4-wheel disc brakes with 4-wheel antilock braking system; 17.2 gal. capacity fuel tank; body-colored front and rear mud flaps, side impact bars; liftback rear cargo door; trailer harness; front and rear colored bumpers with rear step; colored bodyside cladding; monotone paint; aero-composite halogen fully auto headlamps with daytime running lights, delay-off feature; additional exterior lights include front fog/driving lights; driver's and passenger's power remote body-colored folding outside mirrors; front and rear 16" x 6.5" silver alloy wheels; P225/70SR16 M&S BSW front and rear tires; inside under cargo mounted full-size steel spare wheel; air conditioning with climate control, rear heat ducts; AM/FM stereo, seek-scan, cassette, CD changer pre-wiring, in-dash CD pre-wiring, 7 speakers, amplifier, auto equalizer, theft deterrent, and power retractable diversity antenna; cruise control; power door locks with 2 stage unlock, remote keyless entry, child safety rear door locks, power remote hatch/trunk release, remote fuel release; cell phone pre-wiring, 3 power accessory outlets, driver's foot rest, retained accessory power, smokers' package; instrumentation display includes tachometer, water temperature gauge, in-dash clock, exterior temp, trip computer, trip odometer; warning indicators include oil pressure, battery, lights on, key in ignition, low fuel, low washer fluid, bulb failure, door ajar; driver's and passenger's front airbags, driver's and front passenger's seat mounted side airbags; ignition disable, panic alarm, security system; deep tinted windows, power front and rear windows with front and rear 1-touch down, fixed 1/4 vent windows; variable intermittent front windshield wipers, sun visor strip, fixed interval rear wiper, rear window defroster; seating capacity of 5, front bucket seats, adjustable headrests, driver's and passenger's armrests, driver's seat includes 6-way power seat, power 2-way lumbar support, passenger's seat includes 4-way power seat; 60-40 folding rear split-bench seat with reclining adjustable headrests, center armrest; front height adjustable seatbelts with front pretensioners; premium cloth seats, cloth door trim insert, full cloth headliner, full color-keyed carpet floor covering with carpeted floor mats, leather-wrapped gear shift knob; interior lights include dome light, front reading lights, 4 door curb lights, illuminated entry; leather-wrapped steering wheel with tilt adjustment; dual illuminated vanity mirrors, dual auxiliary visors; day/night rearview mirror; partial floor console, mini overhead console with storage, locking glove box with light, front and rear cupholders, instrument panel bin, 2 seat back storage pockets, driver's and passenger's door bins, rear door bins; carpeted cargo floor, carpeted trunk lid, cargo cover, cargo light, cargo concealed storage; chrome grille, black side window moldings, black front windshield molding, black rear window molding and body-colored door handles.

AWD (4A) (in addition to or instead of FWD (4A) equipment): Full-time all-wheel drive and 3.29 axle ratio.

Base Prices

9420	FWD (4A)	28234	32505
9424	AWD (4A)	29450	33905
Destination Charge:		495	495

Accessories

CODE	DESCRIPTION	INVOICE	MSRP
C1	Carpeted Cargo Mat	40	65
DC	6-Disc In-Dash CD Auto-Changer	864	1080
DH	Towing Receiver Hitch	157	248
DR	Roof Rack	149	234
HH	Heated Front Seats *REQUIRES PM or PZ.*	352	440
LA	Leather Trim Package *Includes leather seating surfaces.*	1024	1280
LD	Torsen Rear Limited Slip Differential (AWD)	312	390
NK	Nakamichi Premium Audio System *Includes 6-disc in-dash CD auto-changer.*	1277	1630
PM	Premium Package *Includes leather trim package: leather seating surfaces; driver's seat memory, electrochromic rearview mirror, dual electrochromic heated outside mirrors, programmable garage door opener and air filtration system. NOT AVAILABLE with PZ.*	1536	1920
PZ	Limited Package *Includes leather trim package: leather seating surfaces; driver's seat memory, programmable garage door opener and air filtration system. NOT AVAILABLE with PM.*	1456	1820
RF	Color Keyed Rear Spoiler	224	280
SR	Power Tilt/Slide Moonroof with Sunshade	800	1000
TN	Traction Control System (FWD)	240	300
WL	Wheel Locks	28	42

2000 NAVIGATOR

2000 Lincoln Navigator

What's New?

The 2000 Navigator is now available with a fully integrated satellite navigation system, as well as a reverse-sensing system. Side airbags are standard, while new climate-controlled seats for the driver and front passenger are optional. The 2000 Navigator also features several exterior and interior styling changes.

Review

Based on Ford's hot-selling Expedition, the Navigator is the first truck ever sold by Lincoln. When it first appeared, the Navigator's price tag was hard to swallow because the vehicle offered minimal changes over the Expedition. As opposed to a lot of other luxury-SUV makers, however, Ford has done a good job of adding additional features to distance the Navigator from the Expedition. Last year, the Navigator gained a 300-horsepower, 5.4-liter V8 engine. For 2000, it earns satellite navigation, a reverse-sensing system, side airbags, climate-controlled seats, and exterior and interior styling changes.

Inside, the Navigator has leather-bound seating for seven consisting of bucket seats for the front and second rows and a bench seat in the third row. Seating for eight (with a second-row bench seat) is a no-cost option. Of course, there are luxury touches galore. The new climate-controlled seats can be ordered for both driver and front passenger sides. The system provides both hot and cold air through the specially perforated leather-seat surfaces. The new navigation system utilizes a 5-inch monitor screen that fits neatly into the redesigned center console. New, softer Nudo leather is used on seating surfaces in the first and second row. Also, the use of real wood trim has been increased, and the center console has been redesigned to provide more storage and larger, improved cupholders.

On the outside, the 2000 Navigator features new body cladding integrated into larger side running boards. The antenna whip is removed from the front passenger-side fender and integrated into the passenger-side rear-quarter glass. Standard 17-inch wheels and tires complete the new, freshened exterior.

Using four valves per cylinder (as opposed to the Expedition's two valves per cylinder), the Navigator's V8 produces 300 horsepower and 360 ft-lbs. of torque. Four-wheel-drive models come with Lincoln's adjustable Control-Trac system that can be set in one of three positions by turning a dash-mounted knob. In automatic mode, the system applies power to the front wheels when rear-wheel slippage is detected and maintains it until traction is regained.

Driving this bruiser is actually easy. The powerful Navigator feels light when pulling away from a stop; 300 horses have a way of doing that. Surprisingly, the steering has decent feedback and makes it easy to maintain a true heading on the highway. Highway cruising is relaxed and quiet for such a big, non-aerodynamic box, with little wind or road noise invading the plush cabin. But make no mistake; it takes a while to get used to the Navigator's size, especially when parking.

For people looking for a big luxury SUV, the Navigator is tough to beat. With its 300-horsepower engine, satellite navigation, and climate-controlled seats, Lincoln's SUV offers content worthy of a good luxury sedan. The Toyota Land Cruiser and Lexus LX 470 are arguably better vehicles overall, but they also cost considerably more.

Standard Equipment

2WD (4A): 5.4L V8 DOHC SMPI 32-valve engine, requires premium unleaded fuel; 4-speed electronic OD auto transmission with lock-up; 650-amp battery with run down protection; engine oil cooler; 130-amp alternator; transmission oil cooler; rear-wheel drive, limited slip differential, 3.73 axle ratio; stainless steel exhaust; auto-leveling suspension, front independent suspension with anti-roll bar, front coil springs, rigid rear axle multi-link suspension with anti-roll bar, rear coil springs; power re-circulating ball steering with vehicle speed-sensing assist; 4-wheel disc brakes with 4-wheel antilock braking system; 30 gal. capacity fuel tank; running boards, side impact bars; liftback rear cargo door; HD class III trailering, trailer harness, trailer hitch; roof rack; front and rear body-colored bumpers front with body-colored rub strip, rear step; body-colored bodyside cladding, body-colored wheel well molding; monotone paint; aero-composite halogen fully auto headlamps, delay-off feature; additional exterior lights include front fog/driving lights, underhood light; driver's and passenger's power remote body-colored heated folding outside mirrors; front and rear 17" x 7.5" silver alloy wheels; P275/60SR17 A/S OWL front and rear tires; underbody mounted full-size steel spare wheel; air conditioning with climate control, rear heat ducts; premium AM/FM stereo, seek-scan, cassette, 4 speakers, auto equalizer, and window grid antenna, radio steering wheel controls, rear controls; cruise control with steering wheel controls; power door locks, remote keyless entry, child safety rear door locks, power remote hatch/trunk release; 3 power accessory outlets, driver's foot rest, retained accessory power, garage door opener; instrumentation display includes tachometer, oil pressure gauge, water temperature gauge, volt gauge, in-dash clock, compass, exterior temp, trip computer, trip odometer; warning indicators include oil pressure, water temp, battery, low oil level, lights on, key in ignition, low fuel, low washer fluid, door ajar, trunk ajar; driver's and passenger's front airbags, driver's and front passenger's seat mounted side airbags; ignition disable, panic alarm; deep tinted windows, power front and rear windows with driver's 1-touch down, power 1/4 vent windows; variable intermittent front windshield wipers, sun visor strip, flip-up rear window, fixed interval rear wiper, rear window defroster; seating capacity of 7, front bucket seats, adjustable headrests, center armrest with storage, driver's seat includes 4-way power seat, 8-way direction control, power 2-way lumbar support, power adjustable pedals, passenger's seat includes 4-way power seat, 8-way direction control; 2nd row bucket seat with reclining adjustable headrests, center armrest with storage; removable 3rd row bench seat; front and rear height adjustable seatbelts; leather seats, leather door trim, full cloth headliner, full carpet floor covering with carpeted floor mats, genuine wood trim on instrument panel; memory on driver's seat with 3 memory setting(s) includes settings for exterior mirrors; interior lights include dome light, front and rear reading lights, 2 door curb lights, illuminated entry; steering wheel with tilt adjustment; dual illuminated vanity mirrors, dual auxiliary visors; auto-dimming day/night rearview mirror; full floor console, full overhead console with storage, rear console with storage, glove box with light, front and rear cupholders, instrument panel covered bin, 2 seat back storage pockets, driver's and passenger's door bins, rear door bins; carpeted cargo floor, carpeted trunk lid, cargo net, cargo tie downs, cargo light, cargo concealed storage; chrome grille, chrome side window moldings, black front windshield molding, black rear window molding and chrome door handles.

4WD (4A) (in addition to or instead of 2WD (4A) equipment): Part-time 4 wheel drive, auto locking hub control and electronic shift, limited slip differential; front torsion springs, front torsion bar, front tow hooks and P255/75SR17 AT OWL front and rear tires.

CODE	DESCRIPTION	INVOICE	MSRP

Base Prices

U27	2WD (4A)	37026	42460
U28	4WD (4A)	40213	46210
Destination Charge:		655	655

Accessories

162	Reverse Sensing System *Includes in-cabin speaker for audible feedback. REQUIRES 575.*	208	245
21S	2nd Row Leather 60/40 Bench Seat *Includes removeable third row tip/fold flat/stow bench seat with rollers and rear console delete.*	NC	NC
413	Skid Plate Package (4WD) *Includes fuel tank, transfer case and front differential/suspension protection package.*	89	105
428	High Altitude Principal Use	NC	NC
429	Non-High Altitude Principal Use	NC	NC
43M	Power Moonroof *Includes mini overhead console. REQUIRES 575. NOT AVAILABLE with 65N.*	1271	1495
516	Hands-Free Portable Cellular Telephone *Located in front floor console. REQUIRES 91P.*	553	650
549	Power Folding Side View Exterior Mirrors	123	145
575	Auxiliary Climate Control	599	705
64C	Wheels: 17" x 7.5" Chrome Aluminum	506	595
65N	Navigation System *Includes 5" color display and CD ROM. REQUIRES 91P. NOT AVAILABLE with 43M.*	1696	1995
902	Climate Controlled Front Seats *Includes driver's and passenger's perforated seat and ability to heat or cool the occupant.*	421	495
90H	Heated Front Seats *Includes driver's and passenger's seats.*	247	290
916	Radio: Alpine Audio System *Includes cassette, 7 premium speakers, subwoofer and speed compensated volume control.*	484	570
91P	6-Disc CD Changer *Located in front floor console.*	506	595

2000 B-SERIES

2000 Mazda B-Series Pickup

What's New?

Two B3000 regular-cab models are added—SX and SE. The B2500 Troy Lee edition has been discontinued. Fog lights are standard on all 4x4 models. A CD-equipped audio system is standard on all B4000 models. P225/70R15 tires are standard on SX models, and air conditioning is standard on SE and Troy Lee edition models. A 6,000-pound trailer hitch is standard on B4000 4x4s and optional on B4000 4x2 models. B3000 and B4000 Troy Lee editions get standard leather-wrapped steering wheels. Bucket seats are optional on B4000 models (except the Troy Lee edition).

Review

For people who need the functionality of a pickup but think a full-size truck is too big, there's the Mazda B-Series. Along with its mechanical twin, the Ford Ranger, the Mazda offers a wide range of configurations, four-cylinder and V6 engines, and good reliability.

The different B-Series designations—B2500, B3000 and B4000—refer to the three different engine choices available. The B2500 uses a 2.5-liter four-cylinder engine that develops 119 horsepower and 146 foot-pounds of torque. The B3000 gets a 3.0-liter V6 that makes 150 horsepower and 185 foot-pounds of torque. The top-level B4000 features a 4.0-liter V6 with 160 horsepower and 225 foot-pounds of torque. All three models are available with a manual or automatic transmission (B2500s and B3000s have a four-speed automatic; B4000s get a five-speed automatic). The B2500 is fine for cargo hauling or light towing duties, but you'll want to step up to the B4000 equipped with the automatic transmission if you plan to use your truck to tow heavier toys (maximum trailer rating for the B4000 is 9,500 pounds).

The current B-Series truck has a stylish exterior, and it looks arguably better than the Ranger. This is especially true when the vehicle is fitted with the optional 16-inch wheels. For each series, Mazda offers a regular cab, an extended cab, or a four-door extended cab. The four-door extended cab is our favorite as it increases the functionality of the interior considerably. The side-facing rear seats on this model are by no means comfortable for adults, but they can be used in a pinch. The rest of the interior is clean and well laid-out. The B2500 SX base model is pretty bare bones, but B2500 and B3000 SEs can be ordered with convenience and power packages. Combined, these add items like a tilt steering wheel, cruise control, a bedliner, a sliding rear window, power windows and locks, and remote keyless entry. B4000 4x4 models get all of this standard.

On the road, the B-Series truck provides a stable ride. It's not quite Lexus RX 300 quality, of course, but the overall ride is comfortable for a compact pickup. Four-wheel drive is an option on B3000s and B4000s. This shift-on-the-fly system features pulse vacuum hub-lock technology, allowing the driver to engage four-wheel drive at speeds up to 70 mph. No stopping or backing up is required when shifting into or out of 4-Lo.

With a rugged design, solid good looks and an excellent warranty, Mazda has done truck buyers right with its latest B-Series. If you're in the market for a fun and practical pickup, give these trucks a close look.

Standard Equipment

B2500 SX 2WD REGULAR CAB (5M): 2.5L I4 SOHC MPI 8-valve engine; 5-speed OD manual transmission; HD radiator; 95-amp alternator; rear-wheel drive, 3.73 axle ratio; steel exhaust; front independent double wishbone suspension with anti-roll bar, front coil springs, gas-pressurized front shocks, rigid rear axle suspension with rear leaf springs, gas-pressurized rear shocks; power rack-and-pinion steering; front disc/rear drum brakes with rear wheel antilock braking system; 16.5 gal. capacity fuel tank; front and rear mud flaps, side impact bars; trailer harness; front and rear black bumpers with rear step; clearcoat monotone paint; aero-composite halogen headlamps; driver's and passenger's manual black folding outside mirrors; front and rear 15" x 7" silver styled steel wheels; P225/70SR15 A/S BSW front and rear tires; underbody mounted full-size steel spare wheel; AM/FM stereo, clock, seek-scan, 4 speakers, and fixed antenna; 1 power accessory outlet, driver's foot rest, retained accessory power; instrumentation display includes oil pressure gauge, water temperature gauge, volt gauge, trip odometer; warning indicators include oil pressure, battery, lights on, key in ignition, door ajar; driver's front airbag, passenger's cancelable front airbag; tinted windows; variable intermittent front windshield wipers, sun visor strip; seating capacity of 3, bench front seat, fixed headrests, driver's seat includes 2-way direction control, passenger's seat includes 2-way direction control; front height adjustable seatbelts; vinyl seats, vinyl door trim insert, full cloth headliner, full vinyl floor covering, plastic/rubber gear shift knob; interior lights include dome light; day/night rearview mirror; partial floor console, glove box with light, front cupholder, instrument panel bin; cargo net; black grille, black side window moldings, black front windshield molding, black rear window molding and black door handles.

B3000 SX 2WD REGULAR CAB (5M) (in addition to or instead of B2500 SX 2WD REGULAR CAB (5M) equipment): 3.0L V6 OHV MPI 24-valve engine.

B2500 SE 2WD REGULAR CAB (5M) (in addition to or instead of B2500 SX 2WD REGULAR CAB (5M) equipment): Front and rear chrome bumpers with black rub strip; additional exterior lights include pickup cargo box light; front and rear 15" x 7" alloy wheels; air conditioning; AM/FM stereo, clock, seek-scan, single CD, 4 speakers, and fixed antenna; instrumentation display includes tachometer; 60-40 split-bench front seat, fixed headrests, center armrest with storage, driver's seat includes 4-way direction control, passenger's seat includes 4-way direction control; cloth seats, full carpet floor covering with floor mats; interior lights include front reading lights and driver's and passenger's door bins.

B2500 SE 2WD CAB PLUS (5M) (in addition to or instead of B2500 SE 2WD REGULAR CAB (5M) equipment): 19.5 gal. capacity fuel tank; fixed rear windows; seating capacity of 5; driver's seat includes 4-way direction control, easy entry, passenger's seat includes 4-way direction control, easy entry; 50-50 folding side facing rear jump seats; leather-wrapped gear shift knob; passenger's side vanity mirror; chrome grille and chrome side window moldings.

B3000 SE (5M) (in addition to or instead of B2500 SE (5M) equipment): 3.0L V6 OHV MPI 24-valve engine; HD radiator and chrome bodyside molding.

B4000 (5A) (in addition to or instead of B3000 (5M) equipment): 4.0L V6 OHV MPI 24-valve engine; 5-speed electronic OD auto transmission with lock-up; battery with run down protection; 3.55 axle ratio; additional exterior lights include front fog/driving lights; driver's and passenger's power remote black folding outside mirrors; AM/FM stereo, clock, seek-scan, single CD, 6 speakers, and fixed antenna; cruise control with steering wheel controls; power door locks, remote keyless entry; ignition disable; power windows with driver's 1-touch down; sliding rear window; full carpet floor covering with carpeted floor mats; cabback insulator; leather-wrapped steering wheel with tilt adjustment; 2 seat back storage pockets and carpeted cargo floor.

TROY LEE (in addition to or instead of SE equipment): Rear stabilizer bar (B4000), black fender flares; clearcoat monotone paint with bodyside accent stripe; additional exterior lights include front fog/driving lights (B3000); front and rear 16" x 7" silver alloy wheels; P245/75SR16 AT OWL front and rear tires; premium cloth seats and leather-wrapped steering wheel (B3000).

4WD (in addition to or instead of 2WD equipment): HD radiator; part-time 4-wheel drive, auto locking hub control and electronic shift, 3.73 axle ratio (SE); 4.11 axle ratio (TL); front torsion springs, front torsion bar, rigid rear axle suspension with anti-roll bar, front and rear tow hooks; black fender flares (SE); P235/75SR15 A/S OWL front and rear tires (B3000) and P265/75SR15 A/S OWL front and rear tires (B4000).

Base Prices

Code	Description	Invoice	MSRP
B25SSX2P	B2500 SX 2WD Regular Cab SB (5M)	10764	11495
B30SSX2P	B3000 SX 2WD Regular Cab SB (5M)	11132	11890
B25SSE2P	B2500 SE 2WD Regular Cab SB (5M)	12489	13805
B30SSE2P	B3000 SE 2WD Regular Cab SB (5M)	12846	14200
B25CSE2P	B2500 SE 2WD Cab Plus SB (5M)	14469	15995
B30CSE2P	B3000 SE 2WD Cab Plus SB (5M)	14892	16465
B304SE2P	B3000 SE 2WD Cab Plus 4 SB (5M)	15559	17205
B3XSSEXP	B3000 SE 4WD Regular Cab SB (5M)	16025	17725
B304TL2P	B3000 TL 2WD Cab Plus 4 SB (5M)	16827	18610
B3X4SEXP	B3000 SE 4WD Cab Plus 4 SB (5M)	18270	20010
B404SE2A	B4000 SE 2WD Cab Plus 4 SB (5A)	18649	20630
B4X4SEXP	B4000 SE 4WD Cab Plus 4 SB (5M)	20370	22540
B4X4TLXP	B4000 TL 4WD Cab Plus 4 SB (5M)	21362	23640
Destination Charge:		510	510

Accessories

Code	Description	Invoice	MSRP
1CP	Convenience Package (B3000 SE) *Includes tilt steering wheel, cruise control, bedliner and sliding rear window.*	574	700
1PO	Power Package (B2500 SE Reg Cab/2WD B3000 SE) *Includes power windows, power door locks, power mirrors and remote keyless entry. REQUIRES 1CP.*	439	535
1TC	Traction Package (B4000 4WD) *Includes 4-wheel antilock brakes and limited slip differential.*	492	600
AA1	Stripe Delete (TL) *Reflective flames only.*	(164)	(200)
AC1	Air Conditioning (SX) *Includes 4-speed fan, warm/cool air temperature selection, a choice of recirculating or outside air ventilation and super engine cooling radiator.*	660	805
AT1	Transmission: 4-Speed Automatic (B2500/B3000)	898	1095
AT1	Transmission: 5-Speed Automatic (B4000 4WD)	939	1145

CODE	DESCRIPTION	INVOICE	MSRP
SB2	Bucket Seats (B4000 SE)	295	360
TTH	Class III Trailer Hitch (B4000 2WD)	115	140

2000 MPV

2000 Mazda MPV

What's New?

The MPV has been completely redesigned from top to bottom. Several unique features, like hinged rear doors and all-wheel drive, have disappeared. At the same time, items like roll-down windows in the sliding doors and tailgate seating in the third-row seats certify the MPV as a standout vehicle.

Review

After a one-year hiatus, the MPV returns as an all-new minivan poised for battle with today's best from Chrysler, Ford, Honda and Nissan. Despite Mazda's more conventional approach with their newest minivan, the company still insists that the MPV offers "no compromise" travel in a world filled with boring "box-on-wheels" people movers.

Drivetrain choices for the MPV are limited to a 2.5-liter, DOHC, 24-valve V6 engine that bears much in common with the Ford Duratec V6 of the same size. Creating 170 horsepower (160 in LEV states) and 165 foot-pounds of torque, the MPV will never be mistaken for a performance vehicle, at least in terms of acceleration. Shifting duty comes via a four-speed automatic lifted from Mazda's 626 sedan.

Underneath the MPV you'll find a MacPherson strut front suspension and a torsion beam axle rear suspension, along with front and rear stabilizer bars and a power-assisted rack-and-pinion steering system. Standard brakes are front disc and rear drum with optional ABS. An electronic brake force distribution (EBFD) system is included with ABS to keep stopping distances consistent whether the van is near empty or fully loaded.

Overall size, both inside and out, is down, compared to the largest offerings from Chrysler, Ford and Honda. But Mazda worked hard to make the most of the MPV's interior space. Seating for seven adults is adequate, if not commodious. The tumble-under third-row seat can be folded backwards to allow for tail gate-style seating and the second-row captain's seats can be slid together quickly for bench seating.

Trim levels start with the base DX model that includes 15-inch wheels, dual sliding doors with roll-down windows, de-powered front airbags, removable second-row seats, tumble-under third-row seat, AM/FM/CD player and air conditioning. Step up to the LX and you'll get such niceties as ABS, body-colored bumpers and door handles, dual heated and powered outside mirrors, power windows, cruise control, and privacy glass. The top-of-the-line ES models get 16-inch wheels, leather-trimmed upholstery, side airbags, remote keyless entry and a thundering nine-speaker sound system. Options like a power sunroof, six-disc in-dash CD changer, exterior body cladding and a rear heater can increase your MPV's fun and functionality. It is worth noting, however, that power-sliding side doors are not an option.

Despite climbing SUV sales, the minivan continues as a staple of the automotive industry. If your needs for family toting in style and fun outweigh your requirements for space and power, the MPV deserves a close look.

Standard Equipment

DX (4A): 2.5L V6 DOHC SMPI 24-valve engine; 4-speed electronic OD automatic transmission with lock-up; 356-amp battery; 100-amp alternator; front-wheel drive, 4.38 axle ratio; steel exhaust; front independent strut suspension with anti-roll bar, front coil springs, semi-independent torsion suspension with anti-roll bar, rear coil springs; power rack-and-pinion steering with engine speed-sensing assist; front disc/rear drum brakes; 18.5 gal. capacity fuel tank; side impact bars; 4 doors with sliding left rear passenger door, sliding right rear passenger door, liftback rear cargo door; front and rear argent bumpers; monotone paint; aero-composite halogen headlamps; driver's and passenger's manual black folding outside mirrors; front and rear 15" x 6" steel wheels; P205/65SR15 A/S BSW front and rear tires; underbody mounted compact steel spare wheel; air conditioning, air filter, rear heat ducts; AM/FM stereo, clock, seek-scan, single CD, 4 speakers, and fixed antenna; child safety rear door locks; 2 power accessory outlets, driver's foot rest; instrumentation display includes tachometer, water temperature gauge, trip odometer; warning indicators include oil pressure, battery, lights on, key in ignition, low fuel, door ajar, trunk ajar; driver's and passenger's front airbags; tinted windows, manual front and rear windows, manual 1/4 vent windows; variable intermittent front windshield wipers, fixed interval rear wiper; seating capacity of 7, front captain's seats, adjustable headrests, driver's and passenger's armrests, driver's seat includes 4-way direction control, passenger's seat includes 4-way direction control; removable 50-50 folding split-bench 2nd row seat with reclining adjustable headrests, center armrest; removable 3rd row bench seat with reclining adjustable headrest; front and rear height adjustable seatbelts; cloth seats, cloth door trim insert, full cloth headliner, full vinyl floor covering, deluxe sound insulation; interior lights include dome light; steering wheel with tilt adjustment; vanity mirrors; day/night rearview mirror; locking glove box with light, front cupholder, interior concealed storage, driver's and passenger's door bins; vinyl cargo floor, plastic trunk lid, cargo light; chrome grille, black side window moldings, black front windshield molding, black rear window molding and black door handles.

LX (4A) (in addition to or instead of DX (4A) equipment): 70-amp alternator; front disc/rear drum brakes with 4-wheel antilock braking system, electronic brake force distribution; roof rack; front and rear body-colored bumpers with rear step; body-colored bodyside molding; driver's and passenger's power remote black heated folding outside mirrors; underbody mounted full-size steel spare wheel; cruise control; deep tinted windows, power front and rear windows with driver's 1-touch down; sun visor strip; driver's seat includes 8-way direction control; full carpet floor covering; interior lights include 2 door curb lights; dual illuminated vanity mirrors; 1 seat back storage pocket, front underseat tray and carpeted cargo floor.

ES (4A) (in addition to or instead of LX (4A) equipment): Front and rear 16" x 6" silver alloy wheels; P215/60SR16 A/S BSW front and rear tires; rear air conditioning with separate controls; premium AM/FM stereo, clock, seek-scan, single CD, 9 performance speakers, and fixed antenna; power door locks with 2 stage unlock, remote keyless entry; driver's and front passenger's seat mounted side airbags; ignition disable, panic alarm; leather seats, vinyl door trim insert; simulated wood trim on instrument panel; interior lights include illuminated entry and leather-wrapped steering wheel with tilt adjustment.

CODE	DESCRIPTION	INVOICE	MSRP
	Base Prices		
MP2DX	DX (4A)	18379	19995
MP2LX	LX (4A)	20151	22050
MP2ES	ES (4A)	23343	25550
Destination Charge:		480	480
	Accessories		
—	Alaska Destination Surcharge	200	200
1CO	4-Seasons Package (LX/ES) *Includes rear heater, larger washer tank, HD battery, HD rear window defogger, auxiliary transmission oil cooler, larger radiator and additional cooling fan. REQUIRES 1LX or 2LX (LX).*	344	400
1DX	DX Power Package (DX) *Includes wheels: 15" alloy with locks, power windows, power door locks, power heated mirrors, cruise control, body side moldings, under seat tray and carpeted floor mats.*	1140	1325
1GT	GFX Package (LX/ES) *Includes front spoiler, side sill extentions, rear under spoiler and fog lights. REQUIRES 2LX (LX).*	774	900
1LX	LX Security Package (LX) *Includes wheels: 15" alloy with locks, front side airbags, remote keyless entry, anti-theft alarm with immobilizer, illuminated entry system and carpeted floor mats. NOT AVAILABLE with 2LX, FLM. INCLUDED in 2LX.*	946	1100
2GT	GFX Package (LX) *Includes tires: P215/60HR A/S, wheels: 16" alloy with locks, front spoiler, side sill extentions, rear under spoiler and fog lights. REQUIRES 1LX.*	1032	1200
2LX	LX Touring Package (LX) *Includes LX security package: front side airbags, remote keyless entry, anti-theft alarm with immobilizer, illuminated entry system, carpeted floor mats; tires: P215/60HR A/S, wheels: 16" alloy with locks, wood tone trim and 9-speaker super sound system. NOT AVAILABLE with 1LX, FLM.*	1699	1975
AC8	Rear Air Conditioning (DX/LX) *REQUIRES 1DX (DX).*	512	595
CD2	6-Disc In-Dash CD Changer (LX/ES) *REQUIRES 2LX (LX).*	516	600
CE1	NLEV Emissions	129	150
CGM	Cargo Mat	43	50
CGN	Cargo Net	34	40
ENT	Rear Seat Entertainment System	1372	1595
FLM	Floor Mats (LX) *REQUIRES 2GT or 1GT. NOT AVAILABLE with 1LX, 2LX.*	86	100
FOG	Fog Lights *INCLUDED in 1GT, 2GT.*	215	250
HAND	Great Lakes Handling Charge	65	NC
MG	Great Lakes Administration Fee	81	NC

CODE	DESCRIPTION	INVOICE	MSRP
MGD	Mud Guards	56	65
MR1	Power Moonroof (LX/ES) *REQUIRES 2LX (LX).*	602	700
RBS	Rear Bumper Step Plate	43	50
RCK	Roof Rack	172	200

2000 M-CLASS

2000 Mercedes-Benz ML430

What's New?

All M-Class models get an interior facelift available in one of three new colors, optional third-row seating and a Touch Shift automanual transmission. ML320 buyers get body-color bumpers and trim, real walnut inside, leather-wrapped steering wheel and gearshift knob, revised interior fabric, seatback map pockets and footwell lamps. In addition to these items, a standard navigation system, higher-grade leather, and heated seats come on all ML430s.

Review

Though a runaway sales success, Mercedes-Benz did not hit the bull's-eye with the M-Class sport utility when it was introduced in the fall of 1997 as a 1998 model. The Alabama-built SUV had buyers lined up for months and demand was greater than supply for a long time. But the quality of the vehicle, in terms of the bits and pieces and the way they were assembled, didn't meet the standards of the company or the wealthy clientele that bought them in droves. The vehicle landed last on J. D. Power quality surveys, an embarrassing standing for a German engineering firm that had prided itself for years on vault-like construction and impeccable quality.

The ML320, powered by a peppy 3.2-liter V6 and equipped with drab, gray bumpers and body trim, was priced to steal buyers of loaded Grand Cherokees and 4Runners, though most of the good stuff like leather and wood and everything that makes a Mercedes a Mercedes was optional. Prices for the ML320 rose easily into the low 40s well equipped. The SUV took hits from the public and media for resembling a minivan and performing about as capably as one off-road, but Mercedes knew that if they built them, buyers would come.

In 1999, Mercedes added standard equipment like Electronic Stability Control, Brake Assist, and BabySmart to the ML320 and introduced the opulently outfitted, V8-powered ML430. With a 268-horsepower 4.3-liter motor under the hood and 17-inch tires at each corner, the 430 leaned toward the sporting end of the SUV spectrum. Fast and good-looking with body-colored bumpers and exterior trim, the 430 was a big improvement over the pedestrian 320.

For 2000, Mercedes has improved the recipe once more. All M-Class models get an interior facelift available in one of three new colors in an effort to silence critics who've called the cabin cheap. Optional third-row seating bumps passenger capacity to seven and a Touch Shift automanual transmission makes driving the M more fun. ML320 buyers get body-color bumpers and trim so neighbors don't immediately surmise that they couldn't afford the V8. The 320 also gets real walnut inside, a leather-wrapped steering wheel and gearshift knob, and other goodies for improved ambiance. In addition to these items, a standard navigation system, higher-grade leather, and heated seats come on all ML430s for 2000.

M-Class is equipped with a four-wheel independent double-wishbone suspension for superior on-road ride and outstanding maneuverability. Fast-acting ABS, combined with both traction and stability control, make the M-Class unstoppable in the snow. Blend this inherent ability on pavement and in the slippery stuff with the M's cavernous 80.2 cubic feet of maximum cargo space and long list of standard equipment, and the ingredients for a perfect luxury sport-ute are in place. But true off-road aficionados will want to shop elsewhere for wheels, because the M-Class, despite its boxed frame and four-wheel drive, is much more suited to Chicago's Dan Ryan Expressway than a two-track draped across the Continental Divide.

Standard Equipment

ML320 (5A): 3.2L V6 SOHC SMPI 18-valve engine, requires premium unleaded fuel; 5-speed electronic OD auto transmission with lock-up; engine oil cooler; full-time 4-wheel drive, traction control, 3.69 axle ratio; stainless steel exhaust; auto ride control front independent double wishbone suspension with anti-roll bar, front torsion springs, front torsion bar, rear independent double wishbone suspension with anti-roll bar, rear coil springs; power rack-and-pinion steering; 4-wheel disc brakes with 4-wheel antilock braking system; 19 gal. capacity fuel tank; side impact bars; liftback rear cargo door; roof rack; front and rear body-colored bumpers; body-colored bodyside molding rocker panel extensions; monotone paint; aero-composite halogen headlamps with delay-off feature; driver's and passenger's power remote body-colored heated folding outside mirrors; front and rear 16" x 8" silver alloy wheels; P255/65TR16 M&S BSW front and rear tires; inside under cargo mounted compact steel spare wheel; air conditioning, air filter, rear heat ducts; AM/FM stereo, seek-scan, cassette, CD changer pre-wiring, in-dash CD pre-wiring, 4 speakers, amplifier, theft deterrent, and window grid diversity antenna; cruise control; power door locks with 2 stage unlock, remote keyless entry, child safety rear door locks, power remote hatch/trunk release, power remote fuel release; cell phone pre-wiring, 3 power accessory outlets, driver's foot rest, retained accessory power, garage door opener; instrumentation display includes tachometer, water temperature gauge, in-dash clock, exterior temp, systems monitor, trip odometer; warning indicators include water temp, battery, low oil level, low coolant, lights on, key in ignition, low fuel, low washer fluid, bulb failure, service interval, brake fluid; driver's and passenger's front airbags, driver's and front passenger's door mounted side airbags; ignition disable, panic alarm, security system; tinted windows, power front and rear windows with driver's and passenger's 1-touch down, fixed 1/4 vent windows; variable intermittent front windshield wipers, fixed interval rear wiper, rear window defroster; seating capacity of 5, front bucket seats, adjustable tilt headrests, center armrest with storage, driver's seat includes 6-way direction control, passenger's seat includes 6-way direction control; folding rear split-bench seat with tilt headrests; front and rear height adjustable seatbelts with front and rear pretensioners; cloth seats, leather door trim insert, full cloth headliner, full carpet floor covering with carpeted floor mats, genuine wood trim on instrument panel and doors, leather-wrapped gear shift knob; interior lights include dome light with fade, front and rear reading lights, illuminated entry; leather-wrapped steering wheel with tilt adjustment; dual illuminated vanity mirrors; day/night rearview mirror; full floor console, glove box, front and rear cupholders, instrument panel bin, driver's and passenger's door bins, rear door bins; carpeted cargo floor, plastic trunk lid, cargo cover, cargo tie downs, cargo light; black grille, black side window moldings, black front windshield molding, black rear window molding and black door handles.

ML430 (5A) (in addition to or instead of ML320 (5A) equipment): 4.3L V8 SOHC SMPI 24-valve engine, requires premium unleaded fuel; 3.46 axle ratio; front and rear 17" x 8.5" silver alloy wheels; P275/55TR17 M&S BSW front and rear tires; instrumentation display includes trip computer, navigation system; deep tinted windows; heated-cushion front bucket seats, driver's seat includes 6-way power seat, passenger's seat includes 6-way power seat; leather seats and auto-dimming day/night rearview mirror.

CODE	DESCRIPTION	INVOICE	MSRP

Base Prices

CODE	DESCRIPTION	INVOICE	MSRP
ML320	ML320 (5A)	32829	35300
ML430	ML430 (5A)	40688	43750
Destination Charge:		595	595

Accessories

CODE	DESCRIPTION	INVOICE	MSRP
—	Metallic Paint	442	475
—	Special Order Personalization Charge	930	1000
101	Luxury Package M1 (ML320) *Includes power seats, leather seat trim and privacy glass. REQUIRES 414 or 417. NOT AVAILABLE with 107, 102.*	1395	1500
102	Convenience Package M2 (ML320) *Includes power seat with memory, map lamps, auto-dimming driver's side mirror, auto-dimming interior mirror, power folding side mirrors, safe box and digital trip computer. REQUIRES 107. NOT AVAILABLE with 101.*	925	995
103	Convenience Package M3 (ML430) *Includes power front seats with memory and power folding side mirrors. REQUIRES 414 or 417.*	460	495
104	Off Road Package M4 *Includes polished stainless steel front brush guard, skid plate, mud flaps and side runner bars. REQUIRES 414 or 417.*	1483	1595
107	Luxury Package M1 (ML320) *Includes power seats, leather seat trim and privacy glass. REQUIRES 102 and (414 or 417). NOT AVAILABLE with 101.*	1395	1500
151	Third Row Seat Package M7 with Cloth (ML320) *Includes power rear quarter windows. REQUIRES 414 or 417. NOT AVAILABLE with 152.*	1070	1150
152	Third Row Seat Package M7 with Leather *Includes power rear quarter windows. REQUIRES 414 or 417. NOT AVAILABLE with 151.*	1256	1350
168	Bose Premium Audio System *Includes integrated 6-disc CD changer. REQUIRES 101 or 107.*	977	1050
414	Sunroof, Power Tilt/Sliding Glass *NOT AVAILABLE with 417.*	1018	1095
417	Skyview Top *NOT AVAILABLE with 414.*	2227	2395
873	Heated Seats (ML320)	563	605

2000 MOUNTAINEER

2000 Mercury Mountaineer

What's New?

Mountaineer is available with new Premier and Monterey trim packages, which include tan leather upholstery, special paint, upgraded alloy wheels and wood tone dash trim.

Review

The Explorer-based Mountaineer changes little for 2000. Marketed as an upscale SUV for women and families, the Mountaineer comes with either a 4.0-liter SOHC V6 or a 5.0-liter V8. While horsepower ratings are similar (the V6 makes 210; the V8 produces 215), the V8 does produce more useable torque. Transmission choices still include a five-speed automatic for the V6 and a four-speed automatic with the V8.

Last year, the Mountaineer received new safety features in the form of optional side airbags and an optional reverse parking aid that warns of impending collision with an audible beep. Braking was also improved in '99 with a larger brake booster and upgraded rear-brake calipers. For 2000, the only major change is the addition of Premier and Monterey packages.

There's nothing really new included with the packages, but they do group a large selection of luxury features together. To differentiate Mountaineers with the Premier package, Mercury offers this vehicle only in a Spruce Green exterior color with Medium Prairie Tan interior. The grille, body-side moldings, liftgate molding and license plate shield, rear-quarter extension, running boards and front and rear bumpers are color-keyed to the Spruce Green exterior. Mountaineer Monterey has two tone paint, chrome wheels, and luxury interior touches.

If one orders a new-for-2000 package, the interior (already good in its own right) changes with the addition of special floor mats, leather-trimmed power-adjustable sport bucket seats, and a wood-grain instrument panel.

Both Mountaineers and Explorers retain a distinctly trucklike character, which could be a bonus or a demerit. They're tough and solid, though steering is a little slow and ponderous and the body leans through tight corners. Braking is excellent and the suspension has a compliant attitude, but they can bounce around over rough pavement. For those living in cold-weather climates, or for those who actually intend to make use of the vehicle's off-road capabilities, there is a Control-Trac four-wheel-drive option (with the V6) or a full-time all-wheel-drive option.

Like a lot of Mercury products and their Ford siblings, the Mountaineer's offerings aren't very different than the Explorer's. But that doesn't negate the fact that the Mountaineer is one of the best SUVs currently on the market. It has plenty of space for hauling people and gear through the suburban jungle. The Mercury's abundant standard features provide a great deal of comfort, and the strong engine choices are a bonus when passing at freeway speeds. If you like the Explorer but don't want to see your own vehicle every 10 minutes while driving, Mercury offers a unique alternative.

Standard Equipment

2WD (5A): 4.0L V6 SOHC SMPI 12-valve engine; 5-speed electronic OD auto transmission; 650-amp battery with run down protection; engine oil cooler, HD radiator; 95-amp alternator; rear-wheel drive, 3.55 axle ratio; steel exhaust; front independent suspension with anti-roll bar, front coil springs, front torsion bar, HD front shocks, rigid rear axle suspension with anti-roll bar, rear leaf springs, HD rear shocks; power rack-and-pinion steering; 4-wheel disc brakes with 4-wheel antilock braking system; 21 gal. capacity fuel tank; running boards, side impact bars; liftback rear cargo door; roof rack; front and rear body-colored bumpers with body-colored rub strip, rear step; body-colored bodyside molding; lower accent two-tone paint; aero-composite halogen headlamps; additional exterior lights include front fog/driving lights; driver's and passenger's power remote black folding outside mirrors; front and rear 15" x 7" silver alloy wheels; P225/70SR15 A/S BSW front and rear tires; underbody mounted full-size steel spare wheel; air conditioning, rear heat ducts; AM/FM stereo, clock, seek-scan, cassette, 4 speakers, and fixed antenna; cruise control with steering wheel controls; power door locks, child safety rear door locks; 2 power accessory outlets, retained accessory power, smokers' package; instrumentation display includes tachometer, oil pressure gauge, water temperature gauge, volt gauge, trip odometer; warning indicators include oil pressure, battery, lights on, key in ignition; driver's and passenger's front airbags; ignition disable; deep tinted windows, power front and rear windows with driver's 1-touch down; variable intermittent front windshield wipers, sun visor strip, flip-up rear window, variable intermittent rear wiper, rear window defroster; seating capacity of 5, front captain's seats, fixed headrests, center armrest with storage, driver's seat includes 4-way direction control, passenger's seat includes 4-way direction control; 60-40 folding rear bench seat with adjustable headrests; front height adjustable seatbelts; premium cloth seats, vinyl door trim insert, full cloth headliner, full carpet floor covering with carpeted floor mats, deluxe sound insulation; interior lights include dome light with fade, front reading lights, 2 door curb lights, illuminated entry; leather-wrapped steering wheel with tilt adjustment; dual illuminated vanity mirrors; day/night rearview mirror; full floor console, glove box with light, front and rear cupholders, driver's and passenger's door bins; carpeted cargo floor, plastic trunk lid, cargo cover, cargo tie downs, cargo light; chrome grille, black side window moldings, black front windshield molding, black rear window molding and body-colored door handles.

4WD (5A) (in addition to or instead of 2WD (5A) equipment): Automatic full-time 4-wheel drive, auto locking hub control and electronic shift.

AWD (4A) (in addition to or instead of 4WD (4A) equipment): 5.0L V8 OHV SMPI 16-valve engine; 4-speed electronic OD auto transmission with lock-up; full-time all-wheel drive, limited slip differential, 3.73 axle ratio and P235/75SR15 AT OWL front and rear tires

Base Prices

U66	2WD (5A)	24790	27465
U76	4WD (5A)	26550	29465
U86	AWD (4A)	26960	29930
Destination Charge:		550	550

CODE	DESCRIPTION	INVOICE	MSRP

Accessories

CODE	DESCRIPTION	INVOICE	MSRP
21A	Side Air Bags *REQUIRES 66A.*	336	395
41H	Engine Block Heater	30	35
428	High Altitude Principal Use	NC	NC
429	Non-High Altitude Principal Use	NC	NC
439	Power Moonroof *Includes sunshade, 1-touch open, overhead console, outside temperature and compass display, 2nd row map/dome light. Deletes overhead storage bin and second seat rear reading lamps. REQUIRES 66A.*	680	800
44U	Transmission: 4-Speed Automatic with Overdrive (2WD/AWD)	NC	NC
474	Premier Package (2WD/AWD) *Includes Prairie Tan leather interior, Premier embroidery front floor mats, monotone spruce green clearcoat metallic paint, spruce green grille with chrome Mercury badge logo, running boards, bumpers; Premier badge, steering wheel audio controls, leather-wrapped steering wheel, message center, woodgrain dash center finish panel, spruce green grille, color-keyed body side moldings, wheels: 16" 5-spoke machined aluminum and tires: P255/70R16 OWL. REQUIRES 66A and 66B. NOT AVAILABLE with 646.*	506	595
47U	Monterey Package *Leather seat surfaces in Prairie Tan, lower two-tone paint, wheels: 15" cast aluminum deep dish, wood trim, unique Monterey badging, leather sport bucket seats and embroidered floor mats. REQUIRES 66A and 66B. NOT AVAILABLE with 646.*	421	495
573	Electronic Automatic Temperature Control *Includes message center and steering wheel audio controls. REQUIRES 916 and 66A.*	502	590
646	Wheels: 15" Bright Chrome *NOT AVAILABLE with 474, 47U.*	421	495
66A	Convenience Group *Includes cloth sport bucket seats, remote keyless entry, panic button, electronics package, driver's door keypad, puddle lamps, autolock/relock system, premium AM/FM stereo with CD and cassette, auto on/off headlamps, overhead console, outside temperature and compass display, 2nd row map/dome light, high series floor console, rear heater and A/C fan controls and rear audio controls.*	1016	1195
66B	Luxury Group *Includes leather sport bucket seats, electronic auto temperature control, message center, steering wheel audio controls, unique paint treatment and Ford Mach audio system. REQUIRES 66A.*	1271	1495
67H	Travel Note/Homelink	182	215
68L	Rear Load Leveling (4WD) *REQUIRES 66A and F.*	336	395
76R	Reverse Sensing System *REQUIRES 66A.*	217	255

CODE	DESCRIPTION	INVOICE	MSRP
87K	Skid Plates (4WD/AWD) *Includes transfer case and fuel tank plates.*	107	125
916	Radio: Ford MACH Audio System *Includes AM/FM stereo, cassette, single CD player, 7 premium speakers with 8" subwoofer, 290-watt peak power amplifier and personal audio system. REQUIRES 66A.*	374	440
91P	6-Disc CD Changer *REQUIRES 66A.*	336	395
99P	Engine: 5.0L OHV V8 (2WD) *Includes V8 fender badges, tires: P235/75R15 AT OWL, limited slip with 3.73 axle ratio and trailer tow group. REQUIRES 44U.*	395	465
B3C	Regional No-Charge Leather Program *Available to residents in the following cities/regions: Boston, New York, Philadelphia, Memphis, Orlando, Atlanta, Washington, Chicago, Twin Cities, Cincinnati, California, Denver, Seattle, Kansas City, Southwest Regions, selected counties of Pittsburgh and Detroit.*	(808)	(950)
F	Leather Sport Bucket Seats *Includes 6-way power driver's and passenger's seats and dual manual lumbar supports. REQUIRES 66A.*	808	950
T7R	Tires: P235/75R15 AT OWL (2WD/4WD) *NOT AVAILABLE with 474.*	196	230
XD4	Limited Slip with 3.73 Axle Ratio (2WD/4WD) *Includes trailer tow group.*	302	355

2000 VILLAGER

What's New?

The convenience, comfort, and luxury option packages have been simplified. All 2000 Villagers meet federal low-emission vehicle status and come standard with a child seat-anchor system.

Review

Mercury's entry into the crowded minivan market is the Villager. Redesigned in 1999, the Villager is the twin of the Nissan Quest. Both are designed by Nissan and make use of a Nissan engine, but they're built at a Ford manufacturing plant and sold under two nameplates. The Villager differs from the Nissan Quest only in name, a few interior pieces and some exterior badges. The Villager comes in a base trim level, a mid-level Sport, or a top-level Estate.

All Villagers ride on a relatively short 112.2-inch wheelbase. Suspension components were tweaked in 1999 for a smoother, more controlled ride. Second-generation airbags for driver and front passenger are standard and antilock brakes are optional. Villager scores poorly in offset crash testing.

The interior is functional, but the vehicle's shorter wheelbase means that the Villager doesn't have as big of an interior as other minivans. The Villager has dual sliding doors (non-power operated) to make removing the Villager Sport's second-row chairs (a bench unit on the base model) easy. Once the second row is removed, the third-row bench seat can be pulled forward toward the front seats. The Villager's available cargo space is adequate for most duties, but it's not able to swallow really big items like 4x8 sheets of plywood.

The Villager comes standard with a 3.3-liter V6, which provides 170 horsepower and 200 foot-pounds of torque. This is the same engine you'll find under the hoods of Nissan Pathfinder sport-utes and Frontier pickups, and it's adequate in the performance department when mated to a four-speed automatic transmission.

While the Villager is a decent minivan, it would be wise in your shopping adventures to check out the Honda Odyssey or one of the Chrysler minivans. Both offer more substance for a very similar price.

2000 Mercury Villager

Standard Equipment

BASE (4A): 3.3L V6 SOHC SMPI 24-valve engine; 4-speed electronic OD auto transmission with lock-up; battery with run down protection; HD radiator; 125-amp alternator; front-wheel drive, 3.8 axle ratio; partial stainless steel exhaust; front independent strut suspension with anti-roll bar, front coil springs, rear non-independent suspension with rear leaf springs; power rack-and-pinion steering; front disc/ rear drum brakes; 20 gal. capacity fuel tank; side impact bars; 4 doors with sliding left rear passenger's door, sliding right rear passenger door's, liftback rear cargo door; roof rack; front and rear body-colored bumpers; body-colored bodyside molding; monotone paint; aero-composite halogen headlamps; additional exterior lights include cornering lights; driver's and passenger's power remote black folding outside mirrors; front and rear 15" x 5.5" steel wheels; P215/70SR15 A/S BSW front and rear tires; underbody mounted compact steel spare wheel; air conditioning, rear heat ducts; AM/FM stereo, clock, seek-scan, cassette, 4 speakers, and fixed antenna; cruise control with steering wheel controls; power door locks, remote keyless entry, child safety rear door locks, remote fuel release; 3 power accessory outlets, retained accessory power; instrumentation display includes tachometer, water temperature gauge, trip odometer; warning indicators include water temp, battery, lights on, key in ignition, low fuel, low washer fluid, door ajar, brake fluid; driver's and passenger's front airbags; ignition disable, panic alarm, security system; tinted windows, power windows with driver's 1-touch down, manual 1/4 vent windows; variable intermittent front windshield wipers, sun visor strip, fixed interval rear wiper, rear window defroster; seating capacity of 7, front captain's seats, adjustable headrests, driver's and passenger's armrests, driver's seat includes 4-way direction control, passenger's seat includes 4-way direction control; removable 2nd row full folding bench seat with reclining adjustable headrests; removable full folding 3rd row bench seat with reclining adjustable headrest; front height adjustable seatbelts; cloth seats, cloth door trim insert, full cloth headliner, full carpet floor covering with carpeted floor mats; interior lights include dome light with delay, illuminated entry; steering wheel with tilt adjustment; dual illuminated vanity mirrors; day/night rearview mirror; glove box with light, front and rear cupholders, instrument panel covered bin, dashboard storage, interior concealed storage, 1 seat back storage pocket, driver's and passenger's door bins, front underseat tray; carpeted cargo floor, plastic trunk lid, cargo net, cargo light; chrome grille, black side window moldings, black front windshield molding, black rear window molding and body-colored door handles.

SPORT (4A) (in addition to or instead of BASE (4A) equipment): Touring ride suspension, rear non-independent suspension with anti-roll bar; lower accent two-tone paint with badging; front and rear 16" x 6" silver alloy wheels; P225/60SR16 A/S BSW front and rear tires; rear air conditioning with separate controls, air filter; radio steering wheel controls, rear stereo controls; deep tinted windows, power 1/4 vent windows; flip-up rear window, driver's seat includes 4-way power seat, 8-way direction control, lumbar support; removable full folding 2nd row captain seat with reclining adjustable headrests; interior lights include front and rear reading lights, 2 door curb lights; leather-wrapped steering wheel with tilt adjustment; mini overhead console with storage, 2 seat back storage pockets and front underseat tray.

ESTATE (4A) (in addition to or instead of SPORT (4A) equipment): Body-colored bodyside molding with colored bodyside insert; aero-composite halogen fully auto headlamps, delay-off feature; driver's and passenger's power remote black heated folding outside mirrors; premium AM/FM stereo, clock, seek-scan, cassette, 4 speakers, and fixed antenna; garage door opener; passenger's seat includes 4-way power seat; leather seats and memory on driver's seat with 2 memory setting(s) includes settings for exterior mirrors.

Base Prices

Code	Description	Invoice	MSRP
V11	Base (4A)	20314	22510
V12	Sport (4A)	22954	25510
V14	Estate (4A)	24366	27115
Destination Charge:		605	605

Accessories

Code	Description	Invoice	MSRP
15A	Electronic Instrument Cluster (Estate) *Includes digital speedometer, odometer, dual trip odometers, trip computer with instantaneous fuel economy, average fuel economy, distance-to-empty and outside temperature reading. REQUIRES 573 and 58K.*	251	295
428	High Altitude Principal Use	NC	NC
429	Non-High Altitude Principal Use	NC	NC
439	Power Moonroof (Sport/Estate) *Includes sliding sunshade and fixed air deflector.*	659	775
505	Rear Seat Entertainment System *Includes retractable 6.4 inch color LCD screen, video cassette player, video game plug and play capability, remote control of video cassette player, 2 sets of headphones, 3 headphone jacks, rear passenger controls and floor mounted console.*	1101	1295
534	Trailer Tow Prep Package *Includes trailer tow module and jumper harness.*	213	250
573	Electronic Automatic Temperature Control (Estate) *Controls cabin temperature at desired preset temperature.*	208	245
574	Auxiliary Air Conditioning (Base) *Includes rear audio/fan controls and odor/particulate air filter.*	421	495
586	Radio: Premium AM/FM Stereo with Cassette (Base/Sport) *Includes personal audio system. NOT AVAILABLE with 58K.*	263	310

CODE	DESCRIPTION	INVOICE	MSRP
58K	Radio: Supersound AM/FM Stereo with Cassette and CD (Sport/Estate) .... *Includes 7 speakers, personal audio system and 6-disc CD changer. NOT AVAILABLE with 586.*	735	865
64J	Wheels: 15" Deluxe Aluminum (Base)	336	395
66A	Convenience Group (Base) .... *Includes 6-way power driver's seat, privacy glass, light group, front overhead dual maplights, flip open liftgate window, overhead console and power rear vent windows.*	846	995
67B	Antilock Braking System	502	590
91P	6-Disc CD Changer	314	370
952	Two-Tone Paint (Base)	251	295
M	Leather Seat Trim (Sport) .... *Includes memory driver's seat.*	676	795

2000 MONTERO

2000 Mitsubishi Montero

What's New?

The Montero's list of standard features has been lengthened, and a new Endeavor package adds even more luxury items to Mitsubishi's largest SUV.

Review

Marketed since 1983, Mitsubishi's full-size sport utility ranks as an old-timer in its field, especially since the current four-door, seven-passenger version has been around since '92. To keep up with the burgeoning luxury SUV market, Mitsubishi's veteran mountain machine gains a short list of standard equipment items for 2000. These include a security system with keyless entry, a CD player, a roof rack, a spare-tire cover and, in an amazing show of generosity by Mitsubishi, floor mats!

If the floor mats aren't enough to satisfy your luxury demands, a new Endeavor package can be ordered to further enhance your Montero's opulence. Check this option and you'll be greeted by an interior featuring wood trim, leather-trimmed seats, heated front seats, a power driver's seat, a power sunroof, and an eight-speaker Infinity sound system. You'll also get heated outside mirrors and headlight washers.

Powered by a 3.5-liter, 200-horsepower V6 engine, the Montero moves adequately when asked to do so. It's 228 ft-lbs. of maximum torque help it to power over obstacles when off-roading and its ActiveTrac four-wheel drive can be shifted "on the fly" or set up to operate all the time. A variable shock-absorber system is included on all Monteros and has three settings: hard, medium and soft. These features conspire to make the Montero a capable off-road warrior. And while its 5,000-pound towing capacity looks impressive on paper, in the real world this SUV needs more power. A larger and/or supercharged V6 is in the works, but for now the 3.5-liter engine feels a bit overwhelmed by the Montero's 4,500-pound curb weight.

The interior design has a distinctively trucklike feel, despite its soft-touch surfaces and wood trim. The seating positions are high and upright, even by SUV standards, and the seats themselves are not as comfy as we've come to expect from vehicles in this class. A busy dash layout, featuring a multitude of buttons, switches and knobs, can make simple tasks somewhat daunting.

The Montero does get credit for having one of the largest sunroof openings available on an SUV. We also like its easy-to-use rear seats that quickly turn the Montero from a five-passenger vehicle into a seven-passenger vehicle...as long as children or small adults fill in those last two slots.

CODE	DESCRIPTION	INVOICE	MSRP

Mitsubishi's Montero is an interesting blend of luxurious conveniences, go-anywhere capability and unique styling. A few short years ago, that was enough to be competitive in the SUV market. Today, however, a weak engine and an overall lack of refinement make the Montero a tough sell. With companies like Jeep and Land Rover now offering a generous combination of advanced off-road ability and highly civilized on-road manners, the Montero is simply outclassed. We recommend either shopping elsewhere or waiting for the upcoming redesign.

Standard Equipment

MONTERO (4A): 3.5L V6 SOHC MPI 24-valve engine; 4-speed electronic OD auto transmission with lock-up; 490-amp battery; engine oil cooler; 85-amp alternator; driver's selectable multi-mode transmission, transmission oil cooler; part-time 4-wheel drive, auto locking hub control and manual shift, 4.27 axle ratio; stainless steel exhaust; front independent double wishbone suspension with anti-roll bar, front torsion springs, front torsion bar, rigid rear axle multi-link suspension with anti-roll bar, rear coil springs; power re-circulating ball steering; 4-wheel disc brakes with 4-wheel antilock braking system; 24.3 gal. capacity fuel tank; body-colored front and rear mud flaps, running boards, skid plate(s), side impact bars; conventional rear cargo door; roof rack; front and rear chrome bumpers with body-colored rub strip, front and rear tow hooks, rear step; lower accent two-tone paint; aero-composite halogen headlamps; additional exterior lights include front fog/driving lights; driver's and passenger's power remote black folding outside mirrors; front and rear 15" x 7" silver alloy wheels; P265/70SR15 M&S BSW front and rear tires; outside rear mounted full-size steel spare wheel; air conditioning, rear heat ducts; AM/FM stereo, seek-scan, single CD, 6 speakers, theft deterrent, and power retractable diversity antenna; cruise control; power door locks, remote keyless entry, child safety rear door locks, remote fuel release; 3 power accessory outlets; instrumentation display includes tachometer, oil pressure gauge, water temperature gauge, volt gauge, in-dash clock, compass, exterior temp, trip odometer; warning indicators include oil pressure, battery, low fuel, low washer fluid, door ajar, service interval; driver's and passenger's front airbags; security system; deep tinted windows with driver's 1-touch down, fixed 1/4 vent windows; variable intermittent front windshield wipers, fixed interval rear wiper, rear window defroster; seating capacity of 7, front bucket seats, adjustable tilt headrests, center armrest with storage, driver's seat includes 4-way direction control, passenger's seat includes 4-way direction control; 50-50 folding rear split-bench 2nd row seat with reclining adjustable headrests; 50-50 folding 3rd row split-bench seat with adjustable headrests; front height adjustable seatbelts; cloth seats, cloth door trim insert, full cloth headliner, full carpet floor covering with carpeted floor mats; interior lights include dome light, front and rear reading lights, 2 door curb lights; leather-wrapped sport steering wheel with tilt adjustment; dual illuminated vanity mirrors, dual auxiliary visors; day/night rearview mirror; full floor console, locking glove box, front and rear cupholders, 2 seat back storage pockets, driver's and passenger's door bins, front underseat tray; carpeted cargo floor, plastic trunk lid, cargo tie downs, cargo light; black grille, black side window moldings, black front windshield molding, black rear window molding and black door handles.

Base Prices

MP45-B	Montero (4A)	28938	31807
Destination Charge:		455	455

Accessories

DEST	Alaska Additional Destination Charge	120	120
P2	Montero Endeavor *Includes Mitsubishi/Infinity AM/FM stereo with CD, headlamp washers, leather trimmed seats, heated front seats, power driver's seat, power sunroof, heated mirrors and wood trim.*	2964	3620

2000 MONTERO SPORT

2000 Mitsubishi Montero Sport

What's New?

The 2000 Montero Sport receives significant interior and exterior styling updates like a new grille, revised headlights, body-colored bumpers and new center console design, as well as several technical improvements, including a limited-slip differential on XLS and Limited models, and 16-inch alloy wheels.

Review

Mitsubishi was in the vanguard at the beginning of the sport-utility boom. Way back in 1989, when the Explorer was yet to be introduced and the Grand Cherokee was little more than scribbles in a designer's notebook, the Montero had already evolved into a wonderfully practical four-door design that offered excellent utility and go-anywhere capability. As the years passed, however, the Montero moved further and further up-market as Mitsubishi lavished additional equipment and expensive gee-whiz components on its only sport-ute.

Realizing that they were losing sales because of the Montero's high price, Mitsubishi penned a newly shaped truck, placed it on a proven platform and came up with a not very original name for a smaller, less-expensive SUV in 1997 - the Montero Sport. The Sport shares a frame with the larger Montero, which is good news for those seeking off-road capability, but it is shorter overall due to decreased front and rear overhangs. The Montero Sport's cabin holds five passengers instead of seven but the Sport's cargo space actually surpasses that of the full-size Montero.

Today, the Montero Sport is available in four trim levels: ES, LS, XLS and Limited. Each trim level comes with two- or four-wheel drive except the ES, which is available only as a 2WD model. All 2000 Montero Sports are powered by one of two 24-valve, SOHC V6 engines: the 3.0-liter model or the 3.5-liter version.

Mitsubishi revamped the Montero Sport's exterior and interior for the millennium, adding a new center console with two cupholders, additional power outlets, new seats with lumbar support, two-tone interiors and new fabrics. Outside, the vehicle receives a new body-colored front bumper, cross-hatch black grille, black tailgate garnish, new headlights and bezel, bodyside molding, 16-inch alloy wheels, and 255/70 tires for the LS, XLS and Limited. For 2000, Mitsubishi offers a limited-slip differential for both 2WD and 4WD models - available as part of the XLS premium package or standard on the Limited.

Standard on all but the Limited models is the smaller, 3.0-liter, 173-horsepower engine. ES buyers receive power windows and door locks, AM/FM/CD tuner, rear window wiper/washer and an overhead console with digital clock, map lights and compartments for sunglasses, garage door openers and security cards. Consumers stepping up to the LS will get three-spoke, 16-inch alloy wheels, tube-style side steps, a luggage rack, antilock brakes, driver's seat-height adjuster, 60/40 split-folding rear seat and tinted privacy glass. Montero Sport XLS adds integrated fog lamps, eight-spoke alloy wheels, auto-dimming rearview mirror with compass and outside thermometer, leather-wrapped steering wheel and remote keyless entry.

The Limited trim level comes standard with a 3.5-liter, 200-horsepower V6 engine. Other standard features on the Limited include body-colored door handles, mirrors and fender flares, integrated side steps, power sunroof, machine-finished alloy wheels and rear seat heaters.

Even with the larger engine, we found the Montero Sport to be underpowered when gaining elevation at a steady pace, with its four-speed transmission hunting for the appropriate gears. Slipping into four-wheel drive on-the-fly is easy with Montero Sport's well-placed shift lever, and there are seven available grab handles when the road gets rough. The interior layout is ergonomically sound and user-friendly, though door handles seem small and the stereo buttons are cluttered. Overall, the 2000 Montero Sport is significantly improved and worth looking into.

Standard Equipment

ES 2WD (4A): 3.0L V6 SOHC MPI 24-valve engine; 4-speed electronic OD auto transmission with lock-up; 60-amp alternator; transmission oil cooler; rear-wheel drive, 4.64 axle ratio; stainless steel exhaust; front independent double wishbone suspension with anti-roll bar, front torsion springs, front torsion bar, rigid rear axle suspension with anti-roll bar, rear coil springs; power re-circulating ball steering; front disc/rear drum brakes; 19.5 gal. capacity fuel tank; front and rear mud flaps, skid plate(s), side impact bars; tailgate rear cargo door; front and rear body-colored bumpers with front and rear tow hooks, rear step; monotone paint; aero-composite halogen headlamps; driver's and passenger's power remote black folding outside mirrors; front and rear 15" x 6" silver styled steel wheels; P235/75SR15 M&S BSW front and rear tires; underbody mounted full-size steel spare wheel; air conditioning; AM/FM stereo, clock, seek-scan, single CD, 4 speakers, and fixed antenna; power door locks, remote fuel release; 2 power accessory outlets, driver's foot rest, smokers' package; instrumentation display includes tachometer, water temperature gauge, trip odometer; warning indicators include oil pressure, battery, lights on, key in ignition, door ajar, brake fluid; driver's and passenger's front airbags; ignition disable; tinted windows, power front and rear windows with driver's 1-touch down, fixed 1/4 vent windows; fixed interval front windshield wipers, flip-up rear window, rear window wiper, rear window defroster; seating capacity of 5, front bucket seats, adjustable headrests, center armrest with storage, driver's seat includes 4-way direction control, lumbar support, passenger's seat includes 4-way direction control; full folding rear bench seat with reclining adjustable headrests, center armrest with storage; front height adjustable seatbelts; cloth seats, cloth door trim insert, full cloth headliner, full carpet floor covering; interior lights include dome light, front reading lights, 2 door curb lights; steering wheel with tilt adjustment; vanity mirrors; day/night rearview mirror; full floor console, full overhead console with storage, locking glove box, front cupholder, 2 seat back storage pockets, driver's and passenger's door bins; carpeted cargo floor, plastic trunk lid, cargo tie downs, cargo light; black grille, black side window moldings, black front windshield molding, black rear window molding and black door handles.

LS 2WD (4A) (in addition to or instead of ES 2WD (4A) equipment): 85-amp alternator; front disc/rear drum brakes with 4-wheel antilock braking system; black bodyside molding, black fender flares; front and rear 16" x 7" silver alloy wheels; P255/70SR16 M&S BSW front and rear tires; AM/FM stereo, clock, seek-scan, single CD, 6 speakers, and fixed antenna; cruise control; deep tinted windows; driver's seat includes 6-way direction control, lumbar support; 60-40 folding rear bench seat with reclining adjustable headrests; front and rear cupholders and interior concealed storage.

XLS 2WD (4A) (in addition to or instead of LS 2WD (4A) equipment): Running boards; roof rack; body-colored bodyside molding, body-colored fender flares; lower accent two-tone paint; additional exterior lights include front fog/driving lights; AM/FM stereo, clock, seek-scan, single CD, 6 speakers, theft deterrent, and power retractable antenna; remote keyless entry; instrumentation display includes exterior temp; panic alarm, security system; leather-wrapped steering wheel with tilt adjustment; auto-dimming day/night rearview mirror; cargo cover, cargo concealed storage and chrome grille.

LIMITED 2WD (4A) (in addition to or instead of XLS 2WD (4A) equipment): 3.5L V6 SOHC MPI 24-valve engine; limited slip differential; driver's and passenger's power remote black heated folding outside mirrors; front power sliding and tilting glass sunroof with sunshade; monotone paint; rear heater; premium AM/FM stereo, clock, seek-scan, single CD, 8 premium speakers, amplifier, theft deterrent, and power retractable antenna.

4WD (4A) (in addition to or instead of 2WD (4A) equipment): Part-time 4-wheel drive, auto locking hub control and manual shift and 4-wheel disc brakes with 4-wheel antilock braking system.

Base Prices

MT45-B	ES 2WD 4A)	20493	22527
MT45-D	LS 2WD (4A)	22534	24777
MT45-F	LS 4WD (4A)	24384	26807
MT45-G	XLS 2WD (4A)	24936	27417
MT45-K	XLS 4WD (4A)	26678	29327
MT45-P	Limited 2WD (4A)	27203	29907
MT45-X	Limited 4WD (4A)	28524	31357
Destination Charge:		455	455

Accessories

—	Alaska Destination Surcharge	120	120
KS	Security System (LS) *Includes keyless entry.*	250	305
P3	Leather Seating Package (Limited) *Includes leather trimmed seats and heated front seats.*	1008	1235
P4	Premium Package (XLS) *Includes premium AM/FM stereo with CD, amplifier and 8 speakers; leather seats, power sunroof and limited slip differential.*	2171	2655
P9	Preferred Package (LS) *Includes roof rack, side steps and rear deflector.*	505	755

2000 FRONTIER

2000 Nissan Frontier

What's New?

Nissan's pickup line expands to 11 models, including the new Desert Runner and four-door Frontier Crew Cab.

Review

Nissan has been selling trucks in this country for more than 40 years. In 1998, they decided to redesign the pickup and for the first time ever, gave it a name: the Frontier. Today, Frontiers range from the entry-level, two-wheel-drive XE Regular Cab to the top-of-the-line, four-wheel-drive Crew Cab SE V6. There are 11 Frontier models available for 2000, including the new Desert Runner King Cab and Frontier Crew Cab.

The Desert Runner is a two-wheel-drive V6 King Cab pickup truck, and Nissan expects to sell it to "style-conscious buyers who do occasional off-roading." Built on the four-wheel-drive Frontier chassis, the Desert Runner offers the same rigidity, ride height, ground clearance and rugged looks as the 4WD pickups, but at a lesser price. Available in XE or SE trim levels, the Desert Runner comes equipped with a full-size spare tire, extended passenger compartment with dual jump seats, large fender flares with mud guards and special badging. Weighing 500 pounds less than the 4WD pickup and powered by Nissan's 170-horsepower, 3.3-liter V6 engine, the Desert Runner makes 200 foot-pounds of torque at 1,500 rpm. The truck can be had with a five-speed manual transmission, which can tow 3,500 pounds, or a four-speed automatic transmission, which can tow 5,000 pounds.

For 2000, Nissan Crew Cab buyers will be the first in the U.S. to own a pickup with four full-sized, forward-hinged doors. The four-door configuration allows five passengers to climb aboard easily. The Crew Cab's bed is about 18 inches shorter than the standard Frontier, but an optional bed extender is available. Built on the same chassis as the Desert Runner, the Crew Cab is also powered by the 3.3-liter V6 and comes as a two- or four-wheel-drive model. The 4WD Crew Cab features automatic locking hubs, a shift-on-the-fly feature and an optional limited-slip differential. Standard equipment includes ABS, air conditioning, rear privacy glass, AM/FM/cassette stereo and heavy-duty skid plates. A tubular-style roof rack that can be fitted to carry skis, mountain bikes, kayaks or luggage is optional.

Other Frontiers are available in a multitude of configurations: Regular Cab or Extended King Cab in basic XE or uplevel SE trim powered by either a 143-horsepower, 2.4-liter inline four or the aforementioned 3.3-liter V6 (the latter available in King Cab only). A five-speed manual transmission and four-speed automatic are the transmission choices, and all Frontiers (except Desert Runner) can be selected with two- or four-wheel drive. Four-wheel-drive systems are of the shift-on-the-fly variety on V6 Frontiers, allowing the driver to select it at speeds up to 50 mph.

Inside, the Frontier has a user-friendly, if somewhat dated-looking, control layout. Seats are reasonably comfortable for front passengers, but only children or pets will want to ride in the rear section of the King Cab. Surprisingly, Nissan has not seen fit to offer a third or fourth door on the King Cab, making use of the rear quarters a pain in the butt, at best.

With a relatively tame on-road ride, credible off-road credentials and the deepest cargo bed in the class, the 2000 Frontier promises comfort, utility and a model to suit nearly any pickup buyer's needs. And now, you can use all four doors to crawl inside.

Standard Equipment

XE 2WD REGULAR CAB (5M): 2.4L I4 DOHC SMPI 16-valve engine; 5-speed overdrive manual transmission; 490-amp battery; 70-amp alternator; rear-wheel drive, 3.55 axle ratio; steel exhaust; front independent double wishbone suspension with anti-roll bar, front torsion springs, front torsion bar, rigid rear axle suspension with rear leaf springs; power re-circulating ball steering; front disc/rear drum brakes with rear wheel antilock braking system; 15.9 gal. capacity fuel tank; front and rear mud flaps, skid plate(s), side impact bars; black bumpers; monotone paint; aero-composite halogen headlamps; manual black folding outside mirrors; front and rear 15" x 6" silver styled steel wheels; P215/65RS15 A/S BSW front and rear tires; underbody mounted compact steel spare wheel; 2 power accessory outlets, driver's foot rest; instrumentation display includes tachometer, water temp gauge, trip odometer; warning indicators include oil pressure, battery, lights on, key in ignition, low fuel, brake fluid; driver's front airbag, passenger's cancelable front airbag; tinted windows; fixed interval front windshield wipers; seating capacity of 3, bench front seat fixed headrests, driver's and passenger's seat includes 2-way direction control; front height adjustable seatbelts with front pretensioners; cloth seats, cloth door trim insert, full cloth headliner, full carpet floor covering, plastic/rubber gear shift knob, cabback insulator; interior lights include dome light; day/night rearview mirror; glove box, front cupholder, instrument panel bin, driver's and passenger's door bins; black grille.

XE 2WD KING CAB (5M) (in addition to or instead of XE 2WD REGULAR CAB (5M) equipment): 3.7 axle ratio; rear black bumper with step; P235/70SR15 A/S BSW front and rear tires; vented rear windows; seating capacity of 5, 60-40 split-bench front seat with adjustable headrests, center armrest with storage, driver's and passenger's seat includes 4-way direction control with easy entry; folding rear side facing jump seats and premium cloth seats.

DESERT RUNNER XE-V6 2WD KING CAB (5M) (in addition to or instead of XE 2WD KING CAB (5M) equipment): 3.3L V6 SOHC SMPI 12-valve engine; front disc/rear drum brakes with 4-wheel antilock braking system; 19.4 gal. capacity fuel tank; front and rear mud flaps; black fender flares; underbody mounted full-size steel spare wheel; seating capacity of 4, front bucket seats with adjustable headrests and partial floor console.

DESERT RUNNER SE-V6 2WD KING CAB (5M) (in addition to or instead of DESERT RUNNER XE-V6 2WD KING CAB (5M) equipment): Body-colored fender flares; additional exterior lights include front fog/driving lights; manual body-colored folding outside mirrors; front and rear 16" x 7" silver alloy wheels; P255/65SR16 A/S BSW front and rear tires; AM/FM stereo, clock, seek-scan, single CD, 4 speakers, and fixed antenna; deep tinted windows; variable intermittent front windshield wipers, sliding rear window; front sports seats with adjustable headrests, leather-wrapped gear shift knob; interior lights include front reading lights; leather-wrapped steering wheel with tilt adjustment; passenger's side vanity mirror; cargo light; chrome grille.

XE-V6 2WD CREW CAB (5M) (in addition to or instead of DESERT RUNNER XE-V6 2WD KING CAB (5M) equipment): Rigid rear axle suspension with anti-roll bar, rear leaf springs; chrome bumpers with rear step; front and rear 15" x 7" silver styled steel wheels; air conditioning; deep tinted windows, manual rear windows; sliding rear window; seating capacity of 5; full folding rear bench seat; interior lights include front reading lights and chrome grille.

SE-V6 2WD CREW CAB (5M) (in addition to or instead of XE-V6 2WD KING CAB (5M) equipment): Body-colored fender flares; additional exterior lights include front fog/driving lights; manual body-colored folding outside mirrors; front and rear 16" x 7" silver alloy wheels; P255/65SR16 A/S BSW front and rear tires; underbody mounted full-size alloy spare wheel; AM/FM stereo, clock, seek-scan, single CD, 6 speakers, and fixed antenna; variable intermittent front windshield wipers; front sports seats with adjustable headrests, premium cloth seats; leather-wrapped gear shift knob and steering wheel with tilt adjustment and passenger's side vanity mirror.

XE 4WD KING CAB (5M) (in addition to or instead of XE 2WD KING CAB (5M) equipment): Part-time 4 wheel drive, manual locking hub control and manual shift, 4.38 axle ratio; front disc/rear drum brakes with 4-wheel antilock braking system; black fender flares; front and rear 15" x 7" silver styled steel wheels and underbody mounted full-size steel spare wheel.

XE-V6/SE-V6 4WD KING CAB (5M) (in addition to or instead of DESERT RUNNER XE-V6/SE-V6 2WD KING CAB (5M) equipment): Part-time 4 wheel drive, manual locking hub control and manual shift, 4.38 axle ratio, front and rear 15" x 7" silver styled steel wheels (XE-V6) and running boards and pickup cargo box light (SE-V6).

4WD CREW CAB (5M) (in addition to or instead of 2WD CREW CAB (5M) equipment): Part-time 4 wheel drive, manual locking hub control and manual shift and 4.38 axle ratio.

Base Prices

03050	XE 2WD Regular Cab (5M)	10900	11590
13050	XE 2WD King Cab (5M)	12594	13540
33050	Desert Runner XE-V6 2WD King Cab (5M)	14639	15740
53050	XE-V6 2WD Crew Cab (5M)	16061	17290
23050	XE 4WD King Cab (5M)	15946	17340
33150	Desert Runner SE-V6 2WD King Cab (5M)	16451	17890
43050	XE-V6 4WD King Cab (5M)	16665	18340
53150	SE-V6 2WD Crew Cab (5M)	17095	18590
63050	XE-V6 4WD Crew Cab (5M)	18291	19890
43150	SE-V6 4WD King Cab (5M)	18628	20490
63150	SE-V6 4WD Crew Cab (5M)	19265	21190
Destination Charge:		520	520

Accessories

—	Transmission: 4-Speed Automatic (Desert Runner SE-V6)	966	1050
—	Transmission: 4-Speed Automatic (SE-V6 2WD Crew Cab)	965	1050
—	Transmission: 4-Speed Automatic (SE-V6 4WD Crew Cab)	954	1050
—	Transmission: 4-Speed Automatic (SE-V6 4WD X-Cab)	955	1050
—	Transmission: 4-Speed Automatic (XE 2WD Reg Cab)	988	1050
—	Transmission: 4-Speed Automatic (XE 2WD X-Cab/Desert Runner)	976	1050
—	Transmission: 4-Speed Automatic (XE-V6 2WD Crew Cab)	997	1050
—	Transmission: 4-Speed Automatic (XE-V6 4WD Crew Cab)	975	1050
—	Transmission: 4-Speed Automatic (XE-V6 4WD X-Cab)	966	1050
A01	Air Conditioning (XE 2WD Reg Cab) *NOT AVAILABLE with G02.*	825	950
B10	Limited Slip Differential (SE-V6 Except 2WD Crew Cab)	173	200

CODE	DESCRIPTION	INVOICE	MSRP
F05	Power Package (Crew Cab) *Includes power windows, power door locks, power mirrors, vehicle security system, remote keyless entry and cruise control.*	936	1080
F05	Power Package (XE/SE - Reg Cab/X-Cab) *Includes power windows, power door locks, power mirrors, vehicle security system, remote keyless entry and cruise control. REQUIRES G03 (XE) or B10 (SE).*	849	980
G02	Value Truck Package (XE 2WD Reg Cab) *Includes air conditioning, chrome grille, chrome bumpers and AM/FM cassette with 4 speakers. NOT AVAILABLE with A01, S01.*	516	549
G03	Value Truck Package (XE - X-Cab/Desert Runner) *Includes air conditioning, AM/FM cassette with 4 speakers, alloy wheels, sliding rear window, flip down cargo area light and privacy glass. NOT AVAILABLE with W01, P04.*	893	949
H92	Single Disc CD Player (XE)	231	469
H93	3-Disc CD Player (XE-V6)	196	295
J02	SE Sport Package (SE-V6) *Includes pop-up sunroof, premium AM/FM stereo with cassette, CD and subwoofer. REQUIRES B10 and F05.*	650	749
J92	Fender Flares/Splash Guards (XE 4-Cyl) *NOT AVAILABLE with U04, U05.*	157	209
L92	Floor Mats (All Except Crew Cab)	47	69
L92	Floor Mats (Crew Cab)	58	79
M92	Over Rail Bedliner (Crew Cab)	148	299
M93	Under Rail Bedliner (Crew Cab)	145	299
M94	Under Rail Bedliner (X-Cab)	145	299
M95	Over Rail Bedliner (X-Cab) *NOT AVAILABLE with X92.*	148	299
M96	Under Rail Bedliner (XE 2WD Reg Cab)	145	299
M97	Over Rail Bedliner (XE 2WD Reg Cab) *NOT AVAILABLE with X92.*	148	299
N09	16" Wheel Delete (SE X-Cab)	(86)	(100)
P04	Popular Equipment Package (XE X-Cab) *Includes air conditioning and AM/FM stereo with cassette and 4 speakers. NOT AVAILABLE with G03.*	1213	1399
S01	Chrome and Audio Package (XE 2WD Reg Cab) *Includes chrome grille, chrome bumpers and AM/FM stereo with cassette and 4 speakers. NOT AVAILABLE with G02.*	390	449
U04	Value Plus Package (XE 2WD Reg Cab) *Includes front bucket seats, console with storage, alloy wheels, fender flares, passenger assist grip and sliding rear window. REQUIRES G02. NOT AVAILABLE with J92.*	563	649
U05	Value Plus Package (XE 2WD X-Cab) *Includes front bucket seats, console with storage, alloy wheels, fender flares, tilt steering, variable intermittent windshield wipers, passenger's vanity mirror, tailgate finisher and map lights. REQUIRES G03. NOT AVAILABLE with J92.*	303	349

CODE	DESCRIPTION	INVOICE	MSRP
U06	Value Plus Package (XE-V6 2WD Crew Cab) *Includes tires: P265/70R15, alloy wheels, tilt steering, variable intermittent windshield wipers, passenger's vanity mirror and tailgate finisher.*	519	599
U06	Value Plus Package (XE-V6 4WD Crew Cab) *Includes tires: P265/70R15, alloy wheels, tilt steering, variable intermittent windshield wipers, passenger's vanity mirror, tailgate finisher, limited slip differential and off-road decal.*	693	799
U08	Off-Road Package (XE-V6 4WD X-Cab) *Includes tires: P265/70R15, limited slip differential, tilt steering, variable intermittent windshield wipers, passenger's vanity mirror, tailgate finisher and 4x4 decal.*	563	649
U08	Value Plus Package (Desert Runner XE-V6) *Includes tires: P265/70R15, limited slip differential, tilt steering, variable intermittent windshield wipers, passenger's vanity mirror and tailgate finisher. REQUIRES G03.*	606	699
V10	Utility Package (SE-V6 2WD Crew Cab) *Includes tubular roof rack.*	217	250
V10	Utility Package (SE-V6 4WD Crew Cab) *Includes tubular roof rack and limited slip differential.*	391	450
W01	Appearance Package (XE X-Cab) *Includes alloy wheels, cargo lamp, sliding rear window and privacy glass. NOT AVAILABLE with G03.*	564	650
X92	Bed Extender *NOT AVAILABLE with M97, M95.*	166	229

2000 PATHFINDER

What's New?

After a substantial update in the middle of the 1999 model year, the Pathfinder soldiers into the new millennium without change. However, rumor has it that later in 2000 the Pathfinder will get a massive power upgrade.

Review

Now 5 years old, the current-generation Nissan Pathfinder still sports one of the friendliest interiors of any SUV on the market, and drives very much like a car without sacrificing much capability to travel off the beaten path.

Front passenger space is ample, but the rear seat can be cramped for larger adults. Though the Pathfinder appears to be on the small side of the midsize-SUV continuum, it actually is capable of carting 85 cubic feet of detritus. For comparison purposes, a Dodge Durango can hold only 3 more cubic feet of stuff.

Our main complaints about the Pathfinder revolve around the weak 3.3-liter V6 engine and the tight entry and exit afforded by small rear doors. Last year, Nissan slightly boosted power output to 170 horsepower and 200 ft-lbs. of torque, but the truck still feels winded as the revs climb. Low rpm grunt is acceptable, however, so urban commutes and four-wheeling don't tax the powertrain. Look for a big power boost in the middle of the 2000 model year. The rumors we're hearing involve a 230-hp, 3.5-liter V6.

Other changes last year included revised styling that gives the Pathfinder a more rugged and substantial appearance, new colors, improved NVH performance, revised suspension tuning for better on-road ride and handling, bigger tires and a wider track. Interiors got a makeover with new fabrics, white or titanium gauge clusters, standard CD sound system with cassette player and six speakers, optional side airbags and an ignition immobilizer.

Three trim levels are available with either rear-wheel drive or part-time four-wheel drive. Basic XE models come decently equipped with ABS, automatic transmission, air conditioning, alloy wheels, privacy glass and an anti-theft system. Step up to the SE and enjoy the option of shifting gears manually, tubular step rails, leather-wrapped steering wheel, titanium gauges, suede-look cloth trim, power windows and locks, heated power mirrors, driver's seat height adjustment and lumbar control, and remote keyless entry. Top-of-the-line LE models are loaded with running boards, fog lights, chrome exterior accents, automatic climate control, Bose audio, exterior temperature readout, integrated compass, and fake wood interior accents.

Dealers will likely be getting huge incentives to move underpowered 2000 Pathfinders off the lot until the more powerful V6 arrives. Adding to this consumer-friendly market climate is the incredible popularity of the smaller Xterra, which is cannibalizing Pathfinder intenders with its more hip, youthful image and cheaper price tag. Screaming deals are available on this aging yet still capable sport-ute, and for this reason alone, this truck deserves your attention.

2000 Nissan Pathfinder

Standard Equipment

XE 2WD (4A): 3.3L V6 SOHC SMPI 12-valve engine; 4-speed electronic OD auto transmission with lock-up; 90-amp alternator; rear-wheel drive, 4.36 axle ratio; stainless steel exhaust; front independent strut suspension with anti-roll bar, front coil springs, rigid rear axle multi-link suspension with anti-roll bar, rear coil springs; power rack-and-pinion steering; front disc/rear drum brakes with 4-wheel antilock braking system; 21 gal. capacity fuel tank; front and rear mud flaps, skid plate(s), side impact bars; liftback rear cargo door; roof rack; front and rear black bumpers with chrome bumper insert, rear step; monotone paint; aero-composite halogen headlamps; driver's and passenger's manual black folding outside mirrors; front and rear 16" x 7" polished alloy wheels; P245/70SR16 M&S BSW front and rear tires; underbody mounted full-size steel spare wheel; air conditioning; AM/FM stereo, clock, seek-scan, single CD, 6 speakers, and fixed diversity antenna; child safety rear door locks, remote fuel release; 2 power accessory outlets, driver's foot rest, retained accessory power; instrumentation display includes tachometer, water temperature gauge, trip odometer; warning indicators include oil pressure, water temp, battery, lights on, key in ignition, low fuel, low washer fluid, door ajar, brake fluid;

CODE	DESCRIPTION	INVOICE	MSRP

driver's and passenger's front airbags; ignition disable; deep tinted windows, manual front and rear windows, fixed 1/4 vent windows; variable intermittent front windshield wipers, flip-up rear window, fixed interval rear wiper, rear window defroster; seating capacity of 5, front bucket seats, adjustable headrests, center armrest with storage, driver's seat includes 4-way direction control, passenger's seat includes 4-way direction control; 60-40 folding rear bench seat with reclining adjustable headrests; front height adjustable seatbelts with front pretensioners; cloth seats, cloth door trim insert, full cloth headliner, full carpet floor covering, plastic/rubber gear shift knob; interior lights include dome light, front reading lights; steering wheel with tilt adjustment; passenger's side vanity mirror; day/night rearview mirror; full floor console, mini overhead console with storage, locking glove box with light, front and rear cupholders, 1 seat back storage pocket, driver's and passenger's door bins, rear door bins; carpeted cargo floor, plastic trunk lid, cargo tie downs, cargo light, cargo concealed storage; body-colored grille, black side window moldings, black front windshield molding, black rear window molding and black door handles.

SE 2WD (5M) (in addition to or instead of XE 2WD (5M) equipment): 5-speed OD manual transmission; 4.64 axle ratio; front and rear tow hooks; black fender flares; driver's and passenger's power remote black heated folding outside mirrors; P255/65SR16 M&S BSW front and rear tires; cruise control with steering wheel controls; power door locks with 2 stage unlock, remote keyless entry; panic alarm, security system; power front and rear windows with driver's 1-touch down; driver's seat includes 8-way direction control, lumbar support, rear center armrest; leather-wrapped gear shift knob; leather-wrapped steering wheel with tilt adjustment; cargo cover and black grille.

LE 2WD (4A) (in addition to or instead of SE 2WD (4A) equipment): Four-speed electronic OD auto transmission with lock-up; transmission oil cooler; 4.64 axle ratio; body-colored front and rear mud flaps, running boards; front and rear body-colored bumpers with chrome bumper insert; body-colored fender flares; additional exterior lights include front fog/driving lights; driver's and passenger's power remote body-colored heated folding outside mirrors; air conditioning with climate control; premium AM/FM stereo, clock, seek-scan, single CD, 6 premium speakers, and power retractable diversity antenna; garage door opener; instrumentation display includes compass, exterior temp; simulated wood trim on instrument panel; dual illuminated vanity mirrors and chrome grille.

4WD (in addition to or instead of 2WD equipment): Part-time 4-wheel drive and auto locking hub control and manual shift.

Base Prices

CODE	DESCRIPTION	INVOICE	MSRP
09210	XE 2WD (4A)	24001	26399
09450	SE 2WD (5M)	24865	27349
09610	XE 4WD (4A)	25819	28399
09310	LE 2WD (4A)	26637	29299
09750	SE 4WD (5M)	26683	29349
09810	LE 4WD (4A)	28455	31299
Destination Charge:		520	520

Accessories

CODE	DESCRIPTION	INVOICE	MSRP
4AT	Transmission: 4-Speed Automatic (SE)	909	1000
B10	Limited Slip Differential (4WD - SE/LE) *REQUIRES J03.*	216	249
F92	Floor Mats	58	79

CODE	DESCRIPTION	INVOICE	MSRP
G02	Popular Package (XE) *Includes large door armrests, power windows with driver's auto down, power door locks, vehicle security system, remote keyless entry, cruise control, retractable cargo area cover, cargo net, power heated mirrors, leather-wrapped steering wheel and leather-wrapped shift knob.*	1085	1250
G03	Popular Package (SE) *Includes Bose AM/FM stereo with CD and cassette, power antenna, cargo net, halogen fog lights and rear window deflector.*	NC	NC
H94	6-Disc CD Autochanger	338	719
J03	Sunroof Package (LE) *Includes power tilt and slide glass sunroof.*	NC	NC
J03	Sunroof Package (SE) *Includes power tilt and slide glass sunroof, dual driver's side sunvisors, integrated Homelink transmitter, digital compass, outside temperature display and dual illuminated visor vanity mirrors. REQUIRES G03.*	953	1099
P92	Tow Hitch III	305	389
R94	Body Color Side Moldings	73	99
W94	Gold Badging (XE)	123	389
W97	Gold Badging (LE)	123	389
X03	Leather Package (2WD - SE/LE) *Includes simulated leather door trim, power driver's and passenger's seats and side airbags. REQUIRES J03 and 4AT (SE).*	1560	1799
X03	Leather Package (4WD - SE/LE) *Includes simulated leather door trim, power driver's and passenger's seats and side airbags. REQUIRES J03 and 4AT (SE).*	1734	1999

2000 QUEST

What's New?

A stabilizer bar is now standard on the GLE model while new titanium-colored pockets have been added to the 16-inch SE and 15-inch GXE alloy wheels. The SE gets auto on/off headlights and all Quests now come with a video entertainment system at no extra cost.

Review

Nissan completely redesigned the Quest in 1999 in an attempt to keep pace with superior vans from Honda, Chrysler and Ford. The current van's exterior is larger than the previous-generation Quest, with 4.6 more inches in length and 1.2 more inches in width. These dimensions provide an extra 9.6 cubic feet of cargo volume for a total of 135.6 cubic feet. Stylistically, the Quest's front end is rounded with a chrome grille and multiparabola headlights with crystalline lenses. A standard driver's side rear sliding door is one of its many features, making entry and exit easier for the kiddies.

Under the hood is a 3.3-liter, 170-horsepower V6 engine that makes 200 foot-pounds of torque. This engine is mated to a four-speed automatic transmission that changes gears neatly, without a hint of harshness due to electronic controls. Antilock brakes and power steering are standard on all Quest models and the suspension provides a smooth, quiet, sedan-like ride.

For 2000, the minivan is available in three flavors: value-oriented GXE, sporty SE with larger 16-inch alloy wheels, and luxurious GLE trim, featuring leather seating and the Quest Trac flexible seating system. Versatile passenger space is the Quest's stock-in-trade with a third-row limousine seating option among its many features. With seven-passenger Quest Trac Flexible Seating, you can get 24 different combinations with the bench seat and 66 with the second-row captain's chairs. Second-row seats can fold down into a table, or be removed completely. The third-row seat also folds into a table, folds further for more cargo space, or slides forward on integrated tracks—all the way to behind the driver's seat. Storage compartments total 31 and cupholders will hold 13 drinks throughout. To enhance storage even more, buyers can add an optional multi-adjustable Quest Smart Shelf with mesh net located behind the third row.

The Quest's dashboard has a functional layout with the audio unit located above the climate controls for easier access. An automatic headlight on/off switch (standard on GLE and SE) can be set to sense the onset of darkness and automatically turn the headlights on. Visibility is great, too, from upright but comfortable seating that's tempting for a long trek. Gauges are small, but acceptable, and controls are pleasing to operate. The standard entertainment system features a new, larger screen for 2000 to better pacify rambunctious rear passengers.

Distinctive in shape and enjoyable on the road, Quests perform adequately, though more engine power would be appreciated. Except for the upright seating position, this Nissan's handling traits make it easy to forget that you're inside a minivan. Unfortunately, especially since this is a family-minded vehicle, the Quest's crash test scores are sub par. If you're seeking transportation for loved ones, the Windstar or Odyssey are a "safer" bet.

2000 Nissan Quest

Standard Equipment

GXE (4A): 3.3L V6 SOHC SMPI 12-valve engine; 4-speed electronic OD auto transmission with lock-up; battery with run down protection; 125-amp alternator; front-wheel drive, 3.79 axle ratio; stainless steel exhaust; front independent strut suspension with anti-roll bar, front coil springs, rear non-independent suspension with rear leaf springs; power rack-and-pinion steering with vehicle speed-sensing assist; front disc/rear drum brakes with 4-wheel antilock braking system; 20 gal. capacity fuel tank; side impact bars; 4 doors with sliding left rear passenger's door, sliding right rear passenger's door, liftback rear cargo door; roof rack; front and rear body-colored bumpers with rear step; body-colored bodyside molding; monotone paint; aero-composite halogen headlamps with; additional exterior lights include cornering lights; driver's and passenger's power remote black heated folding outside mirrors; front and rear 15" x 5.5" steel wheels; P215/70SR15 A/S BSW front and rear tires; underbody mounted full-size steel spare wheel; air conditioning, rear heat ducts; AM/FM stereo, clock, seek-scan, cassette, CD changer pre-wiring, in-dash CD pre-wiring, 4 speakers, and fixed antenna;

cruise control with steering wheel controls; power door locks with 2 stage unlock, remote keyless entry, child safety rear door locks, remote hatch/trunk release, remote fuel release; 1 power accessory outlet, driver's foot rest, retained accessory power; instrumentation display includes tachometer, water temperature gauge, trip odometer; warning indicators include oil pressure, battery, lights on, key in ignition, low fuel, low washer fluid, door ajar, brake fluid; driver's and passenger's front airbags; panic alarm, security system; deep tinted windows, power windows with driver's 1-touch down, manual 1/4 vent windows; variable intermittent front windshield wipers, sun visor strip, fixed interval rear wiper, rear window defroster; seating capacity of 7, front bucket seats, adjustable headrests, driver and passenger armrests, driver's seat includes 4-way direction control, passenger's seat includes 4-way direction control; removable full folding 2nd row bench seat with reclining adjustable headrests; full folding 3rd row bench seat with reclining adjustable headrests; front height adjustable seatbelts; cloth seats, cloth door trim insert, full cloth headliner, full carpet floor covering with carpeted floor mats, plastic/rubber gear shift knob; interior lights include dome light with fade, 2 door curb lights, illuminated entry; steering wheel with tilt adjustment; dual illuminated vanity mirrors; day/night rearview mirror; locking glove box with light, front and rear cupholders, instrument panel covered bin, 1 seat back storage pocket, driver's and passenger's door bins, front underseat tray; carpeted cargo floor, plastic trunk lid, cargo net, cargo light; chrome grille, black side window moldings, black front windshield molding, black rear window molding and body-colored door handles.

SE-CLOTH (4A) (in addition to or instead of GXE (4A) equipment): HD battery with run down protection; sport ride suspension, rear non-independent suspension with anti-roll bar; aero-composite halogen fully auto headlamps; front and rear 16" x 6" machined alloy wheels; P225/60SR16 A/S BSW front and rear tires; rear air conditioning with separate controls, air filter; premium AM/FM stereo, clock, seek-scan, cassette, single CD, 7 speakers, and fixed antenna, radio steering wheel controls, rear controls; 2 power accessory outlets; removable 2nd row captain's seat with reclining adjustable headrests; interior lights include front and rear reading lights; leather-wrapped steering wheel with tilt adjustment and mini overhead console with storage.

GLE (4A) (in addition to or instead of SE-CLOTH (4A) equipment): Aero-composite halogen fully auto headlamps with delay-off feature; front and rear 15" x 6" machined alloy wheels; P215/70SR15 A/S BSW front and rear tires; air conditioning with climate control; garage door opener; power 1/4 vent windows; driver's seat includes 6-way power seat, lumbar support, passenger's seat includes 4-way power seat; leather seats, leatherette door trim insert; simulated wood trim on instrument panel; memory on driver's seat with 2 memory setting(s) includes settings for exterior mirrors and 2 seat back storage pockets.

SE-LEATHER (4A) (in addition to or instead of GLE (4A) equipment): Front and rear 16" x 6" machined alloy wheels; P225/60SR16 A/S BSW front and rear tires; underbody mounted full-size steel spare wheel; manual air conditioning; premium AM/FM stereo, clock, seek-scan, cassette, single CD, 4 speakers, and fixed antenna and Smart Shelf.

Base Prices

10310	GXE (4A)	20236	22259
10410	SE-Cloth (4A)	21927	24399
10610	GLE (4A)	23725	26399
10510	SE-Leather (4A)	23994	26699
Destination Charge:		520	520

Accessories

E10	Two-Tone Paint *REQUIRES N07.*	259	299

CODE	DESCRIPTION	INVOICE	MSRP
F05	SE Convenience Package (SE-Cloth) *Includes multi-adjustable Quest Smart shelf, 6-way power driver's seat, power flip-out rear quarter windows, flip-up rear hatch glass and Homelink universal transceiver.*	693	799
G94	Nissan Video Entertainment System	NC	NC
H08	GXE Audio Upgrade Package (GXE) *Includes deluxe AM/FM stereo with CD and cassette. REQUIRES N07. NOT AVAILABLE with K06.*	303	349
H09	SE Audio Upgrade Package (SE) *Includes 6-disc CD autochanger. REQUIRES J01 and F05.*	311	359
J01	Sunroof Package (SE/GLE) *Includes power sliding glass sunroof and wind deflector. REQUIRES F05 or R09.*	779	899
K06	Integrated Child Safety Seat Bench (GXE) *REQUIRES N07. NOT AVAILABLE with H08.*	199	229
M92	Splash Guards (4 Piece Set)	77	99
M93	Splash Guards (2 Piece Set)	39	49
N07	GXE Comfort Plus Package (GXE) *Includes multi-adjustable Quest Smart shelf, overhead conversation mirror, garage door opener storage, wheels: 15" aluminum alloy, leather-wrapped steering wheel, rear air conditioning, rear audio controls, dual overhead map lights, 12V DC power outlet and heavy duty battery.*	779	899
P95	Fog Lights (SE/GLE)	287	389
P96	Fog Lights (GXE)	283	379
R09	GLE Popular Package (GLE) *Includes multi-adjustable Quest Smart shelf, flip-up rear hatch glass, 6-disc CD autochanger, spare tire: conventional and trailer wiring harness.*	433	500
S92	Running Boards and Rear Bumper Pad	373	529
W92	Tow Hitch II (Pkg. I) *NOT AVAILABLE with R09.*	305	419
W93	Tow Hitch II (Pkg. II) (GLE) *REQUIRES R09.*	202	289

2000 XTERRA

What's New?

A truck-based mini-SUV, the athletic, new Xterra competes with several smaller vehicles built on car platforms.

Review

A so-called mini SUV doesn't have to be a compromise, and for proof, look no further than the 2000 Xterra ("terra for the land it crosses and "X" for the generation it intends to target). This new sport-ute from Nissan sits squarely on the large side of the mini-SUV scale, but don't be alarmed by the truck's physical size: the price is tiny by comparison. It is not so cheap that it undercuts all the other "mini-cutes" with which it competes (Honda CR-V, Kia Sportage, Toyota RAV4, Jeep Cherokee and Suzuki Grand Vitara), but you get a lot for your money.

Unlike many of its small SUV competitors, the new Xterra is based on a real truck—Nissan's Frontier compact pickup. And if the Xterra looks familiar, it's because it shares the same hood, front fascia, A-pillars, windshield and front doors with its genetic source. Designed at Nissan Design International (NDI) in La Jolla, Calif., and assembled in Smyrna, Tenn., the vehicle has a 104.3-inch wheelbase, an independent front suspension and a leaf-spring setup at the rear. Taillights form geometric shapes, with white, angled reverse lights appearing out of place. The spare tire is located underneath but still in view from behind–not the choice location for heavy-duty off-road aficionados. Still, the truck looks beefy and solid overall, with unique styling that screams ruggedness. The powder-coated, tubular roof rack comes with adjustable rails for carrying cargo of all shapes and sizes. For smaller items, there's even a plastic cargo tray up front that will hold 30 pounds of odds-'n-ends.

The Xterra is being marketed as a mini-SUV to avoid treading on the toes of its bigger brother, the Pathfinder, but how well it does that is questionable. The Xterra is 178 inches long, only 0.3 of an inch shorter than the Pathfinder. Both offer the same V6 engine, and the Xterra offers an inch more legroom for rear passengers. The Pathfinder will be marketed to a more upscale audience with more options, but that only serves to make the Xterra the better bargain. Nissan has certainly stirred up an interesting option in this market, while the definition of a "mini-SUV" gets murkier all the time.

Offered in two trim levels, the Xterra can be purchased as a base XE or sporty SE model with either two-or four-wheel drive, a four-cylinder or V6 engine, and a five-speed manual or four-speed automatic transmission.

Xterra's standard motivation comes from a 2.4-liter inline four that makes 143 horsepower and 154 foot-pounds of torque. An optional 170-horsepower, 3.3-liter V6 gets 200 accessible foot-pounds of torque and moves the Xterra from zero to 60 in 10.8 seconds. Off-road, the Xterra and its big, all-season tires come in handy, though on-road handling suffers for this trail-blazing perk. Outdoor enthusiasts can tow up to 5,000 pounds with the new Nissan as long as it has an automatic transmission, and antilock brakes are standard on all trim levels.

Inside, five seating positions are offered, but it's a squeeze to fit three adults on the rear-seat bench. With the cargo area folded flat, though, four cross-legged adults can fit in the back without touching knees. The instrument panel and secondary controls are well-laid out and easy-to-use, and the cabin is not cluttered with lots of gee-whiz gadgetry.

Here's our vote for which direction we'd like to see the mini-SUV market turn: Instead of squaring off wagons and raising up cars, the industry would do well to downsize real trucks and make them behave as much like cars as possible. The mini-SUV gene pool would be a lot less mixed up and more Xterra-like 'utes would be produced-which would be a good thing.

2000 Nissan Xterra

Standard Equipment

XE I4 2WD (5M): 2.4L I4 DOHC SMPI 16-valve engine; 5-speed overdrive manual transmission; rear-wheel drive, 4.38 axle ratio; stainless steel exhaust; front independent double wishbone suspension with anti-roll bar, front coil springs, rigid rear axle suspension with anti-roll bar, rear leaf springs; power re-circulating ball steering; front disc/rear drum brakes with 4-wheel antilock braking system; 19.4 gal. capacity fuel tank; front and rear mud flaps, skid plate(s), side impact bars; liftback rear cargo door; front and rear black bumpers with rear tow hooks, rear step; monotone paint; aero-composite halogen headlamps; driver's and passenger's manual black folding outside mirrors; front and rear 15" x 6.5" silver styled steel wheels; P235/70RS15 M&S BSW front and rear tires; underbody mounted full-size steel spare wheel; air conditioning, rear heat ducts; AM/FM stereo, seek-scan, cassette, 4 speakers, and fixed antenna; child safety rear door locks; driver's foot rest; instrumentation display includes tachometer, water temp gauge, in-dash clock, trip odometer; warning indicators include oil pressure, water temp, battery, lights on, key in ignition, low fuel, low washer fluid, door ajar; driver's and passenger's front airbags; deep tinted windows, manual rear windows fixed 1/4 vent windows; fixed interval front windshield wipers, flip-up rear window, rear window defroster; seating capacity of 5, front bucket seats, adjustable headrests, center armrest with storage, driver's seat includes 4-way direction control, passenger's seat includes 4-way direction control; 50-50 folding rear bench seat with reclining fixed headrests; front height adjustable seatbelts with front pretensioners; cloth seats, full cloth headliner, full carpet floor covering; interior lights include dome light; day/night rearview mirror; full floor console, mini overhead console with storage, locking glove box, front and rear cupholders, 1 seat back storage pocket, driver's and passenger's door bins, rear door bins; carpeted cargo floor, plastic trunk lid, cargo tie downs, cargo light, cargo concealed storage; black grille, black side window moldings, black front windshield molding, black rear window molding and black door handles.

XE 2WD (5M) (in addition to or instead of XE I4 2WD (5M) equipment): 3.3L V6 SOHC SMPI 12-valve engine; 4.36 axle ratio; AM/FM stereo, seek-scan, single CD, 6 speakers, and fixed antenna.

SE 2WD (5M) (in addition to or instead of XE 2WD (5M) equipment): Limited slip differential, 4.64 axle ratio; front manual pop-up glass sunroof; roof rack; front tow hooks; black bodyside molding, black wheel well molding; additional exterior lights include front fog/driving lights; driver's and passenger's power remote black folding outside mirrors; P265/70RS15 M&S BSW front and rear tires; premium AM/FM stereo, seek-scan, cassette, single CD, 6 speakers, and fixed antenna; cruise control; power door locks, remote keyless entry; 2 power accessory outlets; panic alarm, security system; deep tinted windows, power front windows with driver's 1-touch down, power rear windows; variable intermittent front windshield wipers, rear window wiper; front sports seats, adjustable headrests; cloth door trim insert; interior lights include front reading lights; leather-wrapped steering wheel with tilt adjustment; passenger's side vanity mirror and; cargo cover.

XE/SE 4WD (5M) (in addition to or instead of XE/SE 2WD (5M) equipment): Part-time 4-wheel drive and auto locking hub control and manual shift.

Base Prices

04050	XE I4 2WD (5M)	16368	17599
04150	XE 2WD (5M)	17438	18749
04250	XE 4WD (5M)	19298	20749
04350	SE 2WD (5M)	20966	22799
04450	SE 4WD (5M)	22805	24799
Destination Charge:		520	520

Accessories

CODE	DESCRIPTION	INVOICE	MSRP
4AT	Transmission: 4-Speed Automatic (SE) *NOT AVAILABLE with N92.*	919	1000
4AT	Transmission: 4-Speed Automatic (XE) *NOT AVAILABLE with N92.*	930	1000
H92	Single Disc CD Player (XE I4)	310	469
L92	Floor Mats	58	79
M92	Alloy Wheels (XE)	434	599
N92	Tow Hitch M/T *NOT AVAILABLE with N93.*	294	399
N93	Tow Hitch A/T (SE) *REQUIRES 4AT. NOT AVAILABLE with N92.*	238	349
N93	Tow Hitch A/T (XE) *REQUIRES 4AT. NOT AVAILABLE with N92.*	238	349
P01	Power Package (XE) *Includes cruise control, fabric door inserts, map lamps, power mirrors, power windows, power door locks, security system and remote keyless entry. REQUIRES U01.*	1126	1299
R92	6-Disc CD Autochanger (XE V6)	338	719
S01	Sport Package (XE) *Includes alloy wheels, fog lamps and limited slip differential. REQUIRES U01.*	693	799
U01	Utility Package (XE I4) *Includes front and rear auxiliary 12V power points, 6 ceiling clips, rear wiper, first aid kit, tilt steering, tubular roof rack, tubular step rails and front variable intermittent wipers.*	779	889
U01	Utility Package (XE V6) *Includes front and rear auxiliary 12V power points, 6 ceiling clips, rear wiper, first aid kit, retractable cargo cover, tilt steering, tubular roof rack, tubular step rails and front variable intermittent wipers.*	866	999
W93	Splash Guards	42	79

See page 6 for details.

2000 BRAVADA

2000 Oldsmobile Bravada

What's New?

GM's OnStar communications system is now available as a dealer-installed option, and a new cargo management system is expected this year. Special color treatments include a new Jewel Coat Red option that features a deep red base color finished with a red-tinted final top coat in place of the usual clearcoat. There's also a Platinum Edition option that adds pewter-colored lower body cladding.

Review

After a major freshening both inside and out in 1998, the Oldsmobile Bravada soldiers on with a few minor revisions this year. Not only must Bravada do battle in the hotly contested luxury compact-SUV market, but it is up against similarly equipped GM sister trucks, the Chevrolet Blazer and GMC Jimmy, which are based on the same S-Series platform.

Styling is similar to the Blazer and Jimmy. But Bravada gets a unique grille and headlamp treatment, bumper trim and some body cladding. As a luxury sport-ute, Bravada comes loaded with nearly every conceivable feature to battle a world full of Ford Explorers and Jeep Grand Cherokees. And its options list includes such extras as a six-disc CD changer, redundant radio and climate controls for the steering wheel, heated seats and a power sunroof, just to name a few. The downside is that this may not be your best choice to go bounding down a rocky trail. In fact, Oldsmobile makes no bones about designing Bravada to be a comfortable on-road SUV.

GM has improved its 4.3-liter Vortec V6 this year to make it quieter running and more durable with better fuel economy and lower emissions. Horsepower remains at 190, and despite sending a stout 250 foot-pounds of torque through the Bravada's four wheels, we find the V6 not up to par with V8-equipped Jeeps and Fords. The Explorer-based Mercury Mountaineer also has all-wheel drive, like the Bravada, but can be had with V8 power. The Oldsmobile's four-wheel disc brakes provide very good stopping ability, though we could do without the mushy feel to the brake pedal.

The Bravada has its strong points. The leather-lined interior offers one of the most comfortable driver's seats in an SUV. The sound system is outstanding. Controls are easy to see and use (though they still look and feel flimsy). Bravada's SmartTrak all-wheel-drive system makes finding grip in a variety of road conditions carefree. Best of all, this is one comfy, fun-to-drive truck that can easily swallow a full-size dryer. Truly, the Bravada is what a luxury compact SUV is all about.

But you need to ask yourself if the extra cost for the Bravada is worth the price of admission over the Blazer and the Jimmy. Better seating and the addition of GM's AutoTrac electronic transfer case in the Chevy and GMC variants have diminished the appeal of the Olds' exclusive front seats and SmartTrak all-wheel-drive system. There's not much left to differentiate Bravada from its corporate twins. In fact, most of the standard equipment on the Bravada is also available on the Chevy or the GMC, with an end result that may be less expensive than the Oldsmobile.

Standard Equipment

BRAVADA (4A): 4.3L V6 OHV SMPI 12-valve engine; 4-speed electronic OD auto transmission with lock-up; 100-amp battery with run down protection; engine oil cooler; 525-amp alternator; auto full-time 4-wheel drive, limited slip differential, 3.73 axle ratio; stainless steel exhaust; front independent suspension with anti-roll bar, front torsion springs, front torsion bar, gas-pressurized front shocks, rigid rear axle suspension with anti-roll bar, rear leaf springs, gas-pressurized rear shocks; power re-circulating ball steering with vehicle speed-sensing assist; 4-wheel disc brakes with 4-wheel antilock braking system; 17.5 gal. capacity fuel tank; front license plate bracket, side impact bars; liftback rear cargo door; roof rack; front and rear body-colored bumpers with front tow hooks, rear step; body-colored bodyside cladding, rocker panel extensions, body-colored wheel well molding; monotone paint with bodyside accent stripe; aero-composite halogen fully auto headlamps with daytime running lights, delay-off feature; additional exterior lights include front fog/driving lights, underhood light; driver's and passenger's power remote black heated folding outside mirrors; front and rear 15" x 7" silver alloy wheels; P235/70SR15 A/S BSW front and rear tires; underbody mounted full-size steel spare wheel; air conditioning with climate control, rear heat ducts; AM/FM stereo, clock, seek-scan, cassette, single CD, 6 speakers, auto equalizer, and fixed antenna; cruise control; power door locks with 2 stage unlock, remote keyless entry, child safety rear door locks, power remote hatch/trunk release; 3 power accessory outlets, retained accessory power, garage door opener; instrumentation display includes tachometer, oil pressure gauge, water temperature gauge, volt gauge, compass, exterior temp, trip computer, trip odometer; warning indicators include battery, lights on, key in ignition, trunk ajar; driver's and passenger's front airbags; ignition disable, panic alarm, security system; deep tinted windows, power front and rear windows with driver's 1-touch down, fixed 1/4 vent windows; variable intermittent front windshield wipers, sun visor strip, flip-up rear window, fixed interval rear wiper, rear window defroster; seating capacity of 5, front bucket seats, adjustable tilt headrests, center armrest with storage, driver's seat includes 6-way power seat, power 2-way lumbar support, passenger's seat includes 4-way direction control, power 2-way lumbar support; 60-40 folding rear split-bench seat with adjustable headrests; leather seats, leatherette door trim insert, full cloth headliner, full carpet floor covering with carpeted floor mats, leather-wrapped gear shift knob; interior lights include dome light with delay, front and rear reading lights, illuminated entry; leather-wrapped steering wheel with tilt adjustment; dual illuminated vanity mirrors; auto-dimming day/night rearview mirror; partial floor console, full overhead console with storage, glove box with light, front cupholder, 2 seat back storage pockets, driver's and passenger's door bins, rear door bins; carpeted cargo floor, carpeted trunk lid, cargo cover, cargo net, cargo tie downs, cargo light, cargo concealed storage; body-colored grille, black side window moldings, black front windshield molding, black rear window molding and black door handles.

Base Prices

HT10506	Bravada (4A)	28505	31498
Destination Charge:		550	550

Accessories

1SA	Option Package 1SA *Includes vehicle with standard equipment.*	NC	NC
86U	Premium Jewel Coat Red	82	95
AG0	Driver's Seat Memory Control *Includes driver-side seat adjuster. INCLUDED in R9B and R9E.*	73	85

CODE	DESCRIPTION	INVOICE	MSRP
AH8	8-Way Power Passenger's Seat Adjuster	215	250
	Includes power recliner. INCLUDED in R9B and R9E.		
B94	Gold Package	150	175
	Includes gold emblems on vehicle and wheels and a gold accent stripe. NOT AVAILABLE with R9E.		
CF5	Electric Sliding Glass Sunroof	645	750
	Includes gray tint with sunshade and mini overhead console.		
DD0	Electrochromic Heated Driver's-Side Mirror	66	77
	INCLUDED in R9B and R9E.		
K05	Engine Block Heater	28	33
KA1	Driver's and Passenger's Heated Seats	215	250
	REQUIRES R9B or R9E.		
QBG	Tires: P235/70R15 AS WOL	116	135
	Use of chains is not recommended with these tires.		
R6M	New Jersey Cost Surcharge	70	NC
R9B	Convenience Package	651	757
	Manufacturer Discount	(602)	(700)
	Net Price	49	57
	Includes 8-way power passenger's seat adjuster, driver's seat memory control, HD towing package, electrochromic heated driver's-side mirror and tires: P235/70R15 A/S WOL. NOT AVAILABLE with R9E.		
R9E	Platinum Edition Package	808	939
	Manufacturer Discount	(602)	(700)
	Net Price	206	239
	Includes platinum colored lower body cladding, 8-way power passenger's seat adjuster, driver's seat memory control, HD towing package, electrochromic heated driver's-side mirror, tires: P235/70R15 A/S WOL and standard stripe delete. NOT AVAILABLE with B94, R9B.		
RAE	Cargo Management System	108	125
U1F	Radio: Bose AM/FM Stereo with CD	426	495
	Includes seek-scan, auto-reverse cassette, digital clock and 6-speaker Bose sound system powered by a 6-channel amplifier.		
U1Z	6-Disc CD Changer	340	395
	Console-mounted.		
UK3	Steering Wheel Radio Controls	108	125
Z82	HD Towing Package	181	210
	Includes weight-distributing platform hitch, heavy-duty flasher and 8-wire electrical harness. Towing capacity is 5,000 lbs.		

2000 SILHOUETTE

What's New?

Olds has canned its 112-inch wheelbase GS, meaning all 2000 Silhouettes (GL, GLS and Premiere) are now extended-length (120-inch wheelbase), seven-passenger models. The traction-control system has been improved, and heated front seats are available in leather. There's also a redesigned instrument cluster with dual trip odometers, as well as upgraded radios, interior lighting and electrical system functions.

2000 Oldsmobile Silhouette

Review

Why do we like this Oldsmobile minivan so much? Because you name the feature, and Olds has it. Want a sliding driver-side door? You get one here. Wish that passenger-side sliding door was power operated? Olds has you covered. Want leather? A CD player? Separate audio controls for rear passengers? Full-function traction control? A powerful V6? How about easy-to-swap flip/fold seats that can be configured in a variety of ways? Maybe a touring suspension with automatic leveling and an air-inflation kit? It's all here, depending on the model you pick. There's even a TV/VCP for rear-seat passengers.

Silhouette is available in three flavors (all with dual sliding doors standard): a well-equipped GL, an uplevel GLS, and the top-of-the-line Premiere. All are powered by a 185-horsepower 3.4-liter V6 that drives the front wheels via an electronically controlled four-speed automatic transmission. Side-impact airbags are included, to go along with Silhouette's reduced-force frontal airbag system, four-wheel antilock brakes, fog lamps and GM's PASSKEY III anti-theft system. Added to the standard equipment list this year are convenience features such as retained accessory power and rear reading lamps.

GL models come with a second-row, 60/40 split bench seat, and boast standard items such as air-conditioning, power windows and locks, cruise control, interior air filter, and a rooftop luggage carrier. The GLS adds such niceties as aluminum wheels, traction control, a power passenger-side door, power leather seats with second-row captain's chairs, overhead console, rear heat/air and steering-wheel radio controls.

Move all the way up to the Premiere, and you get nearly every goodie standard, including the aforementioned combination television and video cassette player for rear-seat passengers and the touring suspension. Among the few options are a 3,500-pound towing package, OnStar communications, an engine block heater and the obligatory gold package.

Every time we've driven the Silhouette, we've come away quite impressed. These well-equipped Oldsmobile minivans are smooth and powerful. Thanks to excellent road feel provided by precise steering and easily modulated brakes, they are actually fun to drive, something that can't be said about many of today's best-selling makes. Our complaints are limited to uncomfortable rear seating and a noticeable amount of cheap-looking plastic inside the cabin.

As you've probably guessed, we like the Oldsmobile Silhouette, and find its exterior styling to be the most attractive of GM's trio of sister minivans. Even in today's hotly contested minivan market, where the latest entries from Honda and Mazda have upped the ante to new heights, the Silhouette remains a solid choice.

Standard Equipment

GL (4A): 3.4L V6 OHV SMPI 12-valve engine; 4-speed electronic OD auto transmission with lock-up; 600-amp battery with run down protection; 105-amp alternator; front-wheel drive, 3.29 axle ratio; stainless steel exhaust; front independent strut suspension with anti-roll bar, front coil springs, rear semi-independent suspension with rear coil springs; power rack-and-pinion steering; front disc/rear drum brakes with 4-wheel antilock braking system; 25 gal. capacity fuel tank; body-colored front and rear mud flaps, side impact bars; 4 doors with sliding left rear passenger door, sliding right rear passenger door, liftback rear cargo door; roof rack, 68; front and rear body-colored bumpers with rear step; body-colored bodyside molding rocker panel extensions; monotone paint; aero-composite halogen fully auto headlamps with daytime running lights; additional exterior lights include front fog/driving lights, underhood light; driver's and passenger's power remote black heated folding outside mirrors; front and rear 15" x 6" steel wheels; P215/70SR15 A/S BSW front and rear tires; underbody mounted compact steel spare wheel; air conditioning, air filter; AM/FM stereo, clock, seek-scan, cassette, 4 speakers, auto equalizer, and window grid antenna; cruise control; power door locks, child safety rear door locks; 3 power accessory outlets, retained accessory power; instrumentation display includes tachometer, water temperature gauge, trip odometer; warning indicators include battery, low oil level, low coolant, lights on, key in ignition; driver's and passenger's front airbags, driver's and front passenger's seat mounted side airbags; ignition disable; deep tinted windows, power front and rear windows with driver's 1-touch down, power 1/4 vent windows; variable intermittent front windshield wipers, sun visor strip, fixed interval rear wiper, rear window defroster; seating capacity of 7, front bucket seats, adjustable headrests, driver's and passenger's armrests, driver's seat includes 6-way direction control, lumbar support, passenger's seat includes 4-way direction control, lumbar support; removable 60-40 folding split-bench 2nd row seat with reclining adjustable headrests; removable 50-50 folding 3rd row split-bench seat with reclining adjustable headrest; front height adjustable seatbelts with front pretensioners; cloth seats, cloth door trim insert, full cloth headliner, full carpet floor covering with carpeted floor mats; interior lights include dome light, front and rear reading lights; steering wheel with tilt adjustment; vanity mirrors; day/night rearview mirror; locking glove box with light, front and rear cupholders, instrument panel covered bin, dashboard storage, 2 seat back storage pockets, driver's and passenger's door bins, front underseat tray; carpeted cargo floor, plastic trunk lid, cargo net, cargo light; body-colored grille, black side window moldings, black front windshield molding, black rear window molding and body-colored door handles.

GLS (4A) (in addition to or instead of GL (4A) equipment): Traction control; front and rear 15" x 6" aluminum wheels; P215/70SR15 touring A/S BSW front and rear tires; rear air conditioning with separate controls, rear heater; radio steering wheel controls, rear audio controls; power sliding passenger's door, power door locks with 2 stage unlock, remote keyless entry; instrumentation display compass, exterior temp, trip computer; ignition disable, panic alarm, security system; front captain's seats, adjustable headrests, driver's seat includes 4-way power seat, 8-way direction control, lumbar support, passenger's seat includes 4-way power seat, 8-way direction control, lumbar support; removable 2nd row captain seat with reclining adjustable headrests; leather seats, leatherette door trim insert; interior lights include illuminated entry; leather-wrapped steering wheel with tilt adjustment; dual illuminated vanity mirrors and full overhead console with storage.

PREMIERE EDITION (4A) (in addition to or instead of GLS (4A) equipment): Touring ride suspension, auto-leveling suspension; AM/FM stereo, clock, seek-scan, cassette, single CD, 4 speakers, auto equalizer, theft deterrent, and window grid antenna, video cassette player, overhead fold-down LCD color monitor and video input jack.

CODE	DESCRIPTION	INVOICE	MSRP
	Base Prices		
3UM16	GL (4A)	22801	25195
3UM16	GLS (4A)	26150	28895
3UM16	Premiere Edition (4A)	28593	31595
Destination Charge:		605	605
	Accessories		
—	Cloth Seat Trim (Premiere) *NOT AVAILABLE with KA1.*	NC	NC
1SA	Option Package 1SA (GL) *Includes vehicle with standard equipment.*	NC	NC
1SC	Option Package 1SC (GLS) *Includes vehicle with standard equipment.*	NC	NC
1SD	Option Package 1SD (Premiere) *Includes vehicle with standard equipment.*	NC	NC
ABD	Captains Chairs (Second Row) (GL) *INCLUDED in 1SC, 1SD.*	254	295
AG9	6-Way Power Driver's and Passenger's Seat Adjuster (GL) *INCLUDED in 1SC, 1SD.*	494	575
C34	Auxiliary Rear A/C and Heater (GL) *REQUIRES UK6. INCLUDED in 1SC, 1SD.*	387	450
DK6	Overhead Extended Console (GL) *Includes storage for sunglasses and garage door opener, compass, outdoor temperature readout and driver's information center. INCLUDED in 1SC, 1SD.*	150	175
E58	Power Sliding Passenger's Side Door (GL)	387	450
FE3	Touring Suspension Group (GL/GLS) *Includes air inflation kit, auto level control and tires: P215/70R15 touring. REQUIRES PH3. INCLUDED in 1SD.*	232	270
K05	Engine Block Heater	17	20
KA1	Heated Front Seats (GLS/Premiere)	168	195
NW9	Traction Control System (GL) *Full function engine and brakes. INCLUDED in 1SC, 1SD.*	168	195
PH3	Wheels: 15" Aluminum (GL) *INCLUDED in 1SC, 1SD.*	254	295
R6M	New Jersey Cost Surcharge	71	NC
R8Q	Personal Convenience Package (GL) *Includes captain's chairs (second row), 6-way power driver's and passenger's seat adjuster, Delco AM/FM stereo with RDS and keyless remote entry system. NOT AVAILABLE with UN0.*	1122	1305
UA6	Keyless Remote Entry System (GL) *Includes key-chain transmitter with panic button. INCLUDED in 1SC, 1SD.*	202	235
UK6	Rear Seat Audio Controls (GL) *Provides choice of music source (AM/FM, cassette tapes or CDs). Includes rear headphones and volume control. INCLUDED in 1SC, 1SD.*	108	125

CODE	DESCRIPTION	INVOICE	MSRP
UN0	Radio: Delco AM/FM Stereo with RDS (GL/GLS) *Includes seek-scan, CD, auto tone control, digital display clock and coaxial speaker system. NOT AVAILABLE with UN7, R8Q, UP0.*	86	100
UP0	Radio: Delco AM/FM Stereo with RDS (GL/GLS) *Includes seek-scan, CD, auto-reverse cassette, auto tone control, digital display clock and coaxial speaker system. NOT AVAILABLE with UN0.*	172	200
V92	Towing Package (3500 Lb) Capacity (GL/GLS) *Includes engine oil cooler, 5-wire electrical harness, HD radiator and touring suspension group: auto level control and tires: P215/70R15 touring.*	318	370
V92	Towing Package (3500 Lb) Capacity (Premiere) *Includes HD radiator, engine oil cooler and 5-wire electrical harness.*	86	100
Y11	Gold Package *Includes gold emblems and gold wheel accents. REQUIRES PH3.*	129	150

2000 GRAND VOYAGER / VOYAGER

2000 Plymouth Voyager

What's New?

Four new colors and a new T-Plus option package that includes a V6 and power goodies for about $20,000 are new this year.

Review

Chrysler used to be the minivan champion. They pioneered the concept of a seven-passenger box-on-wheels way back in 1984, and have effectively dominated this market until last year, when competition from Ford and Honda finally caught up and surpassed them in terms of features, power and crashworthiness.

Plymouth renderings of Chrysler's popular front-drive minivans have been virtual clones of the Dodge Caravan in terms of engineering and design since day one. However, Plymouth is pushing low pricing, aiming squarely at entry-level buyers who are shopping for their first minivans. Voyagers for 2000 are lightly equipped value-leaders for the company, and with the demise of the Plymouth brand, will soldier on with Chrysler nameplates.

For now, leftover Plymouths exist in short- (Voyager) and long-wheelbase (Grand Voyager) versions in two levels of trim: the base model and the step-up SE. A 2.4-liter four-cylinder engine is standard on base models, but these sizable vans benefit from a little extra oomph when an optional V6 is selected. Acceleration with the 3.3-liter, 158-horsepower engine is pretty strong from startup, but sometimes unimpressive when merging onto an expressway. Automatic transmission shifts are neat and smooth. Engine and tire sounds are virtually absent.

Though tautly suspended, the ride is seldom harsh or jarring, unless you get onto truly rough surfaces. Handling is exceptional for a minivan. You might even call it fun. Combined with light steering wheel response and great visibility, the Voyager and Grand Voyager are easy to handle in urban traffic and suburban shopping centers.

So, how does Plymouth improve on this package for 2000? By keeping the price low and the value high. Four new colors debut, and a new T-Plus package is available. Vans equipped with T-Plus include a V6 engine, power windows, locks and mirrors, cruise control, a tilt steering wheel, and a cloth interior. T-Plus models are expected to sell for about $20,000.

Newly revised minivans from Honda, Ford, Mazda and GM are the strongest challengers, but the Voyager holds its own when it comes to value. Where else can you get a commodious and decently equipped minivan for 20 grand?

Standard Equipment

VOYAGER BASE (3A): 2.4L I4 DOHC SMPI 16-valve engine; 3-speed auto transmission; 600-amp battery; 90-amp alternator; front-wheel drive, 3.9 axle ratio; stainless steel exhaust; front independent strut suspension with anti-roll bar, front coil springs, rear non-independent suspension with rear leaf springs; power rack-and-pinion steering; front disc/rear drum brakes; 20 gal. capacity fuel tank; front mud flaps, rear lip spoiler, side impact bars; 3 doors with sliding right rear passenger's door, liftback rear cargo door; front and rear colored bumpers with rear step; colored bodyside molding; monotone paint; aero-composite halogen headlamps; driver's and passenger's manual black folding outside mirrors; front and rear 14" x 6" steel wheels; P205/75SR14 A/S BSW front and rear tires; underbody mounted compact steel spare wheel; AM/FM stereo, clock, seek-scan, cassette, 4 speakers, and fixed antenna; child safety rear door locks; 2 power accessory outlets, driver's foot rest; instrumentation display includes water temperature gauge, trip odometer; warning indicators include oil pressure, water temp, battery, lights on, key in ignition, low fuel, low washer fluid, door ajar, trunk ajar; driver's and passenger's front airbags; tinted windows, fixed rear windows, manual 1/4 vent windows; variable intermittent front windshield wipers, sun visor strip, variable intermittent rear wiper; seating capacity of 5, front bucket seats, fixed headrests, driver's and passenger's armrests, driver's seat includes 4-way direction control, passenger's seat includes 4-way direction control; removable 2nd row bench seat with adjustable headrests; front and rear height adjustable seatbelts; cloth seats, vinyl door trim insert, full cloth headliner, full carpet floor covering; interior lights include dome light, front reading lights; vanity mirrors; day/night rearview mirror; glove box, front and rear cupholders, instrument panel bin, interior concealed storage; carpeted cargo floor, vinyl trunk lid, cargo light; body-colored grille, black side window moldings, black front windshield molding, black rear window molding and body-colored door handles.

GRAND VOYAGER BASE (4A) (in addition to or instead of VOYAGER BASE (4A) equipment): 3.0L V6 SOHC SMPI 12-valve engine; 4-speed electronic OD auto transmission with lock-up; air conditioning; seating capacity of 7; removable full folding 2nd row bench seat with adjustable headrests; removable 3rd row bench seat with adjustable headrests and interior lights include dome light with delay.

SE (4A) (in addition to or instead of BASE equipment): 3.3L V6 OHV SMPI 12-valve engine, flexible fuel capable; 4-speed electronic OD auto transmission with lock-up (VOYAGER BASE); 500-amp battery; front disc/rear drum brakes with 4-wheel antilock braking system; driver's and passenger's power remote black heated folding outside mirrors; front and rear 15" x 6.5" steel wheels; P215/65SR15 A/S BSW front and rear tires; air conditioning (VOYAGER BASE), rear heat ducts; cruise control with steering wheel controls; instrumentation display includes tachometer; power windows with driver's 1-touch down, power 1/4 vent windows; heated variable intermittent front windshield wipers, rear window defroster; removable full folding 2nd row bench seat with reclining adjustable headrests; removable full folding 3rd row bench seat with reclining adjustable headrests; cloth door trim insert, full carpet floor covering with carpeted floor mats, deluxe sound insulation; steering wheel with tilt adjustment; dual illuminated vanity mirrors; glove box with light, front underseat tray and cargo net.

Base Prices

NSHL52	Voyager Base (3A)	17123	18850
NSHL53	Grand Voyager Base (4A)	19895	21955
NSHH52	Voyager SE (4A)	20995	23250
NSHH53	Grand Voyager SE (4A)	21911	24245
Destination Charge:		590	590

CODE	DESCRIPTION	INVOICE	MSRP

Accessories

CODE	DESCRIPTION	INVOICE	MSRP
22S	Quick Order Package 22S (Voyager Base)	NC	NC
	Includes vehicle with standard equipment. REQUIRES (HAA or 4XA) and EDZ and DGA. NOT AVAILABLE with CYK, AAA, AAC, AAE, TBB, GKD, MWG, EFA, EGA, DGB, AAF, EGM, ALD, AAG.		
22T	Quick Order Package 22T (Voyager Base)	1084	1275
	Manufacturer Discount	(1084)	(1275)
	Net Price	NC	NC
	Includes air conditioning, front seat cargo net, 7-passenger seating, rear floor silencer pad and underseat lockable storage drawer. REQUIRES EDZ and DGA. NOT AVAILABLE with 4XA, EFA, EGA, DGB, EGM, ALD, AAG.		
25D	Quick Order Package 25D (SE)	NC	NC
	Includes vehicle with standard equipment. REQUIRES EGM and DGB and (AAB or 4XN). NOT AVAILABLE with EGA.		
25L	Quick Order Package 25L (Voyager SE)	1228	1445
	Manufacturer Discount	(85)	(100)
	Net Price	1143	1345
	Includes overhead console with trip computer, door courtesy lamps, second row reading lamps, manual driver's lumbar adjust, 8-way power driver's seat, 7-passenger quad buckets and premium cloth low back bucket seats. REQUIRES EGM and DGB. NOT AVAILABLE with CYR, EGA, CYT.		
26T	Quick Order Package 26T (Grand Voyager Base)	NC	NC
	Includes vehicle with standard equipment. REQUIRES EFA and DGB. NOT AVAILABLE with EGA.		
26T	Quick Order Package 26T (Voyager Base)	1084	1275
	Manufacturer Discount	(646)	(760)
	Net Price	438	515
	Includes air conditioning, front seat cargo net, 7-passenger seating, rear floor silencer pad and underseat lockable storage drawer. REQUIRES EFA and DGB. NOT AVAILABLE with 4XA, AAC, EDZ, EGA, DGA, EGM, AAE, AAF, AAG.		
28D	Quick Order Package 28D (SE)	NC	NC
	Includes vehicle with standard equipment. REQUIRES EGA and DGB and (AAB or 4XN). NOT AVAILABLE with EGM.		
28L	Quick Order Package 28L (Voyager SE)	1228	1445
	Manufacturer Discount	(85)	(100)
	Net Price	1143	1345
	Includes overhead console with trip computer, door courtesy lamps, second row reading lamps, manual driver's lumbar adjust, 8-way power driver's seat, 7-passenger quad buckets and premium cloth low back bucket seats. REQUIRES EGA and DGB. NOT AVAILABLE with CYR, EGM, CYT.		
28T	Quick Order Package 28T (Grand Voyager Base)	NC	NC
	Includes vehicle with standard equipment. REQUIRES EGA and DGB. NOT AVAILABLE with EFA.		

CODE	DESCRIPTION	INVOICE	MSRP
28T	Quick Order Package 28T (Voyager Base)	1084	1275
	Manufacturer Discount	(646)	(760)
	Net Price	438	515
	Includes air conditioning, front seat cargo net, 7-passenger seating, rear floor silencer pad and underseat lockable storage drawer. REQUIRES EGA and DGB. NOT AVAILABLE with 4XA, AAC, EDZ, EFA, DGA, EGM, AAE, AAF, AAG.		
4XA	Air Conditioning Bypass (Voyager Base)	NC	NC
	NOT AVAILABLE with 22T, 26T, 28T, 25T, HAA, AAA, EFA, EGA.		
4XN	Rear Air Conditioning Bypass (Grand Voyager SE)	NC	NC
	NOT AVAILABLE with AAB.		
AAA	Climate Group II (Grand Voyager)	383	450
	Includes windshield wiper de-icer and sunscreen glass. REQUIRES 26T or 28T. NOT AVAILABLE with 22S, 25S, 4XA.		
AAB	Climate Group III (Grand Voyager SE)	1046	1230
	Manufacturer Discount	(383)	(450)
	Net Price	663	780
	Includes dual zone temperature control, rear air conditioning with heater, 125-amp alternator, overhead console with trip computer, sunscreen glass and second row reading lamps. NOT AVAILABLE with 4XN, ALR, AHT.		
AAB	Climate Group III (Grand Voyager SE)	991	1165
	Manufacturer Discount	(383)	(450)
	Net Price	608	715
	Includes dual zone temperature control, rear air conditioning with heater, 125-amp alternator, overhead console with trip computer, sunscreen glass and second row reading lamps. NOT AVAILABLE with 4XN, ALR.		
AAC	Convenience Group I (Voyager Base)	370	435
	Includes power fold-away mirrors with exterior heating elements, speed control and tilt steering column. NOT AVAILABLE with 22S, 25S, 25T, 26T, 28T, AAG, ALD, GFA.		
AAE	Convenience Group II (Voyager Base)	638	750
	Includes speed sensitive power locks and Convenience Group I: power fold-away mirrors with exterior heating elements, speed control and tilt steering column. REQUIRES 22T. NOT AVAILABLE with 22S, 25S, AAC, 25T, 26T, 28T, AAG, ALD, GFA.		
AAF	Convenience Group III (Voyager Base)	952	1120
	Includes Convenience Group II: speed sensitive power locks and Convenience Group I: power fold-away mirrors with exterior heating elements, speed control and tilt steering column; power quarter vent windows and power windows with driver's one-touch down. REQUIRES 22T. NOT AVAILABLE with 22S, 25S, AAC, 25T, 26T, 28T, AAG, ALD, GFA.		
AAG	Convenience Group IV (SE)	204	240
	Includes keyless entry, illuminated entry and headlamp off time delay.		
AAH	Convenience Group V (SE)	332	390
	Includes Convenience Group IV: keyless entry, illuminated entry and headlamp off time delay and security alarm.		
AAP	Loading Group (SE)	166	195
	Includes tire: full size spare and heavy duty suspension. NOT AVAILABLE with AHT.		

CODE	DESCRIPTION	INVOICE	MSRP
AHT	Trailer Tow Prep Group (Grand Voyager SE)	370	435
	Includes 125-amp alternator, 600-amp maintenance free battery, engine oil cooler, HD transmission oil cooler, HD radiator, tire: full-size spare, HD suspension and trailer tow wiring harness. NOT AVAILABLE with AAP.		
ALD	Value Plus V6 Group (Base)	995	1170
	Manufacturer Discount	(425)	(500)
	Net Price	570	670
	Includes deluxe door trim panel, speed sensitive power locks, power fold-away mirrors, speed control, tilt steering column, power quarter vent windows and power windows with driver's one-touch down. NOT AVAILABLE with AAG, GFA, 22S, 25S, 22T, 25T, AAC, AAE, AAF.		
ALR	Value Plus Climate Group (SE)	383	450
	Manufacturer Discount	(383)	(450)
	Net Price	NC	NC
	Includes sunscreen glass. NOT AVAILABLE with AAB.		
ATB	Radio: AM/FM Stereo with Cassette and CD (SE)	612	720
	Includes equalizer and 10 Infinity speakers and 200-watt amplifier.		
AWS	Smokers' Group (Grand Voyager)	17	20
	Includes front and rear ash receivers and cigar lighter.		
BGF	Antilock Brakes (Base Voyager)	480	565
CYE	7-Passenger Seating (Base Voyager)	319	375
	NOT AVAILABLE with CYK. INCLUDED in 22T, 25T, 26T, 28T.		
CYK	7-Passenger Seating with 2 Child Seats (Base)	200	235
	NOT AVAILABLE with 22S, 25S, CYE.		
CYR	7-Passenger Deluxe Seating with 2 Child Seats (SE)	191	225
	REQUIRES 25D or 28D. NOT AVAILABLE with CYS, CYT, 25L, 28L.		
CYS	7-Passenger Quad Buckets (SE)	591	695
	NOT AVAILABLE with CYR, CYT. INCLUDED in 25L, 28L.		
CYT	7-Passenger Quad Buckets with Child Seat (Voyager SE)	106	125
	NOT AVAILABLE with CYR, CYS, 25D, 28D.		
CYT	7-Passenger Quad Buckets with Child Seat (Voyager SE)	697	820
	NOT AVAILABLE with CYR, CYS, 25L, 28L.		
CYT	7-Passenger Seating with Quads and Child Seat (Grand Voyager SE)	697	820
	NOT AVAILABLE with CYS, CYR.		
DGA	Transmission: 3-Speed Automatic (Voyager Base)	NC	NC
	NOT AVAILABLE with 28T, EFA, EGA, 25S, 26T, EGM, 25T.		
DGB	Transmission: 4-Speed Automatic (All Except Voyager Base)	NC	NC
DGB	Transmission: 4-Speed Automatic (Voyager Base)	170	200
	NOT AVAILABLE with 22S, 22T, EDZ.		
EDZ	Engine: 2.4L 4 Cyl. DOHC 16V SMPI (Voyager Base)	NC	NC
	NOT AVAILABLE with 28T, 26T, DGB, 25S, 25T.		
EFA	Engine: 3.0L MPI V6 (Voyager Base)	680	800
	NOT AVAILABLE with 22S, 22T, 28T, DGA, 25S, 25T, 4XA.		
EFA	Engine: 3.0L V6 MPI (Grand Voyager Base)	NC	NC
	NOT AVAILABLE with 28T.		
EGA	Engine: 3.3L MPI V6 (Grand Voyager Base)	145	170
	NOT AVAILABLE with 26T.		

CODE	DESCRIPTION	INVOICE	MSRP
EGA	Engine: 3.3L MPI V6 (SE)	NC	NC
	NOT AVAILABLE with 25D, 25L.		
EGA	Engine: 3.3L MPI V6 (Voyager Base)	825	970
	NOT AVAILABLE with 22S, 25S, 22T, 25T, 26T, DGA, 4XA.		
EGM	Engine: 3.3L V6 FFV (SE)	NC	NC
	NOT AVAILABLE with 28D, 28L.		
EGM	Engine: 3.3L V6 FFV (Voyager Base)	825	970
	NOT AVAILABLE with 22S, 22T, 26T, 28T, DGA.		
GFA	Rear Window Defroster (Base)	166	195
	NOT AVAILABLE with ALD, AAC, AAE, AAF.		
GFA	Rear Window Defroster (Base)	196	230
GKD	Driver's Side Sliding Door (Voyager Base)	506	595
	REQUIRES 22T or 25T or 26T or 28T. NOT AVAILABLE with 22S, 25S.		
HAA	Air Conditioning (Voyager Base)	731	860
	NOT AVAILABLE with 4XA. INCLUDED in 22T, 25T, 26T, 28T.		
MWG	Roof Rack	183	215
	REQUIRES 22T or 25T or 26T or 28T. NOT AVAILABLE with 22S, 25S.		
NHK	Engine Block Heater	30	35
RF8	Speaker Delete Credit (SE)	(251)	(295)
	Deletes 10 Infinity speakers and amplifier. REQUIRES ATB.		
SER	Load Leveling and Height Control (All Except Grand Voyager Base)	247	290
	REQUIRES BGF.		
TBB	Tire: Full Size Spare	106	125
	REQUIRES 26T or 28T (Base). NOT AVAILABLE with 22S, 25S, AAP.		
WJB	Wheels: 15" Aluminum (SE)	353	415

2000 MONTANA

2000 Pontiac Montana

What's New?

The 2000 Montana boasts improvements to its V6 and antilock brakes, an upgraded electrical system, a revised instrument cluster and radios, a quieter climate-control blower motor, the addition of heated leather seats, reading lamps and oil-life monitoring as well as new paint schemes.

Review

Ever since it took on the Montana name last year, Pontiac's fun-to-drive minivan has been gaining attention as a worthy challenger to its domestic rivals. Like Chrysler, Pontiac offers driver's-side sliding doors on both wheelbase sizes, but Montana adds a power option for the passenger-side door. And Pontiac's minivan can accommodate eight-passenger seating (in both the 112- and 120-inch wheelbase vans), while Chrysler and Ford minivans cannot. Yes, Chrysler vans do feature roll-away bench seats, but they're heavy suckers to unload. The Montana can be equipped with modular seats that weigh just 38 pounds each and are relatively easy to remove.

For motivation, Montana features a standard 3.4-liter, 185-horsepower V6 that has been redesigned for better durability, reduced noise, lower emissions and improved fuel economy (to an EPA rating of 19 city, 26 highway). Around town, Montana feels downright spunky, with good throttle response and car-like handling. Its four-speed automatic is seamless and braking is excellent for a 4,000-pound vehicle. Front seats are comfy, and controls are easy to see and use.

In the safety column, dual front and side airbags are standard, as are antilock brakes and daytime running lights that operate the parking lamps rather than the headlights. Puncture-sealant type tires and a rear window defogger are standard, as is a ventilation system that features a replaceable pollen filter. Rear-seat audio controls can be had with uplevel radios or a CD unit, and extended-wheelbase models can be fitted with MontanaVision, a factory integrated rear-seat entertainment system that includes an overhead LCD monitor, a VCP, and video-game inputs. For soccer dads (and moms) who are sport sedan wannabes, there's an optional sport performance and handling package that offers upgraded tires on racy wheels, a luggage rack, special storage and a sport-tuned suspension with automatic load leveling and traction control.

Montana is, indeed, well-packaged and versatile. But it isn't perfect. If you opt for the modular flip-fold seats, know that they provide little in the way of thigh and leg support. And while the automatic sliding door is great, it doesn't work exactly like a typical elevator door. Designed to reverse direction when it determines that an object is blocking its closure path, it needs a stern reminder that you are in its way. Teach kids that they are, indeed, strong enough to push it back.

Marketers would like you to think that Montana bridges the gap between sport utility and minivan. While we think it takes more than body-cladding, white-letter tires and traction control to match an SUV when it comes to capability, we applaud what Pontiac is doing with Montana. Nobody will confuse this Pontiac with a Jeep, but thanks to a vast array of features and surprising fun-to-drive demeanor, at least they won't have to battle the boredom that most minivan drivers must endure.

Standard Equipment

REGULAR 7-PASSENGER (4A): 3.4L V6 OHV SMPI 12-valve engine; 4-speed electronic OD auto transmission with lock-up; 600-amp battery with run down protection; 105-amp alternator; front-wheel drive, 3.29 axle ratio; stainless steel exhaust; front independent strut suspension with anti-roll bar, front coil springs, rear non-independent suspension with anti-roll bar, rear coil springs; power rack-and-pinion steering with vehicle speed-sensing assist; front disc/rear drum brakes with 4-wheel antilock braking system; 20 gal. capacity fuel tank; front license plate bracket, side impact bars; 4 doors with sliding left rear passenger door, sliding right rear passenger door, liftback rear cargo door; front and rear body-colored bumpers with rear step; body-colored bodyside molding, body-colored bodyside cladding, rocker panel extensions; monotone paint; aero-composite halogen fully auto headlamps with daytime running lights; additional exterior lights include front fog/driving lights, underhood light; driver's and passenger's power remote black heated folding outside mirrors; front and rear 15" x 6" steel wheels; P215/70TR15 self sealing A/S BSW front and rear tires; inside under cargo mounted compact steel spare wheel; air conditioning, air filter; AM/FM stereo, clock, seek-scan, cassette, 4 speakers, and window grid antenna; cruise control; power door locks, child safety rear door locks, power remote hatch/trunk release; 2 power accessory outlets, driver's foot rest; instrumentation display includes tachometer, water temperature gauge, volt gauge, trip odometer; warning indicators include oil pressure, water temp, battery, low oil level, low coolant, lights on, key in ignition, low fuel, door ajar; driver's and passenger's front airbags, driver's and front passenger's seat mounted side airbags; ignition disable; tinted windows, vented rear windows, manual 1/4 vent windows; variable intermittent front windshield wipers, sun visor strip, fixed interval rear wiper, rear window defroster; seating capacity of 7, front bucket seats, adjustable tilt headrests, driver's and passenger's armrests, driver's seat includes 6-way direction control, lumbar support, passenger's seat includes 4-way direction control, lumbar support; removable 60-40 folding split-bench 2nd row seat with adjustable headrests; removable 50-50 folding 3rd row split-bench seat with adjustable headrest; front height adjustable seatbelts with front pretensioners; cloth seats, leatherette door trim insert, full cloth headliner, full carpet floor covering with carpeted floor mats; interior lights include dome light with fade, front reading lights; sport steering wheel with tilt adjustment; vanity mirrors; day/night rearview mirror; mini overhead console, engine cover console with storage, locking glove box with light, front and rear cupholders, instrument panel covered bin, interior concealed storage, 2 seat back storage pockets, driver's and passenger's door bins, rear door bins, front underseat tray; carpeted cargo floor, plastic trunk lid, cargo net, cargo light; body-colored grille, black side window moldings, black front windshield molding, black rear window molding and body-colored door handles.

REGULAR 6-PASSENGER (4A) (in addition to or instead of REGULAR 7-PASSENGER (4A) equipment): Roof rack; deep tinted windows, power windows with driver's 1-touch down, power 1/4 vent windows; seating capacity of 6; removeable 2nd row bucket seats with adjustable headrests and removable 3rd row bucket seats with adjustable headrest.

EXTENDED (4A) (in addition to or instead of REGULAR 7-PASSENGER (4A) equipment): 25 gal. capacity fuel tank.

CODE	DESCRIPTION	INVOICE	MSRP

Base Prices

2UN16	Regular 7-Passenger (4A)	21200	23425
2UV16	Regular 6-Passenger (4A)	21372	23615
2UM16	Extended (4A)	22204	24535
Destination Charge:		605	605

Accessories

—	Prado Leather Seat Trim (7-Passenger) *Includes leather-wrapped steering wheel and steering wheel mounted radio controls. REQUIRES AG1 and ABD. NOT AVAILABLE with 1SA, ZP8, U1P, U1Q, AG9, 1SB.*	1202	1350
1SA	Option Package 1SA (7-Passenger) *Includes vehicle with standard equipment. NOT AVAILABLE with DK6, ABD, AG1, AG2, AG9, V92, UA6, B4U, Leather Seat Trim, KA1, U1Q, U1P, ZY7, ZP8, C34, U42.*	NC	NC
1SB	Option Package 1SB (7-Passenger) *Includes heated outside rearview mirrors, AM/FM stereo with cassette, deep tinted glass, remote keyless entry, power windows with driver's express down, perimeter lighting and two-tone paint with charcoal lower accent. NOT AVAILABLE with AG2, AG9, Leather Seat Trim.*	690	775
1SC	Option Package 1SC (Extended) *Includes heated outside rearview mirrors, AM/FM stereo cassette, deep tint glass, remote keyless entry, power windows with driver's express down, perimeter lighting, illuminated visor vanity mirrors, overhead console, 6-way power driver's seat, luggage rack, two-tone paint with charcoal lower accent and front and rear air conditioning.*	1722	1935
1SC	Option Package 1SC (Regular 7-Passenger) *Includes heated outside rearview mirrors, AM/FM stereo cassette, deep tint glass, remote keyless entry, power windows with driver's express down, perimeter lighting, illuminated visor vanity mirrors, overhead console, 6-way power driver's seat, luggage rack and two-tone paint with charcoal lower accent. NOT AVAILABLE with B4U.*	1322	1485
1SV	Marketing Option Package 1SV (6-Passenger) *Includes vehicle with standard equipment.*	NC	NC
ABD	2nd Row Captain's Chairs (7-Passenger) *Includes 50/50 modular third row split bench seat. NOT AVAILABLE with 1SA, ZP8, AN2.*	263	295
AG1	6-Way Power Driver's Seat (7-Passenger) *REQUIRES leather seat trim or ABD. NOT AVAILABLE with 1SA. INCLUDED in 1SC.*	240	270
AG2	6-Way Power Passenger's Seat (7-Passenger) *REQUIRES leather seat trim. NOT AVAILABLE with 1SA, 1SB, AG9.*	271	305
AG9	6-Way Power Driver's and Passenger's Seats (Regular 7-Passenger) *REQUIRES 1SC. NOT AVAILABLE with 1SA, 1SB, AG2, leather seat trim.*	271	305
AG9	6-Way Power Passenger's Seat (Extended) *REQUIRES 1SC and (ABD or ZP8). NOT AVAILABLE with 1SA, 1SB, AN2, AG2.*	271	305

CODE	DESCRIPTION	INVOICE	MSRP
AJ1	Deep Tint Glass (7-Passenger) *NOT AVAILABLE with 1SA. INCLUDED in 1SV, 1SB, 1SC.*	245	275
AN2	Integral Child Seat (7-Passenger) *Available in gray or neutral interior color only. NOT AVAILABLE with ABD, AG9.*	111	125
B4U	Sport Performance and Handling Package (Regular 7-Passenger, Extended) *Includes luggage rack, wheels: 15" silver painted aluminum, tires: P215/70R15 RWOL touring, traction control, auto level control, saddle bag storage and ugraded suspension. REQUIRES 1SB. NOT AVAILABLE with 1SA, 1SC.*	983	1105
B4U	Sport Performance and Handling Package (Regular 7-Passenger, Extended) *Includes luggage rack, wheels: 15" silver painted aluminum, tires: P215/70R15 RWOL touring, traction control, auto level control, saddle bag storage and upgraded suspension. REQUIRES 1SC. NOT AVAILABLE with 1SA, 1SB.*	828	930
C34	Front and Rear Air Conditioning (Extended) *NOT AVAILABLE with 1SA. INCLUDED in 1SC.*	400	450
D84	Two-Tone Paint with Taupe Lower (7-Passenger) *With light taupe metallic lower accent. NOT AVAILABLE with ZY7.*	134	150
DK6	Overhead Console (7-Passenger) *REQUIRES AU0. NOT AVAILABLE with 1SA. INCLUDED in 1SC.*	156	175
E58	Power Sliding Door (7-Passenger) *REQUIRES 1SB or 1SC.*	400	450
G67	Automatic Level Control (7-Passenger) *Includes saddle bag storage. REQUIRES PH3.*	178	200
K05	Engine Block Heater (7-Passenger)	31	35
KA1	Heated Driver's and Passenger's Seats (7-Passenger) *REQUIRES (AG1 or ABD) and Leather Seat Trim and NW9. NOT AVAILABLE with ZP8, 1SA.*	174	195
NW9	Traction Control (7-Passenger) *REQUIRES G67.*	174	195
PH3	Wheels: 15" Silver Painted Aluminum	249	280
R6M	New Jersey Cost Surcharge	71	NC
U1P	Radio: AM/FM Stereo with CD and EQ (7-Passenger) *Includes leather-wrapped steering wheel, steering wheel mounted radio controls, rear seat audio controls with jacks and extended range coaxial speakers. NOT AVAILABLE with U1Q, 1SA, Leather Seat Trim.*	400	450
U1P	Radio: AM/FM Stereo with CD and EQ (7-Passenger) *Includes leather-wrapped steering wheel, steering wheel mounted radio controls, rear seat audio controls with jacks and extended range coaxial speakers. REQUIRES Leather Seat Trim. NOT AVAILABLE with U1Q, 1SA.*	236	265
U1Q	Radio: AM/FM Stereo with CD, Cassette and EQ (7-Passenger) *Includes leather-wrapped steering wheel, steering wheel mounted radio controls, rear seat audio controls with jacks and extended range coaxial speakers. NOT AVAILABLE with U1P, 1SA, Leather Seat Trim.*	490	550
U1Q	Radio: AM/FM Stereo with CD, Cassette and EQ (7-Passenger) *Includes leather-wrapped steering wheel, steering wheel mounted radio controls, rear seat audio controls with jacks and extended range coaxial speakers. REQUIRES Leather Seat Trim. NOT AVAILABLE with U1P, 1SA.*	325	365

CODE	DESCRIPTION	INVOICE	MSRP
U42	Montana Vision Package (Extended) *Includes video cassette player, fold-down overhead LCD color monitor, rear seat headphone jacks with separate audio controls and video input. REQUIRES U1Q, UA6 and PH3. NOT AVAILABLE with 1SA.*	2310	2595
UA6	Theft Deterrent System (7-Passenger) *REQUIRES AUO. NOT AVAILABLE with 1SA.*	53	60
UK3	Leather-Wrapped Steering Wheel (7-Passenger) *Includes steering wheel mounted radio controls.*	165	185
V54	Luggage Rack (7-Passenger) *INCLUDED in 1SV, 1SC.*	156	175
V92	Trailer Provisions (3,500 Lbs) (7-Passenger) *Does not include hitch. Includes HD radiator cooler, HD transmission oil cooler, engine oil cooler and wiring provisions. REQUIRES G67 or B4U. NOT AVAILABLE with 1SA.*	147	165
ZP8	8-Passenger Seating (7-Passenger) *Includes 3 modular second row buckets and 50/50 modular third row split bench. NOT AVAILABLE with ABD, Leather Seat Trim, KA1, 1SA.*	249	280

2000 FORESTER

2000 Subaru Forester

What's New?

This year, Forester L gets standard cruise control and Forester S receives a viscous limited-slip rear differential at base price increases of $100.

Review

What do you do when sport-utility buyers won't drive home in your all-wheel-drive station wagon, which is dressed up like an SUV, because it looks too "wagony"? If you're gutsy like Subaru, you put a taller, more squared-off body on your wagon chassis, and call it good. The Forester is a Subaru parts-bin exercise, and since the parts bin is rather small at Fuji Heavy Industries, which owns the upstart all-wheel-drive automaker, the car is cobbled together from a mixture of Impreza and previous-generation Legacy bits.

Based on the rally-proven Impreza platform, the Forester uses the same popular all-wheel-drive system found in other Subaru models. The 2.5-liter boxer engine comes from the Legacy Outback, and makes 165 horsepower in the Forester. And, thanks to its hunkered-down stance, low center of gravity and car-based foundation, the Forester handles better than its primary competitors: the Chevrolet Tracker, Honda CR-V, Suzuki Grand Vitara and Toyota RAV4. The trade-off is lower ground clearance and less capable off-road ability, but you weren't going to go too far off the beaten path anyway, were you? (Wink, wink, nudge, nudge.) Automatic transmissions are available on both models for an extra $800 and feature a hill-holding setup that detects the inclination of a road surface and holds a gear to maximize torque or provide engine braking.

Inside is room for four adults, with a rear center position marked off for a fifth rider in a pinch. Though the Forester offers an accommodating rear seat, low step-in height, and a cavernous cargo area, the interior fabric looks and feels like terrycloth stretched over old cardboard, some secondary controls are placed illogically, and the stereo controls are difficult to operate.

Two Forester models are available this year: the L and the high-end S. Air conditioning, roof rack, rear defogger, tachometer, power windows, tilt steering, rear wiper/washer, cassette stereo, antilock brakes, power door locks and cruise control are standard on the L. The uplevel S adds a toothy chrome grille, alloy wheels, bigger tires, rear disc brakes, and upgraded interior trimmings. A limited-slip rear differential is also standard on the S for 2000. Forester options include CD player, alloy wheels (on L), a trailer hitch and a variety of cosmetic upgrades.

While we are partial to the Impreza Outback Sport and Legacy Outback models, the Forester will attract buyers who want an inexpensive, functional, all-wheel-drive vehicle that looks like a truck and drives like a car. As long as Subaru keeps a lid on pricing, the Foresters pick up right where the Outback Wagons leave off.

Standard Equipment

L (5M): 2.5L H4 SOHC SMPI 16-valve engine; 5-speed OD manual transmission; 520-amp battery; 85-amp alternator; full-time 4-wheel drive, 4.44 axle ratio; steel exhaust; HD ride suspension, front independent strut suspension with anti-roll bar, front coil springs, rear independent strut suspension with anti-roll bar, rear coil springs; power rack-and-pinion steering with engine speed-sensing assist; front disc/rear drum brakes with 4-wheel antilock braking system; 15.9 gal. capacity fuel tank; front and rear mud flaps, side impact bars; liftback rear cargo door; trailer harness; roof rack; front and rear colored bumpers with rear step; colored bodyside cladding, rocker panel extensions; lower accent two-tone paint; aero-composite halogen auto off headlamps; additional exterior lights include front fog/driving lights; driver's and passenger's power remote black folding outside mirrors; front and rear 15" x 6" silver styled steel wheels; P205/70SR15 M&S OWL front and rear tires; inside under cargo mounted full-size steel spare wheel; air conditioning, rear heat ducts; AM/FM stereo, clock, seek-scan, cassette, 4 speakers, and fixed antenna; cruise control; power door locks with 2 stage unlock, child safety rear door locks; 2 power accessory outlets, driver's foot rest; instrumentation display includes tachometer, water temperature gauge, trip odometer; warning indicators include oil pressure, battery, key in ignition, low fuel, door ajar, trunk ajar; driver's and passenger's front airbags; tinted windows, power front and rear windows with driver's 1-touch down, fixed 1/4 vent windows; fixed interval front windshield wipers, rear window wiper, rear window defroster; seating capacity of 5, front bucket seats, adjustable headrests, driver's seat includes 6-way direction control, lumbar support, passenger's seat includes 4-way direction control; 55-45 folding rear bench seat with reclining adjustable headrests; front height adjustable seatbelts; cloth seats, cloth door trim insert, full cloth headliner, full carpet floor covering with carpeted floor mats, plastic/rubber gear shift knob; interior lights include dome light, front reading lights; steering wheel with tilt adjustment; day/night rearview mirror; full floor console, mini overhead console with storage, locking glove box with light, front and rear cupholders, instrument panel bin, driver's and passenger's door bins; carpeted cargo floor, plastic trunk lid, cargo cover, cargo tie downs, cargo light, cargo concealed storage; black grille, black side window moldings, black front windshield molding, black rear window molding and black door handles.

S (5M) (in addition to or instead of L (5M) equipment): Viscous limited slip differential; 4-wheel disc brakes with 4-wheel antilock braking system; power remote black folding driver's and passenger's heated outside mirrors; front and rear 16" x 6.5" silver alloy wheels; P215/60HR16 M&S OWL front and rear tires; AM/FM stereo, clock, seek-scan, cassette, 4 speakers, and window grid antenna; heated fixed interval front windshield wipers; heated-cushion front bucket seats, center armrest with storage; vanity mirrors; 2 seat back storage pockets and chrome grille.

Base Prices

YCA	L (5M)	18324	20095
YCC	S (5M)	20506	22595
Destination Charge:		495	495

Accessories

4AT	Transmission: 4-Speed Automatic	719	800
DWA	Upgraded Speakers	127	195
DWB	Subwoofer/Amplifier	202	310
DXB	Tweeter Kit (Pair)	65	100
EWB	CD Player	264	350

CODE	DESCRIPTION	INVOICE	MSRP
F06	Security Group	237	365
	Manufacturer Discount	(12)	NC
	Net Price	225	365
	Includes keyless entry and security system upgrade kit.		
F1*	Outdoor Package I (Beige/Gray)	863	1208
	Manufacturer Discount	(145)	(383)
	Net Price	718	825
	Includes brush guard, side underguard bar, rear diffential protector, gauge pack and beige/gray gauge pack housing.		
F12	Premium Sound Package I	625	905
	Manufacturer Discount	(100)	(210)
	Net Price	525	695
	Includes CD player, tweeter kit (pair), upgraded speakers and subwoofer/amplifier.		
F20	Outdoor Package II (Beige)	635	858
	Manufacturer Discount	(91)	(233)
	Net Price	544	625
	Includes brush guard, rear differential protector, gauge pack and beige gauge pack housing.		
F21	Outdoor Package II (Gray)	635	858
	Manufacturer Discount	(91)	(233)
	Net Price	544	625
	Includes brush guard, rear differential protector, gauge pack and gray gauge pack housing.		
F3A	Feature Group III (Beige)	389	596
	Manufacturer Discount	(20)	NC
	Net Price	369	596
	Includes keyless entry, woodgrain trim kit, beige luggage compartment cover and custom tail pipe cover. REQUIRES 4AT.		
F3B	Feature Group III (Gray)	389	596
	Manufacturer Discount	(20)	NC
	Net Price	369	596
	Includes keyless entry, woodgrain trim kit, gray luggage compartment cover and custom tail pipe cover. NOT AVAILABLE with 4AT.		
F3C	Feature Group III (Gray)	389	596
	Manufacturer Discount	(20)	NC
	Net Price	369	596
	Includes keyless entry, woodgrain trim kit, gray luggage compartment cover and custom tail pipe cover. REQUIRES 4AT.		
F3D	Feature Group III (Beige)	389	596
	Manufacturer Discount	(20)	NC
	Net Price	369	596
	Includes keyless entry, woodgrain trim kit, beige luggage compartment cover and custom tail pipe cover. NOT AVAILABLE with 4AT.		

CODE	DESCRIPTION	INVOICE	MSRP
F4A	Feature Group IV (Beige)	343	526
	Manufacturer Discount	(17)	NC
	Net Price	326	526
	Includes keyless entry, security system upgrade kit, beige luggage compartment cover and custom tail pipe cover.		
F4B	Feature Group IV (Gray)	343	526
	Manufacturer Discount	(17)	NC
	Net Price	326	526
	Includes keyless entry, security system upgrade kit, gray luggage compartment cover and custom tail pipe cover.		
F5A	Feature Group V (Beige)	252	386
	Manufacturer Discount	(13)	NC
	Net Price	239	386
	Includes keyless entry, beige luggage compartment cover and custom tail pipe cover.		
F5B	Feature Group V (Gray)	252	386
	Manufacturer Discount	(13)	NC
	Net Price	239	386
	Includes keyless entry, gray luggage compartment cover and custom tail pipe cover.		
F6A	Feature Group VI (Beige)	145	221
	Manufacturer Discount	(8)	NC
	Net Price	137	221
	Includes air filter, air filter cover, cargo net and beige armrest extension.		
F6B	Feature Group VI (Gray)	145	221
	Manufacturer Discount	(8)	NC
	Net Price	137	221
	Includes air filter, air filter cover, cargo net and gray armrest extension.		
HWA	Wheels: 15" Alloy (L)	447	595
	Includes attachment set.		
IWC	Leather Shift Knob - M/T	30	45
IWD	Leather Shift Knob - A/T	50	77
	REQUIRES 4AT.		
IWE	Beige Leather Seats	975	1295
IWF	Gray Leather Seats	975	1295
IWG	Woodgrain Trim Kit - A/T	137	210
	REQUIRES 4AT.		
IWH	Woodgrain Trim Kit - M/T	137	210
KWA	Air Filter	56	85
	Includes air filter cover.		
KWB	Beige Armrest Extension	61	94
KWC	Gray Armrest Extension	61	94
LWB	Custom Tail Pipe Cover	26	39
LWC	Rear Window Dust Deflector	74	114
LWG	Trailer Hitch	192	295
MSV	Wheel Locks	22	34
MWA	Cargo Net	28	42
NWC	Gauge Pack	296	395
	Includes beige gauge pack housing.		

CODE	DESCRIPTION	INVOICE	MSRP
NWD	Gauge Pack *Includes gray gauge pack housing.*	296	395
NWE	Dual Power Outlet Socket (L)	58	88
OWA	Beige Luggage Compartment Cover	80	122
OWB	Gray Luggage Compartment Cover	80	122
PWD	Side Underguard Bar	228	350
PWE	Brush Guard	282	375
PXB	Rear Differential Protector	57	88
RWA	Keyless Entry	146	225
RWB	Security System Upgrade Kit	91	140

2000 GRAND VITARA

2000 Suzuki Grand Vitara

What's New?

The 2000 Limited Edition Grand Vitara comes with leather seats, privacy glass, fog lamps, a hard spare tire cover, an armrest, gold emblems, and a special black-and-white paint scheme. The spare tire cover on regular Grand Vitaras features a new design. The '99 model's base trim levels (JS and JS+) have been renamed JLS and JLS+. A CD changer is standard equipment on JLS+ and JLX+ models.

Review

With a title that sounds more like a sprawling Spanish estate (or maybe a new, super-potency drug) than a mini-SUV, the Grand Vitara is Suzuki's bold entrant in the rapidly growing mini-SUV segment. Based off the four-door Suzuki Vitara, the big selling point about the Grand Vitara is its V6 engine. Most other mini-SUVs feature four-cylinder engines. Suzuki's 2.5-liter V6 makes 155 horsepower and 160 foot-pounds of torque. Harnessing those 155 horses is either a five-speed manual or four-speed automatic. Four-wheel drive is optional.

The interior offers several amenities not common in this class. These include two reading lights in addition to the main dome light, extended sun-block slats on the visors, plenty of small cargo bins for storing assorted doodads, and comfortable front seats covered in a soft cloth. The Grand Vitara also has a useful large, single door that swings open to access the rear cargo area. The rear seat, however, is essentially useless for anyone over 4-feet tall, particularly if the front passengers are over 5-feet tall.

There's also plenty of luxury with standard air conditioning, power windows, cruise control, keyless entry and daytime running lamps included on every Grand Vitara. Higher levels of trim offer 16-inch alloy wheels and antilock brakes.

Once moving, the Grand Vitara's V6 provides plenty of grunt. Its styling gets attention, especially when equipped with the 16-inch wheels. But the Suzuki is let down by long braking distances and a suspension that doesn't work as well as it should. The Grand Vitara is harsh over broken pavement, and that harshness doesn't seem to translate to substantial benefits off-highway.

The Grand Vitara does have plenty to offer consumers, however. Four-wheel-drive models come with a low-range transfer case, something many other mini SUVs don't have. The 2000 Limited Edition model should further the Grand Vitara's exclusivity. But the '99 Grand Vitara's trump card—V6 power—

has recently been eclipsed by the V6 found in the new 2000 Nissan Xterra. The Xterra's V6 is more powerful, and it's wrapped in an arguably better package.

Standard Equipment

JLS 2WD (5M): 2.5L V6 DOHC MPI 24-valve engine; 5-speed OD manual transmission; 550-amp battery; 80-amp alternator; rear-wheel drive, 4.3 axle ratio; stainless steel exhaust; front independent strut suspension with anti-roll bar, front coil springs, rigid rear axle multi-link suspension with rear coil springs; power rack-and-pinion steering; front disc/rear drum brakes; 17.4 gal. capacity fuel tank; skid plate(s), side impact bars; conventional rear cargo door; roof rack; front and rear body-colored bumpers with front and rear tow hooks, rear step; body-colored bodyside cladding, rocker panel extensions, body-colored fender flares; monotone paint; aero-composite halogen auto on headlamps with daytime running lights; driver's and passenger's power remote body-colored folding outside mirrors; front and rear 16" x 7" silver styled steel wheels; P235/60SR16 A/S BSW front and rear tires; outside rear mounted full-size steel spare wheel; air conditioning, air filter, rear heat ducts; premium AM/FM stereo, clock, seek-scan, cassette, 4 speakers, and fixed antenna; cruise control; power door locks, remote keyless entry, child safety rear door locks, remote fuel release; 2 power accessory outlets; instrumentation display includes tachometer, water temperature gauge, trip odometer; warning indicators include oil pressure, water temp, battery, key in ignition, low fuel; driver's and passenger's front airbags; tinted windows, power front and rear windows with driver's 1-touch down, fixed 1/4 vent windows; variable intermittent front windshield wipers, rear window wiper, rear window defroster; seating capacity of 5, front bucket seats, adjustable headrests, driver's seat includes 4-way direction control, passenger's seat includes 4-way direction control; 50-50 folding rear bench seat with adjustable headrests; front height adjustable seatbelts with front pretensioners; cloth seats, cloth door trim insert, full cloth headliner, full carpet floor covering, plastic/rubber gear shift knob; interior lights include dome light, front reading lights; steering wheel with tilt adjustment; dual auxiliary visors, passenger's side vanity mirror; day/night rearview mirror; full floor console, locking glove box, front cupholder, 2 seat back storage pockets, driver's and passenger's door bins, rear door bins, front underseat tray; carpeted cargo floor, plastic trunk lid, cargo cover, cargo tie downs, cargo light; chrome grille, black side window moldings, black front windshield molding, black rear window molding and black door handles.

JLS+ 2WD (5M) (in addition to or instead of JLX 2WD (5M) equipment): Front disc/rear drum brakes with 4-wheel antilock braking system; front and rear 16" x 7" alloy wheels; premium AM/FM stereo, clock, seek-scan, cassette, trunk-mounted 6-disc CD changer, 4 speakers, and fixed antenna.

LIMITED 2WD (4A) (in addition to or instead of JLS+ 2WD (5M) equipment): Four-speed electronic OD auto transmission with lock-up; monotone paint with bodyside accent gold trim package; additional exterior lights include front fog/driving lights; deep tinted windows and leather seats..

4WD (in addition to or instead of 2WD equipment): Part-time 4-wheel drive and auto locking hub control and manual shift.

Base Prices

LFN86FY	JLS 2WD (5M)	16835	18299
LJN86FY	JLX 4WD (5M)	17755	19299
LFN86TY	JLS+ 2WD (5M)	17939	19499
LJN86TY	JLX+ 4WD (5M)	18859	20499
LFN89WY	Limited 2WD (4A)	19963	21699
LJN89WY	Limited 4WD (4A)	20883	22699
Destination Charge:		450	450

CODE	DESCRIPTION	INVOICE	MSRP

Accessories

—	Transmission: 4-Speed Automatic (All Except Limited) *Includes driving mode switch (Power Normal) and 4.88 axle ratio.*	920	1000

2000 VITARA

2000 Suzuki Vitara

What's New?

Four-door models receive a new luggage cover. The Vitara two-door JLS/JLX will be equipped with air conditioning as standard equipment. There are three new paint colors, and four-wheel-drive models have a "4x4" sticker in the rear-quarter windows.

Review

Now in its second year of production, the Suzuki Vitara competes in the increasingly crowded mini-SUV market. Here, you will find vehicles such as the Toyota RAV4, the Honda CR-V, and the Kia Sportage.

The Vitara comes in two variations: a two-door soft top and a four-door model. Both are built on a trucklike ladder frame and both can be ordered with either two-wheel drive or four-wheel drive. The four-wheel-drive system features a two-speed transfer case (as found in real trucks), which improves performance in extreme off-highway conditions. An independent MacPherson strut front suspension and five-link coil-spring rear suspension is used throughout the Vitara line.

Powering the rear wheels is either a 1.6-liter or a 2.0-liter four-cylinder engine. The smaller engine produces 97 horsepower at 5,200 rpm and 103 foot-pounds of torque at 4,000 rpm. The larger 2.0-liter engine generates 127 horsepower at 6,000 rpm and 134 foot-pounds of torque at 3,000 rpm. Both engines are mated to a standard five-speed manual transmission or an optional four-speed automatic transmission.

The styling of the Vitara is clean with smooth curves and rounded features. The front end features large, multi-reflector headlights and a monotone grille. The two-door Vitara allows you to fold back the durable, canvas drop top like a sunroof, or take it completely off to get your daily dose of solar radiation.

The two-door soft-top model does lack valuable room for cargo, however. Suzuki says there's only 9.9 cubic feet of space for your stuff. If you fold the rear seat down, that number goes to 33.7. The four-door model does slightly better, with a maximum cargo load of 44.6. A Honda CR-V, by comparison, can hold a maximum cargo load of 67.2 cubic feet.

The truck genes found in the Suzuki Vitara might appeal to you that have a big desire to pound the dirt. But if that's really the case, you'd probably be better served with a Jeep Wrangler. On all other fronts, the Vitara competes dismally against other mini SUVs. You also might want to price out the Chevrolet Tracker. Both the Vitara and the Tracker are built at the same assembly plant and are nearly identical underneath and Chevy often provides big rebates to move the metal.

Standard Equipment

JS 1.6 2WD CONVERTIBLE (5M): 1.6L I4 SOHC MPI 16-valve engine; 5-speed OD manual transmission; 390-amp battery; 60-amp alternator; rear-wheel drive, 4.63 axle ratio; stainless steel exhaust; front independent strut suspension with anti-roll bar, front coil springs, rigid rear axle multi-link suspension with rear coil springs; power rack-and-pinion steering; front disc/rear drum brakes; 14.8 gal. capacity fuel tank; side impact bars; conventional rear cargo door; manual convertible roof with roll-over protection; front and rear body-colored bumpers with front and rear tow hooks, rear step; monotone paint; aero-composite halogen auto on headlamps with daytime running lights; driver's and passenger's manual black folding outside mirrors; front and rear 15" x 5.5" silver styled steel wheels; P195/75SR15 A/S BSW front and rear tires; outside rear mounted full-size steel spare wheel; AM/FM stereo, clock, seek-scan, cassette, 2 speakers, and manual retractable antenna; 1 power accessory outlet; instrumentation display includes tachometer, water temperature gauge, trip odometer; warning indicators include oil pressure, water temp, battery, key in ignition, low fuel; driver's and passenger's front airbags; tinted windows; variable intermittent front windshield wipers; seating capacity of 4, front bucket seats, adjustable headrests, driver's seat includes 4-way direction control, easy entry, passenger's seat includes 4-way direction control, easy entry; full folding rear bench seat with adjustable headrests; front height adjustable seatbelts with front pretensioners; cloth seats, full carpet floor covering, plastic/rubber gear shift knob; interior lights include dome light, front reading lights; steering wheel with tilt adjustment; dual auxiliary visors, passenger's side vanity mirror; day/night rearview mirror; full floor console, glove box, front cupholder, 2 seat back storage pockets, driver's and passenger's door bins; carpeted cargo floor, plastic trunk lid; body-colored grille, black side window moldings, black front windshield molding and black door handles.

JLS 2.0 2WD CONVERTIBLE (5M) (in addition to or instead of JS 1.6 2WD CONVERTIBLE (5M) equipment): 2.0L I4 DOHC MPI 16-valve engine; 550-amp battery; 70-amp alternator; driver's and passenger's power remote black folding outside mirrors; front and rear 16" x 6.5" silver styled steel wheels; P215/65SR16 A/S BSW front and rear tires; air conditioning; 50-50 folding rear bench seat with adjustable headrests.

JS 2WD 4-DOOR (5M) (in addition to or instead of JS 1.6 2WD CONVERTIBLE (5M) equipment): 2.0L I4 DOHC MPI 16-valve engine; 550-amp battery; 70-amp alternator; 17.4 gal. capacity fuel tank; roof rack; body-colored bodyside molding; front and rear 16" x 6.5" silver styled steel wheels; P215/65SR16 A/S BSW front and rear tires; rear heat ducts; AM/FM stereo, clock, seek-scan, cassette, 4 speakers, and manual retractable antenna; child safety rear door locks; manual front and rear windows, fixed 1/4 vent windows; rear window wiper, rear window defroster; seating capacity of 5, front sports seats, adjustable headrests, driver's seat includes 4-way direction control, passenger's seat includes 4-way direction control; 50-50 folding rear bench seat with adjustable headrests; cloth door trim insert, full cloth headliner; cargo cover and cargo light.

JLS 2WD 4-DOOR (5M) (in addition to or instead of JS 2WD 4-DOOR (5M) equipment): Driver's and passenger's power remote black folding outside mirrors; air conditioning; cruise control; power door locks, remote keyless entry and power front and rear windows.

4WD (in addition to or instead of 2WD equipment): Part-time 4-wheel drive, auto locking hub control and manual shift and skid plate(s).

CODE	DESCRIPTION	INVOICE	MSRP
	Base Prices		
FME66CY	JS 1.6 2WD Convertible (5M)	12959	13499
FME83FY	JLS 2.0 2WD Convertible (5M)	14399	14999
FGE66CY	JX 1.6 4WD Convertible (5M)	14381	15299
LLN83CY	JS 2WD 4-Door (5M)	14569	15499
LLN83EY	JLS 2WD 4-Door (5M)	15321	16299
FGE83FY	JLX 2.0 4WD Convertible (5M)	15791	16799
LKN83CY	JX 4WD 4-Door (5M)	15731	17099
LKN83EY	JLX 4WD 4-Door (5M)	16467	17899
Destination Charge:		450	450
	Accessories		
—	Alloy Wheels (JLS 2WD 4-Door)	376	400
—	Alloy Wheels (JLX 4WD 4-Door)	368	400
—	Transmission: 4-Speed Automatic (1.6L 2WD Conv.)	960	1000
—	Transmission: 4-Speed Automatic (2.0L 2WD Conv.)	960	1000
—	Transmission: 4-Speed Automatic (2.0L 4WD Conv.)	940	1000
—	Transmission: 4-Speed Automatic (2WD 4-Door/1.6L 4WD Conv.)	940	1000
—	Transmission: 4-Speed Automatic (4-Door 4WD)	920	1000

2000 4RUNNER

2000 Toyota 4Runner

What's New?

Optional color-coordinated fender flares are available on the SR5. An AM/FM/Cassette/CD is now available on base models, and is standard on SR5 and Limited models. Daytime running lights are now included with the antilock brake package.

Review

In 1996, Toyota separated this high-volume SUV from its pickup-truck roots. Thus, the current 4Runner shares little with the Tacoma pickup. As a result, engineers have created a refined vehicle without sacrificing tough off-road ability. In terms of Toyota's lineup, the 4Runner is more expensive than the Tacoma, but less expensive than the Land Cruiser.

The interior is quite roomy, and a low floor and wide doors help make getting into and out of the 4Runner less of an exercise in contortionism. Gauges are clearly marked and legible. 4Runner Limiteds receive walnut wood inserts on the dash, though this can also be gained on base and SR5 models through an option package. Toyota has thoughtfully provided rear passengers with heat and air conditioning ducts that can be operated independently to adjust fan speed and temperature.

There are two engines available on the 4Runner. The base model is propelled by a 2.7-liter inline four cylinder that makes 150 horsepower at 4,800 rpm and 177 foot-pounds of torque at 4,000 rpm. Both the SR5 and Limited models receive a 3.4-liter V6, producing 183 horsepower at 4,800 rpm and 217 foot-pounds of torque at 3,600 rpm. While the V6's numbers are acceptable, both the Ford Explorer and Jeep Grand Cherokee have optional V8 engines that produce considerably more horsepower and torque. Suspension-wise, the 4Runner is near the top of the pack. An optional locking rear differential (4WD models only) allows for effortless trips off highway, and the 4Runner is equally at home cruising suburban asphalt.

Overall, the 4Runner is a nice truck which provides the sophistication that we have come to expect from Toyota products with the overall ruggedness more often associated with Jeeps. Prices are high, however, running from approximately $21,000 for a 2WD four-cylinder base model to over $36,000 for a fully loaded Limited. This lands the top 4Runner right smack dab in Mercedes-Benz ML320, Lexus RX300, and Jeep Grand Cherokee Limited territory. The competition in this segment is getting fierce and there are plenty of good choices for your money, definitely something worth considering when shelling out such a large chunk of change

Standard Equipment

BASE 2WD (5M): 2.7L I4 DOHC MPI 16-valve engine; 5-speed OD manual transmission; 582-amp HD battery; engine oil cooler; 70-amp alternator; rear-wheel drive, 3.73 axle ratio; stainless steel exhaust; front independent double wishbone suspension with anti-roll bar, front coil springs, rigid rear axle multi-link suspension with anti-roll bar, rear coil springs; power rack-and-pinion steering with engine speed-sensing assist; front disc/rear drum brakes; 18.5 gal. capacity fuel tank; front and rear mud flaps, skid plate(s), side impact bars; liftback rear cargo door; front and rear chrome bumpers with front tow hooks, rear step; monotone paint; aero-composite halogen auto off headlamps; driver's and passenger's manual black folding outside mirrors; front and rear 15" x 7" silver styled steel wheels; P225/75SR15 M&S BSW front and rear tires; underbody mounted full-size steel spare wheel; AM/FM stereo, seek-scan, cassette, 4 speakers, and fixed antenna; child safety rear door locks, remote fuel release; 3 power accessory outlets, driver's foot rest; instrumentation display includes tachometer, water temperature gauge, trip odometer; warning indicators include oil pressure, battery, lights on, key in ignition, low fuel, bulb failure, door ajar, trunk ajar; driver's and passenger's front airbags; tinted windows, manual front and rear windows, fixed 1/4 vent windows; fixed interval front windshield wipers, sun visor strip, power rear window; seating capacity of 5, front bucket seats, adjustable headrests, center armrest with storage, driver's seat includes 4-way direction control, passenger's seat includes, 4-way direction control; 60-40 folding rear bench seat with adjustable headrests; front height adjustable seatbelts with front pretensioners; cloth seats, cloth door trim insert, full cloth headliner, full carpet floor covering, plastic/rubber gear shift knob; interior lights include dome light; passenger's side vanity mirror; day/night rearview mirror; full floor console, locking glove box, front and rear cupholders, instrument panel bin, 2 seat back storage pockets, driver's and passenger's door bins, rear door bins; carpeted cargo floor, plastic trunk lid, cargo tie downs, cargo light; chrome grille, black side window moldings, black front windshield molding, black rear window molding and black door handles.

SR5 V6 2WD (4A) (in addition to or instead of BASE 2WD (4A) equipment): 3.4L V6 DOHC SMPI 24-valve engine; 4-speed electronic OD auto transmission with lock-up; 356-amp HD battery; engine oil cooler, HD starter; 80-amp alternator; driver's selectable multi-mode transmission; rear-wheel drive; front disc/rear drum brakes with 4-wheel antilock braking system; aero-composite halogen auto off headlamps with daytime running lights; driver's and passenger's power remote body-colored heated folding outside mirrors; AM/FM stereo, seek-scan, cassette, single CD, 4 speakers, and fixed antenna; cruise control; instrumentation display in-dash clock; deep tinted windows; variable intermittent front windshield wipers, fixed interval rear wiper, rear window defroster; interior lights include front reading lights; steering wheel with tilt adjustment; mini overhead console and locking glove box with light.

LIMITED V6 2WD (4A) (in addition to or instead of SR5 V6 2WD (4A) equipment): 4.1 axle ratio; running boards; front and rear body-colored bumpers with front tow hooks; body-colored bodyside cladding, body-colored fender flares; lower accent two-tone paint; additional exterior lights include front fog/driving lights; front and rear 16" x 7" silver alloy wheels; P265/70SR16 M&S BSW front and rear tires; air conditioning with climate control; premium AM/FM stereo, seek-scan, cassette, single CD, 6 speakers, graphic equalizer, theft deterrent, and power retractable diversity antenna; power door locks with 2 stage unlock, remote keyless entry; retained accessory power; instrumentation display exterior temp; ignition disable, security system; power front and rear windows with driver's and passenger's 1-touch down; front sports seats, adjustable tilt headrests, driver's seat includes 6-way power seat, power 2-way lumbar support, passenger's seat includes 6-way power seat; leather seats, leather door trim insert, carpeted floor mats, simulated wood trim on instrument panel; leather-wrapped steering wheel with tilt adjustment; passenger's side illuminated vanity mirror and cargo cover.

BASE 4WD (5M) (in addition to or instead of BASE 2WD (5M) equipment): Part-time 4-wheel drive, auto locking hub control and manual shift and 4.1 axle ratio.

SR5 V6 4WD (5M) (in addition to or instead of SR5 V6 2WD (4A) equipment): 5-speed OD manual transmission; auto full-time 4-wheel drive, auto locking hub control and manual shift and 3.91 axle ratio.

CODE	DESCRIPTION	INVOICE	MSRP

LIMITED V6 4WD (4A) (in addition to or instead of LIMITED V6 2WD (4A) equipment): 582-amp HD battery; auto full-time 4-wheel drive, auto locking hub control and manual shift and 4.1 axle ratio.

Base Prices

8641	Base 2WD (5M)	19205	21938
8657	Base 4WD (5M)	21096	24098
8642	SR5 V6 2WD (4A)	22725	25958
8665	SR5 V6 4WD (5M)	23732	27108
8648	Limited V6 2WD (4A)	29738	33968
8668	Limited V6 4WD (4A)	31926	36468
Destination Charge:		480	480

Accessories

4AT	Transmission: 4-Speed Automatic (Base 2WD/SR5 4WD)	789	900
AA	Wheels: 16" x 7" Aluminum (SR5 4WD) *Includes 13" brakes, tires: P265/70R16, rear differential lock and 4.30 rear differential. REQUIRES 4AT and (JU or JZ). NOT AVAILABLE with GK, AW, GU, SX.*	1009	1250
AB	Antilock Brakes (Base 4WD) *REQUIRES AW or SV. NOT AVAILABLE with AY.*	539	630
AW	Wheels: 16" x 7" Aluminum (Base 4WD) *Includes 13" brakes, tires: P265/70R16, chrome wheel arch molding and 4.10 rear differential. REQUIRES AB. NOT AVAILABLE with AY, SV.*	784	980
AW	Wheels: 16" x 7" Aluminum (SR5) *Includes 13" brakes, tires: P265/70R16, chrome wheel arch molding and 4.10 rear differential. REQUIRES JU or JZ. NOT AVAILABLE with AY, GJ, GK, AA, GU, SX.*	728	910
AY	Wheels: 15" x 7"Aluminum (2WD - Base/SR5) *NOT AVAILABLE with AW, GJ, GK, JU, JZ.*	292	365
AY	Wheels: 15" x 7" Aluminum (Base 4WD) *NOT AVAILABLE with AW, SV, AB.*	292	365
BM	Body Side Molding (Base/SR5) *Color-keyed.*	89	139
BN	Black Pearl Emblems (2WD - Base/SR5)	139	209
BN	Black Pearl Emblems (4WD - Base/SR5)	159	239
BN	Black Pearl Emblems (Limited 2WD)	225	339
BN	Black Pearl Emblems (Limited 4WD)	245	369
C1	Cargo Mat	44	73
C7	Discount Convenience Package *Includes rear wind deflector, towing receiver hitch, roof rack and cargo mat.*	427	669
C9	Exterior Package (Base/SR5) *Includes chrome running boards and fender flares. NOT AVAILABLE with JZ, SX.*	510	845
CB	Color Keyed Bumpers (Limited) *Includes full body color with cladding and overfender (Millennium Silver M only).*	NC	NC
CD	Tonneau Cover (Base)	72	90

CODE	DESCRIPTION	INVOICE	MSRP
CF	Carpeted Floor Mats (Base/SR5) *Includes a 4-piece set. NOT AVAILABLE with GH, GI.*	51	84
CR	Chrome Running Boards (Base/SR5)	284	470
DD	Rear Wind Deflector	71	118
DH	Towing Receiver Hitch	215	305
DL	Rear Differential Lock (Limited 4WD) *Includes 4.30 rear differential.*	281	340
DR	Roof Rack	165	275
DU	Walnut Wood Dash (Base/SR5)	287	549
EL	Elite Package (Base/SR5) *Includes body side molding, walnut wood dash and hood protector.*	369	1176
ET	Black Elite Package (Base/SR5) *Includes body side molding, walnut wood dash and hood protector.*	349	1076
FN	Fender Flares *NOT AVAILABLE with JZ, SX.*	243	405
GH	Upgrade Value Package #1 (Base) *Includes tilt wheel, variable intermittent wipers, deluxe 3-in-1 combo radio, overhead console, map light, power windows, power door locks, black power mirrors, cruise control and carpeted floor mats.*	1321	1468
GI	Upgrade Value Package #2 (SR5) *Includes power windows, sun visor, keyless entry, premium 3-in-1 combo radio and carpeted floor mats. NOT AVAILABLE with GJ, GK, GU.*	1168	1298
GJ	Upgrade Value Package #3 (SR5 2WD) *Includes Upgrade Value Package #2: power windows, sun visor, keyless entry, premium 3-in-1 combo radio, carpeted floor mats; air conditioner, tonneau cover, sport seat, 4-way adjustable headrest, cloth door trim and leather-wrapped steering wheel cover. NOT AVAILABLE with GK, GI, LA, AW, AY, JU, JZ.*	1870	2078
GK	Upgrade Value Package #4 (SR5) *Includes Upgrade Value Package #2: power windows, sun visor, keyless entry, premium 3-in-1 combo radio, carpeted floor mats; air conditioner, tonneau cover, sport seat, 4-way adjustable headrest, cloth door trim and leather-wrapped steering wheel cover; wheels: 16" aluminum, tires: P265/70R16, chrome wheel arch molding and 4.10 rear differential. REQUIRES JU or JZ or 4AT. NOT AVAILABLE with GI, GJ, LA, AY, AW, GU, AA, SX.*	2361	2623
GN	Cargo Net	27	42
GP	Gold Package (2WD - Base/SR5)	149	224
GP	Gold Package (4WD - Base/SR5)	169	254
GP	Gold Package (Limited 2WD)	229	344
GP	Gold Package (Limited 4WD)	249	374
GU	Upgrade Value Package #5 (4WD SR5) *Includes upgrade value package #4: Includes Upgrade Value Package #2: power windows, sun visor, keyless entry, premium 3-in-1 combo radio, carpeted floor mats; air conditioner, tonneau cover, sport seat, 4-way adjustable headrest, cloth door trim and leather-wrapped steering wheel cover; wheels: 16" aluminum, tires: P265/70R16, chrome wheel arch molding and 4.10 rear differential and rear differential lock. REQUIRES 4AT and (JU or JZ). NOT AVAILABLE with AA, LA, GI, GK, AW, SX.*	2675	2963

CODE	DESCRIPTION	INVOICE	MSRP
HP	Hood Protector *NOT AVAILABLE with SX.*	55	89
JU	Chrome Wheel Molding (SR5) *REQUIRES AW or GK or AA or GU. NOT AVAILABLE with GJ, JZ, AY, SX.*	56	70
JZ	Large Painted Overfender (SR5) *REQUIRES AW or GK or AA or GU. NOT AVAILABLE with GJ, JU, AY, C9, FN, SX.*	184	230
LA	Leather Package (SR5) *Includes 4-way adjustable headrest, leather door trim and leather-wrapped steering wheel cover. REQUIRES 4AT. NOT AVAILABLE with GJ, GK, GU, SX.*	1000	1250
P5	Compact Disc Deck (Base/SR5)	185	264
P9	6-Disc CD Changer	385	550
PG	Privacy Glass (Base) *Gray window glass on rear doors, rear quarter panels and back window.*	248	310
R1	Color-Keyed Running Boards (Base/SR5)	384	649
RB	Black Running Boards (Base/SR5)	209	345
RH	Rear Heater *Includes rear console box with dual cupholders.*	136	170
SD	Sunroof Wind Deflector (SR5/Limited)	33	55
SP	Sport Package (SR5) *Includes 13" brakes, hood scoop, tires: P265/70R16, wheels: 16" x 7" aluminum, 4.10 rear differential, sport seat, 4-way adjustable headrest, cloth door trim, leather-wrapped steering wheel cover, fog lamps, color keyed bumpers and color-keyed grille. REQUIRES 4AT. NOT AVAILABLE with AY, LA, GJ, GK, AW, JU, JZ, FN, HP, C9, AA, GU, SX.*	1300	1625
SR	Power Moonroof (SR5/Limited)	652	815
SV	Wheels: 16" x 7" Steel (Base 4WD) *Includes 13" brakes, tires: P265/70R16, large wheel arch moldings and 4.10 rear differential. REQUIRES AB. NOT AVAILABLE with AW, AY.*	480	600
SX	Sport Package and DL (SR5 4WD) *Includes sport package: 13" brakes, hood scoop, tires: P265/70R16, wheels: 16" x 7" aluminum, 4.10 rear differential, sport seat, 4-way adjustable headrest, cloth door trim, leather-wrapped steering wheel cover, fog lamps, color keyed bumpers and color-keyed grille and rear differential lock. REQUIRES 4AT. NOT AVAILABLE with HP, FN, AA, AW, JU, JZ, GK, GU, LA, C9.*	1581	1965
V3	V.I.P. RS3200 Deluxe Security System *REQUIRES GH or GI or GJ or GK or GU.*	249	399
V5	RS3200 Plus Alarm System *REQUIRES GH or GI or GJ or GK or GU.*	155	249
WL	Alloy Wheel Locks (All Except Limited 2WD) *REQUIRES AY or AW or GJ or GK or SV or AA or SX or GU.*	31	52
WS	Steel Wheel Locks (Base/SR5)	31	52

NOTE: Toyotas sold in AL, FL, GA, NC and SC may be equipped with option packages not listed in this guide. You can expect to haggle 25% off the window sticker price of these packages.

2000 LAND CRUISER

2000 Toyota Land Cruiser

What's New?

The Land Cruiser receives new standard equipment features, such as vehicle skid control and an Active TRAC electronic four-wheel-drive system with torque transfer capability. Additional new standard equipment includes illuminated entry to the remote keyless-entry system. Previously optional equipment including power tilt/slide moonroof and leather interior are now standard equipment. The optional third-row seat now includes rear air conditioning.

Review

There's no such thing as too much of a good thing, right? If this is your personal mantra, Toyota has a vehicle for you: the 2000 Land Cruiser. It's big. It's powerful. It's comfortable. It hauls people and cargo through rough terrain just as easily as it hauls them to the local gigaplex. Yes, the Land Cruiser doesn't skimp on anything. Perhaps that's why it costs close to $50,000.

Coming in only one version with a handful of options, the Toyota Land Cruiser offers one of the best on-road performances of any truck in this segment. The Cruiser's long wheelbase contributes to a supple ride that is well damped at all four corners, and its steering is nicely balanced and weighted for such a heavy vehicle. The Land Cruiser is able to tackle the hardest terrain of the day without breaking a sweat. This ability doesn't hamper the truck's level of control and ease of operation on the freeway and two-lane roads.

Power comes from a 4.7-liter V8 that creates 230 horsepower and 320 foot-pounds of torque. Based on the Lexus LS 400's engine and reworked for duty in this large truck, it provides the Land Cruiser with a definite edge in power delivery, quietness and fuel economy. Acceleration and passing maneuvers are quite easy. ABS is standard, as are front driver and passenger airbags. The new vehicle skid control system (it works by applying the brakes to spinning wheels and transferring torque to the wheels with the most traction) should further the SUV's safety.

The Land Cruiser can seat seven people when equipped with the optional third-row seat. When not in use, this row can be split and folded toward the side of the vehicle. Maximum cargo capacity is 97.5 cubic feet and maximum payload is 1,745 pounds. Other amenities include an easy step-in height, heated and power-adjustable front seats, and the typical Toyota allotment of quality ergonomics and switchgear.

Obviously, the reason that everybody and their dog don't own a Land Cruiser is the price. This year, the Land Cruiser faces renewed competition from a 300-horsepower Lincoln Navigator, a new Ford Excursion, and redesigned full-size utes from General Motors. You might want to check out these new vehicles before putting down the money required to purchase a new Land Cruiser.

Standard Equipment

LAND CRUISER (4A): 4.7L V8 DOHC SMPI 32-valve engine, requires premium unleaded fuel; 4-speed electronic OD auto transmission with lock-up; driver's selectable multi-mode transmission; full-time 4-wheel drive, permanent locking hub control and manual shift, traction control, 4.3 axle ratio; stainless steel exhaust; electronic stability, front independent double wishbone suspension with anti-roll bar, front torsion springs, front torsion bar, rigid rear axle multi-link suspension with anti-roll bar, rear coil springs; power rack-and-pinion steering with engine speed-sensing assist; 4-wheel disc brakes with 4-wheel antilock braking system; 25.4 gal. capacity fuel tank; front and rear mud flaps, skid plate(s), side impact bars; tailgate rear cargo door; front express open sliding and tilting glass sunroof with sunshade; front and rear colored bumpers with front and rear tow hooks, rear step; colored bodyside molding with colored bodyside insert; monotone paint; aero-composite halogen fully auto headlamps with daytime running lights; additional exterior lights include front fog/driving lights; driver's and passenger's power remote body-colored heated folding outside mirrors; front and rear 16" x 8" silver alloy wheels; P275/70SR16 M&S BSW front and rear tires; underbody mounted full-size alloy spare wheel; air conditioning with climate control, air filter, rear heat ducts, rear heater; premium AM/FM stereo, seek-scan, cassette 6-disc CD changer, 7 speakers, theft deterrent, and power retractable diversity antenna; cruise control; power door locks with 2 stage unlock, remote keyless entry, child safety rear door locks, remote fuel release; 3 power accessory outlets, driver's foot rest, retained accessory power; instrumentation display includes tachometer, oil pressure gauge, water temperature gauge, volt gauge, in-dash clock, exterior temp, trip odometer; warning indicators include battery, low oil level, key in ignition, low fuel, door ajar, trunk ajar; driver's and passenger's front airbags; ignition disable, security system; deep tinted windows, power front and rear windows with driver's 1-touch down, fixed 1/4 vent windows; variable intermittent front windshield wipers, sun visor strip, flip-up rear window, fixed interval rear wiper, rear window defroster; seating capacity of 5, heated-cushion front captain's seats, adjustable headrests, center armrest with storage, driver's seat includes 6-way power seat, power 2-way lumbar support, passenger's seat includes 6-way power seat; 60-40 folding rear split-bench seat with adjustable headrests, center armrest; front and rear height adjustable seatbelts with front pretensioners; leather seats, leatherette door trim insert, full cloth headliner, full carpet floor covering, leather-wrapped gear shift knob; interior lights include dome light, front and rear reading lights, 4 door curb lights; leather-wrapped steering wheel with tilt adjustment; dual illuminated vanity mirrors, dual auxiliary visors; day/night rearview mirror; full floor console, mini overhead console with storage, locking glove box with light, front and rear cupholders, 2 seat back storage pockets, driver's and passenger's door bins, rear door bins; carpeted cargo floor, carpeted trunk lid, cargo light; chrome grille, black side window moldings, black front windshield molding, black rear window molding and body-colored door handles.

Base Prices

CODE	DESCRIPTION	INVOICE	MSRP
6156	Land Cruiser (4A)	43713	50828
Destination Charge:		480	480

Accessories

CODE	DESCRIPTION	INVOICE	MSRP
BG	Third Rear Seat *Includes foldaway/removable, leather trimmed 50/50 split rear jump seats with outboard headrests, 3 rear cupholders, assist grips, child protector rear hatch lock, power rear quarter windows and rear climate control.*	1854	2265
BN	Black Pearl Emblems	173	458

CODE	DESCRIPTION	INVOICE	MSRP
C7	Convenience Package *Includes rear wind deflector, towing receiver hitch, roof rack and color-keyed running boards.*	1109	1771
CF	Carpet/Cargo Mat Set (5-Piece set)	109	179
DD	Rear Wind Deflector	155	259
DH	Towing Receiver Hitch	255	365
DR	Roof Rack	274	449
DU	Burlwood Wood Dash	343	549
GN	Cargo Net	27	42
GP	Gold Package	229	599
HP	Hood Protector	59	96
RB	Color-Keyed Running Boards	496	799
SD	Sunroof Wind Deflector	47	78
WI	Spare Tire Lock	33	55
WL	Alloy Wheel Locks	31	52

NOTE: Toyotas sold in AL, FL, GA, NC and SC may be equipped with option packages not listed in this guide. You can expect to haggle 25% off the window sticker price of these packages.

2000 RAV4

2000 Toyota RAV4

What's New?

The RAV4 SUV remains largely unchanged for 2000. RAV4 L models will continue to feature a monochrome paint scheme, while base RAV4 models equipped with extra value packages will come with painted bodyside cladding in a contrasting silver color. All RAV4 models feature a new cupholder design. The two-door RAV4 convertible is no longer available.

Review

The mini-SUV business continues to grow with more manufacturers jumping into the fray every year. Largely comprised of car-based AWD vehicles, the territory of this market has been staked out by Chevrolet, Honda, Isuzu, Kia, Nissan, Subaru, and Suzuki. Toyota, too, recognized this potential boom early on and jumped into the action with the introduction of the '96 RAV4.

A 2.0-liter, 127-horsepower engine hooked to either a five-speed manual or four-speed automatic transmission powers the front or all four wheels of the different RAV4 models. All-wheel-drive models use powertrain components from the long-defunct Celica All-Trac. Four-wheel antilock brakes are optional on all RAV4s. Minimum ground clearance is 7.5 inches on the four-door models.

The RAV4 is an adequate around-town driver, handling more like the car from which its platform is derived than a traditional SUV. Power is on the low side, however. It offers some initial pep when pulling away from stoplights, but any serious attempt at acceleration results in nothing more than noise and vibration. The engine gets particularly obnoxious above 4,500 rpm where underhood clatter is enough to stifle conversation between passengers. This would be more acceptable if accompanied by even a modest form of forward thrust. Unfortunately, it's not.

The interior is not a bad place to spend time. The ventilation controls are easy to understand, the stereo outstanding, and the individual bucket seats are quite comfortable. Even with the rear seat up, cargo space is a healthy 26.8 cubic feet. Fold down the second seat and that number jumps to 57.9 "moving-into-my-first-dorm-room" cubic feet. Adults placed in back will most likely whine about a lack of legroom, however.

While the RAV4 was never a hot rod, its lack of power when first introduced was forgivable in a world of Sidekicks and used Amigos. But with Honda bumping the CR-V to 145 horsepower and Suzuki offering a V6 Grand Vitara, the RAV4 is rapidly becoming an "also ran" in this burgeoning market. Throw in upcoming V6 competitors from Mazda and Ford, and Toyota could find themselves in a rare position for this company: at the bottom of the heap.

Standard Equipment

FWD (5M): 2.0L I4 DOHC SMPI 16-valve engine; 5-speed OD manual transmission; 325-amp battery; 80-amp alternator; front-wheel drive, 4.56 axle ratio; stainless steel exhaust; front independent strut suspension with anti-roll bar, front coil springs, rear independent double wishbone suspension with rear coil springs; power rack-and-pinion steering; front disc/rear drum brakes; 15.3 gal. capacity fuel tank; side impact bars; conventional rear cargo door; front and rear black bumpers with front tow hooks; black bodyside cladding; monotone paint; aero-composite halogen headlamps; driver's and passenger's manual black folding outside mirrors; front and rear 16" x 6" silver styled steel wheels; P215/70SR16 M&S BSW front and rear tires; outside rear mounted full-size steel spare wheel; radio prep, 4 speakers; child safety rear door locks, remote fuel release; 2 power accessory outlets, driver's foot rest, smokers' package; instrumentation display includes tachometer, water temperature gauge, in-dash clock, trip odometer; warning indicators include oil pressure, battery, lights on, key in ignition, low fuel, door ajar; driver's and passenger's front airbags; tinted windows, manual front and rear windows, fixed 1/4 vent windows; fixed interval front windshield wipers, fixed interval rear wiper, rear window defroster; seating capacity of 5, front bucket seats, adjustable headrests, driver's seat includes 4-way direction control, passenger's seat includes 4-way direction control; 50-50 folding rear bench seat with reclining adjustable headrests; front height adjustable seatbelts with front pretensioners; cloth seats, cloth door trim insert, full cloth headliner, full carpet floor covering, plastic/rubber gear shift knob; interior lights include dome light, front reading lights; steering wheel with tilt adjustment; passenger's side vanity mirror; day/night rearview mirror; full floor console, locking glove box, front cupholder, instrument panel bin, 2 seat back storage pockets, driver's and passenger's door bins; carpeted cargo floor, plastic trunk lid, cargo light; black grille, black side window moldings, black front windshield molding, black rear window molding and black door handles.

AWD (5M) (in addition to or instead of FWD (5M) equipment): Full-time 4-wheel drive, auto locking hub control and manual shift, 4.93 axle ratio and skid plate(s).

CODE	DESCRIPTION	INVOICE	MSRP
	Base Prices		
4417	2WD (5M)	15193	16668
4427	AWD (5M)	16199	18078
Destination Charge:		480	480
	Accessories		
—	Transmission: 4-Speed Automatic (2WD) *Includes 3.18 axle ratio.*	956	1050
—	Transmission: 4-Speed Automatic (AWD) *Includes 4.40 axle ratio.*	940	1050
1B	Sport Side Bars	165	275
5A	Cargo Cover	33	55
AB	4-Wheel Antilock Brakes *Includes daytime running lights.*	539	630
AK	Cladding Graphic	49	82
AW	Wheels: Aluminum *Includes P215/70R16 M/S tires, aluminum wheel cap and spare steel wheel. NOT AVAILABLE with VR, VL, SS.*	392	490
C1	Cargo Mat	30	48
C7	Convenience Package (2WD) *Includes removable rear door storage bags, center console box and cargo mat. NOT AVAILABLE with GN.*	169	241
C7	Convenience Package (AWD) *Includes removable rear door storage bags, center console box and cargo mat. NOT AVAILABLE with GN.*	169	241
CF	Carpet Floor Mats *NOT AVAILABLE with VL, VP, VR.*	43	68
DD	Rear Wind Deflector	69	115
DR	Removable Roof Rack	95	155
FG	Rear Step Bumper *Includes tow hitch and mudguards (rears only).*	171	285
GN	Cargo Net *NOT AVAILABLE with N9, C7.*	27	42
LD	Limited Slip Differential (AWD)	322	390
MF	Mudguards (4 Piece Set)	61	85
MI	Mudguards (Fronts Only) *REQUIRES FG or Q4.*	26	38
MJ	Mudguards (Rears Only) *REQUIRES 1B.*	36	52
N9	Removable Rear Door Storage Bags *NOT AVAILABLE with GN.*	83	139
P5	Compact Disc Deck *REQUIRES VP.*	235	335
P6	6-Disc In-Dash CD Changer	279	399
P9	6-Disc CD Changer	385	550
PG	Privacy Glass	248	310

CODE	DESCRIPTION	INVOICE	MSRP
Q4	Active Package *Includes cladding graphic, removeable roof rack, rear step bumper, tow hitch and mudguards (rears only).*	315	450
SD	Sunroof Wind Deflector	33	55
SK	Center Console Box	56	95
SR	Power Sunroof	652	815
SS	Wheels: Alloy *NOT AVAILABLE with AW, VR, VL.*	600	795
V3	V.I.P. RS3000 Deluxe Security System *REQUIRES VL or VP or VR.*	249	399
VL	Value Package #3 with Special Edition and Leather *Includes vinyl headrests, air conditioner, CD combo radio, cruise control, upgrade package: power windows, power door locks, power color-keyed mirrors; color-keyed door handles, cladding and bumpers, privacy glass, wheels: bradley alloy, steel spare wheel, leather seats and carpet floor mats. NOT AVAILABLE with VP, VR, AW, SS.*	2726	3029
VP	Value Package #1 *Includes cloth front and rear headrests, painted silver bumper and cladding, air conditioner, deluxe cassette radio, cruise control, upgrade package: power windows, power door locks, power mirrors and carpet floor mats. NOT AVAILABLE with VR, VL.*	1392	1547
VR	Value Package #2 with EV Special Edition *Includes cloth front and rear headrests, air conditioner, CD combo radio, cruise control, upgrade package: power windows, power door locks, power color-keyed mirrors; color-keyed door handles, cladding and bumpers, privacy glass, wheels: bradley alloy, steel spare wheel and carpet floor mats. NOT AVAILABLE with VP, VL, AW, SS.*	2159	2399
WL	Alloy Wheel Locks	31	52
WS	Steel Wheel Locks	31	52
WZ	Alloy Wheel Locks *REQUIRES SS.*	31	52

NOTE: Toyotas sold in AL, FL, GA, NC and SC may be equipped with option packages not listed in this guide. You can expect to haggle 25% off the window sticker price of these packages.

2000 SIENNA

What's New?

New for Sienna are two exterior colors and standard and optional audio enhancements. All grades feature a standard AM/FM/cassette/CD audio system. XLE models will offer an optional in-dash six-disc changer.

Review

Now in its third model year, the Toyota Sienna is one of the top competitors in the minivan market. With the Sienna, Toyota has placed an emphasis on safety, comfort, quality, and performance.

There are three models: the base CE, the midlevel LE, and the top-level XLE. The CE can be ordered with four or five doors. The LE and XLE come standard with five doors. Under the hood are a standard 3.0-liter V6 and a four-speed automatic transmission. This same powertrain setup can also be found in the Toyota Camry, as the Sienna is built on a stretched and modified Camry platform. In the Sienna, the engine produces 194 horsepower and 209 foot-pounds of torque.

This rigid and lightweight unitized body does exceptionally well in government crash testing. Front driver and passenger airbags are standard, though no side airbags are offered. Other safety features include ABS, front seatbelts with pre-tensioners and force limiters, front height-adjustable seatbelt anchors, and daytime running lights. A low tire-pressure warning system is also a standard feature. The ABS wheel-speed sensors measure each wheel's rotational speed relative to the other wheels, allowing the stem to detect low pneumatic pressure in the tires.

The Sienna's driving experience is similar to the Camry's in that it's pleasantly non-confrontational. Steering is sure if not quite nimble. The suspension does a good job of soaking up road imperfections, and wind noise is kept to a minimum. Acceleration from the V6 is acceptable for almost all situations.

Sienna was designed to offer optimum interior roominess in a compact, easy-to-maneuver package. The interior has a definite Camry feel to it. Removable modular seating allows for custom configurations to accommodate a variety of cargo requirements. Second-row bench seats or captain's chairs and third-row seats can be folded or removed to accommodate bulkier cargo items. Third-row seats also add a 50/50 split-folding and tumble feature for additional cargo space. A power-operated passenger-side sliding door is optional.

Overall, Toyota does not make the biggest minivan, but it does make a convenient alternative to either Chrysler-designed family-haulers or the Honda Odyssey. Need to trade in your old Camry to make room for another member of the family? Toyota has a built-in answer to your dilemma. And it's hoping you see it that way, too.

2000 Toyota Sienna

Standard Equipment

CE 4-DOOR (4A): 3.0L V6 DOHC SMPI 24-valve engine; 4-speed electronic OD auto transmission with lock-up; 582-amp HD battery with run down protection; 100-amp HD alternator; front-wheel drive; stainless steel exhaust; front independent strut suspension with anti-roll bar, front coil springs, rear semi-independent torsion suspension with rear coil springs; power rack-and-pinion steering with engine speed-sensing assist; front disc/rear drum brakes with 4-wheel antilock braking system; 20.9 gal. capacity fuel tank; side impact bars; 3 doors with sliding right rear passenger's door, liftback rear cargo door; front and rear black bumpers; black bodyside cladding; monotone paint; aero-composite halogen fully auto headlamps with daytime running lights; driver's and passenger's manual black folding outside mirrors; front and rear 15" x 6.5" steel wheels; P205/70SR15 A/S BSW front and rear tires; inside under cargo mounted compact steel spare wheel; air conditioning, rear heat ducts, rear heater; AM/FM stereo, seek-scan, cassette, 4 speakers, and fixed antenna, radio steering wheel controls; child safety rear door locks, remote hatch/trunk release, remote fuel release; 2 power accessory outlets, driver's foot rest; instrumentation display includes water temperature gauge, in-dash clock, trip odometer; warning indicators include oil pressure, battery, key in ignition, low fuel, low washer fluid, door ajar; driver's and passenger's front airbags; tinted windows, manual front and rear windows, manual 1/4 vent windows; variable intermittent front windshield wipers, fixed interval rear wiper; seating capacity of 7, front bucket seats, adjustable headrests, driver's and passenger's armrests, driver's seat includes 6-way direction control, passenger's seat includes 4-way direction control; removable 2nd row bench seat with reclining adjustable headrests; removable 3rd row 50-50 folding split-bench seat with reclining adjustable headrest; front height adjustable seatbelts with front pretensioners; cloth seats, cloth door trim insert, full cloth headliner, full carpet floor covering; interior lights include dome light, rear reading lights; steering wheel with tilt adjustment; vanity mirrors; day/night rearview mirror; mini overhead console with storage, locking glove box with light, front and rear cupholders, instrument panel bin, 1 seat back storage pocket, driver's and passenger's door bins, front underseat tray; carpeted cargo floor, plastic trunk lid, cargo light; body-colored grille, black side window moldings, black front windshield molding, black rear window molding and body-colored door handles.

CE 5-DOOR (4A) (in addition to or instead of CE 4-DOOR (4A) equipment): Rear air conditioning with separate controls and 4 doors with sliding right and left rear passenger's door.

LE 5-DOOR (4A) (in addition to or instead of CE 5-DOOR (4A) equipment): Driver's and passenger's power remote black folding outside mirrors; cruise control; retained accessory power; instrumentation display includes tachometer; deep tinted windows, power front and rear windows with driver's 1-touch down, power 1/4 vent windows; rear window defroster; premium cloth seats; interior lights include front and rear reading lights; dual illuminated vanity mirrors and 2 seat back storage pockets.

XLE 5-DOOR (4A) (in addition to or instead of LE 5-DOOR (4A) equipment): Roof rack; front and rear colored bumpers; colored bodyside cladding; driver's and passenger's power remote black heated folding outside mirrors; P215/65HR15 A/S BSW front and rear tires; inside under cargo mounted full-size steel spare wheel; premium AM/FM stereo, seek-scan, cassette, single CD, 6 speakers, and fixed diversity antenna; power door locks with 2 stage unlock, remote keyless entry; ignition disable, panic alarm, security system; front captain's seats, adjustable headrests, driver's and passenger's armrests, carpeted floor mats; dual auxiliary visors and carpeted trunk lid.

Base Prices

5322	CE 4-Door (4A)	19457	21968
5324	CE 5-Door (4A)	20247	22858
5334	LE (4A)	21797	24898
5344	XLE (4A)	23579	26934
Destination Charge:		480	480

Accessories

AJ	Power Sliding Door (XLE) *Right side only.*	316	395
AW	Wheels: Aluminum (LE) *Includes tires: P215/65R15 and matching spare.*	380	475

CODE	DESCRIPTION	INVOICE	MSRP
BN	Black Pearl Emblems *NOT AVAILABLE with GP.*	79	149
CF	Carpet/Cargo Mat Set (CE/LE)	96	161
DF	Rear Window Defogger (CE) *Includes timer.*	164	205
DH	Towing Receiver Hitch	200	290
DU	Burlwood Dash	236	459
EF	Rear Bumper Protector	33	50
GN	Cargo Net	27	42
GP	Gold Package *NOT AVAILABLE with BN.*	89	164
HE	XLE Upgrade Package #2 (XLE) *Includes power sliding door and power tilt and slide moon roof. NOT AVAILABLE with LL, XE.*	1020	1275
HF	XLE Upgrade Package #1 (XLE) *Includes leather seat trim, second row captain's seats, leather-wrapped steering wheel, 6-way power driver's seat and premium 3-in-1 combo radio with CD changer and 6 speakers. NOT AVAILABLE with LL, XE.*	1278	1610
HJ	Homelink Transmitter	136	199
HV	CE Extra Value Package (CE 4-Door) *Includes dual air conditioning, rear window defogger, power windows, power door locks, heated power mirrors, cruise control, swing-out rear quarter vent windows, privacy glass, full size spare tire and floor and cargo carpeted mats. NOT AVAILABLE with TO.*	1247	1386
HV	CE Extra Value Package (CE 5-Door) *Includes rear window defogger, power windows, power door locks, heated power mirrors, cruise control, swing-out rear quarter vent windows, full size spare tire, privacy glass and floor and cargo carpeted mats.*	847	941
J1	Sienna Sport Package (CE/LE) *Includes alloy wheels, running boards and rear spoiler.*	949	1589
J2	Sienna Convenience Package (CE/LE) *Includes cargo net, center console, rear bumper protector and drop hitch.*	259	399
KE	Keyless Entry (CE) *REQUIRES HV.*	176	220
LE	Leather Seat Trim (XLE) *REQUIRES HF or LL.*	NC	NC
LL	XLE Upgrade Package #4 (XLE) *Includes leather seat trim, second row captain's seat, leather-wrapped steering wheel, 6-way power's driver seat, power tilt and slide moon roof, power sliding door and premium 3-in-1 combo radio with CD changer and 6 speakers. NOT AVAILABLE with HE, HF, XE.*	2298	2885
P5	CD Deck (CE/LE) *NOT AVAILABLE with P6.*	235	335
P6	6-Disc In-Dash CD Changer (CE/LE) *NOT AVAILABLE with P5.*	400	575
PN	Anti-Theft Device (LE) *Includes engine imobilizer. REQUIRES UN.*	256	320

CODE	DESCRIPTION	INVOICE	MSRP
RB	Dark Gray Molded Running Boards (CE/LE)	290	480
RB	Painted Running Boards (XLE)	365	595
RF	Rear Spoiler	170	284
SD	Sunroof Wind Deflector (XLE)	33	55
SK	Center Console Box	80	135
SS	Alloy Wheels (CE 5-Door) *NOT AVAILABLE with WS.*	440	592
SS	Alloy Wheels (LE)	440	592
SS	Alloy Wheels (CE 4-Door) *NOT AVAILABLE with WS.*	440	592
TF	Full Size Spare Tire (CE)	68	85
TO	Towing Package (All Except CE 4-Door) *Includes trailering weight (3500 lb).*	128	160
TO	Towing Package (CE 4-Door) *Includes trailering weight (3500 lb) and dual air conditioning. NOT AVAILABLE with HV.*	504	630
UN	LE Extra Value Package (LE) *Includes keyless entry system, roof rack, heated power mirrors, cloth captain's chairs, second row captain seat, floor and cargo carpeted mats.*	271	301
UP	LE Upgrade Package #1 (LE) *Includes power swing privacy glass, premium 3-in-1 combo radio and power sliding door. REQUIRES UN. NOT AVAILABLE with UR.*	504	645
UR	LE Upgrade Package #2 (LE) *Includes power swing privacy glass, premium 3-in-1 combo radio, power sliding door, wheels: aluminum, tires: P215/65R15 and matching spare. REQUIRES UN. NOT AVAILABLE with UP.*	884	1120
V3	V.I.P. RS3000 Deluxe Security System (CE/LE)	249	399
V5	V.I.P. RS3200 Plus Security System (CE/LE) *REQUIRES KE (CE) or UN (LE).*	155	249
WL	Alloy Wheel Locks (LE/XLE) *REQUIRES AW or XL or UR.*	31	52
WL	Alloy Wheel Locks (LE/XLE) *REQUIRES AW. NOT AVAILABLE with WS.*	31	52
WS	Steel Wheel Locks (CE/LE) *NOT AVAILABLE with WZ, SS, WL.*	31	52
WZ	Alloy Wheel Locks (CE) *REQUIRES SS. NOT AVAILABLE with WS.*	31	52
WZ	Alloy Wheel Locks (CE/LE) *REQUIRES SS.*	31	52
XE	XLE Upgrade Package #3 (XLE) *Includes leather seat trim, second row captain's seat, leather-wrapped steering wheel, 6-way power's driver seat, power sliding door and power tilt and slide moon roof. NOT AVAILABLE with HE, HF, LL.*	2148	2685

NOTE: Toyotas sold in AL, FL, GA, NC and SC may be equipped with option packages not listed in this guide. You can expect to haggle 25% off the window sticker price of these packages.

2000 TACOMA

2000 Toyota Tacoma

What's New?

Tacomas with four-cylinder engines and four-wheel drive achieve improved performance from an enhanced gear ratio. Base-grade Tacomas feature a new interior fabric and receive a new exterior rearview mirror design. Daytime running lights are now included with the antilock brake package. There are also two new colors and a new full-color-keyed option package.

Review

Tacoma. It's supposed to suggest the rugged outdoors, as well as strength and adventure. To this end, any of three potent engines go under the hood. Toyota aimed for aggressive styling, inside and out, and Tacomas sport an excellent selection of interior fittings. Regular- and extended-cab bodies are available, with either two- or four-wheel drive..

Two-wheel-drive Tacomas get a 2.4-liter four-cylinder base engine, rated at 142 horsepower and 160 foot-pounds of torque. Tacoma 4x4s earn a 2.7-liter four with 150 horsepower and 177 foot-pounds of torque. If those won't suffice, however, consider the V6 option: a DOHC, 24-valve unit that whips out 190 horses and 220 foot-pounds of torque. With V6 power (This is the same V6 that can be found in the larger Toyota Tundra pickup), the Tacoma can tow up to 5,000 pounds and soundly trounce most factory sport trucks in the stoplight drag race.

All Tacomas have front coil springs instead of the torsion bars, but 4x4s feature longer suspension travel to improve ride/handling qualities. Manual-shift trucks feature reverse-gear synchronization to reduce gear noise when shifting into reverse. Four-wheel antilock braking is optional on all Tacomas, and all pickups contain dual airbags with a shut-off switch for the passenger's side. In top-of-the-line Limited pickups, a one-touch 4-Hi switch is available for easy, pushbutton engagement of four-wheel drive.

The PreRunner model is set to attract truck buyers who desire, but cannot afford, a 4WD truck, 4WD truck owners who don't use their 4WD as often as they expected, and 2WD truck buyers who take their vehicle off-road. Historically, a "pre-runner" is a truck that pre-runs an off-road racecourse. Toyota's new PreRunner has benefited from considerable suspension tuning and development work with Toyota Motorsports desert racing truck program to produce a 2WD vehicle with 4WD capabilities.

Toyota hopes to attract buyers with the style and image of its Tacoma as well as a lower price tag. We like the Tacoma, but question the value it represents. Most of these Toyota trucks don't come cheap. Guess that's the price you pay for the peace of mind a Toyota provides.

Standard Equipment

BASE 2WD REGULAR CAB (5M): 2.4L I4 DOHC MPI 16-valve engine; 5-speed OD manual transmission; 356-amp HD battery; 70-amp alternator; rear-wheel drive, 3.91 axle ratio; stainless steel exhaust; front independent double wishbone suspension with anti-roll bar, front coil springs, rigid rear axle suspension with rear leaf springs; manual rack-and-pinion steering; front disc/rear drum brakes; 15.1 gal. capacity fuel tank; side impact bars; front black bumper; monotone paint; aero-composite halogen headlamps; driver's and passenger's manual black folding outside mirrors; front and rear 14" x 5" steel wheels; P195/75SR14 A/S BSW front and rear tires; underbody mounted full-size steel spare wheel; 3 power accessory outlets, driver's foot rest; instrumentation display includes water temperature gauge; warning indicators include oil pressure, battery, lights on, key in ignition, low washer fluid; driver's front airbag, passenger's cancelable front airbag; tinted windows; sun visor strip; seating capacity of 3, bench front seat, fixed headrests, driver's seat includes 2-way direction control, passenger's seat includes 2-way direction control; front height adjustable seatbelts; cloth seats, cloth door trim insert, full vinyl headliner, full carpet floor covering; interior lights include dome light; day/night rearview mirror; glove box, front cupholder, instrument panel bin, driver's and passenger's door bins; black grille, black side window moldings, black front windshield molding, black rear window molding and black door handles.

PRERUNNER 2WD REGULAR CAB (4A) (in addition to or instead of BASE 2WD REGULAR CAB (4A) equipment): 4-speed electronic OD auto transmission with lock-up; 582-amp HD battery; power rack-and-pinion steering; 18 gal. capacity fuel tank; front and rear mud flaps, skid plate(s); front and rear black bumpers with rear step; front and rear 15" x 6" styled steel wheels; P225/75SR15 M&S BSW front and rear tires.

BASE 2WD XTRACAB (5M) (in addition to or instead of PRERUNNER 2WD REGULAR CAB (5M) equipment): 5-speed OD manual transmission; 356-amp HD battery; manual rack-and-pinion steering; 15.1 gal. capacity fuel tank; front and rear 14" x 6" steel wheels; P215/70SR14 A/S BSW front and rear tires; vented rear windows; seating capacity of 5, 60-40 split-bench front seat, adjustable headrests, driver's seat includes 4-way direction control, passenger's seat includes 4-way direction control, easy entry; 50-50 folding rear jump seat; cabback insulator; rear cupholders, interior concealed storage andcarpeted cargo floor.

PRERUNNER 2WD XTRACAB (4A) (in addition to or instead of BASE 2WD XTRACAB (5A) equipment): 2.7L I4 DOHC MPI 16-valve engine; 4-speed electronic OD auto transmission with lock-up; 3.91 axle ratio; power rack-and-pinion steering, 18 gal. capacity fuel tank; front and rear 15" x 6" silver styled steel wheels; P225/75SR15 M&S BSW front and rear tires; air conditioning and sliding rear window.

BASE V6 2WD XTRACAB (5M) (in addition to or instead of BASE 2WD XTRACAB (5M) equipment): 3.4L V6 DOHC SMPI 24-valve engine and power rack-and-pinion steering.

PRERUNNER V6 2WD XTRACAB (4A) (in addition to or instead of PRERUNNER 2WD XTRACAB (4A) equipment): 3.4L V6 DOHC SMPI 24-valve engine and HD ride suspension.

BASE 4WD REGULAR CAB (5M) (in addition to or instead of BASE 2WD REGULAR CAB (5M) equipment): 2.7L I4 DOHC MPI 16-valve engine; 582-amp HD battery; part-time 4-wheel drive, manual locking hub control and manual shift, 3.42 axle ratio; front and rear mud flaps, skid plate(s), front and rear black bumpers with front tow hooks, rear step; front and rear 15" x 6" silver styled steel wheels and P225/75SR15 M&S BSW front and rear tires.

CODE	DESCRIPTION	INVOICE	MSRP

BASE 4WD XTRACAB (5M) (in addition to or instead of PRERUNNER 2WD XTRACAB (4A) equipment): 5-speed OD manual transmission; part-time 4-wheel drive, manual locking hub control and manual shift; front and rear black bumpers with front tow hooks and rear step.

BASE V6 4WD XTRACAB (5M) (in addition to or instead of BASE 4WD XTRACAB (5M) equipment): 3.4L V6 DOHC SMPI 24-valve engine; engine oil cooler.

LIMITED V6 4WD XTRACAB (5M) (in addition to or instead of BASE V6 4WD XTRACAB (5M) equipment): Front and rear chrome bumpers; body-colored fender flares; driver's and passenger's manual chrome folding outside mirrors; front and rear 15" x 7" silver alloy wheels; P265/75SR15 M&S BSW front and rear tires; AM/FM stereo, seek-scan, cassette, single CD, 4 speakers, and fixed antenna; cruise control; instrumentation display includes tachometer, water temperature gauge, in-dash clock, trip odometer; warning indicators include low fuel; power windows with driver's 1-touch down; variable intermittent front windshield wipers; seating capacity of 4, front sports, seats adjustable headrests, center armrest with storage, driver's seat includes 6-way direction control, lumbar support; premium cloth seats; interior lights include front reading lights; steering wheel with tilt adjustment; passenger's side vanity mirror; partial floor console; chrome grille and chrome door handles.

Base Prices

CODE	DESCRIPTION	INVOICE	MSRP
7103	Base 2WD Regular Cab (5M)	10417	11428
7132	PreRunner 2WD Regular Cab (4A)	12196	13518
7113	Base 2WD Xtracab (5M)	12597	13978
7153	Base V6 2WD Xtracab (5M)	13805	15318
7503	Base 4WD Regular Cab (5M)	14137	15868
7162	PreRunner 2WD Xtracab (4A)	15282	16938
7513	Base 4WD Xtracab (5M)	15812	17748
7164	PreRunner V6 2WD Xtracab (4A)	16121	17868
7553	Base V6 4WD Xtracab (5M)	16782	18838
7557	Limited V6 4WD Xtracab (5M)	21630	24278
Destination Charge:		480	480

Accessories

CODE	DESCRIPTION	INVOICE	MSRP
—	Transmission: Electronic 4-Speed Automatic (Base 2WD X-Cab)	649	720
—	Transmission: Electronic 4-Speed Automatic (Base 2WD Reg Cab)	656	720
—	Transmission: Electronic 4-Speed Automatic (Base 4WD 4-Cyl) *NOT AVAILABLE with DL, OF.*	802	900
—	Transmission: Electronic 4-Speed Automatic (Base V6 2WD X-Cab)	810	900
—	Transmission: Electronic 4-Speed Automatic (Base V6 4WD X-Cab)	802	900
—	Transmission: Electronic 4-Speed Automatic (Limited)	801	900
AA	Aluminum Wheels (PreRunner X-Cab/Base 4WD) *Includes wheel arch moldings. NOT AVAILABLE with OF, WS, ST, FT, FV, FX, FY, AL.*	756	945
AB	4-Wheel Antilock Braking System *Includes daytime running lights.*	539	630
AC	Air Conditioning (2WD/4WD Reg Cab) *NOT AVAILABLE with PY, QY, PV, IX, LX.*	788	985
AC	Air Conditioning (4WD X-Cab) *NOT AVAILABLE with LX, IX.*	788	985
AC	Air Conditioning (Base 2WD/PreRunner Reg Cab)	788	985

CODE	DESCRIPTION	INVOICE	MSRP
AL	Wheels: 15" x 7" Aluminum (Base 4WD X-Cab) *Includes P265/75R15 tires. NOT AVAILABLE with OF, ST.*	324	405
AW	Wheels: 14" x 6" Aluminum (Base 2WD X-Cab) *Includes P215/70R14 tires.*	296	370
AW	Wheels: 14" x 6" Aluminum (Base 2WD Reg Cab) *Includes P215/70R14 tires. NOT AVAILABLE with TU.*	440	550
BL	Over Rail Bedliner *NOT AVAILABLE with LU, LB, FV, FY.*	160	299
BM	Body Side Molding	53	85
BT	Tonneau Cover *NOT AVAILABLE with LB.*	200	300
BU	Bucket Seats (Base 2WD Reg Cab) *Includes cloth headrests, center console box and cloth seat trim.*	244	305
BU	Bucket Seats (Base X-Cab) *Includes cloth headrest, cloth seat trim and center console box.*	52	65
BU	Bucket Seats (PreRunner X-Cab) *Includes cloth headrest and center console box.*	60	75
CF	Carpet Floor Mats (4 Piece Set) (X-Cab)	41	69
CH	Chrome Package (Base 4WD X-Cab) *Includes chrome plated rear bumper, chrome front bumper, chrome grille and chrome door handles. NOT AVAILABLE with KX, LX, IX, KP.*	200	250
CH	Chrome Plated Package (2WD X-Cab) *Includes chrome front bumper, chrome grille and chrome door handles. NOT AVAILABLE with KP, KX, PV, LX, IX, VX, VZ.*	200	250
CK	All Weather Guard Package (Reg Cab)	63	75
CL	Cruise Control (All Except Limited)	200	250
CQ	Convenience Package (All Except Limited) *Includes tachometer, digital clock, lighting package and LCD twin tripmeter. NOT AVAILABLE with TA, TW, OF.*	365	440
CT	Carpet Floor Mats (2-Piece Set) (Reg Cab)	31	51
DH	Towing Receiver Hitch	200	285
DL	Differential Locks (4WD Reg Cab) *REQUIRES TA and CQ.*	281	340
DL	Rear Differential Lock (V6 PreRunner/4WD X-Cab) *REQUIRES CQ or TA or FD. NOT AVAILABLE with OF, FX, FY.*	281	340
DQ	Digital Clock (All Except Limited) *Includes lighting package.*	80	100
DQ	Digital Clock (PPO) (All Except Limited)	50	82
DZ	Radio: Deluxe 3-In-1 Combo (X-Cab Except Limited) *Includes AM/FM stereo, cassette, CD, 4 speakers and spiral spring back antenna. NOT AVAILABLE with EX, IX, LX, VX, VZ, P5.*	473	630
EB	Deluxe Painted Rear Bumper (Reg Cab)	128	215
EC	Chrome Plated Rear Bumper (Reg Cab) *NOT AVAILABLE with EB.*	173	290
EU	Radio: AM/FM Stereo with Cassette (Reg Cab) *Includes 2 speakers and spiral spring back antenna. NOT AVAILABLE with RA, PY, QY, PV, P5.*	323	430

CODE	DESCRIPTION	INVOICE	MSRP
EX	**Radio: AM/FM Stereo with Deluxe Cassette (2WD X-Cab Except Limited)** *Includes 4 speakers and spiral spring back antenna. NOT AVAILABLE with DZ, IX, LX, VX, VZ.*	398	530
EX	**Radio: AM/FM Stereo with Deluxe Cassette (4WD X-Cab)** *Includes 4 speakers and spiral spring back antenna. NOT AVAILABLE with DZ, LX, IX.*	398	530
FB	**High 4 Selector Switch (Limited)**	111	135
FD	**4-Wheel Demand (Base 4WD)**	198	240
FJ	**Cloth Seat Trim (X-Cab Except Limited)** *REQUIRES BU.*	NC	NC
FT	**Preferred Equipment Package #1 (PreRunner V6)** *Includes wheels: 7" x 15" styled steel, tires: P265/75R15 ST, wheel arch moldings and over rail bedliner. NOT AVAILABLE with LU, FV, FX, FY, OF, LB, ST.*	576	770
FV	**Preferred Equipment Package #2 (PreRunner V6)** *Includes wheels: 7" x 15" styled steel, tires: P265/75R15 ST, wheel arch moldings and under rail bedliner. NOT AVAILABLE with BL, FT, FX, FY, OF, LB, ST.*	576	770
FX	**Preferred Equipment Package #3 (PreRunner V6)** *Includes TRD offroad package: off-road suspension, wheel arch molding with black overfender, wheels: 15" aluminum, rear differential lock, tachometer and badging and over rail bedliner. NOT AVAILABLE with FT, FV, FY, LU, OF, LB, KX, ST, DL.*	1481	1890
FY	**Preferred Equipment Package #4 (PreRunner V6)** *Includes TRD offroad package: off-road suspension, wheel arch molding with black overfender, wheels: 15" aluminum, rear differential lock, tachometer and badging and under rail bedliner. NOT AVAILABLE with FT, FV, FX, BL, OF, LB, KX, ST, DL.*	1481	1890
GN	**Cargo Net**	27	42
HP	**Hood Protector**	55	89
IX	**SR5 Package with KP (4WD X-Cab Except Limited)** *Includes SR5 badging, sliding rear window, gray privacy glass, sunvisor with mirror and pocket, deluxe 3-in-1 combo radio and air conditioning. REQUIRES PX. NOT AVAILABLE with EX, DZ, AC, LX, WR, KP, KX, P4.*	1111	1235
IX	**SR5 Package with KP (Base 4-Cyl 2WD X-Cab)** *Includes SR5 badging, power steering, sliding rear window, gray privacy glass, sunvisor with mirror and pocket, deluxe 3-in-1 combo radio and air conditioner. REQUIRES PX. NOT AVAILABLE with LX, EX, DZ, AC, PS, WR, KP, KX, P4.*	1575	1750
IX	**SR5 Package with KP (Base V6 2WD X-Cab)** *Includes SR5 badging, sliding rear window, gray privacy glass, sunvisor with mirror and pocket, deluxe 3-in-1 combo radio and air conditioner. REQUIRES PX. NOT AVAILABLE with LX, EX, DZ, AC, WR, KX, KP, P4.*	1381	1535
KP	**Color Keyed Package (All Except Base 2WD Reg Cab)** *Includes color keyed valance panel, color-keyed front bumper and color keyed grille. REQUIRES PX. NOT AVAILABLE with KX, PV, LX, IX, VX, VZ.*	140	175
KP	**Color Keyed Package (Base 2WD Reg Cab)** *Includes color keyed valance panel, color-keyed front bumper, color keyed grille and chrome plated rear bumper. REQUIRES PX. NOT AVAILABLE with PY, KX, QY.*	260	325

CODE	DESCRIPTION	INVOICE	MSRP
KX	**Full Color Keyed Package (Base 2WD Reg Cab)** *Includes color keyed valance panel, color-keyed front bumper, color keyed grille, color keyed handles, color-keyed mirrors and color-keyed rear bumper. REQUIRES PX. NOT AVAILABLE with KP, QY.*	260	325
KX	**Full Color Keyed Package (Base 2WD X-Cab)** *Includes color keyed valance panel, color-keyed front bumper, color keyed grille, color keyed handles, color-keyed mirrors and color-keyed rear bumper. REQUIRES PX. NOT AVAILABLE with KP, LX, IX.*	140	175
KX	**Full Color Keyed Package (PreRunner/4WD Except Limited)** *Includes color keyed valance panel, color-keyed front bumper, color keyed grille and color-keyed mirrors. REQUIRES PX. NOT AVAILABLE with KP, PV, VX, VZ, OF, FX, FY, IX, LX.*	164	205
LB	**Tonneau Cover and Under The Rail Bedliner** *NOT AVAILABLE with BL, BT, LU, FT, FV, FX, FY.*	370	623
LU	**Under Rail Bedliner** *NOT AVAILABLE with BL, LB, FT, FX.*	160	299
LX	**SR5 Package (4WD X-Cab Except Limited)** *Includes SR5 badging, chrome package, chrome plated rear bumper, chrome front bumper, chrome grille, chrome door handles, sliding rear window, gray privacy glass, sunvisor with mirror and pocket, deluxe 3-in-1 combo radio and air conditioning. NOT AVAILABLE with EX, DZ, AC, KP, IX, WR, KX, P4.*	1179	1310
LX	**SR5 Package (Base 4-Cyl 2WD X-Cab)** *Includes SR5 badging, power steering, sliding rear window, gray privacy glass, sunvisor with mirror and pocket, deluxe 3-in-1 combo radio and air conditioner. NOT AVAILABLE with KX, KP, IX, EX, DZ, AC, PS, WR, P4.*	1597	1775
LX	**SR5 Package (Base V6 2WD X-Cab)** *Includes SR5 badging, sliding rear window, gray privacy glass, sunvisor with mirror and pocket, deluxe 3-in-1 combo radio and air conditioner. NOT AVAILABLE with KP, IX, EX, DZ, AC, WR, KX, P4.*	1449	1610
MF	**Mudguards (2WD)**	30	50
OF	**TRD Offroad Package (4WD X-Cab Except Limited)** *Includes off-road suspension, aluminum wheels, wheel arch moldings, tires: 31X10.5R15, black overfenders, rear differential lock, tachometer and badging. REQUIRES FD. NOT AVAILABLE with TA, AL, ST, DL, KX, CQ.*	1337	1660
OF	**TRD Offroad Package (Limited)** *Includes off-road suspension, aluminum wheels, wheel arch moldings, tires: 31X10.5R15 and badging. NOT AVAILABLE with DL.*	357	435
OF	**TRD Offroad Package (PreRunner 2WD 4-Cyl X-Cab)** *Includes off-road suspension, wheel arch moulding with black overfender, wheels: 15" aluminum, tachometer and badging. NOT AVAILABLE with CQ, ST, TA, KX.*	1056	1320
OF	**TRD Offroad Package (PreRunner V6)** *Includes off-road suspension, wheel arch moulding with black overfender, wheels: 15" aluminum, rear differential lock, tachometer and badging. NOT AVAILABLE with CQ, FT, FV, FX, FY, ST, TA, DL, KX.*	1281	1590
P4	**Auto Reverse Cassette Deck** *NOT AVAILABLE with P5, IX, LX.*	145	207

CODE	DESCRIPTION	INVOICE	MSRP
P5	**Compact Disc Deck (All Except Limited)** *NOT AVAILABLE with EU, P4, DZ.*	185	264
PO	**Power Package (2WD X-Cab/4WD Except Limited)** *Includes power windows and power door locks. REQUIRES CL or CQ.*	376	470
PS	**Power Steering (Base 2WD 4-Cyl - Reg Cab/X-Cab)** *NOT AVAILABLE with PY, QY, IX, LX.*	269	315
PV	**Value Edition Plus (PreRunner Reg Cab)** *Includes AM/FM stereo with cassette, air conditioner, aluminum wheels, wheel arch moldings, tires: P265/75R15, sunvisor with mirror and pocket, chrome plated package, chrome plated rear bumper, chrome front bumper, chrome grille, chrome door handles, sliding rear window, bucket seats, center console box, cloth seat trim and carpeted floor mats. NOT AVAILABLE with AC, KP, KX, EU, RA, ST.*	1840	2045
PV	**Value Edition Plus with AC (Base 4WD Reg Cab)** *Includes AM/FM stereo with cassette, air conditioner, aluminum wheels, wheel arch moldings, tires: P265/75R15 ST, chrome plated package: chrome plated rear bumper, chrome front bumper, chrome grille, chrome door handles; sliding rear window, sunvisor with mirror and pocket, bucket seats, cloth seat trim, center console box and carpet floor mats (2-piece set). NOT AVAILABLE with RA, EU, AC, KX, WR, ST, KP.*	1336	1485
PX	**Metallic Paint** *Color related accessory.*	NC	NC
PY	**Value Edition Package Plus with AC and CH (Base 2WD Reg Cab)** *Includes power steering, AM/FM stereo with cassette, air conditioner, chrome plated package: chrome plated rear bumper, chrome front bumper, chrome grille, chrome door handles and carpeted floor mats. NOT AVAILABLE with AC, EU, KP, PS, QY, RA.*	1467	1630
QY	**Value Edition Package Plus with KP (Base 2WD Reg Cab)** *Includes power steering, AM/FM stereo with cassette, air conditioner, color keyed package: color-keyed front bumper, color keyed grille; chrome plated rear bumper and carpeted floor mats. REQUIRES PX. NOT AVAILABLE with AC, EU, KP, PS, PY, RA, KX.*	1444	1605
RA	**Radio: AM/FM Stereo with 2 Speakers (Reg Cab)** *Includes spiral spring back antenna. NOT AVAILABLE with EU, QY, PY, PV.*	225	300
RB	**Running Boards (Base Reg Cab)**	244	400
RB	**Running Boards (Base X-Cab)**	270	450
SR	**Manual Pop-Up Sunroof (X-Cab)** *Moon roof with sunshade.*	312	390
ST	**Wheels: Styled Steel (PreRunner/4WD Except Limited)** *Includes wheel arch moldings. NOT AVAILABLE with PV, OF, FT, FV, FX, FY, AL.*	376	470
TA	**Tachometer (All Except Limited)** *NOT AVAILABLE with CQ, OF.*	76	95
TU	**Upgraded Tire Package (Base 2WD Reg Cab)** *Includes tires: P215/70R14. NOT AVAILABLE with AW.*	144	180
TW	**Tilt Steering Wheel (All Except PreRunner Reg Cab/Limited)** *NOT AVAILABLE with CQ.*	209	245
TW	**Tilt Wheel (Compact Type) (2WD/4WD Reg Cab)** *NOT AVAILABLE with CQ.*	209	245

CODE	DESCRIPTION	INVOICE	MSRP
V3	V.I.P. RS3000 Deluxe Security System (2WD X-Cab/4WD) *REQUIRES PO.*	249	399
VX	Value Package (PreRunner X-Cab) *Includes deluxe 3-in-1 combo radio, sliding rear window, gray privacy glass, sunvisor with mirror and pocket. NOT AVAILABLE with VZ, EX, DZ, KP, KX, WR.*	540	600
VZ	Value Package with KP (PreRunner X-Cab) *Includes deluxe 3-in-1 combo radio, sliding rear window, gray privacy glass, sunvisor with mirror and pocket, color keyed package: color-keyed front bumper and color keyed grille. REQUIRES PX. NOT AVAILABLE with VX, EX, DZ, KP, KX, WR.*	540	600
WI	Spare Tire Lock	30	49
WL	Alloy Wheel Locks *NOT AVAILABLE with WS.*	31	52
WR	Sliding Rear Window (Base 4WD Reg Cab) *NOT AVAILABLE with PV.*	128	160
WR	Sliding Rear Window (X-Cab Except Limited) *Includes gray privacy glass. NOT AVAILABLE with VX, VZ, IX, LX.*	228	285
WS	Steel Wheel Locks (All Except Limited) *NOT AVAILABLE with WL.*	31	52

NOTE: Toyotas sold in AL, FL, GA, NC and SC may be equipped with option packages not listed in this guide. You can expect to haggle 25% off the window sticker price of these packages.

2000 TUNDRA

What's New?

This is an all-new, full-size pickup truck designed to compete with the Ford F-150, Chevrolet Silverado 1500, GMC Sierra 1500 and Dodge Ram 1500. It features an optional V8 engine and can be ordered in a two or four-door, regular- or extended-cab configuration.

Review

As the maker of America's best-selling automobile (the Camry), it must have been frustrating for Toyota to learn that trucks are now outselling cars in this country. Especially since the closest thing to a full-size pickup truck previously offered by Toyota was the anemic and poorly received T100.

With the introduction of the Tundra in spring of 1999, as a 2000 model, Toyota has finally crafted a full-fledged, maximum-sized pickup, capable of running with the big dogs. Topping its pedigree is an optional 4.7-liter, I-Force V8 engine lifted directly from the Land Cruiser/LX 470 sport utility twins. This powerplant makes 245 horsepower and 315 foot-pounds of torque and is available only with a four-speed automatic transmission. Payload capacity is 2,000 pounds and towing capacities for the V8 start at 5,000 pounds (it goes up to 7,000 pounds with an optional tow package). A 3.4-liter V6, making 190 horsepower and 220 foot-pounds of torque is standard on base model Tundras, which may be mated to either a four-speed automatic or five-speed manual transmission.

Toyota has also met the demand of current truck buyers when it comes to configuration. The Tundra is available in regular and extended-cab versions, the latter with two rear-facing doors for easier rear-seat access (which, by the way, is what Toyota call its four door Tundra layout: Access Cab). Unfortunately, regular-cab versions come in longbed form only while Access cab models come only as shortbeds.

Inside, the Tundra feels a bit more compact than its American counterparts, but not uncomfortably so for front-seat passengers. Rear seating is another matter, with legroom at a premium for anyone of average height. With the exception of rear seating, the Tundra cabin is an excellent place to spend the day. It offers a quiet ride that surpasses competing trucks, as well as many cars. Options like leather seating and a 10-disc CD changer further contribute to the Tundra's relaxing internal environment.

We wish Toyota offered more variety in areas like configuration and option packages, and an increase in rear-seat legroom would help the Tundra better compete with the extended cab models from GM, Ford and Dodge. Still, the very fact that a V8-powered, full-size pickup can now be had with a Toyota nameplate on it means there's a whole new set of rules for America's truck buyer.

2000 Toyota Tundra

Standard Equipment

BASE 2WD REGULAR CAB (5M): 3.4L V6 DOHC SMPI 24-valve engine; 5-speed OD manual transmission; rear-wheel drive, 4.08 axle ratio; stainless steel exhaust; front independent double wishbone suspension with anti-roll bar, front coil springs, gas-pressurized front shocks, rigid rear axle suspension with rear leaf springs, gas-pressurized rear shocks; power rack-and-pinion steering with engine speed-sensing assist; front disc/rear drum brakes; 26.4 gal. capacity fuel tank; side impact bars; front argent bumper with black rub strip; monotone paint; aero-composite halogen auto off headlamps; additional exterior lights include pickup cargo box light; driver's and passenger's manual black folding outside mirrors; front and rear 16" x 7" steel wheels; P245/70SR16 A/S BSW front and rear tires; underbody mounted full-size steel spare wheel; AM/FM stereo, seek-scan, cassette, 4 speakers, and fixed antenna; 3 power accessory outlets, driver's foot rest, smokers' package; instrumentation display includes water temperature gauge, in-dash clock, trip odometer; warning indicators include oil pressure, battery, low oil level, lights on, key in ignition, low fuel, low washer fluid; driver's front airbag, passenger's cancelable front airbag; tinted windows; fixed interval front windshield wipers, rear window defroster; seating capacity of 3, bench front seat, adjustable headrests, center armrest with storage, driver's seat includes 2-way direction control, passenger's seat includes 2-way direction control; front height adjustable seatbelts with front pretensioners; cloth seats, cloth door trim insert, full cloth headliner, full carpet floor covering, plastic/rubber gear shift knob; interior lights include dome light; day/night rearview mirror; locking glove box, front cupholder, driver's and passenger's door bins; black grille, black side window moldings, black front windshield molding, black rear window molding and black door handles.

SR5 2WD ACCESS CAB (5M) (in addition to or instead of BASE 2WD REGULAR CAB (5M) equipment): Font and rear mud flaps; front and rear chrome bumpers with black rub strip, rear step; black bodyside molding with chrome bodyside insert; driver's and passenger's manual chrome folding outside mirrors; air conditioning; instrumentation display includes tachometer, oil pressure gauge, volt gauge; vented rear windows; variable intermittent front windshield wipers; seating capacity of 5, front captain's seats, adjustable headrests, driver's and passenger's armrests, driver's seat includes 4-way direction control, passenger's seat includes 4-way direction control, easy entry; 60-40 folding rear bench seat with adjustable headrests, center armrest with storage; cabback insulator; steering wheel with tilt adjustment; dual auxiliary visors; partial floor console, front and rear cupholders, rear door bins, rear underseat tray; chrome grille and body-colored door handles.

SR5 V8 2WD ACCESS CAB (4A) (in addition to or instead of SR5 2WD ACCESS CAB (5M) equipment): 4.7L V8 DOHC SMPI 32-valve engine; 4-speed electronic OD auto transmission with lock-up; 3.92 axle ratio; cruise control; seating capacity of 6, 60-40 split-bench front seat, adjustable headrests and center armrest with storage.

LIMITED V8 2WD ACCESS CAB (4A) (in addition to or instead of SR5 V8 2WD ACCESS CAB (4A) equipment): Front and rear chrome bumpers, front body-colored rub strip, rear black rub strip, rear step; body-colored bodyside molding with chrome bodyside insert, body-colored fender flares; additional exterior lights include front fog/driving lights; driver's and passenger's power remote body-colored folding outside mirrors; front and rear 16" x 7" alloy wheels; P265/70SR16 M&S BSW front and rear tires; AM/FM stereo, seek-scan, cassette, single CD, 6 speakers, and fixed antenna; deep tinted windows, power windows with driver's 1-touch down; sliding rear window and dual illuminated vanity mirrors.

SR5 4WD REGULAR CAB (5M) (in addition to or instead of SR5 2WD ACCESS CAB (5M) equipment): Part-time 4-wheel drive, auto locking hub control and manual shift, 4.1 axle ratio; skid plate(s); seating capacity of 3, bench front seat, adjustable headrests, center armrest with storage, driver's seat includes 2-way direction control, passenger's seat includes 2-way direction control.

SR5 V8 4WD REGULAR CAB (4A) (in addition to or instead of SR5 4WD REGULAR CAB (5M) equipment): 4.7L V8 DOHC SMPI 32-valve engine; 4-speed electronic OD auto transmission with lock-up; 60-40 split-bench front seat, adjustable headrests, center armrest with storage, driver's seat includes 4-way direction control and passenger's seat includes 4-way direction control.

SR5 4WD ACCESS CAB (5M) (in addition to or instead of SR5 2WD ACCESS CAB (5M) equipment): Part-time 4-wheel drive, auto locking hub control and manual shift, 4.1 axle ratio; front and rear mud flaps and skid plate(s).

V8 4WD ACCESS CAB (4A) (in addition to or instead of V8 2WD ACCESS CAB (4A) equipment): Part-time 4 wheel drive, auto locking hub control and electronic shift, 3.91 axle ratio; front and rear mud flaps and skid plate(s).

Base Prices

7711	Base 2WD Regular Cab (5M)	13359	14995
7721	SR5 2WD Access Cab (5M)	17974	20175
7811	SR5 4WD Regular Cab (5M)	17992	20195
7728	SR5 V8 2WD Access Cab (4A)	19822	22250
7818	SR5 V8 4WD Regular Cab (4A)	20232	22710
7821	SR5 4WD Access Cab (5M)	20825	23375
7738	Limited V8 2WD Access Cab (4A)	21822	24495
7828	SR5 V8 4WD Access Cab (4A)	22794	25585
7838	Limited V8 4WD Access Cab (4A)	24794	27830
Destination Charge:		480	480

Accessories

CODE	DESCRIPTION	INVOICE	MSRP
4AT	Transmission: 4-Speed Automatic (Base Reg Cab)	747	840
4AT	Transmission: 4-Speed Automatic (SR5 2WD Reg Cab)	801	900
4AT	Transmission: 4-Speed Automatic (SR5 2WD X-Cab)	682	765
4AT	Transmission: 4-Speed Automatic (SR5 4WD X-Cab)	735	825
9Z	Wire Harness For Bumper (V8)	99	159
AA	Wheels: 16" Aluminum (SR5) *Includes 5-spoke cast aluminum wheels, front and rear contoured mudguards, wheel ornament and black overfenders. NOT AVAILABLE with AL, AY, ST, SV, LO, OF.*	584	730
AB	Antilock Brake System *Includes 4-wheel ABS and daytime running lights. NOT AVAILABLE with LO.*	539	630
AC	Air Conditioner (Base Reg Cab)	788	985
AL	Wheels: 16" Aluminum (4WD/SR5 2WD) *Includes 1-piece 5-spoke cast aluminum wheels, wheel ornament and chrome-lined wheel arch moulding. NOT AVAILABLE with AA, AY, ST, SV, LO, OF.*	480	600
AY	Wheels: 16" Aluminum (4WD/SR5 2WD) *Includes P245/70R16 tires. NOT AVAILABLE with AA, AL, ST, SV, LO, OF.*	304	380
BL	Over The Rail Bedliner	160	299
BT	Tonneau Cover (Reg Cab)	267	445
BT	Tonneau Cover (X-Cab)	241	402
CB	Painted Bumper (Base Reg Cab)	120	150
CC	Cloth Captain's Chairs (Limited) *Includes power driver's seat. NOT AVAILABLE with LA.*	316	395
CC	Cloth Captain's Chairs (SR5 2WD/SR5 - 4WD X-Cab/4WD Reg Cab V8) *REQUIRES 4AT. NOT AVAILABLE with LO.*	60	75
CC	Cloth Captain's Chairs (SR5 4WD Reg Cab) *REQUIRES 4AT. NOT AVAILABLE with SB.*	244	305
CF	Carpet Floor Mats (4-Piece Set) (X-Cab)	48	80
CK	All Weather Guard Package *Includes anti-chip paint, heavy duty starter and heavy duty heater. REQUIRES MG.*	59	70
CQ	Convenience Package (SR5 V6 X-Cab) *Includes lighting package, power door locks, driver and passenger double sunvisor, chrome power mirrors, sliding rear window with privacy glass and cruise control.*	1048	1310
CQ	Convenience Package (SR5 V8) *Includes lighting package, power door locks, driver and passenger double sunvisor, chrome power mirrors and sliding rear window with privacy glass. NOT AVAILABLE with LO.*	848	1060
CT	Carpet Floor Mats (2-Piece Set) (Reg Cab)	38	63
DH	Towing Receiver Hitch (All Except Limited)	259	379
DO	Delete Package (Base Reg Cab) *Includes vinyl floor mats and vinyl seats.*	(72)	(90)
DZ	Radio: Deluxe 3-In-1 Combo (SR5 2WD X-Cab) *Includes AM/FM stereo, cassette, CD player and 4 speakers. NOT AVAILABLE with LO.*	188	250
DZ	Radio: Deluxe 3-In-1 Combo (SR5 4WD Reg Cab) *Includes AM/FM stereo, cassette, CD player and 4 speakers.*	75	100

CODE	DESCRIPTION	INVOICE	MSRP
EJ	Radio: Premium 3-In-1 with Changer (Limited)	150	200
	Includes AM/FM stereo, cassette, CD player, 6 disc in-dash CD changer, 6 speakers and power amplifier.		
FW	Full Wheel Covers (Base Reg Cab)	80	100
GN	Interior Cargo Net	27	42
HP	Hood Protector	79	129
LA	Leather Package (Limited)	1136	1420
	Includes leather captain's chairs with power driver's seat and synthetic wood trim. NOT AVAILABLE with CC.		
LB	Tonneau Cover/Under The Rail Bedliner (Reg Cab)	427	744
LB	Tonneau Cover/Under The Rail Bedliner (X-Cab)	401	701
LF	Front Fog Lamps (All Except Limited)	80	100
	NOT AVAILABLE with LO.		
LO	Payload Package (SR5 2WD V8)	364	455
	Includes increased payload to 2,011 lbs and tires: P245/70R16. NOT AVAILABLE with AA, AB, AL, AY, CC, CQ, DZ, LF, ST, SV.		
LU	Under The Rail Bedliner	160	299
MG	Black Mudguards (Base Reg Cab)	48	60
OF	Off Road Package (Limited 4WD)	76	95
	Includes front and rear contoured mudguards, wheel ornament, front fog lamps, black overfenders, tires: BF Goodrich P265/70, Bilstein shocks and off-road tuned suspension.		
OF	Off Road Package (SR5 4WD X-Cab)	740	925
	Includes front and rear contoured mudguards, wheel ornament, front fog lamps, black overfenders, tires: BF Goodrich P265/70, Bilstein shocks and off-road tuned suspension. NOT AVAILABLE with AA, AL, AY, ST, SV.		
P5	Compact Disc Deck	185	264
	NOT AVAILABLE with DZ or EJ.		
RB	Color-Keyed Running Boards (X-Cab)	426	699
SB	40/60 Split Bench Seat (SR5 4WD Reg Cab)	184	230
	REQUIRES 4AT. NOT AVAILABLE with CC.		
ST	Wheels: 16" Styled Steel (SR5)	176	220
	Includes wheel ornament and chrome-lined wheel arch molding. NOT AVAILABLE with AA, AL, AY, SV, LO, OF.		
SV	Wheels: Styled Steel (SR5 X-Cab)	280	350
	Includes wheel ornament, front and rear contoured mudguards and black overfenders. NOT AVAILABLE with AA, AL, AY, ST, LO, OF.		
TW	Tilt Steering Wheel (Base Reg Cab)	171	200
	Includes variable intermittent wipers with timer.		
TX	Two-Tone Paint (Limited)	292	365
V3	V.I.P.-RS3000 Deluxe Alarm System	249	399
	REQUIRES CQ (Base/SR5).		
WI	Spare Tire Lock	33	55
WL	Alloy Wheel Locks	31	52
WR	Sliding Rear Window (Base Reg Cab)	128	160
WS	Steel Wheel Locks	31	52

NOTE: Toyotas sold in AL, FL, GA, NC and SC may be equipped with option packages not listed in this guide. You can expect to haggle 25% off the window sticker price of these packages.

2000 EUROVAN

2000 Volkswagen EuroVan

What's New?

During its second year back in the U.S., Volkswagen's EuroVan receives minor equipment updates.

Review

Despite myriad shortcomings, or perhaps because of them, the Volkswagen Vanagon and its successor, the EuroVan, became people-mover cult favorites. Last marketed to Americans in non-RV guise in 1993, the EuroVan returned in 1999 with several improvements designed to make the oddball entry more palatable to American tastes. The comeback was both successful and a failure, depending on whom you ask.

Those who lamented the disappearance of the van six years ago are happy as clams to have it back. People who have become fond of petite, smooth-riding, affordable minivans, however, may find the chunky EuroVan boorish, unrefined and overpriced. Everyone seems happy about the vehicle's engine, though.

Powered by a 140-horsepower, VR6 six-cylinder engine, this motor makes 177 foot-pounds of torque at 3,200 rpm and allows the EuroVan to finally get out of its own way! Charged with motivating more than 2 tons of steel, plastic and glass, the EuroVan is no drag-strip performer, but we'll take what we can get. This engine requires premium fuel and returned just 16.7 mpg during our testing, but we were consoled by the knowledge that the EuroVan can handle up to a 4,500-pound trailer or nearly 1,000 pounds of cargo, not to mention several passengers in the spacious rear seats. Engineers also strengthened the EuroVan's body, reinforced the floor panels and stiffened the B- and C-pillars. And, thicker sound insulation cuts unwanted road and engine noise from filtering into the cabin.

Another surprise is the EuroVan's competent handling. In parking lots, a 38.4-foot turning circle and power rack-and-pinion steering mean easy maneuverability. On the highway, a four-wheel independent suspension keeps the van planted solidly on the ground, despite a large amount of body roll.

Two trim levels are available: GLS and Multivan (MV). Order a GLS and you get seating for seven forward-facing passengers. The MV also seats seven, but two riders are looking out the back window and the third-row bench converts into a bed. An optional Weekender package is available on the MV and should prove quite popular. It includes a pop-up roof with a two-person bed, a small refrigerator, swiveling captain's chairs, side sliding windows with screens and an additional battery.

CODE	DESCRIPTION	INVOICE	MSRP

Standard equipment includes dual front airbags, daytime running lights, power windows and locks, air conditioning with pollen filtration, cruise control, cassette stereo, heated washer nozzles, rear wiper with defroster, power mirrors, and an automatic transmission. A sliding sunroof is available as long as you don't opt for the Weekender package, and GLS buyers can get leather trim with heated front seats.

For 2000, Volkswagen outfitted the EuroVan with a brake-wear indicator, dark tinted glass on the side and rear windows, and remote central locking. The GLS model receives additional reading lights in the rear and optional single seats instead of a bench seat in the second row.

EuroVans are covered by a five-year/50,000-mile powertrain warranty, and all scheduled maintenance for the first two years is free. Pull the seats out and the GLS is capable of moving 150 cubic feet of cargo. While some might find the price prohibitively high, many of you have been waiting patiently for the revival of the quirky VW van. As George Costanza exclaimed on his way to the Hamptons, Let's get nuts!

Standard Equipment

GLS (4A): 2.8L V6 SOHC SMPI 12-valve engine; 4-speed electronic OD auto transmission with lock-up; 150-amp alternator; front-wheel drive, traction control, 3.68 axle ratio; stainless steel exhaust; front independent double wishbone suspension with anti-roll bar, front torsion springs, front torsion bar, rear independent suspension with rear coil springs; power rack-and-pinion steering; 4-wheel disc brakes with 4-wheel antilock braking system; 21.1 gal. capacity fuel tank; front license plate bracket, side impact bars; 3 doors with sliding right rear passenger door, liftback rear cargo door; front and rear body-colored bumpers; monotone paint; aero-composite halogen headlamps with daytime running lights; driver's and passenger's power remote body-colored heated folding outside mirrors; front and rear 15" x 7" silver alloy wheels; P205/65SR15 A/S BSW front and rear tires; inside under cargo mounted full-size steel spare wheel; air conditioning with climate control, rear air conditioning with separate controls, air filter, rear heat ducts; premium AM/FM stereo, seek-scan, auto-reverse cassette, 6 speakers, theft deterrent, and manual retractable antenna; cruise control; power door locks, remote keyless entry, child safety rear door locks; 3 power accessory outlets, driver's foot rest; instrumentation display includes tachometer, water temperature gauge, in-dash clock, trip odometer; warning indicators include oil pressure, water temp, battery, lights on, key in ignition, low fuel; driver's and passenger's front airbags; deep tinted windows, power windows with driver's and passenger's 1-touch down, fixed 1/4 vent windows; fixed interval front windshield wipers with heated jets, sun visor strip, fixed interval rear wiper, rear window defroster; seating capacity of 7, front bucket seats, adjustable tilt headrests, driver's and passenger's armrests, driver's seat includes 4-way direction control, passenger's seat includes 4-way direction control; full folding 2nd row bench seat with tilt headrests, center armrest; full folding 3rd row bench seat with tilt headrest; front height adjustable seatbelts with front pretensioners; cloth seats, cloth door trim insert, full vinyl headliner, full carpet floor covering; interior lights include dome light with delay, front and rear reading lights; dual illuminated vanity mirrors; day/night rearview mirror; glove box, front and rear cupholders, dashboard storage, 2 seat back storage pockets, driver's and passenger's door bins; carpeted cargo floor, plastic trunk lid, cargo cover, cargo tie downs, cargo light; body-colored grille, black side window moldings, black front windshield molding, black rear window molding and black door handles.

MV (4A) (in addition to or instead of GLS (4A) equipment): Removeable full folding 2nd row bucket seat facing rear with reclining adjustable headrests; removable full folding 3rd row bench seat convertabed with adjustable headrest and snap on curtains for side windows.

Base Prices

7DC2L3	GLS (4A)	28417	31300
7DCML3	MV (4A)	29772	32800
Destination Charge:		590	590

CODE	DESCRIPTION	INVOICE	MSRP
	Accessories		
—	Clearcoat Pearl Paint	243	275
3EF/ZD1	Power Sunroof *Topslider. NOT AVAILABLE with W28.*	873	1000
3UE	Second Row Single Seats (GLS) *Replaces bench seat and deltes ISOFIX (child seat anchors).*	163	185
4A3	Heated Seats	353	400

Specifications and EPA Mileage Ratings

2000/2001 New Trucks

Contents

SPECIFICATIONS & EPA MILEAGE RATINGS

	BMW X5	CADILLAC Escalade	CHEVROLET Astro AWD	CHEVROLET Astro RWD	CHEVROLET Blazer 2WD 2-Door	CHEVROLET Blazer 2WD 4-Door	CHEVROLET Blazer 4WD 2-Door
Turning Circle (in.)	39.7	44.6	40.5	39.5	34.8	36.6	35.2
Length (in.)	183.5	201.2	189.8	189.8	176.8	183.3	176.8
Width (in.)	73.6	77	77.5	77.5	67.8	67.8	67.8
Height (in.)	67.7	74.3	76	76	64.9	64.3	67.8
Curb Weight (lbs.)	4828	5573	4397	4187	3536	3692	3418
Wheelbase (in.)	111	117.5	111.2	111.2	100.5	107	100.5
Front Head Room (in.)	38.9	39.9	39.2	39.2	39.6	39.5	39.6
Rear Head Room (in.)	38.5	38.9	37.9	37.9	38.3	38.3	38.3
Front Leg Room (in.)	39.3	41.7	41.6	41.6	42.4	42.4	42.4
Rear Leg Room (in.)	35.4	36.4	36.5	36.5	35.6	36.3	35.6
Maximum Seating	5	5	8	8	5	6	5
Max Cargo Capacity (cu ft.)	54.4	118	170	170	67	74	67
Maximum Payload (lbs.)	NA	933	1649	1763	950	1196	1025
Number of Cylinders	8	8	6	6	6	6	6
Displacement (liters)	4.4	5.7	4.3	4.3	4.3	4.3	4.3
Horsepower @ RPM	282@ 5400	255@ 4600	190@ 4400	190@ 4400	190@ 4400	190@ 4400	190@ 4400
Torque @ RPM	324@ 3600	330@ 2800	250@ 2800	250@ 2800	250@ 2800	250@ 2800	250@ 2800
Fuel Capacity	24.3	30	27	27	19	18	19
Towing Capacity	6000	6500	5000	5500	4900	4900	5600
EPA City (mpg) - Manual	NA	NA	NA	NA	17	NA	15
EPA Hwy (mpg) - Manual	NA	NA	NA	NA	23	NA	18
EPA City (mpg) - Auto	13	12	15	16	16	16	16
EPA Hwy (mpg) - Auto	17	16	19	20	21	21	20

SPECIFICATIONS & EPA MILEAGE RATINGS

	Blazer 4WD 4-Door	C/K2500 2WD Crew Cab HD	C/K2500 2WD Reg Cab HD	C/K2500 2WD X-Cab HD	C/K2500 4WD Crew Cab HD	C/K2500 4WD Reg Cab HD	C/K2500 4WD X-Cab LB HD	C/K2500 4WD X-Cab SB HD	C/K3500 2WD Crew Cab LB	C/K3500 2WD Crew Cab SB
Turning Circle (in.)	39.5	53.8	43.8	50.2	55.7	44.6	52.2	47.6	53.8	53.8
Length (in.)	183.3	231.8	213.4	237.4	231.8	213.4	237.4	218.5	250.9	231.9
Width (in.)	67.8	76.8	76.8	76.8	76.8	76.8	76.8	76.8	76.8	94.3
Height (in.)	64.2	73.9	71.2	72.6	74.5	76	74	74	73.9	73.9
Curb Weight (lbs.)	4023	5641	4737	5107	6554	5165	5470	5217	5509	5509
Wheelbase (in.)	107	154.4	131.5	155.5	154.5	131.5	155.5	141.5	168.5	154.5
Front Head Room (in.)	39.5	39.9	39.9	39.9	39.9	39.9	39.9	39.9	39.9	39.9
Rear Head Room (in.)	38.3	40.8	NA	37.5	40.8	NA	37.5	37.5	40.8	40.8
Front Leg Room (in.)	42.4	41.7	41.7	41.7	41.7	41.7	41.7	41.7	41.7	41.7
Rear Leg Room (in.)	36.3	37.9	NA	34.8	37.9	NA	34.8	34.8	37.9	37.9
Maximum Seating	6	6	3	6	6	3	6	6	6	6
Max Cargo Capacity (cu ft.)	74	56	69	69	56	69	69	56	69	56
Maximum Payload (lbs.)	1293	2959	3516	3516	2367	3435	3130	3383	3499	2944
Number of Cylinders	6	8	8	8	8	8	8	8	8	8
Displacement (liters)	4.3	5.7	5.7	5.7	5.7	5.7	5.7	5.7	5.7	7.4
Horsepower @ RPM	190@ 4400	255@ 4600	255@ 4600	255@ 4600	255@ 4600	255@ 4600	255@ 4600	255@ 4600	255@ 4600	290@ 4000
Torque @ RPM	250@ 2800	330@ 2800	330@ 2800	330@ 2800	330@ 2800	330@ 2800	330@ 2800	330@ 2800	330@ 2800	410@ 3200
Fuel Capacity	18	25	34	34	25	34	34	25	34	26
Towing Capacity	5600	8000	8000	8000	7500	7500	7500	7500	7000	10000
EPA City (mpg) - Manual	NA	NA	NA	NA	NA	NA	NA	NA	NA	NA
EPA Hwy (mpg) - Manual	NA	NA	NA	NA	NA	NA	NA	NA	NA	NA
EPA City (mpg) - Auto	16	NA	NA	NA	NA	NA	NA	NA	NA	NA
EPA Hwy (mpg) - Auto	20	NA	NA	NA	NA	NA	NA	NA	NA	NA

specifications

SPECIFICATIONS & EPA MILEAGE RATINGS	C/K3500 2WD Reg Cab LB	C/K3500 2WD X-Cab LB	C/K3500 4WD Crew Cab LB	C/K3500 4WD Crew Cab SB	C/K3500 4WD Reg Cab LB	C/K3500 4WD X-Cab LB	Express G1500	Express G2500	Express G2500 Extended	Express G3500
Turning Circle (in.)	43.4	50.5	55.8	55.8	45	52	45.3	47.4	53.4	47.4
Length (in.)	213.4	237.4	250.9	231.9	213.4	237.4	218.7	218.7	238.7	218.8
Width (in.)	76.8	94.3	76.8	76.8	76.8	94.3	79.4	79.2	79.2	79.4
Height (in.)	70	72.6	74.5	94.3	74	73.4	80.7	82.7	81.3	83.3
Curb Weight (lbs.)	4838	5427	5893	5893	5229	5836	5166	5857	5844	5996
Wheelbase (in.)	131.5	155.5	168.5	154.5	131.5	155.5	135	135	155	135
Front Head Room (in.)	39.9	39.9	39.9	39.9	39.9	39.9	40.6	40.6	40.6	40.6
Rear Head Room (in.)	NA	37.5	40.8	40.8	NA	37.5	39	39	39	39
Front Leg Room (in.)	41.7	41.7	41.7	41.7	41.7	41.7	41.1	41.1	41.1	41.1
Rear Leg Room (in.)	NA	34.8	37.9	37.9	NA	34.8	38.5	38.5	38.5	38.5
Maximum Seating	3	6	6	6	3	6	8	12	12	15
Max Cargo Capacity (cu ft.)	69	69	69	56	69	69	267	267	317	267
Maximum Payload (lbs.)	4171	4583	3327	2239	3988	4184	1958	2777	2555	3504
Number of Cylinders	8	8	8	8	8	8	6	8	8	8
Displacement (liters)	5.7	5.7	5.7	7.4	5.7	5.7	4.3	5.7	5.7	5.7
Horsepower @ RPM	255@ 4600	255@ 4600	255@ 4600	290@ 4000	255@ 4600	255@ 4600	200@ 4400	255@ 4600	255@ 4600	255@ 4600
Torque @ RPM	330@ 2800	330@ 2800	330@ 2800	410@ 3200	330@ 2800	330@ 2800	250@ 2800	330@ 2800	330@ 2800	330@ 2800
Fuel Capacity	34	34	34	26	34	34	30.9	30.9	30.9	30.9
Towing Capacity	7500	9000	6500	10000	7000	7000	7300	8900	8300	10000
EPA City (mpg) - Manual	NA	NA	NA	NA	NA	NA	NA	NA	NA	NA
EPA Hwy (mpg) - Manual	NA	NA	NA	NA	NA	NA	NA	NA	NA	NA
EPA City (mpg) - Auto	NA	NA	NA	NA	NA	NA	14	14	14	NA
EPA Hwy (mpg) - Auto	NA	NA	NA	NA	NA	NA	18	18	18	NA

SPECIFICATIONS & EPA MILEAGE RATINGS

	Express G3500 Extended	S-10 2WD Reg Cab LB	S-10 2WD Reg Cab SB	S-10 2WD X-Cab SB	S-10 4WD Reg Cab SB	S-10 4WD X-Cab SB	Silverado 1500 2WD Reg Cab LB	Silverado 1500 2WD Reg Cab SB	Silverado 1500 2WD X-Cab LB	Silverado 1500 2WD X-Cab SB
Turning Circle (in.)	53.5	39.8	36.9	41.3	37.3	41.6	43.8	40.1	50.4	46.6
Length (in.)	238.7	206.1	190.1	204.7	190.1	204.7	222.2	203.3	246.7	227.6
Width (in.)	79.2	67.9	67.9	67.9	67.9	67.9	78.5	78.5	78.5	78.5
Height (in.)	82.1	62.9	63.2	62.7	63.4	62.7	71	71.2	71.2	71.2
Curb Weight (lbs.)	6204	3204	3029	3053	3556	3754	4023	3923	4442	4235
Wheelbase (in.)	155	117.9	108.3	122.9	108.3	122.9	133	119	157.5	143.5
Front Head Room (in.)	40.6	39.5	39.5	39.6	39.5	39.6	41	41	41	41
Rear Head Room (in.)	39	NA	NA	NA	NA	NA	NA	NA	38.4	38.4
Front Leg Room (in.)	41.1	42.4	42.4	42.4	42.4	42.4	41.3	41.3	41.3	41.3
Rear Leg Room (in.)	38.5	NA	NA	NA	NA	NA	NA	NA	33.7	33.7
Maximum Seating	15	3	3	5	3	4	3	3	6	6
Max Cargo Capacity (cu ft.)	317	48	39	39	39	39	71	57	71	57
Maximum Payload (lbs.)	3296	1533	1212	1158	1094	900	2368	2177	1757	1965
Number of Cylinders	8	4	4	4	6	6	6	6	8	6
Displacement (liters)	5.7	2.2	2.2	2.2	4.3	4.3	4.3	4.3	4.8	4.3
Horsepower @ RPM	255@ 4600	120@ 5000	120@ 5000	120@ 5000	190@ 4400	190@ 4400	200@ 4400	200@ 4400	270@ 5200	200@ 4400
Torque @ RPM	330@ 2800	140@ 3600	140@ 3600	140@ 3600	250@ 2800	250@ 2800	250@ 2800	250@ 2800	285@ 4000	250@ 2800
Fuel Capacity	30.9	19	19	19	19	19	34	26	34	26
Towing Capacity	10000	2000	2000	2000	3500	3500	8200	8200	8200	8200
EPA City (mpg) - Manual	NA	23	23	23	17	17	17	17	16	17
EPA Hwy (mpg) - Manual	NA	29	29	29	21	21	23	23	20	23
EPA City (mpg) - Auto	NA	19	19	19	16	16	16	16	16	16
EPA Hwy (mpg) - Auto	NA	26	26	26	21	21	20	20	21	20

specifications

SPECIFICATIONS & EPA MILEAGE RATINGS	Silverado 1500 4WD Reg Cab LB	Silverado 1500 4WD Reg Cab SB	Silverado 1500 4WD X-Cab LB	Silverado 1500 4WD X-Cab SB	Silverado 1500 LT 2WD X-Cab LB	Silverado 1500 LT 2WD X-Cab SB	Silverado 1500 LT 4WD X-Cab LB	Silverado 1500 LT 4WD X-Cab SB	Silverado 2500 2WD Reg Cab LB	Silverado 2500 2WD Reg Cab LB HD
Turning Circle (in.)	44.5	40.7	51.1	47.3	50.4	46.6	51.1	47.3	45.4	45.4
Length (in.)	222.2	203.3	246.7	227.6	246.7	227.6	246.7	227.6	222.2	222.2
Width (in.)	78.5	78.5	78.5	78.5	78.5	78.5	78.5	78.5	78.5	78.5
Height (in.)	72.7	72.7	72.7	72.7	71.2	71.2	72.7	72.7	73.7	73.8
Curb Weight (lbs.)	4365	4248	4748	4621	4442	4235	4748	4621	4586	4586
Wheelbase (in.)	133	119	157.5	143.5	157.5	143.5	157.5	143.5	133	133
Front Head Room (in.)	41	41	41	41	41	41	41	41	41	41
Rear Head Room (in.)	NA	NA	38.4	38.4	38.4	38.4	38.4	38.4	NA	NA
Front Leg Room (in.)	41.3	41.3	41.3	41.3	41.3	41.3	41.3	41.3	41.3	41.3
Rear Leg Room (in.)	NA	NA	33.7	33.7	33.7	33.7	33.7	33.7	NA	NA
Maximum Seating	3	3	6	6	5	5	5	5	3	3
Max Cargo Capacity (cu ft.)	71	57	71	57	71	57	71	57	71	71
Maximum Payload (lbs.)	2035	1852	1652	1779	1757	1965	1652	1779	2614	2614
Number of Cylinders	6	6	8	8	8	8	8	8	8	8
Displacement (liters)	4.3	4.3	4.8	4.8	5.3	5.3	5.3	5.3	5.3	6
Horsepower @ RPM	200@ 4400	200@ 4400	270@ 5200	200@ 4600	285@ 5200	285@ 5200	285@ 5200	285@ 5200	270@ 5000	300@ 4800
Torque @ RPM	250@ 2800	250@ 2800	285@ 4000	260@ 2800	325@ 4000	325@ 4000	325@ 4000	325@ 4000	315@ 4000	355@ 4000
Fuel Capacity	34	26	34	26	34	26	34	26	34	34
Towing Capacity	8000	8000	8000	8000	8200	8200	8000	8000	8500	10500
EPA City (mpg) - Manual	15	15	15	15	NA	NA	NA	NA	NA	NA
EPA Hwy (mpg) - Manual	18	18	19	19	NA	NA	NA	NA	NA	NA
EPA City (mpg) - Auto	16	16	15	15	16	16	15	15	15	NA
EPA Hwy (mpg) - Auto	20	20	18	18	20	20	18	18	19	NA

SPECIFICATIONS & EPA MILEAGE RATINGS

	Silverado 2500 2WD X-Cab LB	Silverado 2500 2WD X-Cab SB	Silverado 2500 4WD Reg Cab LB	Silverado 2500 4WD X-Cab LB	Silverado 2500 4WD X-Cab SB	Suburban 1500 2WD	Suburban 1500 4WD	Suburban 2500 2WD	Suburban 2500 4WD	Tahoe 2WD
Turning Circle (in.)	52.2	48.2	45.2	52.4	48.4	43.3	43.3	44.5	44.3	38.3
Length (in.)	246.7	227.6	222.2	246.7	227.6	219.3	219.3	219.3	219.3	198.9
Width (in.)	78.5	78.5	78.5	78.5	78.5	78.8	78.8	78.8	78.8	78.9
Height (in.)	74.1	74	74.2	74.5	74.4	73.3	73.2	74.2	74.7	74.1
Curb Weight (lbs.)	5485	4766	5266	5523	5485	4194	5123	5447	5760	4828
Wheelbase (in.)	157.5	143.5	133	157.5	143.5	130	130	130	130	116
Front Head Room (in.)	41	41	41	41	41	40.7	40.7	40.7	40.7	40.7
Rear Head Room (in.)	38.4	38.4	NA	38.4	38.4	39	39	39	39	39.4
Front Leg Room (in.)	41.3	41.3	41.3	41.3	41.3	41.3	41.3	41.3	41.3	41.3
Rear Leg Room (in.)	33.7	33.7	NA	33.7	33.7	39.1	39.1	39.1	39.1	38.6
Maximum Seating	6	6	3	6	6	3	3	3	3	6
Max Cargo Capacity (cu ft.)	71	57	71	71	57	138	138	138	138	108
Maximum Payload (lbs.)	3287	2434	3334	3077	3115	1886	2077	3153	2839	1472
Number of Cylinders	8	8	8	8	8	8	8	8	8	8
Displacement (liters)	6	5.3	6	6	6	5.3	5.3	6	6	4.8
Horsepower @ RPM	300@ 4800	285@ 5200	300@ 4800	300@ 4800	300@ 4800	285@ 5200	285@ 5200	300@ 4800	300@ 4800	275@ 5200
Torque @ RPM	355@ 4000	325@ 4000	355@ 4000	355@ 4000	355@ 4000	325@ 4000	325@ 4000	355@ 4000	355@ 4000	290@ 4000
Fuel Capacity	34	26	34	34	26	32.5	32.5	38.5	38.5	26
Towing Capacity	10500	8500	10000	10000	10000	6500	6000	7516	7013	7013
EPA City (mpg) - Manual	NA	NA	NA	NA	NA	NA	NA	NA	NA	NA
EPA Hwy (mpg) - Manual	NA	NA	NA	NA	NA	NA	NA	NA	NA	NA
EPA City (mpg) - Auto	12	15	NA	NA	NA	14	14	NA	NA	14
EPA Hwy (mpg) - Auto	16	19	NA	NA	NA	18	16	NA	NA	18

specifications

SPECIFICATIONS & EPA MILEAGE RATINGS

	Tahoe 4WD	Tahoe Limited 2WD	Tahoe/Z71 4WD	Tracker 2WD Convertible	Tracker 2WD Hard Top	Tracker 4WD Convertible	Tracker 4WD Hard Top	Venture Extended	Venture SWB
Turning Circle (in.)	38.3	39.8	40.6	31.5	34.8	31.5	34.8	39.7	37.4
Length (in.)	198.9	199.6	199.6	151.6	162.6	151.6	162.6	200.9	186.9
Width (in.)	78.9	76.8	76.8	67.3	67.3	67.3	67.3	72	72
Height (in.)	74	70.3	72.4	66.5	65.6	66.5	66.3	68.1	67.4
Curb Weight (lbs.)	5050	4874	5280	2602	2866	2639	2987	3792	3671
Wheelbase (in.)	116	117.5	117.5	86.6	97.6	86.6	97.6	120	112
Front Head Room (in.)	40.7	39.9	39.9	40.9	39.9	40.9	39.9	39.9	39.9
Rear Head Room (in.)	39.4	38.9	38.9	39.5	39.6	39.6	39.6	39.3	39.3
Front Leg Room (in.)	41.3	41.7	41.7	41.4	41.4	41.4	41.4	39.9	39.9
Rear Leg Room (in.)	38.6	36.4	36.4	35.9	35.9	35.9	35.9	36.9	36.9
Maximum Seating	6	5	5	4	5	4	5	7	7
Max Cargo Capacity (cu ft.)	108	118	118	34	45	34	45	156	127
Maximum Payload (lbs.)	1751	1437	1534	771	884	948	937	1457	1612
Number of Cylinders	8	8	8	4	4	4	4	6	6
Displacement (liters)	4.8	5.7	5.7	1.6	2	1.6	2	3.4	3.4
Horsepower @ RPM	275@ 5200	255@ 4600	255@ 4600	97@ 5200	120@ 6000	97@ 5200	120@ 6000	185@ 5200	185@ 5200
Torque @ RPM	290@ 4000	330@ 2800	330@ 2800	103@ 4000	134@ 3000	103@ 4000	134@ 3000	210@ 4000	210@ 4000
Fuel Capacity	26	30	30	14.8	17.4	14.8	17.4	25	20
Towing Capacity	6512	6000	5500	1000	1500	1000	1500	3500	3500
EPA City (mpg) - Manual	NA	NA	NA	25	23	25	22	NA	NA
EPA Hwy (mpg) - Manual	NA	NA	NA	28	25	27	25	NA	NA
EPA City (mpg) - Auto	14	14	12	23	24	23	23	18	18
EPA Hwy (mpg) - Auto	18	18	16	25	26	25	25	25	25

SPECIFICATIONS & EPA MILEAGE RATINGS

CHRYSLER

	Town and Country LX AWD/LXi AWD	Town and Country LX FWD/LXi FWD	Town and Country Limited AWD	Town and Country Limited FWD	Grand Voyager Base	Grand Voyager SE	Voyager Base	Voyager SE
Turning Circle (in.)	39.5	39.4	39.5	39.4	39.4	39.4	37.6	37.6
Length (in.)	199.6	199.6	199.6	199.6	199.6	199.6	186.3	186.3
Width (in.)	75	75	75	75	76.8	76.8	76.8	76.8
Height (in.)	68.5	68.5	68.5	68.5	68.5	68.5	68.5	68.5
Curb Weight (lbs.)	4155	4042	4155	4042	3836	3836	3528	3696
Wheelbase (in.)	119.3	119.3	119.3	119.3	119.3	119.3	113.3	113.3
Front Head Room (in.)	39.8	39.8	39.8	39.8	39.8	39.8	39.8	39.8
Rear Head Room (in.)	40	40	40	40	40	40	40.1	40.1
Front Leg Room (in.)	41.2	41.2	41.2	41.2	41.1	41.1	41.2	41.2
Rear Leg Room (in.)	39.6	39.6	39.6	39.6	39.6	39.6	36.6	36.6
Maximum Seating	7	7	7	7	7	7	5	7
Max Cargo Capacity (cu ft.)	163	163	163	163	172	172	143	143
Maximum Payload (lbs.)	NA	NA	NA	NA	NA	NA	NA	NA
Number of Cylinders	6	6	6	6	6	6	4	6
Displacement (liters)	3.8	3.3	3.8	3.8	3	3.3	2.4	3.3
Horsepower @ RPM	180@ 4400	158@ 4850	180@ 4400	180@ 4400	150@ 5200	158@ 4850	150@ 5200	158@ 4850
Torque @ RPM	240@ 3200	203@ 3250	240@ 3200	240@ 3200	176@ 4000	203@ 3250	167@ 4000	203@ 3250
Fuel Capacity	20	20	20	20	20	20	20	20
Towing Capacity	2000	2000	2000	2000	3500	3500	2000	3500
EPA City (mpg) - Manual	NA	NA	NA	NA	NA	NA	NA	NA
EPA Hwy (mpg) - Manual	NA	NA	NA	NA	NA	NA	NA	NA
EPA City (mpg) - Auto	16	18	16	17	18	18	20	18
EPA Hwy (mpg) - Auto	23	24	23	24	25	25	26	25

SPECIFICATIONS & EPA MILEAGE RATINGS

DODGE

	Caravan Base	Caravan SE	Grand Caravan AWD	Grand Caravan Base/SE FWD	Grand Caravan ES FWD	Grand Caravan LE FWD	Dakota 2WD Club Cab SB	Dakota 2WD Quad Cab SB	Dakota 2WD Reg Cab SB
Turning Circle (in.)	37.6	37.6	39.5	39.5	39.5	39.5	41.2	41.3	36
Length (in.)	186.3	186.3	199.6	199.6	199.6	199.6	215	215.1	196
Width (in.)	76.8	76.8	76.8	75.6	75.6	75.6	71.5	71.6	71.5
Height (in.)	68.5	68.5	68.5	68.5	68.5	68.5	65.6	66.3	65.2
Curb Weight (lbs.)	3533	3533	3706	3706	3706	3706	3557	4124	3335
Wheelbase (in.)	113.3	113.3	119.3	119.3	119.3	119.3	131	131	112
Front Head Room (in.)	39.8	39.8	39.8	39.8	39.8	39.8	40	39.8	40
Rear Head Room (in.)	40.1	40.1	40	40	40	40	38	38.4	NA
Front Leg Room (in.)	41.2	41.2	41.2	41.2	41.2	41.2	41.9	41.9	41.9
Rear Leg Room (in.)	36.6	36.6	39.6	39.6	39.6	39.6	32.1	36	NA
Maximum Seating	7	7	7	7	7	7	6	6	3
Max Cargo Capacity (cu ft.)	143	143	169	169	169	169	47	38	47
Maximum Payload (lbs.)	NA	NA	NA	NA	NA	2000	1275	1450	1275
Number of Cylinders	4	6	6	6	6	6	4	6	4
Displacement (liters)	2.4	3.3	3.8	3	3.8	3.3	2.5	3.9	2.5
Horsepower @ RPM	150@ 5200	158@ 4850	180@ 4400	150@ 5200	180@ 4400	158@ 4850	120@ 5200	175@ 4800	120@ 5200
Torque @ RPM	167@ 4000	203@ 3250	240@ 3200	176@ 4000	240@ 3200	203@ 3250	145@ 3250	225@ 3200	145@ 3250
Fuel Capacity	20	20	20	20	20	20	22	24	22
Towing Capacity	1000	2000	2000	1000	2000	2000	2000	3250	2000
EPA City (mpg) - Manual	NA	NA	NA	NA	NA	NA	20	17	20
EPA Hwy (mpg) - Manual	NA	NA	NA	NA	NA	NA	24	23	24
EPA City (mpg) - Auto	20	18	16	19	17	18	16	16	16
EPA Hwy (mpg) - Auto	26	24	23	26	24	24	21	21	21

SPECIFICATIONS & EPA MILEAGE RATINGS

SPECIFICATIONS & EPA MILEAGE RATINGS	Turning Circle (in.)	Length (in.)	Width (in.)	Height (in.)	Curb Weight (lbs.)	Wheelbase (in.)	Front Head Room (in.)	Rear Head Room (in.)	Front Leg Room (in.)	Rear Leg Room (in.)	Maximum Seating	Max Cargo Capacity (cu ft.)	Maximum Payload (lbs.)	Number of Cylinders	Displacement (liters)	Horsepower @ RPM	Torque @ RPM	Fuel Capacity	Towing Capacity	EPA City (mpg) - Manual	EPA Hwy (mpg) - Manual	EPA City (mpg) - Auto	EPA Hwy (mpg) - Auto
Dakota 4WD Club Cab SB	41	215	71.5	68.1	4025	131	40	38	41.9	32.1	6	47	1450	6	3.9	175@ 4800	225@ 3200	22	3800	15	19	14	18
Dakota 4WD Quad Cab SB	42.2	215.1	71.6	68.8	4391	131	39.8	38.4	41.9	36	6	38	1450	6	3.9	175@ 4800	225@ 3200	24	3450	15	19	14	18
Dakota 4WD Reg Cab SB	35.8	196	71.5	67.9	3808	112	40	NA	41.9	NA	3	47	1450	6	3.9	175@ 4800	225@ 3200	22	4100	15	19	14	18
Durango 2WD	38.9	193.5	71.7	71	4394	115.7	39.8	40.6	41.9	35.4	6	88	1656	8	5.2	230@ 4400	300@ 3200	25	4100	NA	NA	14	19
Durango 4WD	38.9	193.5	71.7	72.5	4689	115.9	39.8	40.6	41.9	35.4	6	88	1900	8	4.7	235@ 4800	295@ 3200	25	7600	NA	NA	13	17
Ram 1500 2WD Club Cab SB	46.9	224.2	79.3	71.6	4470	138.7	40.2	39.4	41	33.2	6	56	1695	8	5.2	230@ 4400	300@ 3200	26	3300	13	18	13	19
Ram 1500 2WD Quad Cab LB	51.6	244.1	79.3	72.7	4953	154.7	40.2	39.4	41	33.2	6	72	1450	8	5.2	230@ 4400	300@ 3200	35	2700	13	18	13	19
Ram 1500 2WD Quad Cab SB	46.9	224.2	79.3	71.6	4790	138.7	40.2	39.4	41	33.2	6	56	1610	8	5.2	230@ 4400	300@ 3200	26	3600	13	18	13	19
Ram 1500 2WD Reg Cab LB	45.2	224.1	79.3	72	4330	134.7	40.2	NA	41	NA	3	72	1970	6	3.9	175@ 4800	230@ 3200	35	3600	15	21	15	20
Ram 1500 2WD Reg Cab SB	40.6	204.1	79.3	72	4260	118.7	40.2	NA	41	NA	3	NA	2148	6	3.9	175@ 4800	230@ 3200	26	3600	15	21	15	20

specifications

SPECIFICATIONS & EPA MILEAGE RATINGS	Ram 1500 4WD Club Cab SB	Ram 1500 4WD Quad Cab LB	Ram 1500 4WD Quad Cab SB	Ram 1500 4WD Reg Cab LB	Ram 1500 4WD Reg Cab SB	Ram 2500 2WD Quad Cab LB	Ram 2500 2WD Quad Cab SB	Ram 2500 2WD Reg Cab LB	Ram 2500 4WD Quad Cab LB	Ram 2500 4WD Quad Cab SB
Turning Circle (in.)	45.4	51.6	45.4	45.2	40.6	51.6	51.6	45.7	51.6	51.6
Length (in.)	224.2	244.1	224.2	224.1	204.1	244	224	224.2	244	224
Width (in.)	79.3	79.3	79.3	79.3	79.3	79.3	79.3	79.3	79.3	79.3
Height (in.)	74.6	76.9	74.6	75.4	75.4	72.7	71.6	72	76.9	77.1
Curb Weight (lbs.)	4778	5328	5114	4845	4585	5283	5130	5035	5794	5410
Wheelbase (in.)	138.7	154.7	138.7	134.7	118.7	154.7	138.7	134.7	154.7	138.7
Front Head Room (in.)	40.2	40.2	40.2	40.2	40.2	40.2	40.2	40.2	40.2	40.2
Rear Head Room (in.)	39.4	39.4	39.4	NA	NA	39.4	39.4	NA	39.4	39.4
Front Leg Room (in.)	41	41	41	41	41	41	41	41	41	41
Rear Leg Room (in.)	33.2	33.2	33.2	NA	NA	33.2	33.2	NA	33.2	33.2
Maximum Seating	6	6	6	3	3	6	6	3	6	6
Max Cargo Capacity (cu ft.)	56	72	56	72	56	72	56	72	72	56
Maximum Payload (lbs.)	1560	1315	1475	1555	1715	3355	3465	3765	2905	3015
Number of Cylinders	8	8	8	8	8	8	8	8	8	8
Displacement (liters)	5.2	5.2	5.2	5.2	5.2	5.9	5.9	5.9	5.9	5.9
Horsepower @ RPM	230@ 4400	230@ 4400	230@ 4400	230@ 4400	230@ 4400	245@ 4000	245@ 4000	245@ 4000	245@ 4000	245@ 4000
Torque @ RPM	300@ 3200	300@ 3200	300@ 3200	300@ 3200	300@ 3200	335@ 3200	335@ 3200	335@ 3200	335@ 3200	335@ 3200
Fuel Capacity	26	35	26	35	26	35	34	35	35	34
Towing Capacity	4800	7000	4200	5200	5200	8600	8800	8900	8100	8400
EPA City (mpg) - Manual	13	13	13	13	13	NA	NA	NA	NA	NA
EPA Hwy (mpg) - Manual	17	17	17	17	17	NA	NA	NA	NA	NA
EPA City (mpg) - Auto	12	12	12	12	12	NA	NA	NA	NA	12
EPA Hwy (mpg) - Auto	16	16	16	16	16	NA	NA	NA	NA	16

SPECIFICATIONS & EPA MILEAGE RATINGS	EPA Hwy (mpg) - Auto	EPA City (mpg) - Auto	EPA Hwy (mpg) - Manual	EPA City (mpg) - Manual	Towing Capacity	Fuel Capacity	Torque @ RPM	Horsepower @ RPM	Displacement (liters)	Number of Cylinders	Maximum Payload (lbs.)	Max Cargo Capacity (cu ft.)	Maximum Seating	Rear Leg Room (in.)	Front Leg Room (in.)	Rear Head Room (in.)	Front Head Room (in.)	Wheelbase (in.)	Curb Weight (lbs.)	Height (in.)	Width (in.)	Length (in.)	Turning Circle (in.)
Ram 2500 4WD Reg Cab LB	16	12	NA	NA	8600	35	335@ 3200	245@ 4000	5.9	8	3315	72	3	NA	41	NA	40.2	134.7	5485	77.1	79.3	224.1	45.3
Ram 3500 2WD Quad Cab	NA	NA	NA	NA	8900	35	345@ 3200	245@ 4000	5.9	8	4760	72	6	33.2	41	39.4	40.2	154.7	5904	72.9	93.8	244.1	52.5
Ram 3500 2WD Reg Cab	NA	NA	NA	NA	9300	35	345@ 3200	245@ 4000	5.9	8	5045	72	3	NA	41	NA	40.2	134.7	5455	72.7	93.8	224.1	45.4
Ram 3500 4WD Quad Cab	NA	NA	NA	NA	8600	35	345@ 3200	245@ 4000	5.9	8	4820	72	6	33.2	41	39.4	40.2	154.7	6215	77	93.8	244.1	52.4
Ram 3500 4WD Reg Cab	NA	NA	NA	NA	9000	35	345@ 3200	245@ 4000	5.9	8	4595	72	3	NA	41	NA	40.2	134.7	5905	77.1	93.8	224.1	52.5
Ram Wagon 1500	16	14	NA	NA	5700	32	230@ 3200	175@ 4800	3.9	6	2040	209	8	40.6	39	39.2	38.9	109.6	4245	79.6	78.8	192.6	39.4
Ram Wagon 2500	15	12	NA	NA	7700	35	300@ 3200	230@ 4400	5.2	8	2520	241	8	40.6	39	39.2	38.9	127.6	4290	80	78.8	208.5	46.2
Ram Wagon 3500	NA	NA	NA	NA	7900	35	300@ 3200	230@ 4400	5.2	8	3125	300	15	40.6	39	39.2	38.9	127.6	4645	83.6	78.8	234.5	52.4
FORD																							
Econoline Wagon E-150	18	14	NA	NA	6500	35	250@ 3000	195@ 4750	4.2	6	2165	230	8	36.9	40	40.2	42.5	138	5087	80.9	79.3	211.9	46.7

specifications

SPECIFICATIONS & EPA MILEAGE RATINGS

	Econoline Wagon E-350 SD	Econoline Wagon E-350 SD Extended	Excursion 2WD	Excursion 4WD	Expedition 2WD	Expedition 4WD 4.6L	Expedition 4WD 5.4L	Explorer 4.0L OHC 2WD	Explorer 4.0L OHC 4WD	Explorer V8 AWD
Turning Circle (in.)	48	48	NA	NA	40.4	40.5	40.5	37.3	37.3	37.3
Length (in.)	211.9	231.9	226.7	226.7	204.6	204.6	204.6	190.7	190.7	190.7
Width (in.)	79.3	79.3	80	80	78.7	78.7	78.7	70.2	70.2	70.2
Height (in.)	83.4	84.1	76.5	79.5	78.4	76.5	78.4	67.7	67.5	67.5
Curb Weight (lbs.)	5840	6174	6610	7150	4808	5177	5177	3876	4113	4113
Wheelbase (in.)	138	138	137.1	137.1	119	119	119	111.6	111.6	111.6
Front Head Room (in.)	42.5	42.5	41	41	39.8	39.8	39.8	39.9	39.9	39.9
Rear Head Room (in.)	40.2	40.2	41.1	41.1	39.8	39.8	39.8	39.3	39.3	39.3
Front Leg Room (in.)	40	40	42.3	42.3	40.9	40.9	40.9	42.4	42.4	42.4
Rear Leg Room (in.)	36.9	36.9	40.5	40.5	38.9	38.9	38.9	36.8	36.8	36.8
Maximum Seating	12	15	8	8	8	8	8	5	5	5
Max Cargo Capacity (cu ft.)	230	276	65	65	118	118	118	80	80	81
Maximum Payload (lbs.)	4160	3915	1990	1744	1800	1800	1800	900	900	900
Number of Cylinders	8	8	8	10	8	8	8	6	6	8
Displacement (liters)	5.4	5.4	5.4	6.8	4.6	4.6	5.4	4	4	5
Horsepower @ RPM	235@ 4250	235@ 4250	260@ 4500	310@ 4250	240@ 4750	240@ 4750	260@ 4500	210@ 5250	210@ 5250	215@ 4200
Torque @ RPM	335@ 3000	335@ 3000	345@ 2300	410@ 2650	293@ 3500	293@ 3500	345@ 2300	240@ 3250	240@ 3250	288@ 3300
Fuel Capacity	35	35	44	44	26	30	30	21	21	21
Towing Capacity	10000	10000	6200	9700	5900	7400	6900	4799	5600	5600
EPA City (mpg) - Manual	NA	NA	NA	NA	NA	NA	NA	NA	NA	NA
EPA Hwy (mpg) - Manual	NA	NA	NA	NA	NA	NA	NA	NA	NA	NA
EPA City (mpg) - Auto	NA	NA	13	12	13	12	12	16	16	14
EPA Hwy (mpg) - Auto	NA	NA	18	16	18	16	16	21	20	20

SPECIFICATIONS & EPA MILEAGE RATINGS	Explorer 4.0L OHV 2WD	Explorer 4.0L OHV 4WD	Explorer Sport 2WD	Explorer Sport 4WD	F-150 2WD Reg Cab Flareside	F-150 2WD Reg Cab LB	F-150 2WD Reg Cab SB	F-150 2WD X-Cab LB 4.2L	F-150 2WD X-Cab LB 4.6L	F-150 2WD X-Cab SB 4.2L
Turning Circle (in.)	37.3	37.3	34.6	34.7	40.5	45.9	40.5	51.3	51.3	45.9
Length (in.)	190.7	190.7	180.8	180.8	205.9	224.2	205.6	242.8	242.8	220.8
Width (in.)	70.2	70.2	70.2	70.2	79.1	78.4	78.4	78.4	78.4	78.4
Height (in.)	67.7	67.5	67.1	67	72.7	72.4	72.7	72.5	72.5	72.8
Curb Weight (lbs.)	3876	4113	3680	3903	3949	4041	3923	4393	4393	4216
Wheelbase (in.)	111.6	111.6	101.7	101.7	120	138.5	120	157.1	157.1	138.5
Front Head Room (in.)	39.9	39.9	39.9	39.9	40.8	40.8	40.8	40.8	40.8	40.8
Rear Head Room (in.)	39.3	39.3	39.3	39.3	NA	NA	NA	37.8	37.8	37.8
Front Leg Room (in.)	42.4	42.4	42.4	42.4	40.9	40.9	40.9	40.9	40.9	40.9
Rear Leg Room (in.)	36.8	36.8	34.5	34.5	NA	NA	NA	32.2	32.2	32.2
Maximum Seating	5	5	4	4	3	3	3	6	6	6
Max Cargo Capacity (cu ft.)	80	80	70	70	50	73	59	73	73	59
Maximum Payload (lbs.)	900	900	750	750	1650	1555	1675	1605	1575	1780
Number of Cylinders	6	6	6	6	6	6	6	6	8	6
Displacement (liters)	4	4	4	4	4.2	4.2	4.2	4.2	4.6	4.2
Horsepower @ RPM	160@ 4200	160@ 4200	160@ 4200	160@ 4200	205@ 4750	205@ 4750	205@ 4750	205@ 4750	220@ 4500	205@ 4750
Torque @ RPM	225@ 2750	225@ 2750	225@ 2750	225@ 2750	250@ 3000	250@ 3000	250@ 3000	250@ 3000	290@ 3250	250@ 3000
Fuel Capacity	21	21	17.5	17.5	25	30	25	30	30	25.1
Towing Capacity	5000	5000	2000	1799	2300	2300	2300	2100	3300	2100
EPA City (mpg) - Manual	18	15	18	15	16	16	16	16	NA	16
EPA Hwy (mpg) - Manual	23	19	23	19	21	21	21	21	NA	21
EPA City (mpg) - Auto	16	16	16	16	16	16	16	16	15	16
EPA Hwy (mpg) - Auto	20	20	20	20	20	20	20	20	19	20

specifications

SPECIFICATIONS & EPA MILEAGE RATINGS

SPECIFICATIONS & EPA MILEAGE RATINGS	F-150 2WD X-Cab SB 4.6L	F-150 4WD Reg Cab Flareside	F-150 4WD Reg Cab LB	F-150 4WD Reg Cab SB	F-150 4WD X-Cab Flareside SB	F-150 4WD X-Cab LB	F-150 4WD X-Cab SB	F-150 SVT Lightning	F-250 2WD SD Reg Cab LB	F-250 2WD SD Crew Cab LB
Turning Circle (in.)	45.9	40.5	45.9	40.5	45.9	51.3	45.9	44.3	48.2	58.4
Length (in.)	220.8	207.4	225.7	207.1	226	244.3	225.7	208	222.2	257.6
Width (in.)	78.4	79.5	79.5	79.5	79.5	79.5	79.5	79.1	80	80
Height (in.)	72.6	75.4	75.1	75.1	75.5	75.5	75.1	70.9	76.2	77.2
Curb Weight (lbs.)	4216	4325	4216	4299	4638	4806	4613	4670	4956	5576
Wheelbase (in.)	138.5	120	138.5	120	138.8	157.4	138.8	119.8	137	172.4
Front Head Room (in.)	40.8	40.8	40.8	40.8	40.8	40.8	40.8	40.8	41.3	41.4
Rear Head Room (in.)	37.8	NA	NA	NA	37.8	37.8	37.8	NA	NA	41
Front Leg Room (in.)	40.9	40.9	40.9	40.9	40.9	40.9	40.9	40.9	40.7	40.7
Rear Leg Room (in.)	32.2	NA	NA	NA	32.2	32.2	32.2	NA	NA	42.5
Maximum Seating	6	3	6	3	6	6	6	3	3	6
Max Cargo Capacity (cu ft.)	59	50	59	59	50	73	59	50	78	78
Maximum Payload (lbs.)	1755	1670	1780	1700	1610	1440	1635	800	3722	3144
Number of Cylinders	8	6	6	6	8	8	8	8	8	8
Displacement (liters)	4.6	4.2	4.2	4.2	4.6	4.6	4.6	5.4	5.4	5.4
Horsepower @ RPM	220@ 4500	205@ 4750	205@ 4750	205@ 4750	220@ 4500	220@ 4500	220@ 4500	360@ 4750	260@ 4500	260@ 4500
Torque @ RPM	290@ 3250	250@ 3000	250@ 3000	250@ 3000	290@ 3250	290@ 3250	290@ 3250	440@ 3000	350@ 2500	350@ 2500
Fuel Capacity	25.1	24.5	25.1	24.5	25.1	30	25.1	25	38	38
Towing Capacity	2000	1900	2100	1900	3000	3000	3000	5000	9800	9100
EPA City (mpg) - Manual	NA	15	16	15	14	14	14	NA	NA	NA
EPA Hwy (mpg) - Manual	NA	18	21	18	17	17	17	NA	NA	NA
EPA City (mpg) - Auto	15	15	16	15	14	14	14	13	NA	NA
EPA Hwy (mpg) - Auto	19	18	20	18	17	17	17	17	NA	NA

SPECIFICATIONS & EPA MILEAGE RATINGS	F-250 2WD SD Crew Cab SB	F-250 2WD SD X-Cab LB	F-250 2WD SD X-Cab SB	F-250 4WD SD Crew Cab LB	F-250 4WD SD Crew Cab SB	F-250 4WD SD Reg Cab	F-250 4WD SD X-Cab LB	F-250 4WD SD X-Cab SB	F-350 2WD Reg Cab DRW LB	F-350 2WD Reg Cab SRW LB
Turning Circle (in.)	53.7	54.2	49.6	61.6	56.6	50.4	57.2	52	48.2	48.2
Length (in.)	241.4	243.2	227	257.6	241.4	222.2	243.2	227	222.2	222.2
Width (in.)	80	80	80	80	80	80	80	80	95.5	80
Height (in.)	77.2	76.5	76.6	80.8	80.8	79.7	80.4	80.4	76.2	76.2
Curb Weight (lbs.)	5487	5278	5189	6021	5932	5439	5724	5635	5221	4966
Wheelbase (in.)	156.2	158	141.8	172.4	156.2	137	158	141.8	137	137
Front Head Room (in.)	41.4	41.4	41.4	41.4	41.4	41.3	41.4	41.4	41.3	41.3
Rear Head Room (in.)	41	38.5	38.5	41	41	NA	38.5	38.5	NA	NA
Front Leg Room (in.)	40.7	40.7	40.7	40.7	40.7	40.7	40.7	40.7	40.7	40.7
Rear Leg Room (in.)	42.5	32.4	32.4	42.5	42.5	NA	32.4	32.4	NA	NA
Maximum Seating	6	6	6	6	6	3	6	6	3	3
Max Cargo Capacity (cu ft.)	65	78	65	78	65	78	78	65	78	78
Maximum Payload (lbs.)	3313	3443	3661	2770	2860	3360	3070	3160	5859	4796
Number of Cylinders	8	8	8	8	8	8	8	8	8	8
Displacement (liters)	5.4	5.4	5.4	5.4	5.4	5.4	5.4	5.4	5.4	5.4
Horsepower @ RPM	260@ 4500	260@ 4500	260@ 4500	260@ 4500	260@ 4500	260@ 4500	260@ 4500	260@ 4500	260@ 4500	260@ 4500
Torque @ RPM	350@ 2500	350@ 2500	350@ 2500	350@ 2500	350@ 2500	350@ 2500	350@ 2500	350@ 2500	350@ 2500	350@ 2500
Fuel Capacity	29	38	29	38	29	38	38	29	38	38
Towing Capacity	9100	9400	9400	8700	8700	9300	9000	9000	5500	10000
EPA City (mpg) - Manual	NA	NA	NA	NA	NA	NA	NA	NA	NA	NA
EPA Hwy (mpg) - Manual	NA	NA	NA	NA	NA	NA	NA	NA	NA	NA
EPA City (mpg) - Auto	NA	NA	NA	NA	NA	NA	NA	NA	NA	NA
EPA Hwy (mpg) - Auto	NA	NA	NA	NA	NA	NA	NA	NA	NA	NA

specifications

SPECIFICATIONS & EPA MILEAGE RATINGS	F-350 2WD SD CC DRW LB	F-350 2WD SD CC DRW SB	F-350 2WD SD CC SRW LB	F-350 2WD SD CC SRW SB	F-350 2WD X-Cab DRW LB	F-350 2WD X-Cab SRW LB	F-350 2WD X-Cab SRW SB	F-350 4WD CC DRW LB	F-350 4WD CC DRW SB	F-350 4WD CC SRW LB
Turning Circle (in.)	58.4	53.7	58.4	53.7	54.2	54.2	49.6	61.6	56.6	61.6
Length (in.)	257.6	241.4	257.6	241.4	243.2	243.2	227	257.6	241.4	257.6
Width (in.)	95.5	95.5	80	80	95.5	80	80	95.5	95.5	80
Height (in.)	77.2	77.2	77.2	77.2	76.5	76.5	76.6	80.8	80.8	80.8
Curb Weight (lbs.)	6049	5960	5586	5497	5543	5288	5199	6491	6402	6031
Wheelbase (in.)	172.4	156.2	172.4	156.2	158	158	141.8	172.4	156.2	172.4
Front Head Room (in.)	41.4	41.4	41.4	41.4	41.4	41.4	41.4	41.4	41.4	41.4
Rear Head Room (in.)	41	41	41	41	38.5	38.5	38.5	41	41	41
Front Leg Room (in.)	40.7	40.7	40.7	40.7	40.7	40.7	40.7	40.7	40.7	40.7
Rear Leg Room (in.)	42.5	42.5	42.5	42.5	32.4	32.4	32.4	42.5	42.5	42.5
Maximum Seating	6	6	6	6	6	6	6	6	6	6
Max Cargo Capacity (cu ft.)	78	65	78	65	78	78	65	78	65	78
Maximum Payload (lbs.)	5289	5448	4387	4387	5592	4517	4735	4775	5035	3838
Number of Cylinders	10	10	8	8	8	8	8	10	10	8
Displacement (liters)	6.8	6.8	5.4	5.4	5.4	5.4	5.4	6.8	6.8	5.4
Horsepower @ RPM	310@ 4250	310@ 4250	260@ 4500	260@ 4500	260@ 4500	260@ 4500	260@ 4500	310@ 4250	310@ 4250	260@ 4500
Torque @ RPM	425@ 3250	425@ 3250	350@ 2500	350@ 2500	350@ 2500	350@ 2500	350@ 2500	425@ 3250	425@ 3250	350@ 2500
Fuel Capacity	38	29	38	29	38	38	29	38	29	38
Towing Capacity	10000	10000	10000	10000	10000	10000	10000	10000	10000	10000
EPA City (mpg) - Manual	NA	NA	NA	NA	NA	NA	NA	NA	NA	NA
EPA Hwy (mpg) - Manual	NA	NA	NA	NA	NA	NA	NA	NA	NA	NA
EPA City (mpg) - Auto	NA	NA	NA	NA	NA	NA	NA	NA	NA	NA
EPA Hwy (mpg) - Auto	NA	NA	NA	NA	NA	NA	NA	NA	NA	NA

SPECIFICATIONS & EPA MILEAGE RATINGS	F-350 4WD CC SRW SB	F-350 4WD Reg Cab DRW LB	F-350 4WD Reg Cab SRW LB	F-350 4WD X-Cab DRW LB	F-350 4WD X-Cab SRW LB	F-350 4WD X-Cab SRW SB	Ranger 2WD Reg Cab LB	Ranger 2WD Reg Cab SB	Ranger 2WD X-Cab SB	Ranger 4WD Reg Cab LB
Turning Circle (in.)	56.6	50.4	50.4	57.2	57.2	52	39.8	37.7	42.7	41.1
Length (in.)	241.4	222.2	222.2	243.2	243.2	227	200.7	187.5	202.9	200.7
Width (in.)	80	95.5	80	95.5	80	80	69.4	69.4	69.4	69.4
Height (in.)	80.8	79.7	79.7	80.4	80.4	80.4	64.9	64.9	64.8	67.6
Curb Weight (lbs.)	5942	5704	5449	5900	5734	5645	3086	3030	3210	3505
Wheelbase (in.)	156.2	137	137	158	158	141.8	117.5	111.6	125.7	117.5
Front Head Room (in.)	41.4	41.3	41.3	41.4	41.4	41.4	39.2	39.2	39.2	39.2
Rear Head Room (in.)	41	NA	NA	38.5	38.5	38.5	NA	NA	35.6	NA
Front Leg Room (in.)	40.7	40.7	40.7	40.7	40.7	40.7	42.4	42.4	42.2	42.4
Rear Leg Room (in.)	42.5	NA	NA	32.4	32.4	32.4	NA	NA	40.3	NA
Maximum Seating	6	3	3	6	6	6	3	3	5	3
Max Cargo Capacity (cu ft.)	65	78	78	78	78	65	43	37	37	43
Maximum Payload (lbs.)	3974	5375	4390	5164	4097	4328	1260	1260	1260	1260
Number of Cylinders	8	8	8	8	8	8	4	4	4	6
Displacement (liters)	5.4	5.4	5.4	5.4	5.4	5.4	2.5	2.5	2.5	3
Horsepower @ RPM	260@ 4500	260@ 4500	260@ 4500	260@ 4500	260@ 4500	260@ 4500	119@ 5000	119@ 5000	119@ 5000	152@ 4750
Torque @ RPM	350@ 2500	350@ 2500	350@ 2500	350@ 2500	350@ 2500	350@ 2500	146@ 3000	146@ 3000	146@ 3000	192@ 3750
Fuel Capacity	29	38	38	38	38	29	20	16.5	19.5	20
Towing Capacity	10000	10000	10000	10000	10000	10000	1600	1600	1440	2400
EPA City (mpg) - Manual	NA	NA	NA	NA	NA	NA	22	22	22	18
EPA Hwy (mpg) - Manual	NA	NA	NA	NA	NA	NA	27	27	27	21
EPA City (mpg) - Auto	NA	NA	NA	NA	NA	NA	20	20	20	15
EPA Hwy (mpg) - Auto	NA	NA	NA	NA	NA	NA	25	25	25	19

SPECIFICATIONS & EPA MILEAGE RATINGS	Turning Circle (in.)	Length (in.)	Width (in.)	Height (in.)	Curb Weight (lbs.)	Wheelbase (in.)	Front Head Room (in.)	Rear Head Room (in.)	Front Leg Room (in.)	Rear Leg Room (in.)	Maximum Seating	Max Cargo Capacity (cu ft.)	Maximum Payload (lbs.)	Number of Cylinders	Displacement (liters)	Horsepower @ RPM	Torque @ RPM	Fuel Capacity	Towing Capacity	EPA City (mpg) - Manual	EPA Hwy (mpg) - Manual	EPA City (mpg) - Auto	EPA Hwy (mpg) - Auto
Ranger 4WD Reg Cab SB	39.1	187.5	69.4	67.6	3445	111.6	39.2	NA	42.4	NA	3	37	1260	6	3	152@ 4750	192@ 3750	16.5	2400	18	21	15	19
Ranger 4WD X-Cab SB	43	202.9	69.4	67.5	3606	125.7	39.2	35.6	42.2	40.3	5	37	1260	6	3	152@ 4750	192@ 3750	19.5	2240	18	21	15	19
Windstar Base/LX	40.4	200.9	76.6	66.1	3761	120.7	39.3	41.1	40.7	36.8	7	146	1831	6	3	150@ 5000	186@ 3750	26	2000	NA	NA	17	24
Windstar SE/SEL	40.4	200.9	76.6	65.8	4194	120.7	39.3	40.7	40.7	38.6	7	149	1831	6	3.8	200@ 4900	240@ 3600	26	2000	NA	NA	17	24
GMC																							
C/K2500 2WD Crew Cab SB	53.8	231.9	76.8	73.9	5416	154.5	40	40.8	41.5	37.9	6	56	3184	8	5.7	255@ 4600	330@ 2800	26	8000	NA	NA	NA	NA
C/K2500 2WD Reg Cab LB	43.7	213.4	76.8	71.2	4820	131.5	40	NA	41.5	NA	3	69	3779	8	5.7	255@ 4600	330@ 2800	34	8000	NA	NA	NA	NA
C/K2500 2WD X-Cab LB	46.6	237.4	76.8	73.1	5084	155.5	40	38	41.5	28.7	6	69	3516	8	5.7	255@ 4600	330@ 2800	34	8000	NA	NA	NA	NA
C/K2500 4WD Crew Cab SB	55.7	231.9	76.8	74.5	5707	154.5	40	40.8	41.5	37.9	6	56	2893	8	5.7	255@ 4600	330@ 2800	26	7500	NA	NA	NA	NA
C/K2500 4WD Reg Cab LB	44.7	213.4	76.8	76	5178	131.5	40	NA	41.5	NA	3	69	3422	8	5.7	255@ 4600	330@ 2800	34	7500	NA	NA	NA	NA

SPECIFICATIONS & EPA MILEAGE RATINGS

SPECIFICATIONS & EPA MILEAGE RATINGS	C/K2500 4WD X-Cab LB	C/K2500 4WD X-Cab SB	C/K3500 2WD CC DRW SB	C/K3500 2WD CC SRW LB	C/K3500 2WD Reg Cab SRW LB	C/K3500 2WD X-Cab DRW LB	C/K3500 4WD CC DRW SB	C/K3500 4WD CC SRW LB	C/K3500 4WD Reg Cab SRW LB	C/K3500 4WD X-Cab DRW LB
Turning Circle (in.)	52.2	47.6	53.8	53.8	43.4	50.5	55.8	55.8	45	52
Length (in.)	237.4	218.5	231.9	250.9	213.4	237.4	231.9	250.9	213.4	237.4
Width (in.)	76.8	76.8	94.3	76.8	76.8	94.3	76.8	76.8	76.8	94.3
Height (in.)	74	73.7	73.9	73.9	73.4	72.6	94.3	74.5	74	73.4
Curb Weight (lbs.)	5507	5300	5509	5509	4838	5427	5893	5893	5229	5836
Wheelbase (in.)	155.5	141.5	154.5	168.5	131.5	155.5	168.5	168.5	131.5	155.5
Front Head Room (in.)	40	40	40	40	40	40	39.9	39.9	40	40
Rear Head Room (in.)	38	38	40.8	40.8	NA	38	40.8	40.8	NA	38
Front Leg Room (in.)	41.5	41.5	41.5	41.5	41.5	41.5	41.7	41.7	41.5	41.5
Rear Leg Room (in.)	28.7	28.7	37.9	37.9	NA	28.7	37.9	37.9	NA	28.7
Maximum Seating	6	6	6	6	3	6	6	6	3	6
Max Cargo Capacity (cu ft.)	69	56	56	69	69	69	56	69	69	69
Maximum Payload (lbs.)	3092	3299	2944	3499	4171	4583	2239	3327	3988	4184
Number of Cylinders	8	8	8	8	8	8	8	8	8	8
Displacement (liters)	5.7	5.7	7.4	5.7	5.7	5.7	7.4	5.7	5.7	5.7
Horsepower @ RPM	255@ 4600	255@ 4600	290@ 4000	255@ 4600	255@ 4600	255@ 4600	290@ 4000	255@ 4600	255@ 4600	255@ 4600
Torque @ RPM	330@ 2800	330@ 2800	410@ 3200	330@ 2800	330@ 2800	330@ 2800	410@ 3200	330@ 2800	330@ 2800	330@ 2800
Fuel Capacity	34	25	26	34	34	34	26	34	34	34
Towing Capacity	7500	7500	10000	7000	7500	9000	10000	6500	7000	7000
EPA City (mpg) - Manual	NA	NA	NA	NA	NA	NA	NA	NA	NA	NA
EPA Hwy (mpg) - Manual	NA	NA	NA	NA	NA	NA	NA	NA	NA	NA
EPA City (mpg) - Auto	NA	NA	NA	NA	NA	NA	NA	NA	NA	NA
EPA Hwy (mpg) - Auto	NA	NA	NA	NA	NA	NA	NA	NA	NA	NA

specifications

SPECIFICATIONS & EPA MILEAGE RATINGS	Envoy	Jimmy 2WD 2-Door	Jimmy 2WD 4-Door	Jimmy 4WD 2-Door	Jimmy 4WD 4-Door	Safari AWD	Safari RWD	Savana G1500	Savana G2500	Savana G2500 Extended
Turning Circle (in.)	39.4	34.8	36.6	34.6	36.8	40.5	39.4	45.2	47.4	53.4
Length (in.)	183.8	177.3	183.8	177.3	183.8	189.8	189.8	218.8	218.8	238.8
Width (in.)	67.8	67.8	67.8	67.8	67.8	77.5	77.5	79.2	79.2	79.2
Height (in.)	64.4	65.6	64.8	65.1	64.4	75	75	81.4	82.7	81.3
Curb Weight (lbs.)	4049	3518	3671	3848	4049	4428	4187	5142	5823	6045
Wheelbase (in.)	107	100.5	107	100.5	107	111.2	111.2	135	135	155
Front Head Room (in.)	39.5	39.5	39.5	39.5	39.5	39.2	39.2	40.6	40.6	40.6
Rear Head Room (in.)	38.1	38.3	38.1	38.3	38.1	37.9	37.9	39	39	39
Front Leg Room (in.)	42.4	42.4	42.4	42.4	42.4	41.6	41.6	41.1	41.1	41.1
Rear Leg Room (in.)	36.3	35.6	36.3	35.6	36.3	36.5	36.5	38.5	38.5	38.5
Maximum Seating	5	5	5	5	5	8	8	8	12	15
Max Cargo Capacity (cu ft.)	74	67	74	67	74	170	170	267	267	317
Maximum Payload (lbs.)	1301	932	1329	1002	1301	1672	1763	1958	2776	2555
Number of Cylinders	6	6	6	6	6	6	6	6	8	8
Displacement (liters)	4.3	4.3	4.3	4.3	4.3	4.3	4.3	4.3	5.7	5.7
Horsepower @ RPM	190@ 4400	190@ 4400	190@ 4400	190@ 4400	190@ 4400	190@ 4400	190@ 4400	200@ 4400	255@ 4600	255@ 4600
Torque @ RPM	250@ 2800	250@ 2800	250@ 2800	250@ 2800	250@ 2800	250@ 2800	250@ 2800	250@ 2800	330@ 2800	330@ 2800
Fuel Capacity	18	19	18	19	18	27	27	31	31	31
Towing Capacity	5000	4500	4500	4000	4000	5000	5500	7300	8900	8300
EPA City (mpg) - Manual	NA	17	NA	15	NA	NA	NA	NA	NA	NA
EPA Hwy (mpg) - Manual	NA	23	NA	18	NA	NA	NA	NA	NA	NA
EPA City (mpg) - Auto	16	16	16	16	16	15	16	15	14	14
EPA Hwy (mpg) - Auto	20	21	21	20	20	19	20	19	18	18

SPECIFICATIONS & EPA MILEAGE RATINGS

SPECIFICATIONS & EPA MILEAGE RATINGS	Savana G3500	Savana G3500 Extended	Sierra 1500 2WD Reg Cab LB	Sierra 1500 2WD Reg Cab SB	Sierra 1500 2WD X-Cab LB	Sierra 1500 2WD X-Cab SB	Sierra 1500 4WD Reg Cab LB	Sierra 1500 4WD Reg Cab SB	Sierra 1500 4WD X-Cab LB	Sierra 1500 4WD X-Cab SB
Turning Circle (in.)	47.5	53.5	43.6	40	50.4	46.6	44.5	40.7	51.1	47.3
Length (in.)	218.8	238.8	222.1	203.2	246.6	227.7	222.1	203.2	246.6	227.7
Width (in.)	79.2	79.2	78.5	78.5	78.5	78.5	78.5	78.5	78.5	78.5
Height (in.)	81.3	82.1	71	71.2	70.8	71.2	73.7	73.8	72.7	72.7
Curb Weight (lbs.)	5987	6205	4023	3923	4442	4235	4365	4248	4748	4621
Wheelbase (in.)	135	155	133	119	157.5	143.5	133	119	157.5	143.5
Front Head Room (in.)	40.6	40.6	41	41	41	41	41	41	41	41
Rear Head Room (in.)	39	39	NA	NA	38.4	38.4	NA	NA	38.4	38.4
Front Leg Room (in.)	41.1	41.1	41.3	41.3	41.3	41.3	41.3	41.3	41.3	41.3
Rear Leg Room (in.)	38.5	38.5	NA	NA	33.7	33.7	NA	NA	33.7	33.7
Maximum Seating	12	15	3	3	6	6	3	3	6	6
Max Cargo Capacity (cu ft.)	267	317	71	57	71	57	71	57	71	57
Maximum Payload (lbs.)	3513	3294	2368	2177	1757	1965	2035	1852	1652	1779
Number of Cylinders	8	8	6	6	8	8	6	6	8	8
Displacement (liters)	5.7	5.7	4.3	4.3	4.8	4.8	4.3	4.3	4.8	4.8
Horsepower @ RPM	255@ 4600	255@ 4600	200@ 4600	200@ 4600	275@ 5200	275@ 5200	200@ 4600	200@ 4600	275@ 5200	275@ 5200
Torque @ RPM	330@ 2800	330@ 2800	260@ 2800	260@ 2800	290@ 4000	290@ 4000	260@ 2800	260@ 2800	290@ 4000	290@ 4000
Fuel Capacity	31	31	34	26	34	26	34	26	34	26
Towing Capacity	10000	10000	3500	3500	6000	6000	4000	4000	6500	6500
EPA City (mpg) - Manual	NA	NA	17	17	NA	NA	15	15	NA	NA
EPA Hwy (mpg) - Manual	NA	NA	23	23	NA	NA	18	18	NA	NA
EPA City (mpg) - Auto	14	14	16	16	16	16	16	16	15	15
EPA Hwy (mpg) - Auto	18	18	20	20	21	21	20	20	18	18

specifications

SPECIFICATIONS & EPA MILEAGE RATINGS

	Sierra 2500 2WD Reg Cab HD LB	Sierra 2500 2WD Reg Cab LB	Sierra 2500 2WD X-Cab HD LB	Sierra 2500 2WD X-Cab SB	Sierra 2500 4WD Reg Cab HD LB	Sierra 2500 4WD X-Cab HD LB	Sierra 2500 4WD X-Cab SB	Sonoma 2WD Reg Cab LB	Sonoma 2WD Reg Cab SB	Sonoma 2WD X-Cab SB
Turning Circle (in.)	45.3	45.3	52.1	48.2	45.3	52.3	48.2	39.9	36.9	41.3
Length (in.)	222	222	246.5	227.6	222	246.7	227.6	206.6	190.6	205.3
Width (in.)	78.5	78.5	78.5	78.5	78.5	78.5	78.5	67.9	67.9	67.9
Height (in.)	73.7	73.7	74.1	74	74.2	74.5	74.4	62.9	62	62.7
Curb Weight (lbs.)	4999	4586	5318	4766	5266	5523	5485	3058	3031	3240
Wheelbase (in.)	133	133	157.5	143.5	133	157.5	143.5	117.9	108.3	122.9
Front Head Room (in.)	41	41	41	41	41	41	41	39.5	39.5	39.5
Rear Head Room (in.)	NA	NA	38.4	38.4	NA	38.4	38.4	NA	NA	NA
Front Leg Room (in.)	41.3	41.3	41.3	41.3	41.3	41.3	41.3	42.4	42.4	42.4
Rear Leg Room (in.)	NA	NA	33.7	33.7	NA	33.7	33.7	NA	NA	NA
Maximum Seating	3	3	6	6	3	6	6	3	3	5
Max Cargo Capacity (cu ft.)	71	71	71	57	71	71	57	48	39	39
Maximum Payload (lbs.)	3601	2614	3282	2434	3334	3070	3115	1509	1171	1168
Number of Cylinders	8	8	8	8	8	8	8	4	4	4
Displacement (liters)	6	5.3	6	5.3	6	6	6	2.2	2.2	2.2
Horsepower @ RPM	300@ 4800	285@ 5200	300@ 4800	285@ 5200	300@ 4800	300@ 4800	300@ 4800	120@ 5000	120@ 5000	120@ 5000
Torque @ RPM	355@ 4000	325@ 4000	355@ 4000	325@ 4000	355@ 4000	355@ 4000	355@ 4000	140@ 3600	140@ 3600	140@ 3600
Fuel Capacity	34	34	34	26	34	34	26	19	19	19
Towing Capacity	8700	8700	8700	8700	9400	9400	9400	2000	2000	2000
EPA City (mpg) - Manual	NA	NA	NA	NA	NA	NA	NA	23	23	23
EPA Hwy (mpg) - Manual	NA	NA	NA	NA	NA	NA	NA	29	29	29
EPA City (mpg) - Auto	12	15	12	15	NA	NA	NA	19	19	19
EPA Hwy (mpg) - Auto	16	19	16	19	NA	NA	NA	26	26	26

SPECIFICATIONS & EPA MILEAGE RATINGS

SPECIFICATIONS & EPA MILEAGE RATINGS	Sonoma 4WD Reg Cab SB	Sonoma 4WD X-Cab SB	Yukon 2WD	Yukon 4WD	Yukon Denali	Yukon XL 1500 2WD	Yukon XL 1500 4WD	Yukon XL 2500 2WD	Yukon XL 2500 4WD
Turning Circle (in.)	37.3	41.6	39	40.7	40.7	43.6	44.6	43.4	45
Length (in.)	190.6	205.3	198.9	198.9	201.4	219.3	219.3	219.3	219.3
Width (in.)	67.9	67.9	78.9	78.9	78.8	78.8	78.8	78.8	78.8
Height (in.)	63.4	63.4	76.7	76.5	74.3	75.8	75.7	76.7	77.1
Curb Weight (lbs.)	3564	3757	4471	4827	5867	4769	5226	4769	4769
Wheelbase (in.)	108.3	122.9	116	116	117.5	130	130	130	130
Front Head Room (in.)	39.5	39.5	40.7	40.7	39.9	40.7	40.7	40.7	40.7
Rear Head Room (in.)	NA	NA	39.4	39.4	38.9	39	39	39	39
Front Leg Room (in.)	42.4	42.4	41.3	41.3	41.7	41.3	41.3	41.3	41.3
Rear Leg Room (in.)	NA	NA	38.6	38.6	36.2	39.1	39.1	39.1	39.1
Maximum Seating	3	4	6	6	5	9	9	9	9
Max Cargo Capacity (cu ft.)	39	39	108	108	118	138	138	138	138
Maximum Payload (lbs.)	1094	896	1629	1423	933	1905	1836	3357	2914
Number of Cylinders	6	6	8	8	8	8	8	8	8
Displacement (liters)	4.3	4.3	4.8	4.8	5.7	5.3	5.3	6	6
Horsepower @ RPM	180@ 4400	180@ 4400	275@ 5200	275@ 5200	255@ 4600	285@ 5200	285@ 5200	300@ 4800	300@ 4800
Torque @ RPM	245@ 2800	245@ 2800	290@ 4000	290@ 4000	330@ 2800	325@ 4000	325@ 4000	355@ 4000	355@ 4000
Fuel Capacity	19	19	26	26	29.5	32.5	32.5	38	38
Towing Capacity	5500	5500	6000	5500	6500	6500	6000	7516	7013
EPA City (mpg) - Manual	17	17	NA	NA	NA	NA	NA	NA	NA
EPA Hwy (mpg) - Manual	21	21	NA	NA	NA	NA	NA	NA	NA
EPA City (mpg) - Auto	16	16	14	14	12	14	14	NA	NA
EPA Hwy (mpg) - Auto	21	21	18	18	16	18	16	NA	NA

SPECIFICATIONS & EPA MILEAGE RATINGS

HONDA

	EPA Hwy (mpg) - Auto	EPA City (mpg) - Auto	EPA Hwy (mpg) - Manual	EPA City (mpg) - Manual	Towing Capacity	Fuel Capacity	Torque @ RPM	Horsepower @ RPM	Displacement (liters)	Number of Cylinders	Maximum Payload (lbs.)	Max Cargo Capacity (cu ft.)	Maximum Seating	Rear Leg Room (in.)	Front Leg Room (in.)	Rear Head Room (in.)	Front Head Room (in.)	Wheelbase (in.)	Curb Weight (lbs.)	Height (in.)	Width (in.)	Length (in.)	Turning Circle (in.)
CR-V AWD	25	22	25	22	1000	15.3	133@ 4500	146@ 6200	2	4	NA	67	5	36.7	41.5	39.2	40.5	103.2	3210	65.9	68.9	177.6	34.8
CR-V FWD	25	23	NA	NA	1000	15.3	133@ 4500	146@ 6200	2	4	NA	67	5	36.7	41.5	39.2	40.5	103.2	3126	65.9	68.9	177.6	34.8
Odyssey EX	26	18	NA	NA	2000	20	229@ 4300	210@ 5200	3.5	6	NA	163	7	40	41	40	41.2	118.1	4288	69.7	75.6	201.2	37.7
Odyssey LX	26	18	NA	NA	2000	20	229@ 4300	210@ 5200	3.5	6	NA	163	7	40	41	40	41.2	118.1	4211	68.5	75.6	201.2	37.7
Passport EX 2WD	21	16	NA	NA	4500	21.1	214@ 3000	205@ 5400	3.2	6	NA	81	5	35	42.1	37.9	37.8	106.4	3857	68.8	70.4	178.2	38.4
Passport EX 4WD	20	16	NA	NA	4500	21.1	214@ 3000	205@ 5400	3.2	6	NA	81	5	35	42.1	37.9	37.8	106.4	4102	68.8	70.4	178.2	38.4
Passport LX 4WD	20	16	20	16	4500	21.1	214@ 3000	205@ 5400	3.2	6	NA	81	5	35	42.1	38.3	38.9	106.4	4041	68.8	70.4	184.2	38.4
Passport LX 2WD	21	16	20	16	4500	21.1	214@ 3000	205@ 5400	3.2	6	NA	81	5	35	42.1	38.3	38.9	106.4	3774	68.6	70.4	184	38.4

SPECIFICATIONS & EPA MILEAGE RATINGS

SPECIFICATIONS & EPA MILEAGE RATINGS	EPA Hwy (mpg) - Auto	EPA City (mpg) - Auto	EPA Hwy (mpg) - Manual	EPA City (mpg) - Manual	Towing Capacity	Fuel Capacity	Torque @ RPM	Horsepower @ RPM	Displacement (liters)	Number of Cylinders	Maximum Payload (lbs.)	Max Cargo Capacity (cu ft.)	Maximum Seating	Rear Leg Room (in.)	Front Leg Room (in.)	Rear Head Room (in.)	Front Head Room (in.)	Wheelbase (in.)	Curb Weight (lbs.)	Height (in.)	Width (in.)	Length (in.)	Turning Circle (in.)
INFINITI																							
QX4	19	15	NA	NA	5000	21.1	200@ 2800	170@ 4800	3.3	6	1130	85	5	31.8	41.7	37.5	39.5	106.3	4320	70.7	72.4	183.9	37.4
ISUZU																							
Hombre 4-Cyl 2WD Reg Cab	26	19	29	23	2000	22.2	140@ 3600	120@ 5000	2.2	4	1176	39	3	NA	42.4	NA	39.5	108.3	3024	63.2	67.9	187.1	37
Hombre 4-Cyl 2WD X-Cab	26	19	29	23	2000	22.2	140@ 3600	120@ 5000	2.2	4	1122	39	5	NA	42.4	NA	39.6	122.9	3278	63.3	67.9	201.7	41.3
Hombre 4WD Reg Cab	21	16	22	17	5500	18.5	240@ 2800	180@ 4400	4.3	6	1067	39	3	NA	42.4	NA	39.5	108.3	3583	63.9	67.9	187.1	37.3
Hombre 4WD X-Cab	21	16	22	17	5500	18.5	240@ 2800	180@ 4400	4.3	6	1067	39	5	NA	42.4	NA	39.6	122.9	3583	63.9	67.9	201.7	41.6
Hombre V6 2WD X-Cab	22	17	NA	NA	5500	22.2	240@ 2800	175@ 4400	4.3	6	1122	39	5	NA	42.4	NA	39.6	122.9	3278	63.3	67.9	201.7	41.3
Rodeo 4-Cyl 2WD	NA	NA	23	20	2500	21.1	144@ 4000	130@ 5200	2.2	4	1079	81	5	35	42.1	38.3	38.9	106.4	3471	66.1	70.4	176.7	38.4
Rodeo V6 2WD	21	16	20	16	4500	21.1	214@ 3000	205@ 5400	3.2	6	1049	81	5	35	42.1	38.3	38.9	106.4	3651	68.5	70.4	176.7	38.4

SPECIFICATIONS & EPA MILEAGE RATINGS	EPA Hwy (mpg) - Auto	EPA City (mpg) - Auto	EPA Hwy (mpg) - Manual	EPA City (mpg) - Manual	Towing Capacity	Fuel Capacity	Torque @ RPM	Horsepower @ RPM	Displacement (liters)	Number of Cylinders	Maximum Payload (lbs.)	Max Cargo Capacity (cu ft.)	Maximum Seating	Rear Leg Room (in.)	Front Leg Room (in.)	Rear Head Room (in.)	Front Head Room (in.)	Wheelbase (in.)	Curb Weight (lbs.)	Height (in.)	Width (in.)	Length (in.)	Turning Circle (in.)
Rodeo V6 4WD	20	16	20	16	4500	21.1	214@ 3000	205@ 5400	3.2	6	989	81	5	35	42.1	38.3	38.9	106.4	3863	68.5	70.4	176.7	38.4
JEEP																							
Cherokee 2.5L 2WD 2-Door	22	18	25	21	2000	20	150@ 3250	125@ 5400	2.5	4	1151	69	5	35	41.4	38	37.8	101.4	2979	63.8	69.4	167.5	35.8
Cherokee 2.5L 2WD 4-Door	22	18	25	21	2000	20	150@ 3250	125@ 5400	2.5	4	1151	69	5	35	41.4	38	37.8	101.4	3032	63.8	69.4	167.5	35.8
Cherokee 2.5L 4WD 2-Door	NA	NA	20	18	2000	20	150@ 3250	125@ 5400	2.5	4	1151	69	5	35	41.4	38	37.8	101.4	3125	63.8	69.4	167.5	35.8
Cherokee 2.5L 4WD 4-Door	NA	NA	20	18	2000	20	150@ 3250	125@ 5400	2.5	4	1151	69	5	35	41.4	38	37.8	101.4	3181	63.9	69.4	167.5	35.8
Cherokee 4.0L 2WD 2-Door	22	16	24	18	5000	20	225@ 3000	190@ 4600	4	6	1151	69	5	35	41.4	38	37.8	101.4	2979	63.8	69.4	167.5	35.8
Cherokee 4.0L 2WD 4-Door	22	16	24	18	5000	20	225@ 3000	190@ 4600	4	6	1151	69	5	35	41.4	38	37.8	101.4	3032	63.8	69.4	167.5	35.8
Cherokee 4.0L 4WD 2-Door	21	16	22	17	5000	20	225@ 3000	190@ 4600	4	6	1151	69	5	35	41.4	38	37.8	101.4	3125	63.8	69.4	167.5	35.8
Cherokee 4.0L 4WD 4-Door	21	16	22	17	5000	20	225@ 3000	190@ 4600	4	6	1151	69	5	35	41.4	38	37.8	101.4	3181	63.9	69.4	167.5	35.8

SPECIFICATIONS & EPA MILEAGE RATINGS

SPECIFICATIONS & EPA MILEAGE RATINGS	Grand Cherokee 2WD	Grand Cherokee 4WD	Wrangler SE	Wrangler Sport/Sahara	KIA	Sportage 2WD 4-Door	Sportage 2WD Convertible	Sportage 4WD 4-Door	Sportage 4WD Convertible
Turning Circle (in.)	37.5	37.5	33.6	33.6		34.8	32.2	34.8	32.2
Length (in.)	181.5	181.5	152	152		162.5	150.4	162.5	150.4
Width (in.)	72.3	72.3	66.7	66.7		68.1	68.1	68.1	68.1
Height (in.)	69.4	69.4	70.9	70.9		65	65	65	65
Curb Weight (lbs.)	3880	4130	3045	3202		3186	3108	3352	3230
Wheelbase (in.)	105.9	105.9	93.4	93.4		104.3	92.9	104.3	92.9
Front Head Room (in.)	39.7	39.7	42.3	42.3		39.6	39.6	39.6	39.6
Rear Head Room (in.)	39.5	39.5	NA	40.6		37.8	38.2	37.8	38.2
Front Leg Room (in.)	41.4	41.4	41.1	41.1		44.5	41.3	44.5	41.3
Rear Leg Room (in.)	35.3	35.3	NA	34.9		31.1	31	31.1	31
Maximum Seating	5	5	4	4		5	5	5	5
Max Cargo Capacity (cu ft.)	72	72	55	55		55	39	55	39
Maximum Payload (lbs.)	1150	1150	800	800		860	838	860	838
Number of Cylinders	6	6	4	6		4	4	4	4
Displacement (liters)	4	4	2.5	4		2	2	2	2
Horsepower @ RPM	195@ 4600	195@ 4600	120@ 5400	195@ 4600		130@ 5500	130@ 5500	130@ 5500	130@ 5500
Torque @ RPM	230@ 3000	230@ 3000	140@ 3500	230@ 3000		127@ 4000	127@ 4000	127@ 4000	127@ 4000
Fuel Capacity	20.5	20.5	19	19		15.8	14	15.8	14
Towing Capacity	5000	5000	2000	2000		2000	2000	2000	2000
EPA City (mpg) - Manual	NA	NA	18	16		20	NA	20	20
EPA Hwy (mpg) - Manual	NA	NA	20	19		23	NA	22	22
EPA City (mpg) - Auto	16	16	16	15		18	18	19	NA
EPA Hwy (mpg) - Auto	21	21	18	18		21	21	22	NA

specifications

SPECIFICATIONS & EPA MILEAGE RATINGS

Model	Turning Circle (in.)	Length (in.)	Width (in.)	Height (in.)	Curb Weight (lbs.)	Wheelbase (in.)	Front Head Room (in.)	Rear Head Room (in.)	Front Leg Room (in.)	Rear Leg Room (in.)	Maximum Seating	Max Cargo Capacity (cu ft.)	Maximum Payload (lbs.)	Number of Cylinders	Displacement (liters)	Horsepower @ RPM	Torque @ RPM	Fuel Capacity	Towing Capacity	EPA City (mpg) - Manual	EPA Hwy (mpg) - Manual	EPA City (mpg) - Auto	EPA Hwy (mpg) - Auto
LAND ROVER																							
Discovery Series II	39	185.2	74.4	76.4	4576	100	40.1	40.1	42.5	34	5	63	1488	8	4	188@ 4750	250@ 2600	24.6	5500	NA	NA	13	17
LEXUS																							
RX300 AWD	41.3	180.1	71.5	65.7	3900	103	39.5	39.2	40.7	36.4	5	75	1050	6	3	220@ 5800	222@ 4400	17.2	3500	NA	NA	19	22
RX300 FWD	41.3	180.1	71.5	65.7	3692	103	39.5	39.2	40.7	36.4	5	75	1258	6	3	220@ 5800	222@ 4400	17.2	3500	NA	NA	19	24
LINCOLN																							
Navigator 2WD	42.2	204.8	79.9	75.4	4805	119	39.8	39.8	41	39.7	7	118	1800	8	5.4	300@ 5000	355@ 2750	30	8850	NA	NA	13	17
Navigator 4WD	42.2	204.8	79.9	76.6	5198	119	39.8	39.8	41	39.7	7	118	1600	8	5.4	300@ 5000	355@ 2750	30	8700	NA	NA	12	16
MAZDA																							
B-Series 2.5L 2WD Reg Cab	37.8	187.5	69.4	64.9	3025	111.6	39.2	NA	42.4	NA	3	NA	1260	4	2.5	119@ 5000	146@ 3000	13.6	2180	22	27	25	20

SPECIFICATIONS & EPA MILEAGE RATINGS	EPA Hwy (mpg) - Auto	EPA City (mpg) - Auto	EPA Hwy (mpg) - Manual	EPA City (mpg) - Manual	Towing Capacity	Fuel Capacity	Torque @ RPM	Horsepower @ RPM	Displacement (liters)	Number of Cylinders	Maximum Payload (lbs.)	Max Cargo Capacity (cu ft.)	Maximum Seating	Rear Leg Room (in.)	Front Leg Room (in.)	Rear Head Room (in.)	Front Head Room (in.)	Wheelbase (in.)	Curb Weight (lbs.)	Height (in.)	Width (in.)	Length (in.)	Turning Circle (in.)
B-Series 2.5L 2WD X-Cab	25	20	27	22	1380	16.3	146@ 3000	119@ 5000	2.5	4	1260	NA	5	40.3	42.2	35.6	39.2	125.7	3207	64.7	69.4	202.9	42.8
B-Series 3.0L 2WD Reg Cab	22	17	23	17	4120	13.6	185@ 3750	150@ 5000	3	6	1260	NA	3	NA	42.4	NA	39.2	111.6	3025	64.9	69.4	187.5	37.8
B-Series 3.0L 2WD X-Cab	22	17	23	17	2500	16.3	185@ 3750	150@ 5000	3	6	1620	NA	5	40.3	42.2	35.6	39.2	125.7	3355	64.7	69.4	202.9	42.8
B-Series 3.0L 4WD Reg Cab	20	15	21	17	2700	13.6	185@ 3750	150@ 5000	3	6	1260	NA	3	NA	42.4	NA	39.2	111.6	3423	67.5	70.3	187.7	39.2
B-Series 3.0L 4WD X-Cab	20	15	21	17	2700	16.3	185@ 3750	150@ 5000	3	6	1260	NA	5	40.3	42.2	35.6	39.2	125.9	3616	67.5	70.3	201.7	43
B-Series 4.0L 2WD X-Cab	20	15	21	17	3420	16.3	225@ 3000	160@ 4200	4	6	1620	NA	5	40.3	42.2	35.6	39.2	125.7	3355	64.7	69.4	202.9	42.8
B-Series 4.0L 4WD X-Cab	20	16	20	16	3180	16.3	225@ 3000	160@ 4200	4	6	1500	NA	5	40.3	42.2	35.6	39.2	125.9	3616	67.5	70.3	201.7	43
MPV DX/LX/ES	23	18	NA	NA	2600	18.5	165@ 4250	170@ 6250	2.5	6	NA	127	7	37	40.8	39.3	41	111.8	3657	68.7	72.1	187	37.4
MERCEDES-BENZ																							
M-Class ML320	21	17	NA	NA	5000	19	233@ 3000	215@ 5500	3.2	6	1684	85	5	38	44.3	39.7	39.8	111	4387	69.9	72.2	180.6	37.1

specifications

SPECIFICATIONS & EPA MILEAGE RATINGS	EPA Hwy (mpg) - Auto	EPA City (mpg) - Auto	EPA Hwy (mpg) - Manual	EPA City (mpg) - Manual	Towing Capacity	Fuel Capacity	Torque @ RPM	Horsepower @ RPM	Displacement (liters)	Number of Cylinders	Maximum Payload (lbs.)	Max Cargo Capacity (cu ft.)	Maximum Seating	Rear Leg Room (in.)	Front Leg Room (in.)	Rear Head Room (in.)	Front Head Room (in.)	Wheelbase (in.)	Curb Weight (lbs.)	Height (in.)	Width (in.)	Length (in.)	Turning Circle (in.)
M-Class ML430	18	15	NA	NA	5000	19	288@ 3000	268@ 5500	4.3	8	1684	85	5	38	44.3	39.7	39.8	111	4552	69.9	72.2	180.6	37.1
MERCURY																							
Mountaineer 2WD	20	15	NA	NA	4500	21	240@ 3250	210@ 5250	4	6	NA	80	5	35.8	42.4	39.3	39.9	111.6	3876	70.5	70.2	190.1	37.3
Mountaineer 4WD	19	15	NA	NA	4860	21	240@ 3250	210@ 5250	4	6	NA	80	5	35.8	42.4	39.3	39.9	111.6	4113	70.3	70.2	190.1	37.3
Mountaineer AWD	19	14	NA	NA	6400	21	288@ 3300	215@ 4200	5	8	NA	80	5	35.8	42.4	39.3	39.9	111.6	4348	70.3	70.2	190.1	37.3
Villager Base/Sport/Estate	24	17	NA	NA	2000	20	200@ 2800	170@ 4800	3.3	6	1290	136	7	36.4	39.9	39.9	39.7	112.2	3944	70.1	74.9	194.7	39.9
MITSUBISHI																							
Montero	19	16	NA	NA	5000	24.3	228@ 3500	200@ 5000	3.5	6	1320	67	7	37.6	40.3	40	40.9	107.3	4520	74.8	69.9	186.6	38.7
Montero Sport ES/LS/XLS - 2WD	21	18	NA	NA	5000	19.5	188@ 4000	173@ 5250	3	6	1220	79	5	33.5	42.8	37.3	38.9	107.3	3510	65.6	66.7	178.3	38.8
Montero Sport LS/XLS - 4WD	21	18	NA	NA	5000	19.5	188@ 4000	173@ 5250	3	6	1365	79	5	33.5	42.8	37.3	38.9	107.3	3985	65.6	66.7	178.3	38.8

SPECIFICATIONS & EPA MILEAGE RATINGS

	Montero Sport Limited 2WD	Montero Sport Limited 4WD	NISSAN	Frontier 2WD 4-Cyl Reg Cab	Frontier 2WD 4-Cyl X-Cab	Frontier 2WD Crew Cab	Frontier 2WD V6 X-Cab	Frontier 4WD 4-Cyl X-Cab	Frontier 4WD Crew Cab	Frontier 4WD V6 X-Cab
Turning Circle (in.)	38.8	38.8		33.4	36.8	36.8	36.8	39	39	39
Length (in.)	178.3	178.3		184.3	196.1	193.1	196.1	196.1	193.1	196.1
Width (in.)	69.9	69.9		66.5	66.5	71.9	66.5	71.9	71.9	71.9
Height (in.)	66.2	66.2		62.8	62.6	65.9	62.6	65.9	65.9	65.9
Curb Weight (lbs.)	3955	4195		2911	3173	3813	3217	3599	4108	3726
Wheelbase (in.)	107.3	107.3		104.3	116.1	116.1	116.1	116.1	116.1	116.1
Front Head Room (in.)	38.9	38.9		39.3	39.3	39.3	39.3	39.3	39.3	39.3
Rear Head Room (in.)	37.3	37.3		NA	NA	37.8	NA	NA	37.8	NA
Front Leg Room (in.)	42.8	42.8		40.9	41.4	41.4	41.4	41.4	41.4	41.4
Rear Leg Room (in.)	33.5	33.5		NA	NA	30.7	NA	NA	30.7	NA
Maximum Seating	5	5		3	5	5	4	5	5	4
Max Cargo Capacity (cu ft.)	79	79		46	44	NA	44	44	NA	44
Maximum Payload (lbs.)	1045	1155		1400	1330	1200	1330	1400	1200	1200
Number of Cylinders	6	6		4	4	6	6	4	6	6
Displacement (liters)	3.5	3.5		2.4	2.4	3.3	3.3	2.4	3.3	3.3
Horsepower @ RPM	200@ 5000	200@ 5000		143@ 5200	143@ 5200	170@ 4800	170@ 4800	143@ 5200	170@ 4800	170@ 4800
Torque @ RPM	228@ 3500	228@ 3500		154@ 4000	154@ 4000	200@ 2800	200@ 2800	154@ 4000	200@ 2800	200@ 2800
Fuel Capacity	19.5	19.5		15.9	15.9	19.4	19.4	15.9	19.4	19.4
Towing Capacity	5000	5000		3500	3500	3500	3500	3500	5000	5000
EPA City (mpg) - Manual	NA	NA		22	22	16	16	18	16	16
EPA Hwy (mpg) - Manual	NA	NA		26	26	19	19	21	19	19
EPA City (mpg) - Auto	17	16		20	20	15	15	18	15	15
EPA Hwy (mpg) - Auto	20	20		24	24	19	19	21	19	19

SPECIFICATIONS & EPA MILEAGE RATINGS	Turning Circle (in.)	Length (in.)	Width (in.)	Height (in.)	Curb Weight (lbs.)	Wheelbase (in.)	Front Head Room (in.)	Rear Head Room (in.)	Front Leg Room (in.)	Rear Leg Room (in.)	Maximum Seating	Max Cargo Capacity (cu ft.)	Maximum Payload (lbs.)	Number of Cylinders	Displacement (liters)	Horsepower @ RPM	Torque @ RPM	Fuel Capacity	Towing Capacity	EPA City (mpg) - Manual	EPA Hwy (mpg) - Manual	EPA City (mpg) - Auto	EPA Hwy (mpg) - Auto
Pathfinder 2WD	37.4	182.6	71.7	68.1	3907	106.3	39.5	37.5	41.7	31.8	5	85	1175	6	3.3	170@ 4800	200@ 2800	21	5000	17	19	16	20
Pathfinder 4WD	37.4	182.6	71.7	68.1	4158	106.3	39.5	37.5	41.7	31.8	5	85	1165	6	3.3	170@ 4800	200@ 2800	21	5000	16	18	15	19
Quest GXE/SE/GLE	40	194.8	74.9	67.3	3991	112.2	39.7	39.9	39.9	36.4	7	111	1290	6	3.3	170@ 4800	200@ 2800	20	3500	NA	NA	17	24
Xterra 4-Cyl 2WD	35.4	178	70.4	69.4	3504	104.3	38.6	37.8	41.4	32.8	5	66	1300	4	2.4	143@ 5200	154@ 4000	19.4	3500	19	24	NA	NA
Xterra SE 2WD	35.4	178	70.4	73.6	3821	104.3	38.6	37.8	41.4	32.8	5	66	1000	6	3.3	170@ 4800	200@ 2800	19.4	3500	17	19	16	19
Xterra SE 4WD	35.4	178	70.4	73.4	4092	104.3	38.6	37.8	41.4	32.8	5	66	1000	6	3.3	170@ 4800	200@ 2800	19.4	3500	16	18	15	19
Xterra XE 2WD	35.4	178	70.4	69.4	3668	104.3	38.6	37.8	41.4	32.8	5	66	1000	6	3.3	170@ 4800	200@ 2800	19.4	3500	17	19	16	19
Xterra XE 4WD	35.4	178	70.4	69.4	3933	104.3	38.6	37.8	41.4	32.8	5	66	1000	6	3.3	170@ 4800	200@ 2800	19.4	3500	16	18	15	19
OLDSMOBILE																							
Silhouette GL/GLS/Premiere	39.7	201.4	72.2	68.1	3948	120	39.9	39.3	39.9	39	7	156	1409	6	3.4	185@ 5200	210@ 4000	25	2000	NA	NA	18	25

SPECIFICATIONS & EPA MILEAGE RATINGS

	Turning Circle (in.)	Length (in.)	Width (in.)	Height (in.)	Curb Weight (lbs.)	Wheelbase (in.)	Front Head Room (in.)	Rear Head Room (in.)	Front Leg Room (in.)	Rear Leg Room (in.)	Maximum Seating	Max Cargo Capacity (cu ft.)	Maximum Payload (lbs.)	Number of Cylinders	Displacement (liters)	Horsepower @ RPM	Torque @ RPM	Fuel Capacity	Towing Capacity	EPA City (mpg) - Manual	EPA Hwy (mpg) - Manual	EPA City (mpg) - Auto	EPA Hwy (mpg) - Auto
PLYMOUTH																							
Grand Voyager Base	39.4	199.6	76.8	68.5	3836	119.3	39.8	40	41.1	39.6	7	172	NA	6	3	150@ 5200	176@ 4000	20	3500	NA	NA	18	25
Grand Voyager SE	39.4	199.6	76.8	68.5	3836	119.3	39.8	40	41.1	39.6	7	172	NA	6	3.3	158@ 4850	203@ 3250	20	3500	NA	NA	18	25
Voyager Base	37.6	186.3	76.8	68.5	3528	113.3	39.8	40.1	41.2	36.6	5	143	NA	4	2.4	150@ 5200	167@ 4000	20	2000	NA	NA	20	26
Voyager SE	37.6	186.3	76.8	68.5	3696	113.3	39.8	40.1	41.2	36.6	7	143	NA	6	3.3	158@ 4850	203@ 3250	20	3500	NA	NA	18	25
PONTIAC																							
Montana Extended	40.6	201.3	72.7	68.7	3920	120	39.9	39.3	39.9	39	7	155	1415	6	3.4	185@ 5200	210@ 4000	25	2000	NA	NA	18	25
Montana Regular 6-Pass	38.6	187.3	72.7	67.4	3702	112	39.9	39.3	39.9	36.9	6	133	1627	6	3.4	185@ 5200	210@ 4000	20	2000	NA	NA	18	25
Montana Regular 7-Pass	38.6	187.3	72.7	67.4	3702	112	39.9	39.3	39.9	36.9	7	133	1627	6	3.4	185@ 5200	210@ 4000	20	2000	NA	NA	18	25

SPECIFICATIONS & EPA MILEAGE RATINGS

SPECIFICATIONS & EPA MILEAGE RATINGS	Turning Circle (in.)	Length (in.)	Width (in.)	Height (in.)	Curb Weight (lbs.)	Wheelbase (in.)	Front Head Room (in.)	Rear Head Room (in.)	Front Leg Room (in.)	Rear Leg Room (in.)	Maximum Seating	Max Cargo Capacity (cu ft.)	Maximum Payload (lbs.)	Number of Cylinders	Displacement (liters)	Horsepower @ RPM	Torque @ RPM	Fuel Capacity	Towing Capacity	EPA City (mpg) - Manual	EPA Hwy (mpg) - Manual	EPA City (mpg) - Auto	EPA Hwy (mpg) - Auto
SUBARU																							
Forester L/S	35.4	175.2	68.3	65	3125	99.4	40.6	39.6	43	33.4	5	65	1045	4	2.5	165@ 5600	166@ 4000	15.9	2000	21	27	21	26
SUZUKI																							
Grand Vitara 2WD	34.8	164.6	70.1	68	3064	97.6	39.9	39.6	41.4	35.9	5	45	750	6	2.5	155@ 6500	160@ 4000	17.4	1500	19	22	19	21
Grand Vitara 4WD	34.8	164.6	70.1	68.5	3197	97.6	39.9	39.6	41.4	35.9	5	45	727	6	2.5	155@ 6500	160@ 4000	17.4	1500	19	21	18	20
Vitara 1.6L 2WD Conv.	31.6	152	67.3	66.5	2601	86.6	40.9	39.5	41.4	35.9	4	34	772	4	1.6	97@ 5200	103@ 4000	14.8	1000	25	28	25	27
Vitara 1.6L 4WD Conv.	34.8	152	67.3	66.5	2723	86.6	40.9	39.5	41.4	35.9	4	34	760	4	1.6	97@ 5200	103@ 4000	14.8	1000	22	24	23	25
Vitara 2.0L 2WD Conv.	31.6	152	67.3	66.5	2690	86.6	40.9	39.5	41.4	35.9	4	34	793	4	2	127@ 6000	134@ 3000	14.8	1000	22	24	23	25
Vitara 2.0L 4WD Conv.	34.8	152	67.3	66.5	2811	86.6	40.9	39.5	41.4	35.9	4	34	782	4	2	127@ 6000	134@ 3000	14.8	1000	22	24	23	25
Vitara 2WD 4-Door	34.8	163	67.3	68	2866	97.6	39.9	39.6	41.4	35.9	5	45	948	4	2	127@ 6000	134@ 3000	17.4	1500	22	25	23	25

SPECIFICATIONS & EPA MILEAGE RATINGS	EPA Hwy (mpg) - Auto	EPA City (mpg) - Auto	EPA Hwy (mpg) - Manual	EPA City (mpg) - Manual	Towing Capacity	Fuel Capacity	Torque @ RPM	Horsepower @ RPM	Displacement (liters)	Number of Cylinders	Maximum Payload (lbs.)	Max Cargo Capacity (cu ft.)	Maximum Seating	Rear Leg Room (in.)	Front Leg Room (in.)	Rear Head Room (in.)	Front Head Room (in.)	Wheelbase (in.)	Curb Weight (lbs.)	Height (in.)	Width (in.)	Length (in.)	Turning Circle (in.)
Vitara 4WD 4-Door	25	23	25	22	1500	17.4	134@ 3000	127@ 6000	2	4	937	45	5	35.9	41.4	39.6	39.9	97.6	2987	68.5	67.3	163	34.8
TOYOTA																							
4Runner 4-Cyl 2WD	24	20	23	18	3500	18.5	177@ 4000	150@ 4800	2.7	4	1810	80	5	34.9	42.6	38.7	39.3	105.3	3440	67.5	66.5	183.3	38.2
4Runner 4-Cyl 4WD	21	18	21	17	3500	18.5	177@ 4000	150@ 4800	2.7	4	1525	80	5	34.9	42.6	38.7	39.3	105.3	3725	67.5	66.5	183.3	38.2
4Runner V6 2WD	21	17	NA	NA	5000	18.5	217@ 3600	183@ 4800	3.4	6	1650	80	5	34.9	42.6	38.7	39.3	105.3	3600	67.5	66.5	183.3	38.2
4Runner V6 4WD	20	17	19	17	5000	18.5	217@ 3600	183@ 4800	3.4	6	1365	80	5	34.9	42.6	38.7	39.3	105.3	3885	67.5	66.5	183.3	38.2
Land Cruiser	16	13	NA	NA	6500	25.4	320@ 3400	230@ 4800	4.7	8	1745	98	5	34.3	42.3	39.8	40.6	112.2	5115	73.2	76.4	192.5	39.7
RAV4 2WD	29	24	29	24	1500	15.3	132@ 4600	127@ 5400	2	4	1245	58	5	33.9	39.5	39	40.3	94.9	2668	65.4	66.7	163.8	36.1
RAV4 AWD	26	22	25	22	1500	15.3	132@ 4600	127@ 5400	2	4	1157	58	5	33.9	39.5	39	40.3	94.9	2844	65.4	66.7	163.8	36.1
Sienna CE/LE	24	18	NA	NA	1000	20.9	209@ 4400	194@ 5200	3	6	NA	143	7	36.5	41.9	40.3	40.6	114.2	3880	67.3	73.4	193.5	40

specifications

SPECIFICATIONS & EPA MILEAGE RATINGS

	Sienna XLE	Tacoma 4-Cyl 4WD Reg Cab	Tacoma 4-Cyl 2WD Reg Cab	Tacoma 4-Cyl 2WD X-Cab	Tacoma 4-Cyl 4WD X-Cab	Tacoma PreRunner 2WD X-Cab	Tacoma V6 2WD X-Cab	Tacoma V6 4WD X-Cab	Tundra V6 2WD Reg Cab	Tundra V6 2WD X-Cab
Turning Circle (in.)	40	34.4	35.4	41.4	40	40	41.4	40	44.9	44.9
Length (in.)	193.5	183.8	178.7	203.1	202.3	202.3	203.1	202.3	217.5	217.5
Width (in.)	73.4	66.5	66.5	66.5	66.5	66.5	66.5	66.5	75.2	75.2
Height (in.)	67.3	67.5	62	62.2	67.7	66.9	62.2	67.7	70.5	70.7
Curb Weight (lbs.)	3890	3215	2580	2760	3360	3175	2910	3425	3795	4088
Wheelbase (in.)	114.2	103.3	103.3	121.9	121.9	121.9	121.9	121.9	128.3	128.3
Front Head Room (in.)	40.6	38.2	38.2	38.4	38.4	38.4	38.4	38.4	40.3	40.3
Rear Head Room (in.)	39.8	NA	NA	35.5	35.5	35.5	35.5	35.5	NA	37
Front Leg Room (in.)	41.9	41.7	41.7	42.8	42.8	42.8	42.8	42.8	41.5	41.5
Rear Leg Room (in.)	36.6	NA	NA	27.2	27.2	27.2	27.2	27.2	NA	29.6
Maximum Seating	7	3	3	5	5	5	5	5	3	6
Max Cargo Capacity (cu ft.)	143	44	44	44	44	44	44	44	NA	NA
Maximum Payload (lbs.)	NA	1889	1664	1738	1744	1929	1588	1679	1705	1612
Number of Cylinders	6	4	4	4	4	4	6	6	6	6
Displacement (liters)	3	2.7	2.4	2.4	2.7	2.7	3.4	3.4	3.4	3.4
Horsepower @ RPM	194@ 5200	150@ 4800	142@ 5000	142@ 5000	150@ 4800	150@ 4800	190@ 4800	190@ 4800	190@ 4800	190@ 4800
Torque @ RPM	209@ 4400	177@ 4000	160@ 4000	160@ 4000	177@ 4000	177@ 4000	220@ 3600	220@ 3600	220@ 3600	220@ 3600
Fuel Capacity	20.9	18	15.1	15.1	18	18	15.1	18	26.4	26.4
Towing Capacity	1000	3500	3500	3500	3500	3500	5000	5000	5250	4950
EPA City (mpg) - Manual	NA	17	22	22	17	NA	19	17	16	16
EPA Hwy (mpg) - Manual	NA	21	27	27	21	NA	24	19	20	20
EPA City (mpg) - Auto	18	18	21	21	18	19	19	17	16	16
EPA Hwy (mpg) - Auto	24	21	24	24	21	21	23	20	19	19

SPECIFICATIONS & EPA MILEAGE RATINGS	Tundra V6 4WD Reg Cab	Tundra V6 4WD X-Cab	Tundra V8 2WD X-Cab	Tundra V8 4WD Reg Cab	Tundra V8 4WD X-Cab	VOLKSWAGEN	EuroVan GLS/MV
Turning Circle (in.)	44.3	44.3	44.9	44.3	44.3		38.4
Length (in.)	217.5	217.5	217.5	217.5	217.5		188.5
Width (in.)	75.2	75.2	75.2	75.2	75.2		72.4
Height (in.)	71.1	71.5	70.5	71.1	71.3		76.4
Curb Weight (lbs.)	4123	4133	4276	4321	4518		4220
Wheelbase (in.)	128.3	128.3	128.3	128.3	128.3		115
Front Head Room (in.)	40.3	40.3	40.3	40.3	40.3		39.3
Rear Head Room (in.)	NA	37	37	NA	37		41.3
Front Leg Room (in.)	41.5	41.5	41.5	41.5	41.5		37.8
Rear Leg Room (in.)	NA	29.6	29.6	NA	29.6		28.3
Maximum Seating	3	6	6	3	6		7
Max Cargo Capacity (cu ft.)	NA	NA	NA	NA	NA		41
Maximum Payload (lbs.)	1377	1612	1924	1879	1532		990
Number of Cylinders	6	6	8	8	8		6
Displacement (liters)	3.4	3.4	4.7	4.7	4.7		2.8
Horsepower @ RPM	190@ 4800	190@ 4800	245@ 4800	245@ 4800	245@ 4800		140@ 4500
Torque @ RPM	220@ 3600	220@ 3600	315@ 3400	315@ 3400	315@ 3400		177@ 3000
Fuel Capacity	26.4	26.4	26.4	26.4	26.4		21.1
Towing Capacity	4123	5000	7200	7200	7100		4500
EPA City (mpg) - Manual	16	16	NA	NA	NA		NA
EPA Hwy (mpg) - Manual	18	18	NA	NA	NA		NA
EPA City (mpg) - Auto	16	16	15	14	14		14
EPA Hwy (mpg) - Auto	18	18	19	17	17		19

CRASH TEST DATA

In 1994, the National Highway Traffic Safety Administration (NHTSA — http://www.nhtsa.dot.gov) changed the way they rate frontal crash-test performances of the cars and trucks they run into a fixed barrier at 35 mph. Instead of the confusing numerical scale that had been in place for years, NHTSA decided to make the data more user-friendly for interested consumers by converting to a five-star rating system. This system is just like the one used by the movie reviewer in your local paper and the lucky folks AAA employs to travel around the world eating and sleeping in the best restaurants and hotels. Boy, they've got it rough, don't they?

For frontal-impact NHTSA crash tests, the scale is as follows:

1 Star	46 percent or better chance of life-threatening injury
2 Stars	a 36-45 percent chance of life-threatening injury
3 Stars	a 21-35 percent chance of life-threatening injury
4 Stars	a 11-20 percent chance of life-threatening injury
5 Stars	10 percent or less chance of life-threatening injury

We convert the NHTSA scale as follows:

1 Star	Very Poor
2 Stars	Poor
3 Stars	Average
4 Stars	Good
5 Stars	Excellent

In 1997, NHTSA began testing side-impact protection as well as frontal-impact protection. For side-impact testing, NHTSA runs a deformable barrier into the side of a car twice, once at the front passenger's level and once at the rear passenger's level. As with frontal-impact testing, the side-impact test is conducted at 5 mph above the federal standard, which means the deformable barrier hits the car at 38 mph.

For side-impact NHTSA crash tests, the scale is as follows:

1 Star	26 percent or better chance of life-threatening injury
2 Stars	a 21-25 percent chance of life-threatening injury
3 Stars	a 11-20 percent chance of life-threatening injury
4 Stars	a 6-10 percent chance of life-threatening injury
5 Stars	5 percent or less chance of life-threatening injury

We convert the NHTSA scale as follows:

1 Star	Very Poor
2 Stars	Poor
3 Stars	Average
4 Stars	Good
5 Stars	Excellent

The Insurance Institute for Highway Safety (IIHS — http://www.hwysafety.org) began conducting offset frontal crash tests in 1995. The offset test is conducted at 40 mph, and vehicles crash into a fixed barrier just like in the NHTSA testing, but only half of the front of the vehicle contacts the barrier. The IIHS claims this test, at this speed, more accurately reflects the most deadly real-world crash situations. Offset crash tests do not conform to the scale listed above. Instead, the IIHS rates a vehicle good, acceptable, marginal or poor. There are currently no federally mandated offset crash standards that automakers must meet by law.

The IIHS also conducts bumper-bashing tests. They run cars and trucks into barriers at 5 mph to see how much damage results, in terms of dollars. Front ends are smacked into flat and angled barriers, and they back vehicles into poles and angled barriers. Each vehicle is crashed four times; the lower the total cost for repair after all four tests, the better the vehicle scores. Federal law requires bumpers on passenger cars that can withstand an impact at 2.5 mph. Light trucks are not required to meet bumper-strength standards.

Following are the results of crash testing conducted since 1994, presented in alphabetical order by make and model. All test results are applicable to the 2000 equivalent of the listed model, with one caveat. Most of the models tested before 1998 come equipped with depowered airbags now, and until the vehicle is re-tested by NHTSA, it is unknown how the presence of a depowered airbag will affect occupant safety.

Crash Scores for 2000 Cars and Trucks

Acura Integra

NHTSA Frontal Crash Driver	Good
NHTSA Frontal Crash Passenger	Average
NHTSA Side Crash Front Occupant	Not Tested
NHTSA Side Crash Rear Occupant	Not Tested
IIHS Offset	Not Tested
IIHS Bumper Bash	Not Tested

Acura RL	
NHTSA Frontal Crash Driver	Good
NHTSA Frontal Crash Passenger	Good
NHTSA Side Crash Front Occupant	Not Tested
NHTSA Side Crash Rear Occupant	Not Tested
IIHS Offset	Not Tested
IIHS Bumper Bash	Not Tested
Audi A4	
NHTSA Frontal Crash Driver	Good
NHTSA Frontal Crash Passenger	Excellent
NHTSA Side Crash Front Occupant	Not Tested
NHTSA Side Crash Rear Occupant	Not Tested
IIHS Offset	Not Tested
IIHS Bumper Bash	Not Tested
Audi A8	
NHTSA Frontal Crash Driver	Excellent
NHTSA Frontal Crash Passenger	Excellent
NHTSA Side Crash Front Occupant	Not Tested
NHTSA Side Crash Rear Occupant	Not Tested
IIHS Offset	Not Tested
IIHS Bumper Bash	Not Tested
Audi S4	
NHTSA Frontal Crash Driver	Good
NHTSA Frontal Crash Passenger	Excellent
NHTSA Side Crash Front Occupant	Not Tested
NHTSA Side Crash Rear Occupant	Not Tested
IIHS Offset	Not Tested
IIHS Bumper Bash	Not Tested
BMW 5 Series	
NHTSA Frontal Crash Driver	Not Tested
NHTSA Frontal Crash Passenger	Not Tested
NHTSA Side Crash Front Occupant	Not Tested
NHTSA Side Crash Rear Occupant	Not Tested
IIHS Offset	Good
IIHS Bumper Bash	Poor
Buick Century	
NHTSA Frontal Crash Driver	Good
NHTSA Frontal Crash Passenger	Average
NHTSA Side Crash Front Occupant	Average
NHTSA Side Crash Rear Occupant	Average
IIHS Offset	Acceptable
IIHS Bumper Bash	Acceptable
Buick LeSabre	
NHTSA Frontal Crash Driver	Not Tested
NHTSA Frontal Crash Passenger	Not Tested

NHTSA Side Crash Front Occupant	Not Tested
NHTSA Side Crash Rear Occupant	Not Tested
IIHS Offset	Good
IIHS Bumper Bash	Marginal
Buick Park Avenue	
NHTSA Frontal Crash Driver	Not Tested
NHTSA Frontal Crash Passenger	Not Tested
NHTSA Side Crash Front Occupant	Not Tested
NHTSA Side Crash Rear Occupant	Not Tested
IIHS Offset	Good
IIHS Bumper Bash	Acceptable
Buick Regal	
NHTSA Frontal Crash Driver	Good
NHTSA Frontal Crash Passenger	Average
NHTSA Side Crash Front Occupant	Average
NHTSA Side Crash Rear Occupant	Average
IIHS Offset	Acceptable
IIHS Bumper Bash	Acceptable
Cadillac Escalade	
NHTSA Frontal Crash Driver	Good
NHTSA Frontal Crash Passenger	Good
NHTSA Side Crash Front Occupant	Not Tested
NHTSA Side Crash Rear Occupant	Not Tested
IIHS Offset	Not Tested
IIHS Bumper Bash	Not Tested
Cadillac Eldorado	
NHTSA Frontal Crash Driver	Good
NHTSA Frontal Crash Passenger	Good
NHTSA Side Crash Front Occupant	Not Tested
NHTSA Side Crash Rear Occupant	Not Tested
IIHS Offset	Not Tested
IIHS Bumper Bash	Not Tested
Cadillac Seville	
NHTSA Frontal Crash Driver	Not Tested
NHTSA Frontal Crash Passenger	Not Tested
NHTSA Side Crash Front Occupant	Not Tested
NHTSA Side Crash Rear Occupant	Not Tested
IIHS Offset	Good
IIHS Bumper Bash	Marginal
Chevrolet Astro	
NHTSA Frontal Crash Driver	Average
NHTSA Frontal Crash Passenger	Good
NHTSA Side Crash Front Occupant	Not Tested
NHTSA Side Crash Rear Occupant	Not Tested

IIHS Offset	Poor
IIHS Bumper Bash	Poor
Chevrolet Blazer	
NHTSA Frontal Crash Driver	Average
NHTSA Frontal Crash Passenger	Good
NHTSA Side Crash Front Occupant	Excellent
NHTSA Side Crash Rear Occupant	Excellent
IIHS Offset	Poor
IIHS Bumper Bash	Poor
Chevrolet Camaro	
NHTSA Frontal Crash Driver	Good
NHTSA Frontal Crash Passenger	Excellent
NHTSA Side Crash Front Occupant	Average
NHTSA Side Crash Rear Occupant	Good
IIHS Offset	Not Tested
IIHS Bumper Bash	Not Tested
Chevrolet Cavalier	
NHTSA Frontal Crash Driver	Average (Cpe.); Good (Sdn.)
NHTSA Frontal Crash Passenger	Good
NHTSA Side Crash Front Occupant	Very Poor
NHTSA Side Crash Rear Occupant	Poor (Cpe.); Average (Sdn.)
IIHS Offset	Poor
IIHS Bumper Bash	Acceptable
Chevrolet Impala	
NHTSA Frontal Crash Driver	Excellent
NHTSA Frontal Crash Passenger	Excellent
NHTSA Side Crash Front Occupant	Good
NHTSA Side Crash Rear Occupant	Good
IIHS Offset	Good
IIHS Bumper Bash	Marginal
Chevrolet Lumina	
NHTSA Frontal Crash Driver	Good
NHTSA Frontal Crash Passenger	Excellent
NHTSA Side Crash Front Occupant	Good
NHTSA Side Crash Rear Occupant	Average
IIHS Offset	Good
IIHS Bumper Bash	Marginal
Chevrolet Malibu	
NHTSA Frontal Crash Driver	Good
NHTSA Frontal Crash Passenger	Good
NHTSA Side Crash Front Occupant	Poor
NHTSA Side Crash Rear Occupant	Good
IIHS Offset	Not Tested
IIHS Bumper Bash	Not Tested

Chevrolet Metro	
NHTSA Frontal Crash Driver	Good
NHTSA Frontal Crash Passenger	Good
NHTSA Side Crash Front Occupant	Not Tested
NHTSA Side Crash Rear Occupant	Not Tested
IIHS Offset	Not Tested
IIHS Bumper Bash	Not Tested
Chevrolet Prizm	
NHTSA Frontal Crash Driver	Good
NHTSA Frontal Crash Passenger	Good
NHTSA Side Crash Front Occupant	Average (w/o side airbag); Good (w/side airbag)
NHTSA Side Crash Rear Occupant	Average
IIHS Offset	Acceptable
IIHS Bumper Bash	Good
Chevrolet S-10 Pickup	
NHTSA Frontal Crash Driver	Poor
NHTSA Frontal Crash Passenger	Average
NHTSA Side Crash Front Occupant	Average
NHTSA Side Crash Rear Occupant	Not Applicable
IIHS Offset	Marginal
IIHS Bumper Bash	Marginal
Chevrolet Silverado Extended Cab Pickup	
NHTSA Frontal Crash Driver	Average
NHTSA Frontal Crash Passenger	Good
NHTSA Side Crash Front Occupant	Not Tested
NHTSA Side Crash Rear Occupant	Not Tested
IIHS Offset	Not Tested
IIHS Bumper Bash	Not Tested
Chevrolet Tahoe (Limited and Z71 only)	
NHTSA Frontal Crash Driver	Good
NHTSA Frontal Crash Passenger	Good
NHTSA Side Crash Front Occupant	Not Tested
NHTSA Side Crash Rear Occupant	Not Tested
IIHS Offset	Not Tested
IIHS Bumper Bash	Not Tested
Chevrolet Tracker	
NHTSA Frontal Crash Driver	Not Tested
NHTSA Frontal Crash Passenger	Not Tested
NHTSA Side Crash Front Occupant	Not Tested
NHTSA Side Crash Rear Occupant	Not Tested
IIHS Offset	Acceptable (4-door)
IIHS Bumper Bash	Poor

Chevrolet Venture	
NHTSA Frontal Crash Driver	Good
NHTSA Frontal Crash Passenger	Average
NHTSA Side Crash Front Occupant	Excellent
NHTSA Side Crash Rear Occupant	Excellent
IIHS Offset	Poor
IIHS Bumper Bash	Poor
Chrysler 300M	
NHTSA Frontal Crash Driver	Good
NHTSA Frontal Crash Passenger	Good
NHTSA Side Crash Front Occupant	Good
NHTSA Side Crash Rear Occupant	Average
IIHS Offset	Poor
IIHS Bumper Bash	Marginal
Chrysler Cirrus	
NHTSA Frontal Crash Driver	Average
NHTSA Frontal Crash Passenger	Good
NHTSA Side Crash Front Occupant	Average
NHTSA Side Crash Rear Occupant	Poor
IIHS Offset	Poor
IIHS Bumper Bash	Marginal
Chrysler Concorde	
NHTSA Frontal Crash Driver	Good
NHTSA Frontal Crash Passenger	Good
NHTSA Side Crash Front Occupant	Good
NHTSA Side Crash Rear Occupant	Average
IIHS Offset	Marginal
IIHS Bumper Bash	Marginal
Chrysler LHS	
NHTSA Frontal Crash Driver	Good
NHTSA Frontal Crash Passenger	Good
NHTSA Side Crash Front Occupant	Good
NHTSA Side Crash Rear Occupant	Average
IIHS Offset	Poor
IIHS Bumper Bash	Marginal
Chrysler Sebring Convertible	
NHTSA Frontal Crash Driver	Good
NHTSA Frontal Crash Passenger	Good
NHTSA Side Crash Front Occupant	Not Tested
NHTSA Side Crash Rear Occupant	Not Tested
IIHS Offset	Not Tested
IIHS Bumper Bash	Not Tested
Chrysler Sebring Coupe	
NHTSA Frontal Crash Driver	Excellent
NHTSA Frontal Crash Passenger	Excellent

NHTSA Side Crash Front Occupant	Not Tested
NHTSA Side Crash Rear Occupant	Not Tested
IIHS Offset	Not Tested
IIHS Bumper Bash	Not Tested
Chrysler Town and Country	
NHTSA Frontal Crash Driver	Good
NHTSA Frontal Crash Passenger	Good
NHTSA Side Crash Front Occupant	Excellent
NHTSA Side Crash Rear Occupant	Average
IIHS Offset	Marginal
IIHS Bumper Bash	Poor
Dodge Avenger	
NHTSA Frontal Crash Driver	Excellent
NHTSA Frontal Crash Passenger	Excellent
NHTSA Side Crash Front Occupant	Not Tested
NHTSA Side Crash Rear Occupant	Not Tested
IIHS Offset	Not Tested
IIHS Bumper Bash	Not Tested
Dodge Caravan/Grand Caravan	
NHTSA Frontal Crash Driver	Good
NHTSA Frontal Crash Passenger	Good
NHTSA Side Crash Front Occupant	Excellent (Grand Caravan); Not Tested (Caravan)
NHTSA Side Crash Rear Occupant	Average (Grand Caravan); Not Tested (Caravan)
IIHS Offset	Marginal
IIHS Bumper Bash	Poor
Dodge Dakota	
NHTSA Frontal Crash Driver	Good
NHTSA Frontal Crash Passenger	Good
NHTSA Side Crash Front Occupant	Excellent
NHTSA Side Crash Rear Occupant	Not Applicable
IIHS Offset	Poor
IIHS Bumper Bash	Poor
Dodge Durango	
NHTSA Frontal Crash Driver	Poor
NHTSA Frontal Crash Passenger	Good
NHTSA Side Crash Front Occupant	Not Tested
NHTSA Side Crash Rear Occupant	Not Tested
IIHS Offset	Acceptable
IIHS Bumper Bash	Poor
Dodge Intrepid	
NHTSA Frontal Crash Driver	Good
NHTSA Frontal Crash Passenger	Good
NHTSA Side Crash Front Occupant	Good

NHTSA Side Crash Rear Occupant	Average
IIHS Offset	Marginal
IIHS Bumper Bash	Marginal
Dodge Neon	
NHTSA Frontal Crash Driver	Good
NHTSA Frontal Crash Passenger	Good
NHTSA Side Crash Front Occupant	Average
NHTSA Side Crash Rear Occupant	Average
IIHS Offset	Marginal
IIHS Bumper Bash	Acceptable
Dodge Ram Pickup	
NHTSA Frontal Crash Driver	Good (X-cab); Avg. (Quad Cab)
NHTSA Frontal Crash Passenger	Good
NHTSA Side Crash Front Occupant	Not Tested
NHTSA Side Crash Rear Occupant	Not Tested
IIHS Offset	Not Tested
IIHS Bumper Bash	Not Tested
Dodge Stratus	
NHTSA Frontal Crash Driver	Average
NHTSA Frontal Crash Passenger	Good
NHTSA Side Crash Front Occupant	Average
NHTSA Side Crash Rear Occupant	Poor
IIHS Offset	Poor
IIHS Bumper Bash	Marginal
Ford Contour	
NHTSA Frontal Crash Driver	Excellent
NHTSA Frontal Crash Passenger	Good
NHTSA Side Crash Front Occupant	Average
NHTSA Side Crash Rear Occupant	Good
IIHS Offset	Poor
IIHS Bumper Bash	Poor
Ford Crown Victoria	
NHTSA Frontal Crash Driver	Excellent
NHTSA Frontal Crash Passenger	Excellent
NHTSA Side Crash Front Occupant	Good
NHTSA Side Crash Rear Occupant	Good
IIHS Offset	Not Tested
IIHS Bumper Bash	Not Tested
Ford Econoline	
NHTSA Frontal Crash Driver	Good
NHTSA Frontal Crash Passenger	Good
NHTSA Side Crash Front Occupant	Not Tested
NHTSA Side Crash Rear Occupant	Not Tested
IIHS Offset	Not Tested
IIHS Bumper Bash	Not Tested

Ford Escort ZX2	
NHTSA Frontal Crash Driver	Not Tested
NHTSA Frontal Crash Passenger	Not Tested
NHTSA Side Crash Front Occupant	Very Poor
NHTSA Side Crash Rear Occupant	Good
IIHS Offset	Not Tested
IIHS Bumper Bash	Not Tested
Ford Expedition	
NHTSA Frontal Crash Driver	Good
NHTSA Frontal Crash Passenger	Good
NHTSA Side Crash Front Occupant	Not Tested
NHTSA Side Crash Rear Occupant	Not Tested
IIHS Offset	Not Tested
IIHS Bumper Bash	Not Tested
Ford Explorer	
NHTSA Frontal Crash Driver	Good
NHTSA Frontal Crash Passenger	Good
NHTSA Side Crash Front Occupant	Excellent
NHTSA Side Crash Rear Occupant	Excellent
IIHS Offset	Acceptable
IIHS Bumper Bash	Poor
Ford F-150	
NHTSA Frontal Crash Driver	Good
NHTSA Frontal Crash Passenger	Good
NHTSA Side Crash Front Occupant	Excellent
NHTSA Side Crash Rear Occupant	Not Tested
IIHS Offset	Not Tested
IIHS Bumper Bash	Not Tested
Ford Mustang	
NHTSA Frontal Crash Driver	Good
NHTSA Frontal Crash Passenger	Good
NHTSA Side Crash Front Occupant	Average
NHTSA Side Crash Rear Occupant	Average
IIHS Offset	Not Tested
IIHS Bumper Bash	Not Tested
Ford Ranger	
NHTSA Frontal Crash Driver	Good
NHTSA Frontal Crash Passenger	Good
NHTSA Side Crash Front Occupant	Excellent (Reg. Cab); Not Tested (X-Cab)
NHTSA Side Crash Rear Occupant	Not Applicable
IIHS Offset	Acceptable
IIHS Bumper Bash	Marginal

CRASH TEST DATA

Ford Taurus	
NHTSA Frontal Crash Driver	Not Tested
NHTSA Frontal Crash Passenger	Not Tested
NHTSA Side Crash Front Occupant	Average
NHTSA Side Crash Rear Occupant	Average
IIHS Offset	Good
IIHS Bumper Bash	Good
Ford Windstar	
NHTSA Frontal Crash Driver	Excellent
NHTSA Frontal Crash Passenger	Excellent
NHTSA Side Crash Front Occupant	Excellent
NHTSA Side Crash Rear Occupant	Excellent
IIHS Offset	Good
IIHS Bumper Bash	Acceptable
GMC Denali	
NHTSA Frontal Crash Driver	Good
NHTSA Frontal Crash Passenger	Good
NHTSA Side Crash Front Occupant	Not Tested
NHTSA Side Crash Rear Occupant	Not Tested
IIHS Offset	Not Tested
IIHS Bumper Bash	Not Tested
GMC Envoy	
NHTSA Frontal Crash Driver	Average
NHTSA Frontal Crash Passenger	Good
NHTSA Side Crash Front Occupant	Excellent
NHTSA Side Crash Rear Occupant	Excellent
IIHS Offset	Poor
IIHS Bumper Bash	Poor
GMC Jimmy	
NHTSA Frontal Crash Driver	Average
NHTSA Frontal Crash Passenger	Good
NHTSA Side Crash Front Occupant	Excellent
NHTSA Side Crash Rear Occupant	Excellent
IIHS Offset	Poor
IIHS Bumper Bash	Poor
GMC Safari	
NHTSA Frontal Crash Driver	Average
NHTSA Frontal Crash Passenger	Good
NHTSA Side Crash Front Occupant	Not Tested
NHTSA Side Crash Rear Occupant	Not Tested
IIHS Offset	Poor
IIHS Bumper Bash	Poor

GMC Sierra Extended Cab Pickup	
NHTSA Frontal Crash Driver	Average
NHTSA Frontal Crash Passenger	Good
NHTSA Side Crash Front Occupant	Not Tested
NHTSA Side Crash Rear Occupant	Not Tested
IIHS Offset	Not Tested
IIHS Bumper Bash	Not Tested
GMC Sonoma	
NHTSA Frontal Crash Driver	Poor
NHTSA Frontal Crash Passenger	Average
NHTSA Side Crash Front Occupant	Average
NHTSA Side Crash Rear Occupant	Not Applicable
IIHS Offset	Marginal
IIHS Bumper Bash	Marginal
GMC Yukon Denali	
NHTSA Frontal Crash Driver	Good
NHTSA Frontal Crash Passenger	Good
NHTSA Side Crash Front Occupant	Not Tested
NHTSA Side Crash Rear Occupant	Not Tested
IIHS Offset	Not Tested
IIHS Bumper Bash	Not Tested
Honda Accord	
NHTSA Frontal Crash Driver	Good
NHTSA Frontal Crash Passenger	Good
NHTSA Side Crash Front Occupant	Average (Cpe.); Good (Sdn.)
NHTSA Side Crash Rear Occupant	Good (w/o side airbag); Excellent (w/side airbag)
IIHS Offset	Acceptable
IIHS Bumper Bash	Acceptable
Honda Civic	
NHTSA Frontal Crash Driver	Good
NHTSA Frontal Crash Passenger	Good
NHTSA Side Crash Front Occupant	Poor (Coupe); Average (Sedan)
NHTSA Side Crash Rear Occupant	Average
IIHS Offset	Acceptable
IIHS Bumper Bash	Acceptable
Honda CR-V	
NHTSA Frontal Crash Driver	Good
NHTSA Frontal Crash Passenger	Excellent
NHTSA Side Crash Front Occupant	Excellent*
NHTSA Side Crash Rear Occupant	Excellent*
IIHS Offset	Marginal
IIHS Bumper Bash	Poor

*Note — CR-V rolled one-quarter turn in side-impact testing.

Honda Odyssey	
NHTSA Frontal Crash Driver	Excellent
NHTSA Frontal Crash Passenger	Excellent
NHTSA Side Crash Front Occupant	Not Tested
NHTSA Side Crash Rear Occupant	Not Tested
IIHS Offset	Good
IIHS Bumper Bash	Acceptable
Honda Passport	
NHTSA Frontal Crash Driver	Good
NHTSA Frontal Crash Passenger	Good
NHTSA Side Crash Front Occupant	Excellent*
NHTSA Side Crash Rear Occupant	Excellent*
IIHS Offset	Not Tested
IIHS Bumper Bash	Not Tested
*Note — Passport rolled one-quarter turn in side-impact testing.	
Hyundai Elantra	
NHTSA Frontal Crash Driver	Excellent
NHTSA Frontal Crash Passenger	Good
NHTSA Side Crash Front Occupant	Average
NHTSA Side Crash Rear Occupant	Very Poor
IIHS Offset	Acceptable
IIHS Bumper Bash	Acceptable
Hyundai Sonata	
NHTSA Frontal Crash Driver	Not Tested
NHTSA Frontal Crash Passenger	Not Tested
NHTSA Side Crash Front Occupant	Not Tested
NHTSA Side Crash Rear Occupant	Not Tested
IIHS Offset	Acceptable
IIHS Bumper Bash	Marginal
Infiniti I30	
NHTSA Frontal Crash Driver	Not Tested
NHTSA Frontal Crash Passenger	Not Tested
NHTSA Side Crash Front Occupant	Good
NHTSA Side Crash Rear Occupant	Good
IIHS Offset	Not Tested
IIHS Bumper Bash	Not Tested
Infiniti Q45	
NHTSA Frontal Crash Driver	Not Tested
NHTSA Frontal Crash Passenger	Not Tested
NHTSA Side Crash Front Occupant	Not Tested
NHTSA Side Crash Rear Occupant	Not Tested
IIHS Offset	Marginal
IIHS Bumper Bash	Poor

Infiniti QX4	
NHTSA Frontal Crash Driver	Good
NHTSA Frontal Crash Passenger	Excellent
NHTSA Side Crash Front Occupant	Excellent
NHTSA Side Crash Rear Occupant	Excellent
IIHS Offset	Marginal
IIHS Bumper Bash	Poor
Isuzu Amigo	
NHTSA Frontal Crash Driver	Not Tested
NHTSA Frontal Crash Passenger	Not Tested
NHTSA Side Crash Front Occupant	Not Tested
NHTSA Side Crash Rear Occupant	Not Tested
IIHS Offset	Poor
IIHS Bumper Bash	Poor
Isuzu Hombre	
NHTSA Frontal Crash Driver	Poor
NHTSA Frontal Crash Passenger	Average
NHTSA Side Crash Front Occupant	Average
NHTSA Side Crash Rear Occupant	Not Applicable
IIHS Offset	Marginal
IIHS Bumper Bash	Marginal
Isuzu Rodeo	
NHTSA Frontal Crash Driver	Good
NHTSA Frontal Crash Passenger	Good
NHTSA Side Crash Front Occupant	Excellent*
NHTSA Side Crash Rear Occupant	Excellent*
IIHS Offset	Not Tested
IIHS Bumper Bash	Not Tested
*Note — Rodeo rolled one-quarter turn in side-impact testing.	
Isuzu Trooper	
NHTSA Frontal Crash Driver	Average
NHTSA Frontal Crash Passenger	Average
NHTSA Side Crash Front Occupant	Not Tested
NHTSA Side Crash Rear Occupant	Not Tested
IIHS Offset	Not Tested
IIHS Bumper Bash	Not Tested
Jeep Cherokee	
NHTSA Frontal Crash Driver	Average
NHTSA Frontal Crash Passenger	Average
NHTSA Side Crash Front Occupant	Average
NHTSA Side Crash Rear Occupant	Excellent
IIHS Offset	Marginal
IIHS Bumper Bash	Poor

Jeep Grand Cherokee	
NHTSA Frontal Crash Driver	Average
NHTSA Frontal Crash Passenger	Average
NHTSA Side Crash Front Occupant	Good
NHTSA Side Crash Rear Occupant	Excellent
IIHS Offset	Marginal
IIHS Bumper Bash	Poor
Jeep Wrangler	
NHTSA Frontal Crash Driver	Good
NHTSA Frontal Crash Passenger	Good
NHTSA Side Crash Front Occupant	Not Tested
NHTSA Side Crash Rear Occupant	Not Tested
IIHS Offset	Acceptable
IIHS Bumper Bash	Marginal
Kia Sephia	
NHTSA Frontal Crash Driver	Not Tested
NHTSA Frontal Crash Passenger	Not Tested
NHTSA Side Crash Front Occupant	Not Tested
NHTSA Side Crash Rear Occupant	Not Tested
IIHS Offset	Poor
IIHS Bumper Bash	Marginal
Kia Sportage	
NHTSA Frontal Crash Driver	Average
NHTSA Frontal Crash Passenger	Average
NHTSA Side Crash Front Occupant	Not Tested
NHTSA Side Crash Rear Occupant	Not Tested
IIHS Offset	Marginal (4-door)
IIHS Bumper Bash	Poor
Land Rover Discovery Series II	
NHTSA Frontal Crash Driver	Not Tested
NHTSA Frontal Crash Passenger	Not Tested
NHTSA Side Crash Front Occupant	Not Tested
NHTSA Side Crash Rear Occupant	Not Tested
IIHS Offset	Acceptable
IIHS Bumper Bash	Poor
Lexus ES 300	
NHTSA Frontal Crash Driver	Not Tested
NHTSA Frontal Crash Passenger	Not Tested
NHTSA Side Crash Front Occupant	Excellent
NHTSA Side Crash Rear Occupant	Good
IIHS Offset	Not Tested
IIHS Bumper Bash	Not Tested
Lexus GS 300	
NHTSA Frontal Crash Driver	Not Tested
NHTSA Frontal Crash Passenger	Not Tested

NHTSA Side Crash Front Occupant	Not Tested
NHTSA Side Crash Rear Occupant	Not Tested
IIHS Offset	Good
IIHS Bumper Bash	Poor
Lexus GS 400	
NHTSA Frontal Crash Driver	Not Tested
NHTSA Frontal Crash Passenger	Not Tested
NHTSA Side Crash Front Occupant	Not Tested
NHTSA Side Crash Rear Occupant	Not Tested
IIHS Offset	Good
IIHS Bumper Bash	Poor
Lexus LS 400	
NHTSA Frontal Crash Driver	Not Tested
NHTSA Frontal Crash Passenger	Not Tested
NHTSA Side Crash Front Occupant	Not Tested
NHTSA Side Crash Rear Occupant	Not Tested
IIHS Offset	Good
IIHS Bumper Bash	Poor
Lexus RX 300	
NHTSA Frontal Crash Driver	Not Tested
NHTSA Frontal Crash Passenger	Not Tested
NHTSA Side Crash Front Occupant	Not Tested
NHTSA Side Crash Rear Occupant	Not Tested
IIHS Offset	Good
IIHS Bumper Bash	Poor
Lincoln Continental	
NHTSA Frontal Crash Driver	Not Tested
NHTSA Frontal Crash Passenger	Not Tested
NHTSA Side Crash Front Occupant	Not Tested
NHTSA Side Crash Rear Occupant	Not Tested
IIHS Offset	Acceptable
IIHS Bumper Bash	Good
Lincoln Navigator	
NHTSA Frontal Crash Driver	Good
NHTSA Frontal Crash Passenger	Good
NHTSA Side Crash Front Occupant	Not Tested
NHTSA Side Crash Rear Occupant	Not Tested
IIHS Offset	Not Tested
IIHS Bumper Bash	Not Tested
Lincoln Town Car	
NHTSA Frontal Crash Driver	Good
NHTSA Frontal Crash Passenger	Good
NHTSA Side Crash Front Occupant	Good
NHTSA Side Crash Rear Occupant	Good

IIHS Offset	Not Tested
IIHS Bumper Bash	Not Tested
Mazda 626	
NHTSA Frontal Crash Driver	Good
NHTSA Frontal Crash Passenger	Excellent
NHTSA Side Crash Front Occupant	Average
NHTSA Side Crash Rear Occupant	Average
IIHS Offset	Not Tested
IIHS Bumper Bash	Not Tested
Mazda B-Series Pickup	
NHTSA Frontal Crash Driver	Good
NHTSA Frontal Crash Passenger	Good
NHTSA Side Crash Front Occupant	Excellent (Reg. Cab); Not Tested (X-Cab)
NHTSA Side Crash Rear Occupant	Not Applicable
IIHS Offset	Acceptable
IIHS Bumper Bash	Marginal
Mazda Millenia	
NHTSA Frontal Crash Driver	Good
NHTSA Frontal Crash Passenger	Excellent
NHTSA Side Crash Front Occupant	Not Tested
NHTSA Side Crash Rear Occupant	Not Tested
IIHS Offset	Acceptable
IIHS Bumper Bash	Marginal
Mazda MPV	
NHTSA Frontal Crash Driver	Not Tested
NHTSA Frontal Crash Passenger	Not Tested
NHTSA Side Crash Front Occupant	Excellent
NHTSA Side Crash Rear Occupant	Excellent
IIHS Offset	Not Tested
IIHS Bumper Bash	Not Tested
Mazda Protege	
NHTSA Frontal Crash Driver	Good
NHTSA Frontal Crash Passenger	Good
NHTSA Side Crash Front Occupant	Average
NHTSA Side Crash Rear Occupant	Good
IIHS Offset	Acceptable
IIHS Bumper Bash	Poor
Mercedes-Benz C-Class	
NHTSA Frontal Crash Driver	Not Tested
NHTSA Frontal Crash Passenger	Not Tested
NHTSA Side Crash Front Occupant	Average
NHTSA Side Crash Rear Occupant	Good
IIHS Offset	Not Tested
IIHS Bumper Bash	Not Tested

Mercedes-Benz E-Class	
NHTSA Frontal Crash Driver	Not Tested
NHTSA Frontal Crash Passenger	Not Tested
NHTSA Side Crash Front Occupant	Not Tested
NHTSA Side Crash Rear Occupant	Not Tested
IIHS Offset	Acceptable
IIHS Bumper Bash	Poor
Mercedes-Benz M-Class	
NHTSA Frontal Crash Driver	Good
NHTSA Frontal Crash Passenger	Excellent
NHTSA Side Crash Front Occupant	Not Tested
NHTSA Side Crash Rear Occupant	Not Tested
IIHS Offset	Good
IIHS Bumper Bash	Marginal
Mercury Grand Marquis	
NHTSA Frontal Crash Driver	Excellent
NHTSA Frontal Crash Passenger	Excellent
NHTSA Side Crash Front Occupant	Good
NHTSA Side Crash Rear Occupant	Good
IIHS Offset	Not Tested
IIHS Bumper Bash	Not Tested
Mercury Mountaineer	
NHTSA Frontal Crash Driver	Good
NHTSA Frontal Crash Passenger	Good
NHTSA Side Crash Front Occupant	Excellent
NHTSA Side Crash Rear Occupant	Excellent
IIHS Offset	Acceptable
IIHS Bumper Bash	Poor
Mercury Mystique	
NHTSA Frontal Crash Driver	Excellent
NHTSA Frontal Crash Passenger	Good
NHTSA Side Crash Front Occupant	Average
NHTSA Side Crash Rear Occupant	Good
IIHS Offset	Poor
IIHS Bumper Bash	Poor
Mercury Sable	
NHTSA Frontal Crash Driver	Not Tested
NHTSA Frontal Crash Passenger	Not Tested
NHTSA Side Crash Front Occupant	Average
NHTSA Side Crash Rear Occupant	Average
IIHS Offset	Good
IIHS Bumper Bash	Good
Mercury Villager	
NHTSA Frontal Crash Driver	Not Tested
NHTSA Frontal Crash Passenger	Not Tested

NHTSA Side Crash Front Occupant	Not Tested
NHTSA Side Crash Rear Occupant	Not Tested
IIHS Offset	Poor
IIHS Bumper Bash	Good
Mitsubishi Galant	
NHTSA Frontal Crash Driver	Good
NHTSA Frontal Crash Passenger	Good
NHTSA Side Crash Front Occupant	Excellent
NHTSA Side Crash Rear Occupant	Good
IIHS Offset	Acceptable
IIHS Bumper Bash	Acceptable
Mitsubishi Mirage	
NHTSA Frontal Crash Driver	Not Tested
NHTSA Frontal Crash Passenger	Not Tested
NHTSA Side Crash Front Occupant	Not Tested
NHTSA Side Crash Rear Occupant	Not Tested
IIHS Offset	Poor
IIHS Bumper Bash	Marginal
Mitsubishi Montero	
NHTSA Frontal Crash Driver	Not Tested
NHTSA Frontal Crash Passenger	Not Tested
NHTSA Side Crash Front Occupant	Not Tested
NHTSA Side Crash Rear Occupant	Not Tested
IIHS Offset	Acceptable
IIHS Bumper Bash	Poor
Mitsubishi Montero Sport	
NHTSA Frontal Crash Driver	Average
NHTSA Frontal Crash Passenger	Average
NHTSA Side Crash Front Occupant	Not Tested
NHTSA Side Crash Rear Occupant	Not Tested
IIHS Offset	Poor
IIHS Bumper Bash	Poor
Nissan Altima	
NHTSA Frontal Crash Driver	Not Tested
NHTSA Frontal Crash Passenger	Not Tested
NHTSA Side Crash Front Occupant	Average
NHTSA Side Crash Rear Occupant	Average
IIHS Offset	Not Tested
IIHS Bumper Bash	Not Tested
Nissan Frontier	
NHTSA Frontal Crash Driver	Average
NHTSA Frontal Crash Passenger	Good
NHTSA Side Crash Front Occupant	Good
NHTSA Side Crash Rear Occupant	Not Applicable

IIHS Offset	Poor
IIHS Bumper Bash	Poor
Nissan Maxima	
NHTSA Frontal Crash Driver	Not Tested
NHTSA Frontal Crash Passenger	Not Tested
NHTSA Side Crash Front Occupant	Good
NHTSA Side Crash Rear Occupant	Good
IIHS Offset	Not Tested
IIHS Bumper Bash	Not Tested
Nissan Pathfinder	
NHTSA Frontal Crash Driver	Good
NHTSA Frontal Crash Passenger	Excellent
NHTSA Side Crash Front Occupant	Excellent
NHTSA Side Crash Rear Occupant	Excellent
IIHS Offset	Marginal
IIHS Bumper Bash	Poor
Nissan Quest	
NHTSA Frontal Crash Driver	Not Tested
NHTSA Frontal Crash Passenger	Not Tested
NHTSA Side Crash Front Occupant	Not Tested
NHTSA Side Crash Rear Occupant	Not Tested
IIHS Offset	Poor
IIHS Bumper Bash	Good
Nissan Xterra	
NHTSA Frontal Crash Driver	Good
NHTSA Frontal Crash Passenger	Good
NHTSA Side Crash Front Occupant	Not Tested
NHTSA Side Crash Rear Occupant	Not Tested
IIHS Offset	Not Tested
IIHS Bumper Bash	Not Tested
Oldsmobile Alero	
NHTSA Frontal Crash Driver	Good
NHTSA Frontal Crash Passenger	Good
NHTSA Side Crash Front Occupant	Average (Sedan)
NHTSA Side Crash Rear Occupant	Average (Sedan)
IIHS Offset	Not Tested
IIHS Bumper Bash	Not Tested
Oldsmobile Bravada	
NHTSA Frontal Crash Driver	Average
NHTSA Frontal Crash Passenger	Good
NHTSA Side Crash Front Occupant	Excellent
NHTSA Side Crash Rear Occupant	Excellent
IIHS Offset	Poor
IIHS Bumper Bash	Poor

Oldsmobile Intrigue	
NHTSA Frontal Crash Driver	Good
NHTSA Frontal Crash Passenger	Poor
NHTSA Side Crash Front Occupant	Average
NHTSA Side Crash Rear Occupant	Very Poor
IIHS Offset	Acceptable
IIHS Bumper Bash	Acceptable
Oldsmobile Silhouette	
NHTSA Frontal Crash Driver	Good
NHTSA Frontal Crash Passenger	Average
NHTSA Side Crash Front Occupant	Excellent
NHTSA Side Crash Rear Occupant	Excellent
IIHS Offset	Poor
IIHS Bumper Bash	Poor
Plymouth Breeze	
NHTSA Frontal Crash Driver	Average
NHTSA Frontal Crash Passenger	Good
NHTSA Side Crash Front Occupant	Average
NHTSA Side Crash Rear Occupant	Poor
IIHS Offset	Poor
IIHS Bumper Bash	Marginal
Plymouth Neon	
NHTSA Frontal Crash Driver	Good
NHTSA Frontal Crash Passenger	Good
NHTSA Side Crash Front Occupant	Average
NHTSA Side Crash Rear Occupant	Average
IIHS Offset	Marginal
IIHS Bumper Bash	Acceptable
Plymouth Voyager/Grand Voyager	
NHTSA Frontal Crash Driver	Good
NHTSA Frontal Crash Passenger	Good
NHTSA Side Crash Front Occupant	Excellent (Grand Voyager); Not Tested (Voyager)
NHTSA Side Crash Rear Occupant	Average (Grand Voyager); Not Tested (Voyager)
IIHS Offset	Marginal
IIHS Bumper Bash	Poor
Pontiac Bonneville	
NHTSA Frontal Crash Driver	Not Tested
NHTSA Frontal Crash Passenger	Not Tested
NHTSA Side Crash Front Occupant	Not Tested
NHTSA Side Crash Rear Occupant	Good
IIHS Offset	Good
IIHS Bumper Bash	Marginal

Pontiac Firebird	
NHTSA Frontal Crash Driver	Good
NHTSA Frontal Crash Passenger	Excellent
NHTSA Side Crash Front Occupant	Average
NHTSA Side Crash Rear Occupant	Good
IIHS Offset	Not Tested
IIHS Bumper Bash	Not Tested
Pontiac Grand Am	
NHTSA Frontal Crash Driver	Good
NHTSA Frontal Crash Passenger	Good
NHTSA Side Crash Front Occupant	Average (Sedan)
NHTSA Side Crash Rear Occupant	Average (Sedan)
IIHS Offset	Not Tested
IIHS Bumper Bash	Not Tested
Pontiac Grand Prix	
NHTSA Frontal Crash Driver	Good
NHTSA Frontal Crash Passenger	Good
NHTSA Side Crash Front Occupant	Not Tested
NHTSA Side Crash Rear Occupant	Not Tested
IIHS Offset	Acceptable
IIHS Bumper Bash	Acceptable
Pontiac Montana	
NHTSA Frontal Crash Driver	Good
NHTSA Frontal Crash Passenger	Average
NHTSA Side Crash Front Occupant	Excellent
NHTSA Side Crash Rear Occupant	Excellent
IIHS Offset	Poor
IIHS Bumper Bash	Poor
Pontiac Sunfire	
NHTSA Frontal Crash Driver	Average (Cpe.); Good (Sdn.)
NHTSA Frontal Crash Passenger	Good
NHTSA Side Crash Front Occupant	Very Poor
NHTSA Side Crash Rear Occupant	Poor (Coupe); Average (Sedan)
IIHS Offset	Poor
IIHS Bumper Bash	Acceptable
Saab 9-3	
NHTSA Frontal Crash Driver	Good
NHTSA Frontal Crash Passenger	Good
NHTSA Side Crash Front Occupant	Not Tested
NHTSA Side Crash Rear Occupant	Not Tested
IIHS Offset	Acceptable
IIHS Bumper Bash	Acceptable
Saturn LS	
NHTSA Frontal Crash Driver	Good
NHTSA Frontal Crash Passenger	Excellent

NHTSA Side Crash Front Occupant	Poor
NHTSA Side Crash Rear Occupant	Good
IIHS Offset	Not Tested
IIHS Bumper Bash	Not Tested
Saturn SL	
NHTSA Frontal Crash Driver	Not Tested
NHTSA Frontal Crash Passenger	Not Tested
NHTSA Side Crash Front Occupant	Not Tested
NHTSA Side Crash Rear Occupant	Not Tested
IIHS Offset	Acceptable
IIHS Bumper Bash	Good
Saturn SW	
NHTSA Frontal Crash Driver	Excellent
NHTSA Frontal Crash Passenger	Excellent
NHTSA Side Crash Front Occupant	Average
NHTSA Side Crash Rear Occupant	Average
IIHS Offset	Acceptable
IIHS Bumper Bash	Good
Subaru Forester	
NHTSA Frontal Crash Driver	Good
NHTSA Frontal Crash Passenger	Good
NHTSA Side Crash Front Occupant	Not Tested
NHTSA Side Crash Rear Occupant	Not Tested
IIHS Offset	Good
IIHS Bumper Bash	Marginal
Subaru Impreza	
NHTSA Frontal Crash Driver	Good
NHTSA Frontal Crash Passenger	Good
NHTSA Side Crash Front Occupant	Not Tested
NHTSA Side Crash Rear Occupant	Not Tested
IIHS Offset	Not Tested
IIHS Bumper Bash	Not Tested
Subaru Legacy	
NHTSA Frontal Crash Driver	Good
NHTSA Frontal Crash Passenger	Good
NHTSA Side Crash Front Occupant	Not Tested
NHTSA Side Crash Rear Occupant	Not Tested
IIHS Offset	Not Tested
IIHS Bumper Bash	Not Tested
Subaru Outback Sport	
NHTSA Frontal Crash Driver	Good
NHTSA Frontal Crash Passenger	Good
NHTSA Side Crash Front Occupant	Not Tested
NHTSA Side Crash Rear Occupant	Not Tested

IIHS Offset	Not Tested
IIHS Bumper Bash	Not Tested
Suzuki Grand Vitara	
NHTSA Frontal Crash Driver	Not Tested
NHTSA Frontal Crash Passenger	Not Tested
NHTSA Side Crash Front Occupant	Not Tested
NHTSA Side Crash Rear Occupant	Not Tested
IIHS Offset	Acceptable
IIHS Bumper Bash	Poor
Suzuki Swift	
NHTSA Frontal Crash Driver	Good
NHTSA Frontal Crash Passenger	Good
NHTSA Side Crash Front Occupant	Not Tested
NHTSA Side Crash Rear Occupant	Not Tested
IIHS Offset	Not Tested
IIHS Bumper Bash	Not Tested
Suzuki Vitara	
NHTSA Frontal Crash Driver	Not Tested
NHTSA Frontal Crash Passenger	Not Tested
NHTSA Side Crash Front Occupant	Not Tested
NHTSA Side Crash Rear Occupant	Not Tested
IIHS Offset	Acceptable (4-door)
IIHS Bumper Bash	Poor
Toyota 4Runner	
NHTSA Frontal Crash Driver	Good
NHTSA Frontal Crash Passenger	Excellent
NHTSA Side Crash Front Occupant	Excellent
NHTSA Side Crash Rear Occupant	Excellent
IIHS Offset	Good
IIHS Bumper Bash	Poor
Toyota Camry	
NHTSA Frontal Crash Driver	Good
NHTSA Frontal Crash Passenger	Excellent
NHTSA Side Crash Front Occupant	Average
NHTSA Side Crash Rear Occupant	Average
IIHS Offset	Good
IIHS Bumper Bash	Good
Toyota Camry Solara	
NHTSA Frontal Crash Driver	Not Tested
NHTSA Frontal Crash Passenger	Not Tested
NHTSA Side Crash Front Occupant	Average
NHTSA Side Crash Rear Occupant	Excellent
IIHS Offset	Not Tested
IIHS Bumper Bash	Not Tested

Toyota Corolla	
NHTSA Frontal Crash Driver	Good
NHTSA Frontal Crash Passenger	Good
NHTSA Side Crash Front Occupant	Average (w/o side airbag); Good (w/side airbag)
NHTSA Side Crash Rear Occupant	Average
IIHS Offset	Acceptable
IIHS Bumper Bash	Good
Toyota RAV4	
NHTSA Frontal Crash Driver	Good
NHTSA Frontal Crash Passenger	Good
NHTSA Side Crash Front Occupant	Excellent (4-door)
NHTSA Side Crash Rear Occupant	Excellent (4-door)
IIHS Offset	Marginal (4-door)
IIHS Bumper Bash	Poor
Toyota Sienna	
NHTSA Frontal Crash Driver	Excellent
NHTSA Frontal Crash Passenger	Excellent
NHTSA Side Crash Front Occupant	Good
NHTSA Side Crash Rear Occupant	Excellent
IIHS Offset	Good
IIHS Bumper Bash	Marginal
Toyota Tacoma	
NHTSA Frontal Crash Driver	Good
NHTSA Frontal Crash Passenger	Good
NHTSA Side Crash Front Occupant	Very Poor
NHTSA Side Crash Rear Occupant	Not Applicable
IIHS Offset	Acceptable
IIHS Bumper Bash	Poor
Toyota Tundra	
NHTSA Frontal Crash Driver	Good
NHTSA Frontal Crash Passenger	Average
NHTSA Side Crash Front Occupant	Not Tested
NHTSA Side Crash Rear Occupant	Not Tested
IIHS Offset	Not Tested
IIHS Bumper Bash	Not Tested
Volkswagen Golf	
NHTSA Frontal Crash Driver	Not Tested
NHTSA Frontal Crash Passenger	Not Tested
NHTSA Side Crash Front Occupant	Not Tested
NHTSA Side Crash Rear Occupant	Not Tested
IIHS Offset	Acceptable
IIHS Bumper Bash	Good

Volkswagen Jetta	
NHTSA Frontal Crash Driver	Excellent
NHTSA Frontal Crash Passenger	Excellent
NHTSA Side Crash Front Occupant	Not Tested
NHTSA Side Crash Rear Occupant	Not Tested
IIHS Offset	Acceptable
IIHS Bumper Bash	Good
Volkswagen New Beetle	
NHTSA Frontal Crash Driver	Good
NHTSA Frontal Crash Passenger	Good
NHTSA Side Crash Front Occupant	Excellent
NHTSA Side Crash Rear Occupant	Average
IIHS Offset	Good
IIHS Bumper Bash	Good
Volkswagen Passat	
NHTSA Frontal Crash Driver	Excellent
NHTSA Frontal Crash Passenger	Excellent
NHTSA Side Crash Front Occupant	Not Tested
NHTSA Side Crash Rear Occupant	Not Tested
IIHS Offset	Good
IIHS Bumper Bash	Good
Volvo S70	
NHTSA Frontal Crash Driver	Excellent
NHTSA Frontal Crash Passenger	Excellent
NHTSA Side Crash Front Occupant	Good
NHTSA Side Crash Rear Occupant	No Data
IIHS Offset	Good
IIHS Bumper Bash	Marginal
Volvo S80	
NHTSA Frontal Crash Driver	Not Tested
NHTSA Frontal Crash Passenger	Not Tested
NHTSA Side Crash Front Occupant	Excellent
NHTSA Side Crash Rear Occupant	Excellent
IIHS Offset	Not Tested
IIHS Bumper Bash	Not Tested
Volvo V70	
NHTSA Frontal Crash Driver	Excellent
NHTSA Frontal Crash Passenger	Excellent
NHTSA Side Crash Front Occupant	Good
NHTSA Side Crash Rear Occupant	No Data
IIHS Offset	Good
IIHS Bumper Bash	Marginal

WARRANTIES & ROADSIDE ASSISTANCE

All new vehicles sold in America come with at least two warranties, and many include roadside assistance. Described below are the major types of warranties and assistance provided to consumers:

Basic: Your basic warranty covers everything except items subject to wear and tear, such as oil filters, wiper blades, and the like. Tires and batteries often have their own warranty coverage, which will be outlined in your owner's manual. Emissions equipment is required to be covered for five years or 50,000 miles by the federal government.

Drivetrain: Drivetrain coverage takes care of most of the parts that make the car move, like the engine, transmission, drive axles and driveshaft. Like the basic warranty, parts subject to wear and tear like hoses and belts are not covered. However, most of the internal parts of the engine, such as the pistons and bearings, which are subject to wear and tear are covered by the drivetrain warranty. See your owner's manual or local dealer for specific coverage.

Rust or Corrosion: This warranty protects you from rust-through problems with the sheetmetal. Surface rust doesn't count. The rust must make a hole to be covered. Keep your car washed and waxed, and rust shouldn't be a problem.

Roadside Assistance: Most manufacturers provide a service that will rescue you if your car leaves you stranded, even if it's your fault. Lock yourself out of the car? Somebody will come and open it up. Run out of gas? Somebody will deliver some fuel. Flat tire? Somebody will change it for you. See your owner's manual for details, or ask the dealer about specifics.

Make	Basic (yrs/mi)	Drivetrain (yrs/mi)	Rust/Corrosion (yrs/mi)	Roadside Assistance (yrs/mi)
Acura	4/50,000	4/50,000	5/Unlimited	4/50,000
AM General	3/36,000	3/36,000	6/100,000	None Available
Audi	3/50,000	3/50,000	12/Unlimited	3/Unlimited
BMW	4/50,000	4/50,000	6/Unlimited	4/50,000

WARRANTIES & ROADSIDE ASSISTANCE

Make	Basic (yrs/mi)	Drivetrain (yrs/mi)	Rust/Corrosion (yrs/mi)	Roadside Assistance (yrs/mi)
Buick	3/36,000	3/36,000	6/100,000	3/36,000
Cadillac	4/50,000	4/50,000	6/100,000	4/50,000
Chevrolet	3/36,000	3/36,000	6/100,000	3/36,000
Chrysler	3/36,000	3/36,000	5/100,000	3/36,000
Daewoo	3/36,000	5/60,000	5/Unlimited	3/36,000
Dodge	3/36,000	3/36,000	5/100,000	3/36,000
Ford	3/36,000	3/36,000	5/Unlimited	3/36,000
GMC	3/36,000	3/36,000	6/100,000	3/36,000
Honda	3/36,000	3/36,000	5/Unlimited	None Available
Hyundai	5/60,000	10/100,000	5/100,000	5/Unlimited
Infiniti	4/60,000	6/70,000	7/Unlimited	4/Unlimited
Isuzu	3/50,000	10/120,000 (except Hombre)	6/100,000	5/60,000
Jaguar	4/50,000	4/50,000	6/unlimited	4/50,000
Jeep	3/36,000	3/36,000	5/100,000	3/36,000
Kia	3/36,000	5/60,000	5/100,000	3/36,000
Land Rover	4/50,000	4/50,000	6/Unlimited	4/50,000
Lexus	4/50,000	6/70,000	6/Unlimited	4/Unlimited
Lincoln	4/50,000	4/50,000	5/Unlimited	4/50,000
Mazda	3/50,000	3/50,000	5/Unlimited	3/50,000
Mercedes	4/50,000	4/50,000	4/50,000	Unlimited
Mercury	3/36,000	3/36,000	5/Unlimited	3/36,000
Mitsubishi	3/36,000	5/60,000	7/100,000	3/36,000
Nissan	3/36,000	5/60,000	5/Unlimited	None Available
Oldsmobile	3/36,000	3/36,000	6/100,000	3/36,000
Plymouth	3/36,000	3/36,000	5/100,000	3/36,000
Pontiac	3/36,000	3/36,000	6/100,000	3/36,000
Porsche	4/50,000	4/50,000	10/Unlimited	4/50,000
Saab	4/50,000	4/50,000	6/Unlimited	4/50,000
Saturn	3/36,000	3/36,000	6/100,000	3/36,000
Subaru	3/36,000	5/60,000	5/Unlimited	3/36,000
Suzuki	3/36,000	3/36,000	3/Unlimited	None Available
Toyota	3/36,000	5/60,000	5/Unlimited	None Available
Volkswagen	2/24,000	10/100,000 (except EuroVan)	12/Unlimited (except Cabrio)	2/Unlimited
Volvo	4/50,000	4/50,000	8/Unlimited	4/Unlimited

** All data sourced directly from manufacturer customer assistance telephone operatives and Automotive News.*

DEALER HOLDBACKS

There's plenty of talk these days about dealer holdback, and we suppose we're to blame for some of the hype over this manufacturer kickback to dealers. We've been reporting holdback data for years. But many consumers don't understand what the dealer holdback is, what it is used for, and what the holdback's role is in the deal-making process. Let's try to clear up some of the confusion.

What is Dealer Holdback?

Dealer holdback is a percentage of the MSRP or invoice of a new vehicle that is paid to the dealer by the manufacturer to assist with the dealership's financing of the vehicle. It is almost always non-negotiable, because it is designed to help the dealer cover some of the extraordinary costs of doing business. However, by knowing about the holdback, you can use it as a negotiating tool in some cases. First, a little more background.

The total invoice cost of the car is due to the manufacturer, payable by the dealership, when the vehicle is ordered, not when it is sold. Since car dealerships (or any retail operation, for that matter) must have an inventory on hand which the consumer can browse and ultimately select a vehicle, they must borrow money from the bank to pay for that inventory. The manufacturer pays for financing and maintenance for the first 90 days the vehicle is on the lot, in the form of a quarterly check called a holdback. After the first 90 days, the dealership dips into its own pocket, and into its own profit, to finance the car. Fortunately, most cars don't stay on the lot for three full months.

This amount is "invisible" to the consumer because, unlike the destination charge, it does not appear as an itemized fee on the window sticker and is included in the invoice cost of the car (except in the case of Mitsubishi, where the manufacturer allows dealers to charge the customer directly for the holdback.) If the car sells within 90 days of arrival on the dealer's lot, he is guaranteed a profit even if the vehicle is sold to you at cost. Because of the holdback, the dealer can advertise a car at $1 over invoice and still make hundreds of dollars on the sale.

For example, let's say you're interested in a Ford with a Manufacturer's Suggested Retail Price (MSRP) of $20,500, including optional equipment and destination charge. Dealer invoice on this hypothetical Ford is $18,000, including optional equipment. The invoice includes a dealer holdback that, in the case of all Ford vehicles, amounts to 3 percent of the total MSRP. (The $500 destination charge should not be included when figuring the holdback.) So, on this particular Ford, the true dealer cost is actually $17,400, plus destination charges. Even if the dealer sells you the car for invoice, which is unlikely, he would still be making as much as $600 on the deal when his quarterly check arrived. That is profit to the dealer only; the sales staff doesn't see any of it.

So, if you follow Edmunds.com's advice and offer the dealership 3 percent over invoice for this Ford, or $18,540 plus the destination charge, the dealer and the sales staff are making as much as $1,140 and you're still getting a good deal by paying $1,460 less than the MSRP. (Remember that this price doesn't include destination or advertising charges, additional fees, tax, or license plates.)

However, the true "profit" of holdback money depends on how long the car has been on the lot. If our hypothetical Ford had been sitting there for 45 days before you bought it, the dealer's holdback profit is only half of what it could have been, or only $300, cutting total profit on the deal to $840.

Dealer holdback allows dealers to advertise big sales. Often, ads promise that your new car will cost you just "$1 over/under invoice!" Additionally, the dealer stands to reap further benefits if there is some sort of dealer incentive or customer rebate on the car. Generally, sale prices stipulate that all rebates and incentives go to the dealer. Using the example above, let's see what happens when there is a rebate.

Suppose the car described above has a $1,000 rebate in effect. You need to subtract that $1,000 rebate (remember, the dealer is keeping the rebate) from the dealer invoice of $18,000, which results in a new dealer invoice of just $17,000. Now, you must calculate a fair price. In this example, 3 percent of dealer invoice is $510, which means that the price you should try to buy the car for is $17,510, plus destination, advertising, taxes*, and fees. The dealer is still making as much as $1,110 and you're paying $2,490 less than the MSRP. Remember, the longer the car has been in the dealer's inventory, the less money the dealer is making.

Almost all dealerships consider holdback money sacred, and are unwilling to share any portion of it with the consumer. Don't push the issue. Your best strategy is to avoid mentioning that you know the holdback amount and what it is during negotiations. Mention holdback only if the dealer gives you some song-and-dance about not making any money at 3 percent over invoice.

DEALER HOLDBACKS

So how can you truly benefit from this information? Well, if the dealership doesn't have that pretty green color you're interested in, and they can't find it at another dealership in the area, they have to order it directly from the manufacturer. If that's the case, make sure that they know that you know about the holdback. If a vehicle is special-ordered, holdback money is pure profit, and you will need to factor this into price negotiations.

Domestic manufacturers (Chrysler, Ford and GM) generally offer dealers a holdback equaling 3 percent of the total sticker price, or MSRP, of the car. Import manufacturers (Honda, Nissan, Toyota, etc.) provide varying holdback amounts that are equal to a percentage of total MSRP, base MSRP, total invoice or base invoice.

When calculating a holdback, use the following guidelines.

If a holdback is off the:

- Total MSRP, consumers must include the MSRP price of all options before figuring the holdback.
- Base MSRP, consumers must figure the holdback before adding desired options.
- Total Invoice, consumer must include the invoice price of all options before figuring the holdback.
- Base Invoice, consumers must figure the holdback before adding desired options.

Following is a current list of makes and the amount of the 2000 dealer holdback.

Make	Holdback
Acura	2% of the Base MSRP
Audi	No Holdback
BMW	No Holdback
Buick	3% of the Total MSRP
Cadillac	3% of the Total MSRP
Chevrolet	3% of the Total MSRP
Chrysler	3% of the Total MSRP
Daewoo	One-price sales. Customer pays MSRP.
Dodge	3% of the Total MSRP
Eagle	3% of the Total MSRP
Ford	3% of the Total MSRP

DEALER HOLDBACKS

GMC	3% of the Total MSRP
Honda	2% of the Base MSRP (except Prelude, which has no holdback)
Hyundai	2% of the Total Invoice
Infiniti	1% of the Base MSRP (holdback) + 2% of the Base Invoice (floorplanning allowance)
Isuzu	3% of the Total MSRP
Jaguar	2% of the Base Invoice
Jeep	3% of the Total MSRP
Kia	3% of the Total Invoice
Land Rover	No Holdback
Lexus	2% of the Base MSRP
Lincoln	3% of the Total MSRP
Mazda	2% of the Base MSRP
Mercedes-Benz	3% of the Total MSRP
Mercury	3% of the Total MSRP
Mitsubishi	2% of the Total MSRP
Nissan	2% + 1% of the Total Invoice (holdback + floorplanning allowance)
Oldsmobile	3% of the Total MSRP
Plymouth	3% of the Total MSRP
Pontiac	3% of the Total MSRP
Porsche	No Holdback
Saab	3% of the Base MSRP
Saturn	One-price sales. Customer pays MSRP.
Subaru	2% of the Total MSRP (Amount may differ inNortheastern U.S.)
Suzuki	2% of the Base MSRP
Toyota	2% of the Base Invoice (Amount may differ in Southern U.S.)
Volkswagen	No Holdback
Volvo	$300 Flat Amount

* Incentives and rebates are actually deducted from the transaction price after Uncle Sam has collected taxes. We have taken editorial license with the process in this example for the sake of keeping it simple.

Edmunds.com solicits email queries from consumers who visit our Web site at http://www.edmunds.com. Below are 25 commonly asked questions regarding new cars and the buying process.

FAQ

---

1. How do I figure a fair deal?

Use this formula: Dealer Invoice of car and options + 3 percent Fair Profit + Destination Charge + Advertising Fees + Tax - Incentives and/or Rebates = Fair Deal

2. Why won't the dealer accept my offer of 3 percent over dealer cost?

The dealer doesn't have to sell you a car. If demand for the model is high, if supplies are short, or if the dealer enjoys making a healthy profit, you won't be able to buy the car for a fair price. Don't argue the point, just find another dealer. If all the dealers you contact refuse to sell the car at this price, then your offer is too low, and you must start over at a higher value.

3. How can a dealer sell a new car for less than the invoice price Edmunds.com publishes?

Auto manufacturers will often subsidize volume-sellers to keep sales and production up by offering car dealers hefty cash rewards for meeting monthly or quarterly sales goals. In other words, the dealer will take a slight loss on the car in anticipation of larger cash rewards if sales goals are met. It has been our experience that when a dealer sells a vehicle for less than invoice, the manufacturer is in one form or another always subsidizing the deal. In print ads, always look for phrases such as "all incentives and/or rebates assigned to dealer."

Also, since profit can be made on other parts of the deal, a dealer may be willing to take a loss on the price of the car in exchange for profit gleaned from a low-ball trade-in value, high-interest financing, rustproofing, an extended warranty, and aftermarket or dealer-installed accessories. We once met a Plymouth salesman who bragged that he sold a Neon for invoice, but with the undervalued trade-in, high-interest financing and dealer-installed items factored into the deal, the buyer actually paid more than $20,000 for the car. Keep in mind that there is more to a good deal than a low price.

4. How can I find out what customer rebates or dealer incentives are currently available?

Rebates to customers are clearly announced in advertising. Incentives to dealers, commonly known as "back-end monies," are not. Edmunds.com publishes current national and large regional rebate and incentive programs online at **http://www.edmunds.com**. Local rebate and incentive programs also exist on occasion, but Edmunds.com doesn't have access to this information. Ask your dealer if the local automobile dealer association or advertising association is sponsoring any rebates or incentives in your area. They might actually share this information with you, and it never hurts to ask.

5. Why do some dealer incentives on specific models have a range of values?

Sometimes, the manufacturer will tell the dealer that he must sell a certain number of cars to qualify for an incentive. For example, let's say Nissan offered dealers an incentive of $100-1,000 on the Altima. This is a quota-based incentive. It means that to get the $100 per car, the dealer might have to sell 10 cars before a certain date. To get $500 per car, the dealer might have to sell 50 cars before a certain date. To get $1,000 per car, the dealer might have to sell 100 cars before a certain date. The more cars the dealer sells, the more money he makes, because quota-based rebates are retroactive.

With these types of quota-based incentives, you have leverage. With your sale, the dealer is one car closer to clearing the next hurdle and making more money. We recommend that you request half of the maximum quota-based incentive while negotiating your deal, unless the dealer or salesperson bungles and admits that your sale will put them into the next tier of incentive qualification. In this case, demand the maximum incentive.

6. What is a carryover allowance?

At the beginning of a new model year, some manufacturers provide dealers with a carryover allowance in addition to the dealer holdback. The carryover allowance is applied to cars from the previous model year, and is designed to assist dealers in lowering prices and clearing out old stock. Currently, the only domestic automaker that gives its dealers a carryover allowance is Ford Motor Company. The amounts can vary, but they average 5 percent of the MSRP. General Motors and Chrysler target slow sellers with heavy incentives and rebates. Most import manufacturers subscribe to the incentive and rebate philosophy as well.

7. I want to pay cash for my new car. Do I have an advantage?

Not necessarily. You must remember that no matter how you pay for your car, it's all cash to the dealer. In the old days when dealers carried your note, you could save money by paying cash because there was no risk to the dealer. Today, dealerships finance through one of several lending institutions (banks, credit unions, or the automaker's captive financing division) that pay them cash when the contract is presented. In fact, if dealerships do the financing on your behalf, they tend to make more money on your contract in the form of a reserve; anywhere from ½ to 1 point spread on the interest. For example, if the published rate is 8.75 percent, the lender to dealer rate may be discounted to 8 percent; the .75 percent is the reserve held by the dealer as additional profit. This may not sound like much, but it adds up to hundreds of thousands of dollars a year at larger dealerships. This is the reason you should always arrange financing before going to the dealership, and then ask the dealer if they can beat your pre-approved rate. In most cases, they cannot, because of the reserve.

Paying cash is an advantage if you suffer from poor credit or bankruptcy, because it allows you to avoid the higher interest rates charged on loans to people with past credit problems. The bottom line is that if you think you can invest your money at a higher return than the interest rate of the car loan, you could actually save money by not paying cash.

8. Do factory orders cost more than buying from dealer stock?

All things considered equal, ordered vehicles cost no more than vehicles in dealer stock and, in some cases, may actually cost less. When you buy from dealer stock, you may have to settle for a vehicle with either more or less equipment or your second or third color choice. Moreover, the dealership pays interest on stocked vehicles at a predetermined monthly rate to the manufacturer. This interest is called floor plan, and is subsidized by the dealer holdback. When you factory order, you get exactly what you want, in the color you want, and the dealer should eliminate the floor plan cost. In most cases, the dealer passes the savings on to the customer, and the savings could amount to several hundred dollars.

The downside to ordering is that incentives and rebates are good only on the day of delivery, unless stated otherwise (in writing) by the dealer. If an incentive or rebate plan was in effect when the vehicle was ordered, but not in effect the day of delivery, the customer is usually not eligible for the incentive or rebate. If you order a vehicle, and the delivery date is very close to the expiration date of a rebate or incentive program, beware that the dealer may try to delay delivery until after the rebate or incentive has expired.

From a negotiation standpoint, dealers may be more likely to offer a better price on a vehicle in stock, particularly if the monthly floor plan payments have exceeded the holdback amount and are now chewing into the dealer's profit.

9. Can I order a car directly from the factory?

No you cannot. Dealerships are franchisees of the factory, and are protected as such. However, a few manufacturers are buying large groups of dealerships in some areas to test the idea that a factory-owned store can serve the customer's needs better than individually owned and operated stores. Ford is testing this philosophy in several markets, and Daewoo originally intended to sell cars exclusively through factory owned stores until some states reminded the company that factory dealerships were *verboten.* Even stalwart General Motors is trying to consolidate dealerships in L.A.'s massive San Fernando Valley, but with little success. But signs exist that in the future, factory-owned stores may become commonplace.

10. Why are destination charges the same for every dealer around the country?

Auto manufacturers will average the cost to ship a car from the factory to the furthest dealership with the cost to ship a car from the factory to the closest dealership. Some manufacturers do this for each model, others average costs across an entire make. Sometimes, shipping costs to Hawaii and Alaska may be higher than the averaged amount for the contiguous 48 states.

11. Can I avoid paying the destination charge by picking up a car at the factory?

Currently, the only North American factories that allow customers to take delivery the minute a car rolls off the assembly line are the Corvette plant in Bowling Green, Ky., the Dodge Viper plant in Detroit, and the BMW plant in Spartanburg, S.C. Buyers who opt to travel to pick up their new Corvette, Viper or M Roadster still pay the dealer they bought it from the destination charge.

12. Why should I pay advertising fees?

Most vehicles carry a legitimate advertising fee levied by either the manufacturer or by regional dealer groups. National or regional advertising fees, when charged, should not exceed 1.5 percent of the vehicle's MSRP. Because individual dealership advertising is a cost of doing business, you should never pay an advertising fee levied by the dealer rather than a regional dealer association or the manufacturer.

13. Can I negotiate price on a Saturn, Daewoo or at a no-haggle dealership?

You cannot negotiate price on a Saturn, but you can haggle over your trade-in and shop aggressively for the lowest-rate financing to keep costs down. Daewoo dealers also use a one-price philosophy, but the company wants to expand quickly and sell lots of cars, and there are often incentives and rebates available on these models, so the climate is favorable for negotiation.

No-haggle dealerships might wiggle a little on price, but if they're smart, they'll tell you to get lost. If you want to duke it out over $100, why would you shop at a no-haggle dealership wasting their time and yours? Think about this. If the no-haggle dealer caves and drops the price to sell you the car, you're gonna tell your buddies, and they're gonna tell their buddies, and pretty soon the whole town will be haggling over cars with the no-haggle dealer, and the no-haggle dealer isn't a no-haggle dealer anymore. Get it?

14. Why won't the dealer give me wholesale value for my trade-in?

When a dealership takes a car in on trade, it is responsible for the car. Before the trade-in can be sold, it must be inspected and often repaired. Sometimes, emissions work is necessary. All this inspection and repair work costs the dealership money. If the trade is in good condition and has low miles, the dealer will put the car on the used-car lot for retail price. When the car sells, it is rarely for retail price, so the profit margin is shaved. The less you accept for the trade-in, the more room the dealer has to make a deal with a prospective buyer, and the more money the dealer will make thanks to increased profit margins.

If the car doesn't sell, if it has high miles, or it is in poor condition, the dealer will have to wholesale it. The dealer will likely sell the car for below wholesale value at the auction, and expects to recoup some of the money spent reconditioning and inspecting the car. If the dealer offered you wholesale price when you traded in the car, he wouldn't make the money back in the event that the trade-in went to auction.

Regardless of the condition of your car, the dealer will anticipate taking the car to auction, and will leave room to make money in that event. Your best bet is to sell your car on your own to a private party, and forget about trading in.

15. Should I buy rustproofing, fabric protection packages, paint sealant, and other dealer-installed items?

Of course not. Most new cars are covered against rust perforation for several years and up to 100,000 miles. Want to protect your fabric? Go to an auto parts store and buy a can or two of Scotchgard. New cars have clearcoat paint, which offers protection from the elements. A little elbow grease and a jar of carnauba wax will keep the finish protected and looking great. By investing a little time and effort into your automobile, you can save hundreds on these highly profitable dealer protection packages.

16. How much does an extended warranty cost the warranty company?

The cost of an extended warranty is based upon the degree of probability that any given vehicle will require repairs during the extended warranty period. Reliability records and repair cost information for a vehicle are evaluated to forecast potential future repair costs, and the extended warranty company will then charge a premium adequate enough to cover the potential cost of repairing the vehicle during the warranty period, while still making a profit. It is important to note that the cost of an extended warranty includes administrative costs for handling paperwork and claims, and insurance to guarantee that claims will be paid.

Extended warranty costs are based on averages, so the cost of applying an extended warranty to any given make and model of car can vary from consumer to consumer. Let's say you bought a $1,000 extended warranty for two identical Brand X vehicles: Car A and Car B. During the extended warranty period, Car A never breaks, so the extended warranty is never used. At the same time, Car B suffers bills amounting to $1,200 for transmission and valve problems. Profit on the warranty sold for Car A will counterbalance the loss suffered on Car B. Extended warranty companies sell thousands of warranties annually, and are able to make a profit when the actual loss experience is lower than the forecast potential for future repair. In other words, when sales exceed overhead the company makes money.

17. Who sets the residual value for a lease?

The financing institution that is handling the lease for the dealership sets the residual value, which can be affected by market forces and vehicle popularity. When shopping leases, it is important to shop different financing institutions for the highest residual value and the lowest interest rate.

18. When I use Edmunds.com's formula to calculate a lease, I get a payment that is substantially higher than what the dealer quoted me. Why is this?

The manufacturer subsidizes most nationally advertised leases. This means that the manufacturer gives the dealer incentive money to lower the capitalized cost (selling price) listed on the lease, or that the financing institution owned by the manufacturer has artificially inflated the residual value to lower the monthly payment, or both. Dealers may not inform you of these adjustments in the numbers.

Another problem with advertised lease payments seen in newspapers and on television is that consumers don't read the terms of the lease carefully. Sometimes, a substantial capitalized cost reduction (down payment) is required. Sometimes hefty deposits and other drive-off fees are involved. Mileage limits may be ridiculously low. Payments may be required for 39, 48 or 60 months rather than the conventional 24- or 36-month term. Read the fine print carefully!

Also, keep in mind that there are more than 250 different lending institutions across the country, and each one sets its own residual values for lease contracts. Don't be surprised if you go to three different dealers and get three different lease payments for the same vehicle over the same term.

19. When is the best time to purchase a car from a dealer?

There's as much advice about when to visit a dealer as there are days in a year. Some say that Mondays are good because business is slower on Monday than on the weekend. Some say holidays like Thanksgiving are good for the same reason: nobody else will be there, and the sales team will be hungry for a sale. Others advise to go when it's raining or snowing; after all, who wants to look at a car and get wet? Then there's the advice that the end of the month is the best time because the dealership needs to make its "quota" of car sales and will be more willing to cut a deal. Still others advise not to buy a car until the end of the model year, or in slow months like August or December when people are busy thinking about going back to school or shopping for Christmas gifts rather than buying a new car.

Our advice is don't buy a car until you're ready. That's usually the best time. By then you have saved enough for a substantial down payment, and you've had plenty of time to do your research for the lowest interest rate, and you know all the current incentives and rebates. There is no way to tell when is the best time to buy other than personal need.

If a dealer has already made his target sales for the month, you're not going to have any advantage by showing up on the 31st of the month. While there may be something to say for going to a dealership on a weekday near the end of the month on Thanksgiving at five o'clock during a raging blizzard, your best bet is to track incentives and rebates, don't buy hot new models, and do your research first.

20. How soon after a price increase does Edmunds.com modify its data?

This depends on how soon our sources are notified. Sometimes, it's a matter of days; other times, it can take longer. Rest assured that we painstakingly attempt to maintain the most up-to-date pricing. If a dealer disputes the accuracy of our pricing, ask them to prove it by showing you the invoice so you can compare. If prices have indeed increased, the amount will not be substantial: the new figures should easily be within a few percentage points of those published in this guide.

21. Why is the car I'm looking at on the West Coast or in the Southern tier of states priced differently than what's listed in this guide?

California, Oregon, Washington and Idaho are the testing grounds for different pricing and option schemes. Because of the popularity of imported makes in this market, domestic manufacturers will often slash dealer profit margins and offer better-equipped cars at lower prices than those available in other parts of the country. This is why some dealer incentives and customer rebates do not apply on the West Coast, and why some option packages available in those states may not be listed in this guide.

In the Southeast, large distributors control Toyota pricing, and take advantage of this monopoly by charging more money for destination and advertising fees. They also front-load many cars with worthless packages of cosmetic items that you don't need. Similarly, in the Northeast, a single distributor, who may charge differently for fees and options than dealers in the rest of the United States, handles Subaru products.

22. Why doesn't Edmunds.com list option prices for some makes and models?

Almost all Acura, Honda, and Suzuki options are dealer-installed. Some manufacturers, like Nissan, Subaru, Toyota and Volvo, will offer both factory- and dealer-installed options. Pricing for these items can vary depending on region and dealer. Therefore, it is impossible for Edmunds.com to list an accurate price for these items. Our experience shows that these items often carry a 100 percent markup in dealer profit. We recommend that you avoid buying dealer-installed options if you can help it.

23. When should a car be considered used?

Technically, a vehicle is considered used if it has been titled. However, some dealers can rack up hundreds or thousands of miles on a new car without titling it. In these cases, the ethical definition of a used car should include any car used for extensive demonstration or personal use by dealership staff members. The only miles a new car should have on the odometer when purchased are those put on during previous test drives by prospective buyers (at dealerships where demonstrators are not used), and any miles driven during a dealer trade, within a reasonable limit. If the new car you're considering has more than 300 miles on the odometer, you should question how the car accumulated so many miles, and request a discount for the excessive mileage. We think a discount amounting to a dime a mile is a fair charge for wear and tear inflicted by the dealership.

A car should not be considered used if it is a brand-new leftover from a previous model year. However, it should be discounted, because many manufacturers offer dealers incentives designed to help the dealer lower prices and clear out old stock.

24. What's the difference between a demo car and a program car?

A demo car is one used by the dealership as a demonstrator to potential buyers. Often, dealership personnel will use the car as personal transportation. A program car is a former rental car, purchased at auction by the dealership. Either type of car is more likely to have been abused than a brand-new car or a used car offered for sale by a private owner.

25. Is it fair for a dealer to ask if my trade has ever been wrecked, or damaged in any way?

Certainly. If you were buying a car from a used-car dealer, you'd want to know the same thing, wouldn't you?

You've seen the ads: Honda Civic for $189 a month. Jeep Grand Cherokee for $289 a month. GMC Yukon for $389 a month. Wow! You can't believe your eyes. Visions of shiny new golf clubs in your trunk, a big-screen TV in your living room and two weeks of prime vacationing in Vail release endorphins at twice the Surgeon General's recommended level in anticipation of big savings.

But be careful, because you probably shouldn't believe your eyes when you read such banner ads, not until they're grazing over the fine print. See where it says "Capitalized Cost Reduction"? That's lease-speak for down payment. See where it says "30,000 miles over three-year term"? That's lease-speak for "You're going to the Safeway and back — and that's all folks." Want the car for zero down? That's gonna cost you. You drive someplace more than twice a month? That's gonna cost you, too.

Like most consumers, you want to know how to buy or lease the car of your choice for the best possible price. Buyers are attracted to leasing by low payments and the prospect of driving a new car every two or three years. Many people figure that a car payment is an unavoidable fact of budgetary life, and they might as well drive 'new' rather than 'old.' True, leasing is an attractive alternative, but there are some things you need to understand about leasing before jumping in feet first without a paddle. Whatever. You know what we mean.

How to Lease

Never walk into a dealership and announce that you want to lease a car. Don't talk payment, either. Once a salesperson identifies you as a payment shopper, you're a dead duck. Any competent dealer can find a way to make a car fit your budget while maximizing profit simultaneously. Concentrate on finding a car you like, and know before you go into the dealership what you can afford in terms of sticker price.

Lease payments are based on the capitalized cost, which is the selling price of the car. The residual value is the predicted value of the vehicle at the end of the lease term, and can be expressed as a percentage of the MSRP. Sometimes, the residual value is not the predicted value of the car at the end of the lease, but a number that allows the leasing company to lower the cost of the lease as much as possible without incurring excessive risk when it comes time to sell the off-lease vehicle. A money factor, which is lease-speak for 'interest rate,' is also involved in the calculation of a lease payment. If the money factor is expressed as a percentage, convert the percentage to the money factor by dividing the number by 24 (yes, it's 24 regardless of the term of the lease). For example, a 7 percent (.07) interest rate converts to a .0029 money factor. Then, of course, there are associated taxes and fees that are added. Accept the fact that if the car you want to lease is not a popular model, your lease may be a bit higher than you anticipated.

LEASING TIPS

Calculating an actual lease payment beforehand is nearly impossible, particularly when the lease is subsidized by the automaker, but you can arrive at a ballpark figure by using the following formula, which we will illustrate using a 2000 Honda Accord EX V6 as an example. Remember that if you put any money down, or trade in your old car, you must deduct this amount from the capitalized cost. This deduction is called the capitalized cost reduction. We recommend paying the destination charge, the acquisition fee, the security deposit, and any taxes up front rather than rolling them into the lease.

2000 Honda Accord EX V6

MSRP	$24,550
Capitalized Cost (negotiated fair price)	$22,490
Destination Charge	$415
Acquisition Fee	$450
Security Deposit	$450 (refunded at end of lease)
Capitalized Cost Reduction	$900 (security deposit + acquisition fee)
Total Payment Due at Lease Signing*	$1,315 (destination charge + cap. reduction)
Residual Value after 3 years	(57% of MSRP in this example) $24,550 x .57 = $13,993.50
Term Depreciation	(Capitalized Cost - Residual Value) $22,490 - $13,993.50 = $8,496.50
Money Factor	(Interest Rate divided by 24) 7.5% divided by 24 = .0031
Monthly Lease Rate	(Capitalized Cost + Residual Value x .0031) ($22,490 + $13,993.50) x .0031 = $113.10
Monthly Depreciation	(Term Depreciation divided by Lease Term) $8,496.50 divided by 36 = $236.01
State Sales Tax on Payment	([Monthly Depreciation + Monthly Lease Rate] x Sales Tax Rate [6.5% in this ex.) $236.01 + $113.10 x .065 = $22.69
State Sales Tax on Cap Reduction	(Cap Cost Reduction x Sales Tax Rate [6.5% in this ex.]) $900 x .065 = $1.63
Monthly Payment	(Monthly Depreciation + Monthly Lease Rate + State Sales Tax) $236.01 + $113.10 + $24.32 = $373.43

* Most leases also require that the first monthly payment be made at lease signing.

For comparison purposes, we used Honda's Web site lease calculator (http://www.honda2000.com/models/calculators/index.html) to see what American Honda Finance Corp. (AHFC) would quote us using as many of the same parameters as possible from our example above. The Web site calculator told us on October 6, 1999, that this sample Accord EX V6 would run

run $339.80 per month (including tax), for a 36-month lease with 15,000 miles allowed per year and $1,350 down on a cap cost of $22,490. AHFC reported a residual value at the end of the lease of $14,479.70, which is $486.20 higher than our estimate, and a disclaimer indicated the AHFC quote was based on a net capital cost of $21,590, which is $900 lower than our example. This lower cap cost, according to the disclaimer, is dependent on dealer participation, which tells us Honda is subsidizing Accord leases to the tune of $900 in dealer cash and that it's the dealer's prerogative whether or not the consumer shares in that factory money. The bottom line is that a 2000 Accord EX V6 should run between $340 per month and $375 per month with little money down. If this fits your budget, so does the Accord EX V6.

Keep in mind that every vehicle will have a unique residual value, based on its popularity, its resale value and its reputation for reliability and dependent of the term of the lease. Also remember that the above formula doesn't take the following into account: delivery and handling (D&H fees), documentation fees, the cost of license plates, city or county sales tax (if applicable in your part of the country), or trade-in values. The trade-in value and any cash down payment should be deducted from the capitalized cost before calculating the lease.

If you're upside down on your trade, which means the car is worth less than you owe on the loan, you'll need to add the difference between the balance due on the loan and the trade-in value to the capitalized cost.

The example we illustrated is a straightforward lease with no factory subsidy. This formula will not account for subsidized leases, as evidenced by the subsidized payment the Honda Web site calculated. Subsidized leases allow dealers to lower payments by artificially raising residual values or lowering the capitalized cost through dealer incentives. You can easily recognize a subsidized lease. Any nationally or regionally advertised lease is generally subsidized by the manufacturer to keep lease payments low. The $289 per month Jeep Grand Cherokee popular in TV and newspaper advertising is an example of a subsidized lease payment.

Actual lease payments are affected by negotiation of the sticker price on the vehicle, term of the lease, available incentives, residual values, and layers of financial wizardry that even sales managers can't interpret without divine intervention. Once you find a car you can afford, negotiate the sticker price and then explore leasing based on the negotiated price. Ask what the residual value is and subtract any rebates or incentives from the capitalized cost, and remember that you'll need to pay tax to Uncle Sam for that discount. Use the formula above to calculate a ballpark figure, and if the dealer balks at your conclusion, ask them to explain the error of your ways.

Your best bet when leasing is to choose a model with a subsidized lease. Payments are low, terms are simple to understand, and they are the only true bargain in the world of leasing.

Low Payments

Low payments aren't a fallacy with leasing, when taken in proper context. Let's look at our Honda Accord EX V6 example again. To lease for three years with a minimal capitalized cost reduction (down payment) of $1,350, it'll cost you about $350 per month (plus tax and fees). To buy that Accord, financed for 36 months at a 9 percent annual percentage rate (APR) with $1,350 down, you would pay about $685 per month (plus tax and fees). So you see, leasing is cheaper in terms of a monthly payment when compared to financing for the same term.

There are two flaws here. First, 60-month financing is now the standard, and 72-month financing is becoming more popular. Using the same APR and down payment, the Accord will cost right around $445 per month (plus tax and fees) for 5 years and still be worth a good chunk of change at the end of the loan if cared for properly. Second, ownership is far less restrictive, even if the bank holds the title until 2005. You can drive as far as you want, paint the thing glow-in-the-dark orange with magenta stripes, and spill coffee on the seats without sweating a big wear-and-tear bill down the road. Leasing for three years costs about $13,500 (assuming you get the entire security deposit back), and you don't own the car at lease-end. Financing for three years costs about $26,000, but you own a car worth about $14,000 when the payment book is empty (unless, of course, you've actually painted it orange with magenta stripes and spilled coffee all over the interior), which makes your actual cost close to $12,000. Is leasing cheaper? Monthly payments, when compared to financing over the same term, are lower. But in most cases, leasing is actually more expensive.

Let's compare the longer-term effects of leasing vs. buying, over the same term and under identical conditions. By leasing the Accord in this example for three years, and then buying the car for its $13,993.50 residual value with two-year financing at a higher interest rate than you would have paid new (interest rates rise as the vehicle gets older), you pay thousands more for the car. Assume the interest rate for 24 months on a 3-year-old Accord is 11 percent. Payments for the loan would total about $650 per month, or right around $15,600 for the life of the loan. Added to the cost of the three-year lease, the $23,000 Accord has cost you $29,100 (plus tax) with average payments over 60 months of $500 per month (plus tax). Had you bought the Accord outright, financing for 60 months at 9 percent interest, the Accord would have cost $26,700 (plus tax) with monthly outlays of $445 (plus tax).

But there are several factors that should be kept in mind. When leasing, tax is calculated on the payment; when buying, tax is calculated on the selling price. At a 6.5 percent sales tax rate, the Accord costs the buyer using conventional 60-month financing roughly $300 less in sales tax than the buyer who leases and then purchases the car at the residual value. Other factors, like fluctuating interest rates, down payments, and contractual obligations can also affect the lease vs. loan scenario. Additionally, vehicle condition can have a tremendous affect on value. A few dents, dings or scratches could easily make a lease the more expensive proposition, with charges for worn tires, excessive mileage and cosmetic repair likely to top $1,000 at the end of the contract.

When trying to determine if leasing or buying is right for you, carefully weigh all the factors that can affect payments over the term of the lease or loan, including the way you drive and maintain a vehicle.

Restrictions

Leasing severely restricts your use of a vehicle. Mileage allowances are limited, modifications to the vehicle can result in hefty fines at the end of the lease, and if the vehicle is not in top condition when it is returned, excessive wear-and-tear charges may be levied. Many dealers and financing institutions will be more lenient if you buy or lease another vehicle from them at the end of your term, but if you drop off the car and walk, prepare yourself for some lease-end misery.

Be sure to define these limitations at the beginning of the lease so that you know what you're getting yourself into. Find out what will be considered excessive in the wear-and-tear department and try to negotiate a higher mileage limit.

Benefits

By leasing, you get to drive a new vehicle every two or three years. This also means that, in most cases, the only time the car will be in the shop is for routine maintenance. And, as long as you lease only for the term of the original manufacturer's warranty, you're not liable for catastrophic repair bills. Additionally, leasing can allow a buyer to make that dream car fit the budget when conventional financing will not. Finally, and perhaps for some people this is the most important benefit, you're never again upside-down on a car loan, unless you try to end the lease early.

Lease-end

Studies show that consumers generally like leases, right up until they end. The reason for their apprehension is rooted in the dark days of open-end leasing, when Joe Lessee was dealt a sucker punch by the lessor on the day Joe returned the car to the leasing agent. Back then, residual values were established at the beginning of the lease, but the lessee was responsible for the difference between the residual value and the fair market value at the end of the lease. The resulting lease-end charges maxed out credit cards and dealers laughed all the way to the bank.

LEASING TIPS

Leasing has evolved, and with today's closed-end leases (the only type of lease you should consider), the lease-end fees are generally reasonable, unless the car has 100,000 miles on it, a busted-up grille and melted chocolate smeared into the upholstery. Dealers and financial institutions want you to buy or lease another car from them, and can be rather lenient regarding excess mileage and abnormal wear. After all, if they hit you with a bunch of trumped up charges you're not going to remain a loyal customer, are you?

Additionally, closed-end leasing establishes a set, non-negotiable residual value for the car in advance, at the beginning of the lease. Also, any fees or charges you may incur at the lease-end are spelled out in detail before you sign the lease. All the worry is removed by the existence of concrete figures. But keep in mind that if you take your business elsewhere, you're going to be facing a bill for items like worn tires, paint chips, door dings, and the like.

Another leasing benefit is the myriad of choices you have at the end of the term. Well, maybe not a myriad, but there are four, which is more than you have after two or three years of financing. They are:

1.) **Return the car to the dealer and walk away from it** after paying any applicable charges like a termination fee, wear-and-tear repairs, or excessive mileage bills. Of course, if you don't plan to buy or lease another car from the dealer, you may get hit for every minor thing, but those are the risks.

2.) **Buy the car** from the dealer for the residual value established at the beginning of the lease. If the car is in good shape, the residual value is probably lower than the true value of the car, making it a bargain, and many leasing companies will guarantee financing at the lowest interest rate available at the time your lease ends. If you've trashed the lease car, compare the lease-end wear-and-tear charges to the devaluation in worth the vehicle has suffered while in your care. You might be surprised to find that it's easier and less expensive to just give the car back and pay the fines.

3.) **Use any equity in the car as leverage in a new deal** with the dealer. Since residual values are sometimes set artificially high, the car is not likely to be worth more than the residual value at lease-end under these circumstances. But a well-maintained, low-mileage lease car might allow the dealer to knock up to a couple of thousand bucks off your next deal.

4.) **Sell the car yourself** and pay off the residual value, pocketing whatever profit you make.

Conclusion

Closed-end leasing is a win-win situation for everybody except people who want to keep their cars for a good long time. The manufacturer sells more cars, the dealer sells more cars, and you get low payments and a new car every couple of years. However, it is important to stress that you never own the car and leasing can be quite restrictive. If you're a low-mileage driver who maintains cars in perfect condition, don't like tying up capital in down payments and don't mind never-ending car payments, leasing is probably just right for you. If you're on the road all day every day, beat the stuffing out of your wheels, enjoy a 'customized' look or drive your cars until the wheels fall off, buy whatever it is you're considering, because it will be less expensive in the long run.

2000 Honda Accord EX V6

"Parking... requires planning."

"...12.4 miles per gallon..."

"...biggest SUV on the planet."

Overdoing it has become a national pastime in the United States. We eat too much, spend lavishly on credit, and buy extravagant houses. Talk shows tell us that size does indeed matter, and we believe that he who dies with the most toys wins. Want proof that our culture is deeply stained by wretched excess? Check out Howard Stern's extreme Saturday night television shows. The extravaganza that is Las Vegas. Obesity in children who do nothing but play expensive video games hour after hour. Record numbers of bankruptcies during one of the most extensive economic booms this country has ever witnessed. The inexplicable success of Pamela Anderson Lee's "VIP." Execrable gold packages and fake interior wood trim kits on Toyota Corolla CEs. This excursive road test, from which many words should have been expurgated. The fact that the Ford Excursion exists, and is selling briskly.

"Geez, Wally! Get outta the way of the maniac in the Kenworth, will ya?"

WRETCHED EXCE$$

"...for more than 40 grand..."

By Christian J. Wardlaw

photography courtesy of Ford Motor Company

Excrescence, which also fits Ford's ex post facto nomenclature scheme for its lineup of SUVs, might have been a better name for this monstrous outgrowth of the sport-ute craze. Our dictionary says "excursion" means a short journey or outing made for pleasure or a trip at a special reduced fare. Since this truck isn't pleasurable to pilot, costs more than 40 large and slurps fuel like a wino does Boone's Farm, excursion is not exactly accurate.

Ostensibly designed for those who tow large loads or shuttle eight passengers on a regular basis, the Excursion is Ford's new entry in the expanding full-size sport-utility arena. Based on the heavy-duty F-250/350 pickup truck frame and sharing sheetmetal with the rugged Super Duty trucks from the A-pillar forward, Excursion officially breaks General Motors' lock on the super-size SUV market and dethrones the General at the same time. Exalted to king of what many consider to be (Expletive) Mountain, Ford now claims bragging rights to the biggest SUV on the planet.

It's larger than the redesigned Chevrolet Suburban and GMC Yukon XL — much larger. To the extent that it must be parked outside in the weather because it won't fit in a standard garage. So have fun scraping the ice off the windows in the winter and scrubbing bird excrement and tree sap off the roof in the summer. In comparison, the shorter (in length and height) Suburban and Yukon XL squeeze into most covered spaces attached to modern homes.

Adding insult to injury, the big GM utes will also tow more weight when properly equipped (10,500 pounds vs. the Excursion's 10,000-pound limit) while carrying the same number of passengers. And who transports eight passengers on a regular basis besides airport shuttles and couples doing their part to overpopulate the earth? If indeed you do need that many seats,

vans provide superior entry and exit for travelers. Aside from ski resorts that operate express transport from Vail to Denver's airport, we can't think of a single hotel or taxi service that would prefer the pricey Excursion over an economical Econoline.

Furthermore, Ford is exploiting Excursion's status as a low-emission vehicle and the existence of a patented Blocker Beam as exculpatory evidence exonerating the company from responsibility for damage to both the environment and motorists involved in an accident with the new SUV. Allow us to expatiate. Because the Excursion's earth-crushing 8,600-pound gross vehicle weight rating (GVWR) exempts it from meeting stringent light-duty truck emissions standards, the Excursion can legally expel twice as many pollutants* through the exhaust pipe than the light-duty Suburban and Yukon XL 1500. Still, 20 percent of

Exempt from light-duty truck emissions standards, the Excursion only appears to be environmentally friendly in Ford's promotional materials.

each Excursion is comprised of discarded consumer trash, and all but 15 percent of this SUV can be recycled when the truck expires.

But all those used two-liter soda pop bottles, bottle caps and rubber tires add up to an excessive 6,610-pound curb weight (2WD with 5.4-liter V8 — the 4WD Diesel weighs 7,648 pounds). When meeting up with an Excel sedan barely one-third as heavy, Excursion will certainly expunge the Hyundai driver's beliefs in existentialism. For reference, a 2WD Suburban 1500 weighs 4,194 pounds and the 4WD 2500 tops out at 5,760.

Expounding on Ford's exclusive Blocker Beam, we can tell you it consists of a hollow steel crossmember hung from the front edge of the frame that is designed to "catch" passenger cars in a collision, theoretically keeping them from becoming subjects of extrication for paramedics. At the rear, a standard trailer-towing hitch keeps regular Joes from sliding beneath the vehicle, though we wonder if the system was properly tested for effectiveness. In most rear-end collisions, the driver doing the colliding is on the brakes hard, which pitches the vehicle's nose forward and down. If the Excursion's trailer hitch isn't low enough, it'll just dig a trench in the hood of the car ramming it until the rear bumper is introducing itself to the wayward driver's windshield.

Despite Ford's predictions about who will buy the Excursion, we're seeing them pop up in exurbia like Boxsters in May. Wealthy soccer moms and dads concerned about the safety of their families on road-rage ravaged highways are just as excited about this truck as retirees with an Airstream to haul to Florida for the winter. So, as good citizens interested in helping consumers find the vehicle that fits their needs, we obtained an Excursion Limited for a two-week test in Denver.

Exorbitant fuel expenditures may cause extrasensory levels of disbelief. For example, our 4WD V10-powered Ford averaged 12.4 miles per gallon in city and highway driving on the pavement. That translated to $1 for every 8.7 miles traveled during the test period, not including maintenance and insurance. Filling the 44-gallon tank at $1.30 per gallon would cost $57.20. Off-road, we got 10.1 mpg. Excruciating, huh?

Though the 6.8-liter, single-overhead-cam V10 engine makes 300 horsepower at 4,250 rpm and 430 ft-lbs. of torque at 3,250 rpm (maximum torque output measures 383 ft-lbs. at an extraordinarily low 1,500 rpm), our truck accelerated lethargically despite a heavy foot on the throttle. Mated to a four-speed overdrive automatic transmission, power delivery is smooth and refined, though on hills the tranny can hunt for the right gear, sometimes shifting harshly. An overdrive-off button on the end of the shift column lets you use engine braking to help slow the Excursion on steep declines, saving the brakes for when you really need them.

Fuel expenses and snail's pace motorvating aside, there are other reasons to leave the hulking Excursion to that small percentage of the population that actually needs it.

Exhilarating is not how we would describe the Excursion driving experience. Despite leather seats and a full load of luxury-like conveniences, this truck drives like a Super Duty pickup loaded with 1,500 pounds of metal, rubber and glass. Ride quality and steering response, like fuel economy, are oxymora. The archaic yet sturdy front suspension (Twin I-Beam on 2WD and beam axle with leaf springs on 4WD) transmits via shock wave impacts encountered by either of the front tires directly to the driver's arms. Ride harshness is quite evident, and over dips, such as those traversed on expressway overpasses, the Excursion porpoises fore and aft. Exacerbating ride comfort problems are long stretches of broken pavement that unsettle the underpinnings, making the truck feel like it's about to change course whether you want it to or not.

RuPaul's sexual preference is less vague than the Excursion's recirculating ball-type steering gear, and this exacts a toll on any feeling of stability. Around turns, the rear end seems to change direction only after a momentary pause. Though equipped with large front disc/rear drum four-wheel antilock brakes, our test truck dove left under hard braking and wavered all over the lane in panic stops. Riding on 265/75R16 light-truck all-season tires, the overwhelming Excursion couldn't exit a cloverleaf off-ramp at more than the posted speed without scaring the bejesus out of the driver and passengers.

As expected, modern strip-mall parking lots are exceptionally difficult to navigate, and it's not easy to judge distances in close quarters. In fact, our Excursion didn't fit into any of the slots at the Barnes & Noble near Park Meadows mall in suburban Denver. We considered testing to see if we could stuff it into the underground parking area at downtown's Pavillions shopping and entertainment complex, but we thought better of it after trying to cram it into our editor's garage. Parking this truck, whether at home, work or when out for a night on the town, requires planning.

An off-road expedition takes just that, too. Planning. Not because you'll need to worry about packing light. There's no need to be concerned about exiguous cargo space with this expansive beast. You'll just need to make sure the Excursion will fit where you want to go. This vehicle is 6-and-a-half feet wide at the mirrors, and with nearly 19 feet of sheetmetal between the tips of the bumpers and an extremely wide turning circle, it would be simple to get wedged into a tight spot that would require deforestation to extract the truck.

We went off-road in the foothills of Colorado's Rocky Mountains, keeping to well-traveled paths to avoid getting in over our heads. On these trails, the Excursion performed remarkably competently, with brush scratching the paintwork only occasionally. Wheel articulation was impressive, and we didn't bottom the truck or scrape the trailer hitch during any part of our maneuvers. The Super Duty pickup's ultra-stiff underpinnings helped in this regard, but plowing over successive dips and whoops was akin to riding a bucking bronco.

Power folding mirrors would have come in handy on a couple of tighter sections of two-track, and the gargantuan hood hides everything on the other side of hills, requiring that the driver stop to check what's on the other side before proceeding. Once, when we were engaging in exactly this behavior, we found a Blazer, an Explorer and a Pathfinder headed out of the hills for home. Backing the Excursion along narrow trails is no treat. Finding a spot to move it out of the way without excoriating exterior extremities is even more challenging.

Exhibiting an exceedingly obnoxious thrumming reverberation on washboard roads, the Excursion also emitted a cacophony of rattles and squeaks over rutted roadway. On a positive note, the

ABS is not at all intrusive on dirt, offering excellent pedal feel, progressive rates of travel and easy modulation. The thirsty V10 grunts the giant truck up and over all obstacles, proving the benefits of tremendous low-end torque.

After our trek into the mountains, we decided to wash the Excursion in the driveway. Using two buckets of suds. And a stepladder. We didn't want to

risk damage to the test truck in an automated car wash. After the lengthy task was complete, we noticed how handsome the Excursion is. As mentioned previously, it shares components with the Super Duty pickup from the A-pillars forward, giving it a rugged, real-truck image. But from the front doors rearward, it reminded us of an Econoline van. In back, you get a cleanly finished three-portal dutch-door arrangement, flanked by simple taillights. Our two-tone Limited model (why not Eddie Bauer, we wonder?) was equipped with useful illuminated running boards necessary to board and disembark the vehicle.

Once inside, you'll find an all-work-and-no-play dash design lifted intact from the Super Duty truck. Industrial hard plastic surfaces coat the cabin throughout, but materials are generally good with fine fit and finish. Fake wood accents help richen the ambiance a bit, as does embroidered "Limited" script on the seatbacks. Phoenix and Vegas residents beware that the power window switches, when left exposed to direct sunlight, get too hot to touch, making it hard to air out the truck on hot summer days.

Our Limited model was equipped with a basic trip computer that offered readouts for exterior temperature, compass, average miles per gallon, and all-important in a gas hog like this, distance to empty. We also got comfy, well-placed armrests for both front seats, power rear quarter windows, and air-conditioning vents for all three rows of seats.

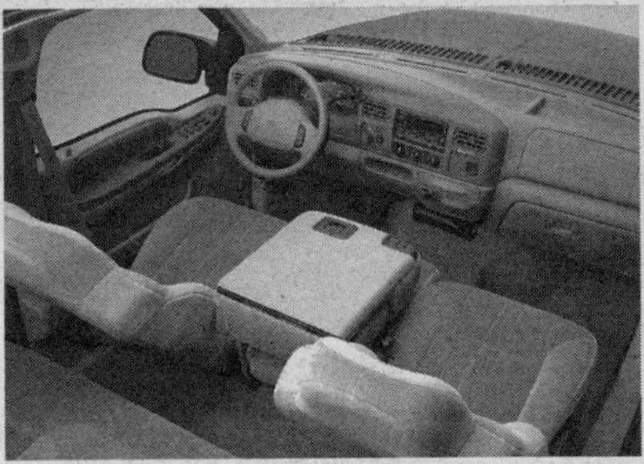

What we didn't get, and expected for more than 40 grand, was satellite stereo controls on the steering wheel, especially important on this vehicle since the dash-mounted switchgear is such a long stretch for driver. Other items we'd pay extra for include adjustable pedals, automatic climate control, a rear sensor system, signal arrow mirrors, an interior conversation mirror to spy on the youngsters in the rear seats, and a rear video entertainment system. Oh, wait. We forgot. The Excursion isn't designed to cater to the family-of-four crowd. Give back bumper instead.

Front seats, covered in leather and heated on our Limited model, are quite comfortable and are multi-adjustable to ensure that everyone can find a proper driving position. However, since Ford isn't currently offering its slick adjustable pedal option on the Excursion, shorter drivers will be up close and personal with the steering wheel. Dual door panel bins, a deep dash slot and a gigantic center storage console mean you'll have plenty of space for storage.

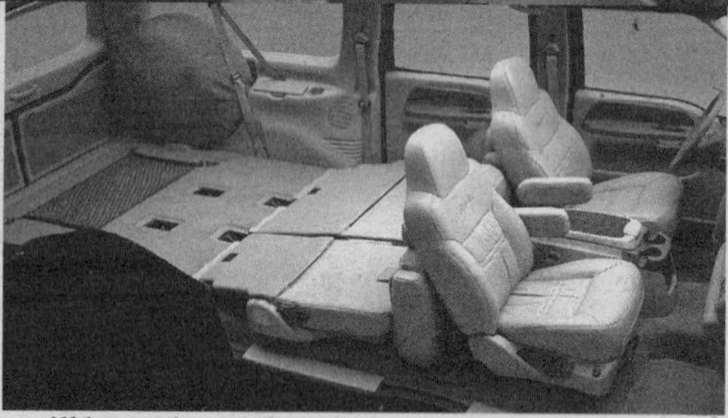

Rear seat riders will be less impressed with the Excursion, despite a rear audio system and separate air-conditioning controls. The rear seat cushion is too flat to support the thighs of longer-limbed adults, and legroom wasn't as generous as we expected. Underseat foot room was also tight beneath the power front chairs. Third-row passengers will be more comfortable, once they clamber aboard and slither past the sectioned second row (which slides generously forward to make back-backseat access easy). There's plenty of room in the last row for legs and feet, as well as a large storage bin.

That third-row bench is easily removable to expand cargo space, thanks to a simple release handle and casters that allow the seat to roll to the back of the truck. But once there, it's too wide to simply roll out through the dutch doors. The heavy bench must be muscled to an angle and then yanked out by two people (one person who wants a hernia can manage the task with considerable exertion). Thanks to 48.6 cubic feet of cargo space with all seats installed, however, removing the rearmost bench will be a rare occurrence for most households.

Make no mistake, it will be households that buy this rig in droves, and not the heavy-duty towing crowd Ford claims will drive most Excursions home. So, for those buyers without Class D certification on their driver's licenses, this expostulation is for you. This is reality without exaggeration.

If you must own an Excursion, exercise great care. You have to drive this vehicle deliberately at all times. Forget the cell phone and Big Macs. Also, you'll have to live with the fact that this is one truck that cannot be threaded through traffic expeditiously. It doesn't respond well to abrupt inputs, proper spacing between the Excursion and the vehicle in front of you must be maintained at all times for maximum

braking room, and the engine isn't powerful enough to fill gaping holes in traffic with expediency. So just sit there in the middle lane and let the more rational drivers among us pass in peace. Fortunately, visibility is outstanding, thanks to the tall driving position, expansive glass area, and large mirrors that can be positioned to reduce blind spots. You won't have any excuses when you're explaining your side to the cops after exterminating the young family in the Civic next to you.

Fuel is going to be a huge expense. Parking is going to be difficult, and you'll probably suffer some dents, dings and scrapes with time. Passing won't be easy. U-turns require forethought and lots of room. The truck gets stored outside unless you have an oversized garage in terms of depth and height. This means you'll need to wax it more often, especially if you're leasing, and you'll need to find a way to scrape snow and ice off the glass without using a stepladder.

On the plus side, it holds up to nine people and a duffel bag for each, it is capable of moving substantial amounts of cargo (maximum capacity measures 165 cubic feet, though this is roughly equivalent to a Honda Odyssey), and it can tow an incredible, if not class-leading, amount of weight. Squatters get out of the left lane when you come blazing up behind them with the lights on (Geez, Wally! Get outta the way of the maniac in the Kenworth, will ya?), and

the huge fuel tank provides exceptional highway range. Perhaps the deal clincher for some buyers will be the fact that the Excursion is exempt from luxury excise taxes.

Urban dwellers will want to avoid this vehicle. This is not an executive commuter (except maybe in Dearborn, Mich.). This is not a Mommobile. This is not an acceptable substitution for a minivan. It is designed to tow. It is designed to move large numbers of people on a regular basis. It is designed to carry bulky and heavy cargo. It requires wide-open expanse and a fat wallet to pay the monthly bill for fuel.

We aren't SUV-bashers, but we execrate the Excursion. The exemplary 2000 Chevrolet Suburban and GMC Yukon XL, thanks to their garageable dimensions, identical passenger-toting ability, and superior payload and tow ratings, are the full-size SUVs to buy, unless you need cargo-carrying space that only the Excursion's 165 cubic feet can offer (the GM utes provide only 138.4 cubes inside). Essentially, Ford has created an alternative to Super Duty pickup trucks for loyal Ford buyers who need the heavy-duty capabilities this beast boasts. In all other applications, Excursion exemplifies wretched excess. ■

*an extrapolation on our part

Vehicle Tested: 2000 Ford Excursion Limited 4WD

Base Price of Test Vehicle: $40,880 (including destination charge)

Options on Test Vehicle: 4.30 Limited-Slip Rear Axle ($250); Heated Seats ($290); Skid Plate Package ($75); LT265/75R16 All-Terrain Tires ($130)

Price of Test Vehicle: $41,625 (including destination charge)

Pros: Tows plenty of weight, provides safe haven for the family, carries lots of stuff.

Cons: Won't fit in a standard garage, drives like a loaded U-Haul, horrific fuel economy, hard to park, can't beat the Suburban at its own game.

Automobile Manufacturers

Customer Assistance Numbers

Acura	1-800-382-2238
Audi	1-800-822-2834
BMW	1-800-831-1117
Buick	1-800-521-7300
Cadillac	1-800-458-8006
Chevrolet	1-800-222-1020
Chrysler	1-800-992-1997
Daewoo	1-888-643-2396
Dodge	1-800-992-1997
Ford	1-800-392-3673
GMC	1-800-462-8782
Honda	1-800-999-1009
Hyundai	1-800-633-5151
Infiniti	1-800-662-6200
Isuzu	1-800-255-6727
Jeep	1-800-992-1997
Kia	1-800-333-4542
Land Rover	1-800-637-6837
Lexus	1-800-255-3987
Lincoln	1-800-392-3673
Mazda	1-800-222-5500
Mercedes-Benz	1-800-222-0100
Mercury	1-800-392-3673
Mitsubishi	1-800-222-0037
Nissan	1-800-647-7261
Oldsmobile	1-800-442-6537
Plymouth	1-800-992-1997
Pontiac	1-800-762-2737
Porsche	1-800-545-8039
Saab	1-800-955-9007
Saturn	1-800-553-6000
Subaru	1-800-782-2783
Suzuki	1-800-934-0934
Toyota	1-800-331-4331
Volkswagen	1-800-822-8987
Volvo	1-800-458-1552

PAYMENT TABLE

*Depicts estimated monthly payment per $1,000 borrowed**

TERM (length of loan)

		12	24	36	48	60
I	4%	85.15	43.40	29.50	22.55	18.45
N	5%	85.60	43.85	29.95	23.00	18.90
T	6%	86.05	44.30	30.40	23.50	19.35
E	7%	86.55	44.75	30.90	23.95	19.80
R	8%	87.00	45.25	31.35	24.40	20.30
E	9%	87.45	45.70	31.80	24.90	20.75
S	10%	87.90	46.15	32.25	25.35	21.25
T	11%	88.40	46.60	32.75	25.85	21.75
	12%	88.85	47.05	33.20	26.35	22.25
R	13%	89.30	47.55	33.70	26.85	22.75
A	14%	89.80	48.00	34.20	27.35	23.25
T	15%	90.25	48.50	34.65	27.85	23.80
E	16%	90.75	48.95	35.15	28.35	24.30

*rounded to nearest nickel

Notes

Notes

Notes

edmunds.com
consumer driven

BUYER'S GUIDES SCHEDULED RELEASE DATES FOR 2000 / 2001*

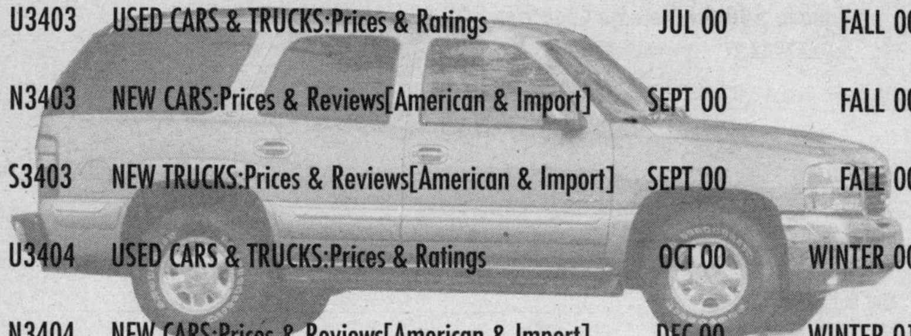

VOL. 34/35		RELEASE DATE	COVER DATE
U3402	USED CARS & TRUCKS:Prices & Ratings	APR 00	SUMMER 00
N3402	NEW CARS:Prices & Reviews[American & Import]	JUN 00	SUMMER 00
S3402	NEW TRUCKS:Prices & Reviews[American & Import]	JUN 00	SUMMER 00
U3403	USED CARS & TRUCKS:Prices & Ratings	JUL 00	FALL 00
N3403	NEW CARS:Prices & Reviews[American & Import]	SEPT 00	FALL 00
S3403	NEW TRUCKS:Prices & Reviews[American & Import]	SEPT 00	FALL 00
U3404	USED CARS & TRUCKS:Prices & Ratings	OCT 00	WINTER 00
N3404	NEW CARS:Prices & Reviews[American & Import]	DEC 00	WINTER 01
S3404	NEW TRUCKS:Prices & Reviews[American & Import]	DEC 00	WINTER 01
U3501	USED CARS & TRUCKS:Prices & Ratings	JAN 01	SPRING 01
N3501	NEW CARS:Prices & Reviews[American & Import]	MAR 01	SPRING 01
S3501	NEW TRUCKS:Prices & Reviews[American & Import]	MAR 01	SPRING 01

**Subject to Change*